Butterworths New Law Guides

The Proceeds of Crime Act 2002

Butterworths New Law Guides

The Proceeds of Crime Act 2002

Stuart Biggs MA (Cantab), Barrister at 9–12 Bell Yard

Simon Farrell MA (Cantab), Diploma in Law (City), Barrister at 3 Raymond Buildings, Gray's Inn

Nicola Padfield MA (Oxon), Dip Crim (Cantab), DES (Aix-Marseille), Barrister, Lecturer, Institute of Criminology, Fellow of Fitzwilliam College, Cambridge

Butterworths
LexisNexis™

Members of the LexisNexis Group worldwide

United Kingdom	LexisNexis Butterworths Tolley, a Division of Reed Elsevier (UK) Ltd, Halsbury House, 35 Chancery Lane, LONDON, WC2A 1EL, and 4 Hill Street, EDINBURGH EH2 3JZ
Argentina	LexisNexis Argentina, BUENOS AIRES
Australia	LexisNexis Butterworths, CHATSWOOD, New South Wales
Austria	LexisNexis Verlag ARD Orac GmbH & Co KG, VIENNA
Canada	LexisNexis Butterworths, MARKHAM, Ontario
Chile	LexisNexis Chile Ltda, SANTIAGO DE CHILE
Czech Republic	Nakladatelství Orac sro, PRAGUE
France	Editions du Juris-Classeur SA, PARIS
Hong Kong	LexisNexis Butterworths, HONG KONG
Hungary	HVG-Orac, BUDAPEST
India	LexisNexis Butterworths, NEW DELHI
Ireland	Butterworths (Ireland) Ltd, DUBLIN
Italy	Giuffré Editore, MILAN
Malaysia	Malayan Law Journal Sdn Bhd, KUALA LUMPUR
New Zealand	LexisNexis Butterworths, WELLINGTON
Poland	Wydawnictwo Prawnicze LexisNexis, WARSAW
Singapore	LexisNexis Butterworths, SINGAPORE
South Africa	LexisNexis Butterworths, DURBAN
Switzerland	Stämpfli Verlag AG, BERNE
USA	LexisNexis, DAYTON, Ohio

© Reed Elsevier (UK) Ltd 2002

A CIP Catalogue record for this book is available from the British Library.

Stuar Biggs, Simon Farrell and Nicola Padfield, have asserted their rights under the Copyrights, Designs and Patents Act 1988 to be identified as the authors of this work.

ISBN 0 406 95653 7

Printed and bound in Great Britian by Thomson Litho Ltd, East Kilbride, Scotland.

Visit Butterworths LexisNexis *direct* **at www.butterworths.com**

Preface

Jack Straw, whilst Home Secretary described the draft Proceeds of Crime Bill as 'large, complex and innovative'. Others have described it as problematic, disproportionate and lacking in procedural safeguards. What is certainly true is that the new Act reflects a determined effort on the part of the government to encourage more effective recovery of the proceeds of crime from its perpetrators. The key features of the Act are—

   —the creation of the Assets Recovery Agency (the "ARA");

   —a strengthened scheme for the making and enforcement of, confiscation orders in criminal proceedings;

   —a civil law confiscations regime of general application;

   —the delegation of revenue collection powers to the ARA;

   —extended anti-money laundering laws.

Whilst no one argues with the main principle, that criminals should not be able to retain their ill-gotten gains, the Act does raise serious problems as follows—it reproduces many of the inconsistencies of the existing law; it undermines the human rights of those suspected of benefiting from crime; it poses an onerous duty on the law abiding to police the activities of other people.

Perhaps most importantly it is vital to remember that passing legislation is only the first step. Whether or not the ARA will have the resources to achieve what the government hopes for remains to be seen.

Meanwhile, we hope that this book may serve as a useful guide to this new chapter in the 'war against crime'. We have attempted to comment on the Act section by section, highlighting in particular those sections which we believe may pose greatest difficulties in practice.

Many provisions of the Act require regulations to be made before coming into force. To enable readers of this book to keep up to date, the secondary legislation and other relevant material (including codes of practice) will be accessible on the Butterworths website; see inside front cover for details.

The necessary password is—assets

The manuscript was submitted to the publishers in early October and so is only up-to-date up until that time.

Stuart Biggs
Simon Farrell
Nicola Padfield

October 2002

Contents

Contents

Table of Statutes

Table of Statutory Instruments

Table of Cases

Table of cases

Table of cases

1 Introduction

SIGNIFICANCE OF NEW ACT

Background

1.1   The last 30 years have witnessed a steady march towards powers of forfeiture matched in scale only by those that existed a century ago. Under the system that operated until the late nineteenth century forfeiture of a defendant's property (and often that of his relatives) was automatic upon conviction for most serious criminal offences. The main difference now (and strengthened under the new Act) is that a person convicted of a serious offence involving financial benefit is frequently required to show that all his property is legitimately owned. Failure to do so will lead to the property being confiscated.

International procedure

1.2   The Proceeds of Crime Act 2002 ('PCA 2002') brings the UK into line with the US by the introduction of a civil power[1] which allows the High Court to order the forfeiture of property in the absence of any conviction for a criminal offence. If the property is 'or represents property obtained through unlawful conduct'[2] it will be liable to forfeiture. The successful operation of similar civil forfeiture laws in New South Wales and the Republic of Ireland were also behind the Government's decision to introduce the new Act.[3]

---

[1]   In 1970 the US Congress introduced criminal and civil forfeiture in an attempt to deal with organised crime. This marked the reintroduction of forfeiture in the US which had not been applied for 180 years. These new powers were part of the Racketeer Influenced and Corrupt Organizations Act (RICO) and the Continuing Criminal Enterprises Act (CCE). RICO and CCE were enacted by Congress in October 1971. The present RICO offences are contained in 18 USC Ch 96, sec 1962 (a) to (d). Most states have also passed forfeiture laws similar to the federal ones. For example Florida passed the Contraband Forfeiture Act in 1980 to deal with drug trading and, in 1983, amended the Act to allow forfeiture in relation to all felonies.

[2]   See s 240(1)(a).

[3]   See Performance and Innovation Unit Report (hereinafter 'PIU Report'), June 2000, paras 5.6–5.11 for some international comparisons.

Confiscation

1.3   The new Act also revises the system of confiscation following criminal conviction. Although the existing confiscation laws are tough, they have been underused. For example, confiscation orders were made in only 0.3% of non-drug-related cases in 1998. Although orders were made in a higher proportion of drug-related cases (17.8% in 1998) recovery rates were low.[1] PCA 2002 represents a sea change in the way that the authorities intend to deal with criminals and criminal assets. There is likely to be a significant increase in Crown Court business, with many powers formerly exercised by the High Court being transferred there. All restraint proceedings and ancillary matters will now be dealt with by the Crown Court. Complex confiscation hearings will become more common, often with more at stake for the defendant given the terms of imprisonment in default of payment. It remains to be seen whether the Crown Court is able to deal with this extra work.

---

[1]   PIU Report, para 4.21 and Table 4.4.

The new law

1.4   PCA 2002 consolidates, updates and strengthens existing legislation and brings in sweeping new powers. It transfers many confiscation powers to the Crown Court, and establishes an Assets Recovery Agency (ARA). It also makes money laundering offences stricter by the introduction of a negligence based criminal offence, which will apply not only to financial institutions but also to solicitors and other professionals who manage or deal with clients' money, introduces civil forfeiture in the High Court and empowers the Director of the ARA to tax the proceeds of criminal conduct. The new money laundering provisions, which criminalise negligent conduct, will be especially important to financial institutions, banks, lawyers and accountants. The City was described in the House of Commons by Ian Davidson, MP in the following terms—

> 'We should understand that there are people in British banking who are crooks. They have benefited from crime for a considerable period. Some of us have travelled to other jurisdictions, where we are told that Britain is good at telling them how they should improve their systems. However, they say the City is the dirtiest washing machine in the world in terms of the amount of illicit money that goes through it.' . . . 'I hope that the Bill's provisions will be applied vigorously to identify lawyers, bankers and accountants involved in concealing assets, punish them severely and send a message to others'.[1]

---

[1]   HC 2R, 30 October 2001, col 792.

1.5   One of the effects of the new Act is that financial institutions and those professionals who manage assets will swiftly have to establish proper systems to avoid falling foul of the new money laundering provisions.

A BRIEF HISTORY OF FORFEITURE

1.6   Forfeiture of property upon conviction of criminal offences has its origins in Saxon times. William Blackstone wrote in the late eighteenth century that the forfeiture of 'lands and tenements to the Crown' for treason was 'transmitted from our Saxon ancestors' and formed part of 'the ancient Scandinavian constitution'.[1] Where a person violated the fundamental contract between the King and his people he was no longer entitled to enjoy the benefits of being a member of the community and of holding property.[2] This principle of protection by the King and/or lord in return for rights was central to feudal society. William I took the legal ownership of all the land after the Conquest and distributed it in return for military services (or the equivalent in money).

---

[1]   Blackstone W *Commentaries on the Laws of England* Book IV, Ch 29, p 377 (1979) University of Chicago Press.
[2]   *Blackstone's Commentaries* Book IV, Ch 29, p 375.

1.7   Forfeiture of property subsequently extended to anyone convicted of a felony.[1] By the seventeenth century felonies included murder, manslaughter, witchcraft, larceny, abduction of an heiress with intent to marry her, forgery of a deed or testimonial, and malicious cutting of another man's tongue or eyes. Most felonies were punishable by death, but there were further penalties.

---

[1]   *Stroud* (2nd edn) quoting Termes de la Ley 'It seemeth that they [serious crimes] are called felonies of the ancient English word fell or fierce because that they are intended to be done with a cruell, bitter, fell, fierce or mischievous minde' (Medieval Latin *fello, onis* a traitor). The term *felonia* first appears in 1108 during the reign of Henry 1 (1100–1135) and is used to describe a vassal's breach of contract with his lord.

1.8   The concept of breach of trust between citizen and King extended to citizen and lord. By breaching his allegiance to his lord, a felon forfeited his rights to the land that he held for that lord. As it was held feudally, the land, or its profits, would then pass back to the lord. If the felony were a treason, the land would pass directly to the King. Upon an indictment for treason, the Crown could also seize the accused's chattels, which were not returned following an acquittal. The rules of forfeiture, and their application, were complex, and they varied over time.[1] Nevertheless, forfeiture consistently provided feudal lords and the Crown with substantial income, and the question of which offences amounted to treason, and which to more limited felonies was therefore a matter of great dispute between the King and his barons.

---

[1] For an article on the history of forfeiture in both the US and England see Cecil Greek 'Drug Control and Asset Seizures: A Review of the History of Forfeiture in England and Colonial America' in Mieczkowski T (ed) *Drugs Crime and Social Policy* Allyn and Bacon, Boston. See also the Hodgson Committee Report 'The Profits of Crime and their Recovery' (1984) Heineman, Ch 2 ('the Hodgson Report').

1.9   A felony did not only lead to loss of life and land. The felon's blood was deemed to have corrupted his wife and descendants. Through this concept of 'corruption of blood' the felon's family lost its rights to inherit his land and chattels. The widow could not keep her 'dower', which was normally one-third of her husband's property. The felon's widow and children would also be unable to inherit from the felon's parents. Property lost in this way again passed to the lord.

1.10   Forfeiture and corruption of blood only took place after conviction by a jury after a trial. There were however two ways that an accused could preserve his property for his family. One was *peine forte et dure*, the other was benefit of clergy.

Peine forte et dure

1.11   When an accused was arraigned and stood mute, he would undergo '*peine forte et dure*', a development of the more ancient trial by ordeal. Initially, *peine forte et dure* meant that the accused would be imprisoned and fed only bread and stagnant water, on alternate days, until he decided to enter a plea. However, over the years, too many people who undertook this regime starved to death, thus depriving their lords and the King of their property. The law was therefore changed to help the accused make up his mind more quickly about how to plead at arraignment. From the reign of Henry IV, those who decided to stand mute were no longer subjected to prison and a restricted diet; instead, they were 'pressed'. Large stones were placed on top of them until they entered a plea or died. When pressing killed them, and they had not pleaded, their families would not be subject to corruption of blood, neither would their land be forfeited.[1]

---

[1] Hale Sir M *The History of the Pleas of the Crown* (1736 edn reproduced in 1987) Professional Books Ltd, vol 2, p 319. As Hale put it: 'the severity of the judgment is to bring men to put themselves upon their legal trial, and though sometimes it hath been given and executed, yet for the most part men bethink themselves and plead'. The judgment of the court was particularly unpleasant: 'that he be sent to the prison . . . and put into a dark, lower room, and there laid naked upon the bare ground . . . his arms and legs drawn and extended with cords . . . and upon his body laid as great a weight of iron, as he can bear and more . . . till he die'.

Benefit of clergy

1.12   An accused could claim benefit of clergy if he could show that he was connected to the Church. He could then be tried in a Church court, where acquittals were common. In some cases, a man found guilty in a criminal court could claim benefit of clergy before he was sentenced, and thus go to a Church court to be punished. Church courts did not have the sentencing powers of their secular counterparts: a Church court could not impose the death penalty, and it could not order the seizure of lands or corruption of blood.

1.13   From the fourteenth century until 1707, an accused could claim benefit of clergy if he could read. The court tested his reading by presenting him with a Bible and asking him to read Psalm 51 aloud. If he could, he received the benefit. Many defendants simply memorised the Psalm. It became known as the 'neck verse', because that, along with the defendant's property, was what it saved.

Other types of forfeiture

1.14   There were other types of forfeiture. When an individual's property (animate or inanimate) caused the death of another individual, whether accidentally or intentionally, (including by way of self-defence), the property, or its value, was forfeited to the King as 'deodand'. Also, where a murderer could not be found, the local community had to pay the Crown a fine, the 'murdrum'.

1.15   These practices remained in English law for hundreds of years. *Peine forte et dure* was abolished in 1772 and the last recorded pressing took place in 1741.[1] In 1772 standing mute came to be taken as a guilty plea (standing mute was made equivalent to a not guilty plea in 1827). Corruption of blood was eliminated for all felonies except murder in 1814.[2] Benefit of clergy was abolished in 1827. Forfeiture as a penalty for felony or treason was abolished in 1870.

---

[1]   See Lyon B *A Constitutional and Legal History of Medieval England* (1960) Harper Brothers, New York, p 451. Although the last recorded pressing took place in 1741, the assembly place for criminals at Newgate in London was still known as the 'press yard' at the end of the eighteenth century and was so called because accused who had refused to enter a plea had been pressed to death here in earlier times; see James Boswell's journal entry for 29 May 1785 in J Boswell 'The Applause of the Jury' (ed by Lustig and Pottle, 1982) Heineman.

[2]   Kent J *Commentaries on American Law* (4 vols) (1971) DaCapo Press, New York, vol 2, p 319.

1.16   Except for a limited number of specific offences, where the possession of the object was itself an offence (for example, tools for making counterfeit currency, the coins themselves, pornography and offensive weapons), and as a means of enforcing fiscal policies by the Inland

Revenue and Customs and Excise, the use of forfeiture disappeared from late Victorian times until the 1970s. Felons often had little to forfeit and during the period of transportation, it was considered inappropriate.[1]

---

[1]   See Ekirch R *Bound for America The Transportation of British Convicts to the Colonies* (1987) Oxford University Press, New York. Between the passing of the Transportation Act 1718 and 1776, 50,000 convicts were sent to America and by 1866 150,000 had been transported to Australia.

THE PERIOD 1970 TO 1986

1.17   It was the recognition that criminals were making substantial sums from crime which they retained even when convicted of serious criminal offences that led to the calls for change. In 1970 a report by the Advisory Council on the penal system recommended that powers of forfeiture on conviction should be made more general in nature. The result was the Powers of Criminal Courts Act 1973, s 43. This introduced a very limited general power of forfeiture. It allowed a Crown Court to order that a convicted defendant forfeit ('be deprived of his rights in') any property which was in his possession or under his control at the time of his arrest and which had been used for 'the purpose of committing, or facilitating the commission of any offence' or 'was intended by him to be used for that purpose'. The Powers of Criminal Courts Act 1973, s 39 gave the power to the Crown Court to make a criminal bankruptcy order. These reforms were described in the Hodgson Report as 'wholly ineffective' and 'infrequently used'.[1]

---

[1]   See The Report of the Committee chaired by Sir Derek Hodgson (1984) Heinemann, p 9 (the Hodgson Report).

1.18   Forfeiture of property was also permitted in drugs-related cases after conviction by virtue of the Misuse of Drugs Act 1971, s 27. The Crown Court had the power to order—

> 'anything shown to the satisfaction of the Court to relate to the offence, to be forfeited and either destroyed or dealt with in such other manner as the Court may order'.

The limitations of this power became clear in 1981 when the House of Lords in *Cuthbertson* ruled 'with considerable regret' that the Misuse of Drugs Act 1971, s 27 did not operate to allow the Crown Court to order the forfeiture of the monetary profits of the drug trade.[1] In that case (the so-called 'Operation Julie' trial) the illegal profits were substantial and, as a result of the public outcry, the Hodgson Committee was set up by the Howard League for Penal Reform in 1980 to—

> 'consider the present law relating to the forfeiture of property associated with crime in the light of . . . [the decision in *Cuthbertson*] . . . to assess how far the powers of criminal courts to impose monetary penalties meet the need to strip offenders of their ill gotten gains, and whether further provisions are necessary to ensure that the fruits of crime are returned either to the innocent owners of the property or to the Crown'.[2]

---

1   *R v Cuthbertson* [1981] AC 470, [1980] 2 All ER 401, HL.
2   See Hodgson Report (1984), p 4.

1.19   The Hodgson Committee Report recommended that—

> 'criminal courts should have the power to order the confiscation of proceeds of an offence of which the defendant has been convicted or asked to be taken into consideration'.[1]

The report was highly influential in the debate that led to the Drug Trafficking Offences Act 1986.

---

1   See Hodgson Report (1984), pp 74 and 151.

THE DRUG TRAFFICKING OFFENCES ACT 1986

1.20   This Act ('DTOA 1986') put into place for the first time a system for the confiscation of assets when a defendant was convicted of a drug trafficking offence. The Crown Court was responsible for making confiscation orders, whilst the High Court dealt with restraint and charging orders, the appointment of receivers and certificates of inadequacy. The magistrates' court was responsible for enforcing payment of the order as if the amount were a fine.[1] DTOA 1986 introduced a 'value confiscation approach' whereby the Crown Court was required to conduct two accounting exercises. First the court assessed the defendant's criminal proceeds (his 'benefit') and secondly, determined the value of any property which he owned or in which he had an interest which was then used to satisfy any order made by the court. Failure to pay led to a term of imprisonment in default and enforcement by the appointment of a receiver in the High Court. The Crown Court was given power to order that the prosecution and defence provide statements of information.

[1]   As to how the magistrates' court should approach a warrant of commitment hearing see *R v Harrow Justices, ex p DPP* [1991] 3 All ER 873, [1991] 1 WLR 385.

1.21   The defendant benefited from drug trafficking if he 'received any payment or reward in connection with drug trafficking'.[1] In making the determination of benefit the court was permitted (but not required) to make statutory assumptions.[2] These were that any property which appeared to have been held by the defendant since his conviction or received by him during the six years prior to the institution of the proceedings against him constituted the proceeds of drug trafficking. The court was also permitted to assume that any expenditure the defendant had incurred during the same period was made out of such proceeds. The Crown Court had a discretion not to apply the assumptions if they would lead to a serious risk of injustice.

[1]   DTOA 1986, s 1(3).
[2]   DTOA 1986, s 2.

1.22   Once the court had determined the amount of the benefit it was required to determine 'the amount to be recovered'.[1] This amount was the value of the defendant's proceeds of drug trafficking unless the court determined that the 'amount that might be realised'[2] was less than this figure. In that case the order would be for the lower amount. It was for the defendant to show that the amount that might be realised was less than the amount assessed by the court as the value of his proceeds of drug trafficking. Realisable property was given a wide definition and included any property held by the defendant and any 'gift caught by this Act'.[3] A gift was 'caught' if it was made by the defendant at any time since the beginning of the period of six years ending when the proceedings were instituted against him, or if it was a gift of property received by the defendant at any time in connection with drug trafficking carried on by him or another person, or which in whole or in part directly or indirectly represented in the defendant's hands property received by him in that connection.[4] The way that 'tainted gifts' are valued under PCA 2002 is similar to the approach under the existing law.[5]

1   DTOA 1986, s 4(1).
2   DTOA 1986, s 4(2).
3   DTOA 1986, s 5(1).

4   DTOA 1986, s 5(9). PCA 2002, ss 9(1)(b) and 77 retain a similar method of calculating the 'available amount' to be recovered under a confiscation order. 'Gifts caught by the (1986) Act' are now called 'tainted gifts' in PCA 2002.
5   See PCA 2002, s 81.

THE PERIOD 1986 TO 1998

1.23   From 1986 until 1998 several statutes extended the court's powers of restraint and confiscation.[1] Confiscation provisions were extended to Scotland in 1987 while the Criminal Justice Act 1988 ('CJA 1988') introduced confiscation proceedings for all non-drug indictable offences. The basic structure of CJA 1988 was similar to DTOA 1986, although in its original form less draconian.[2] The Criminal Justice (International Co-operation) Act 1990 introduced mutual assistance provisions, further drug money laundering offences and the power of the authorities to seize cash over £10,000 if it was being imported or exported.[3] The Criminal Justice Act 1993 amended CJA 1988 and introduced non-drug money laundering offences and amended the existing non-drug legislation. The Drug Trafficking Act of 1994 ('DTA 1994'), which applies to a person charged after 3 February 1995, consolidated the provisions relating to confiscation in drug cases.

1   See para 1.25.
2   Unlike DTOA 1986 there were no provisions in the original CJA 1988 allowing the court to make statutory assumptions that property held by the defendant or received by him within the previous six years was the proceeds of or connected with criminal conduct. Under the original CJA 1988 the Crown Court had to be satisfied that the defendant's benefit was at least £10,000 before an order could be made.
3   See DTA 1994, ss 42 and 43.

1.24   The Proceeds of Crime Act 1995, came into force on 1 November 1995 and further amended CJA 1988. It abolished the minimum amount requirement and strengthened investigative and enforcement powers relating to confiscation. It made provision for ordering the defendant to supply the court with relevant information, with the court being entitled to draw adverse inferences from any unreasonable failure to do so. The most significant change was the introduction of statutory assumptions in non-drug cases similar to those created by the drug legislation. Therefore a confiscation order in a non-drugs case could be made on the basis that the defendant had benefited from criminal activity in respect of which there had been no conviction and which had never been taken into consideration by a court.

Confiscation legislation[1]

1.25

Year	Statute	Provisions
1986	Drug Trafficking Offences Act (DTOA)	Confiscation provisions for drug trafficking offences and first drug money laundering offence
1987	Criminal Justice (Scotland) Act	
1988	Criminal Justice Act 1988 (CJA 1988)	Confiscation provisions for all non-drug indictable offences and specified summary offences
1990	Criminal Justice (International Co-operation) Act	Mutual legal assistance, further drug money laundering offences and drug cash seizure on import or export
1993	Criminal Justice Act (CJA 1993)	(Other forms of) money laundering offences and enhancements to all crime confiscation provisions
1994	Drug Trafficking Act (DTA)	Consolidating the drug provisions and removing mandatory confiscation
1994	Criminal Justice and Public Order Act	Bringing forward the date from which CJA 1993 confiscation provisions apply
1995	Proceeds of Crime Act (PCA)	Further alignment of all crime confiscation provisions with DTA 1994; notably use of assumptions . . . in crime lifestyle cases
1995	Proceeds of Crime (Scotland) Act	
1996	Proceeds of Crime (NI) Order	
1998	Crime and Disorder Act	Amendment to CJA for confiscation orders on committal for sentence

---

[1]   PIU Report, Table 4.1.

OUTLINE OF DOMESTIC CASE LAW UNDER EXISTING LEGISLATION

1.26   The Court of Appeal has made it clear that the trial judge who deals with the confiscation issue has a wide discretion which will not be interfered with unless the judge—

— has taken something into account which he should not have done;
— left something out of account that should have been included; or
— proceeded on an incorrect principle.[1]

Although findings of fact are difficult to challenge this has not prevented a torrent of appeals.

---

[1] *R v Judge and Woodridge* (1992) 13 Cr App Rep (S) 685.

Determining value of proceeds

1.27   In computing the value of the defendant's proceeds of drug trafficking the court is required to take account of gross receipts rather than net profits.[1] In determining a defendant's benefit in non-drug cases the court is concerned simply with the value of the property obtained by the defendant in connection with the offence. CJA 1988, s 71(4) defines the defendant's benefit as 'the value of the property so obtained'. The House of Lords held in *Smith*[2] that it makes no difference in calculating the benefit figure if, after the defendant had obtained relevant property, it was destroyed or damaged or even forfeited to customs officers. What matters is the value of the property in determining the amount of the benefit. One of the draconian aspects of the forfeiture legislation is that the amount of legal benefit determined by the court often bears little relation to the defendant's real profits from crime. The way in which benefit is calculated has the effect of stripping the defendant of legitimate as well as illegitimate assets.

---

[1] *R v Smith* (1989) 11 Cr App Rep, (S) 55, CA; *R v Simons* (1993) 15 Cr App Rep (S) 126, CA; and *R v Banks* (1997) 2 Cr App Rep (S) 110, CA.
[2] *R v Smith (David)* [2001] UKHL 68, [2002] 1 All ER 366, [2002] 1 WLR 54.

1.28   Under CJA 1988, s 71(4) the defendant benefits from an offence if 'he obtains' property as a result of or in connection with its commission. The phrase 'he obtains' has been the subject of judicial attention. Despite some dicta to the contrary the better view appears to be that the phrase means an obtaining of property by the defendant himself rather than an obtaining by him for another or enabling another to obtain or retain property.[1] The amount of benefit does not take account of the deduction of expenses.[2]

---

[1] *R v Rees* (19 July 1990, unreported) per Auld J; *R v Gokal CCC* (7 May 1997, unreported) Case No T950223, per Buxton J; *R v Saia* (20 April 1999, unreported) per Langley J; *R v Patel (Assesh)* (3 November 1999, unreported) Case No 99/01946/Y5, per Douglas Brown J; and *R v Ahmed* (8 February 2000, unreported).
[2] *R v Smith* [1989] 2 All ER 948, [1989] 1 WLR 765, CA; *R v Taylor (RJM)* [1996] 2 Cr App Rep 64, [1996] 2 Cr App Rep (S) 96, CA.

1.29   A defendant is also liable to a confiscation order when he has obtained a pecuniary advantage 'as a result of or in connection with an offence'.[1] The phrase 'pecuniary advantage' should be given its ordinary and natural meaning. It includes situations where a debt is evaded or deferred.[2] In a case where tax has been evaded the 'pecuniary advantage' obtained by the defendant was the amount represented by the underpayment of tax resulting from his failure fully to disclose his profits together with interest, but does not extend to the balance of the undeclared profits which were the product of lawful trading.[3]

---

[1]   CJA 1988, s 71(5).
[2]   *R v Smith (David)* [2001] UKHL 68, [2002] 1 All ER 366, [2002] 1 WLR 54.
[3]   *R v Moran* [2001] EWCA Crim 1770, [2002] 1 WLR 253, [2002] 1 Cr App Rep (S) 413; *R v Dimsey* [2000] 2 All ER 142, [2000] 1 Cr App Rep (S) 497, CA.

1.30   Any assets in which the defendant has an interest are 'realisable property' within the meaning of CJA 1988 and DTA 1994, even if lawfully held and not connected with any criminal offence.[1] A defendant's contingent interest under a trust for example, is 'property' for the purposes of confiscation.[2] It is the value of the defendant's interest in realisable property at the time that the confiscation order is made which is important. Under DTOA 1986 and CJA 1988 the court had a discretion whether the defendant's interest in the family home could be realised.[3] This was removed by the later legislation. Under PCA 2002 only the Scottish courts are given a discretion not to order the sale of the family home and to take into account the interests of others.[4] As PCA 2002 passed through the House of Commons in late February 2002 an unsuccessful attempt was made to extend this discretion to the courts in England and Wales.[5]

---

[1]   *R v Currey* (1994) 16 Cr App Rep (S) 421, CA; *R v Chrastny (No 2)* [1992] 1 All ER 192, [1991] 1 WLR 1385, CA.
[2]   *R v Walbrook and Glasgow* (1994) 15 Cr App Rep (S) 783, CA. See also the interesting discussion of conflicting priorities of confiscation order and property adjustment order under the Magistrates' Courts Act 1973 in *Customs and Excise Comrs v A* [2002] EWCA Civ 1039, [2002] All ER (D) 312 (Jul), (2002) Times, 25 July.
[3]   See *R v Lee* [1996] 1 Cr App Rep (S) 135, CA and *R v Taigel* [1998] 1 Cr App Rep (S) 328, CA.
[4]   Section 98 gives the courts in Scotland a discretion not to order the sale of the family home.
[5]   See HC Debates, 26 February 2002, col 626.

Postponement of confiscation order

1.31   Perhaps one of the most troubling provisions of the existing system has been the power of the Crown Court to postpone the issue of confiscation until after sentence. The order must be made within six months from plea of guilty or conviction unless there are exceptional circumstances. A number of important and high-profile confiscation orders have been quashed because of procedural irregularities. The

Court of Appeal has emphasised that the Crown Court can only postpone the issue of confiscation until after sentence if it requires further information.[1] The decision to postpone must involve the court in making an informed decision. A postponement to a date within the six-month statutory period may be adjourned 'administratively' to a further date within the statutory period.[2] Applications to postpone must be made within the period of postponement and not after it has expired. The court must proceed towards a confiscation order if the prosecutor asks it to do so.[3]

---

[1] *R v Shergill* [1999] 2 All ER 485, [1999] 2 Cr App Rep (S) 341, CA; *R v Khan* [2000] 2 Cr App Rep (S) 76, CA; *R v Miranda* [2000] 2 Cr App Rep 164, [2000] 2 Cr App Rep (S) 347, CA; *R v Ross* [2001] EWCA Crim 560, [2001] 2 Cr App Rep (S) 484; *R v Lingham* [2001] 1 Cr App Rep (S) 158, CA; *R v Steele* [2001] 2 Cr App Rep (S) 178, CA; *R v Davies* [2001] EWCA Crim 3902, [2002] 1 WLR 1806, [2002] 2 Cr App Rep 332; *R v Copeland* [2002] Crim LR 507 NB; *R v Martin* [2001] EWCA Crim 2761, [2002] 2 Cr App Rep (S) 122; and see report and commentary in [2002] Crim LR 228. Mantell LJ said that 'because of the manner in which the legislation has been introduced this has proved a troublesome area of law to apply and productive of many appeals'.
[2] *R v Cole* (22 April 1998, unreported) 97/3929/X4.
[3] *R v Stuart and Bonnett* (1989) 11 Cr App Rep (S) 89, CA.

Burden of proof

1.32   The burden of proving the value of the proceeds of drug trafficking falls on the Crown to the criminal standard.[1] If the judge is satisfied by admissible evidence that any given sum is the proceeds of drug trafficking then there is no need for him to proceed by way of the assumptions in DTOA 1986, s 2(2). The judge at a confiscation hearing is entitled to rely on evidence which has already been given at trial, but the defendant must be given the opportunity to give evidence whether or not he has given evidence during the trial.[2]

---

[1] *R v Dickens* [1990] 2 QB 102, 91 Cr App Rep 164, CA.
[2] *R v Jenkins* (1990) 12 Cr App Rep (S) 582, CA.

1.33   If the judge in his discretion makes the assumption with regard to any item or group of items, that will amount to proof to the requisite standard if it is not shown to be incorrect by the defence on the balance of probabilities.[1] Whether a judge should make an assumption with regard to any item or group of items is a matter for his discretion, to be exercised when it is reasonable in all the circumstances to do so. The court must not make the assumption if it considers it unjust to do so in a particular defendant's case.[2] Once the court has decided the amount of benefit or proceeds of drug trafficking (the burden being on the Crown with the assistance of the statutory assumptions) it is for the defendant to satisfy the court that the 'amount that might be realised' is less than this amount to the civil standard.[3] The judge is not limited in determining the amount of a confiscation order by the allegations made by the Crown in their tendered statement. The judge is entitled to find that the amount of benefit is greater than that alleged by the prosecution.[4] Where a defendant has pleaded guilty in the magistrates' court to offences triable either way and is committed to the Crown Court for sentence that court does have the power to make a confiscation order.[5]

---

[1]   *R v Redbourne* [1993] 2 All ER 753, 14 Cr App Rep (S) 162, CA.
[2]   *R v Clark* [1997] 4 All ER 803, [1997] 2 Cr App Rep (S) 99, CA; see also recent cases on ECHR, para 1.39 ff.
[3]   *R v Illsemann* (1990) 12 Cr App Rep (S) 398, CA; *R v Comiskey* (1990) 93 Cr App Rep 227, CA; *R v Carroll* (1991) 13 Cr App Rep (S) 99, CA; and *R v Layode* (12 March 1993, unreported) No 91/3416/Z3.
[4]   *R v Atkinson* (1992) 14 Cr App Rep (S) 182, CA.
[5]   *R v Pope* [2002] UKHL 26, [2002] 3 All ER 889, 1 WLR 1966, thus overruling *R v Whellem* [2000] 1 Cr App Rep (S) 200, CA.

MONEY LAUNDERING LEGISLATION

1.34   The Criminal Justice Act 1993 inserted seven new sections into CJA 1988 entitled 'money laundering and other offences'.[1] Three more sections were introduced by the Proceeds of Crime Act 1995.[2] These give effect to European Directive 91/308/EEC[3] on the prevention of the use of the financial system for the purposes of money laundering. Thus, for example, CJA 1988, s 93A created an offence of 'assisting another to retain the benefit of criminal conduct'. European directives have been the driving force in the development of money laundering legislation. Directive 91/308/EEC gave rise to the original Money Laundering Regulations 1993,[4] which require those carrying on relevant financial businesses to check the identity of their customers, keep records of their transactions, maintain procedures for reporting suspicious transactions and provide training for their employees, both in those procedures and, more generally, in the recognition of money laundering transactions and the law relating to money laundering.

---

[1]   CJA 1988, ss 93A–93G.
[2]   CJA 1988, ss 93H–93J.
[3]   See Appendix 2.
[4]   SI 1993/1933; see Appendix 2.

1.35   The Second Money Laundering Directive[1] led to the Money Laundering Regulations 2001.[2] These supplement the Money Laundering Regulations 1993,[3] extending the definition of 'relevant financial business' to encompass those who operate a bureau de change; those who transmit money, or any representation of monetary value, by any means; and those who cash cheques which are made payable to customers. Thus many more businesses are brought within the system of regulation.

---

1 Directive 2001/97/EC, (amending Directive 91/308/EEC); see Appendix 2.
2 SI 2001/3641; see Appendix 2.
3 SI 1993/1933; see Appendix 2.

1.36 A further effect of the Second Money Laundering Directive,[1] is that many solicitors will become part of the 'regulated sector' for the purposes of PCA 2002, s 330. This section creates an offence of negligently failing to report a suspicion, which arises in the course of a business in the regulated sector, that another is involved in money laundering. It will now not be necessary for the prosecution to show that the defendant *actually* knew or suspected money laundering but only that on an objective basis he *ought to have known or suspected*. This new section applies to the 'regulated sector' as defined by PCA 2002, Sch 9 which largely replicates the Money Laundering Regulations 1993.[2] The position of solicitors has been unclear and their inclusion within the regulated sector is still not expressly set out in Sch 9. However, as firms have been expanding their roles such activities carried out by solicitors may now fall within Sch 9, para 1(2) (see para 8.19). The Government is required to implement the full terms of the Second Money Laundering Directive by 28 June 2003 and by then the definition of the regulated sector must include solicitors carrying on 'relevant financial business' within the meaning of the Directive. Article 6(3) of the Directive provides that a solicitor does not have to report suspicions where he is providing legal advice to clients or representing a client in legal proceedings. The Directive draws a distinction between solicitors carrying out transactional work such as financial, tax and commercial work and solicitors providing advice to clients on their legal position and representing them in legal proceedings. Solicitors 'assisting in the planning and execution of transactions for clients'[3] such as setting up trusts, giving tax advice, setting up and managing companies, managing client money or other assets and buying and selling property will be under a duty to report suspicions of money laundering. Failure to do so may lead to prosecution.[4]

---

1 Directive 2001/97/EC.
2 SI 1993/1933.
3 See Council Directive 91/308/EEC, Art 2a (as inserted by the Second Money Laundering Directive 2001/97/EC); see Appendix 2.
4 See Srivastava A 'Money Laundering: Focus on lawyers and the EU Directives' (2002) 152 NLJ 760.

1.37 The legal privilege which remains in other situations does not, of course, absolve the solicitor from criminal prosecution if he is himself taking part in money laundering activities or providing legal advice for money laundering purposes.

1.38   The Money Laundering Regulations 2001[1] also introduce a requirement for 'money service operators' to apply for registration with the Commissioners of Customs and Excise and provides Customs with extensive powers of entry, search and inspection of premises which they have reasonable cause to believe are being used in connection with 'money service business'.

---

[1]   SI 2001/3641.

1.38A   The effect of the new scheme will be that where a solicitor is carrying out 'transactional' work and he suspects money laundering he must report the suspicion. He should not tell his client as this would make him liable under the 'tipping off' provisions in s 333. The professional adviser in these circumstances would find it difficult to continue acting and would be well advised to seek guidance from the Law Society and the National Criminal Intelligence Service ('NCIS'). Where a solicitor is 'providing legal advice to a client or representing a client in legal proceedings' he need not report his suspicion. However in these circumstances the solicitor should be careful not to become involved in the money laundering himself.

THE EUROPEAN CONVENTION FOR THE PROTECTION OF HUMAN RIGHTS ('ECHR')

1.39   Powers of criminal confiscation under DTOA 1986 in general were approved by the European Court of Human Rights in 1995 in *Welch v UK*,[1] although it was held that the retrospective effect of DTOA 1986 in that individual case amounted to a breach of ECHR, Art 7. Since the Human Rights Act 1998 came into force the legislation has been tested against the ECHR by domestic courts. The Privy Council in *McIntosh v Lord Advocate*[2] had to consider whether the application of the statutory assumptions created a reverse persuasive burden on the defendant and was in breach of ECHR, Art 6(2). They held that since confiscation proceedings are civil and not criminal in nature, Art 6(2) was of no application.[3] Lord Bingham concluded that the result did not leave a defendant unprotected since confiscation proceedings were subject to the right to a fair trial guaranteed by ECHR, Art 6(1). He stressed that 'in making a confiscation order the court had to act with scrupulous fairness in making its assessment to ensure that the accused nor any third person suffered any injustice'.[4] It was emphasised that the reverse onus provisions may fall foul of ECHR, Art 6(1) depending on the facts of each particular case.

---

[1] *Welch v United Kingdom* (1995) 20 EHRR 247, [1996] Crim LR 276.
[2] *McIntosh v Lord Advocate* [2001] UKPC D1, [2001] 2 All ER 638, [2001] 3 WLR 107.
[3] ECHR, Art 6(1) applies 'in the determination of his civil rights and obligations' in addition to purely criminal matters. ECHR, Art 6(2) states that: 'Everyone charged with a criminal offence shall be presumed innocent until proved guilty according to law.'
[4] *McIntosh v Lord Advocate* [2001] 3 WLR 107, per Lord Bingham at 119C.

1.40 Lord Bingham suggested that it was only if—

'a significant discrepancy was shown between the property and the expenditure of the accused on the one hand and his "known sources of income" on the other that the court would think it right to make the extended benefit assumptions'

and unless 'the accounting details reveal such a discrepancy the prosecutor will not in practice apply for an order'.[1] What Lord Bingham appeared to be saying was that it was for the prosecution first of all to show that there was unexplained income and/or assets which only the defendant could explain. It was not unreasonable in those circumstances for him to explain where he had acquired the income/assets.

---

[1] *McIntosh v Lord Advocate* [2001] 3 WLR 107, per Lord Bingham at 121G–H.

1.41 *McIntosh* was followed by the House of Lords in *R v Benjafield*[1] where it was again held that a defendant against whom a confiscation order was sought was not 'charged with a criminal offence' and that therefore Art 6(2) of the Convention was of no application. The defendant was entitled to the benefit of the full protection of a fair hearing under Art 6(1). It was further held that the application of the statutory assumptions were not wider than necessary to achieve the legitimate aim in the public interest of depriving professional and habitual criminals of the proceeds of their criminal conduct and were not, in putting a persuasive burden on the defendant, disproportionate to the objective so as to be incompatible with the defendant's Convention rights. Lord Steyn emphasised that the judge administering the confiscation procedure had to stand back and decide whether there was any serious or real risk of injustice to the defendant.

---

[1] *R v Benjafield* [2002] UKHL 2, [2002] 2 WLR 235, and see 245, paras E–F.

1.42 The European Court of Human Rights in the case of *Phillips v United Kingdom*[1] scrutinised the legislation and the decision of the Court of Appeal in *Benjafield*. The Court held that the ECHR had not been

violated. For the majority, ECHR, Art 6(2) was not applicable to confiscation proceedings and that although Art 6(1) was applicable it had not been violated. They concluded that although the extended benefit assumptions were 'mandatory' to determine benefit, there were sufficient safeguards for a defendant. These included a judicial procedure with a public hearing, advance disclosure of the prosecution case, the opportunity for the defendant to adduce evidence, the fact that the court could only make an order in respect of property which might be realised and that the applicant could rebut the assumption if he could show that he had acquired the property other than through drug trafficking. The Court noted that the judge had a discretion to disapply the assumptions if there was a serious risk of injustice. The conclusion of the majority is set out at para 47 of the judgment and reads as follows—

> 'overall, therefore, the Court finds that the application to the applicant of the relevant provisions of DTA 1994 was confined within reasonable limits given the importance of what was at stake and that the rights of the defence were fully respected.'

It is worth noting that the minority took the view that ECHR, Art 6(2) did apply, but that policy factors were such as to justify the conclusion that the statutory presumptions are within reasonable limits. Doubtless the controversy surrounding the legality of the reverse onus provisions will continue, despite Lord Rooker's endorsement of the Proceeds of Crime Bill as Convention compatible, as required by the Human Rights Act 1998, s 19.[2]

---

[1]   (2001) 11 BHRC 280, [2001] Crim LR 817, Application Number 41087/98, 5 July 2001.

[2]   On 25 March 2002 Lord Rooker, when introducing the Second Reading in the House of Lords, said 'We have looked carefully at the Joint Committee's suggestion that civil recovery will amount to a criminal penalty under the ECHR. However, we continue to believe that a better view is that civil recovery is a civil remedy.'

BACKGROUND TO PCA 2002

1.43   The Government announced a commitment in the Queen's Speech at the opening of Parliament on 6 December 2000 that a Bill would be published to increase the powers against money laundering and make it easier to recover the proceeds of crime. The origins of the Bill are to be found in two main documents, which we now consider in turn.

Criminal assets

1.44 The Third Report of the Home Office Organised and International Crime Directorate Working Group on Confiscation,[1] entitled *Criminal Assets*, and published in November 1998, recommended radical extensions to the confiscation legislation as well as a national confiscation agency. It was a consultation document which sought responses by February 1999.

---

[1] This report is available at http://www.homeoffice.gov.uk/oicd/jcu/wgconf.htm.

Recovering the proceeds of crime

1.45 A report by the Performance and Innovation Unit of the Cabinet Office, entitled *Recovering the Proceeds of Crime*, was published in June 2000.[1] The Prime Minister had commissioned this Report in October 1998, though the report itself states that it was the product of nine months' study. In the introduction to the report, the Prime Minister wrote—

> '. . . this government is determined to create a fair and just society in which crime does not pay . . . . For too long we paid insufficient attention to the financial aspects of crime. We must remember that many criminals are motivated by money and profit. Leaving illegal assets in the hands of criminals damages society. First, these assets can be used to fund further criminal activity, leading to a cycle of crime that plagues communities. Second, arrest and conviction alone are not enough to clamp down on crime; they leave criminals free to return to their illegal enterprises, or even to continue their 'businesses' from prison. And third, it simply is not right in modern Britain that millions of law-abiding people work hard to earn a living, whilst a few live handsomely off the profits of crime. The undeserved trappings of success enjoyed by criminals are an affront to the hard-working majority . . . . The criminal justice system is not designed to take away from criminals the gains they have made from crime. Typically a court order is made to recover assets following under 1% of convictions. And the amounts recovered fall far short of those sought by the courts . . . . The conclusions of this report represent agreed government policy. Through implementing the recommendations in this report, we shall help turn the tide against criminals. We will deter people from crime by ensuring that criminals do not hang on to their unlawful gains. We will

enhance confidence in the law by demonstrating that nobody is beyond its reach. We will make it easier for courts to recover the proceeds of crime from convicted criminals. And we will return to society the assets that have been unlawfully taken. All this will need to be achieved in a way that respects civil liberties; we will ensure that is the case.'

---

[1] This report is available at http://www.cabinet-office.gov.uk/innovation/2000/crime/recovering.

1.46 The PIU Report concluded that a new Act was necessary because of 'anomalies in the [existing] legal regime' and because of 'significant deficiencies'[1] in its use. It highlighted the piecemeal nature of existing legislation, and pointed out that in the previous five years confiscation orders had been made in only 20% of drugs cases and a mere 0.3% of other crime cases. The collection rate was only 40% of the amounts ordered to be paid. The report therefore concluded that pursuit and recovery of criminal assets in the UK was failing to deliver the intended attack on the proceeds of crime. The aims of the new Act would be—

(1) to achieve a more strategic approach with joined up action from all relevant parts of the criminal justice system;
(2) a simpler and more robust legal regime including extended civil forfeiture power;
(3) greater efforts to stem the laundering of criminal assets;
(4) better trained and supported law enforcement officers;
(5) full use of existing tax powers;
(6) a higher international standard; and
(7) new structures to underpin these changes.

---

[1] PIU Report, para 1.5.

1.47 The PIU Report concluded by reaching 68 'conclusions' which form the basis of the Act.

THE PROCEEDS OF CRIME BILL

Draft Bill

1.48 The Proceeds of Crime Bill was first published, unusually, in draft form. The draft Bill was announced in the government's paper

'Criminal Justice: the Way Ahead', published in February 2001.[1] This stated the intention of the government as follows—

'We will deprive criminals of their assets.

3.214   Justice demands that we should stop criminals profiting from their crimes. Confiscating assets and preventing money laundering also reduces the incentives for crime, and removes an important source of finance for the continued operation and expansion of criminal enterprises.

3.215   We will ensure that powers to deprive criminals of their assets are used more extensively, so that criminals know that they face a greater likelihood of losing the proceeds of their crimes. A new assets recovery agency will be established to pursue the confiscation of criminal assets both at home and abroad. We will channel more of the resulting receipts into a fund for crime fighting and reduction, and into drugs prevention. We also plan to extend powers to seize drug related cash at frontiers to non-drug cases.

3.217   The government is improving the effectiveness of this partnership. It will provide £1.8 million of additional funding for the NCIS Economic Crime Unit each year for the next three years. New powers for the FSA in the Financial Services and Markets Act 2000 will improve the consistency with which banks report suspicious transactions. Future steps will include introducing a light touch regulatory regime for bureau de change and money transmission agents.'

[1]   Cm 5074.

1.49   Responses to the Draft Bill were requested before 29 May 2001. Those received are available on the Home Office website.[1]

[1]   http://www.homeoffice.gov.uk/atoz/consult_papers.htm.

Passage through Parliament

1.50   The Bill received its First Reading in the House of Commons on 18 October 2001 and its Second Reading on 30 October 2001. The House of Commons Standing Committee B examined the Bill in detail from 13 November 2001 to 5 February 2002. Bob Ainsworth MP, as Parliamentary Under Secretary for Anti-drugs Co-ordination and

Organised Crime, was responsible for steering the legislation through the House of Commons. The Report Stage took place on 26 and 27 February 2002. It was as the Bill was leaving the House of Commons in late February that an unsuccessful attempt was made to amend it by the introduction of a judicial discretion over the sale of the matrimonial home in England and Wales. Such a power is preserved in Scotland. The proposed amendment was defeated.

1.51   The Bill received its First Reading in the House of Lords on 28 February 2002, its Second Reading on 25 March 2002 and went into committee from 22 April 2002 until 27 May 2002. Report Stage was on 25 June 2002 and the Third Reading on 11 July 2002.

1.52   The House of Commons considered the Lords' amendments on 18 July 2002 and the House of Lords looked at the Commons' reasons on 22 July 2002. The Commons considered the Lords' reasons on 24 July 2002 and on that date the Act received Royal Assent.

Confiscation

1.53   In Committee in the House of Commons concerns were raised about the mandatory nature of the confiscation procedure. However, no amendments diluting this aspect of the legislation were passed in the Commons. In the House of Lords, when the Bill reached the Report Stage on 25 June 2002, several key amendments were passed including a power for the court not to proceed with confiscation where it found that there were 'exceptional circumstances' for not doing so. A new provision was added by the Lords giving protection to the defendant's unsecured creditors.

1.54   These two amendments did not survive the return of the Bill to the House of Commons on 18 and 24 July although other, mainly Government, amendments did. Criticism was made in the Lords of the way in which the Bill passed through Parliament with so many government amendments coming so late in the day. Lord Goodhart said during the Report Stage in the House of Lords that Parliament was—

> '. . . getting back to the bad old days of two or three years ago, when major Bills kept appearing with hundreds of government amendments. That has happened again on this occasion. It suggests serious overload on parliamentary counsel. I hope that we shall not see that happening again.'[1]

---

[1]   HL Report Stage, 25 June 2002, col 1207.

1.55 The confiscation provisions applicable in criminal cases were consolidated and extended by the Bill. The 'criminal lifestyle' confiscation procedure is triggered upon conviction if the benefit is more than £5,000 and where the offences constitute conduct forming part of a course of criminal activity or where one offence is committed over a period of at least six months. It is also triggered where the defendant is convicted of an offence listed in Sch 2 (or Schs 4 and 5 for Scotland and Northern Ireland respectively) whatever the benefit figure.

1.56 One of the difficulties which will arise is that in practice a large proportion of those convicted of offences involving a benefit will be caught by the criminal lifestyle confiscation procedure. There will be a proliferation of confiscation work in the Crown Court. Orders in excess of £1m will lead to sentences of up to ten years in default in addition to the sentence for the offence. Those convicted will frequently be required to show that all property they hold at the time of conviction and any property they have received or spent in the six years prior to the start of the proceedings is not the proceeds of criminal conduct. It is important to remember how unfair this type of legislation can be in practice and how difficult it is for the defendant to deal with confiscation proceedings because—

   (1) the benefit figure arrived at by the court is often not the defendant's profits of or proceeds from crime;

   (2) the realisable property figure is frequently an amount, in reality, unavailable to the defendant either because of the 'gift' provisions or because of the way that property is valued;

   (3) a defendant in practice often finds it difficult to prove the legitimacy of six years' worth of receipts and spending; and

   (4) the defendant is required to prove a negative (ie that he does not have money to pay the amount of the benefit). The burden is on the defendant to do this once benefit is established. If he fails then the confiscation order will be for the full amount of benefit.

1.57 A simplified version of the facts in the case of *R v Sissen*[1] provides a good example. The defendant was convicted of four counts of smuggling nine rare parrots, for which he paid £59,000. The authorities seized the parrots on his arrest. His sentence was 18 months' imprisonment. His simple 'benefit' was assessed at £59,000.[2] This in no real sense could be said to be his proceeds of or profits from the crime. He had in fact lost £59,000, which he used to pay for the parrots. The authorities had seized them and they were to be forfeited. In addition, and because of the extended benefit provisions, the defendant was required to show that all his receipts for the previous six years were legitimate. He was also required to show that all property he currently held was legitimate whenever acquired. He had been a breeder of parrots for 35 years. He is dyslexic and had kept poor records.

---

[1]   *R v Sissen* [2001] 1 WLR 902. The conviction was unsuccessfully appealed on a jurisdictional point.
[2]   On the basis of the judgment in *R v Smith (David)* [2001] UKHL 68, [2002] 1 All ER 366, [2002] 1 WLR 55.

1.58   The defendant could avoid paying the extended benefit figure if he proved the legitimacy of all his current assets (including his parrots) and six years' worth of receipts. He claimed to have bred most of his parrots and purchased the rest. For the defendant to prove what he must was on any view very difficult. The trial judge ruled that the six years' worth of spending was not benefit but found that 60% of the value of the remaining parrots was. This figure was £100,000. A confiscation order for £150,000 was made which had to be met out of the legitimately held assets.

1.59   If a criminal prosecution fails or is felt to be inappropriate then civil recovery under PCA 2002, Pt 5 can take place. Not only does this have the lower civil standard of proof, but on the face of the Act the particular offence need not be specified: simply that the property is or represents property obtained through unlawful conduct.

1.60   If there is any property left it may fall to be taxed under PCA 2002, Pt 6 which gives the Director the powers of the Inland Revenue but with the important difference that there is no need to establish the source of income or assets before taxing them.

PCA 2002

1.61   The main changes brought in by the new Act are as follows: It—
    (1)   consolidates the existing legislation;
    (2)   extends the powers of the criminal courts to make confiscation orders;
    (3)   brings within the Crown Court powers formerly exercised by the High Court and the magistrates' courts;
    (4)   introduces enhanced post-conviction confiscation powers;
    (5)   establishes a national Assets Recovery Agency (ARA);

(6) introduces new and stricter money laundering offences involving negligence (creating a criminal offence of failing to make a disclosure where there are reasonable grounds for knowing or suspecting that another is engaged in money laundering); and

(7) introduces civil proceedings in the High Court allowing for the forfeiture of assets if it can be shown on the balance of probabilities that there are 'reasonable grounds' for 'suspecting' that the assets to be forfeited are the proceeds of, or to be used in, criminal activities.

1.62 The Act is in 12 parts which are briefly summarised at paras 1.63–1.89.

Part 1: Assets Recovery Agency

1.63 PCA 2002 establishes a national Assets Recovery Agency ('ARA'). The Director is given wide-ranging powers and duties (including establishing a system for the accreditation of financial investigators and giving advice and assistance to the Home Secretary).

Parts 2, 3 and 4: Confiscation in England and Wales, Scotland and Northern Ireland

1.64 These Parts consolidate earlier legislation on restraint, confiscation, receivership and related matters. Parts 3 (Scotland) and 4 (Northern Ireland) mirror Pt 2 to a great extent. Part 2, relating to England and Wales, brings within the Crown Court powers formerly exercised by the High Court and the magistrates' courts (though it leaves enforcement in the hands of magistrates' courts).

1.65 Under s 6, where a defendant is convicted in the Crown Court of any offence, or is committed from the magistrates' court under s 70 with a view to a confiscation order being considered, and either the Director of the ARA asks the court to proceed or the court believes it appropriate to do so, the court must—

(1) decide whether the defendant has a 'criminal lifestyle';
(2) if so, it must decide whether he has benefited from his 'general criminal conduct';
(3) if not, it must decide whether he has benefited from his 'particular criminal conduct'.

1.66 The court then decides the recoverable amount and makes a confiscation order. These questions are decided only on a balance of probabilities. Once the court has decided that the defendant has a 'criminal lifestyle' a number of assumptions come into play. It will not be difficult for the court to find a criminal lifestyle: either the defendant must have been convicted of one of an eclectic list of offences specified in Sch 2, which may be amended by the Home Secretary (Schs 4 and 5 apply in Scotland and Northern Ireland respectively), *or* the offence of which he has been convicted 'constitutes conduct forming part of a course of criminal activity' *or* 'it is an offence committed over a period of at least six months and the defendant has benefited from the conduct which constitutes the offence'. Conduct forms part of a course of criminal activity if the defendant has benefited from the conduct and either was convicted of three or more such offences in the proceedings or has two separate convictions in the previous six years of offences constituting conduct from which he has benefited. At present, where there is conduct over at least six months or where there has been a course of criminal activity, the relevant benefit must be of not less than £5,000 for there to be a 'criminal lifestyle'.

Part 5: Civil recovery of the proceeds of unlawful conduct

1.67   Part 5 introduces civil proceedings in the High Court (and in the Court of Session in Scotland) allowing for the forfeiture of assets if it can be shown on the balance of probabilities that the assets to be forfeited are the proceeds of unlawful conduct. These proceedings will be against property which has been obtained through unlawful conduct or property which represents property obtained through unlawful conduct. PCA 2002 also broadens DTA 1994, Pt II providing for the seizure of cash which is reasonably suspected of having been obtained through unlawful conduct or of being intended for use in such conduct, and for the forfeiture of such cash in proceedings before a magistrates' court, sheriff or justice of the peace. This scheme for the recovery of cash in summary proceedings is currently subject to a consultation exercise, as required by s 292(3). The proposed Code of Practice explains the procedure as well as the standard forms which will be used in applications for a search warrant under s 289.

Part 6: Revenue functions

1.68   Part 6 empowers the Director of the ARA to exercise functions of the Inland Revenue in relation to income, gains and profits arising from or accruing as a result of criminal conduct. The Government claims that the Director will be more efficient than the Revenue in focusing on collecting tax from those who have gained from unlawful conduct. The Director has the advantage over the Revenue that he will not have to specify or prove the source of income which he taxes.

Part 7: Money laundering

1.69 PCA 2002 reproduces much of the current money laundering regime but also extends it, introducing most notably a new offence involving negligence for the regulated sector. Solicitors will find themselves within the definition of the regulated sector when the Second Money Laundering Directive[1] is brought into effect. The deadline for this is June 2003 but it may be earlier. This will mean that solicitors providing tax and/or trust advice and those managing or dealing in property or assets will be required to report suspicions under s 330.

---

[1]   Directive 2001/97/EC.

1.70 A person is guilty of an offence if he conceals, disguises, converts, transfers, or removes criminal property (s 327). A person commits an offence if he enters into or 'becomes concerned in an arrangement' which he knows or suspects facilitates the acquisition, retention, use or control of criminal property by or behalf of another person (s 328). A person also commits an offence if he acquires, uses or possesses criminal property. PCA 2002 also creates three separate criminal offences of failing to make a disclosure where there are reasonable grounds for knowing or suspecting that another is engaged in money laundering, which apply to persons working in the regulated sector, nominated officers in the regulated sector and other nominated officers (ss 330–332). The ARA will not need to link the property to a specific criminal offence: it will only be necessary to prove that the property was 'criminal property' defined to include property which represents a person's benefit from criminal conduct (in whole or in part and whether directly or indirectly).

1.71 The main offences are not committed where a person has made an authorised disclosure and he has the appropriate consent. Part 7 deals explicitly with the issue of consent and with protected and authorised disclosure to 'NCIS'.

Part 8: Investigations

1.72 Part 8 sets out a series of orders which may be obtained from the courts for investigations into money laundering or for the purposes of civil recovery or of confiscation following criminal conviction. These are production orders, search warrants, disclosure orders, customer information orders and account monitoring orders.

Part 9: Insolvency

1.73 Part 9 deals with the relationship between confiscation and insolvency proceedings.

Part 10: Information

1.74 Part 10 provides for the disclosure of information to and by the Director of ARA and the Scottish ministers. It also allows the exchange of information between the Scottish ministers and the Lord Advocate.

Part 11: Co-operation

1.75 Part 11 provides for co-operation in investigation and enforcement between the jurisdictions of the UK and with overseas authorities.

Part 12: Miscellaneous and general

1.76 Finally, Pt 12 deals with miscellaneous matters, most notably the use of pseudonyms for the protection of staff of the ARA and Scottish ministers.

Implementation

1.77 The provisional date for the Act to come into force is February 2003. However, the provisions relating to the recovery of cash in summary proceedings[1] and money laundering[2] have provisional commencement dates in December 2002. The Second Money Laundering Directive[3] which will have the effect of including solicitors in the 'regulated sector' for the purposes of s 330 is expected to be implemented by June 2003.

---

[1] Part 5, Ch 3.
[2] Part 7.
[3] Directive 2001/97/EC.

1.78 The post of Director of the ARA was advertised in early August.

1.79 As well as the consultation papers already mentioned above, a number of other Codes are out to consultation. In Scotland, under s 293 the Scottish ministers are required to 'make' a Code of Practice in connection with the exercise by constables of their powers of search contained in s 289.[1] There is a similar duty on the Secretary of State contained in s 292.

---

[1] http://www.scotland.gov.uk/pages/default.aspx contains the consultation for the Scottish Code of Practice under s 293.

1.80   Section 339 provides that the Secretary of State 'may by order' prescribe the 'form and manner in which a disclosure under ss 330, 331, 332 or 338 must be made'.[1] The Code of Practice required by s 377 to define the functions of the Director of the ARA, members of staff of the Agency, accredited financial investigators, constables and customs officers will go out to consultation at some time in the autumn.

---

[1]   http://www.homeoffice.gov.uk/atoz/consult_papers.htm contains the consultations for the Code of Practice under s 292 and the prescribed form for the making of suspicious transaction reports as required under the money laundering provisions.

CONCLUSION

1.81   Under the existing legal system the large number of different statutes and procedures has caused difficulty. The drugs confiscation laws originally enacted in 1986 have been amended on a number of occasions, as has CJA 1988 for non-drugs-related cases. Each new Act brought with it new rules of procedure (such as the necessity or otherwise of serving a notice in the proper form) and more substantial amendments. Clearly, the new Act is intended to unify and thereby simplify the procedures. However, PCA 2002 contains no express transitional provisions, so there is great danger that existing problems concerning which statute should apply will persist.

2 Assets Recovery Agency

BACKGROUND

2.1 Key to the success of the Proceeds of Crime Act 2002 ('PCA 2002') will be the effectiveness of the ARA. Originally conceived of in the PIU Report as a National Confiscation Agency in order to strengthen the criminal justice system's fight against crime, by the time the draft Bill was published it had become an 'Assets Recovery Agency' created by what are now PCA 2002, Pt 1 (ss 1–5) and Sch 1. The Agency has been sceptically compared to the Child Support Agency. The PIU Report identified annual costs of £20m for the implementation of the conclusion of the Report. The sceptics will be watching the costs involved in setting up and maintaining the new agency. It is perhaps a shame that the functions of the Director are not to be carried out by a central prosecution agency such as the CPS. Their position appears weakened every time that a new agency is set up to carry out 'special' tasks.

The Agency and its Director (s 1 and Sch 1)

2.2 Section 1 provides for the creation of the ARA, headed by a Director appointed by the Secretary of State. The Secretary of State will set the period of the Director's tenure (see Sch 1) and has the power to remove a Director if unfit or unable to carry out the functions of the position. The Explanatory Notes explain that in practice the functions of the Secretary of State relating to the Agency will be carried out by the Home Secretary, in consultation with the Secretary of State for Northern Ireland and the Scottish ministers (for the Director's revenue functions in Scotland), as necessary.[1]

---

[1] Explanatory Notes, para 11.

2.3 The constitutional position of the Director was much discussed: whether he should be a civil servant (as was finally decided) or simply specifically excluded from the House of Commons. Section 1(3) makes clear that he is a corporation sole and as such has legal personality. Section 1(4) enables the Director (in his capacity as office-holder) to employ staff to assist him (or her) in carrying out his functions, and to enter into contractual arrangements for the provision of the ARA's services. The Director as a civil servant must obtain the approval of the Minister for the Civil Service as to the number of staff he appoints. The staff of the ARA will include a deputy Director to carry out the Director's role in his or her absence and a senior official with responsibility for the exercise of the Director's functions in Northern Ireland.[1] Bob Ainsworth explained in Committee Stage in the House of Commons that the senior official for Northern Ireland would be appointed following consultation by the Director with the Secretary of State for Northern Ireland, although this requirement has never been expressed in the Bill or Act.[2] The Government estimated at the time a staff of 100.[3] Section 1(6) enables the Director to delegate the exercise of his functions to his staff and to others working on a contractual basis for him.[4]

---

[1]   Schedule 1, para 3.

[2]   HC SC B, 13 November 2001, col 8.

[3]   HC Debates, 30 October 2001, col 776 (Mr Kidney); interestingly the advertisement for the Director of the ARA published in July 2002 suggested a staff of between 150 and 200.

[4]   Read strictly this section does not prevent the Director delegating powers to the most junior staff.

2.4   Schedule 1, para 5 provides for the funding of the ARA. Schedule 1, paras 6–7 require the Director to draft annual plans for the ARA which must be approved by the Secretary of State and to report to Parliament on the activity and financial management of the Agency. These reports are to be published. Originally Sch 1 had specified that the Director could not be a serving MP or member of the Northern Ireland Assembly, whilst he was the holder of the post. This was no longer required once it was established during Committee Stage in the House of Lords that the Director will be a civil servant and therefore automatically barred from standing for Parliament.

Director's functions: general (s 2)

2.5   Section 2 grants the Director wide powers to 'exercise his functions in the way which he considers is best calculated to contribute to the reduction of crime', subject to the requirement that he has regard to his current annual plan as approved by the Secretary of State (s 2(2)(b)) and to any guidance given to him by the Secretary of State (s 2(5)). Section 2(6) indicates that this guidance 'must indicate that the reduction of crime is in general best secured by means of criminal investigations and criminal proceedings'. This is an interesting statement and implies that the Director should consider criminal over civil recovery proceedings. It is a shame this hierarchy has not been more clearly set out in the Act.

2.6 Section 2(3) empowers the Director to carry out investigations, and take any other steps, which he considers appropriate for facilitating, or incidental or conducive to, the exercise of his functions.

Accreditation and training (s 3)

2.7 The Director must implement a system of accreditation and training for the financial investigators, some of whom will be employed by the ARA. This is an innovative provision. Will the ARA keep the best of those it trains or lose them to the private sector?

Co-operation (s 4)

2.8 Section 4 requires co-operation between the Director and other persons with investigation functions, prosecution functions or other functions relating to crime in the exercise of their respective functions under the Act. Through the Explanatory Notes the Government explained that this is intended to apply to police officers, officers of HM Customs & Excise and members of the Crown Prosecution Service (CPS) and NCIS.[1] However, a strict reading of the wording would seem to encompass courts, requiring them to co-operate with the Director in some administrative or quasi-judicial way.[2] Surely this is sloppy drafting and will not be read strictly by the courts! Concern has been expressed as to how the ARA will share work and interact with the CPS, in particular whether the possibility of civil recovery would effect the decision of law enforcement agencies to continue with a criminal investigation. Lord Lloyd of Berwick feared duplication of work and general confusion.[3] To counter these concerns Bob Ainsworth explained in the House of Commons that a memorandum of understanding will follow the Act, defining the borders of responsibility of the different agencies. He said—

> 'We are looking to the agency to provide the sort of expertise that will be necessary to use some of the powers, to take over the complicated confiscation cases that will be too much for individual crown prosecution services or other law enforcement agencies, and to operate civil recovery and other powers which will be exclusive to the agency.[4]

It is disappointing that this Memorandum of Understanding has not yet been published and we can only rely on the words of ministers that the independence of the CPS will be maintained.[5]

---

[1] Explanatory notes, para 19.

[2] This fault was pointed out by retired High Court judge Sir Edwin Jowitt in his response to the consultation stage of the draft Bill. The document Sir Edwin produced was endorsed by the Lord Chief Justice and by Lord Justice Rose, the Vice-President of the Court of Appeal (Criminal Division).

3 HL 2R, 25 March 2002, col 46.
4 HC Debates, 18 July 2002, cols 481 and 482.
5 HL Committee Stage, 22 April 2002, col 33 (Lord Rooker).

Advice and assistance (s 5)

2.9 The Director is required to give such advice and assistance to the Secretary of State as is reasonably required for the operation of the Act and the reduction of crime. The Explanatory Notes suggest that the Director might, for example, if required to do so, propose amendments to the Government's strategy and targets for recovering the proceeds of crime. He might also be required to advise and assist the Secretary of State on matters connected with his own functions.[1]

1 Explanatory notes, para 20.

3 Confiscation: England and Wales

INTRODUCTION

3.1   The Proceeds of Crime Act 2002 ('PCA 2002'), Pt 2 (ss 6–91) deals
with confiscation orders, restraint orders and their enforcement. The
Act consolidates and extends the confiscation scheme which
presently exists and which is described in the Introduction to this
book. It brings together in one statute many of the concepts contained
in the present drug and non-drug legislation. For example, the
extended benefit assumptions in CJA 1988, s 72AA and DTA 1994,
s 4 become 'benefit from general criminal conduct' from a 'criminal
lifestyle' under the new Act. It also transfers to the Crown Court many
of the powers formerly exercised by the High Court such as restraint,
the appointment of receivers and reconsideration. Much controversy
has surrounded the extension of the confiscation scheme for those
who lead a 'criminal lifestyle' and the survival of the reverse onus
provisions of the earlier legislation. Recent case law on this topic is
discussed at paras 1.57, 1.58.

CONFISCATION ORDERS

Making of order (s 6)

3.2   The Crown Court procedure for the making of an order is set out in
s 6. Confiscation proceedings will happen if two conditions are
satisfied. First, the defendant must have been convicted of an offence
or offences in the Crown Court or committed from the magistrates'
court for sentence or for sentence and confiscation (under a new
procedure set out in s 70).[1] Secondly, the prosecutor or Director must
ask the court to proceed, or the court must think it appropriate to do
so. If these conditions are satisfied the court must proceed to consider
whether a confiscation order should be made.

34

[1] An amendment was proposed in Committee Stage in the House of Commons to limit the operation of this section to matters where conviction was in the Crown Court. This amendment was withdrawn. See s 70 for the provision dealing with committals to the Crown Court by the magistrates' court.

3.3 The Crown Court alone in England and Wales will have the power to make confiscation orders following criminal proceedings. The court has no discretion at this stage if asked to proceed by the prosecution. This was the cause of much debate in Committee Stage in both Houses of Parliament, with a number of amendments being proposed. The concern was that draconian confiscation powers should be mitigated by judicial discretion. Typical of those who argued for such a position was Mr Grieve, a Conservative member of the House of Commons Select Committee, who said during discussion on this topic that 'the normal safeguard that a sensible Parliament introduces is a judicial discretion'.[1]

[1] HC Debates, 18 July 2002, col 488.

3.4 Interestingly the Bill originally included a discretion in its provisions for confiscation in Scotland because, the government explained, Scotland had no history of mandatory confiscation and its procedure had been perceived to be more successful than that in England and Wales. When Opposition members pointed out the inconsistency, the Government, rather than introducing a discretionary power throughout the UK, removed the discretion in Scotland, thus bringing the Scottish provisions in line with those for England, Wales and Northern Ireland.

3.5 In the House of Lords an attempt was made to make the procedure discretionary by the introduction of an amendment allowing the court not to proceed with the confiscation process where it found 'exceptional circumstances'. This amendment was defeated when the Bill returned to the House of Commons by a division of 260 to 149.[1] Bob Ainsworth maintained the Government's line that the Director and the prosecuting authorities would be under a duty to act reasonably and would not mount hearings for inappropriate cases.[1] This complacent attitude has worried those who are also conscious of the reluctance of the High Court to allow judicial reviews of prosecutorial decisions.[2]

[1] HC Debates, 18 July 2002, col 501.
[2] See *R v DPP, ex p Kebilene* [2000] 2 AC 326, [1999] 4 All ER 801, HL.

3.6 The danger of private prosecutors improperly asking the court to make an assessment was also highlighted. In response, Lord Goldsmith simply cited the power of the DPP to take over private prosecutions as a bulwark to this.[1]

---

[1]   HL Committee Stage, 22 April 2002, col 45.

3.7   Once the court has been asked to proceed it must consider whether the defendant has a 'criminal lifestyle'.[1] This choice of words is highly contentious since people can live with the stereotypical trappings of a criminal lifestyle without committing any offence. Alternative phrases such as, 'an habitual criminal for gain' and 'a person living off, or from, the proceeds of crime' were suggested in Committee Stage in the House of Commons. If the court decides that the defendant has a criminal lifestyle, then it must consider whether he has benefited from his general criminal conduct. If it decides that he does not have a criminal lifestyle, the court must decide whether the defendant has benefited from the particular criminal conduct for which he has been convicted.

---

[1]   Defined in s 75.

3.8   Throughout the debate in Parliament complaint was made that the wording of the Act requires the court to come to a definite conclusion as to whether the defendant has or does not have a criminal lifestyle. What if the evidence is not sufficiently clear? Surely it would have been better to phrase the section so that where the court was not satisfied that there was a criminal lifestyle it would then automatically go on to look at benefit from particular criminal conduct. As the wording stands there is a danger, at least in theory, of some cases falling between the two stools.[1]

---

[1]   See, for example, pp 5–6 of a document produced by retired High Court judge Sir Edwin Jowitt as his response to the consultation stage of the draft Bill. This document was endorsed by the Lord Chief Justice and by Lord Justice Rose, the Vice-President of the Court of Appeal (Criminal Division). It may be found on the Home Office website.

3.9   If there is benefit from general conduct or from the particular offence, the court must decide the recoverable amount and make a confiscation order in that sum. The duty of the court to calculate the recoverable amount becomes a discretionary power if it believes that any victim of the criminal conduct has instituted or intends to institute civil proceedings for recovery for loss, injury or damage.

3.10   The court must decide these questions on a balance of probabilities only. The original clause 6 stated that the standard was 'the standard applicable in civil proceedings'. The Government decided to clarify this by specifying the balance of probabilities. However, neither wording will satisfy critics concerned about the use of civil standards of proof in what many see as criminal proceedings.

3.11   If the defendant has absconded different provisions apply.[1]

---
[1]   See s 27.

Recoverable amount, defendant's benefit and available amount (ss 7–9)

3.12   PCA 2002, ss 7–9 should be read together in order to understand how the amount of the confiscation order is to be calculated. The recoverable amount is a sum equal to the benefit obtained by the defendant or the amount available to the defendant at the time of the assessment, whichever is the lower. This replicates the existing law and sadly may result in continuation of existing problems.[1]

---
[1]   For example, the conflicting priorities of confiscation orders and property adjustment orders under the Matrimonial Causes Act 1973; see *Commrs of Customs and Excise Comrs v A* [2002] EWCA Civ 1039, [2002] All ER (D) 312 (Jul).

3.13   'Benefit' is defined in s 76(4). In calculating the defendant's benefit, the court must take account of conduct occurring, and property obtained, up to the time it makes its decision. If the court has found there to be a criminal lifestyle, the provisions of s 10 apply in calculating the benefit figure. If there is no criminal lifestyle the benefit figure will be the amount of benefit from the particular criminal conduct.

3.14   Section 8 states that where the defendant has previously had a confiscation order made against him under PCA 2002 or other listed statutory provisions under which his benefit from general criminal conduct was assessed, that figure must be taken as final for the value of his benefit up to the date of that previous confiscation order. The court must deduct that figure specified as the benefit from general criminal conduct under a previous order from the benefit figure in the new proceedings. The same applies where there are a number of previous orders, save that sums must not be deducted twice. This means that where the benefit under an earlier order has been deducted in calculating a later order it must not be deducted again for the purposes of the present order. In relation to orders made under previous legislation, references here to general criminal conduct mean conduct in respect of which a court was required or entitled to make one or more assumptions for the purpose of assessing the defendant's benefit (s 8(7)).

3.15   The available amount (equivalent to the term 'the amount that might be realised' in the previous legislation) is defined in s 9 as the total of the values (at the time the order is made) of all the free property then held by the defendant minus those amounts payable in pursuance of obligations that have priority over the confiscation order (eg pre-existing fines and other orders of the court and preferential debts within the meaning of the Insolvency Act 1986, s 386), plus the total value of all 'tainted gifts' as defined in s 77.

3.16   There was debate at Committee Stage in both Houses as to whether the law could be drafted so as to protect honest tradesmen and shopkeepers who had given credit to a defendant. An amendment to protect unsecured creditors was passed in the House of Lords. As Lord Goodhart said—

> 'In the case of the builder that we have suggested, the Government are claiming money twice because the state gets the improved value of the defendant's building without having to pay for the cost of the improvement. That is clearly double counting.'[1]

---

[1]   HL Report Stage, 25 June 2002, col 1237.

3.17   However, the amendment was overturned in the Commons in a division of 253 to 136.[1] The Government had earlier agreed in the House of Commons that nothing should be done to encourage the creation by defendants of elaborate schemes to keep monies away from the enforcement agencies.[2] They were not prepared to alter their view in light of the Lords' amendment.

---

[1]   HC Debates, 18 July 2002, col 525.
[2]   HC SC B, 20 November 2001, cols 169–194.

3.18   The recoverable amount is 'an amount equal to the defendant's benefit from the conduct concerned' (s 7(1)). Section 7(2) then places the burden on the defendant to show that the available amount is less than the benefit figure. Where the court decides the available amount it must include a statement of its findings within the confiscation order (s 7(5)). The Explanatory Notes explain that this provision is intended to assist enforcement by alerting the enforcing authorities to the property available for confiscation. [1]

---

[1]   Explanatory Notes, para 25.

3.19   If the available amount is nil, an order for a nominal amount should be made. The court also takes into account any action or anticipated action by any victim of the criminal conduct. Where the court believes that any victim 'has at any time started or intends to start proceedings against the defendant' (s 6(6)) the court has a discretion not to order the defendant to pay the recoverable amount.

Assumptions to be made in case of criminal lifestyle (s 10)

3.20 This section broadly reflects existing law[1] although the statutory assumptions in PCA 2002 can be triggered by one offence rather than the two 'qualifying offences' required under CJA 1988.[2] PCA 2002 requires the court to decide whether a defendant has a 'criminal lifestyle' as a trigger for it to make the assumptions about benefit from general criminal conduct. 'Criminal lifestyle' is defined in PCA 2002, s 75. Assumptions continue to cause much debate. The new Act does not use Lord Woolf's test in the Privy Council case of *A-G of Hong Kong v Lee Kwong-Kut*,[3] which incorporated a minimum test for the application of assumptions. The court may refuse to make the assumption, but only where it is shown to be incorrect or where there would be a serious risk of injustice if it were made (s 10(6)).

---

[1] See CJA 1988, s 72AA and DTA 1994, s 4.
[2] CJA 1988, s 72AA(1)(c).
[3] [1993] AC 951, [1993] 3 All ER 939, PC.

3.21 The assumptions contained in CJA 1988[1] and DTA 1994[2] have survived challenges in the Court of Appeal, the House of Lords, the Privy Council and the European Court of Human Rights, but as David Thomas comments, 'doubtless the whole matter will be re-litigated when the "criminal lifestyle" provisions of the Proceeds of Crime [Act] come into force'.[3]

---

[1] Section 72AA.
[2] Section 4.
[3] [2002] Crim LR 337.

3.22 If the court finds there to be a criminal lifestyle it must make the following four assumptions in deciding whether the defendant has benefited and to what extent—
   (1) any property transferred to the defendant at any time after the relevant date was obtained by him as a result of his general criminal conduct and was obtained at the earliest time he appears to have held it;
   (2) any property held by the defendant at any time after the date of conviction was obtained by him as a result of his general criminal conduct and was obtained at the earliest time he appears to have held it;
   (3) any expenditure incurred by the defendant at any time after the relevant date was met from property obtained by him as a result of his general criminal conduct; and
   (4) any property the court assesses under the above three assumptions is assumed to have been obtained free from other interests in it.

3.23   The court must not make these assumptions if they are shown by the defendant to be incorrect on a balance of probabilities or if the defendant shows on the balance of probabilities that there is a serious risk of injustice in making them (s 10(6)). The meaning of 'serious risk of injustice' is somewhat unclear. However, the principles set out in the cases of *McIntosh*[1] and *Benjafield*[2] described in the Introduction will apply. Section 10 does not state that 'injustice' refers only to injustice to the defendant. In Committee in the House of Commons Mr Ian Lucas (Labour) and Mr Nicholas Hawkins (Conservative) both saw it as being wider than that. Mr Hawkins suggested it be read to cover injustice to, for example, the disabled child of a defendant where money that would otherwise be subject to the assumptions is being used to provide medical care.[3]

[1]   [2001] UKPC D1, [2001] 2 All ER 638, [2001] 3 WLR 107.
[2]   [2002] UKHL 2, [2002] 1 All ER 815, [2002] 2 WLR 235.
[3]   HC SC B, 20 November 2001, col 208.

3.24   The court must give reasons for not applying any assumption. In the House of Lords Lord Goodhart suggested that a court should give reasons whichever way it decides.[1] Good practice will presumably lead to the giving of reasons in most cases.

[1]   HL SC, 22 April 2002, col 66.

3.25   The 'relevant date' for these purposes is the date six years before the day the earliest set of proceedings currently before the court were commenced against the defendant. Property held by the defendant at the relevant time is affected no matter how long ago it was obtained. The point was made at Committee Stage in the House of Commons that people generally keep records for, at most, the seven-year period required by the Inland Revenue. Requiring the defendant to prove to the court the provenance of property purchased many years ago but still held is an onerous burden indeed. The Government's response, voiced by Mr Ainsworth, was—

> 'The convicted criminal will have to show the court, on the balance of probabilities, that the assets are not the proceeds of crime, but he will not have to show proof of a particular transaction from 25 years ago . . . . If the criminal can show that, on the balance of probabilities, it would be a serious injustice if [it] was assumed that his property was the proceeds of crime—or show that, again on the balance of probabilities, it is not the proceeds of crime, the property will not be removed.'[1]

[1]   HC SC B, 22 November 2001, cols 239–240.

3.26 This is only partly correct. When the statutory assumptions are made a defendant will have to show the legality of any property held by him after the date of conviction whenever he acquired the property, even if it was 25 years ago. This would be the case unless the court decided not to make the assumption on the grounds that 'there would be a serious risk of injustice if the assumption were made' (s 10(6)(b)). In practice if a defendant holds property at the time of a confiscation hearing the court is likely to require him to show its legality whenever he obtained it.

3.27 If an earlier confiscation order has been made against the defendant, the relevant day is the date when the defendant's benefit was calculated for the purposes of the last confiscation order. This avoids double recovery. Where there have been convictions on different dates in the proceedings before the court the date of conviction for the purposes of Pt 2 of the Act is the latest.

Time for payment (s 11)

3.28 Payment of the sum specified is due immediately, but the if the defendant shows he needs time to pay the court may specify a period for payment of up to six months. The court may extend the period to a maximum of twelve months from the date of the order if it believes there are exceptional circumstances. Application for extension should be made (although not necessarily heard) within the specified six months. There is no provision for payment by instalment.

Interest on unpaid sums (s 12)

3.29 If the sum due is not paid on time, without an authorised extension, interest accrues as on a civil debt under the Judgments Act 1838, s 17. The payment of interest is mandatory in all cases. Interest charged can be taken into account in s 22 reconsideration.[1] Interest is not payable for a period in which a court is considering an application for an extension of time to pay.

---

[1] That this is the Government's intention was confirmed by Mr Ainsworth, HC SC B, 22 November, col 263.

3.30 This represents a change from the present legislation, which refers to a 'liability' to pay interest. It has been suggested that this may mean that there is a discretion as to whether or not interest is added to a particular unpaid order. Any such doubts are removed by s 10 which makes it clear that if an order is not paid immediately interest 'must' be paid.

Effect of order on court's other powers (s 13)

3.31   Section 13 upholds the basic proportionality principle of English sentencing law, namely that— the appropriate sentence should not be affected by the confiscation order. However the court should take the amount of the confiscation order into account before it imposes a fine or compensation order (s 13(2), (3)). If the court makes both a confiscation order and a compensation order and believes that the defendant will not have sufficient means to satisfy both, the court must direct that whatever amount of the compensation order it believes will not be recoverable should be paid out of the sum recovered under the confiscation order. It is curious that the Act does not simply specify that the compensation order should be factored into the calculation of the available amount.

PROCEDURAL MATTERS

Background

3.32   The original Bill required that the confiscation order be made before sentence unless a postponement was granted. This provision was removed but without any amendment to the following two sections. The assumption must be that the confiscation order will normally be made before sentencing. The extraordinary statement in s 14(11), that a confiscation order must not be quashed solely on the ground that there was a defect or omission in the application of the procedure for postponement makes nonsense of the detailed procedural requirements in the Act.

3.33   It is understandable that MPs were unhappy with the number of confiscation orders that have been quashed for procedural reasons under the existing law. The case of *R v Martin*,[1] for example, concluded in the overturning of a £10m confiscation order due to procedural errors emanating from confusion about the interplay and transitional provisions of the various pieces of legislation that have dealt with confiscation. However, the purpose of the new Act should surely be to consolidate and simplify the law in this area, and mistakes made by the lower courts are no reason to undermine the importance of procedural safeguards.

---

[1]   [2001] EWCA Crim 2761, [2002] 2 Cr App Rep (S) 122, [2002] Crim LR 228.

Postponement (s 14)

3.34 The defendant, prosecutor or Director may apply for postponement of the making of a confiscation order and the court may also postpone the making of the order of its own motion. Whilst the Government was understandably keen to suggest that postponement should not be granted easily,[1] in practice it seems likely that postponements will remain common. Under existing legislation the power to postpone is limited to six months unless an extension was granted in 'exceptional circumstances', but this was seen to have operated as a bar to the making of many justifiably delayed confiscation orders. The PIU Report stated (at para 8.22)—

> 'The practical implications of this limit are that confiscation orders cannot be obtained in a number of cases due to simple administrative delay. For example, lack of court time, unavailability of counsel, judge or defendant, or the ongoing trial of a co-defendant have each caused confiscation hearings to collapse following postponement beyond the time limit. And there have also been cases in which defendants have deliberately delayed the inquiry to take advantage of the six-month time limit.'

[1] HC SC B, 22 November 2001, col 272.

3.35 The problems identified in the PIU may persist. It is not obvious how the Crown Court will be able to deal with the increased business which will be generated by PCA 2002. Proceedings may be postponed for a specified period which must not exceed two years from the date of the latest conviction (s 14(5)). The postponement may be extended further still where the court finds exceptional circumstances. PCA 2002 also provides that further extensions can be granted after the end of the current period so long as the application for extension is made within the existing period (s 14(8)). It is not clear whether this means beyond the two year-period. Mr Ainsworth told the House of Commons Committee—

> 'Under usual circumstances, that postponement can extend for up to two years and, in exceptional circumstances, it can go beyond that'.[1]

[1] HC SC B, 27 November 2001, col 334.

3.36 Extension may be made for any reason and not only, as under previous legislation, in order to obtain further information. Under the current legislation, postponement is a judicial act that must be carried out in open court with all parties present.[1] Presumably, this case law will apply to PCA 2002, although this is not expressly on its face.[2]

1   R v *Steele* and *Shevki* [2001] 2 Cr App Rep (S) 40; see also *R v Martin* [2001] EWCA Crim 2761, [2002] 2 Cr App Rep (S) 122, [2002] Crim LR 228.
2   See the discussion of case law on postponement under existing legislation at para 1.31.

Effect of postponement (s 15)

3.37   If the confiscation order is postponed as discussed above[1] the court may proceed to sentence provided that the sentence does not involve a fine, compensation, forfeiture or deprivation orders. However, the court may vary its sentence to include such an order following the postponed making of the confiscation order, provided that it does so within the period of 28 days from the last day of the postponement period. The Explanatory Notes state that this will, in particular, enable the forfeiture and destruction of drugs to be ordered in a drug trafficking case.[2] Varying a sentence in this way restarts the clock for the time limit for appeal. If the court proceeds to sentence before making the confiscation order and in so doing takes other offences into consideration, those offences are then considered as part of the particular criminal conduct for the purposes of s 6.

1   Explanatory notes, paras 3.34–36.
2   Explanatory notes, para 37.

Statement of information (s 16)

3.38   Where the court proceeds under s 6 on the prosecutor or Director's request (s 6(3)(a)) the prosecutor or Director must give the court a statement of information detailing the defendant's benefit from criminal conduct, within a period set by the court. If the court began proceedings of its own motion (s 6(3)(b)) it may order the prosecutor to provide the information. The Explanatory Notes state that s 16(2), which allows the court to act of its own motion—

> 'is based on the assumption that the court will never hold a confiscation hearing of its own volition in a case in which the Director is involved.'[1]

The prosecutor or Director may make a further statement at any time or the court may order it to do so within a time set by it. The court may vary the orders it makes in respect of the making of statements.

1   Explanatory Notes, para 38.

3.39   If the prosecutor or Director believes that the defendant has had a criminal lifestyle he must include in his statement matters he believes relevant for the court in considering whether the defendant has a criminal lifestyle. It must also include whether he has benefited from general criminal conduct and the extent of his benefit; anything relevant to the s 10 assumptions; and anything the Director or prosecutor believes relevant to the question of whether it would be unjust to make the assumptions. An early draft of the Bill had only required that the prosecutor gave information that he believed might lead to a serious risk of injustice. That wording was severely criticised and the final provision, requiring him to provide all evidence he believes relevant, is clearly wider. If the prosecutor or Director does not believe the defendant has a criminal lifestyle his statement should include information as to whether the defendant has benefited from particular conduct and to what extent.

3.40   In Committee the Government explained that Crown Court Rules will require that all information served on the court is also served on the defendant, but there is no such requirement on the face of the statute.[1]

[1]   HC SC B, 22 November 2001, col 281.

Defendant's response to statement of information (s 17)

3.41   If the prosecutor or Director makes a statement under s 16 and it is served upon the defendant the court may order the defendant to indicate (in a manner ordered by the court) which allegations he accepts and to give particulars of those things upon which he relies in relation to those matters with which he takes issue. Interestingly, the corresponding Scottish provision (s 102) imposes a mandatory requirement on the court. Acceptance of any matters is conclusive of the matters to which that acceptance relates. In general, failure to respond in whole or part is taken to be acceptance of the matters in the report except for any that are responded to. However, silence on the part of the defendant is not taken as acceptance of any allegation that the defendant has benefited from his general or particular criminal conduct because, as the Explanatory Notes state—

   'it is not thought appropriate that the defendant's silence should be conclusive of these matters'.[1]

The court may vary its orders at any time in relation to the defendant's response. In order to comply with the European Court of Human Rights' interpretation of ECHR, no acceptance made under this procedure is admissible as evidence in proceedings for an offence (s 17(6)).

[1]   Explanatory Notes, para 41.

Provision of information by defendant (s 18)

3.42   If the court is proceeding under s 6 following a request by the prosecutor (s 6(3)(a)) or proceeds of its own motion, (s 6(3)(b)) or is considering whether to proceed, it may order the defendant to give it specified information to help it carry out its functions. The order may specify the manner in which and the date by which the information must be supplied. If the defendant fails to comply with the order without reasonable excuse the court may draw such inferences as it believes appropriate. If any allegation made by the defendant in this way, or through any other statement given to the court in any matter relevant to deciding the available amount, is accepted by the prosecutor or Director (in any manner prescribed by the court), that acceptance shall be conclusive of the matters to which it relates. The court may vary the orders it makes in this regard at any time. Again, in order to comply with the requirements of the European Court of Human Rights, no admission of benefit from criminal conduct made under this section is admissible in proceedings for an offence. However, as the Explanatory Notes state, this protection—

> 'does not prevent the authorities from prosecuting the defendant or another person using other evidence which may come to light following such an admission'.[1]

---

[1]   Explanatory Notes, para 45.

3.43   Although the consequence of a failure to provide information is that the court will be entitled to treat facts asserted by the Crown as conclusively proved (under s 17) and it will be allowed to draw inferences adverse to the defendant under s 18. It will also be a contempt of court to fail to provide the information. It may seem a surprising result that remaining silent in the face of an order under ss 17 or 18 is punishable as a contempt, as this might be thought to breach the defendant's right of silence in criminal proceedings (see *Saunders v United Kingdom*).[1] However, s 18(5) provides that even though inferences may be drawn by the confiscating court where information is not provided, this—

> 'does not affect any power of the court to deal with the defendant in respect of a failure to comply with an order under this section'.

It should also be noted that the courts in *McIntosh*[2] and *Benjafield*[3] confiscation proceedings were held to be not criminal but civil in nature, so ECHR, Art 6(2) did not apply. Furthermore, PCA 2002, s 17(6) specifically states that no acceptance by the defendant under this section that he has benefited from conduct is admissible in evidence in proceedings for an offence. It would seem, therefore, that a failure by the defendant to provide information under these sections would be a contempt of court and, as such, separately punishable. The Explanatory Notes state that the power to draw inferences—

> 'does not detract from any other power the court has to deal with the defendant, notably its power to punish the defendant for contempt of court in refusing to comply with the order'.[4]

1   *Saunders v United Kingdom* (1996) 23 EHRR 313, [1997] BCC 872, ECtHR.
2   *McIntosh v Lord Advocate* [2001] UKPC 01, [2001] 2 All ER 638, [2001] 3 WLR 107.
3   *R v Benjafield* [2002] UKHL 2, [2002] 1 All ER 815, [2002] 2 WLR 235.
4   Explanatory Notes, para 44.

RECONSIDERATION

Introduction

3.44   Sections 19–26 deal with reconsideration by the Crown Court of cases after conviction. The sections allow the court to make a confiscation order where no order was originally made, or to increase the amount of the original order. They allow a court to make a confiscation order even though no order was made at the time of sentence where fresh evidence becomes available to the prosecutor.

3.45   Sections 19–20 deal with the reconsideration of a case or of benefit where no order was made.

No order made: reconsideration of case (s 19)

3.46   Section 19 gives the Crown Court the power to make a confiscation order when none was made at the time of the original criminal proceedings. The section applies where evidence which was not available to the prosecutor at the time of the original proceedings has since come to light. First, it must be established that the first condition in s 6 is satisfied (ie that the defendant has been convicted in the Crown Court or has been convicted in the magistrates' court and committed to the Crown Court). The prosecutor or Director must make an application for reconsideration within six years of conviction.[1] In hearing the application the court will consider the new evidence and will institute the procedure for making an order if it believes it is appropriate to do so.

1   After six years there remains the possibility of civil recovery subject to a 12 year limitation period: see s 288 which amends the Limitation Act 1980 by the addition of a new s 27A establishing the 12-year time limit for civil recovery orders.

3.47   Where the defendant has already been sentenced, his particular criminal conduct includes that of the offence itself and any offences that were taken into consideration in sentencing him. In calculating 'b+on, presumably to allow the court to recognise the impact of sentencing. The recoverable amount under s 19 is the amount that the court 'believes is just' but must not exceed the amount found due under s 7. Section 19(7) states that in assessing the recoverable amount regard should be had to financial orders previously imposed in respect of the offences.

3.48   Section 19(5) modifies s 10 so that the reconsideration is genuinely a reconsideration; namely, the court puts itself into the position that the original court would have been in had it had the new evidence. Hence, the first and second assumptions do not apply with regard to property obtained by the defendant on or after the relevant date, the third assumption does not apply with regard to expenditure incurred by him on or after that date and the fourth assumption does not apply with regard to property obtained by him on or after that date. Confusion may be caused by the different meanings of 'the relevant date' in ss 10 and 19.

3.49   Interestingly, s 19 allows the court a flexibility not available at the first consideration, presumably to allow the court to recognise the impact of sentencing. The recoverable amount under s 19 is the amount that the court 'believes is just' but must not exceed the amount found due under s 7. Section 19(7) states that in assessing the recoverable amount regard should be had to financial orders previously imposed in respect of the offences.

No order made: reconsideration of benefit (s 20)

3.50   Section 20 allows the court to reconsider the question of whether the defendant 'benefited' from criminal conduct where a confiscation hearing was held and the court decided that the defendant had a criminal lifestyle but had not benefited from his general criminal conduct or that he did not have a criminal lifestyle and had not benefited from his particular criminal conduct. The fresh evidence must have been unavailable to the prosecutor or Director at the earlier hearing. The new order must still not exceed the available amount. The Explanatory Notes state—

> 'The principle underlying these sections is that a reconsideration should only be applied for where new evidence comes to light. It is not appropriate for an authority to have evidence at the time of the earlier

proceedings, not to apply for a confiscation order on that occasion but to apply for a reconsideration at a later date. Provision is included to reflect this principle'.[1]

---

[1]   Explanatory notes, para 48.

3.51   The application for reconsideration must be made within six years of the date of conviction. Before considering the amount of the defendant's benefit, the court must first conclude that it would have decided that the defendant had benefited from his general or particular criminal conduct had it seen the new evidence at the time. The court will then recalculate the benefit under s 6(4)(b) or (c) and make a new confiscation order.

3.52   In calculating the benefit figure under s 20 the relevant date for calculation is the date of the court's original decision that there was no benefit. From there the court must adopt the same approach as in s 19, disregarding the irrelevant assumptions under s 10 and calculating the 'just amount' (see discussion of s 19 in para 3.46).

3.53   Sections 21 and 22 deal with the reconsideration of benefit and/or of the available amount where an order has been made.

Order made: reconsideration of benefit (s 21)

3.54   This section enables the amount payable under a confiscation order to be increased where the Crown Court made a confiscation order at the original proceedings but the Director or prosecutor believes that the benefit figure ought to be reconsidered. Application must be made to the Crown Court within six years of the original conviction. There must be new evidence that was not available to the prosecutor or the Director at the time of the original order. There is no limit on the number of times benefit can be reconsidered. Further, the use of s 21 is not a bar to the later use of s 22 (reconsideration of available amount). The court is required to make a new calculation of the defendant's benefit (bearing in mind changes in the value of money). The court may increase the original order by 'such amount as it believes just'.[1] The court is not, however, required to increase the amount to the full extent of the benefit determined.[2]

---

[1]   Section 21(7)(b). In the House of Commons Committee the Government said that s 21(7)(b) is not intended to allow the amount in the order to be reduced: HC SC B, 27 November 2001, col 334 (Mr Ainsworth).

[2]   That it was Parliament's intention that the court have a discretion not to increase the order by the full amount of extra benefit now apparent is made clear by the words of Mr Ainsworth: HC SC B, 27 November 2001, col 335.

3.55 Section 21 largely mirrors the existing legislation, except that it recognises the role of the newly created Director. Two provisions are, however, new. First, the court is required to take into account certain orders made against the defendant in the original proceedings (because the court might not have made these other orders in the original proceedings if it had made a confiscation order). However, these earlier orders are not to be taken into account if they have already been taken into account by the court in deciding what is free property for the purposes of revaluation proceedings. This stops the defendant from being given the benefit of a reduction twice in respect of the same property. Offences committed subsequently to the original date of conviction may not be taken into account at the reconvened confiscation hearing.[1]

---

[1] See Mr Ainsworth HC SC B, 27 November 2001, col 334, together with the wording of the Act.

3.56 Secondly, s 21(10) deals with the situation where both a compensation order and a confiscation order have been made in the original proceedings and the court has directed under s 13(6) that the compensation order be paid out of the proceeds of the confiscation order. Clearly, the court cannot take the compensation order into account in reconsidering the defendant's benefit because the defendant would then be able to offset the impact of the compensation order twice.

3.57 Offences to be taken into consideration (TICs) will have been considered under s 6 where it was known at the time of the original confiscation proceedings that the defendant wished them to be taken into consideration in the passing of his sentence (s 76(3)(c)). The House of Commons Standing Committee were told that if the court is only informed that there are TICs after the confiscation proceedings have concluded, they could be included in a reconsideration.[1]

---

[1] HC SC B, 27 November 2001, cols 299–300.

Order made: reconsideration of available amount (s 22)

3.58 Under s 22, where the Crown Court at the original hearing made a confiscation order for an amount lower than the defendant's assessed benefit because there was insufficient recoverable property to satisfy the order which had been made, the prosecutor, the Director, or a receiver appointed in the case may apply to the Crown Court to recalculate the available amount. This is an example of a power which has been transferred from the High Court to the Crown Court.

3.59 There is no limit to the number of reconsiderations. In addition there is no six-year time limit for making the application (in contrast to ss 19–21).

3.60 Where the Crown Court finds that the available amount has increased, it may vary the amount of the original order to an amount that the court 'believes is just' (s 22(4)(a)). The court is to have regard to any fine, ancillary order or compensation order imposed on the defendant following the original conviction (the reason being that the amount the offender is able to pay may be affected) (s 22(5)).

3.61 Section 22(6) contains a provision requiring the court when deciding what is 'just' not to take into account a compensation order if a court had earlier made a direction under s 13(6). This is because the defendant would then be able to offset the impact of the compensation order twice.

3.62 Section 22(7) states that in deciding whether one amount exceeds another the court must take into account of any change in the value of money.

3.63 Sections 23 and 24 deal with variations and discharges of orders where the available amount is inadequate, and we now look at them in detail.

Inadequacy of available amount: variation of order (s 23)

3.64 Under the previous legislation, where a confiscation order had been made and where realisable property was insufficient to satisfy the confiscation order, the defendant or receiver could apply to the High Court for a certificate of inadequacy.[1] Such certificates are only available in limited circumstances and cannot be used as an appeal to go behind the original Crown Court order. It is appropriate to make such an application, for example, where property has been sold for less than the value assessed by the Crown Court at the time the confiscation order was made. Where the High Court issued such a certificate, the matter went back to the Crown Court or magistrates' court and the amount of the confiscation order would then be reduced. The new s 23 simplifies the procedure, abolishing the jurisdiction of the High Court and providing instead for an application to be made directly to the Crown Court by the defendant or a receiver. This section is not intended to change the way the courts should approach the question of inadequacy.[2]

---

[1] See CJA 1988, s.83.

[2] The Government attempted to clarify this in Committee: 'The confiscation system is designed to ensure that orders are not made for more than the value of the property available to justify them. However, it may happen that the realisable property, if assessed by the court at the defendant's request, loses its value before the order is fully satisfied. The clause therefore enables the court to reduce the amount payable. The clause is based on existing legislation . . .': HC SC B, 27 November 2001, col 340.

3.65   The Crown Court is required to calculate the available amount and in doing so must apply s 9 as if references to the time the confiscation order is made were to the time of the calculation, and as if references to the date of the confiscation order were to the date of the calculation. If the court finds that the available amount (as so calculated) is inadequate for the payment of any amount remaining to be paid under a confiscation order it may substitute any amount it 'believes is just'.

3.66   Bankruptcy is dealt with in PCA 2002, Pt 9.[1] If bankruptcy comes before an order and before restraint under the Act then bankruptcy proceedings will take place in the usual way; their hierarchy undisturbed. However, in order that bankruptcy is not used as a tool to avoid a confiscation order, where confiscation proceedings are commenced, subsequent bankruptcy will not prevent the Act biting.[2]

---

[1]   See ch 9.
[2]   HC SC B, 27 November 2001, col 341 (Mr Ainsworth).

Inadequacy of available amount: discharge of order (s 24)

3.67   The present legislation does not allow for the discharge of a confiscation order where it has not been met for purely technical reasons. An example of the sort of situation at which the section is aimed is set out in s 24(4). Where a court makes a confiscation order based on an assessment of realisable property in the form of foreign currency and a shortfall in payment of the order arises later, due entirely to a change in the value of the currency concerned in the period between the order being made and payment, the order cannot be varied under existing legislation unless a certificate of inadequacy is obtained.[1] Section 24 allows the court to vary the order much more easily.

---

[1]   This section is 'designed to provide . . . a simplified way of dealing with a specific problem that has arisen in some Customs and Excise cases. It relates overwhelmingly to currency fluctuations': Mr Ainsworth, HC SC B, 27 November 2001, col 345.

3.68   Section 24(1) provides that, where a justices' chief executive in the magistrates' court is enforcing a confiscation order he may apply to the Crown Court which may write the order off if the outstanding sum is under £1,000. This may only be done if the reason for the shortfall is a fluctuation in exchange rates or some other factor specified in secondary legislation, or some combination of the two.[1] The limit of £1,000 is variable by order. This section does not apply where the Director is enforcing a confiscation order. Such enforcement by the Director always involves the appointment of a receiver. In such circumstances he would have to apply to the Crown Court under s 23.

---

[1]   HC Official Report SC B, 27 November 2001, col 346 (Mr Ainsworth).

3.69 Section 24 is intended to deal with difficulties caused by fluctuating exchange rates for currencies or for property such as gold. Larger variations may be dealt with under ss 22 and 23.

Small amount outstanding: discharge of order (s 25)

3.70 Where a justices' chief executive is enforcing a confiscation order and the confiscation order has been satisfied almost in its entirety, but a sum of £50 or less is outstanding, the justices' chief executive may apply to the Crown Court for the order to be written off. Section 25 thus introduces an exception to the general principle that a confiscation order may not be written off, but its purpose is simply to save expenses and bureaucracy where the outstanding amount is not worth chasing. The Secretary of State may, by order, vary the £50 limit. Curiously there is no equivalent Scottish provision.

Information (s 26)

3.71 The purpose of s 26 is to make clear that the provisions requiring that the prosecution and defence provide information prior to a confiscation hearing after conviction (ss 16–18) also apply to reconsideration proceedings. If the court proceeds to reconsider an original order under s 6 in pursuance of ss 19 or 20, or under s 21, ss 16, 17 and 18, which require statements of information from prosecution and defence, also apply to the reconsideration proceedings.

DEFENDANT ABSCONDS

Changes in the new Act

3.72 Sections 27–31, deal with confiscation orders against defendants who abscond either after conviction or after 'proceedings for an offence or offences are started but not concluded'. Under the present legislation,[1] in drug trafficking cases the High Court may make a confiscation order against an absconded drug trafficker who had either been charged or convicted, or against a convicted drug trafficker who dies after he has been convicted. PCA 2002 now allows the Crown Court to make a confiscation order against a defendant who absconds and who has been convicted of, or charged with, any crime.

---

[1] See DTA 1994, s. 19.

3.73   The existing provision allowing for the High Court in England and Wales to make a confiscation order against a drug trafficker who dies after conviction but before the Crown Court can make a confiscation order is abolished. The reason for this is that the Government believed that recovery of criminal benefit where the defendant had died was better dealt with under the civil recovery procedures in PCA 2002, Pt 5.[1]

---

[1]   See ch 6.

3.74   The Government declared in the House of Commons that criminal proceedings should take priority over civil recovery even where the defendant has absconded and that legal representation would be provided in the form of an *amicus curiae*.[1] The relevant representation provisions will be amended to provide funding.

---

[1]   This was promised on behalf of the Government by Mr Ainsworth: HC SC B, 27 November 2001, col 362.

Defendant convicted or committed (s 27)

3.75   Where a defendant is convicted in the Crown Court and then absconds before sentence and/or the making of a confiscation order, or where the defendant has been convicted in the magistrates' court and has been committed from that court to the Crown Court for sentence and/or the making of a confiscation order, the prosecutor or Director may apply to the Crown Court to proceed under s 27. The court will then consider whether it believes it 'appropriate' to proceed with confiscation (s 27(3)(b)).

3.76   Section 27(5) modifies the procedure under s 6 by entitling any person the court believes is likely to be affected by any order to appear before the court and make representations. No order may be made unless the prosecutor or Director has taken reasonable steps to contact the defendant. If the court does proceed in the absence of the defendant, the assumptions may not be applied, as the defendant, being absent, is not in a position to rebut them.

3.77   Section 27(5)(e) provides that reconsideration, under ss 19–21, is not possible whilst the defendant is still an absconder. However, the reconsideration provisions will apply where a convicted absconder returns.

Defendant neither convicted nor acquitted (s 28)

3.78   Where the defendant has absconded after proceedings have been started against him, a confiscation order may only be made two years after the 'day the court believes he absconded'. The prosecutor or Director makes the application and the court then considers whether it believes it is 'appropriate' to proceed. Under existing law the High Court has power[1] to make such an order, but this power will be transferred to the Crown Court.

---
[1]   See DTA 1994, s 19(4).

3.79   Sections 28(5)(d) and (e) modify the reconsideration provisions in ss 19-21 where the defendant absconds before he has been convicted. There can be no reconsideration by the Crown Court under those sections while the defendant is still an absconder. Section 28(7) states that when a court has made a confiscation order under s 6 on an absconder, it cannot later make a separate order if the defendant returns and is convicted.

Variation of order (s 29)

3.80   Where the Crown Court has made a confiscation order in the absence of an absconder before conviction the order remains even where he ceases to be an absconder. However, within 28 days of conviction he has the right to apply to the Crown Court for the amount of the order to be varied where—

'he believes that the amount to be paid was too large (taking the circumstances prevailing when the amount was found for the purposes of the order)' (s 29(1)(c), (d)).

3.81   The court may vary the order and instead order payment of such amount 'as it believes just'.

3.82   Section 28 alters the present provision, which only allows a confiscation order made in the absence of the defendant to be varied within six months of it being made, regardless of whether the defendant has returned and been convicted.

Discharge of order (s 30)

3.83   The Crown Court must discharge a confiscation order where it was made in the absence of the defendant before he was convicted when he returns and is acquitted on all matters (or the proceedings against him are discontinued).

3.84   The Crown Court has a discretion to discharge such a confiscation order when the defendant ceases to be an absconder and where he has not been 'acquitted of all counts' if there has been undue delay in continuing the proceedings against him, or where the prosecutor does not intend to proceed with the prosecution.

3.85   Section 30(5) provides that where a confiscation order is discharged under this section the court may make appropriate consequential or incidental orders.

APPEALS

Appeals to the Court of Appeal and the House of Lords

3.86   Appeals against confiscation orders to both the Court of Appeal and to the House of Lords are dealt with in ss 31–33.

Appeal by prosecutor or Director (s 31)

3.87   Section 31 provides that either the prosecutor or the Director may appeal against any confiscation order made by the Crown Court, and against any decision of the Crown Court not to make a confiscation order. The appeal is not limited and appears to be available on any ground. The Explanatory Notes give the example that it will be possible to appeal where the prosecutor or the Director believe that the court has failed to take account of property which should be taken account of, or has made some miscalculation concerning the amount of the order.[1]

---

[1]   Explanatory Notes, para 68.

3.88   Section 30 does not allow for an appeal against a decision of the Crown Court under the reconsideration sections (ss 19, 20), nor under those sections allowing confiscation orders to be made against convicted and unconvicted absconders (ss 27, 28).

Court's powers on appeal (s 32)

3.89   The Court of Appeal may confirm, quash or vary the order. It may either itself proceed under s 6 (ignoring s 32(1)–(3)) or direct the Crown Court to proceed afresh.

3.90   The court is required to have regard to any fine or ancillary order imposed on the defendant as part of the sentencing process. When a compensation order has been made against the defendant the court must have regard to the compensation order, but may not order its payment out of confiscated monies. The intention is to ensure that treatment on appeal is the same as in the substantive proceedings.

Appeal to House of Lords (s 33)

3.91   The Court of Appeal's decision may be appealed to the House of Lords, whose powers are similar to those of the Court of Appeal. However, the function of the House of Lords is to review the Court of Appeal's decision, and not the original Crown Court decision. When the Court of Appeal has confirmed a Crown Court decision not to make a confiscation order or when it quashes the Crown Court's order, the House of Lords may confirm the decision or remit the case to the Crown Court, with directions, to proceed afresh. The House of Lords will not itself proceed under s 6.

ENFORCEMENT AUTHORITY (s 34)

3.92   Enforcement under PCA 2002 is carried out either by the Director of the ARA or the magistrates' court with the assistance of the prosecutor. Section 34 dictates who should initiate enforcement proceedings. PCA 2002 generally preserves the present system if the Director is not the enforcement authority. At present the magistrates' court is responsible for enforcing confiscation orders as if they were fines imposed by the Crown Court.[1] Terms of imprisonment in default of payment of a confiscation order originally fixed by the Crown Court are activated by the magistrates' court issuing a warrant of commitment.

---

[1]   See *R v Hastings and Rother Justices, ex p Anscombe* (1988) 162 JP 340, [1998] Crim LR 812.

3.93   If a confiscation order is unpaid, a hearing is normally arranged shortly before the release of the defendant. The magistrates' court, before committing the defendant to prison, decides whether the defendant has the means to pay the order. If he does not he will be sent to prison in default of payment. It is not possible for the defendant at this stage to challenge the original Crown Court order. He must either appeal to the Court of Appeal or seek a certificate of inadequacy from the High Court. Under PCA 2002 the same principles will apply, although any application to vary the original order (ie the new certificate of inadequacy provisions) will be made to the Crown Court under PCA 2002, s 23.

3.94   There are important differences between the current powers of a magistrates' court to enforce a fine and to enforce a confiscation order. For example, when dealing with a confiscation order the magistrates' court does not hold a means enquiry and has no power to remit part or the whole of a confiscation order.[1] Any sentence in default activated by the magistrates' court is served consecutively to the sentence for the offence. Serving the time in default of payment does not extinguish the defendant's liability to pay a confiscation order. The order may also be met by the appointment of a receiver. The position will be the same under the new legislation.

---

[1]   *R v Harrow Justices, ex p DPP* [1991] 3 All ER 873, [1991] 1 WLR 395.

3.95   By virtue of s 34 the court *must* appoint the Director of the ARA as the enforcement authority where—

(a)   it was the Director who had originally applied for the order (this includes applications under the reconsideration and absconder provisions);

(b)   he appeals against a decision made about a confiscation order; or

(c)   before the order is made, he applies to the court to be appointed to enforce it.

Otherwise, the magistrates' court enforces the order with the assistance of the prosecutor.

ENFORCEMENT AS FINES ETC

Director not appointed as enforcement authority (s 35)

3.96   The procedure for the enforcement of confiscation orders by the magistrates' court is not changed by PCA 2002. The order is treated as a Crown Court fine and enforced, as such, using the magistrates' court's fine enforcement powers.[1] As with a Crown Court fine, when the Crown Court makes a confiscation order, it sets a term of imprisonment to be imposed in default of payment. Default terms depend upon the amount payable under the confiscation order. The maximum default term ranges from seven days for £200 or less, to ten years for an amount in excess of £1m (see Powers of Criminal Courts (Sentencing) Act 2000, s 139).

---

[1]   Magistrates' Courts Act 1980, Pt 3.

Director appointed as enforcement authority (s 36)

3.97   The court is required to specify a term of imprisonment in default of payment when the Director enforces the order. Terms of imprisonment in default of payment will be fixed by reference to s the Powers of Criminal Courts (Sentencing) Act 2000, s 139. Section 139(4) of that Act contains a table setting out maximum terms of imprisonment in default. A judge, when fixing a sentence in default, can impose a term up to the maximum allowed for the amount which is to be paid.

Director's application for enforcement (s 37)

3.98   Section 37 creates specific provisions where the Director applies for enforcement. Although based largely on the provisions of the Magistrates' Courts Act 1980, the default term can only be activated after the Director has applied to the Crown Court.

Provisions about imprisonment or detention (s 38)

3.99   As is presently the case,[1] a term of imprisonment to be served in default must be served consecutively to the substantive term imposed for the original offence. Section 38 states that if the defendant serves a term of imprisonment in default the sum due remains outstanding. In a case[2] concerning similar provisions under existing law the Administrative Court held that a defendant was 'liable to serve' the term in default when he was to be released on licence rather than at the end of the full term of his original sentence. Section 38(3) contains similar words to DTA 1994 and CJA 1988 and in particular uses the same phrase 'liable to serve'. Where the prosecution and/or magistrates' court delay(s) in applying for the warrant of commitment, so the defendant is released, this will not prevent him from later serving the sentence in default.[3]

---

[1]   See DTA 1994, s 9(2) and CJA 1988, s 75(3).
[2]   *R v City of London Justices, ex p Chapman* (1998) 162 JP 359.
[3]   *R v Chichester and District Justices, ex p Crowther* [1999] COD 34 (Sedley J) in which there was a gap of four years between release and warrant.

Reconsideration etc: variation of prison term (s 39)

3.100   Section 39 allows the Crown Court to alter the period of imprisonment in default where the court varies the amount due under a confiscation order under the 'reconsideration' provisions of the Act.[1]

---

[1]   See ss 19–30.

3.101   Where the variation of the confiscation order reduces the amount due, so that the new amount falls into a lower bracket of time in default, the court is required to lower the default term. The court has a discretion to increase the term in default where the amount of the order is increased.

3.102   Further, where the amount due under the confiscation order is increased by interest payable under s 12, the Director or the prosecutor may apply to the court to increase the term of imprisonment in default.

RESTRAINT ORDERS

Major changes

3.103   A restraint order freezes property that may be the subject of a confiscation order in criminal proceedings. Existing legislation allows the High Court to make a restraint or charging order where proceedings have been instituted or the defendant is to be charged, or an application in respect of further confiscation proceedings has been made or is to be made (for example, where the court is asked to reopen the question of confiscation where further realisable property is found). PCA 2002 introduces three major changes to the present position—

   (1)   Charging orders are abolished by virtue of Sch 12. This is not surprising as such orders were rarely made given the wide powers of restraint.

   (2)   The Crown Court, rather than the High Court, is given the jurisdiction to make restraint orders. This is in line with the aim of PCA 2002 to consolidate in one court as much confiscation business as possible. It should be noted that confiscation orders will still be enforced by the magistrates' court or by the Director.[1]

   (3)   The time when a restraint order may be made is now at any point after an investigation has been started, rather than when the defendant 'is to be charged' as under the existing system.[2]

---

[1]   See para 3.95.
[2]   DTA 1994, s 25(3).

3.104   A major concern about restraint orders is their continuing potential to limit the lawful use of property. The problem is particularly acute in the case of the defendant who is subsequently acquitted or when third parties have an interest in restrained funds. In the recent case of *Hughes*[1] it was held that receivers were entitled to their costs out of restrained assets even though the defendant was subsequently acquitted. The Court of Appeal in reaching this decision rejected strong arguments that the intention of the legislation was that the prosecution should bear the costs of receivers until there was a conviction and confiscation order.[2] A consequence of this ruling is that third parties whose assets are restrained because, for example, they hold a joint interest in property with the defendant, may be liable to pay a proportion of the receiver's costs because these come out of the restrained funds.

---

1   *Hughes v Customs and Excise Comrs* [2002] EWCA Civ 734, [2002] 4 All ER 633.
2   See commentary in *Criminal Law Week* Issue 21, 3 June 2002.

3.105   In answer to Lord Goodhart who raised the point that there was no provision for compensation for losses caused to the innocent defendant by a restraint order where there has been no serious default on the part of the enforcement authorities, Lord Falconer of Thoroton referred to *Hughes*[1] and said—

> 'It is . . . interesting to note that the courts have recently endorsed that approach in the case of *Hughes and Another and R and another*, which was decided by the Court of Appeal . . . . That case dealt with the issue of whether it was compatible with the European Convention on Human Rights that receivers should be able to pay their expenses out of the assets which they were managing. Lord Justice Simon Brown acknowledged that an acquitted or unconvicted defendant had for those purposes to be treated as an innocent person, but he did not accept that, for that reason, it had to be regarded as disproportionate to leave the defendant against whom restraint and receivership orders had been made uncompensated for such loss as they might have caused him.
>
> He held that because acquitted defendants are not generally entitled to compensation for deprivation of liberty or other loss suffered through prosecution, they should not be entitled to compensation for loss suffered through restraint and receivership action.'[2]

---

1   [2002] EWCA Civ 734, [2002] 4 All ER 633.
2   HL Report Stage, 25 June 2002, col 1254.

3.106   Another concern expressed in the House of Commons at Committee Stage was that the Crown Court would not have the expertise and capacity to deal with restraint orders. An amendment proposed by a Conservative member, Mr Grieve, that the High Court retain the power to make restraint orders was rejected. The argument that the High Court should retain the power was expressed in this way—

> 'it is not possible to magic up new Crown Court judges in 24 hours—or, indeed, in six months—or to identify swiftly where to find the expertise to deal with this kind of application'.[1]

Further concerns were expressed about the Crown Courts finding the time to deal with these complex applications. Mr Ainsworth, for the Government, said that as only 252 restraint orders had been made in 1997 and 247 in 1998 the Crown Courts would be able to cope with the extra business.

---

[1]   HC SC B, 29 November 2001, col 372.

Conditions for exercise of powers (s 40)

3.107   The Crown Court may exercise the powers conferred on it by s 41 to restrain where there is reasonable cause to believe that the alleged offender has benefited from his criminal conduct and one of five conditions applies—

(1)   a criminal investigation has been started in England and Wales with regard to an offence;

(2)   proceedings for an offence have been started and not concluded;

(3)   an application by the prosecutor or Director has been made under ss 19, 20 (no order made: reconsideration), ss 27 or 28 (defendant absconds) and not concluded, or the court believes that such an application is to be made;

(4)   an application has been made by the prosecutor or Director under s 21 (order made: reconsideration of benefit) and not concluded, or the court believes that such an application is to be made. The court must also be satisfied that there is reasonable cause to believe that it will decide under that section that the amount found under the new calculation of the defendant's benefit exceeds the amount found as his benefit for the purposes of the confiscation order; or

(5)   an application has been made by the prosecutor or Director under s 22 (order made: reconsideration of available amount) and not concluded or the court believes that such an application is to be made. There too the court must be satisfied that there is reasonable cause to believe that it will decide under that section that the amount found under the new calculation of the defendant's benefit exceeds the amount found as his benefit for the purposes of the confiscation order.

3.108 Conditions (2), (3), (4) and (5) are not satisfied where the court believes there has been undue delay in continuing the proceedings or the prosecutor or Director does not intend to proceed (s 40(7), (8)). 'Undue delay' is not defined.[1]

---

[1]   Mr Ainsworth acknowledged this: 'There is no definition of "undue". It is at the discretion of the court to decide whether undue delay has occurred.' HC SC B, 29 November 2001, col 374.

Restraint orders (s 41)

3.109 If any condition set out in s 40 is satisfied, the Crown Court may make a restraint order 'prohibiting any specified person from dealing with any realisable property[1] held by him'. A restraint order may be made either against the defendant or person under investigation, and any other person holding realisable property. Section 41(3) gives the court the power to provide for 'exceptions' to the restraint order allowing for reasonable living and legal expenses and for the purpose of enabling a person to carry on any trade, profession or occupation.

---

[1]   Defined in s 83.

3.110 Section 41(4) states that an exception to a restraint order must not make provision for any legal expenses incurred in relation to the offences in respect of which the restraint order is made. The effect of this is that funds under restraint may not be released to the defendant or the recipient of a tainted gift for legal expenses incurred in relation to the offences in respect of which the restraint order is made. Public funding for such legal expenses will be available.[1] This replaces the present rule which allows the court to release restrained assets for the purposes of legal fees to fund the restraint and criminal proceedings. This alteration is curious, given that receivers are entitled to be paid often substantial fees out of restrained assets even where a defendant is acquitted. Mr Ainsworth explained in Committee that the reason for this change was 'because the PIU Report elaborated on the fact that money held under restraint is frequently dissipated on legal fees'.[2] The Explanatory Notes state that a defendant and any recipient of a tainted gift will be entitled to civil public funding.[3] The Access to Justice Act 1999, which governs civil public funding, is amended by PCA 2002, Sch 11.

---

[1]   The Access to Justice Act 1999 is to be amended (Mr Ainsworth: HC SC B, 29 November 2001, col 377).
[2]   See PCA 2002, Sch 11, para 36 for the extent of the amendment made to the Access to Justice Act 1999.
[3]   Explanatory notes, para 88.

3.111   The court has wide powers under s 41(7) to 'make such order as it believes is appropriate for the purpose of ensuring that the restraint order is effective'. The Crown Court is allowed to make ancillary orders, aimed at ensuring that the restraint order is effective. For example, the court can order that any relevant person disclose his or her assets, and failure to do so will amount to a contempt of court. Section 41(8) provides that a restraint order cannot be made in respect of any property subject to a charging order under current legislation: there is little point in making a charging and restraint order in respect of the same property.

Application, discharge and variation (s 42)

3.112   The prosecutor, the Director or an accredited financial investigator[1] may apply for a restraint order. Application may be made ex parte to a judge in chambers. Accredited financial investigators are those accredited by the Director. They will probably be employed by Customs and Excise or be drawn from the police's Financial Investigation Units (FIUs). Section 68 requires that applications will need the authority of a police superintendent or Customs equivalent or be from a financial investigator nominated by the Secretary of State pursuant to s 453.

---

[1]   See ss 3 and 68 (paras 2.7 and para 3.154 respectively).

3.113   The Crown Court may vary or discharge the restraint order. An application for variation or discharge may be made by the 'person who applied for the order'[1] or 'any person affected by' it. PCA 2002 changes the venue for restraint order proceedings from the High Court to the Crown Court and allows an order to be made at an earlier time than under the existing legislation.

---

[1]   What happens where the original applicant is on sick leave or has left his or her post? Contrast s 48 where there is provision for an officer of equal rank to the original applicant to take over the role.

3.114   If the qualifying condition satisfied under s 40 was that proceedings were started or an application was made, the court must discharge the order at the conclusion of those proceedings or application. If the condition was that an investigation was started or that an application was to be made, the court must discharge the order if it forms the view that proceedings for the offence have not commenced or the application has not been made after a reasonable time.

Appeal to Court of Appeal (s 43)

3.115 Under the existing legislation[1] a general right of appeal lies to the Court of Appeal from a decision of the High Court in respect of restraint and ancillary orders. The Supreme Court Act 1981, s 16 does not apply to the Crown Court and therefore it was necessary for PCA 2002 to include a specific right of appeal.

[1] Supreme Court Act 1981, s 16.

3.116 The right to appeal from the Crown Court applies where the court decides not to make a restraint order and against the court's decision to vary or discharge the existing order or not to do so. There is no right to appeal against the Crown Court's decision to make a restraint order in the first place. The way to challenge a restraint order is for the relevant person to apply to the Crown Court for variation or discharge of the original order, and if that application is refused then to apply to the Court of Appeal. The reason for this is that most restraint orders are applied for and dealt with on an ex parte basis. This is also in line with the Government's desire to keep as much of the process as possible in the Crown Court.[1]

[1] In Committee, Mr Ainsworth confirmed that it is intended that the Act be read to allow appeal to the Court of Appeal not only on a 'point of law', but also 'on a refusal to vary or discharge a confiscation order' (HC SC B, 29 November 2001, col 381). Presumably, this means that the Crown Court's interpretation of the facts can be challenged.

Appeal to House of Lords (s 44)

3.117 An appeal to the House of Lords from a decision of the Court of Appeal made under s 43 is allowed under s 44. Only the parties to the Court of Appeal proceedings may appeal further to the House of Lords. On appeal, the House of Lords may confirm the decision of the Court of Appeal or make such order as it believes to be appropriate.

Seizure (s 45)

3.118 Section 45 gives a constable or customs officer the power to seize 'any realisable property' to which a restraint order applies, to prevent its removal from England and Wales. Property seized must be 'dealt with' in accordance with the directions of the court that made the order. At present realisable property may be seized to prevent its removal from England, Scotland or Wales. The current legislation goes back to DTOA 1986 when confiscation legislation was not in force in Scotland. The provision in relation to Scotland is now contained in PCA 2002, Pt 3.

Hearsay evidence (s 46)

3.119   In present High Court proceedings for restraint, hearsay evidence is frequently admitted.[1] Section 46 states that hearsay evidence is admissible in all restraint proceedings. The Civil Evidence Act 1995, ss 2-4 apply in this regard.

---

[1]   *Re a Defendant* (1987) Times, 7 April.

Supplementary (s 47)

3.120   Section 47 mirrors the existing legislation. Where a restraint order affecting land is applied for, an 'inhibition' may be placed on the property at the Land Registry preventing its disposal.

MANAGEMENT RECEIVERS

Appointment (s 48)

3.121   The present legislation allows the High Court to appoint 'a receiver' on the application of the prosecutor to manage assets until conviction and after conviction to dispose of them to satisfy any order made. These receivers are known in practice as 'management' and 'enforcement' receivers, although the terms were not used in the earlier legislation. PCA 2002 gives effect to the current practice and adopts the terms

3.122   A management receiver may be appointed by the Crown Court where a restraint order has been made. A receiver may only be appointed on an application to the Crown Court by the person who applied for the restraint order. However, the proceedings need not be conducted by

the same individual who applied for the restraint order (since s/he may, for example, become ill or have left his or her post after applying for the order).

Powers (s 49)

3.123 The court can confer wide powers on a management receiver, including the power to take possession of property, the power to 'manage or otherwise deal with property' (s 49(2)(b)) the power to start, carry on or defend any legal proceedings in respect of property and the power to realise so much of the property as is necessary to meet the receiver's remuneration and expenses (s 49(2)(d)). The receiver may be authorised to hold property, to enter into contracts, to sue or be sued, to employ agents, to execute powers of attorney and to 'take any steps the court thinks appropriate'.

3.124 The phrase 'managing or otherwise dealing with property' is defined to include selling the property or any part of it or interest in it, carrying on or arranging for another person to carry on any trade or business the assets of which are or are part of the property and incurring capital expenditure in respect of the property (s 49(10)).

3.125 The court may also order any person holding an interest in realisable property to which the order applies to make to the receiver such payment as the court specifies in respect of a beneficial interest held by the defendant or the recipient of a tainted gift. On such payment being made the court may by order transfer, grant or extinguish any interest in the property (s 49(6)).

3.126 The court 'must not' confer the powers in s 49(2)(b), (2)(d) or (6) on the receiver 'unless it gives persons holding interests in the property a reasonable opportunity to make representations to it' (s 49(8)).

3.127 The court may also confer on the receiver power to enter any premises in England and Wales and to carry out a search for 'anything authorised by the court', to make copies, photographs and records of anything found and to remove anything 'which the receiver is required or authorised to take possession of in pursuance of an order of the court' (s 49(3)).

3.128 The powers cannot be used in relation to property subject to a charging order under earlier confiscation legislation in England and Wales or Northern Ireland (there was no provision for charging orders in the Scottish legislation) (s 49(7)).

ENFORCEMENT RECEIVERS

Appointment (s 50)

3.129 Where a confiscation order has been made the magistrates' court will be responsible for its enforcement. The Crown Court may appoint a person to act as enforcement receiver to help enforce the confiscation order where it is not satisfied and it is not subject to appeal. This is another example of jurisdiction which was formerly exercised by the High Court being transferred to the Crown Court. As in the existing legislation the prosecutor must make the application. The enforcement receiver may (but need not) be the same person as the management receiver appointed under s 48.

Powers (s 51)

3.130 The powers which the Crown Court may confer on enforcement receivers are wide ranging and are similar to the provisions for management receivers set out in s 49.[1] The main difference is that enforcement receivers can be given power to realise all property, while management receivers can only do this for the purpose of paying their own remuneration and expenses. The statute has been drafted in this way to reflect the functions of receivers under existing legislation. For the first time these functions are reflected in the titles given to the receivers in the Act.

---
[1]   See para 3.122.

3.131 As enforcement receivers may need to manage property before disposing of it they are given the powers to do so.

DIRECTOR'S RECEIVERS

Appointment (s 52)

3.132 If a confiscation order is made and the Director is appointed as the enforcement authority for the order under s 34, the Crown Court must make an order for the appointment of a receiver in respect of realisable property.

3.133 Where the Director is responsible for the enforcement of a confiscation order this wi11 be carried out by his receiver.

3.134 Section 52(4) states that although the Crown Court makes the order, it is the responsibility of the Director 'to nominate the person who is to be the receiver'. A person nominated may be either a member of the staff of the agency or a person providing services under arrangements made by the Director.

Powers (s 53)

3.135 The Crown Court may confer the same wide powers on the Director's receiver to manage and realise property as those given to enforcement receivers under s 50 on the application of the prosecutor.[1]

---
[1] See para 3.129.

APPLICATION OF SUMS

Enforcement receivers (s 54)

3.136 Where the prosecutor has successfully applied for the appointment of an enforcement receiver under s 50 any sums in the possession of the receiver are to be divided up in the prescribed manner after a confiscation order has been made. They must be applied—
    (1) to discharge such expenses incurred by any person acting as an insolvency practitioner;[1]
    (2) in making payments directed by the Crown Court; and
    (3) on the defendant's behalf towards the satisfaction of the confiscation order. The receiver is required to pay the sum realised (after the two initial deductions) to the enforcing justices' chief executive who is responsible for enforcing the confiscation order.

---
[1] See s 432.

3.137 Section 54(3) sets out what is to happen where the confiscation order has been fully paid but there are sums remaining. The Crown Court must direct that such sums are distributed among such persons 'who held (or hold) interests in the property concerned'[1] as the Crown Court directs and in such proportion as it directs. The Crown Court is required to give those with interests in the property concerned 'a reasonable opportunity to make representations' before making such directions (s 54(4)).

Sums received by justices' chief executive (s 55)

3.138 If a justices' chief executive receives sums in respect of a confiscation order either from a receiver or where the defendant makes voluntary payments, he must deal with them in the prescribed way. He is required to pay the expenses of the insolvency practitioner and the receiver if he has received the money under either ss 50 or 54. If a direction was made that a sum of compensation be paid under s 13(6) the chief executive must pay that amount. However some existing powers have been abolished. First, under existing legislation the justices' chief executive has the power to pay back to the prosecutor out of confiscated monies the sums the prosecutor has paid to a receiver in advance. The money will now be paid to the Consolidated Fund rather than to reimburse the prosecutor. Secondly, the deduction from compensation orders for victims of a share of enforcement costs has been abolished. Where the confiscation order takes precedence over parallel bankruptcy proceedings and the receiver has sums of money left over after the confiscation order has been paid, that money is paid into the bankrupt's estate, rather than disposal being the responsibility of the court making the confiscation order.[1]

---

[1] See Sch 11, para 16 which adds s 306B(1)(d) and (2) to the Insolvency Act 1986.

Director's receivers (s 56)

3.139 Section 56 sets out how the Director's receiver should apply sums obtained by him. The section contains similar provisions to s 54 except that the sums must be paid to the Director rather than the justices' chief executive.

Sums received by Director (s 57)

3.140 Where the Director is responsible for enforcement and where he has received sums pursuant to a confiscation order, he must apply the sums in the prescribed manner. The section is similar to s 55 but there are important differences.

3.141 First, the Director is required to pay the remuneration and expenses of any enforcement receiver appointed in the case (s 57(4)), but s 57(6) makes it clear that this does not apply where the receiver is a member of the Director's own staff or providing services under arrangements made by the Director. Such costs will be paid out of the Director's budget.

3.142 Secondly, the Director must pay any remaining monies received to the Consolidated Fund[1] which will also be the eventual destination of the monies when they are received by a justices' chief executive.

1 See Sch 1, para 5(2).

RESTRICTIONS

Restraint orders (s 58)

3.143 The rights of certain third parties in respect of realisable property which is the subject of a restraint order are limited by s 58 without the leave of the Crown Court. No distress may be levied and no right of forfeiture by peaceable re-entry may be exercised by a landlord or other person to whom rent is payable. The section also makes provision for situations where other proceedings are pending in relation to property which is the subject of restraint. The court is given the power to 'stay the proceedings or allow them to continue on any terms it thinks fit' (s 58(5)). This power applies to any court dealing with the matter. The earlier legislation was silent about this, although in practice the High Court exercising its inherent power often stayed other property proceedings where a restraint order had been made. This section may provide welcome clarification but it was not obviously necessary.

Enforcement receivers; Director's receivers (ss 59 and 60)

3.144 Similar restrictions on the rights of third parties are imposed where an enforcement receiver or the Director's receiver has been appointed after a confiscation order has been made.

RECEIVERS: FURTHER PROVISIONS

Protection (s 61)

3.145 Section 61 provides protection for receivers (whether appointed under ss 48, 50 or 52) from civil liability where they have mistakenly dealt with the property of innocent third parties, unless they have been negligent. The section recreates the existing legislation, and applies where a receiver—

(1) takes action in relation to property which is not realisable property (defined in s 83);

(2) would be entitled to take the action if it were realisable property; and

(3) believes on reasonable grounds that he is entitled to take the action.

In this case he is not liable to any person for loss and damage resulting from that action 'except so far as the loss or damage is caused by his negligence'.

Further applications (s 62)

3.146   Receivers appointed under ss 48, 50 or 52 may apply to the Crown Court for an order giving directions as to the exercise of their powers. The section also allows 'any person' affected by action taken by the receiver and any person who may be affected by any action that the receiver proposes to take to apply to the Crown Court. The court may make any order which it believes to be appropriate. The section is widely drafted and allows 'any person affected' to apply to the court. The 'person affected' may be the defendant, the recipient of a tainted gift from the defendant or any other person affected by the order.

Discharge and variation (s 63)

3.147   Section 63 sets out who may apply for the variation or discharge of a receivership order. The list includes the receiver, Director and any person affected by the order. The section also sets out the circumstances in which the Court is bound to discharge an order appointing a management receiver.

Management receivers: discharge (s 64)

3.148   Section 64 is included because of the new distinction created by the new legislation between management and enforcement receivers. It is aimed at ensuring that any property in the possession of a management receiver is transferred to an enforcement receiver when appointed. This does not of course apply to property realised for the purpose of discharging the receiver's remuneration and expenses.

Appeal to Court of Appeal (s 65)

3.149 Section 65 gives rights of appeal to the Court of Appeal against decisions of the Crown Court relating to receivership orders. The section is necessary because the existing right of appeal to the Court of Appeal from the High Court does not apply to the Crown Court. The persons who may appeal are the person who applied for the order, any person affected by the order and the receiver. The Court of Appeal may confirm the decision or make such order as it believes appropriate.

Appeal to House of Lords (s 66)

3.150 Section 66 provides a right of appeal to the House of Lords against a decision of the Court of Appeal. As with s 44, it is not possible for new parties to join an appeal at this stage. Only those who were parties to the proceedings at the Court of Appeal stage may appeal to the House of Lords.

SEIZED MONEY (s 67)

3.151 Section 67 creates a new power allowing the magistrates' court to order banks and building societies to pay realisable property which is in an account to the justices' chief executive so that a confiscation order can be met. The power is similar in principle to a garnishee order made by the civil courts.

3.152 Section 67 only applies where—
   (1) a restraint order has effect in relation to the money in the account;
   (2) a confiscation order has been made against the person by whom the money is held;
   (3) the Director has not been appointed as the enforcement authority for the confiscation order;
   (4) a receiver has not been appointed under s 50 in respect of the money; and
   (5) any period allowing time to pay (under s 11) has expired).

3.153 The section also allows justices' chief executives to obtain access to money which was originally seized as part of the criminal investigation, either by a constable or by customs officers, and then paid into a bank or building society account. Previously the only way to achieve this where the defendant was not willing to pay was to apply for the appointment of a receiver.

3.154 Section 67(6) provides that if a bank or building society fails to comply with the order that money be paid, then the court may order they pay a sum not exceeding £5000. It states that this sum is to be treated as adjudged to be paid by a conviction of the court (s 67(6)(b)). Thus the fine enforcement powers in the Magistrates' Courts Act 1980, Pt 3, are available to enforce payment of the sum which was ordered to be paid.

FINANCIAL INVESTIGATORS; APPLICATIONS AND APPEALS (s 68)

3.155 No accredited financial investigator may make an application for a restraint order or appeal against a first instance decision unless authorised to do so. Authorisation may be given either by a police officer not below the rank of superintendent or by a customs officer who is not below such grade as is designated by the Commissioners or an accredited financial investigator specified by the Secretary of State pursuant to s 445.

3.156 It is made clear in s 68(3) and (4) that after the initial application subsequent actions need not be taken by the same investigator who made the first application. This is included to avoid the inevitable problems which would arise, for example, due to the ill health of the original accredited financial investigator.

EXERCISE OF POWERS

Powers of Court and Receiver (s 69)

3.157 Section 69 substantially reproduces the existing powers of court and receiver. The powers must be exercised without taking into account any obligation of the defendant or obligations of the recipient of a tainted gift from the defendant.

3.158 New provisions[1] require the court and receivers to exercise their powers where a confiscation order has not been made, with a view to securing that there is no diminution of realisable property. This is designed to allow management receivers to sell assets which are falling in value.

---
[1]   Section 69(2)(b), (3)(c), (4) and (5).

3.159 The defendant or the recipient of a tainted gift has the right to make an application to the court to challenge the management receiver's decision to sell particular assets on the basis that the asset 'cannot be replaced' (s 69(4)). This has been inserted to give some measure of protection to either the defendant or the recipient of a tainted gift prior to a conviction (s 69(3)(c)).[1] If the relevant property cannot be replaced then the court 'may order that it must not be sold'. Section 69(4) does not apply at the enforcement stage as at that time all realisable property in which the defendant has an interest may be realised to meet the order. Section 69(5) allows the court to 'revoke or vary' an order made under s 69(4).

---
[1]   Examples were given by Mr Ainsworth of a house that has been in a family for generations, a work of art or a racehorse. Items of sentimental value are intended to be included (HC SC B, 29 November 2001, cols 405–406).

COMMITTAL

Committal by magistrates' court (s 70)

3.160 A defendant may be committed to the Crown Court for confiscation proceedings to be considered following a conviction of any offence in the magistrates' court (either indictable or summary). Section 70 only applies if the prosecutor 'asks the court to commit the defendant' after conviction. In that event the magistrates' court has no choice but to do so. Section 70(1)(b) only gives the power to seek committal to the 'prosecutor'. The Director therefore does not have the power to seek committal but can take over the confiscation proceedings in the Crown Court. The Explanatory Notes state—

'The power to have a person committed is granted only to the prosecutor, not to the Director of the Agency. However the Director can assume responsibility for the subsequent confiscation proceedings in the Crown Court.'[1]

---

[1]   Explanatory Notes, para 126.

3.161   Where the defendant is convicted of an either way offence, s 70(5) requires the magistrates' court to state whether it would have committed the defendant to the Crown Court for sentence anyway under the Powers of Criminal Courts (Sentencing) Act 2000, s 3(2). The reason for this is that by virtue of PCA 2000, s 71, the Crown Court's sentencing powers following a committal for confiscation are normally limited to the sentencing powers the magistrates' court would have had in the same case.

Sentencing by Crown Court (s 71)

3.162   Where a person is committed to the Crown Court from the magistrates' court under s 70, the Crown Court carries out the sentencing process. This means that where the magistrates' court has certified under s 70(5) that it would have committed the defendant for sentence anyway, the Crown Court must enquire into the circumstances of the case. The Crown Court is given the power to deal with the offender in any way in which it could have dealt with him had he just been convicted of the offence on indictment before it. In any other case the Crown Court must enquire into the circumstances of the case but it may only deal with the defendant in a way in which the magistrates' court could have dealt with him if it had just convicted him of the offence.

COMPENSATION

Serious default (s 72)

3.163   This section allows the Crown Court, in limited circumstances, to order that compensation be paid to a person whose property has been affected by confiscation proceedings where there has been serious default by those involved in the investigation. The Crown Court can order the payment of such compensation as it believes just.[1]

---

[1]   In Standing Committee B the Government saw this provision as giving a court the option of awarding less compensation where it perceived that the defendant had brought the prosecution or proceedings on himself through his own behaviour (HC SC B, 29 November 2001, col 418).

3.164   A compensation order cannot be made, however, unless three conditions are satisfied—

(1)   there has been serious default by investigators (those specified in s 72(9)) and either a criminal investigation was started but no proceedings were ever brought, or the defendant was never convicted of an offence, or his conviction was quashed on appeal, or he receives a pardon;

(2)   either the investigation or the proceedings would not have started or continued but for the serious default; and

(3)   the person making the application must be someone who held realisable property and who has 'suffered loss in consequence of anything done in relation to it' as a result of any order made under PCA 2002, Pt 2.

3.165   Section 72 does not apply to default by receivers as they are not included in the list of relevant persons in s 72(9). The list includes members of the police, Customs, SFO officers of the Inland Revenue and the CPS. The normal rules of the civil law of tort (professional negligence duty of care) apply to receivers' conduct.

3.166   Lord Rooker, speaking on behalf of the Government, said that this section should not apply to negligent default, as had been proposed in an amendment, because this would 'unnecessarily inhibit. . .' the enforcement authorities.[1] This led Lord Kingsland to point out the difference between this approach and the negligence offence of failing to disclose a suspicion contained in Pt 7.[2] Astonishingly PCA 2002 expects more of the regulated sector than of the receivers for whose appointment it makes provision.

---

[1]   HL Committee Stage, 13 May 2002, col 25.
[2]   HL Committee Stage, 13 May 2002, col 27.

3.167   Section 72 does reflect the existing power of the High Court to pay compensation to those who have suffered loss as a result of restraint or forfeiture proceedings if that loss arose out of 'serious default' by those investigating the case.[1] However, no compensation is payable if the proceedings would have been instituted even if the default had not occurred.[2] Section 72 widens the law to reflect the fact that a restraint order is available under PCA 2002 at an earlier stage than before.

1   Terrorism Act 2000, Sch 4, para 9.
2   Terrorism Act 2000, Sch 4, para 9(5).

3.168   The Access to Justice Act 1999 is amended by PCA 2002, Sch 11 to make civil public funding available for s 72 applications.[1]

Order varied or discharged (s 73)

3.169   The Crown Court has the power to award compensation to be paid to 'a person who held realisable property and who suffered loss as a result' (s 73(1)(b)) of a confiscation order being made in cases where the order had originally been made under s 29 (defendant absconds) and then varied or discharged under s 30 or s 31. The court may award such compensation as it 'believes is just'.

3.170   Unlike the power to compensate specified in s 72, this power is not restricted to cases where there has been serious default. The court here is given a wide discretion to award compensation under this section. The reason for this section not being limited to serious default is because the Government considered that the court should be able to—

> 'exercise a more flexible approach in circumstances where a confiscation order has been made without the defendant having been tried'.[1]

1   Explanatory Notes, para 131.

3.171   Civil public funding is made available for s 73 applications.[1]

1   See para 3.167.

ENFORCEMENT ABROAD (s 74)

3.172   Section 74 sets out how the prosecutor or Director in England and Wales should make requests for assistance to other countries when they believe that realisable property is situated there. The section only applies to requests connected with PCA 2002, Pt 2.

3.173 Section 74 reflects the increasing co-operation between states to deal with financial crime and operates within the framework of international law. On 29 May 2000 the UK signed the Convention on Mutual Assistance in Criminal Matters Between Member States of the European Union. A Protocol to the Convention was signed on 16 October 2001. The Protocol requires European member states to—

    (1) locate and provide details of all bank accounts held by a natural or legal person who is the subject of an investigation into serious crime;

    (2) provide details of transactions on specified accounts; and

    (3) monitor account activity in response to a request for mutual assistance.

The UK government has agreed in common with all EU countries that the Protocol will be implemented urgently. Its purpose is to extend the types of mutual assistance available and the circumstances in which it can be provided. The measures will include provision of information on identified bank accounts, the use of customer information orders (s 363) the use of account monitoring orders (s 370) and the provision of information on specific bank accounts. The Home Office is presently consulting the banking industry and associated organisations on how the Protocol should be implemented.

3.174 Treaties exist between the UK and other states outside the European Union. Section 74 allows requests to be made for assistance from other states, but whether there is any prospect of those requests being complied with will of course depend upon the treaties, arrangements and international relations between the UK and the foreign states in question.

3.175 Requests for foreign assistance must be made either by the prosecutor or by the Director and must be sent to the Secretary of State with a view to the request being forwarded to the foreign state by the Secretary of State (s 74(1)(c)). All outgoing requests will in fact go to the UK Central Authority for mutual assistance in criminal matters which is part of the Home Office. The Secretary of State may only forward the request if 'he believes it is appropriate to do so' (s 74(5)).

3.176 The form of the request where no confiscation order has been made is to ask that the receiving country ensure that any person be prohibited from dealing with specified realisable property. Where a confiscation order has been made, in addition to the request above, the Secretary of State may ask the receiving country to 'realise' realisable property and then to apply it 'in accordance with the law of the receiving country' (s 74(3)). Where property is realised in this way the Crown Court is required to reduce the amount of the confiscation order accordingly (s 74(6)).

3.177 A certificate from the requested government certifying that property has been realised in pursuance of a request, the date of realisation and the proceeds of realisation is admissible as evidence in the Crown Court.

3.178 A request may be made where *any* of the conditions in s 40 are satisfied (s 74(1)(a)). This means that the prosecutor or the Director can request that a foreign country freezes an asset before any restraint order has been made in England and Wales. This will enable the prosecutor or the Director to request that a foreign state freeze assets abroad before any restraint order has yet been made in England and Wales, as long as the conditions for making a restraint order are satisfied at the time.

INTERPRETATION

Criminal lifestyle (s 75)

3.179 As the Explanatory Notes state—

> 'The criminal lifestyle regime is based on the principle that an offender who gives reasonable grounds to believe that he is living off crime should be required to account for his assets, and should have them confiscated to the extent that he is unable to account for their lawful origin.'[1]

---
[1] Explanatory Notes, para 135.

3.180 Section 75 defines 'criminal lifestyle'. The phrase, which first appears in s 6, is a highly controversial lynchpin of the Act, as it determines whether a defendant's benefit is to be limited to the offence for which he has been convicted (ie his particular criminal conduct) or whether his benefit is widened to include his general criminal conduct. In the latter situation the court must make the assumptions set out in s 10.

3.181 Offences which are 'lifestyle offences' are set out in PCA 2002, Sch 2. When a defendant is convicted of any offence in Sch 2 the general criminal conduct assumptions will apply. The offences include blackmail, people trafficking, counterfeiting, intellectual property offences under the Copyright, Designs and Patents Act 1988, offences connected with brothels and pimps and arms trafficking. The Secretary of State may by delegated legislation amend this list to add or remove offences when he considers it justified. The list has been much criticised as being too broad. One problem with it is that many types of offence encompass greatly varying sets of facts, a good example being that of blackmail. Lord Goldsmith, speaking on behalf of the Government, made it clear that the inclusion of blackmail was aimed at extortion rather than cases of simple blackmail.[1] His Lordship said in Committee—

> 'However, there are two important safeguards. It is important to bear them in mind when considering that case and certain other cases. First, the order will not be made save where the prosecutor asks for confiscation. One would not expect that to take place if there were a single isolated instance of an opportunistic blackmail . . . . Secondly, . . . the court always has the power not to apply the assumptions if there might be a serious risk of injustice. That is a second safeguard against the instance where there would be an isolated example which, in the court's view, did not justify the finding.'[2]

[1] HL Committee Stage, 22 April 2002, col 20.
[2] HL Committee Stage, 22 April 2002, col 27.

3.182 This again puts great faith in the prosecutor. Rather than relying on these 'safeguards', the list of offences could have been narrowed. That the power to amend is by delegated legislation is equally worrying.

3.183 Where a defendant is convicted in the Crown Court (or is committed from the magistrates' court) the court must first decide whether he has a 'criminal lifestyle'. and if so whether he has benefited from his general criminal conduct'. If he does not have a criminal lifestyle the court must decide whether he benefited from his 'particular criminal conduct'.

3.184 A defendant has a criminal lifestyle if—
  (a) he is convicted of one offence contained in Sch 2; or
  (b) the offence of which he has been convicted 'constitutes conduct forming part of a course of criminal activity' (s 75(2)(b)) and the offences forming that course of criminal activity plus any

taken into consideration by the court on the same occasions have a benefit value of at least £5,000; or

(c) he is convicted of 'an offence committed over a period of at least six months and the defendant has benefited from the conduct which constitutes the offence' (s 75(2)(c)) to the value of at least £5,000 (including any offences taken into consideration by the court on that occasion).

3.185 Conduct forms part of a course of criminal activity if the defendant has benefited from the conduct and either was convicted of three or more such offences in the proceedings or has two separate convictions in the previous six years for offences constituting conduct from which he has benefited. The minimum of £5,000 in conditions (b) and (c) above may be amended by order.

3.186 The experience of many criminal practitioners will certainly be that many defendants who commit a series of thefts which are fairly petty but may total £5,000 in value will be the least able to rebut the assumptions. Even where the available amount is eventually found to be nil the court will have been forced to waste time and money in order to establish this.

3.187 These provisions arise out of the existing drug and non-drug legislation. Under the provisions in CJA 1988 where a defendant is convicted of two or more offences from which he has received a benefit in the present proceedings or of one in the present proceedings and one in the last six years, the court makes the 'extended benefit assumptions'.[1] These assumptions are similar to those relating to 'general criminal conduct' in CJA 1988. In drug cases one offence was enough for the court to make similar statutory assumptions.

---
[1] CJA 1988, s 72AA.

3.188 Justice suggested that a judicial discretion be inserted in s 75 so that the phrase 'criminal lifestyle' would not be applied inappropriately.[1] This suggestion was not adopted.

---
[1] Justice Proposed Amendments, April 2002.

Conduct and benefit (s 76)

3.189 Criminal conduct is defined as conduct which constitutes an offence in England and Wales or which would constitute an offence if it occurred there (s 76(1)). Under existing legislation confiscation is limited to drug trafficking offences, indictable offences and some summary offences. This limitation is removed by PCA 2002, which allows the Crown Court to make a confiscation order in respect of any 'criminal conduct'. All that the Crown Court is required to do is determine whether a defendant has benefited from criminal conduct. Thus, whilst the offence or offences upon conviction for which the confiscation procedure is initiated must postdate the Act coming into force, it is the intention of Government that the Act is retrospective in that the court can then look back at benefit for previous conduct that predates it.

3.190 Mr Ainsworth told the House of Commons in Committee that a confiscation order may be imposed—

> 'only when all offences that are the subject of the present proceedings have been committed after the Bill comes into force' but once that criteria was satisfied 'a confiscation order can be imposed in respect of benefit from conduct, however far back the benefit was derived'.[1]

Whether this breaches ECHR, Art 7 will doubtless be explored in future litigation.

---

[1] HC SC B, 4 December 2001, cols 465–466.

3.191 Section 76 also defines 'general criminal conduct' and 'particular criminal conduct'. These terms are central to the making of confiscation orders as set out in s 6, which allows for confiscation of the defendant's benefit from either his 'general criminal conduct' or his 'particular criminal conduct'. General criminal conduct is defined in s 76 as 'all his criminal conduct' whenever the conduct occurred. Particular criminal conduct is defined by reference to the offences of which the defendant has been convicted in the current proceedings, together with any taken into consideration by the court in passing sentence. Thus, general criminal conduct includes particular criminal conduct.

3.192 A person benefits from criminal conduct if 'he obtains property as a result of or in connection with the conduct' (s 76(4)). This brings together the present legislation relating to drug trafficking and other offences. Under the existing drug trafficking legislation 'benefit' is defined as where a person 'received any payment or other reward in connection with drug trafficking carried on by him or another person'.[1] Under CJA 1988 in non-drug cases a person benefits from an offence 'if he obtains any property as a result of or in connection with its commission'.[2]

---

[1] DTA 1994, s 2(3); see paras 1.27–1.29.
[2] CJA 1988, s 71(4).

3.193 The broad definition that has been given to the word 'payment' under the DTA 1994[1] so as to include money received for use in the criminal enterprise and not just for reward, means that in effect the definition under the new Act does not change the current position.

---

[1]   *R v Osei* [1988] Crim LR 775, (1988) 10 Cr App Rep (S) 289, CA.

3.194   PCA 2002 reflects existing law[1] under which a defendant is considered to have derived a pecuniary advantage and a benefit even though he may never have realised the value of the criminal conduct. As Lord Rooker put it—

> '. . . if an offender steals a television and subsequently drops and breaks it while carrying it to his home, he would still be liable to have the value of the television confiscated from him even though he could not sell the television in order to make any money. There is no reason why a pecuniary advantage that has been lost should be treated any differently. The point is that recovering the proceeds of crime is supposed to have a deterrent as well as a restitutory effect.'[2]

---

[1]   See eg *R v Smith (David)* [2001] UKHL 68, [2002] 1 All ER 366, [2002] 1 WLR 54.
[2]   HL Committee Stage, 22 April 2002, col 58.

3.195   This demonstrates what many see as the underlying unfairness of the old and new law of confiscation. The value of the television would still be a 'benefit' if it had not been dropped and if it had been recovered intact. A defendant benefits from an offence if he obtains property as a result of or in connection with criminal conduct (s 76(4)). PCA 2002, s 76(7) defines the amount of the defendant's benefit as 'the value of the property obtained'. This amount is not diminished even if the property is recovered. The effect of this is that a defendant will not only receive a sentence for stealing the recovered television but will also have to pay the value of it as a confiscation order out of his legitimate assets and/or be imprisoned in default. The legislation does not therefore just strip defendants of their proceeds of crime.

3.196   Where there has been a joint enterprise, or where there are a number of defendants, the issue of joint benefit arises. PCA 2002 is unfortunately silent in this regard. Where all co-conspirators are before the court it may be simple to divide the benefit figure on the basis of the evidence or in equal shares.[1] However, in *Chrastny*[2] the Court of Appeal held that where only one conspirator was before the court there was nothing wrong with making an order for the full amount, provided the defendant had sufficient control over the property identified to be able to realise it. The effect of this is that in a joint benefit case the whole of the benefit made may be attributable to each defendant. This approach will have to be looked at again in the light of ECHR, Protocol 1, Art 1. None of the current cases specifically deal with this issue.

---

[1] *R v Porter* [1990] 3 All ER 784, 92 Cr App Rep 126, CA.
[2] *R v Chrastny* [1992] 1 All ER 189, [1991] 1 WLR 1381, 94 Cr App Rep 283, CA.

3.197 Pecuniary advantage is defined in s 76(5) and (6). Section 76(6) is drafted in very wide terms and is aimed at depriving an offender of the legitimately earned profits which originated from a fraudulent source (for example, if a fraudster successfully invested money obtained by fraud and made a profit it is the intention of the Act that that profit would be confiscated along with the original stake).[1]

---

[1] This was the example cited by Mr Ainsworth on behalf of the Government (HC SC B, 1 December 2001, cols 467–468). Contrast *R v Moran* [2001] EWCA Crim 1770, [2002] 1 WLR 253, [2002] 1 Cr App Rep (S) 413, in which case it was held that the defendant's pecuniary advantage extended to his unpaid tax together with interest, but did not extend to the balance of undeclared profits which were the product of lawful trading. It is unclear whether *Moran* will be followed under the new Act.

3.198 There does seem to have been some confusion in Parliament about the effect of PCA 2002. The House of Commons Committee were reassured by Mr Ainsworth that 'property cannot be confiscated if it is shown not to be the proceeds of crime' and—

> 'we want to stick to the safeguard in the Bill, whereby if the defendant can show that the assets in question are not the proceeds of crime, they are not confiscatable'.[1]

This is plainly incorrect. Legitimate assets are realisable under the confiscation process.

---

[1] Mr Ainsworth, HC SC B, 4 December 2001, col 469.

3.199 The Crown Court, under the existing legislation and under the new Act, has the power to order the confiscation of any assets held by the defendant or in which he has an interest, up to the benefit figure found by the court. A defendant can reduce the benefit figure in a general criminal conduct case (and thus the amount he potentially owes) by showing that the statutory assumptions are incorrect because, for example, the property assumed to be the proceeds of criminal conduct is not such.

Gifts (ss 77 and 78)

3.200 All the existing provisions in drug and non-drug cases which enable gifts made by a defendant to others to be recovered to satisfy a confiscation order are brought together in s 77. (Gifts are called 'gifts caught by the Act' under the existing legislation and 'tainted gifts' in PCA 2002.)

3.201 Under both the existing and new law if a gift is found to be tainted (or caught by the Act) it becomes part of the realisable property of the defendant.[1] This can cause difficulty to a defendant who, by definition, is no longer in control of the property and will often be unable to get it back. If he fails to do so he will serve time in prison in default of payment because the court treats the property as being 'realisable' even if in practice it cannot be recovered. This is another example of the draconian nature of the legislation.

---

[1] See s 83.

3.202 PCA 2002 provides that where the court has concluded that a defendant has a criminal lifestyle, any gift made by the defendant to any person within six years of the beginning of the proceedings is caught, along with any gift made at any time from the proceeds of crime. If the court determines that a defendant does not have a criminal lifestyle, only gifts made since the time of the earliest offence are caught.

3.203 At a restraint hearing the wider definition of tainted gifts applies. However, as the court is required to exercise its discretion at such a hearing, if it is obvious at this stage that the defendant does not have a criminal lifestyle then the court would no doubt be reluctant to apply the wider definition.

3.204 A gift is defined in s 78(1) as a transfer of property to another for a 'consideration whose value is significantly less than the value of the property at the time of the transfer'. For example, if the defendant sold a boat worth £20,000 for £5,000 then this would still be a 'gift' within the meaning of the Act. This provision is new.

Value (ss 79–81)

3.205 Sections 79–81 define how the court is to calculate the value of property held by any relevant person and how it is to decide the value of property obtained from criminal conduct and the value of any tainted gifts. The sections largely recreate the existing legislation. A gift is a transfer of property at a significant undervalue. Transfers of property for market value in bad faith are capable of being a 'gift'.[1]

---

[1] *R v Crown Court at Maidstone, ex p Dickens* (4 March, 1991, unreported).

3.206 The basic rule is that the value of any property held by a person is the market value of the property at the time in question (s 79(2)). The issue is the date applied.

3.207 Sections 80 and 81 are drafted so as to maximise the figure the court calculates as the 'value' of the property obtained or of a tainted gift. The 'value' is the greater of either—
   (a)   the value of the property/ gift at the time it was obtained/given, adjusted to take into account changes in the value of money; or
   (b)   the value of the property held at the time of the court's decision which either is or represents the gift/property originally obtained.
The following examples illustrate the way in which the value rules operate in the same way in relation to both benefit obtained and tainted gifts—
   (a)   D obtains/gives a house worth £100,000 in 1997. At the date of the confiscation hearing in 2002 the house is worth £50,000. The value of the property/gift is £100,000 plus the RPI increase to reflect the increase in the value of money;
   (b)   D obtains/gives a house worth £100,000 in 1997. It increases in value by the time of the confiscation hearing to £200,000. The value of the property/gift is £200,000 (that being greater than its original value plus RPI adjustment);
   (c)   D obtains/gives house worth £100,000 in 1997. Prior to the confiscation hearing the house is exchanged for another property. This new property is worth £200,000 at the time of the confiscation hearing. The value of the property/gift is £200,000 (that being greater than the original value of the original property plus RPI adjustment); or
   (d)   D obtains/gives two houses in 1997 worth £100,000 each. Before the confiscation hearing one of the houses is exchanged for another property (Greenacre) but the other is retained. At the time of the hearing Greenacre is worth £300,000 and the other original property is worth £100,000. The value is £400,000 (that being greater than the original £200,000 plus RPI adjustment).

3.208 These provisions are similar to the existing law and can cause hardship to the defendant. For example in *Foxley*[1] one of the issues was how to value property purchased by the defendant and transferred as a gift by him. The Court of Appeal upheld the trial judge's ruling that the correct valuation of the gift for confiscation purposes was its original value at the time it was made plus an increase calculated by reference to the RPI. The figure arrived at as a result of this calculation was greater than the valuation of the relevant property at the time of the confiscation hearing. As Roch LJ said—

'the greater of the two values is the value of the gift to the
recipient when he received it, adjusted to take account of
the subsequent values of money'.[2]

---

[1]   [1995] 2 Cr App Rep 523, 16 Cr App Rep (S) 879, CA; see also *R v Dickens* [1990] 2 QB
102, 91 Cr App Rep 164, CA for a further example of the law under CJA 1988 and DTA 1994 in
practice.
[2]   *R v Foxley* (1995) 16 Cr App Rep (S) 879 at 883 and 884, CA.

3.209   If the property has been disposed of by the recipient of the gift the
relevant value is either the value of the proceeds of sale or the original
value of the gift, whichever is the higher. The value of the gift is added
to the amount of the defendant's realisable assets even though he by
definition no longer has the property in question. This is another
example of how punitive and draconian confiscation law has
become. A confiscation order can also be enforced against the
recipient of the gift.

3.210   If a defendant has made gifts of expensive holidays and other
expenditure these will be calculated as 'tainted gifts' and therefore
realisable property (s 83) and will become part of the 'available
amount' under s 9 even though the defendant no longer has the
property and obviously cannot get it back.

Property (ss 82–84)

3.211   Section 82 is a new provision. It provides that property which is
already subject to earlier forfeiture and deprivation orders is not 'free
property'. The principle underlying this section is that property
subject to these orders, made in earlier proceedings, should not be
included in the calculation of the available amount for confiscation.

3.212   'Realisable property' is defined as 'any free property held by the
defendant' and 'any free property held by a recipient of a tainted gift'
(s 83(a), (b)). In addition, property is not 'free' if it is subject to orders
under Pt 5 (on civil recovery).

3.213   As under the existing legislation, s 84(1) defines property in very wide
terms to include money, all forms of real or personal property and
things in action and other intangible or incorporeal property. Section
84(2) provides a list of 'rules' which apply in relation to property.
Property is held by a person if he 'holds an interest in it' (s 84(2)(a)).
Property is obtained when a person 'obtains an interest in it'
(s 84(2)(b)). The list also includes a definition of when property
is transferred (where A transfers or 'grants an interest in it' to B)
(s 84(2)(c)).

3.214 In response to a proposed amendment to make it clear that interests in property were 'property' within the meaning of s 84, Lord Bassam of Brighton stated on behalf of the Government—

> '. . . we consider that interests are already covered by the wide definition of property, particularly that given in paragraphs (b) and (c) of Clause 84(1).'[1]

---

[1]   HL Committee Stage, 13 May 2002, col 29.

3.215 Lord Goodhart highlighted the problem that definition of property under PCA 2002 would appear to encompass the interests of other, innocent, parties in property in which the defendant holds an interest.[1]

---

[1]   HL Committee Stage, 13 May 2002, cols 28–30.

Proceedings, applications and confiscation orders (ss 85–87)

3.216 Sections 85–87 define when proceedings for an offence are started and concluded, when applications are concluded, and when confiscation orders are satisfied and are subject to appeal. These sections are new and are necessary to reflect the new rights of appeal contained in PCA 2002. The Explanatory Notes explain that—

> 'The purpose of the new provision is to ensure that proceedings are not concluded where the prosecutor or Director appeals against the Crown Court's decision, and thus to ensure that a restraint order may be made where such an appeal is lodged, and that any restraint order already made in the case does not have to be discharged.'[1]

---

[1]   Explanatory Notes, para 147.

Other interpretative provisions (s 88)

3.217 This section contains a number of interpretative provisions, for example, a criminal investigation is—

> 'an investigation which police officers or other persons have a duty to conduct with a view to it being ascertained whether a person should be charged with an offence' (s 88(2)).

This wide definition is introduced because restraint orders may now be made at the beginning of criminal investigations[1] but it could surely have been more tightly drafted.

---

[1]   See ss 40(2) and 41.

GENERAL

Procedure on appeal to the Court of Appeal (s 89)

3.218   An appeal to the Court of Appeal lies only with leave of that Court. The appeal is subject to the rules of court under the Supreme Court Act 1981, s 53(1).

3.219   The section also allows the Secretary of State to make an order containing provision corresponding to any provisions of the Criminal Appeal Act 1968 to cover procedural matters such as the procedures for obtaining leave to appeal and transcripts.

Procedure on appeal to the House of Lords (s 90)

3.220   Section 90 provides for appeal to the House of Lords. The precise procedure is to be made by order of the Secretary of State. The provisions of the order will correspond to those for the Court of Appeal in the Criminal Appeal Act 1968.

Crown Court Rules (s 91)

3.221   This section allows for the creation of Crown Court Rules to cover restraint and receivership proceedings in the Crown Court. The existing legislation in the High Court is the subject of the Civil Procedure Rules 1998.

4 Confiscation: Scotland

INTRODUCTION

4.1 The system of confiscation in Scotland is set out in the Proceeds of Crime Act 2002 ('PCA 2002') Pt 3 (ss 92–155). Part 3 is very similar in effect to Pt 2, with the necessary changes in terminology. However, in some respects the Scottish provisions differ and those differences are set out below.

CONFISCATION ORDERS

Making of order (s 92)

4.2 The court must proceed to consider confiscation if three conditions are satisfied, namely—
   (1) An accused be convicted of an offence or offences or receives an absolute discharge without conviction in summary proceedings.
   (2) The prosecutor asks the court to act under this section.
   (3) The court must have decided to order some disposal (absolute discharge is a disposal for this purpose) in respect of the accused.

4.3 In other respects s 92 mirrors s 6, save that before making an order under s 92 the court must take into account any representations made by any person whom it thinks likely to be affected by the order, and that for the purposes of any appeal or review an order under s 92 is a sentence.

4.4 References to 'the court' in ss 92–118 mean the High Court of Justiciary or the sheriff court (s 92(13)).

Disposal of family home (s 98)

4.5 Section 98 provides a protection for the family home in Scotland that does not exist in England, Wales or Northern Ireland. The reasoning for this distinction is not entirely clear. In attempting to explain why the Government felt it right to make the Scottish provisions different in this respect Mr Foulkes stated in Committee—

> 'The answer is historical. Prior to the Proceeds of Crime (Scotland) Act 1995, the Scottish Law Commission made certain recommendations. It advised that some protection should be afforded to the parties who may have an interest in the family home . . . . There are arguments in favour of both positions. On one hand, it may be argued that no one should be able to retain the proceeds of crime, and that a confiscation order should always be enforceable against any realisable property regardless of its nature. On the other hand, there is an argument that family circumstances may be so particular that the retention of the value of the proceeds of crime may be permissible. The provisions under Parts 2, 3 and 4 reflect a policy difference between the existing legislation of the three jurisdictions. As the position is settled and is not thought to have given rise to practical problems, we have not thought it necessary to change it in the Bill.'[1]

---

[1]   HC SC B, 6 December 2001, cols 519–520.

4.6   This seems an extraordinary attempt at justification. Why do recommendations of the Scottish Law Commission in this one respect carry so much weight for the Government when the recommendations of so many other organisations in relation to this Act do not?

4.7   Where a confiscation order has been made but the court has not been satisfied that the defendant against whom it has been made acquired his interest in the family home from his criminal conduct, the administrator cannot dispose of the interest (or bring an action for division and sale or an action to obtain vacant possession) without obtaining the consent of the spouse or former spouse. Where the person lives with a child but no spouse the administrator must obtain the consent of the defendant. Alternatively, where consent cannot be obtained the administrator may apply for authority from the court.

4.8   If the administrator applies to the court for authority to dispose of the interest in the home the court must consider all the circumstances of the case, including the needs and financial resources of the spouse or former spouse and any children, and the length of time the property has been home to those people. The court then has a discretion to refuse the application, to postpone it for up to 12 months or to grant the application together with any conditions it wishes to prescribe.

4.9 'Family home' is defined in s 98(5). The definition covers property in which the defendant has a right or interest and which is occupied by—

(a) the defendant and his spouse;

(b) the defendant's spouse or former spouse;

(c) the defendant with a child or grandchild of the defendant, his spouse, or his former spouse; or

(d) the defendant with a person who has been treated by the defendant, his spouse or former spouse, as if she or he were a child of the defendant, his spouse or former spouse.

The age of the child, grandchild or person treated as such is irrelevant.

4.10 A proposed amendment to extend this protection to same-sex partners in relationships of at least six months was unsuccessful. The same effect may come via the forthcoming Scottish Family Law Bill, which is intended to broaden the concept of 'family' across the Scottish legal system.[1]

---

[1] HL Committee Stage, 13 May 2002, cols 35–37.

PROCEDURAL MATTERS

Postponement (s 99)

4.11 Section 99 mirrors s 14, save that in Scotland a period of postponement can overrun the permitted period not only where there are exceptional circumstances, but also where the accused has failed to comply with an order under s 102(1) to respond to the statement of information.

Accused's response to statement of information (s 102)

4.12 The court 'shall' order the accused to respond to the prosecutor's statement of information (s 102(1)). The equivalent provision in s 17 uses the word 'may'.

4.13 The prosecutor should serve a copy of the statement of information on the accused, and when the court is satisfied that this has been done it will order the accused to indicate what within the statement he accepts and, in relation to allegations that he does not accept, which matters he proposes to rely upon. The court will specify a time limit for the accused's response. Where there has been postponement of the making of the order the court must require the accused to provide his response at least six months before the expiration of the permitted postponement period under s 99.

4.14   Acceptance by the accused is conclusive of the matters alleged in the prosecution statement. A failure to respond to an allegation is conclusive of that allegation unless it is an allegation that the accused has benefited from his general or particular criminal conduct. No acceptance by the accused under this section of benefit is admissible against him in proceedings for an offence.

4.15   Where there is dispute either by the accused or by the prosecution over matters relied upon by the accused the court must order a hearing. The judge who presides over the hearing may adjourn the matter for the trial judge to hear if he considers it appropriate.

RECONSIDERATION

Inadequacy of available amount: variation of order (s 108)

4.16   The accused or the prosecutor (as opposed to a receiver under s 23) may apply to the court to vary a confiscation order. The court is required to calculate the available amount and in doing so must apply s 95 as if references to the time the confiscation order is made were to the time of the calculation, and as if references to the date of the confiscation order were to the date of the calculation.

4.17   If the court finds that the available amount (as so calculated) is inadequate for the payment of any amount remaining to be paid under a confiscation order it may substitute any amount it 'believes is just' (s 108(3)).

Inadequacy of available amount: discharge of order (s 109)

4.18   Section 109 mirrors s 24, save that it is the prosecutor who can apply for discharge of the order. It is worth noting that there is no Scottish equivalent to s 25 (ie there is no discretion to discharge an order where there is a small amount outstanding).

APPEAL BY PROSECUTOR (s 115)

4.19 Section 115 amends the Criminal Procedure (Scotland) Act 1995 ('CP(S)A 1995') to give the prosecutor a right of appeal against a decision of the court not to make a confiscation order.

PAYMENT AND ENFORCEMENT

Time for payment (s 116)

4.20 The amount due under a confiscation order is due immediately on the date of the order unless the court is persuaded by the accused that he needs time to pay, in which case it may allow up to six months for payment. During that six months, or later so long as twelve months have not passed since the making of the order, the accused may apply for further time which may be granted up to a maximum of twelve months from the date of the confiscation order. A court may postpone its decision as to whether to allow time pending the exercise of the administrator's functions under Pt 3.

Interest on unpaid sums (s 117)

4.21 Unauthorised late payment incurs interest at the rate payable under a decree of the Court of Session.

Application of provisions about fine enforcement (s 118)

4.22 The provisions as to fine enforcement are set out in s 118 in conjunction with CP(S)A 1995.

Application, recall and variation (s 121)

4.23 Section 121 mirrors s 42, save that only the prosecutor may apply to the court for the order and a duty is placed upon him to intimate an order to every person affected by it. The prosecutor and any person affected by an order may apply to the court to recall or vary the order. Whilst an application for variation or recall is unresolved the property to which the order applies must not be realised.

RESTRAINT ORDERS ETC

Appeals (s 122)

4.24   The prosecutor may reclaim or appeal a decision not to make a restraint order to the Court of Session. The prosecutor or a person affected by an order may appeal against a decision regarding recall or variation under s 122(2) to the Court of Session.

Inhibition of property affected by order (s 123)

4.25   Sections 123 and 124 replicate the powers in existing legislation and give the Lord Advocate and prosecutor a procedure through which they may prevent the dissipation of the accused's heritable or moveable property.

4.26   The Lord Advocate may apply to the Court of Session in relation to any heritable realisable property that is the subject of a restraint order seeking a warrant of inhibition against any person specified in the restraint order. The warrant for inhibition acts as if granted on an action for debt by the Lord Advocate and may be executed, recalled, loosed or restricted accordingly. It has the effect of letters of inhibition and must be registered forthwith by the Lord Advocate in the Register of Inhibitions and Adjudications. The effective date of the inhibition is governed by the Titles to Land Consolidation (Scotland) Act 1868, s 155. The inhibition does not prejudice the powers of the administrator under this Part. The inhibition subsists for as long as the restraint order applies. When the restraint order comes to an end or is altered the Lord Advocate must apply for the recall or restriction of the inhibition and amend the Register of Inhibitions and Adjudications.

Arrestment of property affected by order (s 124)[1]

4.27   The prosecutor may apply to the court for a warrant for arrestment in relation to moveable realisable property to which a restraint order applies. The court may grant the warrant where the property would be arrestable if the person entitled to it were a debtor. The warrant has effect as if granted under an action for debt and may be executed, recalled, loosed or restricted accordingly. The warrant does not prejudice the exercise of the powers of the administrator under this Part. The arrestment subsists so long as and in such respects as the restraint order has effect. When the restraint order comes to an end or is altered the prosecutor must apply to recall or restrict the arrestment accordingly (see para 4.25).

---

[1] See para 4.25.

Management administrators (s 125)

4.28   If the court has made a restraint order the prosecutor may apply to the court requesting that it appoint an administrator to take possession of and manage the realisable property that is the subject of the order and/or order any person with possession of that property to give it to the administrator. The court clerk will notify affected persons of such an order. The court may order a person holding an interest in realisable property to make a payment to the administrator in respect of a beneficial interest held by the accused or a recipient of a tainted gift. The court may also order the transfer of an interest or may grant or extinguish an interest in the property.

4.29   The administrator will then manage the realisable property in accordance with the court's directions until the confiscation order is made.

Seizure (s 126)

4.30   If there is an attempt to remove property which is the subject of a restraint order from Scotland a constable may seize it. The property will then be dealt with as the court directs.

Restraint orders: restriction on proceedings and remedies (s 127)

4.31   Whilst a restraint order is in force the court may sist any other legal proceedings or process in respect of the property concerned. Any court in which those proceedings are taking place may sist the proceedings or allow them to continue on terms it thinks fit, providing that it first hears from the applicant for the restraint order and any administrator appointed.

REALISATION OF PROPERTY: GENERAL

Enforcement administrators (s 128)

4.32   Where the amount due under a confiscation order has not been paid and the period of imprisonment in default has not been served and where the order is not subject to appeal, the prosecutor may apply to the court requesting that it appoints an administrator of realisable property. The court may give this administrator the power to take possession of any realisable property; to manage or otherwise deal with that property; and to realise that property in such a manner as the court may specify. The court may order that the person holding the property hand it over to the administrator and may order a person holding an interest in realisable property to make a payment to the administrator in respect of a beneficial interest held by the accused or a recipient of a tainted gift. The court clerk will notify affected persons of the orders the court makes in this regard and the court must not authorise the administrator to deal with or realise the property without hearing any representations from any persons holding interests in it.

Management administrators: discharge (s 129)

4.33   When an administrator is appointed under s 125 the court orders the s 128 management administrator to transfer all the property held by him to the new administrator. He is then discharged from his duties.

Sums received by clerk of court (s 131)

4.34   Section 131 sets out the way in which the court clerk should apply money he receives. Section 154 states that the term 'clerk of court' includes the sheriff clerk. The clerk must meet the insolvency practitioner's expenses and any compensation order under s 97(6) if these have not been met under s 130 (which mirrors s 54). The clerk must also pay the expenses of and remuneration for the administrator. This is paid out of the amount due under the confiscation order.

ADMINISTRATORS: GENERAL

Protection of administrators (s 133)

4.35   If an administrator deals with property mistakenly, but reasonably believes it to be realisable property, he will not be liable for loss or damage unless negligent. If an administrator incurs expenses before a compensation order is made or if the order is made but the administrator receives nothing or an insufficient amount the Lord Advocate must reimburse him.

Protection of persons affected (s 134)

4.36   Anyone affected by action taken by an administrator, or who may be affected by proposed action, may apply to the court. The court may make any order it considers appropriate including removing the administrator from office.

Recall and variation of order (s 135)

4.37   The prosecutor or any person affected by an order under ss 125 or 128 may apply to the court for its variation or recall.

4.38   Where a s 125 order was made on the basis that proceedings were started or an application was made, it must be recalled at the conclusion of the proceedings or application. Where the application was made on the basis that an investigation had been started or that there was an application to be made, it must be recalled if within a reasonable time no proceedings for an offence have been started or no application made.

Appeals (s 136)

4.39   The following appeals may be made in relations to ss 125, 128, 134 and 135—
   (1)   The prosecutor may appeal to the Court of Session against a decision of a court not to make an order under ss 125 or 128.
   (2)   Where an order is made under ss 125 or 128, the prosecutor or any person affected by the order may appeal to the Court of Session.
   (3)   An applicant for an order under s 134 may appeal to the Court of Session where no order is made.
   (4)   Where a s 134 order is made, the person who applied for the order, any person affected by it, or the administrator, may appeal to the Court of Session.
   (5)   Where there has been an application under s 135 the person who made the application, any person affected by the court's decision, or the administrator may appeal to the Court of Session.

In each case the Court of Session may confirm the decision of the lower court or make such order as it believes is appropriate.

Administrators: further provision (s 137)

4.40   Section 137 introduces Sch 3, which makes further detailed provision on the appointment, functions and powers of an administrator.

Administrators: restriction on proceedings and remedies (s 138)

4.41   Where an administrator is appointed the court may sist any other legal process or proceedings in respect of the property and any court involved in such a process may, if satisfied that an application is made for appointment of an administrator, sist its proceedings or allow them to continue on such terms as it thinks fit.

COMPENSATION

Serious default (s 139)

4.42   Section 139 makes provision for the payment of compensation in certain circumstances to people who have suffered loss as a result either of a criminal investigation into an offence which did not lead to proceedings, or of proceedings for an offence which do not result in conviction or where the defendant's conviction is quashed or he is pardoned. Compensation is available in these circumstances if there has been serious default by a constable, procurator fiscal or agent of the Lord Advocate, customs officer or Inland Revenue officer, without which the investigation would not have continued or the prosecution would not have been instigated or continued. The offence in relation to which there has been serious default may be one of a number of offences for which there is an investigation or proceedings relating to the defendant or suspect. The defendant or suspect must apply to the court and may be awarded a sum the court thinks just to represent the loss to his realisable property caused in consequence of anything done in relation to it under Pt 3. Section 139(9) specifies who is the appropriate body to pay compensation depending on who was at fault.

4.43   Section 139 extends the previous legislation to cover the whole investigation and recognises the effects of the operation of Pt 3 and the danger of injustice as a result of the restraint provisions. It will be interesting to see whether statistics on compensation claims will be published.

Confiscation order varied or discharged (s 140)

4.44   Where a defendant had absconded but returned and a compensation order has been made without a trial, that order may be varied or discharged under ss 113 or 114. Any person who holds realisable property and has suffered loss under the original compensation order may then apply under this section for compensation from the Lord Advocate for loss flowing from the making of the order. The court may award any sum it believes just and is not restricted to awarding compensation for serious default.

INTERPRETATION: CRIMINAL LIFESTYLE (s 142)

4.45　Section 142 mirrors s 75, save that the relevant schedule of 'lifestyle offences' is Sch 4.

GENERAL: RULES OF COURT (s 155)

4.46　Service of documents under Pt 3, the functions set out in Sch 3 and the accounts to be kept by the administrator may be governed by act of sederunt. This is without prejudice to the Sheriff Courts (Scotland) Act 1971, s 32 or the Court of Session Act 1988, s 5.

5 Confiscation: Northern Ireland

CONFISCATION ORDERS

5.1 The system of confiscation in Northern Ireland is set out in the Proceeds of Crime Act 2002 ('PCA 2002') Pt 4 (ss 156-239). It works in a very similar way to that in England and Wales but the differences of substance are discussed in this chapter.

Making of order (s 156)

5.2 The provisions in s 156 are as those in s 6, except that there is no reference to committal for sentence under the Powers of Criminal Court (Sentencing) Act 2000, ss 3, 4 or 6.

Available amount (s 159)

5.3 Section 159 mirrors s 9, except that under s 159(3) 'Preferential debts' has the meaning given by the Insolvency (Northern Ireland) Order 1989.[1]

---

[1] SI 1989/2405 (NI 19), art 346.

DEFENDANT ABSCONDS: AFTER CONVICTION OR ACQUITTAL (s 177)

5.4 Where a defendant absconds after conviction or committal the provisions are as those in s 6, except that there is no reference to committal for sentence under the Powers of Criminal Court (Sentencing) Act 2000, ss 3, 4 or 6.

ENFORCEMENT AS FINES ETC

Enforcement as fines etc (s 185)

5.5   Under s 185 a confiscation order made by the court is to be treated as a Crown Court fine for the purposes of the Criminal Justice Act (Northern Ireland) 1945.[1] However, it is not to be treated as a fine, costs, damages or compensation for the purposes of the Criminal Justice (Northern Ireland) Order 1998,[2] art 35 (parent or guardian to pay fine etc instead of child).

---

[1]   Section 35(1)(c), (2), (4) and (5).
[2]   SI 1998/1504 (NI 9).

Director's application for enforcement (s 186)

5.6   Section 186 replicates s 38, except that a warrant issued under s 186 is issued under the Treatment of Offenders Act (Northern Ireland) 1968, s 5 and that the provisions contained in ss 38(8)–(10) do not apply in Northern Ireland.

Provisions about imprisonment or detention (s 187)

5.7   This section replicates s 38 save for the references to parallel Northern Ireland legislation.

RESTRAINT ORDERS: SUPPLEMENTARY (s 195)

5.8   Section 195 deals with the interrelation of PCA 2002, Pt 4 with the Land Registration Act (Northern Ireland) 1970. For the purposes of the Land Registration Act (Northern Ireland) 1970, s 66 (provisions relating to cautions), the person applying for a restraint order must be treated as a person interested in relation to any registered land to which either the application or a restraint order made in pursuance of the application relates. The applicant should serve a copy of the restraint order on the Land Registrar who will then make an entry on the register in relation to any land to which the restraint order or an application for a restraint order relates. This entry will prevent anyone dealing with the land without the consent of the High Court. The Land Registration Act (Northern Ireland) 1970, s 67(2) and (4) apply to such an entry on the register. An order discharging a restraint order may require that the entry on the register be vacated.

RESTRICTIONS (ss 206–208)

5.9   Provisions regarding restrictions in Northern Ireland (ss 206–208) mirror ss 58–60, save that there are no provisions relating to distress being levied against realisable property.

RECEIVERS: FURTHER APPLICATIONS (s 210)

5.10   Under s 210 a receiver appointed under ss 196, 198 or 200 may apply to the High Court (if appointed under s 196) or the Crown Court (if appointed under ss 198 or 200) for an order giving directions as to the exercise of his powers.

5.11   Any person who is affected by action taken by a receiver, or who will be affected by proposed action, may apply to the High Court (where the receiver is appointed under s 196) or the Crown Court (where the receiver is appointed under ss 198 or 200) and the court may then make such order as it believes fit.

COMMITTAL AND COMPENSATION: SENTENCING BY CROWN COURT AND SERIOUS DEFAULT (ss 218–220)

5.12   The provisions in ss 218–220 mirror those in ss 70–72, save that there is no reference to the power of committal for sentence under the Powers of Criminal Court (Sentencing) Act 2000, s 3.

INTERPRETATION: CRIMINAL LIFESTLYE (s 223)

5.13   Section 223 mirrors s 75, save that the relevant schedule of 'lifestyle offences' is Sch 5.

6 Civil recovery of the proceeds etc of unlawful conduct

INTRODUCTORY

6.1   The Proceeds of Crime Act 2002 ('PCA 2002'), Pt 5 (ss 240–316) is highly controversial. As *Justice* put it—

> 'The action for civil recovery under Part 5 is problematic, in using the form of a civil action, in which the standard of proof is the balance of probabilities, to allow a state agency with extensive investigatory powers to seek a punitive order for forfeiture of assets. There is the risk that, in practice, this mechanism could undermine the safeguards of the criminal law, through the use of the more flexible civil procedures. These civil procedures are designed to regulate relations between private individuals rather than to enforce the criminal law: a state body such as the Criminal Assets Recovery Agency should not be considered as approximating to a private party in a tort action. It is questionable whether the low standard of proof that applies under Part 5 is adequate to protect defendants from the excessive, arbitrary or discriminatory use of these powers.'[1]

---

[1]   *Justice* Briefing for Second Reading, House of Lords March 2002, para 16.

6.2   The Criminal Bar Association in its response to the PIU Report wrote on 4 September 2000 that—

> 'the CBA believes that the new proposals relating to civil forfeiture are unnecessary, are wrong in principle and pose a significant threat to civil liberties'.

6.3   A further concern is the unexplained relationship between civil and criminal proceedings. Will civil proceedings start to take priority over criminal prosecutions? The Government's assurance that this will not happen is hollow whilst a hierarchy of proceedings remains absent from the face of the Act. During the Second Reading of the Bill in the House of Commons Mr Ainsworth, on behalf of the Government, said that—

> 'Civil proceedings will not run parallel to confiscation proceedings or criminal proceedings. If there are criminal proceedings, confiscation proceedings could well be part of that. Civil proceedings will only be instituted when criminal proceedings are not felt to be available or appropriate.'[1]

---
[1]   HC 2R, 30 October 2001, col 846.

6.4   He gave the example of a person being abroad, untraceable or even dead;[1] the Explanatory Notes add that civil proceedings will also be appropriate where there is insufficient evidence for a criminal prosecution.[2] The Government was unmoved by the argument that if civil actions are to be pursued by the State instead of criminal prosecutions, the safeguards applicable in such proceedings should reflect the quasi-criminal nature of the action.

---
[1]   HC 2R, 30 October 2001, col 844.
[2]   Explanatory Notes, para 290.

6.5   Where a conviction has been obtained, property is not recoverable if it has been taken into account in deciding the amount to be paid under a confiscation order. The civil procedure is available even following a criminal trial where there has been no conviction; where there has been a conviction but no confiscation; and where there has been confiscation but not all property now apparent was taken into account. In the House of Lords, Lord Goldsmith stated—

> 'We certainly do not accept that, where a criminal case has not resulted in a conviction, civil recovery action should automatically be barred.'[1]

---
[1]   HL Committee Stage, 13 May 2002, col 77.

6.6   There has been great concern that it is unfair to expose people to civil proceedings when they have come through criminal proceedings and received a not guilty verdict from a jury. There is perceived to be something very much akin to double jeopardy and the reassurance offered (that these are proceedings in rem and not in personam) will provide small comfort in many cases. The response of Lord Goldsmith, speaking on behalf of the Government in the House of Lords, was—

> '. . . there could still be many different reasons why it would be appropriate to continue with the civil recovery.
>
> I do not shrink from the fact that one of those reasons could be, for example, that either new evidence may come to light after a trial which could not be used to bring

further criminal proceedings, or simply that evidence could be available in the civil process which was not available in the criminal one, or that evidence is available in the civil process which would satisfy a court, even though it did not satisfy the criminal process.

Why is that not double jeopardy? So far as the proceeds are concerned, there will not be double jeopardy because the same property cannot be recovered twice. It is not double jeopardy otherwise because the consequence of civil recovery will not be a conviction—a sentence of imprisonment—against the person whose conduct is at issue.

However, I have indicated that there will be cases where the Director may well take the view that, having regard to the way in which the criminal trial proceeded, it would not be appropriate to continue with any form of civil recovery . . . . He is a public authority subject to the Human Rights Act 1998 and he would have to operate in a proportionate manner.'[1]

---

[1]   HL Committee Stage, 13 May 2002, col 79.

6.7   Proceedings under Pt 5 will usually take place in open court. An amendment that all civil recovery proceedings should take place in Chambers was defeated.[1] Under the Civil Procedure Rules ('CPR')[2] any party has the right to apply for the proceedings to be in private. The CPR set out situations in which the court may order a private hearing, such as where children are involved or where the case involves national security. The court may make an order that proceedings be conducted in Chambers where it is in the 'interests of justice to do so'.[3]

---

[1]   HC SC B, 13 December 2001, col 678.
[2]   CPR r 39.3.
[3]   CPR r 39.2(3)(g).

6.8   The breadth of types of property that may be affected by these proceedings, both in the interim stages and/or finally by recovery, have necessitated complex provisions in ss 267–280. Whether these provisions are sufficient is a matter of debate. In particular, the operation of the system of interim receiver is both essential in demarcating and securing property for recovering and apparently open to abuse. The civil recovery procedures will inevitably be subject to serious review under ECHR. The PIU Report conceded that there is a careful balance to be struck between the civil rights of the individual and the need to ensure that the state has the tools to protect society by tackling crime effectively. However, the introduction of the civil forfeiture power may breach ECHR, First Protocol, Art 1, which provides that no one shall be deprived of his possessions except in the public interest and subject to the conditions provided for by law.

6.9   Although ECHR establishes the right to the peaceful enjoyment of one's possessions, it expressly allows a state a wide power to interfere with that right in the public interest. The Republic of Ireland introduced civil forfeiture and established a Criminal Assets Bureau by the Proceeds of Crime Act 1995. In the case of *Murphy*[1] and the linked case of *John Gilligan v CAB* the Irish Supreme Court held that the legislation did not create 'criminal offences' and was 'civil in character'. The Court ruled that the legislation was not unconstitutional. In *Murphy* the Supreme Court ruled that as the ECHR was not part of the domestic law of the state it was—

> 'accordingly unnecessary to express any opinion on whether the legislation is, as alleged, a breach in any way of the convention'.[2]

Any restriction of the ECHR, First Protocol, must satisfy the test of proportionality and by not being arbitrary or unfair. One argument will be that the civil powers are in fact criminal in nature and should attract the full protection of ECHR, Art 6. The ECHR looks beyond the label given to the procedure at the substance of the proceedings. However, given that the Privy Council, the House of Lords and the European Court of Human Rights[3] have held that confiscation proceedings in the Crown Court are not criminal but civil in nature, such an attack will inevitably face difficulties. It is likely that the ECHR will afford the UK authorities a wide margin of appreciation in confiscation and forfeiture cases.

---

[1]   [2001] IESC 63 (18 October 2001). The case contains a useful description of the US case law which upholds civil forfeiture as constitutional. See *US v Ursery* 135 L Ed 2d 549.

[2]   *Murphy v MG* [2001] IESC 63, per Keane CJ at 141.

[3]   See *R v Benjafield* [2002] UKHL 2, [2002] 1 All ER 815, [2002] 2 WLR 235; *McIntosh v Lord Advocate* [2001] UKPC D1, [2001] 2 All ER 638, [2001] 3 WLR 107; *Phillips v United Kingdom* (2001) 11 BHRC 280, [2001] Crim LR 817, App No 41087/98.

General purpose of Pt 5 (s 240)

6.10   PCA 2002 creates two ways in which the authorities may seek the civil recovery of property which is the proceeds of unlawful conduct.[1] First, the Director of the ARA, or in Scotland the Scottish ministers, may bring an action in the High Court or Court of Sessions to recover property which is, or represents, property obtained through unlawful conduct.[2] Secondly, s 240(1)(b) gives a power of forfeiture to magistrates or sheriffs who rule that cash is, or represents, property obtained through unlawful conduct, or which is intended to be used in unlawful conduct (s 240(1)(a)). Except as specifically provided by PCA 2002, court proceedings in the High Court will be governed in the usual way in England and Wales by CPR or in Northern Ireland by Rules of the Supreme Court, and in the Court of Session in Scotland by Petition Rules.

[1] HL Committee Stage, 13 May 2002, cols 58–63 and 65–75.
[2] Section 240(1)(a).

6.11   These powers greatly extend and replace the existing provisions (in DTA 1994, Pt II) which allow for the forfeiture of cash (if over £10,000) discovered on export or import which is reasonably suspected to be derived from, or intended for use in, drug trafficking. In Committee the House of Lords debated whether PCA 2002, Pt 5 is compatible with ECHR, Art 7, as it may be used in relation to property obtained before the Act comes into force.[1] The Joint Committee on Human Rights formed the view that the unlimited retrospective effect Pt 5 may breach Art 7.[2] The retrospective effect survived the passage of the Bill through Parliament but a challenge seems inevitable in the courts.

[1] HL Committee Stage, 13 May 2002, cols 58–63.
[2] Third Report of the Joint Committee on Human Rights, 30 November 2001 (HL 43, HC 405).

'Unlawful conduct' (s 241)

6.12 'Unlawful conduct' is defined by s 241, as—
   (1) including all conduct that is unlawful under the criminal law (s 241(1)); and
   (2) conduct which occurs abroad and which is unlawful under the criminal law of that country and which would be unlawful under the law of the UK if it had happened here (s 241(2)).

6.13 The question of unlawful conduct is central. The authorities must satisfy the tribunal on the balance of probabilities that the relevant property is the proceeds of crime or unlawful conduct or that a person intended to use any cash in unlawful conduct. In the House of Commons during the Second Reading of the Bill, Mr Ainsworth explained—

   'the Agency will have to go to court and show a good, arguable case in the first instance. It will have to prove—yes to the civil standard—that property involved is the proceeds of crime. The individuals concerned will not

> be subject to the necessity of proving that their property is not the proceeds of crime—it will be the other way around.'[1]

---

[1]   HC 2R, 30 October 2001, cols 844–845.

6.14   Thus, the Government refused to heed the calls of those, including *Justice,* to adopt the standard of proof of 'beyond reasonable doubt' in these civil proceedings in order to avoid undermining criminal proceedings. In their briefing to the House of Lords, *Justice* suggested,

> 'that, at a minimum, if civil actions are to be pursued by the State in place of prosecutions, then the safeguards applicable in such proceedings should reflect the quasi-criminal nature of the action'.[1]

---

[1]   Briefing for House of Commons Second Reading, October 2001.

'Property obtained through unlawful conduct' (s 242)

6.15   Section 242 states that property is obtained through unlawful conduct if a person obtains it by his or another's lawful conduct (eg through theft or receiving stolen goods) or in return for his or another's unlawful conduct (eg by being paid to commit murder or arson, or taking a bribe to give false evidence or corruptly award a contract).

6.16   Under s 242(2)(a) property is considered to have been obtained through unlawful conduct regardless of the investment of any legitimately obtained funds into that conduct. Thus, if a person buys illicit drugs with honestly obtained money, and sells them at a profit, the whole of the proceeds of the sale will count as having been obtained through unlawful conduct, and not just the profit. Further, s 242(2)(b) provides that it is not necessary to show that property was obtained though a particular kind of unlawful conduct, so long as it can be shown to have been obtained through unlawful conduct of one kind or another. So it will not matter, for example, that it cannot be established whether certain funds are attributable to drug dealing, money laundering, brothel-keeping or other unlawful activities, provided that it can be shown that they are attributable to some unlawful conduct, either of a single unspecified type or perhaps some combination. At Committee Stage in the House of Commons an amendment which would have required the application for civil recovery to identify the specific criminal conduct relied upon was defeated.[1] The Law Society had prompted the proposed amendment by arguing that—

'Vague assertions should not be sufficient to allow the appointment of interim receivers and/or recovery proceedings or orders to be made.'[2]

---

[1]   HC SC B, 13 December 2001, col 698.
[2]   Mr Hawkins, HC SC B, 13 December 2001, col 698.

6.17   However Mr Ainsworth's response was that the application would be governed by CPR. The effect of this, he explained, was that the claim form would be 'likely to include details of the unlawful conduct that is alleged have generated the recoverable property'.[1]

---

[1]   HC SC B, 13 December 2001, col 695.

CIVIL RECOVERY IN THE HIGH COURT OR COURT OF SESSION

PROCEEDINGS FOR RECOVERY ORDERS AND 'ASSOCIATED PROPERTY' (SS 243–245)

6.18   Sections 243–245 set out in detail the way in which civil recovery is to operate in the High Court and Court of Sessions. Proceedings in England, Wales and Northern Ireland are initiated by the Director of the ARA serving a claim form on the respondent (the person the authority suspects of holding recoverable property) and on any person who the Director thinks holds associated property which the ARA also wishes to recover (s 243). Under the Scottish provisions the Scottish ministers must serve an application on the respondent and any holders of associated property wherever domiciled, resident or present.

6.19   The order for recovery may include property that is 'associated property' as defined by s 245, which sets out the situations in which property will be treated as 'associated property'. The Explanatory Notes give examples for the five different categories of associated property set out in ss 245(1)(a)–(e).[1] Interests in recoverable property may be associated property, such as a tenancy in a recoverable freehold (s 245(1)(a)). Further, where a lease in a freehold block of flats had been purchased with recoverable property, another lease in the same block bought with legitimate money would be associated property (s 245(1)(b)). Where two people buy a car or obtain a tenancy together, one with recoverable cash and one with legitimate cash, the share of the person who bought with legitimate cash is the associated property (s 245(1)(c), (d)). Under s 245(1)(e), where recoverable property is part of a larger property but not a separate part, the remainder of that larger property is associated property. The Explanatory Notes give the somewhat surprising example for this of a painting, which is recoverable property. Where it has been framed using legitimate money, the frame would be associated property.[2] This implies a very narrow definition of 'separate' and a distinction between being 'separate' and being capable of being separated.

---

[1]   Explanatory Notes, para 302.
[2]   Explanatory Notes, para 302.

6.20   Under s 245(3), where the recoverable property consists of rights under a pension scheme, no property is to be treated as associated with that recoverable property. This has the effect that the interests of all those, other than the respondent, who have interests in the pension fund, cannot be made the subject of an interim receiving order or a recovery order.

6.21   The claim form or application (in Scotland) must specify or describe the property and specify whether it is sought as recoverable property or as associated property. Particulars of claim should be served in the usual way and if they are served later than the claim form they should also specify or describe any associated property.

INTERIM RECEIVING ORDERS (ENGLAND AND WALES AND NORTHERN IRELAND)

Application for interim receiving order (s 246)

6.22   In order to ensure that property is not dispersed or hidden during application for its recovery PCA 2002 creates a procedure for obtaining interim receiving orders to restrict the way in which it may be dealt with pending the outcome of proceedings. In England, Wales and Northern Ireland the Director may apply to the High Court for such an order that will provide for the detention, custody or preservation of the property and the appointment of an interim receiver. This may be done before or after commencing the substantive proceedings. The application may be made without notice if to give notice would prejudice the application for recovery (s 246(3)). The test for the court to apply is whether there is 'a good arguable case' that the property concerned is all either recoverable or associated property (s 246(5)). The 'good arguable case' test is already used by the civil courts for applications for injunctions to freeze disputed property during litigation so that ultimate enforcement of judgment cannot be frustrated.

6.23 If any of the property against which the order is sought is associated property the Director must have established the identity of the owner or taken all reasonable steps to do so.

6.24 The Director must nominate a suitably qualified external interim receiver, who is not a member of the staff of the ARA (s 246(7)). One wonders who will put themselves forward as interim receivers for this purpose and how much they will charge. The reason for keeping them independent from the ARA must be to ensure that there is no suggestion that in carrying out their investigatory role (establishing whether the property is recoverable or associated property and whether there is any other property that is recoverable as a result of the same conduct) interim receivers are influenced by the fact that it will be their employer who will receive the property recovered.

6.25 The power of the High Court to make interim receiving orders is not limited by ss 247–255 (s 246(8)). The High Court retains its inherent discretion to make appropriate orders when making interlocutory injunctions.

Functions of interim receiver (s 247)

6.26 The role of the interim receiver will be the key to the effective operation of civil recovery in most cases. The interim receiver makes the first determination of the status of the specified property, may add other property to the proceedings and is responsible for ensuring that property is not dissipated before the court has opportunity to consider it. Unsurprisingly, therefore, the court has been given a wide discretion as to how the interim receiving order is to take effect. The court may authorise an interim receiver to take whatever steps it thinks appropriate to secure the 'detention, custody or preservation' of the specified property. This may include the exercise of those powers set out in detail in Sch 6.[1]

---

[1] See para 6.30.

6.27 The court has no discretion and must require the interim receiver to establish, by any means it thinks necessary, that the specified property is recoverable or associated property (s 247(2)(a)). The interim receiver must also establish whether there is any other property that is recoverable as a result of the same unlawful conduct and, if so, who holds that additional property (s 247(2)(b)). The Explanatory Notes state that the order must require the interim receiver to establish this to his own satisfaction.[1] This gives the interim receiver great control over people's property with no real safeguard against abuse.

---

[1]   Explanatory Note, para 312.

6.28   As soon as an interim receiving order is made or a claim form is issued the Director's civil investigation powers under Pt 8 cease. From that point further investigation to establish the facts about the specified property can only be carried out by the interim receiver acting under the court's direction.

6.29   Some legal protection for the interim receiver is provided (s 247(3)). So long as he is not negligent he cannot be held liable for loss or damage to property that he mistakenly deals with whilst reasonably believing it to be the property specified in the interim receiving order.

Powers of interim receiver or administrator (Sch 6)

6.30   A non-exhaustive list of powers which the court may confer upon an interim receiver is set out in Sch 6. It includes a power to compel people to answer questions irrespective of any restrictions on the disclosure of information which would otherwise apply (Sch 6, para 2). Although it is not apparent on the face of the Schedule, Mr Ainsworth, on behalf of the Government, explained at Committee Stage—

> 'I can confirm that the wording does not affect the position of legal professional privilege. I am assured that the duty to disclose that may be imposed under the Bill is subject to protection in the public interest of legal professional privilege.'[1]

---

[1]   HC SC B, 13 December 2001, col 710.

6.31   As compulsory disclosure under Sch 6 may lead to self-incrimination, in order to comply with the requirements of the European Court of Human Rights,[1] answers obtained may not be used against the person who provides them in criminal proceedings, unless those proceedings are a prosecution for perjury or where the person or his representative adduces evidence or asks a question relating to the answer and in giving evidence makes a statement inconsistent with the answer given to a Sch 6 request. Use of the evidence against that person is, however, permissible in all civil proceedings.[2]

---

[1]   *Saunders v United Kingdom* [1998] 1 BCLC 362, [1997] BCC 872, 23 EHRR 313.
[2]   HC SC B, 18 December 2001, cols 715–722. A Government amendment meant that answers given to the interim receiver can be used in all civil proceedings rather than just civil recovery cases.

6.32 Schedule 6 also sets out powers of entry, search and seizure (Sch 6, para 3) and powers to oblige persons to assist the interim receiver in the exercise of those powers (Sch 6, para 4). Schedule 6, para 5 sets out powers for the interim receiver to carry on a trade or business and to sell perishable goods or depreciating property once it is under his control.

6.33 Much concern was expressed at Committee Stage in the House of Commons as to the extent of the receiver's powers. Mr Ainsworth attempted to allay those fears by emphasising that a receiver would only have such powers as were granted to him by the court—

> 'He will have to convince the court that those [powers] are necessary in the case that he intends to pursue. The court will not grant wide-ranging and general powers, willy-nilly, without being absolutely convinced that they will be necessary to enable the interim receiver to pursue the case.'[1]

---

[1]   HC SC B, 18 December 2001, col 732.

Registration (ss 248 and 249)

6.34 The aim of s 248 is to allow interim receiving orders relating to land to be entered on the Land Registry so that the land in question cannot be transferred.

6.35 Section 248 concerns the application of the Land Registration Act 1925, the Land Charges Act 1972 and the Land Registration Act 2002 to the functions of the interim receiver. These Acts apply to interim receiving orders in the same way that they apply to court orders enforcing judgments or recognisances or to pending land actions. However, no notice may be entered in the register of title under the Land Registration Act 2002 in respect of an interim receiving order. A person applying for an interim receiving order is an interested person for the purposes of the Land Registration Act 1925, s 57.

6.36 The equivalent provisions relating to Northern Ireland are found in PCA 2002, s 249. Thus an applicant for an interim receiving order is an interested person for the purposes of the Land Registration Act (Northern Ireland) 1970, s 66. The registrar must make an entry inhibiting any dealing with land that is the subject of an interim receiving order.

Duties of respondent etc (s 250)

6.37 Any person to whose property the order applies may be required by the order to bring the property and/or documents relating to it to a place specified by the interim receiver or to hand custody of it over to the interim receiver (if either is possible) and to do anything reasonably required by the interim receiver for the preservation of the property.

Supervision of interim receiver and variation of order (s 251)

6.38   In light of the hugely important role of the interim receiver, the court has been given the power, on an application by the interim receiver, respondent or any other person affected,[1] to make further directions as to the exercise of the interim receiver's functions. For example, the court may be asked by the interim receiver to extend the interim receiving order to additional property in respect of which evidence has come to light, or discharge or vary the order, provided that before doing so it gives the parties and the interim receiver an opportunity to make representations. Sir Edwin Jowitt queried at an early stage why there is no power for the court to make such directions of its own motion, given that the interim receiver is an officer of the court.[2]

---

[1]   See HC SC B, 18 December 2001, cols 741–742, where s 251(4) was amended in Committee by deletion of the words 'interested in' and the insertion of 'affected by'. This suggests Parliament intends a wide range of people to have the power to apply to the court seeking further directions for the interim receiver.

[2]   See p 14 of the document produced by retired High Court judge Sir Edwin Jowitt as his response to the consultation stage of the draft Bill. This document was endorsed by the Lord Chief Justice and by Lord Justice Rose, the Vice-President of the Court of Appeal (Criminal Division).

Restrictions on dealing etc with property (s 252)

6.39   An interim receiving order must prohibit any person to whose property it applies from dealing with that property. This is subject to exclusions, which the court may make at any time, to allow that person to meet his reasonable living expenses or to carry on any trade, business, profession or occupation. The exclusion may be subject to conditions and, controversially, must not cover the payment of legal expenses in respect of proceedings under PCA 2002, Pt 5. The Explanatory Notes state confidently that persons involved in civil recovery proceedings will be able to apply to the Community Legal Service scheme, or the Legal Aid scheme which applies in Northern Ireland, for their legal costs, or, of course, to use any unfrozen assets they may have available.[1] There will thus be no need for them to draw from the property subject to the order. The point was made at Committee Stage that third parties with associated property, not themselves suspected of any unlawful conduct, would also be unable to use the property to finance legal expenses. However, this did not lead to any amendment.[2] Section 252 emphasises the importance of recovery of the unlawfully obtained property by the enforcement agency and stresses that the court should ensure so far as is practicable that this is not prejudiced. A person who has notice of the order and contravenes it will be liable to be proceeded against for contempt of court.

---

[1]   Explanatory Notes, para 321.
[2]   HC SC B, 18 December 2001, cols 742–744.

Restriction on proceedings and remedies (s 253)

6.40   Section 253 ensures that no other legal action or right will prejudice the exercise of an interim receiving order. The Court has power to stay any legal 'action, execution or other legal process' regarding the specified property and states that no distress may be levied against the property without the Court's leave (s 253(1)). Section 253(2) applies to other courts which are dealing with the same property in parallel proceedings. This gives a power to those courts, if satisfied that an interim receiving order exists or has been applied for, to stay proceedings or to let them continue on terms the court thinks fit. A court acting under s 253(2) must give the enforcement authority and the interim receiver (if appointed) an opportunity to address it (s 253(3)). In Committee, Mr Ainsworth said that the section—

> 'is intended to cover the situation where a civil recovery procedure and other proceedings are ongoing in respect of the same property. In such circumstances the parties to the other proceedings will have had an automatic right to be heard, before the court exercises any power under subsection (2) to stay the proceedings or to allow them to continue.'[1]

---

[1]   HC SC B, 18 December 2001, col 732.

6.41   The right of landlords to forfeit a tenancy that is property specified in an interim receiving order by peaceable re-entry is removed by PCA 2002, (s 253(4)). Peaceable re-entry may only be affected with the leave of the court and on such terms as it may impose.

Exclusion of property which is not recoverable etc (s 254)

6.42   The court must vary an interim receiving order if it decides that the property to which it relates is neither recoverable nor associated property. The court may at any time release associated property from the remit of the order when it feels it is not necessary to keep it within the order to protect the recoverable property to which it was decided it related (s 254(2)). If the court believes it is necessary or expedient to do so it may, under s 254(3), attach conditions to the release of the associated property from the order so as to satisfy itself that the recoverable property is protected.

Reporting (s 255)

6.43   The interim receiving order must require the interim receiver to inform the court as soon as reasonably practical if he thinks that—
   (1)   any property to which the order applies which is claimed to be recoverable property is not in fact recoverable;
   (2)   any property to which the order applies which is claimed to be associated property is not in fact associated property;
   (3)   any property not subject to the order is in fact recoverable (by virtue of the same unlawful conduct) or is associated property; or
   (4)   any property to which the order applies is held by someone different to the person identified on the claim form.

6.44   The interim receiver must also report any other material change of circumstances and make a formal report of his findings to the court. He must also serve copies of the report on all those who may be affected by it. This report may comprise a comprehensive account of the nature and origins of, and interests in, the property in question. If the report is comprehensive it will be capable of being used as a basis to establish agreed facts and to identify disputed matters that will fall to be resolved at the final hearing.

INTERIM ADMINISTRATION ORDERS (SCOTLAND)

Application for interim administration order (s 256)

6.45   The Scottish provisions regarding interim administration orders largely mirror those for the rest of the UK. Where there are differences in terminology or form they are set out here.

6.46   The Scottish ministers may apply to the Court of Session for an order. The test for the court to apply is that there is '*probabilis causa litigandi*' that the property concerned is all either recoverable or associated property. The enforcement authority must nominate a suitably qualified interim administrator who is not a member of the Scottish Administration. These provisions do not limit the extent of the power to make the order (s 256(8)). Section 256(8) has been included to make it clear that the Court of Session retains the inherent discretion which it has in civil litigation to make appropriate orders when making interlocutory injunctions.

Inhibition of property affected by order (s 258)

6.47 Section 258 allows the enforcement authority to obtain inhibitions in relation to the property concerned against specified persons for the lifetime of the interim administration order.

Restriction on proceedings and remedies (s 262)

6.48 Section 262 ensures that no other legal action or right will prejudice the exercise of an interim receiving order. The court has power to sist any action, execution or other legal process regarding the specified property (s 262(1)). Section 262(2) applies to other courts which are dealing with the same property in parallel proceedings. This gives a power to those courts, if satisfied that an interim receiving order exists or has been applied for, to stay proceedings or to let them continue on terms the court thinks fit. A court acting under s 262(2) is required to give the enforcement authority and the interim receiver (if appointed) an opportunity to address it (s 262(3)).

Arrestment of property affected by interim administration order (s 265)

6.49 Section 265 allows the enforcement authority to obtain arrestment in relation to moveable recoverable property to which an interim administration order applies.

VESTING AND REALISATION OF RECOVERABLE PROPERTY

Recovery orders (s 266)

6.50 Where the court is satisfied that property is recoverable it must make a recovery order vesting the property in the trustee for civil recovery. However, the court may not make such an order if to do so would be incompatible with the Human Rights Act 1998 or if the conditions in s 266(4) or (5) (in Scotland) are all met and it would not be just and equitable to make an order.[1] The conditions set out in s 266(4) relate to the situation where a party has obtained the property in good faith and has taken steps as a result of obtaining the property or in anticipation of obtaining it without notice that it was recoverable property. If a recovery order would be detrimental to him by reason of those steps then the criteria in s 266(4) are fulfilled and the court must consider whether it is just and equitable to make the order. The same test is provided for Scotland (s 266(5)) save that the holder of the property must have 'no reasonable grounds for believing' it to be recoverable, rather than that he had no notice that it was recovered.

It is difficult to see any justification for this difference between the two jurisdictions. The Scottish appear to be held to an objective standard whilst the English, Welsh and Northern Irish need only act in good faith! In considering whether it is just and equitable the court must have regard both to the degree of detriment that would be suffered as well as the interest of the enforcement authority in receiving the proceeds of the property (s 266(6)). The order may sever any property and may impose conditions as to the manner in which the trustee may deal with the property for the purpose of realising it. Section 266(9) states that this section is subject to ss 270–278.

---

[1]   HC SC B, 18 December 2001, cols 768–770.

Functions of the trustee for civil recovery (s 267)

6.51   Where it makes a recovery order, the court must appoint a trustee for civil recovery. The enforcement authority must nominate a trustee who must be suitably qualified but may also be a member of the authority's own staff. The Explanatory Notes explain that this is because, unlike the interim receiver, the trustee acts in the interests of the enforcement authority following the court's judgment in favour of that authority and has no investigative functions.[1] Section 267(3) sets out the functions which the trustee for civil recovery must carry out. These are—

(a)   to secure the property which will be vested in him;

(b)   in Scotland, to register the inhibition in the register of inhibitions and adjudications if he considers it necessary;

(c)   to liquidate non-cash assets for the benefit of the enforcement authority; and

(d)   to perform any other functions conferred upon him by this chapter of the Act.

The trustee acts as such on behalf of the enforcement authority and under its instruction (s 267(4)). He has a duty to deal with the property in such a way as to maximise the amount of money for the enforcement authority (s 267(5)).

---

[1]   Explanatory Notes, para 352.

Powers of trustee for civil recovery (Sch 7)

6.52   Section 267(6) introduces Sch 7 which sets out the powers of the trustee for civil recovery. These are self-explanatory. However, in Committee, Mr Ainsworth stated that this list was not exhaustive, explaining that the trustee 'can do anything else that is necessary and expedient' and 'effectively holds the ring and can settle proceedings involving property'.[1]

---

[1]   HC SC B, 18 December 2001, col 771.

Recording of recovery order (Scotland) (s 268)

6.53   The clerk of the court must send a certified copy of the recovery order to the keeper of the register of inhibitions and adjudications who will record it in the register. This has the effect of an inhibition, effective from the date of the order, against the person in whom the heritable property was previously vested.

Rights of pre-emption, etc (s 269)

6.54   Recovery orders override any provisions that would 'otherwise prevent, penalise or restrict the vesting of the property' (s 269(1)) in the trustee for civil recovery. The effect of s 269(2) is that the property will pass into the control of the trustee without any right of another party to pre-emption, irritancy or return taking effect. However, the combined effect of s 269(2) and (3) is that such rights will not become extinguished. In the Explanatory Notes to the Act it is explained that such rights will continue to have effect when the property is vested in the trustee as if no transfer of property has taken place.[1] Therefore, a person who has the first option to buy property when it changes hands will not be able to exercise his right to prevent the vesting of recoverable property in the trustee by the recovery order but will have first right to buy the property when the trustee comes to sell it on. The same is true of rights or interests created by the order itself.

---

[1]   Explanatory Notes, para 355.

6.55   If a person holding such rights suffers loss as a result of property vesting in the trustee, he may apply to the court for compensation as described below.

Associated and joint property (s 270)[1]

6.56   Section 270 defines the situations in which ss 271 and 272 will apply, namely where the court makes a recovery order in respect of associated property and the owner, not being the respondent in the proceedings, has been served with a claim form or application (in Scotland). Sections 271 and 272 also apply where the recoverable property belongs to joint tenants, one of whom is an 'excepted joint tenant' under s 270(4). Sub-section (4) defines an 'excepted joint tenant' as a person who obtained the property in circumstances that would not make it recoverable (s 270(4)). The share of the property attributable to the excepted joint tenant is that which he would obtain were the property to be severed.

---

[1]   Sections 270–272 (paras 6.57–6.61) were incorporated into PCA 2002 to deal with the difficult issues presented by property held jointly or property that is 'associated property' as defined in s 245.

Agreements about associated and joint property (s 271)

6.57   Section 271 offers one possible way of dealing with the difficult situations presented by associated property and by joint tenancies involving one or more excepted joint tenants. Under s 271 a recovery order may endorse an agreement between the owner(s) of the associated property or excepted joint tenant(s) and the enforcement authority that the property shall not pass to the trustee for civil recovery but that instead the owner or tenant shall pay an agreed sum of money to the enforcement authority. The order may include the necessary provision for 'vesting, creating or extinguishing any interest' (s 271(2)) in the property for the benefit of the paying party. The amount payable should be the amount agreed by the enforcement authority and the payee to represent the value of the recoverable property (where the payee is the owner of associated property) or the value of the recoverable property less the excepted joint tenant's share. This sum may be reduced by an amount that the enforcement authority agrees is reasonable having regard to any loss incurred to the payee during the course of any interim receiving order that had effect over the property and any other relevant circumstances. If there is associated property with different owners or if there are a number of excepted joint tenants all of them should agree with the enforcement authority the total sum to be paid and their respective shares of that payment. A recovery order made under s 271 should make it clear that the property ceases to be recoverable by it.

6.58   Whilst s 271 does allow some flexibility and pragmatism there will surely be many people unable to afford to 'buy out' their joint tenant in this way.

Associated and joint property: default of agreement (s 272)

6.59   Where there is associated property or an excepted joint tenancy as defined in s 270 but there has been no agreement under s 271 the court may, where it considers it to be just and equitable to do so, make a recovery order which provides that the associated property be vested in the trustee for civil recovery, or that the excepted joint tenant's interest be extinguished or severed. Where the property is vested in the trustee or the interest is extinguished the order may require the trustee to pay an amount of money to the holder of the associated property or the excepted joint tenant and/or may create interests in favour of that person or liabilities or conditions in respect of the property vested. The Explanatory Notes give the example that the court might order that a joint owner's interest in a house be extinguished, but might at the same time create a right for him to live in the house for his lifetime, as well, perhaps, as ordering that he be paid compensation.[1] In making such an order the court must weigh the interests of the holder of the property or excepted joint tenant against those of the enforcement authority in receiving the realised proceeds of the recoverable property. Mr Ainsworth explained in Committee—

'The overarching safeguard is that it [the court] can make an order in respect of non-recoverable property only if it thinks it just and equitable to do so.'[2]

[1]   Explanatory Notes, para 362.
[2]   HC SC B, 18 December 2001, col 778.

6.60   Others may feel that this very difficult area is ambiguous and that the panoply of situations that will confront the courts will mean that many innocent property holders will not know what to expect from the courts. It is interesting to note the faith the Government display in judicial discretion here in contrast to PCA 2002, Pts 2–4 where they were determined to make the provisions mandatory. It seems that the Government believe that judges are a sufficient safeguard for the property rights of ordinary people but not of the Government's objectives.

6.61   If the court is satisfied that the holder of associated property or excepted joint tenant has suffered any loss as a result of an interim receiving order in respect of the property it may require the enforcement authority to pay compensation to that person in an amount which the court thinks reasonable having regard to the amount of the loss and to any other relevant circumstances (s 272(5)–(6).

Payments in respect of rights under pension schemes (s 273)

6.62   Section 273 relates to recoverable property consisting of rights under a pension scheme. It provides that instead of vesting the property in the trustee for civil recovery the recovery order should require the trustees or managers of the pension scheme to pay a sum equivalent to the value of the rights under the scheme to the trustee for civil recovery. Regulations may make provision for the assessment of the value of the rights under a pension scheme (s 273(7)).[1] Section 273(5) ensures that no provision in a scheme nor any enactment can override the effect of this section. The court may order that any expense incurred by the trustees or managers of the scheme in complying with the recovery order or providing information, before the order was made, to the enforcement authority, interim receiver or interim administrator, shall be deducted from the sum to be paid by them or recovered in some other way.

---

[1]   The Explanatory Notes to the Bill (para 346) stated that there is already a well established method for valuing the pension rights of members of pension schemes, for example where a person wants to transfer their rights to another scheme and explained that the regulations for the calculation of the 'cash equivalent' in cases brought under this Part will broadly reflect the principles set out for calculating cash equivalents in other cases..

Consequential adjustment of liabilities under pension schemes (s 274)

6.63   Clearly, following payment to the trustee for civil recovery by trustees or managers of a pension scheme under s 273, their liability to their customer must be extinguished or altered. This is provided for by s 274 which states that a recovery order made under s 273 must provide for the liabilities of the scheme to be reduced by the amount to be paid under s 273.

6.64   The order must provide that the liabilities in respect of the respondent cease or be adjusted and may provide that liabilities under the scheme to any other person which derive from the rights of the respondent should cease or be adjusted.

Pension schemes: supplementary (s 275)

6.65   Section 275 which types of pension rights are amenable to a recovery order. Section 275(3) confirms that the regulations referred to above are to be made by the Secretary of State after consultation with the Scottish ministers. The regulations may provide that any values or liabilities be calculated or verified in a manner approved by or in accordance with guidance produced by a person prescribed in the regulations (s 275(1)). Examples given in the Explanatory Notes are the Institute of Actuaries in England and Wales and by the Faculty of Actuaries in Scotland.[1]

---

[1]   Explanatory Notes, para 369

Consent orders (s 276)

6.66   Section 276 for consent orders where all parties involved, namely the enforcement authority, the respondent, the holder of any associated property to be affected and any excepted joint tenant affected, agree on the terms of a recovery order. Before the order can be made the proceedings must have been commenced and all of the above parties must become parties to the proceedings. The order may, under the terms of the agreement, stay or sist the proceedings on terms, make provision for property to cease to be recoverable and/or make any further provisions that the court thinks appropriate.

Consent orders: pensions (s 277)

6.67   Section 277 was added in Committee in the House of Commons in order to highlight the possibility of there being consent orders even where there is a pension scheme in place. Mr Foulkes, speaking on behalf of the Government during Committee Stage explained—

> 'If a civil recovery case involves pension rights, the new clause will ensure that it is possible for an agreement to be reached by the parties in a way that recognises the particular needs of pension schemes.'[1]

---

[1]   HC SC B, 18 December 2001, col 782.

6.68   It is perhaps strange to add a new section to PCA 2002 simply to highlight a process which it seems could have operated under s 273 in any event. Surely a practice direction or Government statement would have sufficed.

6.69   Section 277 provides that there can be a consent order where the recoverable property is a right in a pension scheme. The trustee or managers of the scheme must be party to an agreement with the enforcement authority as to the terms of the order. The trustees or managers are given power to come to such agreements (s 277(4)). The order may provide for recovery by the trustees or managers of the scheme of expenses incurred in complying with the order or providing information before the making of the order to the enforcement authority, interim receiver or interim administrator. In other respects the order will then operate as that under s 273.

Limit on recovery (s 278)

6.70   Section 278 imposes important limitations on the amount of recovery resulting from the application of the above rules. The enforcement authority is of course entitled to trace property obtained through unlawful conduct and to recover property that 'represents' or is related to the original benefit. However, this may result in a situation where the enforcement authority is in a position to recover a large body of property which is disproportionate to the original benefit. Where the original property still exists the court will not allow the enforcement authority to recover both that and representative property. Where the original property cannot be found but there are related items of property the court will control which property (or parts of property) can be recovered so as to satisfy the enforcement authority's right to recover the original property (s 278(3), (4).

6.71   However, profits accruing to property properly subject to recovery are a different matter and nothing in this section prevents a court from ordering their recovery (s 278(5)).

6.72   Where the right of the enforcement authority to recover the original property has already been satisfied by a previous recovery order, summary forfeiture, civil recovery by the victim of the criminal conduct, or confiscation following criminal proceedings, the court is allowed to limit recovery to prevent double recovery(s 278(2), (6)–(9)).

Section 278: supplementary (s 279)

6.73   Section 279 gives examples of the ways in which the enforcement authority's right to recover the original property can be satisfied. It prevents the respondent from thwarting the enforcement authority by exchanging the property. Where property which the enforcement authority has a right to recover is disposed of in whole and other property is obtained in its place, the right of the enforcement authority will be satisfied on recovery of the new property that represents the old. If there is a part disposal of the original property and other property is obtained in place of that part the right of the enforcement authority is to obtain the remainder of the original property together with the new property that represents the part disposed of. Original property has the same meaning as under s 278, and part disposal includes the granting of an interest in the property.[1]

---

[1]   See ss 279(4)(b) and 314(1)).

Applying realised proceeds (s 280)

6.74   The trustee for civil recovery holding sums realised from recovered property and sums of recovered money must deal with that total sum in the following way. First, he must make any payment required of him by s 272. Secondly, he must make any payment due under s 432(10), for expenses of an insolvency practitioner. The remaining sum is then to be paid to the enforcement authority (the Director or the Scottish ministers).

EXEMPTIONS ETC

Victims of theft, etc (s 281)

6.75   Section 281 is designed to protect the interests of victims of theft by ensuring that the provisions of Pt 5 do not prevent them from regaining their property. A person who has been deprived of property by unlawful conduct and finds that his property is now the subject of proceedings under Pt 5 as suspected recoverable property or property representing recoverable property may apply for a declaration under s 281. He must show that he has been deprived of the property and is its owner and that it was not recoverable property before he was deprived of it.[1] Once a declaration is made the property ceases to be recoverable.

---

[1]   The principle of *nemo dat quod non habet* is of course well established; see *National Employers' Mutual General Insurance Association Ltd v Jones* [1990] 1 AC 24, [1988] 2 All ER 425, HL.

6.76   The Explanatory Notes explain that the unlawful conduct by which the applicant was deprived need not be the same conduct as that upon which the authority relies—

> 'So if, for example, a drug trafficker steals money from a person and invests it in drug trafficking, the enforcement authority may bring proceedings in respect of the property that the drug trafficker has obtained through the drug trafficking. But the victim would still be able to claim that part of the property belonged to him, even though the authority was relying on the drug trafficking, rather than the theft.'[1]

---

[1]   Explanatory Notes, para 386.

Other exemptions (s 282)

6.77   Section 282 sets out a series of exemptions from civil recovery proceedings. First, s 282(1) provides that the Secretary of State (following consultation with the Scottish ministers) may make an exempting order to prevent civil recovery against a particular person or class of persons on the basis of who they are or on the basis of what the property consists. Any order proposed under these provisions will be subject to approval by both Houses of Parliament.[1] Section 282(2) sets out the distinction between the civil recovery order and summary proceedings. If the recoverable property is all in the form of cash with no simultaneous recovery of other property from the respondent then civil recovery proceedings may not be used and the summary procedure is the only available option. Particular types of property are exempt from recovery (s 282(3)–(5)): property held by the FSA; property held by an insolvency practitioner; and property subject to specified charges which relate to assets that are intended as security for financial markets. As discussed above, the interrelationships of the ARA with other agencies will be watched with interest, not least amongst these will be its relationship with the FSA.

---

[1]   See s 459(6)(a).

MISCELLANEOUS

Compensation (s 283)

6.78   If property is made the subject of an interim receiving order or an interim administration order (in Scotland), and there is no decision of a court at the end of the proceedings that the property is recoverable or associated property, the owner may make an application to the court for compensation (s 283(1)). This does not apply if a s 281 declaration has been made or if the reason the court has not decided the property is recoverable or associated is because a s 276 consent order has been made. The application must be made within three months from the date of the decision of the court that no order could be made or from the date of discontinuance by the enforcement authority. If on hearing an application the court is satisfied that the applicant has suffered loss as a result of the interim receiving order or interim administration order it may require the enforcement authority to pay compensation.

6.79   If as a result of s 269 any person has suffered a loss in that a right, such as a right of pre-emption, cannot subsequently operate in favour of him or be exercised by him, he may apply for compensation and the court, if satisfied, may require the enforcement authority to pay it. The application must be made within three months of the vesting of the interest referred to in s 269(2).

6.80   In awarding compensation under any part of this section the court should specify such an amount as it thinks reasonable having regard to the loss suffered and any other relevant circumstances.

Payment of interim administrator or trustee (Scotland) (s 284)

6.81   Fees or expenses incurred by interim administrators or trustees for civil recovery in Scotland are to be reimbursed by the Scottish ministers as soon as practicable after they have been incurred.

Effect on diligence of recovery order (Scotland) (s 285)

6.82   Section 285 applies to the situation in Scotland where recoverable property has been vested in the hands of the trustee for civil recovery and a creditor seeks to enforce a judgment against the respondent in respect of that property. Section 285 effectively prevents the creditor from taking such action in respect of property after it has been vested in the trustee for civil recovery. Once recoverable property is vested in the trustee, any other enforcement action (diligence) executed thereafter in relation to that property will be ineffectual.

Scope of powers (Scotland) (s 286)

6.83   The Court of Session may make an order in respect of a person wherever he is domiciled, present or resident and in respect of moveable property wherever it is situated, save that an order may not be made in respect of moveable property if the person to whom the property belongs is not domiciled, resident or present in Scotland and the property is not in Scotland, unless the unlawful conduct took place in Scotland.

Financial threshold (s 287)

6.84   Section 287 allows the Secretary of State to make rules to prevent proceedings being initiated in small cases. Following consultation with the Scottish ministers, he may make an order specifying a minimum amount for the purposes of Pt 5 of the Act. The enforcement authority must not institute proceeding for a recovery order or apply for an interim receiving order unless it reasonably believes that the aggregate value of the recoverable property will be at least the minimum amount. Section 287 does not affect an order which was properly applied for at the time but relates to property that may turn out to be worth less than envisaged or to proceedings which are discontinued in part bringing the value below the limit.

6.85   Not for the first time in PCA 2002 this constitutes what some may see as a worrying obfuscation of responsibility by Parliament. There is nothing on the face of the statute to even hint at what the threshold will be.

Limitation (s 288)

6.86   A limitation period for bringing proceedings for a recovery order is set
        at 12 years from the date that the original property is obtained
        through unlawful conduct. Section 288 makes the appropriate
        amendments to the Limitation Act 1980, the Prescription and
        Limitation (Scotland) Act 1973 and the Limitation (Northern Ireland)
        Order 1989[1] to effect this.

        ---
        [1]   SI 1989/1339 (NI 11).

RECOVERY OF CASH IN SUMMARY PROCEEDINGS

INTRODUCTION

6.87   The second type of action created under PCA 2002, Pt 5 is a summary
        procedure that takes place before a magistrates' court or the sheriff.
        The need for, and appropriateness of, a summary procedure has been
        much questioned and many will watch with interest to see to what
        extent it will be used. In the House of Lords, Lord Goodhart doubted
        the suitability of the magistrates' court for dealing with the complex
        issues that could arise.[1] In essence the powers are an extension of the
        existing powers under DTA 1994 to cover non-drug related offences,
        but this is not a complete answer to the concerns.

        ---
        [1]   HL Committee Stage, 13 May 2002, cols 53–54.

6.88   PCA 2002 provides customs officers (so far as it concerns offences
        that are assigned offences in accordance with the Customs and Excise
        Management Act 1979) and constables with powers of search and
        seizure. It details a procedure by which the court may forfeit cash.
        Cash has a broad definition including cheques, postal orders,
        bankers' drafts, bearer bonds and bearer shares. This is a broader
        definition than that contained in DTA 1994, s 48.

SEARCHES

Searches, prior approval and reports (ss 289–291)

6.89   Sections 289–291 strengthen the already considerable police and
        customs powers of search. If a customs officer or constable is lawfully

on premises and has reasonable grounds for suspecting there is cash on the premises which is recoverable property or is intended by any person for use in unlawful conduct and which is over the minimum amount, he may search for the cash. If an officer or constable has reasonable grounds for suspecting that a person is carrying such cash, he may require the person, so far as it is necessary or expedient, to permit a search of any article he has with him and/or his person, save that the search of the person may not be an intimate or strip search.[1] In order to conduct the search the officer or constable may detain the person as long as necessary. These powers do not extend to items other than cash.

[1]   Within the meaning of Customs and Excise Management Act 1979, s 164.

6.90   Prior approval must be obtained before exercising the above search powers unless it is 'not practicable to obtain that approval before exercising the power' (s 290(1)). It will be interesting to see how this phrase is interpreted by the courts. If 'practicable', approval should be from a justice of the peace or sheriff. If this is not practicable, approval should be from an inspector or the HMCE equivalent. Only if this too would not be practicable should an officer or constable proceed to search without either form of approval. Where there is no approval from a justice of the peace or sheriff the officer or constable must make a written report to the person appointed by the Secretary of State or Scottish ministers in all cases where no cash is seized or any seized is not detained for more than 48 hours. Such a report must set out what led him to believe the power was exercisable and why it was not practicable to seek judicial approval. The appointed person in turn makes annual reports to the Secretary of State or Scottish ministers who must publish it and lay it before Parliament or the Scottish Parliament. This report details the exercise of these search powers in cases where no cash is seized or none is detained beyond 48 hours.

6.91   Clearly there is a risk that this power will be abused. Mr Ainsworth, speaking on behalf of the Government in reference to the search power explained—

> 'We are introducing a power for the use of constables or Customs officers that we intend to be used in situations in which there are clear grounds for suspicion. In the main, it will be used for intelligence-led operations that allow the seizure of cash. The power is not meant to allow speculative searches in circumstances in which there is no justification. The current wording of the clause and the safeguards that exist in this part of the Bill ensure that the power cannot be used in that way.'[1]

[1]   HC SC B, 8 January 2002, col 799.

6.92   However, the difficulty with any 'intelligence-led' power is that secrecy surrounding sources and methods of intelligence is likely to make effective scrutiny of the use of that power very difficult. Those interested in the effect of these provisions will look with interest to see who is appointed to monitor these powers and at the annual reports.

Codes of practice (ss 292 and 293)

6.93   Sections 292 and 293 require the Secretary of State (s 292) and the Scottish ministers (s 293) to publish Codes of Practice setting out how the search powers in s 289 are to be exercised by customs officers and police officers. The exact form of these Codes of Practice is not yet decided, although the matter is subject to consultation.[1]

---

[1]   The consultation document for the Scottish Code of Practice under s 293 can be found at http://www.scotland.gov.uk/pages/default.aspx   while   http://www.homeoffice.gov.uk/atoz/consult_papers.htm contains the consultations for the Code of Practice under s 292.

SEIZURE AND DETENTION

Seizure of cash (s 294)

6.94   Section 294 expands and replaces the scheme set out in DTA 1994, Pt II which provides for the seizure and forfeiture of cash being imported into or exported from the UK, which represents the proceeds of, or is intended for use in, drug trafficking. This scheme is expanded to include cash related to all unlawful conduct rather than just that suspected to relate to drugs offences. It also may be used in relation to cash discovered inland, whilst DTA 1994 relates only to cash being imported into or exported from the UK. A customs officer or constable may seize any cash if he has reasonable grounds for suspecting that it is recoverable property or is intended for use by any person in unlawful conduct. An officer or constable may also seize other cash that it is not reasonably practical to separate from the cash liable to seizure per se. Again, there is a minimum amount that may be seized.[1]

---

[1]   See s 303.

6.95   This extension of an already draconian power brings with it obvious concerns. Mr Ainsworth told Parliament—

> 'We do not intend that powers should be introduced to seize automatically any cash found in the possession of suspicious characters throughout the land. We intend to

give powers to constables and Customs officers to use appropriately when they encounter suspicious cash while performing other duties.'[1]

---
[1]   HC SC B, 10 January 2002, cols 841–842.

6.96   However, *Justice*, amongst others, does not find reassurance in this, and complained that on the face of PCA 2002 the powers of seizure are too broadly defined. *Justice*'s view is that a significant intrusion of privacy, such as is provided for here, should only operate under judicial authorisation.[1]

---
[1]   *Justice* Briefing for Second Reading, House of Lords, March 2002.

Detention of seized cash (s 295)

6.97   A constable or customs officer may hold cash for 48 hours provided he continues to have reasonable grounds for suspicion. Further detention may then be authorised by a magistrates' court or (in Scotland) a sheriff. Further detention may be for a maximum of three months from the date of the order, but further applications may be granted provided the total period from the date of the first order does not exceed two years. The first order for further detention may be granted by a single justice of the peace (s 296(3)). The application must be made by the Commissioners of Customs and Excise or a constable (in England, Wales and Northern Ireland) or by the procurator fiscal (in Scotland). A tribunal granting the period of further detention must be satisfied that there are reasonable grounds for the officer's suspicion and that the continued detention is justified for the purposes of investigating its origin or intended use. The magistrate may also make an order for continued detention if consideration is being given to the bringing of criminal proceedings (in the UK or elsewhere), or if such proceedings have been commenced and not concluded.

6.98   If no application for further detention is made to a court within the 48 hours the cash must be released. Presumably the courts will continue to enforce these time limits rigorously. The case of *R v Uxbridge Magistrates' Court, ex p Henry*[1] concerned detention of cash under the Criminal Justice (International Co-operation) Act 1990, s 25 (the predecessor of DTA 1994, s 42). The Divisional Court held that the time limits in the Act must be read strictly. Time ran from when the officers had first physically detained the cash with the relevant suspicion and not from the later time at which they had served notice. The application for continued detention was, on the facts of that case, held to be out of time. The High Court left open the question as to whether the order for continued detention must actually be made within the 48 hours, presuming the application is in time.

---

[1]   [1994] Crim LR 581.

6.99   An application for further detention may also be made where cash has been seized under s 294(2) and one of the conditions set out above is satisfied in respect of part of the cash, the tribunal being further satisfied that it is not reasonably practicable to separate the cash and detain only that part.

6.100   An order made under s 294(2) must provide for notice to be given to persons affected by it (s 298(8)).

Interest (s 296)

6.101   Monies detained should be paid into an interest-bearing account 'at the first opportunity' (s 296(1)). Interest accrued is added to the sum forfeited or released at the end of proceedings. Monies seized under s 294(2), being money in relation to which the officer has no suspicion but could not separate at the time of seizure from money in relation to which he did have suspicion, must be released once it is in the interest bearing account and can be separated. The requirement to pay monies into an account does not apply if the monies or the part of the monies to which suspicion relates are required as evidence of an offence or as evidence in proceedings under PCA 2002, Pt 5, Ch 3.

Release of detained cash (s 297)

6.102   A person from whom cash has been seized under PCA 2002, Pt 5, Ch 3 of the Act may apply to a magistrates' court or a sheriff for the return of all or part of the cash. To succeed the applicant must satisfy the court that the conditions for detention in s 295 are no longer met. The magistrates' court or sheriff may then direct that the cash be released. The Explanatory Notes state that the fact that only the person from whom the money is seized may apply to the court is intended to prevent the magistrates' court from becoming embroiled in a dispute between the person from whom the cash was seized and the rightful owner of the cash.[1]

---

[1]   Explanatory Notes, para 412.

6.103   A customs officer, constable or (in Scotland) the procurator fiscal may, after notifying the tribunal under whose order cash is being detained, release the whole or part of it if satisfied its detention is no longer justified (s 297(4)).

6.104 However, cash is not to be released by anyone if an application for its forfeiture under s 298, or its release under s 301, is made until any proceedings in pursuance of the application (including appeal proceedings) are concluded.

FORFEITURE

Forfeiture (s 298)

6.105 Whilst cash is detained under s 295 the Commissioners of Customs and Excise or a constable (in England, Wales and Northern Ireland) or the Scottish ministers (in Scotland) may apply to a magistrates' court or a sheriff respectively for forfeiture of the whole or part of the cash. To order forfeiture the tribunal must be satisfied that the cash or part of it is recoverable property or is intended by any person for use in unlawful conduct. However, where recoverable property is held by joint tenants, one of whom is an excepted joint tenant (s 270) the order for forfeiture may not apply to that part of the property that the tribunal thinks is attributable to the excepted joint tenant's share. The Explanatory Notes give the example of a joint bank account into which drug trafficking proceeds (dirty money) has been paid by one signatory and legitimately obtained money by the other.[1] If the former withdraws all the cash and it is subsequently seized, the court can then distinguish between the clean and dirty money. The court has the discretion to return to the 'innocent' partner his share of the money. The civil standard of proof applies to applications for forfeiture.

---

[1] Explanatory Notes, para 414.

Appeal against forfeiture (s 299)

6.106 A party whose property is forfeited may appeal, in England and Wales to the Crown Court, in Northern Ireland to the county court and in Scotland to the Court of Session. In England, Wales and Northern Ireland the appeal must be made within 30 days of the making of the order. The appeal is by way of rehearing and the appeal court may make any order it thinks appropriate. If the appeal court upholds the appeal, it may order the release of the cash.

Application of forfeited cash (s 300)

6.107 Forfeited cash is paid into the appropriate consolidated fund but not before any appeal is determined or time barred.

SUPPLEMENTARY

Victims and other owners (s 301)

6.108 At any time, a person may apply to magistrates or a sheriff for the return of cash to him if it has been forfeited from another person under the above procedure. The applicant must show that he was deprived of the cash or part of it, or of property which it represents, by unlawful conduct (eg it was stolen from him); that it was not recoverable property immediately before he was deprived of it; and that the cash or part belongs to him. The court or sheriff may order the cash or part to be released to the applicant. The application may be made in the course of proceedings under s 295 (further detention) or s 298 (forfeiture) or at any other time.

Compensation (s 302)

6.109 A person whose cash has been detained but then released without forfeiture may apply for compensation. If for any period after the initial 48 hours the cash was not held in an interest-bearing account the court or sheriff may order a sum equivalent to that lost interest to be paid. The court or sheriff may order additional compensation from HMCE or the police if satisfied that the circumstances are exceptional and further loss has been suffered. Compensation may be given in respect of cash returned even if other cash has been forfeited. However, compensation should not be paid following a successful application under s 301.

'The minimum amount' (s 303)

6.110 The minimum amount will be specified by order made by the Secretary of State after consultation with the Scottish ministers. The current minimum in respect of the forfeiture of drug-related cash on import or export is £10,000 and the Government intends that the same level should be imposed in respect of this scheme.[1] Figures from Customs and Excise show that under DTA 1994, s 42 the following amounts of cash were seized: £2.1m in 1996–97, £1.9m in 1997–98, £2.8m in 1998–99 and £4.4m in 1999–2000.[2]

---

[1]   HC SC B, 10 January 2002, col 891.
[2]   Quoted in the PIU Report, June 2000, Table 4.6 at para 4.29.

GENERAL

RECOVERABLE PROPERTY

Property obtained through unlawful conduct, tracing, mixing and accruing profits (ss 304–307)

6.111 Not all property obtained through unlawful conduct is recoverable property for the purposes of ss 304–307. If property, having been obtained through unlawful conduct, is disposed of whether it remains recoverable depends on into whose hands it passes. As soon as property passes to someone from whom it is not recoverable it ceases to be recoverable property for the purposes of s 304. However, recoverable property can pass through a series of hands and remain recoverable (s 304(2)). Property representing the original property is also recoverable, so a person cannot thwart the purpose of the ARA by exchanging his recoverable property for something else to exclude civil proceedings against him for it (s 305).

6.112 If recoverable property is either—
   (1) cash deposited into a bank account to increase funds already in that account,
   (2) used in part payment for an asset,
   (3) used in the restoration or improvement of land or
   (4) used by a person with a leasehold to secure the freehold so that it is mixed with other property and cannot be distinguished,

a portion of the mixed property representing the proportion of the total that was recoverable property shall be recoverable (s 306). If profits are accrued on recoverable property they become recoverable as well (s 307). This is subject to s 280 (payment of joint owners/ tenants and insolvency practitioners).

General exceptions (s 308)

6.113 Title to property will always be a controversial issue. Mr Ainsworth quipped in Committee—

> 'Heaven only knows how we remove the opprobrium from such situations. As the hon Gentleman and I know, people still suggest that the Elgin marbles and the Koh-i-Noor diamond and other items were obtained by semi-legitimate or illegitimate means. Debate will continue about that and about the circumstances in which something is chased because it is the proceeds of crime.'[1]

---
[1] HC SC B, 10 January 2002, col 895.

6.114 Under s 308, property ceases to be recoverable if it—
  (a)   passes into the hands of a bona fide purchaser for value;
  (b)   is vested, forfeited or otherwise disposed of in pursuance of powers conferred by this PCA 2002, Pt 5. (The Explanatory Notes give the example that if property is sold by an interim receiver or interim administrator in the exercise of his powers, although it may still be 'property obtained through unlawful conduct', or representative of such property, it will not be recoverable in the hands of the recipient and may be recycled in the market in the ordinary way);[1]
  (c)   is given in payment in pursuance to a civil judgment in a claim based on the defendant's unlawful conduct;
  (d)   is paid or passed in accordance with a compensation order or restitution order;
  (e)   is the subject of a restraint order (under ss 41, 120, 190 or under a corresponding provision mentioned in s 8(7)(a)–(g)); or
  (f)   has been taken into account in the making of a confiscation order under this or previous legislation.

---

[1]   Explanatory Notes, para 431.

6.115 However, if the property is disposed of in accordance with (a) or (b) above but the person disposing of it receives something in return, that property received in return is recoverable (s 308(10)).

Granting interests (s 310)

6.116 Under s 310 the granting of an interest in recoverable property has the same effect as disposal of that property in that the interest becomes recoverable on its creation unless one of the above exceptions applies.

INSOLVENCY (s 311)

6.117 Section 311 sets out the interrelationship between civil recovery and insolvency proceedings. Where insolvency proceedings[1] are in train, proceedings for a civil recovery order or summary proceedings under s 295 may not be brought without the leave of the appropriate court and then only in accordance with terms imposed by that court. The enforcement authority may apply for leave as provided for in the Insolvency Act 1986 (and its Northern Ireland equivalent, the Insolvency (Northern Ireland) Order 1989). The Explanatory Notes explain that s 311, coupled with existing legislation, means that the enforcement authority will now have to apply for leave from the insolvency court in all circumstances where insolvency proceedings are underway.[2]

---

[1] Defined in s 311(3).
[2] Explanatory Notes, para 437.

6.118 An application to the insolvency court may be made without notice, to prevent a potential civil recovery respondent finding out about the Director's intention to bring proceedings (s 311(4)), but notice must still be given to the insolvency practitioner or to the official receiver where required (s 311(5)).

DELEGATION OF ENFORCEMENT FUNCTIONS (ss 312 AND 313)

6.119 Sections 312 and 313 govern which of the Director's or Scottish ministers' powers may be exercised by police officers assigned to work in civil recovery and which powers are reserved to the Scottish ministers, the Director and other Agency staff.

INTERPRETATION

Obtaining and disposing of property (s 314)

6.120 Section 314 gives a wide interpretation to references to the disposal of property. For the purposes of PCA 2002 a part-disposal of property or the granting of an interest in property is a disposal. Payment is a disposal, as is the passing of property under a will or intestacy or 'by operation of law'. A person does not receive property for value for the purposes of PCA 2002 unless he gives consideration that is executed.

Northern Ireland courts (s 315)

6.121 In relation to Northern Ireland, expressions in Pt 5 are to be read in accordance with rules of court.

General interpretation (s 316)

6.122 Section 316 provides a long list of definitions. Section 316(3) however is of particular note. It states that for the purposes of deciding whether or not property was recoverable at any time (including times before commencement), it is to be assumed that Pt 5 was in force at that and any other relevant time. Thus, civil recovery proceedings under Pt 5, Ch 2 are blatantly and overtly retrospective.

7 Revenue functions

NEW POWERS

7.1 The Proceeds of Crime Act 2002 ('PCA 2002'), Pt 6 deals with Revenue functions delegated from the Inland Revenue. The Government envisages that in spite of the draconian powers in Pts 2 to 5, there will be situations where benefit from unlawful conduct will remain in the hands of the criminal. This benefit, be it income, a capital gain, or inheritance, would be liable to taxation by the Inland Revenue, but the Government believe that the Inland Revenue are not best placed to deal with these situations. Mr Ainsworth stated in Committee—

> '. . . the Revenue also has a massive responsibility that ranges across the whole population of the United Kingdom, and it cannot therefore be expected to focus on the need to recover the proceeds of crime for the taxation system, as the Director can and will be required to do . . . . We are trying to introduce effective powers to use against people who have clearly gained by their criminality – they might own a property or an asset – but we also wish to isolate those [Revenue collection] powers, because it is important to provide the maximum bulwark against their seeping into the rest of the taxation system. If we were to oblige the Inland Revenue to exercise those powers [in respect of benefit from unlawful conduct], we would wind up having to establish an organisation within the Inland Revenue to provide focus, and the gateways would be more difficult to control.'[1]

---

[1]   HC SC B, 15 January 2002, cols 927 and 933.

7.2 The thinking behind these powers was set out in the PIU Report in June 2000—

> '. . . depriving criminal targets of assets by tax means may yield a greater benefit than simply the amount of money recoverable. In addition, application of Inland Revenue powers against individuals who are otherwise perceived to be above the law would send out a strong message that the UK taxation system is indeed fairly applied across sections of society'.[1]

[1] PIU Report, June 200, para 10.8. The Government estimates that between £6.5 billion and £11.1 billion were generated by criminal business in 1996 (PIU Report, para 10.1).

7.3 Under PCA 2002 the Director may obtain the Revenue assessment and collection powers of the Inland Revenue but with the vital difference that he, unlike the Inland Revenue, will not have to prove the source of the monies. This will of course make it easier to tax criminal funds.

7.4 Where the Director takes over Revenue collection he may have to consider a range of types of taxation, including such things as statutory maternity pay and student loans. This led to questions in Committee as to whether the Director was 'biting off more than he can chew'.[1] One assumes that this is not said out of concern for the Director! It is one thing to say that the ARA will be able to focus on criminal conduct but the alternative argument is that they do not have the wealth of experience and will have to acquire or recruit the specialist knowledge necessary to deal fully and fairly with all the issues that may arise.

[1] HC SC B, 15 January 2002, col 938 (Mr Grieve).

GENERAL FUNCTIONS

Director's general Revenue functions (s 317)

7.5 PCA 2002, Pt 6 comes into play where the Director has reasonable grounds to suspect either that in a chargeable period a person has received income chargeable to income tax or a chargeable gain, or that a company is chargeable to corporation tax on its profits and that the income, gain or profit arise or accrue, wholly or partly and directly or indirectly, as a result of any person's 'criminal conduct' (s 317(1)). The phrasing of this test was queried in Committee[1] as the Government claim that the words 'criminal conduct' are indistinguishable from 'unlawful conduct', the phrase employed elsewhere in PCA 2002.[2] If so, why the difference?

[1] The use of two different phrases which no one seemed able to distinguish in effect was criticised in Committee: HC SC B, 15 January 2002, cols 911–923.

7.6   Many will be skeptical about the transfer of powers. Mr Ainsworth attempted to allay concerns as to how often the Director would acquire the Revenue's powers—

> 'If a person has not been involved in criminality, the director will not as a matter of routine become involved. The issue will involve his taxation powers only when it has passed down the hierarchy, having been passed to him because some criminal activity had been pursued. He will be involved only if various investigations have been undertaken as to whether criminal confiscation or civil recovery can be used, and whether a tax liability has been avoided.'[1]

---

[1]   HC SC B, 15 January 2002, col 967.

7.7   Where this condition is satisfied the Director may serve a notice upon the Commissioners of Inland Revenue specifying the person or company concerned and the chargeable period or periods. The notice should set out which of the general Revenue functions the Director intends to use (s 317(2), (5)). By service of this notice the Director acquires those functions subject to s 318.

7.8   The Director can serve a notice of withdrawal upon the Commissioners at any time, divesting himself of those functions. He must serve a notice of withdrawal should the qualifying condition contained in s 317 cease to be satisfied (s 317(4), (6)).

7.9   The Commissioners retain the power to carry out functions that the Director has acquired (s 317(7)). Concern was expressed in Committee that assessments by both the Director and the Inland Revenue would be overly onerous and open to abuse. Mr Ainsworth was unwilling to entertain an amendment to prevent the Director becoming involved in cases where the Inland Revenue had already carried out work. However, he did state—

> 'The amendment implies that the director and the Revenue should not both assess the same tax. I assure the Committee that we do not intend to double-tax in that way, but that only the director will collect the tax, interest and penalties due. If the subject of the inquiry demonstrates that tax on the investigated income and gain was paid to the Inland Revenue, the director will not raise an assessment and he will serve notice of withdrawal.'[1]

---

[1]   HC SC B, 15 January 2002, col 936.

7.10 Once again it seems a shame that the Government offer only oral reassurances rather than statutory protection.

7.11 When the Director acquires a function under s 317 he can carry it out without the authorisation from the Commissioners that may be required by any other function (s 317(8)). The Director has the power to use the Revenue functions he acquires retrospectively in respect of chargeable periods that fall before or partly before the passing of PCA 2002 (s 317(9)).

Revenue functions regarding employment (s 318)

7.12 Section 318 ensures that in respect of income tax, National Insurance and student loan payments paid by a company for its employers, the Director can only take over the functions for which a company is responsible as an employer where the relevant periods for those matters fall wholly within a period or periods for which the Director has served a notice. The same is true in respect of the self-employed and any functions relating to the payment of Class 2 contributions. This is important because these liabilities fall due at different times than those set out in the qualifying condition under s 317(1).

Source of income (s 319)

7.13 Assessments of income tax raised by the Inland Revenue are required to specify the source of the income in question, which the Inland Revenue must be able to prove on the balance of probabilities if required. Section 319 removes the requirement to state or prove the source from the Director when he or she is carrying out the assessment. However, if his assessment is abandoned following the issuing of a notice of withdrawal it will become invalid to the extent that it did not specify a source. It is important to note that monies out of reach of the Revenue authorities because of their undisclosed criminal source can now be demanded by the Director. Where the source is demonstrably criminal there could of course be proceedings under Pt 5 for civil recovery, so in theory the Director will be relying on this section whenever he resorts to using Pt 6. Yet again, however, there is nothing on the face of the Act to prevent the Director from taking the easier option of using Pt 6 and thereby having to prove nothing.

Appeals (s 320)

7.14 A right of appeal in respect of the exercise of the Director's general Revenue functions lies to the Special Commissioners assisted by special assessors nominated by the Lord Chancellor (following consultation with the Scottish ministers). The Explanatory Notes explain that this excludes any right of appeal to the General Commissioners.[1]

---

[1]   Explanatory notes, para 457.

INHERITANCE TAX FUNCTIONS

Director's functions: transfers of value (s 321)

7.15   The Director is allowed to obtain the power to exercise inheritance tax functions on satisfaction of the qualifying condition that he or she has reasonable grounds for believing that there has been a transfer of value (within the meaning of the Inheritance Tax Act 1984), and that the value transferred is in whole or in part attributable to criminal property. Mr Ainsworth explained the Government's logic behind this provision—

> 'People who are involved in drug trafficking or other organised crime may, because of the work in which they are involved, be candidates for a relatively low life expectancy. The issue of pursuing their ill-gotten gains beyond the grave may arise more often than it would in the case of Members of Parliament . . . . The clause may be needed far more often . . . because of the dangerous criminal activity in which such people are involved. Therefore, . . . it is still a necessary tool in the tax-gathering armoury'.[1]

---

[1]   HC SC B, 15 January 2002, col 952.

7.16   The Government also believes that the law of inheritance and trusts are tools used by criminals to protect their unlawful profits.[1]

---

[1]   HC SC B, 15 January 2002, col 940.

7.17   Criminal property is defined in s 326. To obtain this function the Director must serve a notice upon the Commissioners specifying the transfer and stating that the Director intends to carry out functions in respect of it. Withdrawal notices work as above (see paras 7.5–7.11). It is immaterial whether the transfer occurred before or after the passing of PCA 2002.

Director's functions: certain settlements (s 322)

7.18 The Director may use Revenue functions in respect of property comprised in a settlement that is relevant property for the purposes of the Inheritance Tax Act 1984, Pt 3, Ch 3 (settlements without interest in possession), where he or she has reasonable grounds for suspecting that such property exists and is criminal property in whole or part. The procedure mirrors that in s 321.

GENERAL

Functions (s 323)

7.19 Section 323 sets out which general Revenue functions the Director may and may not obtain by the procedures discussed above.

Exercise of Revenue functions (s 324)

7.20 Section 324 regulates the exercise of the Director's functions. Section 1(6)(b) does not apply to the exercise of Revenue functions and so the Director may not delegate these powers to anyone not directly employed by the ARA (sub-contractors), although he may delegate them to his staff. In carrying out Revenue functions the Director must have regard to interpretations of law, concessions, published material and practices of the Commissioners and must provide them with such documents and information as they consider appropriate. They will thus be able to monitor his or her application of their policy.

Declarations (s 325)

7.21 The Director and any member of staff to whom he or she delegates Revenue functions must make a declaration, set out in Sch 5, undertaking not to make any unlawful disclosure of information obtained in the exercise of his Revenue functions.

Interpretation (s 326)

7.22 Definitions for Pt 6 are provided in s 326. Criminal conduct is defined so as to include conduct amounting to any criminal offence in the UK except for Revenue offences. It also includes acts committed outside the jurisdiction that would have constituted offences (other than

Revenue offences) in the UK had they been committed here. The definition covers offences committed before the passing of PCA 2002.

7.23   Criminal property is any property that constitutes or represents, directly or indirectly, benefit from any person's criminal conduct. A person benefits from conduct if he obtains property as a result of or in connection with that conduct. Any pecuniary advantage obtained in this way will be equated with a sum of money of equal value. A pecuniary advantage falls within the definition even if it was obtained by means of a combination of criminal and other conduct.

7.24   Civil recovery under Pt 5 requires the property to be identified. Presumably Pt 6 goes further in that property that has perished or been consumed, for example, will still be liable to taxation.

7.25   The amount of benefit is the amount obtained as a result of or in connection with the conduct. Property is given a non-exhaustive definition and includes intangible or incorporeal property, money and land. Obtaining an interest in property is sufficient to activate PCA 2002, Pt 6. This includes all interests, including an equitable interest or power in land, with the exception of a Scottish lease that is not a long lease.

7.26   Where further definitions are required in this part reference should be made to the Taxes Acts (within the meaning given by the Taxes Management Act 1970, s 118).

8 Money laundering

> 'The proof necessary to convict the enemies of the people is every kind of evidence, either material or moral or verbal or written . . . every citizen has the right to seize conspirators and counter revolutionaries and to arraign them before magistrates. He is required to denounce them when he knows of them.'

(The law established by the Jacobins in their Law of 22 Prairial Year II (June 10 1794))

THE NEED FOR CHANGE

8.1 The Proceeds of Crime Act 2002 ('PCA 2002'), Pt 7 (ss 327–340) significantly alters the law relating to money laundering. The perceived need for the overhaul was set out in the PIU Report—

> 'Much of the profit from major organised crime is moved out of the UK. It is typically invested in bank accounts, properties and luxury vehicles. Similarly, proceeds of crime committed overseas are invested in the UK. Criminal assets can move faster than law enforcement and judicial efforts to trace and recover them. This problem is already acute and is getting worse, mirroring the increase in global transactions in the legitimate economy.'[1]

---

[1] Para 11.1.

8.2 A person commits an offence if he with knowledge or suspicion acquires, uses or possesses criminal property. PCA 2002 also creates three separate criminal offences of failing to make a disclosure where there are reasonable grounds for knowing or suspecting that another is engaged in money laundering, which apply to persons working in the regulated sector, nominated officers in the regulated sector and other nominated officers (ss 330–332). These offences do not even require knowledge or suspicion; negligence will be enough. Solicitors and other professionals who deal with clients' money will find themselves included in the 'regulated sector' by virtue of the Second Money Laundering Directive.[1] The Government is required to implement this Directive by June 2003. For a more detailed discussion of this see Ch 1.

---

[1]   Directive 2001/97/EC; see Appendix 2.

8.3   PCA 2002 creates new (and dangerously wide) offences as well as consolidating the existing law. Of particular concern is the fact that the mens rea for the offences in ss 327 and 329 is contained in the definition of 'criminal property' in s 340(3)(b). All the offences (apart from ss 330 and 331 which can be committed negligently) require the defendant to have knowledge or suspicion. In a response to the consultation for the Draft Bill Sir Edwin Jowitt wrote—

> 'No doubt someone will argue that knowing and suspecting are two different offences. The difference between these two states of mind is perhaps as wide as the difference between reckless and intending which in criminal damage cases calls for two separate counts.'[1]

---

[1]   From a document produced by retired High Court judge Sir Edwin Jowitt as his response to the consultation stage of the draft Bill. The document was endorsed by the Lord Chief Justice and by Lord Justice Rose, the Vice-President of the Court of Appeal (Criminal Division). It may be found through the Home Office website.

8.4   Sir Edwin Jowitt's criticisms of the offence of using criminal property in s 329(1)(b) were particularly apt—

> 'It would catch the man who visits his neighbour and watches his TV, which he suspects was stolen, or wipes his feet on what he suspects is a stolen doormat and does not in either of these cases, make the disclosure required'.[1]

---

[1]   See para 8.3 fn 1.

8.5   One objectionable feature of these offences is that they will lead to an explosion of reports by those who are suspicious in order to avoid the possibility of criminal action against them.

OFFENCES

Concealing etc (s 327)

8.6 It an offence for any person to conceal, disguise, convert or transfer criminal property, or to remove criminal property from England, Wales, Scotland or Northern Ireland. Concealing or disguising includes concealing or disguising the ownership, source, location or disposition of the property or any rights in relation to it (s 327(3)). The mens rea for the offence is not clear. Section 340 defines 'criminal property' in such as way as to require that the offender knows or suspects the property to be criminal property.[1] What is unclear is whether the offender has to perform the act (the concealment etc) intentionally. Despite questions in the House of Lords, Lord Bassam, speaking on behalf of the Government, thought that clarification was not necessary.[2]

---

[1] See discussion of s 340 in para 8.50.
[2] HL Committee Stage, 27 May 2002, cols 1063–1064.

8.7 No offence is committed if a s 338 disclosure has been made in respect of the property[1] before the act is done and he has the appropriate consent, or if a person intended to make a s 338 disclosure but had a reasonable excuse for not doing so. There will be no offence if the act is done in carrying out a function that the person has in relation to the enforcement of any provision of PCA 2002 or similar legislation (s 327(2)), for example officers transferring seized money into an interest-bearing account pending further investigation. If the matter goes to trial it is for the defendant to prove on the balance of probabilities that he made a s 338 disclosure or had a reasonable excuse for not doing so. The Government clearly believes that this would not appear to breach the current law on reverse burdens following *R v Lambert*[2] and *Lynch v DPP*.[3] Doubtless both these reverse onus provisions and the mens rea ingredient of the offences will require clarification in the courts.

---

[1] See para 8.39.
[2] [2001] UKHL 37, [2001] 3 All ER 577, [2001] Cr App Rep 511.
[3] [2001] EWHC Admin 882.

8.8 This offence replaces DTA 1994, s 49 and CJA 1988, s 93C and the corresponding Scottish and Northern Irish provisions. That legislation required that the act be done for the purpose of avoiding prosecution for an offence or the making or enforcement of a confiscation order. The new offence has no such element. This change must be seen as a broadening of scope.

8.9   Lord Bassam of Brighton accepted, on behalf of the Government, that there is some overlap with the offence of handling stolen goods although for the new offence, importantly, suspicion is sufficient.[1]

---
[1]   HL Committee Stage, 27 May 2002, col 1065.

Arrangements (s 328)

8.10   Section 328 creates an offence of entering into or becoming concerned in an arrangement knowing or suspecting that it facilitates the acquisition, retention, use or control of criminal property by or on behalf of another person. Once again, no offence is committed if a s 338 disclosure has been made in respect of the property or if a person intended to make one but had a reasonable excuse for not doing so. Again, it is for the defendant to prove this on the balance of probabilities. There will also be no offence if the act is done in carrying out a function that the person concerned has in relation to the enforcement of any provision of PCA 2002 or similar legislation. Suspicion is a concept now familiar as a component of DTA 1994, s 49 and CJA 1988, s 93C, as well as in DTA 1994, s 50 and CJA 1988, s 93A. Mitchell et al[1] suggested in relation to the old law that one look to the dictionary definition—

> 'act of suspecting: state of being suspected: the imagining of something without evidence or on slender evidence: inkling: mistrust'.[2]

---
[1]   See Mitchell, Taylor and Talbot *Confiscation and the Proceeds of Crime* (2nd edn, 1997), p 187.
[2]   *Chambers English Dictionary* (7th edn).

8.11   DTA 1994, s 50 and CJA 1988, s 93A and the equivalent Scottish and Northern Irish provisions are replaced by the new offence. Under the previous legislation an offence was comitted where the arrangement was entered into and the defendant knew or suspected that the person whose proceeds were involved was involved in criminal activity. There is a defence that the defendant did not know or suspect the arrangement related to proceeds of criminal conduct or did not know or suspect that the arrangement he had entered into would facilitate the retention or control etc of the property. In *R v Butt*[1] the Court of Appeal allowed the appeal where the judge at first instance had confused the mens rea of the CJA 1988, 93A offence with the statutory defence.[2] The judge had erred in not making it clear that the prosecution were required to prove the mens rea of the offence. However, the Court of Appeal read the statute strictly so as to impose the burden of proving the statutory defence upon the defendant. In his commentary to this case in the *Criminal Law Review*, Professor Smith saw this reverse burden as a 'prime candidate for condemnation' under ECHR.[3] The wording of PCA 2002, s 328 appears to have taken on board these concerns and moved the burden to the prosecution.

---

[1] [1999] Crim LR 414, CA.
[2] CJA 1988, s 93A(4).
[3] [1999] Criminal Law Review, p 415.

Acquisition, use and possession (s 329)

8.12 Section 329 represents a major change in the law and, when coupled with other changes in PCA 2002, Pt 7, may have a substantial effect. DTA 1994, s 51, CJA 1988, s 93B and the equivalent Scottish and Northern Irish provisions which this offence replaces did not apply to the original offender, relating only to those secondary parties who assist criminals to deal with the proceeds of their crimes. Almost every person who commits a property offence in English law will now also commit an additional money laundering offence as he, for example, conceals or converts the spoils of his own crime. Together with the offence under s 330, this change places a great burden upon the banking industry.[1] It might also be argued that it is unnecessary and cumbersome to make a separate offence of what is really just the inevitable conclusion of the offender's original property offence.

---

[1] See para 8.16.

8.13 Section 329 creates offences where a person acquires, uses, or has possession of criminal property. The Explanatory Notes to the Bill (para 453) stated that under this section possession means having physical custody of criminal property, although this is not specifically stated in PCA 2002. Again there is no offence where there has been a s 338 disclosure, where there is a reasonable excuse for not making a s 338 disclosure or where the person concerned is carrying out a function under PCA 2002. Again, it is for the defendant to prove these things on the balance of probabilities. There is also a further defence, in s 329(2)(c), of having acquired, used or had possession of the property for adequate consideration. It is interesting to compare this to the usual maxim of 'bona fide purchaser for value'; why is there no requirement that the purchaser has clean hands?

8.14 The effect of the defence of adequate consideration is that persons, such as tradesmen, who are paid for ordinary consumable goods and services in money that comes from crime are not under any obligation to question the source of the money. The consideration must not be significantly less than the value of the property acquired or the value of the use or possession of the property (s 329(3)(a), (b)).

Section 329(3)(c) makes it clear that the provision of goods or services for adequate consideration that help a person to carry out criminal conduct would not be a defence. The burden of proving this defence is on the defendant and the standard is the balance of probabilities.

8.15   This same defence is part of DTA 1994, s 51 and CJA 1988, s 93B, and that the burden is on the defence was made clear in relation to s 93B in *R v Gibson*.[1] As in his commentary to *R v Butt*,[2] here too Professor Smith criticised the use of a reverse burden and suggested it as a 'prime candidate' for condemnation under the Human Rights Act 1998. He argued that the distinction between 'essential ingredients' of an offence and defences employed by the courts is a false one. It seems inevitable, particularly in light of the legislature's capitulation in respect of the s 328 offence, that Professor Smith's argument will be laid before a court in relation to s 329 in the not too distant future.

---

[1]   [2000] Crim LR 479, CA.
[2]   See para 8.11.

Failure to disclose: regulated sector (s 330)

8.16   Section 330 replaces DTA 1994, s 52 and the equivalent Scottish and Northern Irish provisions. There is no corresponding provision under CJA 1988 and so PCA 2002 widens the scope of the offences beyond drug money laundering to the laundering of the proceeds of any criminal conduct.

8.17   The mens rea for the new offence, however, only requires negligence where objectively there are reasonable grounds to suspect. It is an offence aimed at those who work in the regulated sector as defined by PCA 2002, Sch 9, Pt 1. This definition follows closely the equivalent provisions in the Money Laundering Regulations 1993.[1] The definition in Sch 9 provides that a business is in the regulated sector to the extent that it carries out the activities listed in Sch 9, Pt 1. The Explanatory Notes state that where a business carries out some activities which are listed in Sch 9 and some which are not, only employees carrying out the listed activities will be caught.[2] DTA 1994, s 52 did not specify that the trade, business or employment must be in the regulated sector and in that respect was wider than the new offence.

---

[1]   SI 1993/1933; see Appendix 2.
[2]   Explanatory Notes, para 479.

8.18　The Money Laundering Regulations 1993 were updated by virtue of a second EC Directive in 2001,[1] which led to the Money Laundering Regulations 2001.[2] These amend the 1993 Regulations,[3] extending the definition of 'relevant financial business' to encompass those which operate a bureau de change; those who transmit money, or any representation of monetary value, by any means; and those who cash cheques which are made payable to customers. Thus many more businesses are brought within the system of regulation.

---

[1]　Directive 2001/97/EC; see Appendix 2.
[2]　SI 2001/3641; see Appendix 2.
[3]　SI 1993/1933; see Appendix 2.

8.19　A further effect of the Second Money Laundering Directive[1] is that many solicitors will become expressly part of the 'regulated sector' if they carry on 'relevant financial business' within the meaning of the Directive. A solicitor will not have to report suspicions where he is 'providing legal advice to clients or representing a client in legal proceedings'.[2] However, solicitors 'assisting in the planning and execution of transactions for clients' such as establishing trusts, giving tax advice, setting up and managing companies, managing clients' money and buying and selling property, will be under a duty to report suspicions of money laundering. It may be that some solicitors now carry out activities which may take them within PCA 2002, Sch 9, para 1(2) in any event. The position is unclear as the Act stands as the categories in para 1(2) are very broad. Between the coming into force of the Act and the implementation of the Second Money Laundering Directive firms should consider very carefully how far their activities go.

---

[1]　Directive 2001/97/EC; see Appendix 2.
[2]　Directive 2001/97/EC (amending Council Directive 91/308/EEC).

8.20　The legal privilege which remains in other situations does not absolve the solicitor from criminal prosecution if—

> 'the legal counsellor is taking part in money laundering activities, the legal advice is provided for money laundering purposes or the lawyer knows that the client is seeking advice for money laundering purposes'.[1]

The UK Government is required to implement the Second Directive by June 2003.

---

[1]　See Directive 2001/97/EC, Recital; see Appendix 2.

8.21　If, as a result of information received in the course of a business in the regulated sector, a person knows or suspects, or objectively had reasonable grounds for knowing or suspecting that another person was engaged in money laundering and he has not reported this as soon as practicable, then he commits an offence unless he has a reasonable excuse for non-disclosure or can rely on legal professional privilege.

8.22   Reports are to be made to—

(a)   a person authorised by the Director General of NCIS (ie civilian staff of NCIS); or

(b)   an internal nominated officer (within a company, firm, body or association) in accordance with internal procedure.

8.23   In deciding whether this offence has been committed the court must consider whether the defendant followed relevant guidance published by a supervisory authority (defined in Sch 6, Pt 2) or other appropriate body (eg a trade association)[1] in a way so as to come to the attention of those persons likely to be affected by it and approved by the Treasury.

---

[1]   Guidance notes on money laundering have been produced and issued since 1990 to regulated institutions by the industry's Joint Money Laundering Steering Group, which operates under the auspices of the British Bankers' Association.

8.23A   The concept of reasonable grounds for suspecting is well known to law. For example, in order to carry out an arrest without a warrant a constable must have reasonable grounds for suspicion in his own mind.[1] It is important to note that likewise in PCA 2002, s 330 the first condition is that the person *has* reasonable grounds, and not that *there are* reasonable grounds. Further, the second condition states that the information '*came to him* in the course of a business in the regulated sector' (emphasis added). It seems therefore, that the objective test is only to be carried out on the basis of facts of which it is established the person was aware. The prosecution must show that the defendant had learnt the relevant facts upon the basis of which he could objectively be expected to have formed a suspicion. He is then guilty whether he did form a suspicion (but failed to report it) or was negligent in not forming what was a reasonable suspicion. It would seem that, if a person was so incompetent that he did not even discover the relevant facts he would not be guilty. The guidance[2] provided by the Joint Money Laundering Steering Group appears to go further than this and could be read to include negligence in failing to glean the primary facts. It is to be hoped the courts do not interpret the statute in this way.

---

[1]   *O'Hara v Chief Constable of RUC* [1997] AC 286.

[2]   Joint Money Laundering Steering Group Guidance Notes (November 2002), Chapter 5, paras 5.6, 5.7.

8.24   Legal professional privilege is defined in PCA 2002 so as to cover information imparted during the seeking or receipt of legal advice or in connection with legal proceedings or contemplated legal proceedings provided it is not communicated in order to further a criminal purpose. Money laundering is defined in s 340(11) as any act which constitutes an offence under ss 327, 328 or 329, or would constitute an inchoate version of or secondary participation in the same.

8.25   A difficulty concerning, amongst others, the British Bankers' Association is that when combined with s 329, this requires bank employees and others working in the regulated sector to blow the whistle on every one of its customers whom it has reasonable grounds to suspect of effectively any offence. The British Bankers' Association writes—

> 'This reform will in turn lead to a huge increase in the number of reports being made to NCIS. We question whether NCIS has the resources to cope with any significantly increased level in reporting. We understand that NCIS has only recently been able to manage its present workload, and we are concerned that any extension in the scope of the "receiving" offence, could mean that NCIS would have a huge backlog of reports with the result that important "traditional" money laundering disclosures (as defined under current legislation) will be missed. Given that there is no de minimis requirement in the proposed legislation for making reports, this will further exacerbate the position. Even if the proceeds are only £15, a report would still have to be made. In many cases the matter will already have been reported to the police, often without any further development.'[1]

---

[1]   British Bankers' Association Briefing, distributed under cover of letter by Ian Mullen of the Association, dated 12 December 2001.

8.26   A further problem highlighted by the British Bankers' Association is the draconian way in which what is akin to professional negligence in civil law now leads to criminal liability and potential long prison sentences—

> 'Whilst it is easy for anyone using hindsight or working in an investigative role to decide that an action is suspicious, it will not necessarily be so apparent to a member of staff in a line role. Such staff will have many day-to-day pressures and may rarely ever come across a criminal activity. In particular, we firmly believe that criminal sanctions for negligence should not be extended to junior staff. In a number of cases, junior staff will not have

sufficient experience, or information on the background to a transaction, to enable an objective assessment to be made. Internal disciplinary sanctions for a breach of procedures should be sufficient punishment.'[1]

---

[1]   British Bankers' Association Briefing, distributed under cover of letter by Ian Mullen of the Association, dated 12 December 2001.

8.27   The procedural and bureaucratic burdens on NCIS will be enormous, especially since it must respond to requests for consent within seven working days. Section 339 permits the Home Secretary to prescribe the manner and form in which disclosures are to be made. A Consultation Document was published in August 2002 on the proposed order. NCIS's current forms will need adapting to take into account the different parts of the regulated sector (for example, a different form may be required for reporting suspicions of tax evasions to that for reporting banking suspicions).

8.28   Lord Goldsmith's answer in the House of Lords that these concerns overlooked the fact that the prosecution must prove that money laundering was planned or undertaken provide little reassurance for the bank clerk.[1] Concern was also expressed by a number of MPs. Mr Field said—

'The phrase "reasonable grounds" represents a high hurdle for a professional to traverse. My worry about the thinking behind this clause, and others, is that there must be analysis after the event. People will piece together things after money laundering and criminality has come to light. A great burden will be placed on individuals. Indeed the burden of proof will be almost reversed.'[2]

Ms Vera Baird added—

'How does one avoid committing the crime if one is tired or worried? Every time one is worried about something, the only way to avoid committing the crime would be to take the day off.'[3]

---

[1]   HL 2R, 25 March 2002, col 64.
[2]   HC SC B, 22 January 2002, col 1084.
[3]   HC SC B, 22 January 2002, col 1111.

8.29   The problem of widening the scope of money laundering offences is of course that no-one knows exactly how much in the way of resources will be required to cope with the new regime. If the suspicions of the PIU Report[1] are correct one can expect a great burden to fall upon both the regulated sector and the enforcement authorities. Baroness Noakes and others expressed concern that accountants in particular come across many examples of minor conduct that would fall within the broad definition of money laundering (the Baroness gave the example of shoplifting). Reporting every such incident would be an enormous burden on both the person making disclosures and the enforcement authorities receiving them.[2]

---

[1]   Paras 1.45–1.46.
[2]   HL Committee Stage, 27 May 2002, cols 1070–1075.

8.30   Lord Kingsland expressed concern that solicitors would fall foul of this offence if they believed they had the protection of legal professional privilege but were mistaken as to that on the facts of the particular case. Lord Rooker replied—

'. . . it is clear that professional legal advisers ought to know whether legal privilege applies; indeed, if they do not, there are people whom they can consult. The criminal law is quite clear: where a criminal offence is silent as to its mental element, the courts must read in the appropriate mental element. Therefore, in circumstances where a legal adviser did not know that information was not legally privileged, the courts would read in a requirement that he could not be convicted unless he did know. We believe it best to rely on that rule of interpretation, which is the current situation, rather than try to put anything on the face of the Bill.

. . . the definition of "legal privilege" in Clause 330 is already to be found in existing legislation. There is no evidence available to us to show that it is not working satisfactorily.'[1]

---

[1]   HL Committee Stage, 27 May 2002, cols 1077–1078; legal professional privilege has not yet been extended beyond the legal profession as required by the Second European Directive on Money Laundering (Directive 2001/97/EC) (HL Committee Stage, 27 May 2002, col 1080).

8.31   It is difficult to see how his Lordship can be confident that the courts will favour the legal profession by interpreting PCA 2002 in this way when the Act does not expressly state this.

8.32   It should be noted in passing that under the Money Laundering Regulations 1993[1] employers commit an offence if the training they provide is insufficient. However, a lack of training is no defence for employees accused under s 330.

---

[1]   SI 1993/1933; see Appendix 2.

Failure to disclose: nominated officers in the regulated sector (s 331)

8.33   If a nominated officer as a result of a s 330 disclosure to him, knows or suspects, or has reasonable grounds for knowing or suspecting, that a person is engaged in money laundering and the officer does not disclose that information to the person authorised by the Director General of NCIS in the form or manner prescribed (if any) by s 339, then he commits an offence unless he has a reasonable excuse for not doing so. The court must take into consideration whether the nominated officer followed any relevant guidance.

Failure to disclose: other nominated officers (s 332)

8.34   If a nominated officer as a result of a s 337 or s 338 disclosure knows or suspects that another person is engaged in money laundering and the officer does not disclose that information to the person authorised by the Director General of NCIS in the form or manner prescribed (if any) by s 339, then he commits an offence unless he has a reasonable excuse for not doing so.

Tipping off (s 333)

8.35   Section 333 creates an offence of tipping off. Together with s 342 in Pt 8 (offence of prejudicing an investigation), this new offence replaces DTA 1994, s 53(2), CJA 1988, s 93D(2) and the equivalent Scottish and Northern Irish provisions. If a person knows or suspects that a ss 337 or 338 disclosure has been made and then himself passes information to another in such a way as is likely to prejudice any investigation coming out of the ss 337 or 338 disclosure he commits an offence unless one of the following exceptions apply. First, there is no offence if he neither knew nor suspected that his tip off was likely to be prejudicial to an investigation. Secondly, if he passes the information in the course of carrying out a function under PCA 2002 or similar legislation. Finally, there is no offence if he is a professional legal adviser and the passing of information was in the course of giving legal advice or in relation to actual or contemplated legal proceedings so long as, in either case, the information was not passed with a view to furthering a criminal purpose.

8.36   CJA 1988, s 93D(1) and DTA 1994, s 53(1) contain offences of tipping off where there has been no disclosure to a constable but the person giving the tip off knows or suspects the constable is acting or proposing to act in connection with an investigation into money laundering and the tip off is likely to prejudice that investigation are replaced by s 342 in PCA 2002, Pt 8. These are considered below.

8.37 The law in relation to tipping off has already caused problems for financial institutions. In the cases of *Bank of Scotland v A Ltd,*[1] *A Bank v A Ltd (Serious Fraud Office, Interested Party),*[2] and *C v S*[3] consideration was given as to what action a bank should take when faced with conflicting duties under the 'tipping off' legislation on the one hand and orders for disclosure of documents or liabilities under a constructive trust for paying out the proceeds of crime on the other. In summary, the correct approach in such situations would appear to be for the bank to approach the enforcement authority in the first instance and try to agree what could be disclosed (that being effectively a bar to future prosecution, any attempt to prosecute following such a reassurance being likely to be declared an abuse of process). In the absence of agreement an order of the court should be sought on the basis that a decision of a court in possession of the full facts would be a protection from prosecution. This is a complex area and even close examination of the above cases may not be sufficient to ensure compliance with the law.

---

[1] [2001] EWCA Civ 52, [2001] 3 All ER 58, [2001] 1 WLR 751.
[2] (2000) Times, 18 July (CLW/00/28/8).
[3] [1999] 2 All ER 343, [1999] 1 WLR 1551, CA.

Penalties (s 334)

8.38 Offences under ss 327, 328 and 329 are either way matters with a maximum sentence in the Crown Court of 14 years' imprisonment or a fine or both. Failing to disclose and tipping off offences are either way matters with a maximum sentence in the Crown Court of five years' imprisonment or a fine or both.

CONSENT

Appropriate consent (s 335)

8.39 Appropriate consent is consent to proceed granted by the nominated officer, constable or customs officer to whom disclosure was made. In order that practitioners are not left in limbo awaiting consent for too long a period (unable of course to explain to their client for fear of falling foul of the tipping off offence) consent is assumed if the practitioner makes his authorised disclosure to a constable or customs officer and does not receive notice from a constable or customs officer that consent is refused within seven working days starting from the first working day[1] after the practitioner makes the disclosure. A practitioner is also treated as having the appropriate consent if, having made his authorised disclosure to a constable or customs officer, he receives notice that consent is refused within the seven working days notice period but the moratorium period (31 days[2] starting with the day on which the person receives notice that consent is refused) has expired. The idea behind this is that the enforcement authorities have 31 days to carry out further investigations and obtain a restraining order.[3] The practitioner will of course have the difficult task of fending off enquiries from the client for over a month in order to avoid committing the tipping off offence. Whether NCIS will be able to comply with this strict timetable remains to be seen.

---

[1]   Working days are all days other than Saturdays, Sundays, Christmas Day, Good Friday or Bank Holidays (as under the Banking and Financial Dealings Act 1971).
[2]   These are calendar days not working days (HL Committee Stage, 27 May 2002, col 1056, Lord Rooker introducing the offence as an amendment).
[3]   HL Committee Stage, 27 May 2002, col 1056.

Nominated officer: consent (s 336)

8.40   A nominated officer commits an offence if he gives the appropriate consent otherwise than in accordance with this section. He may give appropriate consent to the doing of a prohibited act if he discloses to a person authorised by the Director General of NCIS that property is criminal property and—

   (a)   that person gives consent to the doing of the act;
   (b)   within the notice period of seven working days starting with the first working day[1] after he makes the disclosure he has not received notice from that person that consent is refused; or
   (c)   receives notice within the period that consent is refused and the moratorium period (31 days[2] starting with the day he is given notice of the refusal of consent) has expired.[3]

---

[1]   See para 8.39, fn 1.
[2]   See para 8.39, fn 2.
[3]   The idea behind this is that the enforcement authorities have 31 days to carry out further investigations and obtain a restraining order.

8.41   There is nothing expressly in the statute to prevent NCIS from consistently or automatically withholding consent until the final day of the notice period. Lord Rooker gave what appears to have become the Government's stock answer to the failure of PCA 2002 to provide protections from abuse by the enforcement authorities—

> 'Our answer is that, like any other public body, the National Criminal Intelligence Service must act reasonably and must comply with the European Convention on Human Rights. It would be acting

unlawfully if it withheld consent without good reason. The idea of an unspoken policy within the agency of waiting until the last day before taking action to stop it would not be held as reasonable.'[1]

One can only hope that the courts will take a robust approach to supervising NCIS.

[1] HL Committee Stage, 27 May 2002, col 1056.

8.42 The nominated officer commits the offence if he gives consent to a prohibited act otherwise than as set out here, knowing or suspecting that the act is a prohibited act. Lord Rooker explained—

'. . . it is the nominated officer's responsibility to keep track of the time constraints and notify the employee when it is safe to proceed with the transaction.'[1]

[1] HL Committee Stage, 27 May 2002, col 1056.

8.43 The offence is triable either way with a maximum sentence in the Crown Court of five years' imprisonment and/or a fine.

DISCLOSURES

Protected disclosures (s 337)

8.44 Section 337 protects people carrying out activities in the regulated sector (as defined in Sch 9). The usual statutory and common law rules on dispersing information do not apply to disclosures made as soon as practicable to constables, customs officers or nominated officers (ie nominated by their company and receiving information in accordance with company policy and procedure) of information causing knowledge, suspicion or reasonable grounds for suspicion that another person is engaged in money laundering. The Explanatory Notes state that the protection is very wide so as to be consistent with the UK's obligations under Article 9 of the 1991 European Community Directive[1] on prevention of the use of the financial system for the purpose of money laundering.[2]

[1] Directive 91/308/EEC.
[2] Explanatory Notes, para 492.

8.45 Concern was expressed that the protection is limited to the disclosure of that on which the accountant's knowledge or suspicion was based and that additional information required of accountants by NCIS would not be protected under s 333. The common law public interest defence to a breach of client confidentiality was thought to be a weaker substitute to broadening the statutory protection.[1]

---

[1]   Baroness Noakes, HL Committee Stage, 27 May 20002, cols 1087–1088.

Authorised disclosures (s 338)

8.46   It is a defence to the offences discussed in paras 8.6–8.15 for a defendant to show that he has made a s 338 authorised disclosure or has had a reasonable excuse for not doing so. This is a disclosure to a constable,[1] customs officer or nominated person (ie a person nominated within a company and who receives the information in accordance with company policy, the defendant making the disclosure in the course of his employment) that property is criminal property where either—
   (a)   the disclosure was made before the defendant did the act and the act was then done with the consent of the constable, customs officer or nominated officer; or
   (b)   the disclosure was made after he acted but there was good reason not to make the disclosure before then and the defendant did make the disclosure of his own initiative and as soon as was practicable. An authorised disclosure does not breach any restriction (statutory or otherwise) on the disclosure of information (s 338(4)).

---

[1]   Section 340(13) defines constable so as to include references to a person authorised for the purposes of Pt 7 by the Director General of NCIS.

Form and manner of disclosures (s 339)

8.47   Section 339 gives the Secretary of State the power to specify the manner and form in which disclosures must be made and to require such additional information from the person making the disclosure as is necessary to enable the recipient to decide whether to start a money laundering investigation. Disclosures made under this provision do not breach any restriction on the dissemination of information (ie under the Data Protection Acts).

INTERPRETATION (s 340)

8.48   'Criminal property' is defined in s 340(3) as property constituting a person's benefit from criminal conduct or directly or indirectly representing such benefit. Further, for property to be 'criminal property' the alleged offender must know or suspect the property to be such. Attempts by Opposition MPs to restrict this definition to reduce the burden upon employees and companies in the regulated sector were lampooned by those such as Mr Davidson, who asked—

> 'Is the case being advanced that we should be lenient with money launderers, crooks and rascals so as not to place the City of London at a competitive disadvantage vis-à-vis other jurisdictions?'[1]

---

[1]   HC SC B, 17 January 2002, col 1014.

8.49   Criminal conduct is any conduct that is either an offence in the UK or would be if it occurred here. It is immaterial who carried out the conduct, who benefited from it and whether the conduct predates PCA 2002. To benefit is to obtain property as a result of or in connection with the conduct. The extent of a pecuniary advantage is equated with the equivalent sum of money in value. Property or pecuniary advantage obtained in any part as a result of criminal conduct is treated as if it were completely from that source. The amount of benefit is the amount obtained as a result of or in connection with the conduct. Property is given a non-exhaustive definition and includes intangible or incorporeal property, money and land. Property is obtained for the purposes of PCA 2002, Pt 7 if an interest is obtained in it including an equitable interest or power.

8.50   The Explanatory Notes make it clear that because of the definition of criminal property in s 340, all three principal money laundering offences now apply to an offender laundering the proceeds of his own crime as well as those of a crime committed by another.[1]

---

[1]   Explanatory Notes, para 469.

9 Investigations

INTRODUCTION

General

9.1   The Proceeds of Crime Act 2002 ('PCA 2002'), Part 8 (ss 341–416) provides a number of 'tools' for the investigator. The orders combine with the existing powers, such as those in the Police and Criminal Evidence Act 1984 ('PACE 1984'). The orders available are: production orders, search and seizure warrants, disclosure orders, customer information orders and account monitoring orders. Schedule 11 amends the Access to Justice Act 1999 to provide civil public funding to apply to vary investigative orders made under Pt 8.

9.2   The impact of these orders, in particular on banks, is large. Added to it is the related effect of the Convention on Mutual Assistance in Criminal Matters Between Member States of the EU. The UK became a signatory to the Convention on 29 May 2000 and signed the accompanying protocol on 16 October 2001.[1] The Convention requires that member states—
   (a)   locate and provide details of all bank accounts held by a natural or legal person who is the subject of an investigation into serious crime;
   (b)   provide details of transactions on specified accounts; and
   (c)   monitor account activity in response to a request for mutual legal assistance.

Clearly, banks are to find themselves playing an ever increasing role in the investigation of crime.

---

[1]   See the Protocol at http//www.homeoffice.gov.uk.

Investigation (s 341)

9.3   PCA 2002 identifies three different types of investigations. First, there are 'confiscation investigations' into whether a person has benefited from his criminal conduct or as to the extent or whereabouts of his benefit from his criminal conduct. Secondly, there are 'civil recovery investigations' to examine whether property is recoverable property or associated property, who holds the property and its extent and

164

whereabouts. Section 341(3) defines civil recovery investigations. An investigation is not a civil recovery investigation—

  (a) once proceedings for a civil recovery order have been started;
  (b) if an interim receiving or administration order is in place; or
  (c) if the property is being detained under s 295. Finally, money laundering investigations are investigations into whether a person has committed a money laundering offence for the purposes of Pt 8.

9.4 None of the powers under Pt 8 is available for use in investigations into crEminal offences other than those concerning money laundering. Inevitably, however, evidence pertinent to a criminal prosecution may come to light as a by-product of the use of these orders and, subject to the protection against self-incrimination discussed below, this may make criminal prosecution a possibility.

Offence of prejudicing investigation (s 342)

9.5 Section 342 provides an offence of prejudicing an investigation by knowingly making a disclosure that one knows or suspects is likely to prejudice an investigation or intentionally falsifying, concealing, destroying or otherwise disposing of or causing or permitting the falsification, concealment, destruction or disposal of documents relevant to an investigation knowing or suspecting those documents to be relevant. No offence is committed if the act is done in pursuance of a requirement under PCA 2002 or similar legislation or if it is covered by legal professional privilege as defined above. The offence is triable either way and punishable in the Crown Court with up to five years' imprisonment or a fine or both.

9.6 Section 342 extends the offences in CJA 1988, s 93D(1) and DTA 1994, s 53(1) (which related only to money laundering investigations), to incorporate civil recovery and confiscation investigations. The remainder of ss 93D and 53 are replaced by PCA 2002, s 333. The offence would seem further good reason for accountancy and auditing firms to monitor what their employees are shredding!

ENGLAND AND WALES AND NORTHERN IRELAND

JUDGES AND COURTS (SS 343–344)

9.7 Sections 343–344 state that in England, Wales and Northern Ireland applications in respect of confiscation and money laundering investigations for the orders available under Pt 8 are to be made to a judge entitled to exercise the jurisdiction of the Crown Court sitting in the Crown Court (a Crown Court judge in Northern Ireland). Applications for the orders relating to civil recovery investigations are to be made to a High Court judge sitting in the High Court. Provision is made in Pt 8 for the variation and discharge of orders and the making of rules of court for the Crown Court and High Court in Northern Ireland. No such provision is required in respect of the High Court in England and Wales, which has inherent powers to vary or discharge orders.

PRODUCTION ORDERS

Production orders (s 345)

9.8   Under s 345 an appropriate officer may apply for a production order requiring the person specified therein to produce specified material relating to an investigation. The order will state a period in which the material must be produced, namely seven days, unless the judge finds that to be an inappropriate period. The order may give the officer power to take the material away or restrict him from having access to it.

Requirements for making of production order (s 346)

9.9   To grant a production order the judge must be satisfied that there are reasonable grounds for believing that the specified person is in possession or control of the material and that the material is likely to be of substantial value (whether or not by itself) for the investigation. The judge must be further satisfied that there are reasonable grounds to suspect—
   (a)   in the case of a confiscation investigation, that the specified person has benefited from his criminal conduct; or
   (b)   in the case of a civil recovery investigation, that the specified property is recoverable property or associated property; or
   (c)   in the case of a money laundering investigation, that the specified person has committed a money laundering offence.

9.10   This new production order replaces similar existing powers under CJA 1988, s 93H, DTA 1994, s 55 and the Proceeds of Crime (Northern Ireland) Order 1996,[1] art 50. Section 346(5) contains a public interest test whereby there must be reasonable grounds for believing that it is in the public interest for the material to be produced or for access to it to be given, having regard to—
   (a)   the benefit likely to accrue to the investigation if the material is obtained;

(b)   the circumstances under which the person specified in the application as appearing to be in posession or control of the material holds it.

The original Bill had no such test on its face and for a long time the Government resisted amendment on the basis that the ECHR placed effectively the same responsibility upon judges as a public interest test would. Lord Thomas of Gresford challenged this position, arguing—

'. . . these are applications that, in effect, are made ex parte for a production order. There is no one on the other side. Although [the section] sets out a check list for the judge to go through while he considers whether a production order would be appropriate, it is asking a little of him also to have regard to the European convention and to all the possible provisions that might apply in circumstances such as these — the right to property and so forth.

In those circumstances, the European Convention does not match up to a provision asking the judge to think about the public interest . . . it appears in other legislation and there is no valid reason why it should not be included here.'[2]

Lord Thomas of Gresford and those who backed his view won the day and it is to be hoped that the public interest test is given the importance that it merits following this parliamentary debate.

---

[1]   SI 1996/1299 (NI 9).
[2]   HL Committee Stage, 27 May 2002, cols 1090–1091.

Order to grant entry (s 347)

9.11   A judge has a subsidiary power where he has made a production order. He may make an order requiring any person who appears to an appropriate officer to be a person entitled to grant entry to premises to enable the officer to gain access to the material. Section 347 was intended to clarify the power (repealed by PCA 2002) contained in CJA 1988, s 93H(5), DTA 1994, s 55(5) and the Proceeds of Crime (Northern Ireland) Order 1996,[1] art 50(5).

---

[1]   SI 1996/1299 (NI 9).

Further provisions (s 348)

9.12   A production order overrides any restrictions on the disclosure of information save that it cannot require disclosure of material covered by legal professional privilege or which is excluded material as defined by PACE 1984. An appropriate officer may take copies of material produced under a production order. Material may be retained 'so long as it is necessary' to keep it (rather then a copy) in connection with the investigation (s 348(6)). However, if an appropriate person has reasonable grounds for believing that the material may need to be produced in any legal proceedings and it might be unavailable if not held, it can be held until the proceedings are completed (s 348(7)).

Computer information (s 349)

9.13   Information stored on computers that is made the subject of a production order must be supplied to the officer or he must be given access to it (as specified in the order) in such a way that the information is visible and legible. Sir Edwin Jowitt queried whether this requirement would be satisfied by the provision of a floppy disc or CD.[1]

---

[1]   Page 15 of a document produced by Sir Edwin Jowitt, a retired High Court judge, during the consultation process for the draft Bill. The Lord Chief Justice and Rose LJ endorsed the document.

Government departments (s 350)

9.14   If information required for an investigation is held by an authorised government department (as defined by the Crown Proceedings Act 1947 and including Northern Ireland Departments) it may be obtained by serving a production order upon the department as if one were serving civil proceedings upon it. There is a duty on all those in the department who receive the order to bring it to the attention of the relevant officer within the department. If this is not done within the period stated on the face of the order the person in the department on whom it was served must report his reasons for failing to do this to a judge (the judge must be the same rank as is required to make an order). This is a new provision and, coupled with the provision in s 348 that production orders override data protection legislation, seems particularly significant in the shadow of public debate on the subject of access by different government departments to each other's records.

Supplementary (s 351)

9.15   An application for a production order may be made ex parte to a judge in chambers. Section 351 also provides that rules of court may make provision as to the relevant practice and procedure.

9.16   Application to vary or discharge an order made under Pt 8 may be made by the person who applied for the original order (or a colleague where the applicant was a constable, customs officer or accredited investigator), or by any person affected by the order.

9.17   Section 351(7) provides clumsily that orders to grant entry 'have effect as if they were orders of the court'. This means simply that it is a contempt of court not to comply with an order.

SEARCH AND SEIZURE WARRANTS

The new PCA warrants

9.18   PCA 2002 creates a new procedure for obtaining search and seizure warrants. These go further than warrants under PACE 1984, Pt II (or PACE (NI) Order 1989,[1] Pt III) in that they do not exclude special procedure material.[2] Importantly, warrants will be issued under PCA 2002 on the basis of suspicion of benefit, rather than suspicion of an offence. The reason for this in relation to confiscation investigations is obvious. Presumably, it applies to civil recovery investigations because civil recovery investigations are intended to be mounted where there is suspicion of unlawful conduct producing benefit but no grounds for suspicion of a particular offence. This accords with the general vagueness of the civil procedure. The basis for the test in money laundering investigations is even more controversial; why should the test for warrants in money laundering cases differ from that in relation to other criminal offences?

---

[1]   SI 1989/1341.
[2]   PACE 1984, s 14.

9.19   Another important change is that the new PCA warrants, in contrast with warrants issued under PACE 1984, Sch 1, can be made in relation to special procedure material (as defined by PACE 1984, s 14) without notice to the person whose premises are to be searched. Where no different provision is made explicit in PCA 2002, the general provisions in PACE 1984, Pt II about search warrants apply also to PCA 2002 search warrants.

Search and seizure warrants (s 352)

9.20   An appropriate officer (as defined for each of the different types of investigation in s 378) may apply to a judge for a search and seizure warrant. The judge must be satisfied that a production order made in relation to the material sought has not been complied with and there are reasonable grounds for believing that the material is on the specified premises. The application must specify the person or property that is the subject of the investigation, and must further state that the warrant is sought for the purposes of the investigation and in relation to specified premises. The warrant must either specify the material sought or state that there are reasonable grounds to believe that material falling within s 353(6), (7) or (8) is on the premises. The warrant gives a constable or customs officer (in confiscation or money laundering investigations) or a member of staff of the ARA (in civil recovery investigations) the power to enter and search the specified premises and seize and retain any material found there likely to be of substantial value to the investigation.

Requirements where production order not available (s 353)

9.21   Section 353 permits the granting of search and seizure warrants in situations where there can be no production order.

9.22   A warrant may be issued instead of a production order where it is not practicable to communicate with the person against whom a production order could be made, or any other person who would have to comply with it, and the investigation might be seriously prejudiced unless immediate access to the material is secured. The same criteria as set out at para 9.9 for obtaining production orders must be satisfied. In addition there must be reasonable grounds for suspecting that the material is on the specified premises.

9.23   Alternatively, a warrant may be granted where material is sought which cannot be identified for the purposes of a production order but relates to a specified person or specified property, relates to the question behind the investigation (ie is there benefit, is there recoverable or associated property how much and with whom, has there been a money laundering offence?) and is of substantial value to the investigation. A warrant may only be granted in these circumstances where either it is not practicable to communicate with the person entitled to grant entry to the premises, or that consent will not be given to enter without a warrant, or that the investigation might be seriously prejudiced unless immediate entry can be secured.

Further provisions: general (s 354)

9.24   A search and seizure warrant does not give the right to seize legal professional privileged material, except material containing only the name and address of a lawyer's client. Nor is there a right to seize excluded material (s 379 adopts the definition of 'excluded material' to be found in PACE 1984).

Further provisions: confiscation and money laundering (s 355)

9.25   The Secretary of State may make an order to supplement the provisions relating to search and seizure in respect of confiscation or money laundering investigations by applying the provisions contained in PACE 1984 (or its Northern Ireland equivalent).

Further provisions: civil recovery (s 356)

9.26   Whilst s 355 allows for the application of further provisions to the making of search and seizure warrants in relation to confiscation and money laundering investigations, s 356 sets out further provisions in relation to civil recovery investigations on the face of the Act. Warrants may be used up to one month from the date of issue. A member of the ARA staff carrying out the search may require information held on computer which he believes to be relevant to the investigation to be produced in a visible and legible form in which it can be taken away (ie printed). Copies may be taken of any material seized. A warrant issued for a civil recovery investigation may include conditions and may also give authority to do other specified things necessary to give effect to the warrant. This gives a High Court judge power to authorise the member of staff of the ARA to use reasonable force if he thinks it necessary to make the warrant effective. Material seized under a warrant issued for a civil recovery investigation may be held so long as it is necessary to hold it (as opposed to copies of it) for the purposes of the investigation or, where the Director has reasonable grounds to believe it may need to be produced in any legal proceedings and that if not held it might not be available, the material seized may be held until those proceedings are concluded.

DISCLOSURE ORDERS

Disclosure orders (s 357)

9.27   A disclosure order is an order authorising the Director to send a notice to anyone they believe has information relevant to the investigation requiring them to answer questions where and when specified or at once; to provide specified information in a specified manner and at a specified time or at once; to produce specified or described at a specified time or at once and in a specified manner. A copy of the order (or other evidence of it) should be sent with the notice otherwise it has no authority.

9.28   The Director may apply for such an order in respect of a person who is the subject of a confiscation investigation or of property subject to a civil recovery investigation. The order is not available in relation to money laundering investigations. Given the necessarily invasive nature of such an order, it is not intended for investigations into offences.

9.29   It seems that once a disclosure order is made in relation to an investigation there is no limit on the number of requests the Director can make in respect of the same person or property.

9.30   Similar powers exist in the Terrorism Act 2000 in relation to terrorist offences as well as terrorist funding. A legacy of the troubles in Northern Ireland is that similar powers are currently available in Northern Ireland to court-appointed financial investigators where an investigation is taking place into the proceeds of crime.[1]

_____

[1]   See the Proceeds of Crime (Northern Ireland) Order 1996, SI 1996/1299 (NI 9), Sch 2, para 2.

Requirements for making of disclosure order (s 358)

9.31   To make a disclosure order the court must be satisfied that there are reasonable grounds for suspecting that the specified person has 'benefited from his criminal conduct', or that the specified property is recoverable property or associated property. The judge must also be satisfied that there are reasonable grounds for believing that information sought under the order will be of substantial value to the investigation.

9.32   The Government admits in the Explanatory Notes that judges must address the issue of proportionality in accordance with their obligations under the Human Rights Act 1998[1] and so must consider whether a less intrusive order, such as a production order, would serve the purpose required. Again, Lord Gresford's concerns have been heeded and there is a public interest test in s 358(4).

_____

[1]   Explanatory Notes, para 518.

Offences (s 359)

9.33   Failure to comply with a disclosure order without reasonable excuse is an offence, carrying a maximum of a six months' imprisonment and/or a level 5 fine. If a person purports to comply with a disclosure order but knowingly or recklessly makes a false or misleading statement in respect of a material particular he is guilty of an either way offence, the maximum sentence for which in the Crown Court is two years' imprisonment and/or a fine.

Statements (s 360)

9.34   In general, statements made by persons in response to disclosure orders may not be used against the maker in criminal proceedings. However, this rule does not apply to proceedings under PCA 2002, Pts 2 or 4 or s 359(1) and (3). They may only be used in criminal proceedings for other offences where two conditions are satisfied: (a) the person makes a statement in giving evidence which is inconsistent with a statement it made in response to the disclosure order; *and* (b) in those criminal proceedings the person (or his representative) adduces evidence or asks a question relating to the statement made in response to the disclosure order. This restriction has been introduced to comply with the decision of the European Court of Human Rights in *Saunders v United Kingdom*.[1]

---

[1]   [1998] 1 BCLC 362, [1997] BCC 872, 23 EHRR 313. Note that similar provisions are to be found in the Youth Justice and Criminal Evidence Act 1999, Sch 3.

Further provisions (s 361)

9.35   Disclosure orders do not extend to privileged or excluded material but in all other respects they override restrictions on the disclosure of information. The Director may make copies of any document produced and may retain any document so long as it is necessary to retain the original (as opposed to a copy) in connection with the investigation. Moreover, if the Director has reasonable grounds for believing that the document may need to be produced for the purposes of any legal proceedings and that returning it may lead to it being unavailable for those proceedings, he may retain it until the proceedings are concluded.

Supplementary (s 362)

9.36   Section 362 sets out a number of supplementary or miscellaneous points. Firstly, an application for a production order or an order to grant entry may be made ex parte to a judge in chambers.

9.37 Secondly, s 362 deals with discharge and variation of production orders and orders to grant entry. Except in respect of an order made for the purposes of a civil recovery investigation in England or Wales an order may be varied or discharged by the court on application by the Director or any person affected by it. The Director and any person affected by the order have a right to apply for it to be varied or discharged and the judge, if persuaded, may discharge or vary the order. Rules of the court may be developed to control the procedure for applications to vary or discharge orders.

CUSTOMER INFORMATION ORDERS

Customer information orders (s 363)

9.38 A financial institution (or a number of financial institutions) must provide, when required to do so in writing, any such customer information as it has relating to the person specified in a customer information order. The institution may require sight of the order before providing the information. The application must specify a person who is the subject of a confiscation or money laundering investigation, or specify property which is the subject of a civil recovery investigation and the name of the person who appears to hold that property. The application, to be made by an appropriate officer (s 378), must state that the order is sought for the purposes of that investigation and specify the financial institutions against which it is sought. The order may simply state that it applies to 'all financial institutions' but there is, once again, the issue of proportionality to consider.

Meaning of customer information (s 364)

9.39 It is the appropriate officer who specifies the time and manner in which the information is to be provided. It seems strange that the court must leave the timescale to the officer in this way. Presumably the courts will be willing to judicially review the appropriate officer's decision should he set an unreasonable time limit (s 363(6)). The institution must state whether the person named (which may be a company) holds or has held an account (including a joint account) with that institution. If an account exists or existed further information listed in s 364(2) for a personal account and s 364(3) for the account of a company, limited liability partnership or similar foreign entity must also be provided.

Requirements for making a customer information order (s 365)

9.40   The judge must be satisfied (as in applications for the orders considered above) that—
   (a)   there are reasonable grounds for suspicion that the person specified has benefited from criminal conduct;
   (b)   the property is recoverable or associated property and that the specified person is holding it; or
   (c)   the person specified has committed a money laundering offence. He must further be satisfied that there are reasonable grounds for believing that the customer information that may be provided as a result of the order sought is likely to be of substantial value (whether or not by itself) to the investigation.

Section 365(6) contains a public interest test whereby the judge must have regard to the level of benefit likely to accrue to the investigation.

Offences (s 366)

9.41   The failure of an institution to comply with an order without reasonable excuse is a summary offence with a maximum punishment of a level 5 fine. If misleading or false material is provided knowingly or recklessly an either way offence is committed, punishable by fine.

Statements (s 367)

9.42   Generally, statements made by financial institutions in response to customer information orders may not be used in evidence against the institution in criminal proceedings. They may be used in proceedings under PCA 2002, Pts 2 or 4, or for prosecution of offences under s 366(1) or (3). They may only be used in criminal proceedings for other offences where two conditions are satisfied: (a) the financial institution makes a statement in giving evidence in the criminal proceedings which is inconsistent with a statement it made in response to the customer information order; *and* (b) in those criminal proceedings the financial institution (or its legal representative) adduces evidence or asks a question relating to the statement made in response to the customer information order. This restriction follows the decision in *Saunders v United Kingdom*[1] and the similar provisions in the Youth Justice and Criminal Evidence Act 1999, Sch 3. The Scottish provision (s 401) is the same in relation to Pt 3 but what is not covered is the situation where there is a statement made under s 367 and a later offence under Pt 3 or the reverse position of a statement under the Scottish provisions and an offence under Pts 2 or 4.

---

[1]   [1998] 1 BCLC 362, [1997] BCC 872, 23 EHRR 313.

Disclosure of information (s 368)

9.43   A customer information order overrides all restrictions on the disclosure of information except legal professional privilege.

Supplementary (s 369)

9.44   Section 369 sets out a number of supplementary or miscellaneous points. Firstly, an application for a production order or an order to grant entry may be made ex parte to a judge in chambers.

9.45   Secondly, s 369 deals with discharge and variation of production orders and orders to grant entry. Except in respect of an order made for the purposes of a civil recovery investigation in England or Wales an order may be varied or discharged by the court on application by the Director or any person affected by it. The person who applied for the order (or a colleague senior enough to have applied for the order) and any person affected by the order have a right to apply for it to be varied or discharged and the judge, if persuaded, may discharge or vary the order.

9.46   Section 369 allows for rules of the court to be developed to control the procedure for applications to vary or discharge orders.

9.47   An accredited financial investigator, a constable or a customs officer may not make an application for a customer information order or an application to vary a customer information order unless he is a senior appropriate officer or is authorised to do so by a senior appropriate officer.

9.48   In the Regulatory Impact Assessment for PCA 2002, the Government estimated that the cost of customer information orders for the financial sector will be £250 per order per institution.[1]

---

[1]   See http//www.homeoffice.gov.uk.

ACCOUNT MONITORING ORDERS

Account monitoring orders (s 370)

9.49   A financial institution must, for a stated period not exceeding 90 days, provide account information of the kind specified in an account monitoring order to an appropriate officer in the manner and at the times specified in the order.

9.50 The application, by an appropriate officer (s 378), must state that a specified person is subject to a money laundering or confiscation investigation or that the property specified is subject to a civil recovery investigation and the person specified appears to hold that property. The application must further specify that the order is sought for the purpose of the relevant investigation and must specify the financial institution and account details to which the application applies. The account may be held solely by the specified person or be a joint account held by him and another. The application may simply apply to 'all accounts' held by that person at the specified institution or may be more specific (although the judge must of course consider the issue of proportionality).

9.51 One attraction of the new order for the Government will be that the creation of the account monitoring order will replace the need for multiple applications for production orders in the same investigation. This will, therefore, save money.

Requirements for making of account monitoring order (s 371)

9.52 For an order to be granted, there must be an 'investigation' and the judge must be satisfied that there are reasonable grounds for suspecting that the person specified has benefited from criminal conduct or committed a money laundering offence, or that the property specified is recoverable or associated property and that the specified person holds all or some of the property. The judge must further be satisfied that there are reasonable grounds for believing that the material is likely to be of substantial value (whether or not by itself) to the investigation for the purposes of which the order is sought. Again, there is a public interest test. There must be reasonable grounds for believing that it is in the public interest for the account information to be provided, having regard to the benefit likely to accrue to the investigation if the information is obtained (s 371(6)). It is suggested that within this, and in light of HRA 1998, a judge should consider the issue of proportionality and specifically whether a production order (which is less oppressive than an order lasting for up to 90 days) is sufficient.

Statements (s 372)

9.53 There are limitations on the use of information gathered in criminal proceedings against the provider of the information (the financial institution). Information provided in statements may not be used in criminal proceedings against the maker unless the proceedings are for contempt of court or for offences under Pts 2 or 4 or for other offences as previous inconsistent statement. See para 9.42 for further discussion of this.

Applications (s 373)

9.54   Section 373 states that an application for an account monitoring order may be made ex parte to a judge in chambers. It would seem likely that appropriate officers will take advantage most, if not all, of the time.

Disclosure of information (s 374)

9.55   Legal profession privilege may be invoked but no other restrictions (however imposed) on the provision of information apply. Here again the investigative powers under PCA 2002 override both data protection legislation and common law concepts of confidentiality.

Supplementary (s 375)

9.56   The officer who made the original application or a colleague who is also an appropriate officer may apply to vary the application. He or any person affected by the order may apply for its variation or discharge (except for orders made in respect of civil recovery investigations in England or Wales). Section 375 also makes provision for rules of the court to govern the practice and procedure of applications for account monitoring orders.

9.57   There are no new offences for failure to comply with account monitoring orders or for providing false or misleading information in relation to an account monitoring order. However, the orders are orders of the court (s 375(6)) and so failure to comply is contempt of court.

EVIDENCE OVERSEAS (S 376)

9.58   Section 376 sets out the procedure for obtaining evidence from overseas. Letters of request requiring evidence from abroad may be issued by a judge or the Director of the ARA for the purpose of an investigation into whether a person has benefited from criminal conduct and the extent or whereabouts of that benefit. Letters must go to the appropriate foreign court, tribunal or authority via the Secretary of State unless the case is one of urgency. 'Urgency' is not defined in PCA 2002.

CODES OF PRACTICE (S 377)

9.59 Section 377 provides for the creation of a code of practice to govern the exercise of these investigatory powers. At the time of writing this Code of Practice is in the consultation stage.

INTERPRETATION

Officers (s 378)

9.60 The provisions discussed above use the terms 'appropriate officer' and 'senior appropriate officer'. These are defined as in the table below—

Type of Investigation	Appropriate Officer	Senior Appropriate Officer
Confiscation investigation	the Director of the ARA; an accredited financial investigator; a constable; a customs officer	the Director; a police officer of the rank of superintendent or higher; an equivalent ranking customs officer; an accredited financial investigation of sufficient rank as specified by order of the Secretary of State
Civil recovery investigation	the Director	the Director
Money laundering investigation	an accredited financial investigator; a constable; a customs officer; a person authorised for the purposes of money laundering investigations by the Director General of NCIS (for purposes of s 342 only)	the Director; a police officer of the rank of superintendent or higher; an equivalent ranking customs officer; an accredited financial investigation of sufficient rank as specified by order of the Secretary of State

9.61 A person is not an appropriate officer or a senior appropriate officer in relation to a money laundering investigation if he is a member of the staff of the ARA or a person providing services under arrangements made by the Director.

Miscellaneous (s 379)

9.62   The terms 'document', 'excluded material' and 'premises' have the
same meanings as in PACE 1984 and the PACE (NI) Order 1989.[1]

------
[1]   SI 1989/1341.

SCOTLAND

PRODUCTION ORDERS (SS 380–386)

9.63   In Scotland, the procurator fiscal (in relation to a confiscation or
money laundering investigation) or the Scottish ministers (in relation
to a civil recovery investigation) may apply to a sheriff for a
production order. The criteria for granting the order are the same as in
the rest of the UK. Orders to grant entry may also be made by the
sheriff and enable a constable or customs officer (in relation to
confiscation or money laundering proceedings) or a person
nominated by the Scottish ministers (in relation to a civil recovery
investigation) to gain access to the material. The application for the
order to grant entry may be made ex parte to a sheriff in chambers.
Section 386 again allows for rules of the court to be developed to
control the procedure for applications to vary or discharge orders.
The report setting out reasons for failure of an officer in a government
department to bring an order to the attention of the relevant officer
must be made to the sheriff in the case. In all other respects, save
service, the Scottish legislation mirrors that for England, Wales and
Northern Ireland.

SEARCH WARRANTS (SS 387–390)

9.64   The procedure for the grant of search warrants in Scotland mirrors
that in England, Wales and Northern Ireland. The procurator fiscal (in
relation to a confiscation or money laundering investigation) or the
Scottish ministers (in relation to a civil recovery investigation) may
apply to a sheriff (sitting in his civil jurisdiction) for a search warrant.
The search is made by a customs officer constable or a person
nominated by the Scottish ministers as appropriate.

DISCLOSURE ORDERS (SS 391–396)

9.65 The Lord Advocate may apply to the High Court of Justiciary in relation to a confiscation investigation for a disclosure order and the Scottish ministers may apply to the Court of Session for a disclosure order in relation to a civil recovery investigation. It will be the Lord Advocate or Scottish ministers who send notice as above. The offences in Scotland are contained in s 393 and are identical to those in the rest of the UK.

CUSTOMER INFORMATION ORDERS (SS 397–403)

9.66 The procurator fiscal (in relation to a confiscation or money laundering investigation) or the Scottish ministers (in relation to a civil recovery investigation) may apply to a sheriff (sitting in his civil jurisdiction) for a customer information order. The Scottish offence is contained in s 400 but mirrors that in s 366. In other respects the Scottish provisions reflect those governing the rest of the UK.

ACCOUNT MONITORING ORDERS (SS 404–408)

9.67 The procurator fiscal (in relation to a confiscation or money laundering investigation) or the Scottish ministers (in relation to a civil recovery investigation) may apply to a sheriff (sitting in his civil jurisdiction) for an account monitoring order. The Scottish provisions in these sections reflect the equivalent provisions for the rest of the UK.

GENERAL

Jurisdiction of sheriff (s 409)

9.68 In Scotland the orders may be made by a sheriff who has jurisdiction in relation to property anywhere in Scotland. Orders made by a sheriff in this way may be executed throughout Scotland.

Code of practice (s 410)

9.69 Section 410 makes provision for the creation of a code of practice governing investigation under PCA 2002 in Scotland. At the time of writing, the Code of Practice is not yet completed.

Performance of functions of Scottish ministers by constables in Scotland (s 411)

9.70   Section 411 gives constables engaged in temporary service with the Scottish ministers in connection with their functions under Pt 8 powers to carry out many of the functions of the ministers. A list of powers that are not granted to constables is set out in s 411(2).

Interpretation (s 412)

9.71   It is worth noting that 'premises' is defined to include any place including any vehicle, vessel, aircraft or hovercraft and any offshore installation within the meaning of the Mineral Workings (Offshore Installations) Act 1971, s 1 and any tent or moveable structure, and that 'legal privilege' is defined so as to reflect the current position.

INTERPRETATION

Criminal conduct (s 413)

9.72   Criminal conduct is defined in the same way as in the confiscation provisions.[1]

---

[1]   See PCA 2002, Pts 2–4. See paras 3.189–3.199.

9.73   The effect of s 413(5) is that the powers in Pt 8 may be used from the date of its commencement irrespective of whether the conduct was committed or the property in question was obtained before the commencement of PCA 2002. Thus, Pt 8 has retrospective effect. This will be a cause of great concern for many. The argument that these are proceedings against property rather than the person will be small comfort to those who lose their homes!

Property (s 414)

9.74   Property is given a wide definition and a person obtains property if he obtains an interest in it. Section 414 states that 'recoverable property' has the same meanings as in Pt 5. Presumably, this means that 'recoverable property' is property obtained through unlawful conduct.[1] 'Associated property' has the same definition as in Pt 5.[2]

¹ See ss 240–242.
² See s 245.

Money laundering offences (s 415)

9.75 Offences under ss 327, 328 and 329 are 'money laundering offences' for the purposes of Pt 8 as are inchoate versions of or aiding, abetting, counselling or procuring of the same.

Other interpretive procedures (s 416)

9.76 Section 416 serves as an index to definitions relevant to this Part found elsewhere in PCA 2002.

10 Insolvency etc

INTRODUCTION

10.1   The Proceeds of Crime Act 2002 ('PCA 2002'), Pt 9 (ss 417–434) deals with the interrelation of the statute with the insolvency legislation. The provisions are detailed but self-explanatory. The primary purpose of Pt 9 is to ensure that respondents/defendants cannot use the insolvency legislation to avoid paying money due under PCA 2002.

BANKRUPTCY IN ENGLAND AND WALES (ss 417–419)

10.2   Sections 417–419 concern the application of PCA 2002 and the amendment of the Insolvency Act 1986 where a person is ajudged bankrupt in England and Wales. Where bankruptcy postdates orders made under ss 41, 120, 190, 50, 52, 128(3), 198 or 200 the property subject to those orders is excluded from the estate for the purposes of the bankruptcy. If the property is in Scotland the order under PCA 2002 must be registered for it to take priority. The powers given to an interim receiver under the Insolvency Act 1986, s 286 (debtors) do not apply to property subject to a restraint order under ss 41, 120 or 190.

10.3   Where bankruptcy proceedings predate the confiscation order, certain property may not be the subject of powers conferred upon the court under ss 41–67, 120–136, Sch 3 or ss 190–215; powers of a receiver appointed under ss 48, 50, 52, 196, 198 or 200; or powers of an administrator appointed under ss 125 or 128(3). These same powers must not be exercised in relation to sums that remain in the hands of a receiver (appointed under ss 50, 52, 198 or 200) or an administrator (appointed under s 128) after the amount required to be paid under a confiscation order has been fully paid. In cases where bankruptcy pre-dates the coming into force of the Insolvency Act 1986 the same provisions apply with the necessary changes (s 418(5)).

10.4 Section 419 states that no order made under the Insolvency Act 1986, ss 339, 340 or 423 (or equivalent older provisions) may be made in relation to property that is a tainted gift (see Pts 2, 3 or 4) and is subject to a restraint order under ss 41, 120 or 190, or an order under ss 50, 52, 128(3), 198 or 200. Where one of these orders under PCA 2002 has been discharged an order made under the Insolvency Act 1986, ss 339, 340 or 423 must take into account any realisation under PCA 2002, Pts 2, 3 or 4 of property held by the recipient of the tainted gift.

SEQUESTRATION IN SCOTLAND (ss 420–422) AND BANKRUPTCY IN NORTHERN IRELAND (ss 423–425)

10.5 Sections 420–425 mirror in their effect those for bankruptcy in England and Wales.

WINDING UP (ss 426–429)

10.6 Sections 426–429 detail how PCA 2002 interrelates with the procedure for winding up companies in England and Wales under the Insolvency Act 1986 and in Northern Ireland under the 1989 Order.[1] In relation to England, Wales and Scotland, s 426 gives primacy over the functions of the liquidator to orders made under PCA 2002, ss 41, 120, 190, 50, 52, 128(3), 198 or 200 (in Scotland this is the case only where the order is registered) which predate the date of the winding up order or the passing of the resolution of voluntary winding up. Section 426 also ensures that powers granted under PCA 2002 are not exercised so as to inhibit the liquidator from exercising his functions for the purpose of distributing property to the company's creditors, or so as to prevent the payment out of any property of expenses properly incurred during the winding up. Section 427 gives primacy to specified orders under PCA 2002 over the winding up provisions under the Insolvency Act 1986 in relation to tainted gifts. Sections 428 and 429 mirror these provisions in relation to Northern Ireland.

---

[1] Insolvency (Northern Ireland) Order 1989, SI 1989/2405 (NI 19).

FLOATING CHARGES (ss 430)

10.7 Section 430 details the interrelation of PCA 2002 and the provisions in the Insolvency Act 1986 and the Insolvency (Northern Ireland) Order 1989[1] concerning floating charges. Again the provisions give primacy to PCA 2002 save that the receiver's functions for the purpose of distributing property to the company's creditors must not be inhibited and the powers conferred by PCA 2002 must not be exercised so as to prevent the payment out of any property of expenses properly incurred by the receiver in performing his functions in respect of the property.

---

[1] SI 1989/2405 (NI 19).

LIMITED LIABILITY PARTNERSHIPS (s 431)

10.8 Section 431 states that the provisions in PCA 2002, ss 426, 427 and 430 in relation to companies apply equally to limited liability partnerships.

INSOLVENCY PRACTITIONERS (s 432–433)

10.9 Section 432 reproduces existing legislation and explains what is to happen when an insolvency practitioner takes action against property subject to a restraint order made under PCA 2002, Pts 2, 3 or 4. The provision allows insolvency practitioners to recover their expenses and ensures that they will only be liable for interfering with property subject to a restraint order if they are negligent. Section 433 defines who is an insolvency practitioner for the purposes of s 432.

11 Information

INTRODUCTION

11.1   The Proceeds of Crime Act 2002 ('PCA 2002'), Pt 10 (ss 435–442) provides for the disclosure of information to and by the Director of the ARA and the Scottish ministers. It also allows the exchange of information between the Scottish ministers and the Lord Advocate.

ENGLAND AND WALES AND NORTHERN IRELAND

Use of information by Director (s 435)

11.2   Section 435 allows the Director to use information received by him in respect of one function in relation to another. The example given in the Explanatory Notes was that information obtained in the course of a criminal confiscation investigation may be used by the Director in a civil recovery investigation.[1]

---

[1]   Explanatory Notes, para 577.

Disclosure of information to Director (s 436)

11.3   'Permitted persons', as defined in s 436(5), are allowed to disclose information held by them to the Director so that it may be used by him for the purpose of exercising any of his functions. The permitted persons include 'a constable', which includes any person with the powers of a constable such as MOD or BT police officers.[1] Section 436(6) allows the Secretary of State to designate by order other permitted persons, subject to the approval of both Houses of Parliament by virtue of s 459(6)(a).

---

[1]   Explanatory Notes, para 578.

11.4   Mr Ainsworth explained—

'The power in Part 10 to disclose information to the Director will be permissive; nobody will be required to disclose information . . . .'[1] The hierarchy will work in such a way that the overwhelming majority of the information that comes to the Director comes from the police authorities or the prosecution authorities. In most circumstances, that will occur where they have decided that prosecution is not viable or appropriate, for whatever reason.'[2]

---

[1]   HC Debates, 26 February 2002, col 587.
[2]   HC Debates, 26 February 2002, col 593.

11.5   Section 436(7) requires the Secretary of State, when designating permitted persons under s 436(5), to 'specify the functions' in respect of which the designation is made.

11.6   Under s 436(8) and (9) information must not be disclosed on behalf of the Commissioners of Inland Revenue or Customs and Excise unless they authorise its disclosure. The power of disclosure may be delegated by the Commissioners, in the case of the Inland Revenue, to an officer of the Board of the Inland Revenue, and in the case of Customs and Excise, to a customs officer. The purpose of these provisions is to put in place a safeguard in respect of the disclosure of sensitive information held by those bodies.

11.7   Disclosures that contravene the Data Protection Act 1998, or are prohibited by the Regulation of Investigatory Powers Act 2000, Pt I, are prohibited by s 436(3). The Explanatory Notes state that it is implicit that the provisions of the Human Rights Act 1998 will need to be taken into account before disclosure is made.[1]

---

[1]   Explanatory Notes, para 579.

Further disclosure (s 437)

11.8   Section 437 provides a supposed safeguard in respect of confidential information given to the Director by either Customs and Excise or the Inland Revenue. The Director is prohibited from further disclosing the material except for the purpose connected with the exercise of his functions and with the consent of the relevant Commissioners. Any 'permitted person' who discloses information to the Director may attach conditions as to the further disclosure of the information (s 437(6)). This is to cover the situation where, for example, sensitive operational details may have been disclosed. Regrettably, PCA 2002 makes no provision for sanctions for breach.

Disclosure of information by Director (s 438)

11.9   The Director is permitted to disclose information for the purposes set out in s 438(1)(a) to (i). These include disclosure for the purposes of any criminal investigation or proceedings and the exercise of his functions. Subsections (2) and (3) prevent the Director from disclosing information obtained by him under his Revenue functions[1] except to the Commissioners of Inland Revenue, or to the Lord Advocate for the exercise of his functions under Pt 3.

---

1   PCA 2002, Pt 6.

11.10   These provisions seek to ensure that confidential material about tax affairs is not disclosed except in limited circumstances. The reason for allowing information to be given to the Lord Advocate is for him to be in the same position in respect of his Pt 3 functions as the Director would be in relation to his Pt 2 functions.

11.11   The Lord Advocate is permitted to disclose information received by him under s 438(3)(b) to Scottish ministers for the purpose of the exercise by them of their functions under Pt 5 (s 438(4)).

11.12   The Director may impose conditions on further disclosure of information supplied by him 'as he thinks fit' (s 438(5)). A recipient of such information is prohibited from disclosing it in contravention of the conditions (s 438(6)).

11.13   A designated function is defined as 'a function which the Secretary of State thinks is a function of a public nature and which he delegates by order' (s 438(9)). This will be subject to the approval of both Houses of Parliament (s 459(6)).

11.14   No disclosure which contravenes the Data Protection Act 1998, or which is prohibited by the Regulation of Investigatory Powers Act 2000, Pt I, is permitted (s 438(8)). Any disclosure will, of course, have to comply with the Human Rights Act 1998.

SCOTLAND

Disclosure of information to Lord Advocate and to Scottish Ministers (s 439)

11.15 Section 439 mirrors s 436 and puts in place in Scotland similar rules relating to disclosure as have been introduced in England and Wales. 'Permitted persons', as defined in s 439(5), are allowed to disclose information held by them to the Scottish Ministers or the Lord Advocate so that it may be used for the purpose of exercising any of their functions.

Further disclosure (s 440)

11.16 Section 440 provides the same supposed safeguard in respect of confidential information given to the Lord Advocate or the Scottish ministers as s 437.

Disclosure of information by Lord Advocate and by Scottish Ministers (s 441)

11.17 Section 441 mirrors the provisions of s 438.

RESTRICTION ON DISCLOSURE FOR OVERSEAS PURPOSES (s 442)

11.18 Section 442 states that the Anti-terrorism, Crime and Security Act 2001, s 18 applies to the disclosure of information authorised by PCA 2002, ss 432(1)(a) or (b) or 435(2)(a) or (b). The Anti-terrorism, Crime and Security Act 2001, s 18 gives the Secretary of State power to restrict disclosure of information when criminal proceedings or a criminal investigation is taking place overseas. The power may be exercised where it appears to the Secretary of State that the overseas investigation or proceeding relates to a matter in which it would be more appropriate for any investigation to be carried out by the authorities of the UK or a third country. The section reflects the fact that mutual cooperation in criminal matters is not always straightforward!

12 Co-operation

The UK and overseas authorities

12.1 The Proceeds of Crime Act 2002 ('PCA 2002'), Pt 11 (ss 443–447) provides for co-operation in investigation and enforcement between the various parts of the UK and with overseas authorities. The type of crime that appears to have been foremost in the minds of MPs during their debates in Parliament is large scale. Repeated reference was made to the 'Mr Bigs' in society. Such crime is often no respecter of national boundaries. The PIU Report[1] quoted from responses to its questionnaire of UK financial investigators—

> 'Too many transgressors have assets disappear overseas before restraint, frustrating my role.'
>
> 'Problems with international confiscation action are becoming so acute that assets overseas are being ignored for confiscation purposes.'

---

[1] PIU Report, Box 11.2.

12.2 Financial investigators and others will be keen to see if Pt 11 improves upon this area. As present we know little as, to a large extent, the way ahead suggested in the PIU Report is to be achieved by Orders in Council, for which Pt 11 provides only a framework.

Enforcement in different parts of the UK (s 443)

12.3 Section 443 allows for enforcement of restraint, confiscation, receivership and investigation orders and warrants made in England, Wales, Northern Ireland and Scotland in each of the separate jurisdictions. The detailed arrangements for this enforcement are to be made by Orders in Council. These Orders may amend an enactment or apply an enactment, with or without modifications. The effect of this is of course unpredictable and open-ended.

External requests and orders (s 444)

12.4 Section 444 allows for provisions to be made by Order in Council for any property which is sought by foreign request as the proceeds of crime to be frozen and realised. 'External orders' are defined in s 447. They may be enforced, whether they are orders for the recovery of particular tainted property or orders for specified sums of money that may be satisfied out of any property, legally or illegally obtained.

Such orders are enforceable in the UK. As the Explanatory Notes make clear, such an order could have been made against a person (an 'in personam' order) or an order made against property (an 'in rem' order, as in civil forfeiture proceedings in the US).[1]

---

[1]　Explanatory Notes, para 599.

12.5 Similar powers in the existing legislation are in DTA 1994, ss 39 and 40, CJA 1988, ss 96 and 97, the Proceeds of Crime (Scotland) Act 1995, ss 40 and 41 and the Proceeds of Crime (Northern Ireland) Order 1996, art 42.[1]

---

[1]　SI 1996/1299 (NI 9).

12.6 Under the Criminal Justice (International Co-operation) Act 1990, s 9, and Orders in Council made pursuant to it, forfeiture orders made by foreign jurisdictions can be enforced in the UK. However, these orders are limited to orders for the disposal of 'instrumentalities' of crime (ie items used, or intended for use, in the commission of criminal offences). PCA 2002 makes no change to the Criminal Justice (International Co-operation) Act 1990, s 9, and does not affect the operation of the Orders in Council made under it.

12.7 Certainly the Government envisaged that the Home Secretary would, by Order in Council made under this s 444, allow the UK courts to restrain assets at the request of a foreign jurisdiction at an earlier stage in proceedings than is possible under existing legislation (ie at the commencement of an investigation).

12.8 Under existing legislation the UK will not assist foreign jurisdictions to freeze assets unless the foreign jurisdiction in question has been 'designated'. Section 444 does away with this requirement.

12.9 Section 444 does provide that the Order in Council may include provision—
    (a)　about the registration of external orders,
    (b)　about the authentication of any foreign judgement or order,
    (c)　about evidence and
    (d)　to secure that any person affected by the implementation of an external request to make representations to the UK court.

12.10 While of course it is vitally important that overseas authorities should be able to seek out the proceeds of crime in this country (and for UK authorities to do likewise abroad), the mechanisms for preventing abuses of the process should surely have been included in PCA 2002.

External investigations (s 445)

12.11 Section 445 provides that investigative powers may be created by Order in Council in respect of overseas investigations. These will be subject to annulment in pursuance of a resolution of either House (s 459(4)).

12.12 PCA 2002, Pt 8 of the Act deals with UK orders and warrants. Section 445(1) allows similar orders to be made in respect of external investigations and provides for the creation of offences which are similar to those contained in Pt 8 (ie of prejudicing an investigation and the offence of failing to comply with a customer information or disclosure order in respect of an overseas investigation).

12.13 An external investigation is defined as one by an overseas authority into whether property has been obtained as a result of or in connection with criminal conduct or whether a money laundering offence has been committed (s 447(3)).

12.14 Section 445(3) mirrors s 357(2) in Pt 8. Thus, disclosure orders will not be available for foreign money laundering investigations.

Rules of court (s 446)

12.15 Section 446 states that rules of court may make such provision as is necessary or expedient to give effect to an Order in Council made under this part.

Interpretation (s 447)

12.16 An overseas court is defined as 'a court of a country or territory outside the United Kingdom' (s 447(10)). The court proceedings may be criminal or civil. However, non-court confiscation orders such as 'administrative' confiscation orders made by police officers and similar such authorities are excluded from this scheme.

12.17 An 'overseas authority' is defined in s 447(11).

13 Miscellaneous and general

MISCELLANEOUS

Tax (s 448 and Sch 10)

13.1 The Proceeds of Crime Act 2002 ('PCA 2002'), s 448 introduces Sch 10 which governs the interplay of taxes liabilities under other legislation with PCA 2002.

Sch 10, Pt I: General

13.2 The Taxes Management Act 1970, ss 75 and 77 allow taxes owed by a person, where a receiver has been appointed by the court, to be collected from the receiver. Schedule 10, Pt 1 provides that these sections do not apply to the confiscation legislation.

Sch 10, Pt 2: Provisions relating to Pt 5

13.3 Schedule 10, Pt 2 relates to PCA 2002, Pt 5 (civil recovery orders and the summary forfeiture procedure). The transfer of property to a trustee for civil recovery under a Pt 5 order would, for example, amount to a disposal at market value for capital gains purposes or as a transfer for the purposes of income tax. The same would be true of foreign currency forfeited under Pt 5. Schedule 10 sets out the extent to which the usual consequences of the taxation legislation do not apply to this property.

13.4 As a general rule transfers by vesting or forfeiture do not amount to a chargeable gain.[1] However, where the transferor receives a compensatory payment, tax may be due.

---

[1] Schedule 10, para 3.

13.5 In relation to the following matters tax will not be due unless a compensating payment is made to the transferor[1]—
(a) transfer of securities within the meaning of the Taxes Act 1988, ss 711–728 (transfers with or without accrued interest);

    (b)   transfer of a relevant discounted security within the meaning of the Finance Act 1996, Sch 13;

    (c)   transfer of right to receive amounts stated in certificates of deposit;[2]

    (d)   transfer of material interests in offshore funds;[3]

    (e)   transfer of futures and options;[4] or

    (f)   transfers that would fall within the loan relationship rules for computing a corporation tax charge.[5]

---

[1]   Schedule 10, paras 4–10.
[2]   Taxes Act 1988, ss 56(2), 56A(1).
[3]   Taxes Act 1988, s 757(1)(a) or (b).
[4]   Taxes Act 1988, Sch 5AA, para 4.
[5]   See Finance Act 1996, s 84.

13.6   The tax provisions are disapplied where the relevant property is trading stock of a business.[1] The situation where the relevant property attracts capital allowances is dealt with in Sch 10, paras 12–29. These paragraphs render the vesting of the property concerned free from taxation save that they take into account any compensating payments that have been received by the transferor.

---

[1]   Schedule 10, para 11.

13.7   Employee share schemes are covered in Sch 10, paras 30–33. They cover the situations where an employee has acquired shares, or options over shares, and that interest is recovered as representing the proceeds of crime. Were it not for these provisions there would be a charge to income tax at the time of the disposal in these situations. Tax liabilities that would normally be incurred on the transfer to the trustee for civil recovery are removed even where the tax liability was deferred on purchase of the shares.

Agency staff and pseudonyms (ss 449 and 450)

13.8   Sections 449 and 450 provide that the Director or Scottish Ministers may authorise, where necessary or expedient, the use of pseudonyms by anyone acting under PCA 2002 on behalf of the Director or any staff carrying out civil recovery functions under the Scottish Ministers. Their true identities must not be revealed in proceedings. A certificate signed by the Director or Scottish Ministers that sufficiently identifies the authorised person by reference to the pseudonym is conclusive evidence that the person is authorised to use the pseudonym.

Customs and Excise prosecutions (s 451)

13.9   The Commissioners of Customs and Excise are permitted to bring proceedings for a money laundering offence, an offence of prejudicing an investigation (s 337) and certain inchoate offences in relation to these offences. The provision reflects that in existing legislation (DTA 1994, s 60 and CJA 1988, s 93F), except that it now includes attempts, conspiracies, aiding and abetting.

13.10 Section 451 does not apply to proceedings on indictment in Scotland (s 451(7)), where prosecutions are brought in the name of the Lord Advocate. In Scotland these prosecutions will be brought by the Lord Advocate or Procurator Fiscal.[1]

---

[1]   Explanatory Notes, para 641.

GENERAL

Amendments (s 456)

13.11 Section 456 introduces Sch 11, which amends existing statutes. Not all the implications of the Schedule are considered here but some of the interesting amendments are discussed.

13.12 Schedule 11, para 2 brings the Director's exercise of his Revenue functions within the remit of the Parliamentary Commissioner to the Administration (the Parliamentary Ombudsman). The Commissioner will be able to investigate complaints concerning the Director's handling of tax and related matters so that he is subject to the same scrutiny as the Inland Revenue in this respect. It is disappointing that the Ombudsman cannot investigate all complaints against the Director of the ARA rather than just those relating to his use of Revenue powers.

13.13 Schedule 11, para 14 makes a significant amendment to PACE 1984. It introduces a new power, enabling an officer to delay a detained person's right to have someone informed of their arrest and the right to access to legal advice, provided the officer has reasonable grounds for believing that the person detained has benefited from his criminal conduct and that the recovery of the value of the property constituting the benefit will be hindered by the exercise of those rights.

13.14 Two significant amendments are to be found in Sch 11, paras 17 and 18. Paragraph 17 amends CJA 1988 to give customs the power to arrest bail absconders pursuant to certain criminal offences, including money laundering offences. Paragraph 18 amends the Extradition Act 1989 to make extradition available under the 1988 Vienna Drug Trafficking Convention in relation to money laundering offences. In both cases the old definition of money laundering, including the acquisition offence, applies, rather than the new definition 'criminal lifestyle' contained in PCA 2002, Sch 2.[1]

---

[1] This was explained by Lord Rooker on behalf of the Government: HL Committee Stage, 27 May 2002, col 1106.

13.15 Schedule 11, para 36 concerns the provision of funding for legal representation under the Access to Justice Act 1999.

Repeals and revocations (s 457)

13.16 Section 457 introduces Sch 12 which contains repeals and revocations. The most significant points to note are that CJA 1988, ss 77–102 and DTA 1994, ss 1–54 are repealed.

Commencement (s 458)

13.17 PCA 2002 will come into force as ordered by the Secretary of State following consultation with the Scottish Ministers for the Scottish sections. At the time of writing the provisional commencement date is understood to be February 2003 but the provisions relating to the recovery of cash in summary proceedings (Pt 5, Ch 3) and money laundering (Pt 7) have provisional commencement dates in December 2002, and the provisions enabling the setting up of the ARA and preparation for the new regime will be brought into force significantly earlier.

Appendix 1
Proceeds of Crime Act 2002

Proceeds of Crime Act 2002

(2002 c 29)

ARRANGEMENT OF SECTIONS

PART 1
ASSETS RECOVERY AGENCY

PART 2
CONFISCATION: ENGLAND AND WALES

Confiscation orders

Procedural matters

Reconsideration

Defendant absconds

Appeals

Proceeds of Crime Act 2002

206

PART 5
CIVIL RECOVERY OF THE PROCEEDS ETC OF UNLAWFUL CONDUCT

CHAPTER 1
INTRODUCTORY

CHAPTER 2
CIVIL RECOVERY IN THE HIGH COURT OR COURT OF SESSION

CHAPTER 3
RECOVERY OF CASH IN SUMMARY PROCEEDINGS

Searches

Seizure and detention

Forfeiture

Supplementary

CHAPTER 4
GENERAL

Recoverable property

Insolvency

Delegation of enforcement functions

Interpretation

PART 6
REVENUE FUNCTIONS

General functions

PART 7
MONEY LAUNDERING

Offences

Consent

Disclosures

Interpretation

PART 8
INVESTIGATIONS

CHAPTER 1
INTRODUCTION

CHAPTER 2
ENGLAND AND WALES AND NORTHERN IRELAND

Judges and courts

CHAPTER 3
SCOTLAND

An Act to establish the Assets Recovery Agency and make provision about the appointment of its Director and his functions (including Revenue functions), to provide for confiscation orders in relation to persons who benefit from criminal conduct and for restraint orders to prohibit dealing with property, to allow the recovery of property which is or represents property obtained through unlawful conduct or which is intended to be used in unlawful conduct, to make provision about money laundering, to make provision about investigations relating to benefit from criminal conduct or to property which is or represents property obtained through unlawful conduct or to money laundering, to make provision to give effect to overseas requests and orders made where property is found or believed to be obtained through criminal conduct, and for connected purposes.

[24 July 2002]

Parliamentary debates.
House of Commons:
2nd Reading 30 October 2001: 373 HC Official Report (6th series) col 757.
Committee Stages 13 November 2001–5 February 2002: HC Official Report, SC B (Proceeds of Crime Bill).
Report Stage 26, 27 February 2002: 380 HC Official Report (6th Series) cols 586, 715.
3rd Reading 27 February 2002: 380 HC Official Report (6th Series) col 806.
Consideration of Lords' Amendments 18 July 2002: 389 HC Official Report (6th series) col 480; 24 July 2002: 389 HC Official Report (6th Series) col 1050.
House of Lords:
2nd Reading 25 March 2002: 633 HL Official Report (5th series) cols 12, 44.
Committee Stages 22 April 2002: 634 HL Official Report (5th series) col 10; 13 May 2002: 635 HL Official Report (5th series) col 23; 27 May 2002: 635 HL Official Report (5th series) col 1051.
Report Stage 25 June 2002: 636 HL Official Report (5th series) col 1290.
3rd Reading 11 July 2002: 637 HL Official Report (5th series) col 839.
Consideration of Commons' Amendments 22 July 2002: 638 HL Official Report (5th series) col 42.

PART 1
ASSETS RECOVERY AGENCY

1 The Agency and its Director

(1)   There shall be an Assets Recovery Agency (referred to in this Act as the Agency).

(2)   The Secretary of State must appoint a Director of the Agency (referred to in this Act as the Director).

(3)   The Director is a corporation sole.

(4)   The Director may—
      (a)   appoint such persons as members of staff of the Agency, and
      (b)   make such arrangements for the provision of services,
as he considers appropriate for or in connection with the exercise of his functions.

(5)   But the Director must obtain the approval of the Minister for the Civil Service as to the number of staff appointed under subsection (4)(a).

(6)   Anything which the Director is authorised or required to do may be done by—
      (a)   a member of staff of the Agency, or
      (b)   a person providing services under arrangements made by the Director,
if authorised by the Director (generally or specifically) for that purpose.

(7)   Schedule 1 contains further provisions about the Agency and the Director.

References   See para 2.2.

2 Director's functions: general

(1)   The Director must exercise his functions in the way which he considers is best calculated to contribute to the reduction of crime.

(2)   In exercising his functions as required by subsection (1) the Director must—
      (a)   act efficiently and effectively;
      (b)   have regard to his current annual plan (as approved by the Secretary of State in accordance with Schedule 1).

(3)   The Director may do anything (including the carrying out of investigations) which he considers is—
    (a)   appropriate for facilitating, or
    (b)   incidental or conducive to,
the exercise of his functions.

(4)   But subsection (3) does not allow the Director to borrow money.

(5)   In considering under subsection (1) the way which is best calculated to contribute to the reduction of crime the Director must have regard to any guidance given to him by the Secretary of State.

(6)   The guidance must indicate that the reduction of crime is in general best secured by means of criminal investigations and criminal proceedings.

Definitions   For "the Director", see s 1(2).
References   See paras 2.5, 2.6.

3 Accreditation and training

(1)   The Director must establish a system for the accreditation of financial investigators.

(2)   The system of accreditation must include provision for—
    (a)   the monitoring of the performance of accredited financial investigators, and
    (b)   the withdrawal of accreditation from any person who contravenes or fails to comply with any condition subject to which he was accredited.

(3)   A person may be accredited—
    (a)   in relation to this Act;
    (b)   in relation to particular provisions of this Act.

(4)   But the accreditation may be limited to specified purposes.

(5)   A reference in this Act to an accredited financial investigator is to be construed accordingly.

(6)   The Director may charge a person—
    (a)   for being accredited as a financial investigator, and
    (b)   for the monitoring of his performance as an accredited financial investigator.

(7)   The Director must make provision for the training of persons in—
    (a)   financial investigation, and
    (b)   the operation of this Act.

(8)   The Director may charge the persons who receive the training.

Definitions   For "the Director", see s 1(2).
References   See para 2.7.

4 Co-operation

(1)   Persons who have functions relating to the investigation or prosecution of offences must co-operate with the Director in the exercise of his functions.

(2)   The Director must co-operate with those persons in the exercise of functions they have under this Act.

Definitions   For "the Director", see s 1(2).
References   See para 2.8.

5 Advice and assistance

The Director must give the Secretary of State advice and assistance which he reasonably requires and which—
(a)   relate to matters connected with the operation of this Act, and
(b)   are designed to help the Secretary of State to exercise his functions so as to reduce crime.

Definitions   For "the Director", see s 1(2).
References   See para 2.9.

PART 2
CONFISCATION: ENGLAND AND WALES

Confiscation orders

6 Making of order

(1)   The Crown Court must proceed under this section if the following two conditions are satisfied.

(2)   The first condition is that a defendant falls within any of the following paragraphs—
(a)   he is convicted of an offence or offences in proceedings before the Crown Court;
(b)   he is committed to the Crown Court for sentence in respect of an offence or offences under section 3, 4 or 6 of the Sentencing Act;
(c)   he is committed to the Crown Court in respect of an offence or offences under section 70 below (committal with a view to a confiscation order being considered).

(3)   The second condition is that—
(a)   the prosecutor or the Director asks the court to proceed under this section, or
(b)   the court believes it is appropriate for it to do so.

(4)   The court must proceed as follows—
(a)   it must decide whether the defendant has a criminal lifestyle;
(b)   if it decides that he has a criminal lifestyle it must decide whether he has benefited from his general criminal conduct;
(c)   if it decides that he does not have a criminal lifestyle it must decide whether he has benefited from his particular criminal conduct.

(5)   If the court decides under subsection (4)(b) or (c) that the defendant has benefited from the conduct referred to it must—
(a)   decide the recoverable amount, and
(b)   make an order (a confiscation order) requiring him to pay that amount.

(6)   But the court must treat the duty in subsection (5) as a power if it believes that any victim of the conduct has at any time started or intends to start proceedings against the defendant in respect of loss, injury or damage sustained in connection with the conduct.

(7)   The court must decide any question arising under subsection (4) or (5) on a balance of probabilities.

(8)   The first condition is not satisfied if the defendant absconds (but section 27 may apply).

(9)   References in this Part to the offence (or offences) concerned are to the offence (or offences) mentioned in subsection (2).

Definitions   For "benefits from conduct", see ss 76(4), (7), 88(7); for "criminal conduct", see ss 76(1), 88(7); for "criminal lifestyle", see ss 75, 88(7), Sch 2; for "defendant", see s 88(3), (7); for "the Director", see s 1(2); for "general criminal conduct", see ss 76(2), 88(7); for "particular criminal conduct", see ss 76(3), 88(7); for "Sentencing Act", see s 88(5), (7).
References   See paras 3.2–3.11.

7 Recoverable amount

(1)   The recoverable amount for the purposes of section 6 is an amount equal to the defendant's benefit from the conduct concerned.

(2)   But if the defendant shows that the available amount is less than that benefit the recoverable amount is—
>   (a)   the available amount, or
>   (b)   a nominal amount, if the available amount is nil.

(3)   But if section 6(6) applies the recoverable amount is such amount as—
>   (a)   the court believes is just, but
>   (b)   does not exceed the amount found under subsection (1) or (2) (as the case may be).

(4)   In calculating the defendant's benefit from the conduct concerned for the purposes of subsection (1), any property in respect of which—
>   (a)   a recovery order is in force under section 266, or
>   (b)   a forfeiture order is in force under section 298(2),

must be ignored.

(5)   If the court decides the available amount, it must include in the confiscation order a statement of its findings as to the matters relevant for deciding that amount.

Definitions   For "benefits from conduct", see ss 76(4), (7), 88(7); for "confiscation order", see s 88(6)(a), (7); for "defendant", see s 88(3), (7); for "property", see ss 84(1), 88(7).
References   See paras 3.12–3.19.

8 Defendant's benefit

(1)   If the court is proceeding under section 6 this section applies for the purpose of—
>   (a)   deciding whether the defendant has benefited from conduct, and
>   (b)   deciding his benefit from the conduct.

(2) The court must—

   (a) take account of conduct occurring up to the time it makes its decision;

   (b) take account of property obtained up to that time.

(3) Subsection (4) applies if—

   (a) the conduct concerned is general criminal conduct,

   (b) a confiscation order mentioned in subsection (5) has at an earlier time been made against the defendant, and

   (c) his benefit for the purposes of that order was benefit from his general criminal conduct.

(4) His benefit found at the time the last confiscation order mentioned in subsection (3)(c) was made against him must be taken for the purposes of this section to be his benefit from his general criminal conduct at that time.

(5) If the conduct concerned is general criminal conduct the court must deduct the aggregate of the following amounts—

   (a) the amount ordered to be paid under each confiscation order previously made against the defendant;

   (b) the amount ordered to be paid under each confiscation order previously made against him under any of the provisions listed in subsection (7).

(6) But subsection (5) does not apply to an amount which has been taken into account for the purposes of a deduction under that subsection on any earlier occasion.

(7) These are the provisions—

   (a) the Drug Trafficking Offences Act 1986 (c 32);

   (b) Part 1 of the Criminal Justice (Scotland) Act 1987 (c 41);

   (c) Part 6 of the Criminal Justice Act 1988 (c 33);

   (d) the Criminal Justice (Confiscation) (Northern Ireland) Order 1990 (SI 1990/2588 (NI 17));

   (e) Part 1 of the Drug Trafficking Act 1994 (c 37);

   (f) Part 1 of the Proceeds of Crime (Scotland) Act 1995 (c 43);

   (g) the Proceeds of Crime (Northern Ireland) Order 1996 (SI 1996/1299 (NI 9));

   (h) Part 3 or 4 of this Act.

(8) The reference to general criminal conduct in the case of a confiscation order made under any of the provisions listed in subsection (7) is a reference to conduct in respect of which a court is required or entitled to make one or more assumptions for the purpose of assessing a person's benefit from the conduct.

Definitions For "benefits from conduct", see ss 76(4), (7), 88(7); for "confiscation order", see s 88(6)(a), (7); for "criminal conduct", see ss 76(1), 88(7); for "defendant", see s 88(3), (7); for "general criminal conduct", see ss 76(2), 88(7); for "property", see ss 84(1), 88(7); for "property held", see ss 84(2)(a), (d), 88(7); for "property obtained in connection with conduct", see ss 76(6), 88(7).
References See paras 3.12–3.19.

9 Available amount

(1) For the purposes of deciding the recoverable amount, the available amount is the aggregate of—

      (a)   the total of the values (at the time the confiscation order is made) of all the free property then held by the defendant minus the total amount payable in pursuance of obligations which then have priority, and

      (b)   the total of the values (at that time) of all tainted gifts.

(2)   An obligation has priority if it is an obligation of the defendant—

      (a)   to pay an amount due in respect of a fine or other order of a court which was imposed or made on conviction of an offence and at any time before the time the confiscation order is made, or

      (b)   to pay a sum which would be included among the preferential debts if the defendant's bankruptcy had commenced on the date of the confiscation order or his winding up had been ordered on that date.

(3)   "Preferential debts" has the meaning given by section 386 of the Insolvency Act 1986 (c 45).

Definitions   For "confiscation order", see s 88(6)(a), (7); for "defendant", see s 88(3), (7); for "free property", see ss 82, 88(7); for "property", see ss 84(1), 88(7); for "property held", see ss 84(2)(a), (d), 88(7); for "tainted gift", see ss 77, 88(7).
References   See paras 3.12–3.19.

---

10 Assumptions to be made in case of criminal lifestyle

(1)   If the court decides under section 6 that the defendant has a criminal lifestyle it must make the following four assumptions for the purpose of—

      (a)   deciding whether he has benefited from his general criminal conduct, and

      (b)   deciding his benefit from the conduct.

(2)   The first assumption is that any property transferred to the defendant at any time after the relevant day was obtained by him—

      (a)   as a result of his general criminal conduct, and

      (b)   at the earliest time he appears to have held it.

(3)   The second assumption is that any property held by the defendant at any time after the date of conviction was obtained by him—

      (a)   as a result of his general criminal conduct, and

      (b)   at the earliest time he appears to have held it.

(4)   The third assumption is that any expenditure incurred by the defendant at any time after the relevant day was met from property obtained by him as a result of his general criminal conduct.

(5)   The fourth assumption is that, for the purpose of valuing any property obtained (or assumed to have been obtained) by the defendant, he obtained it free of any other interests in it.

(6)   But the court must not make a required assumption in relation to particular property or expenditure if—

      (a)   the assumption is shown to be incorrect, or

      (b)   there would be a serious risk of injustice if the assumption were made.

(7)   If the court does not make one or more of the required assumptions it must state its reasons.

(8)　The relevant day is the first day of the period of six years ending with—

　　(a)　the day when proceedings for the offence concerned were started against the defendant, or

　　(b)　if there are two or more offences and proceedings for them were started on different days, the earliest of those days.

(9)　But if a confiscation order mentioned in section 8(3)(c) has been made against the defendant at any time during the period mentioned in subsection (8)—

　　(a)　the relevant day is the day when the defendant's benefit was calculated for the purposes of the last such confiscation order;

　　(b)　the second assumption does not apply to any property which was held by him on or before the relevant day.

(10)　The date of conviction is—

　　(a)　the date on which the defendant was convicted of the offence concerned, or

　　(b)　if there are two or more offences and the convictions were on different dates, the date of the latest.

Definitions　For "benefits from conduct", see ss 76(4), (7), 88(7); for "criminal conduct", see ss 76(1), 88(7); for "criminal lifestyle", see ss 75, 88(7), Sch 2; for "defendant", see s 88(3), (7); for "general criminal conduct", see ss 76(2), 88(7); for "interest" in relation to land, see ss 84(2)(f), (g), 88(7); for "interest" in relation to property other than land, see ss 84(2)(h), 88(7); for "offence concerned", see ss 6(9), 88(1), (7); for "offences concerned", see ss 6(9), 88(1), (7); for "proceedings started", see ss 85(1), (2), 88(7); for "property", see ss 84(1), 88(7); for "property held", see ss 84(2)(a), (d), 88(7); for "property obtained", see ss 84(2)(b), 88(7); for "property obtained in connection with conduct", see ss 76(6), 88(7); for "property transferred", see ss 84(2)(c), 88(7).
References　See paras 3.20–3.27.

11　Time for payment

(1)　The amount ordered to be paid under a confiscation order must be paid on the making of the order; but this is subject to the following provisions of this section.

(2)　If the defendant shows that he needs time to pay the amount ordered to be paid, the court making the confiscation order may make an order allowing payment to be made in a specified period.

(3)　The specified period—

　　(a)　must start with the day on which the confiscation order is made, and

　　(b)　must not exceed six months.

(4)　If within the specified period the defendant applies to the Crown Court for the period to be extended and the court believes there are exceptional circumstances, it may make an order extending the period.

(5)　The extended period—

　　(a)　must start with the day on which the confiscation order is made, and

　　(b)　must not exceed 12 months.

(6)　An order under subsection (4)—

　　(a)　may be made after the end of the specified period, but

　　(b)　must not be made after the end of the period of 12 months starting with the day on which the confiscation order is made.

(7)　The court must not make an order under subsection (2) or (4) unless it gives—

　　(a)　the prosecutor, or

(b)   if the Director was appointed as the enforcement authority for the order under section 34, the Director,

an opportunity to make representations.

12 Interest on unpaid sums

(1)   If the amount required to be paid by a person under a confiscation order is not paid when it is required to be paid, he must pay interest on the amount for the period for which it remains unpaid.

(2)   The rate of interest is the same rate as that for the time being specified in section 17 of the Judgments Act 1838 (c 110) (interest on civil judgment debts).

(3)   For the purposes of this section no amount is required to be paid under a confiscation order if—
(a)   an application has been made under section 11(4),
(b)   the application has not been determined by the court, and
(c)   the period of 12 months starting with the day on which the confiscation order was made has not ended.

(4)   In applying this Part the amount of the interest must be treated as part of the amount to be paid under the confiscation order.

13 Effect of order on court's other powers

(1)   If the court makes a confiscation order it must proceed as mentioned in subsections (2) and (4) in respect of the offence or offences concerned.

(2)   The court must take account of the confiscation order before—
(a)   it imposes a fine on the defendant, or
(b)   it makes an order falling within subsection (3).

(3)   These orders fall within this subsection—
(a)   an order involving payment by the defendant, other than an order under section 130 of the Sentencing Act (compensation orders);
(b)   an order under section 27 of the Misuse of Drugs Act 1971 (c 38) (forfeiture orders);
(c)   an order under section 143 of the Sentencing Act (deprivation orders);
(d)   an order under section 23 of the Terrorism Act 2000 (c 11) (forfeiture orders).

(4)   Subject to subsection (2), the court must leave the confiscation order out of account in deciding the appropriate sentence for the defendant.

(5)   Subsection (6) applies if—
(a)   the Crown Court makes both a confiscation order and an order for the payment of compensation under section 130 of the Sentencing Act against the same person in the same proceedings, and

>   (b)   the court believes he will not have sufficient means to satisfy both the orders in full.

(6)   In such a case the court must direct that so much of the compensation as it specifies is to be paid out of any sums recovered under the confiscation order; and the amount it specifies must be the amount it believes will not be recoverable because of the insufficiency of the person's means.

Definitions   For "confiscation order", see s 88(6)(a), (7); for "defendant", see s 88(3), (7); for "offence concerned", see ss 6(9), 88(1), (7); for "offences concerned", see ss 6(9), 88(1), (7); for "Sentencing Act", see s 88(5), (7).
References   See para 3.31.

Procedural matters

14 Postponement

(1)   The court may—
>   (a)   proceed under section 6 before it sentences the defendant for the offence (or any of the offences) concerned, or
>   (b)   postpone proceedings under section 6 for a specified period.

(2)   A period of postponement may be extended.

(3)   A period of postponement (including one as extended) must not end after the permitted period ends.

(4)   But subsection (3) does not apply if there are exceptional circumstances.

(5)   The permitted period is the period of two years starting with the date of conviction.

(6)   But if—
>   (a)   the defendant appeals against his conviction for the offence (or any of the offences) concerned, and
>   (b)   the period of three months (starting with the day when the appeal is determined or otherwise disposed of) ends after the period found under subsection (5),

the permitted period is that period of three months.

(7)   A postponement or extension may be made—
>   (a)   on application by the defendant;
>   (b)   on application by the prosecutor or the Director (as the case may be);
>   (c)   by the court of its own motion.

(8)   If—
>   (a)   proceedings are postponed for a period, and
>   (b)   an application to extend the period is made before it ends,

the application may be granted even after the period ends.

(9)   The date of conviction is—
>   (a)   the date on which the defendant was convicted of the offence concerned, or
>   (b)   if there are two or more offences and the convictions were on different dates, the date of the latest.

(10) References to appealing include references to applying under section 111 of the Magistrates' Courts Act 1980 (c 43) (statement of case).

(11) A confiscation order must not be quashed only on the ground that there was a defect or omission in the procedure connected with the application for or the granting of a postponement.

(12) But subsection (11) does not apply if before it made the confiscation order the court—
    (a)   imposed a fine on the defendant;
    (b)   made an order falling within section 13(3);
    (c)   made an order under section 130 of the Sentencing Act (compensation orders).

Definitions   For "confiscation order", see s 88(6)(a), (7); for "defendant", see s 88(3), (7); for "the Director", see s 1(2); for "offence concerned", see ss 6(9), 88(1), (7); for "offences concerned", see ss 6(9), 88(1), (7); for "Sentencing Act", see s 88(5), (7); for "sentencing the defendant for an offence", see s 88(4), (7).
References   See paras 3.34–3.36.

---

15 Effect of postponement

(1) If the court postpones proceedings under section 6 it may proceed to sentence the defendant for the offence (or any of the offences) concerned.

(2) In sentencing the defendant for the offence (or any of the offences) concerned in the postponement period the court must not—
    (a)   impose a fine on him,
    (b)   make an order falling within section 13(3), or
    (c)   make an order for the payment of compensation under section 130 of the Sentencing Act.

(3) If the court sentences the defendant for the offence (or any of the offences) concerned in the postponement period, after that period ends it may vary the sentence by—
    (a)   imposing a fine on him,
    (b)   making an order falling within section 13(3), or
    (c)   making an order for the payment of compensation under section 130 of the Sentencing Act.

(4) But the court may proceed under subsection (3) only within the period of 28 days which starts with the last day of the postponement period.

(5) For the purposes of—
    (a)   section 18(2) of the Criminal Appeal Act 1968 (c 19) (time limit for notice of appeal or of application for leave to appeal), and
    (b)   paragraph 1 of Schedule 3 to the Criminal Justice Act 1988 (c 33) (time limit for notice of application for leave to refer a case under section 36 of that Act),

the sentence must be regarded as imposed or made on the day on which it is varied under subsection (3).

(6) If the court proceeds to sentence the defendant under subsection (1), section 6 has effect as if the defendant's particular criminal conduct included conduct which constitutes offences which the court has taken into consideration in deciding his sentence for the offence or offences concerned.

(7)   The postponement period is the period for which proceedings under section 6 are postponed.

Definitions   For "criminal conduct", see ss 76(1), 88(7); for "defendant", see s 88(3), (7); for "offence concerned", see ss 6(9), 88(1), (7); for "offences concerned", see ss 6(9), 88(1), (7); for "particular criminal conduct", see ss 76(3), 88(7); for "Sentencing Act", see s 88(5), (7); for "sentencing the defendant for an offence", see s 88(4), (7).
References   See para 3.37.

16 Statement of information

(1)   If the court is proceeding under section 6 in a case where section 6(3)(a) applies, the prosecutor or the Director (as the case may be) must give the court a statement of information within the period the court orders.

(2)   If the court is proceeding under section 6 in a case where section 6(3)(b) applies and it orders the prosecutor to give it a statement of information, the prosecutor must give it such a statement within the period the court orders.

(3)   If the prosecutor or the Director (as the case may be) believes the defendant has a criminal lifestyle the statement of information is a statement of matters the prosecutor or the Director believes are relevant in connection with deciding these issues—
   (a)   whether the defendant has a criminal lifestyle;
   (b)   whether he has benefited from his general criminal conduct;
   (c)   his benefit from the conduct.

(4)   A statement under subsection (3) must include information the prosecutor or Director believes is relevant—
   (a)   in connection with the making by the court of a required assumption under section 10;
   (b)   for the purpose of enabling the court to decide if the circumstances are such that it must not make such an assumption.

(5)   If the prosecutor or the Director (as the case may be) does not believe the defendant has a criminal lifestyle the statement of information is a statement of matters the prosecutor or the Director believes are relevant in connection with deciding these issues—
   (a)   whether the defendant has benefited from his particular criminal conduct;
   (b)   his benefit from the conduct.

(6)   If the prosecutor or the Director gives the court a statement of information—
   (a)   he may at any time give the court a further statement of information;
   (b)   he must give the court a further statement of information if it orders him to do so, and he must give it within the period the court orders.

(7)   If the court makes an order under this section it may at any time vary it by making another one.

Definitions   For "benefits from conduct", see ss 76(4), (7), 88(7); for "criminal conduct", see ss 76(1), 88(7); for "criminal lifestyle", see ss 75, 88(7), Sch 2; for "defendant", see s 88(3), (7); for "the Director", see s 1(2); for "general criminal conduct", see ss 76(2), 88(7); for "particular criminal conduct", see ss 76(3), 88(7).
References   See paras 3.38–3.40.

17 Defendant's response to statement of information

(1)   If the prosecutor or the Director gives the court a statement of information and a copy is served on the defendant, the court may order the defendant—

(a)   to indicate (within the period it orders) the extent to which he accepts each allegation in the statement, and

(b)   so far as he does not accept such an allegation, to give particulars of any matters he proposes to rely on.

(2)   If the defendant accepts to any extent an allegation in a statement of information the court may treat his acceptance as conclusive of the matters to which it relates for the purpose of deciding the issues referred to in section 16(3) or (5) (as the case may be).

(3)   If the defendant fails in any respect to comply with an order under subsection (1) he may be treated for the purposes of subsection (2) as accepting every allegation in the statement of information apart from—

(a)   any allegation in respect of which he has complied with the requirement;

(b)   any allegation that he has benefited from his general or particular criminal conduct.

(4)   For the purposes of this section an allegation may be accepted or particulars may be given in a manner ordered by the court.

(5)   If the court makes an order under this section it may at any time vary it by making another one.

(6)   No acceptance under this section that the defendant has benefited from conduct is admissible in evidence in proceedings for an offence.

Definitions   For "benefits from conduct", see ss 76(4), (7), 88(7); for "criminal conduct", see ss 76(1), 88(7); for "defendant", see s 88(3), (7); for "the Director", see s 1(2); for "general criminal conduct", see ss 76(2), 88(7); for "particular criminal conduct", see ss 76(3), 88(7).
References   See para 3.41.

---

18 Provision of information by defendant

(1)   This section applies if—

(a)   the court is proceeding under section 6 in a case where section 6(3)(a) applies, or

(b)   it is proceeding under section 6 in a case where section 6(3)(b) applies or it is considering whether to proceed.

(2)   For the purpose of obtaining information to help it in carrying out its functions the court may at any time order the defendant to give it information specified in the order.

(3)   An order under this section may require all or a specified part of the information to be given in a specified manner and before a specified date.

(4)   If the defendant fails without reasonable excuse to comply with an order under this section the court may draw such inference as it believes is appropriate.

(5)   Subsection (4) does not affect any power of the court to deal with the defendant in respect of a failure to comply with an order under this section.

(6)   If the prosecutor or the Director (as the case may be) accepts to any extent an allegation made by the defendant—

(a)   in giving information required by an order under this section, or

(b)   in any other statement given to the court in relation to any matter relevant to deciding the available amount under section 9,

the court may treat the acceptance as conclusive of the matters to which it relates.

(7)   For the purposes of this section an allegation may be accepted in a manner ordered by the court.

(8)   If the court makes an order under this section it may at any time vary it by making another one.

(9)   No information given under this section which amounts to an admission by the defendant that he has benefited from criminal conduct is admissible in evidence in proceedings for an offence.

Definitions   For "benefits from conduct", see ss 76(4), (7), 88(7); for "criminal conduct", see ss 76(1), 88(7); for "defendant", see s 88(3), (7); for "the Director", see s 1(2).
References   See para 3.42, 3.43.

Reconsideration

19 No order made: reconsideration of case

(1)   This section applies if—

(a)   the first condition in section 6 is satisfied but no court has proceeded under that section,

(b)   there is evidence which was not available to the prosecutor on the relevant date,

(c)   before the end of the period of six years starting with the date of conviction the prosecutor or the Director applies to the Crown Court to consider the evidence, and

(d)   after considering the evidence the court believes it is appropriate for it to proceed under section 6.

(2)   If this section applies the court must proceed under section 6, and when it does so subsections (3) to (8) below apply.

(3)   If the court has already sentenced the defendant for the offence (or any of the offences) concerned, section 6 has effect as if his particular criminal conduct included conduct which constitutes offences which the court has taken into consideration in deciding his sentence for the offence or offences concerned.

(4)   Section 8(2) does not apply, and the rules applying instead are that the court must—

(a)   take account of conduct occurring before the relevant date;

(b)   take account of property obtained before that date;

(c)   take account of property obtained on or after that date if it was obtained as a result of or in connection with conduct occurring before that date.

(5)   In section 10—

(a)   the first and second assumptions do not apply with regard to property first held by the defendant on or after the relevant date;

- (b) the third assumption does not apply with regard to expenditure incurred by him on or after that date;
- (c) the fourth assumption does not apply with regard to property obtained (or assumed to have been obtained) by him on or after that date.

(6) The recoverable amount for the purposes of section 6 is such amount as—
  - (a) the court believes is just, but
  - (b) does not exceed the amount found under section 7.

(7) In arriving at the just amount the court must have regard in particular to—
  - (a) the amount found under section 7;
  - (b) any fine imposed on the defendant in respect of the offence (or any of the offences) concerned;
  - (c) any order which falls within section 13(3) and has been made against him in respect of the offence (or any of the offences) concerned and has not already been taken into account by the court in deciding what is the free property held by him for the purposes of section 9;
  - (d) any order which has been made against him in respect of the offence (or any of the offences) concerned under section 130 of the Sentencing Act (compensation orders).

(8) If an order for the payment of compensation under section 130 of the Sentencing Act has been made against the defendant in respect of the offence or offences concerned, section 13(5) and (6) above do not apply.

(9) The relevant date is—
  - (a) if the court made a decision not to proceed under section 6, the date of the decision;
  - (b) if the court did not make such a decision, the date of conviction.

(10) The date of conviction is—
  - (a) the date on which the defendant was convicted of the offence concerned, or
  - (b) if there are two or more offences and the convictions were on different dates, the date of the latest.

Definitions   For "criminal conduct", see ss 76(1), 88(7); for "defendant", see s 88(3), (7); for "the Director", see s 1(2); for "free property", see ss 82, 88(7); for "offence concerned", see ss 6(9), 88(1), (7); for "offences concerned", see ss 6(9), 88(1), (7); for "particular criminal conduct", see ss 76(3), 88(7); for "property", see ss 84(1), 88(7); for "property held", see ss 84(2)(a), (d), 88(7); for "property obtained", see ss 84(2)(b), 88(7); for "property obtained in connection with conduct", see ss 76(6), 88(7); for "Sentencing Act", see s 88(5), (7); for "sentencing the defendant for an offence", see s 88(4), (7).
References   See paras 3.46–3.49.

20 No order made: reconsideration of benefit

(1) This section applies if the following two conditions are satisfied.

(2) The first condition is that in proceeding under section 6 the court has decided that—
  - (a) the defendant has a criminal lifestyle but has not benefited from his general criminal conduct, or
  - (b) the defendant does not have a criminal lifestyle and has not benefited from his particular criminal conduct.

(3)   If the court proceeded under section 6 because the Director asked it to, the second condition is that—

    (a)   the Director has evidence which was not available to him when the court decided that the defendant had not benefited from his general or particular criminal conduct,

    (b)   before the end of the period of six years starting with the date of conviction the Director applies to the Crown Court to consider the evidence, and

    (c)   after considering the evidence the court concludes that it would have decided that the defendant had benefited from his general or particular criminal conduct (as the case may be) if the evidence had been available to it.

(4)   If the court proceeded under section 6 because the prosecutor asked it to or because it believed it was appropriate for it to do so, the second condition is that—

    (a)   there is evidence which was not available to the prosecutor when the court decided that the defendant had not benefited from his general or particular criminal conduct,

    (b)   before the end of the period of six years starting with the date of conviction the prosecutor or the Director applies to the Crown Court to consider the evidence, and

    (c)   after considering the evidence the court concludes that it would have decided that the defendant had benefited from his general or particular criminal conduct (as the case may be) if the evidence had been available to it.

(5)   If this section applies the court—

    (a)   must make a fresh decision under section 6(4)(b) or (c) whether the defendant has benefited from his general or particular criminal conduct (as the case may be);

    (b)   may make a confiscation order under that section.

(6)   Subsections (7) to (12) below apply if the court proceeds under section 6 in pursuance of this section.

(7)   If the court has already sentenced the defendant for the offence (or any of the offences) concerned, section 6 has effect as if his particular criminal conduct included conduct which constitutes offences which the court has taken into consideration in deciding his sentence for the offence or offences concerned.

(8)   Section 8(2) does not apply, and the rules applying instead are that the court must—

    (a)   take account of conduct occurring before the date of the original decision that the defendant had not benefited from his general or particular criminal conduct;

    (b)   take account of property obtained before that date;

    (c)   take account of property obtained on or after that date if it was obtained as a result of or in connection with conduct occurring before that date.

(9)   In section 10—

    (a)   the first and second assumptions do not apply with regard to property first held by the defendant on or after the date of the original decision that the defendant had not benefited from his general or particular criminal conduct;

  (b) the third assumption does not apply with regard to expenditure incurred by him on or after that date;
  (c) the fourth assumption does not apply with regard to property obtained (or assumed to have been obtained) by him on or after that date.

(10) The recoverable amount for the purposes of section 6 is such amount as—
  (a) the court believes is just, but
  (b) does not exceed the amount found under section 7.

(11) In arriving at the just amount the court must have regard in particular to—
  (a) the amount found under section 7;
  (b) any fine imposed on the defendant in respect of the offence (or any of the offences) concerned;
  (c) any order which falls within section 13(3) and has been made against him in respect of the offence (or any of the offences) concerned and has not already been taken into account by the court in deciding what is the free property held by him for the purposes of section 9;
  (d) any order which has been made against him in respect of the offence (or any of the offences) concerned under section 130 of the Sentencing Act (compensation orders).

(12) If an order for the payment of compensation under section 130 of the Sentencing Act has been made against the defendant in respect of the offence or offences concerned, section 13(5) and (6) above do not apply.

(13) The date of conviction is the date found by applying section 19(10).

Definitions   For "benefits from conduct", see ss 76(4), (7), 88(7); for "confiscation order", see s 88(6)(a), (7); for "criminal conduct", see ss 76(1), 88(7); for "criminal lifestyle", see ss 75, 88(7), Sch 2; for "defendant", see s 88(3), (7); for "the Director", see s 1(2); for "free property", see ss 82, 88(7); for "general criminal conduct", see ss 76(2), 88(7); for "offence concerned", see ss 6(9), 88(1), (7); for "offences concerned", see ss 6(9), 88(1), (7); for "particular criminal conduct", see ss 76(3), 88(7); for "property", see ss 84(1), 88(7); for "property held", see ss 84(2)(a), (d), 88(7); for "property obtained", see ss 84(2)(b), 88(7); for "property obtained in connection with conduct", see ss 76(6), 88(7); for "Sentencing Act", see s 88(5), (7); for "sentencing the defendant for an offence", see s 88(4), (7).
References   See paras 3.50–3.52.

21 Order made: reconsideration of benefit

(1) This section applies if—
  (a) a court has made a confiscation order,
  (b) there is evidence which was not available to the prosecutor or the Director at the relevant time,
  (c) the prosecutor or the Director believes that if the court were to find the amount of the defendant's benefit in pursuance of this section it would exceed the relevant amount,
  (d) before the end of the period of six years starting with the date of conviction the prosecutor or the Director applies to the Crown Court to consider the evidence, and
  (e) after considering the evidence the court believes it is appropriate for it to proceed under this section.

(2) The court must make a new calculation of the defendant's benefit from the conduct concerned, and when it does so subsections (3) to (6) below apply.

(3)   If a court has already sentenced the defendant for the offence (or any of the offences) concerned section 6 has effect as if his particular criminal conduct included conduct which constitutes offences which the court has taken into consideration in deciding his sentence for the offence or offences concerned.

(4)   Section 8(2) does not apply, and the rules applying instead are that the court must—

    (a)   take account of conduct occurring up to the time it decided the defendant's benefit for the purposes of the confiscation order;

    (b)   take account of property obtained up to that time;

    (c)   take account of property obtained after that time if it was obtained as a result of or in connection with conduct occurring before that time.

(5)   In applying section 8(5) the confiscation order must be ignored.

(6)   In section 10—

    (a)   the first and second assumptions do not apply with regard to property first held by the defendant after the time the court decided his benefit for the purposes of the confiscation order;

    (b)   the third assumption does not apply with regard to expenditure incurred by him after that time;

    (c)   the fourth assumption does not apply with regard to property obtained (or assumed to have been obtained) by him after that time.

(7)   If the amount found under the new calculation of the defendant's benefit exceeds the relevant amount the court—

    (a)   must make a new calculation of the recoverable amount for the purposes of section 6, and

    (b)   if it exceeds the amount required to be paid under the confiscation order, may vary the order by substituting for the amount required to be paid such amount as it believes is just.

(8)   In applying subsection (7)(a) the court must—

    (a)   take the new calculation of the defendant's benefit;

    (b)   apply section 9 as if references to the time the confiscation order is made were to the time of the new calculation of the recoverable amount and as if references to the date of the confiscation order were to the date of that new calculation.

(9)   In applying subsection (7)(b) the court must have regard in particular to—

    (a)   any fine imposed on the defendant for the offence (or any of the offences) concerned;

    (b)   any order which falls within section 13(3) and has been made against him in respect of the offence (or any of the offences) concerned and has not already been taken into account by the court in deciding what is the free property held by him for the purposes of section 9;

    (c)   any order which has been made against him in respect of the offence (or any of the offences) concerned under section 130 of the Sentencing Act (compensation orders).

(10)   But in applying subsection (7)(b) the court must not have regard to an order falling within subsection (9)(c) if a court has made a direction under section 13(6).

(11)   In deciding under this section whether one amount exceeds another the court must take account of any change in the value of money.

(12) The relevant time is—
- (a) when the court calculated the defendant's benefit for the purposes of the confiscation order, if this section has not applied previously;
- (b) when the court last calculated the defendant's benefit in pursuance of this section, if this section has applied previously.

(13) The relevant amount is—
- (a) the amount found as the defendant's benefit for the purposes of the confiscation order, if this section has not applied previously;
- (b) the amount last found as the defendant's benefit in pursuance of this section, if this section has applied previously.

(14) The date of conviction is the date found by applying section 19(10).

Definitions   For "benefits from conduct", see ss 76(4), (7), 88(7); for "confiscation order", see s 88(6)(a), (7); for "criminal conduct", see ss 76(1), 88(7); for "defendant", see s 88(3), (7); for "the Director", see s 1(2); for "free property", see ss 82, 88(7); for "offence concerned", see ss 6(9), 88(1), (7); for "offences concerned", see ss 6(9), 88(1), (7); for "particular criminal conduct", see ss 76(3), 88(7); for "property", see ss 84(1), 88(7); for "property held", see ss 84(2)(a), (d), 88(7); for "property obtained", see ss 84(2)(b), 88(7); for "property obtained in connection with conduct", see ss 76(6), 88(7); for "Sentencing Act", see s 88(5), (7); for "sentencing the defendant for an offence", see s 88(4), (7).
References   See paras 3.54–3.57.

22 Order made: reconsideration of available amount

(1) This section applies if—
- (a) a court has made a confiscation order,
- (b) the amount required to be paid was the amount found under section 7(2), and
- (c) an applicant falling within subsection (2) applies to the Crown Court to make a new calculation of the available amount.

(2) These applicants fall within this subsection—
- (a) the prosecutor;
- (b) the Director;
- (c) a receiver appointed under section 50 or 52.

(3) In a case where this section applies the court must make the new calculation, and in doing so it must apply section 9 as if references to the time the confiscation order is made were to the time of the new calculation and as if references to the date of the confiscation order were to the date of the new calculation.

(4) If the amount found under the new calculation exceeds the relevant amount the court may vary the order by substituting for the amount required to be paid such amount as—
- (a) it believes is just, but
- (b) does not exceed the amount found as the defendant's benefit from the conduct concerned.

(5) In deciding what is just the court must have regard in particular to—
- (a) any fine imposed on the defendant for the offence (or any of the offences) concerned;
- (b) any order which falls within section 13(3) and has been made against him in respect of the offence (or any of the offences) concerned and has not already been taken into account by the court in deciding what is the free property held by him for the purposes of section 9;

(c)   any order which has been made against him in respect of the offence (or any of the offences) concerned under section 130 of the Sentencing Act (compensation orders).

(6)   But in deciding what is just the court must not have regard to an order falling within subsection (5)(c) if a court has made a direction under section 13(6).

(7)   In deciding under this section whether one amount exceeds another the court must take account of any change in the value of money.

(8)   The relevant amount is—
    (a)   the amount found as the available amount for the purposes of the confiscation order, if this section has not applied previously;
    (b)   the amount last found as the available amount in pursuance of this section, if this section has applied previously.

(9)   The amount found as the defendant's benefit from the conduct concerned is—
    (a)   the amount so found when the confiscation order was made, or
    (b)   if one or more new calculations of the defendant's benefit have been made under section 21 the amount found on the occasion of the last such calculation.

Definitions   For "benefits from conduct", see ss 76(4), (7), 88(7); for "confiscation order", see s 88(6)(a), (7); for "defendant", see s 88(3), (7); for "the Director", see s 1(2); for "free property", see ss 82, 88(7); for "offence concerned", see ss 6(9), 88(1), (7); for "offences concerned", see ss 6(9), 88(1), (7); for "property", see ss 84(1), 88(7); for "Sentencing Act", see s 88(5), (7).
References   See paras 3.58–3.62.

---

23 Inadequacy of available amount: variation of order

(1)   This section applies if—
    (a)   a court has made a confiscation order, and
    (b)   the defendant, or a receiver appointed under section 50 or 52, applies to the Crown Court to vary the order under this section.

(2)   In such a case the court must calculate the available amount, and in doing so it must apply section 9 as if references to the time the confiscation order is made were to the time of the calculation and as if references to the date of the confiscation order were to the date of the calculation.

(3)   If the court finds that the available amount (as so calculated) is inadequate for the payment of any amount remaining to be paid under the confiscation order it may vary the order by substituting for the amount required to be paid such smaller amount as the court believes is just.

(4)   If a person has been adjudged bankrupt or his estate has been sequestrated, or if an order for the winding up of a company has been made, the court must take into account the extent to which realisable property held by that person or that company may be distributed among creditors.

(5)   The court may disregard any inadequacy which it believes is attributable (wholly or partly) to anything done by the defendant for the purpose of preserving property held by the recipient of a tainted gift from any risk of realisation under this Part.

(6)   In subsection (4) "company" means any company which may be wound up under the Insolvency Act 1986 (c 45) or the Insolvency (Northern Ireland) Order 1989 (SI 1989/2405 (NI 19)).

Definitions   For "confiscation order", see s 88(6)(a), (7); for "defendant", see s 88(3), (7); for "property", see ss 84(1), 88(7); for "property held", see ss 84(2)(a), (d), 88(7); for "realisable property", see ss 83, 88(7); for "recipient of a tainted gift", see ss 78(3), 88(7); for "tainted gift", see ss 77, 88(7). **References**   See paras 3.64–3.66.

---

24 Inadequacy of available amount: discharge of order

(1)   This section applies if—
- (a)   a court has made a confiscation order,
- (b)   a justices' chief executive applies to the Crown Court for the discharge of the order, and
- (c)   the amount remaining to be paid under the order is less than £1,000.

(2)   In such a case the court must calculate the available amount, and in doing so it must apply section 9 as if references to the time the confiscation order is made were to the time of the calculation and as if references to the date of the confiscation order were to the date of the calculation.

(3)   If the court—
- (a)   finds that the available amount (as so calculated) is inadequate to meet the amount remaining to be paid, and
- (b)   is satisfied that the inadequacy is due wholly to a specified reason or a combination of specified reasons,

it may discharge the confiscation order.

(4)   The specified reasons are—
- (a)   in a case where any of the realisable property consists of money in a currency other than sterling, that fluctuations in currency exchange rates have occurred;
- (b)   any reason specified by the Secretary of State by order.

(5)   The Secretary of State may by order vary the amount for the time being specified in subsection (1)(c).

Definitions   For "confiscation order", see s 88(6)(a), (7); for "property", see ss 84(1), 88(7); for "realisable property", see ss 83, 88(7). **References**   See paras 3.67–3.69.

---

25 Small amount outstanding: discharge of order

(1)   This section applies if—
- (a)   a court has made a confiscation order,
- (b)   a justices' chief executive applies to the Crown Court for the discharge of the order, and
- (c)   the amount remaining to be paid under the order is £50 or less.

(2)   In such a case the court may discharge the order.

(3)   The Secretary of State may by order vary the amount for the time being specified in subsection (1)(c).

Definitions For "confiscation order", see s 88(6)(a), (7).
References See para 3.70.

26 Information

(1) This section applies if—
    (a) the court proceeds under section 6 in pursuance of section 19 or 20, or
    (b) the prosecutor or the Director applies under section 21.

(2) In such a case—
    (a) the prosecutor or the Director (as the case may be) must give the court a statement of information within the period the court orders;
    (b) section 16 applies accordingly (with appropriate modifications where the prosecutor or the Director applies under section 21);
    (c) section 17 applies accordingly;
    (d) section 18 applies as it applies in the circumstances mentioned in section 18(1).

Definitions For "the Director", see s 1(2).
References See para 3.71.

Defendant absconds

27 Defendant convicted or committed

(1) This section applies if the following two conditions are satisfied.

(2) The first condition is that a defendant absconds after—
    (a) he is convicted of an offence or offences in proceedings before the Crown Court,
    (b) he is committed to the Crown Court for sentence in respect of an offence or offences under section 3, 4 or 6 of the Sentencing Act, or
    (c) he is committed to the Crown Court in respect of an offence or offences under section 70 below (committal with a view to a confiscation order being considered).

(3) The second condition is that—
    (a) the prosecutor or the Director applies to the Crown Court to proceed under this section, and
    (b) the court believes it is appropriate for it to do so.

(4) If this section applies the court must proceed under section 6 in the same way as it must proceed if the two conditions there mentioned are satisfied; but this is subject to subsection (5).

(5) If the court proceeds under section 6 as applied by this section, this Part has effect with these modifications—
    (a) any person the court believes is likely to be affected by an order under section 6 is entitled to appear before the court and make representations;
    (b) the court must not make an order under section 6 unless the prosecutor or the Director (as the case may be) has taken reasonable steps to contact the defendant;

(c)   section 6(9) applies as if the reference to subsection (2) were to subsection (2) of this section;

(d)   sections 10, 16(4), 17 and 18 must be ignored;

(e)   sections 19, 20 and 21 must be ignored while the defendant is still an absconder.

(6)   Once the defendant ceases to be an absconder section 19 has effect as if subsection (1)(a) read—

"(a)   at a time when the first condition in section 27 was satisfied the court did not proceed under section 6,".

(7)   If the court does not believe it is appropriate for it to proceed under this section, once the defendant ceases to be an absconder section 19 has effect as if subsection (1)(b) read—

"(b)   there is evidence which was not available to the prosecutor or the Director on the relevant date,".

Definitions   For "defendant", see s 88(3), (7); for "the Director", see s 1(2); for "Sentencing Act", see
s 88(5), (7).
References   See paras 3.75–3.77.

28 Defendant neither convicted nor acquitted

(1)   This section applies if the following two conditions are satisfied.

(2)   The first condition is that—

(a)   proceedings for an offence or offences are started against a defendant but are not concluded,

(b)   he absconds, and

(c)   the period of two years (starting with the day the court believes he absconded) has ended.

(3)   The second condition is that—

(a)   the prosecutor or the Director applies to the Crown Court to proceed under this section, and

(b)   the court believes it is appropriate for it to do so.

(4)   If this section applies the court must proceed under section 6 in the same way as it must proceed if the two conditions there mentioned are satisfied; but this is subject to subsection (5).

(5)   If the court proceeds under section 6 as applied by this section, this Part has effect with these modifications—

(a)   any person the court believes is likely to be affected by an order under section 6 is entitled to appear before the court and make representations;

(b)   the court must not make an order under section 6 unless the prosecutor or the Director (as the case may be) has taken reasonable steps to contact the defendant;

(c)   section 6(9) applies as if the reference to subsection (2) were to subsection (2) of this section;

(d)   sections 10, 16(4) and 17 to 20 must be ignored;

(e)   section 21 must be ignored while the defendant is still an absconder.

(6)   Once the defendant has ceased to be an absconder section 21 has effect as if references to the date of conviction were to—

(a) the day when proceedings for the offence concerned were started against the defendant, or

(b) if there are two or more offences and proceedings for them were started on different days, the earliest of those days.

(7) If—

(a) the court makes an order under section 6 as applied by this section, and

(b) the defendant is later convicted in proceedings before the Crown Court of the offence (or any of the offences) concerned,

section 6 does not apply so far as that conviction is concerned.

Definitions   For "defendant", see s 88(3), (7); for "the Director", see s 1(2); for "offence concerned", see ss 6(9), 88(1), (7); for "offences concerned", see ss 6(9), 88(1), (7); for "proceedings concluded", see ss 85(3)–(8), 88(7); for "proceedings started", see ss 85(1), (2), 88(7).
References   See paras 3.78–3.79.

29 Variation of order

(1) This section applies if—

(a) the court makes a confiscation order under section 6 as applied by section 28,

(b) the defendant ceases to be an absconder,

(c) he is convicted of an offence (or any of the offences) mentioned in section 28(2)(a),

(d) he believes that the amount required to be paid was too large (taking the circumstances prevailing when the amount was found for the purposes of the order), and

(e) before the end of the relevant period he applies to the Crown Court to consider the evidence on which his belief is based.

(2) If (after considering the evidence) the court concludes that the defendant's belief is well founded—

(a) it must find the amount which should have been the amount required to be paid (taking the circumstances prevailing when the amount was found for the purposes of the order), and

(b) it may vary the order by substituting for the amount required to be paid such amount as it believes is just.

(3) The relevant period is the period of 28 days starting with—

(a) the date on which the defendant was convicted of the offence mentioned in section 28(2)(a), or

(b) if there are two or more offences and the convictions were on different dates, the date of the latest.

(4) But in a case where section 28(2)(a) applies to more than one offence the court must not make an order under this section unless it is satisfied that there is no possibility of any further proceedings being taken or continued in relation to any such offence in respect of which the defendant has not been convicted.

Definitions   For "confiscation order", see s 88(6)(a), (7); for "defendant", see s 88(3), (7).
References   See paras 3.80–3.82.

30 Discharge of order

    (1)   Subsection (2) applies if—

        (a)   the court makes a confiscation order under section 6 as applied by section 28,

        (b)   the defendant is later tried for the offence or offences concerned and acquitted on all counts, and

        (c)   he applies to the Crown Court to discharge the order.

    (2)   In such a case the court must discharge the order.

    (3)   Subsection (4) applies if—

        (a)   the court makes a confiscation order under section 6 as applied by section 28,

        (b)   the defendant ceases to be an absconder,

        (c)   subsection (1)(b) does not apply, and

        (d)   he applies to the Crown Court to discharge the order.

    (4)   In such a case the court may discharge the order if it finds that—

        (a)   there has been undue delay in continuing the proceedings mentioned in section 28(2), or

        (b)   the prosecutor does not intend to proceed with the prosecution.

    (5)   If the court discharges a confiscation order under this section it may make such a consequential or incidental order as it believes is appropriate.

Definitions   For "confiscation order", see s 88(6)(a), (7); for "defendant", see s 88(3), (7); for "offence concerned", see ss 6(9), 88(1), (7); for "offences concerned", see ss 6(9), 88(1), (7).
References   See paras 3.83–3.85.

Appeals

31 Appeal by prosecutor or Director

    (1)   If the Crown Court makes a confiscation order the prosecutor or the Director may appeal to the Court of Appeal in respect of the order.

    (2)   If the Crown Court decides not to make a confiscation order the prosecutor or the Director may appeal to the Court of Appeal against the decision.

    (3)   Subsections (1) and (2) do not apply to an order or decision made by virtue of section 19, 20, 27 or 28.

Definitions   For "confiscation order", see s 88(6)(a), (7); for "the Director", see s 1(2).
References   See paras 3.87, 3.88.

---

32 Court's powers on appeal

    (1)   On an appeal under section 31(1) the Court of Appeal may confirm, quash or vary the confiscation order.

    (2)   On an appeal under section 31(2) the Court of Appeal may confirm the decision, or if it believes the decision was wrong it may—

        (a)   itself proceed under section 6 (ignoring subsections (1) to (3)), or

        (b)   direct the Crown Court to proceed afresh under section 6.

(3)   In proceeding afresh in pursuance of this section the Crown Court must comply with any directions the Court of Appeal may make.

(4)   If a court makes or varies a confiscation order under this section or in pursuance of a direction under this section it must—

    (a)   have regard to any fine imposed on the defendant in respect of the offence (or any of the offences) concerned;

    (b)   have regard to any order which falls within section 13(3) and has been made against him in respect of the offence (or any of the offences) concerned, unless the order has already been taken into account by a court in deciding what is the free property held by the defendant for the purposes of section 9.

(5)   If the Court of Appeal proceeds under section 6 or the Crown Court proceeds afresh under that section in pursuance of a direction under this section subsections (6) to (10) apply.

(6)   If a court has already sentenced the defendant for the offence (or any of the offences) concerned, section 6 has effect as if his particular criminal conduct included conduct which constitutes offences which the court has taken into consideration in deciding his sentence for the offence or offences concerned.

(7)   If an order has been made against the defendant in respect of the offence (or any of the offences) concerned under section 130 of the Sentencing Act (compensation orders)—

    (a)   the court must have regard to it, and

    (b)   section 13(5) and (6) above do not apply.

(8)   Section 8(2) does not apply, and the rules applying instead are that the court must—

    (a)   take account of conduct occurring before the relevant date;

    (b)   take account of property obtained before that date;

    (c)   take account of property obtained on or after that date if it was obtained as a result of or in connection with conduct occurring before that date.

(9)   In section 10—

    (a)   the first and second assumptions do not apply with regard to property first held by the defendant on or after the relevant date;

    (b)   the third assumption does not apply with regard to expenditure incurred by him on or after that date;

    (c)   the fourth assumption does not apply with regard to property obtained (or assumed to have been obtained) by him on or after that date.

(10) Section 26 applies as it applies in the circumstances mentioned in subsection (1) of that section.

(11) The relevant date is the date on which the Crown Court decided not to make a confiscation order.

Definitions   For "confiscation order", see s 88(6)(a), (7); for "criminal conduct", see ss 76(1), 88(7); for "defendant", see s 88(3), (7); for "free property", see ss 82, 88(7); for "offence concerned", see ss 6(9), 88(1), (7); for "offences concerned", see ss 6(9), 88(1), (7); for "particular criminal conduct", see ss 76(3), 88(7); for "property", see ss 84(1), 88(7); for "property held", see ss 84(2)(a), (d), 88(7); for "property obtained", see ss 84(2)(b), 88(7); for "property obtained in connection with conduct", see ss 76(6), 88(7); for "Sentencing Act", see s 88(5), (7); for "sentencing the defendant for an offence", see s 88(4), (7).
References   See paras 3.89, 3.90.

33 Appeal to House of Lords

(1)   An appeal lies to the House of Lords from a decision of the Court of Appeal on an appeal under section 31.

(2)   An appeal under this section lies at the instance of—
- (a)   the defendant or the prosecutor (if the prosecutor appealed under section 31);
- (b)   the defendant or the Director (if the Director appealed under section 31).

(3)   On an appeal from a decision of the Court of Appeal to confirm, vary or make a confiscation order the House of Lords may confirm, quash or vary the order.

(4)   On an appeal from a decision of the Court of Appeal to confirm the decision of the Crown Court not to make a confiscation order or from a decision of the Court of Appeal to quash a confiscation order the House of Lords may—
- (a)   confirm the decision, or
- (b)   direct the Crown Court to proceed afresh under section 6 if it believes the decision was wrong.

(5)   In proceeding afresh in pursuance of this section the Crown Court must comply with any directions the House of Lords may make.

(6)   If a court varies a confiscation order under this section or makes a confiscation order in pursuance of a direction under this section it must—
- (a)   have regard to any fine imposed on the defendant in respect of the offence (or any of the offences) concerned;
- (b)   have regard to any order which falls within section 13(3) and has been made against him in respect of the offence (or any of the offences) concerned, unless the order has already been taken into account by a court in deciding what is the free property held by the defendant for the purposes of section 9.

(7)   If the Crown Court proceeds afresh under section 6 in pursuance of a direction under this section subsections (8) to (12) apply.

(8)   If a court has already sentenced the defendant for the offence (or any of the offences) concerned, section 6 has effect as if his particular criminal conduct included conduct which constitutes offences which the court has taken into consideration in deciding his sentence for the offence or offences concerned.

(9)   If an order has been made against the defendant in respect of the offence (or any of the offences) concerned under section 130 of the Sentencing Act (compensation orders)—
- (a)   the Crown Court must have regard to it, and
- (b)   section 13(5) and (6) above do not apply.

(10) Section 8(2) does not apply, and the rules applying instead are that the Crown Court must—
- (a)   take account of conduct occurring before the relevant date;
- (b)   take account of property obtained before that date;
- (c)   take account of property obtained on or after that date if it was obtained as a result of or in connection with conduct occurring before that date.

(11) In section 10—
- (a) the first and second assumptions do not apply with regard to property first held by the defendant on or after the relevant date;
- (b) the third assumption does not apply with regard to expenditure incurred by him on or after that date;
- (c) the fourth assumption does not apply with regard to property obtained (or assumed to have been obtained) by him on or after that date.

(12) Section 26 applies as it applies in the circumstances mentioned in subsection (1) of that section.

(13) The relevant date is—
- (a) in a case where the Crown Court made a confiscation order which was quashed by the Court of Appeal, the date on which the Crown Court made the order;
- (b) in any other case, the date on which the Crown Court decided not to make a confiscation order.

Definitions   For "confiscation order", see s 88(6)(a), (7); for "criminal conduct", see ss 76(1), 88(7); for "defendant", see s 88(3), (7); for "the Director", see s 1(2); for "free property", see ss 82, 88(7); for "offence concerned", see ss 6(9), 88(1), (7); for "offences concerned", see ss 6(9), 88(1), (7); for "particular criminal conduct", see ss 76(3), 88(7); for "property", see ss 84(1), 88(7); for "property held", see ss 84(2)(a), (d), 88(7); for "property obtained", see ss 84(2)(b), 88(7); for "property obtained in connection with conduct", see ss 76(6), 88(7); for "Sentencing Act", see s 88(5), (7); for "sentencing the defendant for an offence", see s 88(4), (7).
References   See para 3.91.

Enforcement authority

34 Enforcement authority

(1)   Subsection (2) applies if a court makes a confiscation order and any of the following paragraphs applies—
- (a) the court proceeded under section 6 after being asked to do so by the Director;
- (b) the court proceeded under section 6 by virtue of an application by the Director under section 19, 20, 27 or 28;
- (c) the court proceeded under section 6 as a result of an appeal by the Director under section 31(2) or 33;
- (d) before the court made the order the Director applied to the court to appoint him as the enforcement authority for the order.

(2)   In any such case the court must appoint the Director as the enforcement authority for the order.

Definitions   For "confiscation order", see s 88(6)(a), (7); for "the Director", see s 1(2).
References   See paras 3.92–3.95.

Enforcement as fines etc

35 Director not appointed as enforcement authority

(1)   This section applies if a court—
- (a) makes a confiscation order, and

(b)   does not appoint the Director as the enforcement authority for the order.

(2)   Sections 139(2) to (4) and (9) and 140(1) to (4) of the Sentencing Act (functions of court as to fines and enforcing fines) apply as if the amount ordered to be paid were a fine imposed on the defendant by the court making the confiscation order.

(3)   In the application of Part 3 of the Magistrates' Courts Act 1980 (c 43) to an amount payable under a confiscation order—
   (a)   ignore section 75 of that Act (power to dispense with immediate payment);
   (b)   such an amount is not a sum adjudged to be paid by a conviction for the purposes of section 81 (enforcement of fines imposed on young offenders) or a fine for the purposes of section 85 (remission of fines) of that Act;
   (c)   in section 87 of that Act ignore subsection (3) (inquiry into means).

Definitions   For "confiscation order", see s 88(6)(a), (7); for "defendant", see s 88(3), (7); for "the Director", see s 1(2); for "Sentencing Act", see s 88(5), (7).
References   See para 3.96.

36 Director appointed as enforcement authority

(1)   This section applies if a court—
   (a)   makes a confiscation order, and
   (b)   appoints the Director as the enforcement authority for the order.

(2)   Section 139(2) to (4) and (9) of the Sentencing Act (functions of court as to fines) applies as if the amount ordered to be paid were a fine imposed on the defendant by the court making the confiscation order.

Definitions   For "confiscation order", see s 88(6)(a), (7); for "defendant", see s 88(3), (7); for "the Director", see s 1(2); for "Sentencing Act", see s 88(5), (7).
References   See para 3.97.

37 Director's application for enforcement

(1)   If the Director believes that the conditions set out in subsection (2) are satisfied he may make an ex parte application to the Crown Court for the issue of a summons against the defendant.

(2)   The conditions are that—
   (a)   a confiscation order has been made;
   (b)   the Director has been appointed as the enforcement authority for the order;
   (c)   because of the defendant's wilful refusal or culpable neglect the order is not satisfied;
   (d)   the order is not subject to appeal;
   (e)   the Director has done all that is practicable (apart from this section) to enforce the order.

(3)   If it appears to the Crown Court that the conditions are satisfied it may issue a summons ordering the defendant to appear before the court at the time and place specified in the summons.

(4)   If the defendant fails to appear before the Crown Court in pursuance of the summons the court may issue a warrant for his arrest.

(5)   If—
    (a)   the defendant appears before the Crown Court in pursuance of the summons or of a warrant issued under subsection (4), and
    (b)   the court is satisfied that the conditions set out in subsection (2) are satisfied,

it may issue a warrant committing the defendant to prison or detention for default in payment of the amount ordered to be paid by the confiscation order.

(6)   Subsection (7) applies if the amount remaining to be paid under the confiscation order when the warrant under subsection (5) is issued is less than the amount ordered to be paid.

(7)   In such a case the court must substitute for the term of imprisonment or detention fixed in respect of the order under section 139(2) of the Sentencing Act such term as bears to the original term the same proportion as the amount remaining to be paid bears to the amount ordered to be paid.

(8)   Subsections (9) and (10) apply if—
    (a)   the defendant has been committed to prison or detention in pursuance of a warrant issued under subsection (5), and
    (b)   a payment is made in respect of some or all of the amount remaining to be paid under the confiscation order.

(9)   If the payment is for the whole amount remaining to be paid the defendant must be released unless he is in custody for another reason.

(10) If the payment is for less than that amount, the period of commitment is reduced so that it bears to the term fixed under section 139(2) of the Sentencing Act the same proportion as the amount remaining to be paid bears to the amount ordered to be paid.

Definitions   For "confiscation order", see s 88(6)(a), (7); for "defendant", see s 88(3), (7); for "the Director", see s 1(2); for "satisfied", see ss 87(1), 88(7); for "Sentencing Act", see s 88(5), (7); for "subject to appeal", see ss 87(2), 88(7).
References   See para 3.98.

38 Provisions about imprisonment or detention

(1)   Subsection (2) applies if—
    (a)   a warrant committing the defendant to prison or detention is issued for a default in payment of an amount ordered to be paid under a confiscation order in respect of an offence or offences, and
    (b)   at the time the warrant is issued the defendant is liable to serve a term of custody in respect of the offence (or any of the offences).

(2)   In such a case the term of imprisonment or of detention under section 108 of the Sentencing Act (detention of persons aged 18 to 20 for default) to be served in default of payment of the amount does not begin to run until after the term mentioned in subsection (1)(b) above.

(3)   The reference in subsection (1)(b) to the term of custody the defendant is liable to serve in respect of the offence (or any of the offences) is a reference to the

term of imprisonment, or detention in a young offender institution, which he is liable to serve in respect of the offence (or any of the offences).

(4)   For the purposes of subsection (3) consecutive terms and terms which are wholly or partly concurrent must be treated as a single term and the following must be ignored—

    (a)   any sentence suspended under section 118(1) of the Sentencing Act which has not taken effect at the time the warrant is issued;

    (b)   in the case of a sentence of imprisonment passed with an order under section 47(1) of the Criminal Law Act 1977 (c 45) (sentences of imprisonment partly served and partly suspended) any part of the sentence which the defendant has not at that time been required to serve in prison;

    (c)   any term of imprisonment or detention fixed under section 139(2) of the Sentencing Act (term to be served in default of payment of fine etc) for which a warrant committing the defendant to prison or detention has not been issued at that time.

(5)   If the defendant serves a term of imprisonment or detention in default of paying any amount due under a confiscation order, his serving that term does not prevent the confiscation order from continuing to have effect so far as any other method of enforcement is concerned.

Definitions   For "confiscation order", see s 88(6)(a), (7); for "defendant", see s 88(3), (7); for "Sentencing Act", see s 88(5), (7).
References   See para 3.99.

---

39 Reconsideration etc: variation of prison term

(1)   Subsection (2) applies if—

    (a)   a court varies a confiscation order under section 21, 22, 23, 29, 32 or 33,

    (b)   the effect of the variation is to vary the maximum period applicable in relation to the order under section 139(4) of the Sentencing Act, and

    (c)   the result is that that maximum period is less than the term of imprisonment or detention fixed in respect of the order under section 139(2) of the Sentencing Act.

(2)   In such a case the court must fix a reduced term of imprisonment or detention in respect of the confiscation order under section 139(2) of the Sentencing Act in place of the term previously fixed.

(3)   Subsection (4) applies if paragraphs (a) and (b) of subsection (1) apply but paragraph (c) does not.

(4)   In such a case the court may amend the term of imprisonment or detention fixed in respect of the confiscation order under section 139(2) of the Sentencing Act.

(5)   If the effect of section 12 is to increase the maximum period applicable in relation to a confiscation order under section 139(4) of the Sentencing Act, on the application of the appropriate person the Crown Court may amend the term of imprisonment or detention fixed in respect of the order under section 139(2) of that Act.

244

(6)   The appropriate person is—
      (a)   the Director, if he was appointed as the enforcement authority for the order under section 34;
      (b)   the prosecutor, in any other case.

Definitions   For "confiscation order", see s 88(6)(a), (7); for "the Director", see s 1(2); for "Sentencing Act", see s 88(5), (7).
References   See para 3.101, 3.102.

Restraint orders

40 Conditions for exercise of powers

(1)   The Crown Court may exercise the powers conferred by section 41 if any of the following conditions is satisfied.

(2)   The first condition is that—
      (a)   a criminal investigation has been started in England and Wales with regard to an offence, and
      (b)   there is reasonable cause to believe that the alleged offender has benefited from his criminal conduct.

(3)   The second condition is that—
      (a)   proceedings for an offence have been started in England and Wales and not concluded, and
      (b)   there is reasonable cause to believe that the defendant has benefited from his criminal conduct.

(4)   The third condition is that—
      (a)   an application by the prosecutor or the Director has been made under section 19, 20, 27 or 28 and not concluded, or the court believes that such an application is to be made, and
      (b)   there is reasonable cause to believe that the defendant has benefited from his criminal conduct.

(5)   The fourth condition is that—
      (a)   an application by the prosecutor or the Director has been made under section 21 and not concluded, or the court believes that such an application is to be made, and
      (b)   there is reasonable cause to believe that the court will decide under that section that the amount found under the new calculation of the defendant's benefit exceeds the relevant amount (as defined in that section).

(6)   The fifth condition is that—
      (a)   an application by the prosecutor or the Director has been made under section 22 and not concluded, or the court believes that such an application is to be made, and
      (b)   there is reasonable cause to believe that the court will decide under that section that the amount found under the new calculation of the available amount exceeds the relevant amount (as defined in that section).

(7)   The second condition is not satisfied if the court believes that—
      (a)   there has been undue delay in continuing the proceedings, or
      (b)   the prosecutor does not intend to proceed.

(8)   If an application mentioned in the third, fourth or fifth condition has been made the condition is not satisfied if the court believes that—

    (a)   there has been undue delay in continuing the application, or

    (b)   the prosecutor or the Director (as the case may be) does not intend to proceed.

(9)   If the first condition is satisfied—

    (a)   references in this Part to the defendant are to the alleged offender;

    (b)   references in this Part to the prosecutor are to the person the court believes is to have conduct of any proceedings for the offence;

    (c)   section 77(9) has effect as if proceedings for the offence had been started against the defendant when the investigation was started.

Definitions   For "application under s 19, 20, 27 or 28 concluded", see ss 86(1), 88(7); for "application under s 21 or 22 concluded", see ss 86(2), 88(7); for "benefits from conduct", see ss 76(4), (7), 88(7); for "confiscation order", see s 88(6)(a), (7); for "criminal conduct", see ss 76(1), 88(7); for "defendant", see s 88(3), (7) (and sub-s (9)(a)); for "the Director", see s 1(2); for "proceedings concluded", see ss 85(3)–(8), 88(7); for "proceedings started", see ss 85(1), (2), 88(7).
References   See paras 3.103–3.108.

---

41 Restraint orders

(1)   If any condition set out in section 40 is satisfied the Crown Court may make an order (a restraint order) prohibiting any specified person from dealing with any realisable property held by him.

(2)   A restraint order may provide that it applies—

    (a)   to all realisable property held by the specified person whether or not the property is described in the order;

    (b)   to realisable property transferred to the specified person after the order is made.

(3)   A restraint order may be made subject to exceptions, and an exception may in particular—

    (a)   make provision for reasonable living expenses and reasonable legal expenses;

    (b)   make provision for the purpose of enabling any person to carry on any trade, business, profession or occupation;

    (c)   be made subject to conditions.

(4)   But an exception to a restraint order must not make provision for any legal expenses which—

    (a)   relate to an offence which falls within subsection (5), and

    (b)   are incurred by the defendant or by a recipient of a tainted gift.

(5)   These offences fall within this subsection—

    (a)   the offence mentioned in section 40(2) or (3), if the first or second condition (as the case may be) is satisfied;

    (b)   the offence (or any of the offences) concerned, if the third, fourth or fifth condition is satisfied.

(6)   Subsection (7) applies if—

    (a)   a court makes a restraint order, and

    (b)   the applicant for the order applies to the court to proceed under subsection (7) (whether as part of the application for the restraint order or at any time afterwards).

(7)   The court may make such order as it believes is appropriate for the purpose of ensuring that the restraint order is effective.

(8)   A restraint order does not affect property for the time being subject to a charge under any of these provisions—

- (a)   section 9 of the Drug Trafficking Offences Act 1986 (c 32);
- (b)   section 78 of the Criminal Justice Act 1988 (c 33);
- (c)   Article 14 of the Criminal Justice (Confiscation) (Northern Ireland) Order 1990 (SI 1990/2588 (NI 17));
- (d)   section 27 of the Drug Trafficking Act 1994 (c 37);
- (e)   Article 32 of the Proceeds of Crime (Northern Ireland) Order 1996 (SI 1996/1299 (NI 9)).

(9)   Dealing with property includes removing it from England and Wales.

Definitions   For "offence concerned", see ss 6(9), 88(1), (7); for "offences concerned", see ss 6(9), 88(1), (7); for "property", see ss 84(1), 88(7); for "property held", see ss 84(2)(a), (d), 88(7); for "property transferred", see ss 84(2)(c), 88(7); for "realisable property", see ss 83, 88(7); for "recipient of a tainted gift", see ss 78(3), 88(7); for "tainted gift", see ss 77, 88(7).
References   See paras 3.109–3.111.

42 Application, discharge and variation

(1)   A restraint order—
- (a)   may be made only on an application by an applicant falling within subsection (2);
- (b)   may be made on an ex parte application to a judge in chambers.

(2)   These applicants fall within this subsection—
- (a)   the prosecutor;
- (b)   the Director;
- (c)   an accredited financial investigator.

(3)   An application to discharge or vary a restraint order or an order under section 41(7) may be made to the Crown Court by—
- (a)   the person who applied for the order;
- (b)   any person affected by the order.

(4)   Subsections (5) to (7) apply to an application under subsection (3).

(5)   The court—
- (a)   may discharge the order;
- (b)   may vary the order.

(6)   If the condition in section 40 which was satisfied was that proceedings were started or an application was made, the court must discharge the order on the conclusion of the proceedings or of the application (as the case may be).

(7)   If the condition in section 40 which was satisfied was that an investigation was started or an application was to be made, the court must discharge the order if within a reasonable time proceedings for the offence are not started or the application is not made (as the case may be).

Definitions   For "accredited financial investigator", see s 3(5); for "the Director", see s 1(2); for "proceedings concluded", see ss 85(3)–(8), 88(7); for "proceedings started", see ss 85(1), (2), 88(7); for "the prosecutor", see s 40(9)(b); for "restraint order", see s 88(6)(b), (7).
References   See paras 3.112–3.114.

43 Appeal to Court of Appeal

(1)   If on an application for a restraint order the court decides not to make one, the person who applied for the order may appeal to the Court of Appeal against the decision.

(2)   If an application is made under section 42(3) in relation to a restraint order or an order under section 41(7) the following persons may appeal to the Court of Appeal in respect of the Crown Court's decision on the application—
     (a)   the person who applied for the order;
     (b)   any person affected by the order.

(3)   On an appeal under subsection (1) or (2) the Court of Appeal may—
     (a)   confirm the decision, or
     (b)   make such order as it believes is appropriate.

Definitions   For "restraint order", see s 88(6)(b), (7).
References   See paras 3.115, 3.116.

44 Appeal to House of Lords

(1)   An appeal lies to the House of Lords from a decision of the Court of Appeal on an appeal under section 43.

(2)   An appeal under this section lies at the instance of any person who was a party to the proceedings before the Court of Appeal.

(3)   On an appeal under this section the House of Lords may—
     (a)   confirm the decision of the Court of Appeal, or
     (b)   make such order as it believes is appropriate.

Definitions   For "customs officer", see s 454; for "property", see ss 84(1), 88(7); for "realisable property", see ss 83, 88(7); for "restraint order", see s 88(6)(b), (7).
References   See para 3.117.

45 Seizure

(1)   If a restraint order is in force a constable or a customs officer may seize any realisable property to which it applies to prevent its removal from England and Wales.

(2)   Property seized under subsection (1) must be dealt with in accordance with the directions of the court which made the order.

References   See para 3.118.

46 Hearsay evidence

(1)   Evidence must not be excluded in restraint proceedings on the ground that it is hearsay (of whatever degree).

(2)   Sections 2 to 4 of the Civil Evidence Act 1995 (c 38) apply in relation to restraint proceedings as those sections apply in relation to civil proceedings.

(3)   Restraint proceedings are proceedings—
     (a)   for a restraint order;

    (b)   for the discharge or variation of a restraint order;

    (c)   on an appeal under section 43 or 44.

(4)   Hearsay is a statement which is made otherwise than by a person while giving oral evidence in the proceedings and which is tendered as evidence of the matters stated.

(5)   Nothing in this section affects the admissibility of evidence which is admissible apart from this section.

Definitions   For "restraint order", see s 88(6)(b), (7).
References   See para 3.119.

47 Supplementary

(1)   The registration Acts—
    (a)   apply in relation to restraint orders as they apply in relation to orders which affect land and are made by the court for the purpose of enforcing judgments or recognisances;
    (b)   apply in relation to applications for restraint orders as they apply in relation to other pending land actions.

(2)   The registration Acts are—
    (a)   the Land Registration Act 1925 (c 21);
    (b)   the Land Charges Act 1972 (c 61);
    (c)   the Land Registration Act 2002 (c 9).

(3)   But no notice may be entered in the register of title under the Land Registration Act 2002 in respect of a restraint order.

(4)   The person applying for a restraint order must be treated for the purposes of section 57 of the Land Registration Act 1925 (inhibitions) as a person interested in relation to any registered land to which—
    (a)   the application relates, or
    (b)   a restraint order made in pursuance of the application relates.

Definitions   For "restraint order", see s 88(6)(b), (7).
References   See para 3.120.

Management receivers

48 Appointment

(1)   Subsection (2) applies if—
    (a)   the Crown Court makes a restraint order, and
    (b)   the applicant for the restraint order applies to the court to proceed under subsection (2) (whether as part of the application for the restraint order or at any time afterwards).

(2)   The Crown Court may by order appoint a receiver in respect of any realisable property to which the restraint order applies.

Definitions   For "property", see ss 84(1), 88(7); for "realisable property", see ss 83, 88(7); for "restraint order", see s 88(6)(b), (7).
References   See paras 3.121, 3.122.

49 Powers

(1)   If the court appoints a receiver under section 48 it may act under this section on the application of the person who applied for the restraint order.

(2)   The court may by order confer on the receiver the following powers in relation to any realisable property to which the restraint order applies—
   (a)   power to take possession of the property;
   (b)   power to manage or otherwise deal with the property;
   (c)   power to start, carry on or defend any legal proceedings in respect of the property;
   (d)   power to realise so much of the property as is necessary to meet the receiver's remuneration and expenses.

(3)   The court may by order confer on the receiver power to enter any premises in England and Wales and to do any of the following—
   (a)   search for or inspect anything authorised by the court;
   (b)   make or obtain a copy, photograph or other record of anything so authorised;
   (c)   remove anything which the receiver is required or authorised to take possession of in pursuance of an order of the court.

(4)   The court may by order authorise the receiver to do any of the following for the purpose of the exercise of his functions—
   (a)   hold property;
   (b)   enter into contracts;
   (c)   sue and be sued;
   (d)   employ agents;
   (e)   execute powers of attorney, deeds or other instruments;
   (f)   take any other steps the court thinks appropriate.

(5)   The court may order any person who has possession of realisable property to which the restraint order applies to give possession of it to the receiver.

(6)   The court—
   (a)   may order a person holding an interest in realisable property to which the restraint order applies to make to the receiver such payment as the court specifies in respect of a beneficial interest held by the defendant or the recipient of a tainted gift;
   (b)   may (on the payment being made) by order transfer, grant or extinguish any interest in the property.

(7)   Subsections (2), (5) and (6) do not apply to property for the time being subject to a charge under any of these provisions—
   (a)   section 9 of the Drug Trafficking Offences Act 1986 (c 32);
   (b)   section 78 of the Criminal Justice Act 1988 (c 33);
   (c)   Article 14 of the Criminal Justice (Confiscation) (Northern Ireland) Order 1990 (SI 1990/2588 (NI 17));
   (d)   section 27 of the Drug Trafficking Act 1994 (c 37);
   (e)   Article 32 of the Proceeds of Crime (Northern Ireland) Order 1996 (SI 1996/1299 (NI 9)).

(8)   The court must not—
   (a)   confer the power mentioned in subsection (2)(b) or (d) in respect of property, or

(b)   exercise the power conferred on it by subsection (6) in respect of property,

unless it gives persons holding interests in the property a reasonable opportunity to make representations to it.

(9)   The court may order that a power conferred by an order under this section is subject to such conditions and exceptions as it specifies.

(10) Managing or otherwise dealing with property includes—
(a)   selling the property or any part of it or interest in it;
(b)   carrying on or arranging for another person to carry on any trade or business the assets of which are or are part of the property;
(c)   incurring capital expenditure in respect of the property.

Definitions   For "defendant", see ss 40(9)(a), 88(3), (7); for "interest" in relation to land, see ss 84(2)(f), (g), 88(7); for "interest" in relation to property other than land, see ss 84(2)(h), 88(7); for "interest held by a person beneficially in property", see ss 84(2)(e), 88(7); for "property", see ss 84(1), 88(7); for "realisable property", see ss 83, 88(7); for "recipient of a tainted gift", see ss 78(3), 88(7); for "restraint order", see s 88(6)(b), (7); for "tainted gift", see ss 77, 88(7).
References   See paras 3.123–3.128.

Enforcement receivers

50 Appointment

(1)   This section applies if—
(a)   a confiscation order is made,
(b)   it is not satisfied, and
(c)   it is not subject to appeal.

(2)   On the application of the prosecutor the Crown Court may by order appoint a receiver in respect of realisable property.

Definitions   For "confiscation order", see s 88(6)(a), (7); for "property", see ss 84(1), 88(7); for "realisable property", see ss 83, 88(7); for "satisfied", see ss 87(1), 88(7); for "subject to appeal", see ss 87(2), 88(7).
References   See para 3.129.

51 Powers

(1)   If the court appoints a receiver under section 50 it may act under this section on the application of the prosecutor.

(2)   The court may by order confer on the receiver the following powers in relation to the realisable property—
(a)   power to take possession of the property;
(b)   power to manage or otherwise deal with the property;
(c)   power to realise the property, in such manner as the court may specify;
(d)   power to start, carry on or defend any legal proceedings in respect of the property.

(3)   The court may by order confer on the receiver power to enter any premises in England and Wales and to do any of the following—
(a)   search for or inspect anything authorised by the court;

     (b)   make or obtain a copy, photograph or other record of anything so authorised;

     (c)   remove anything which the receiver is required or authorised to take possession of in pursuance of an order of the court.

(4)   The court may by order authorise the receiver to do any of the following for the purpose of the exercise of his functions—

     (a)   hold property;

     (b)   enter into contracts;

     (c)   sue and be sued;

     (d)   employ agents;

     (e)   execute powers of attorney, deeds or other instruments;

     (f)   take any other steps the court thinks appropriate.

(5)   The court may order any person who has possession of realisable property to give possession of it to the receiver.

(6)   The court—

     (a)   may order a person holding an interest in realisable property to make to the receiver such payment as the court specifies in respect of a beneficial interest held by the defendant or the recipient of a tainted gift;

     (b)   may (on the payment being made) by order transfer, grant or extinguish any interest in the property.

(7)   Subsections (2), (5) and (6) do not apply to property for the time being subject to a charge under any of these provisions—

     (a)   section 9 of the Drug Trafficking Offences Act 1986 (c 32);

     (b)   section 78 of the Criminal Justice Act 1988 (c 33);

     (c)   Article 14 of the Criminal Justice (Confiscation) (Northern Ireland) Order 1990 (SI 1990/2588 (NI 17));

     (d)   section 27 of the Drug Trafficking Act 1994 (c 37);

     (e)   Article 32 of the Proceeds of Crime (Northern Ireland) Order 1996 (SI 1996/1299 (NI 9)).

(8)   The court must not—

     (a)   confer the power mentioned in subsection (2)(b) or (c) in respect of property, or

     (b)   exercise the power conferred on it by subsection (6) in respect of property,

unless it gives persons holding interests in the property a reasonable opportunity to make representations to it.

(9)   The court may order that a power conferred by an order under this section is subject to such conditions and exceptions as it specifies.

(10) Managing or otherwise dealing with property includes—

     (a)   selling the property or any part of it or interest in it;

     (b)   carrying on or arranging for another person to carry on any trade or business the assets of which are or are part of the property;

     (c)   incurring capital expenditure in respect of the property.

Definitions   For "defendant", see s 88(3), (7); for "interest" in relation to land, see ss 84(2)(f), (g), 88(7); for "interest" in relation to property other than land, see ss 84(2)(h), 88(7); for "interest held by a person beneficially in property", see ss 84(2)(e), 88(7); for "property", see ss 84(1), 88(7); for "realisable property", see ss 83, 88(7); for "recipient of a tainted gift", see ss 78(3), 88(7); for "tainted gift", see ss 77, 88(7).
References   See paras 3.130, 3.131.

Director's receivers

52 Appointment

(1) This section applies if—
    (a) a confiscation order is made, and
    (b) the Director is appointed as the enforcement authority for the order under section 34.

(2) But this section does not apply if—
    (a) the confiscation order was made by the Court of Appeal, and
    (b) when the Crown Court comes to proceed under this section the confiscation order has been satisfied.

(3) If this section applies the Crown Court must make an order for the appointment of a receiver in respect of realisable property.

(4) An order under subsection (3)—
    (a) must confer power on the Director to nominate the person who is to be the receiver, and
    (b) takes effect when the Director nominates that person.

(5) The Director must not nominate a person under subsection (4) unless at the time he does so the confiscation order—
    (a) is not satisfied, and
    (b) is not subject to appeal.

(6) A person nominated to be the receiver under subsection (4) may be—
    (a) a member of the staff of the Agency;
    (b) a person providing services under arrangements made by the Director.

(7) If this section applies section 50 does not apply.

Definitions   For "the Agency", see s 1(1); for "confiscation order", see s 88(6)(a), (7); for "the Director", see s 1(2); for "property", see ss 84(1), 88(7); for "realisable property", see ss 83, 88(7); for "satisfied", see ss 87(1), 88(7); for "subject to appeal", see ss 87(2), 88(7).
References   See paras 3.132–3.134.

---

53 Powers

(1) If the court makes an order for the appointment of a receiver under section 52 it may act under this section on the application of the Director.

(2) The court may by order confer on the receiver the following powers in relation to the realisable property—
    (a) power to take possession of the property;
    (b) power to manage or otherwise deal with the property;
    (c) power to realise the property, in such manner as the court may specify;
    (d) power to start, carry on or defend any legal proceedings in respect of the property.

(3) The court may by order confer on the receiver power to enter any premises in England and Wales and to do any of the following—
    (a) search for or inspect anything authorised by the court;

     (b)   make or obtain a copy, photograph or other record of anything so authorised;

     (c)   remove anything which the receiver is required or authorised to take possession of in pursuance of an order of the court.

(4)   The court may by order authorise the receiver to do any of the following for the purpose of the exercise of his functions—

     (a)   hold property;

     (b)   enter into contracts;

     (c)   sue and be sued;

     (d)   employ agents;

     (e)   execute powers of attorney, deeds or other instruments;

     (f)   take any other steps the court thinks appropriate.

(5)   The court may order any person who has possession of realisable property to give possession of it to the receiver.

(6)   The court—

     (a)   may order a person holding an interest in realisable property to make to the receiver such payment as the court specifies in respect of a beneficial interest held by the defendant or the recipient of a tainted gift;

     (b)   may (on the payment being made) by order transfer, grant or extinguish any interest in the property.

(7)   Subsections (2), (5) and (6) do not apply to property for the time being subject to a charge under any of these provisions—

     (a)   section 9 of the Drug Trafficking Offences Act 1986 (c 32);

     (b)   section 78 of the Criminal Justice Act 1988 (c 33);

     (c)   Article 14 of the Criminal Justice (Confiscation) (Northern Ireland) Order 1990 (SI 1990/2588 (NI 17));

     (d)   section 27 of the Drug Trafficking Act 1994 (c 37);

     (e)   Article 32 of the Proceeds of Crime (Northern Ireland) Order 1996 (SI 1996/1299 (NI 9)).

(8)   The court must not—

     (a)   confer the power mentioned in subsection (2)(b) or (c) in respect of property, or

     (b)   exercise the power conferred on it by subsection (6) in respect of property,

unless it gives persons holding interests in the property a reasonable opportunity to make representations to it.

(9)   The court may order that a power conferred by an order under this section is subject to such conditions and exceptions as it specifies.

(10) Managing or otherwise dealing with property includes—

     (a)   selling the property or any part of it or interest in it;

     (b)   carrying on or arranging for another person to carry on any trade or business the assets of which are or are part of the property;

     (c)   incurring capital expenditure in respect of the property.

Definitions   For "defendant", see s 88(3), (7); for "the Director", see s 1(2); for "interest" in relation to land, see ss 84(2)(f), (g), 88(7); for "interest" in relation to property other than land, see ss 84(2)(h), 88(7); for "interest held by a person beneficially in property", see ss 84(2)(e), 88(7); for "property", see ss 84(1), 88(7); for "realisable property", see ss 83, 88(7); for "recipient of a tainted gift", see ss 78(3), 88(7); for "tainted gift", see ss 77, 88(7).
References   See para 3.135.

Application of sums

54 Enforcement receivers

(1)   This section applies to sums which are in the hands of a receiver appointed under section 50 if they are—
  (a)   the proceeds of the realisation of property under section 51;
  (b)   sums (other than those mentioned in paragraph (a)) in which the defendant holds an interest.

(2)   The sums must be applied as follows—
  (a)   first, they must be applied in payment of such expenses incurred by a person acting as an insolvency practitioner as are payable under this subsection by virtue of section 432;
  (b)   second, they must be applied in making any payments directed by the Crown Court;
  (c)   third, they must be applied on the defendant's behalf towards satisfaction of the confiscation order.

(3)   If the amount payable under the confiscation order has been fully paid and any sums remain in the receiver's hands he must distribute them—
  (a)   among such persons who held (or hold) interests in the property concerned as the Crown Court directs, and
  (b)   in such proportions as it directs.

(4)   Before making a direction under subsection (3) the court must give persons who held (or hold) interests in the property concerned a reasonable opportunity to make representations to it.

(5)   For the purposes of subsections (3) and (4) the property concerned is—
  (a)   the property represented by the proceeds mentioned in subsection (1)(a);
  (b)   the sums mentioned in subsection (1)(b).

(6)   The receiver applies sums as mentioned in subsection (2)(c) by paying them to the appropriate justices' chief executive on account of the amount payable under the order.

(7)   The appropriate justices' chief executive is the one for the magistrates' court responsible for enforcing the confiscation order as if the amount ordered to be paid were a fine.

Definitions   For "confiscation order", see s 88(6)(a), (7); for "defendant", see s 88(3), (7); for "interest" in relation to property other than land, see ss 84(2)(h), 88(7); for "property", see ss 84(1), 88(7).
References   See paras 3.136, 3.137.

55 Sums received by justices' chief executive

(1)   This section applies if a justices' chief executive receives sums on account of the amount payable under a confiscation order (whether the sums are received under section 54 or otherwise).

(2)   The chief executive's receipt of the sums reduces the amount payable under the order, but he must apply the sums received as follows.

(3)   First he must apply them in payment of such expenses incurred by a person acting as an insolvency practitioner as—

    (a)   are payable under this subsection by virtue of section 432, but

    (b)   are not already paid under section 54(2)(a).

(4)   If the justices' chief executive received the sums under section 54 he must next apply them—

    (a)   first, in payment of the remuneration and expenses of a receiver appointed under section 48, to the extent that they have not been met by virtue of the exercise by that receiver of a power conferred under section 49(2)(d);

    (b)   second, in payment of the remuneration and expenses of the receiver appointed under section 50.

(5)   If a direction was made under section 13(6) for an amount of compensation to be paid out of sums recovered under the confiscation order, the justices' chief executive must next apply the sums in payment of that amount.

(6)   If any amount remains after the justices' chief executive makes any payments required by the preceding provisions of this section, the amount must be treated for the purposes of section 60 of the Justices of the Peace Act 1997 (c 25) (application of fines etc) as if it were a fine imposed by a magistrates' court.

(7)   Subsection (4) does not apply if the receiver is a member of the staff of the Crown Prosecution Service or of the Commissioners of Customs and Excise; and it is immaterial whether he is a permanent or temporary member or he is on secondment from elsewhere.

Definitions   For "confiscation order", see s 88(6)(a), (7).
References   See para 3.138.

---

56 Director's receivers

(1)   This section applies to sums which are in the hands of a receiver appointed under section 52 if they are—

    (a)   the proceeds of the realisation of property under section 53;

    (b)   sums (other than those mentioned in paragraph (a)) in which the defendant holds an interest.

(2)   The sums must be applied as follows—

    (a)   first, they must be applied in payment of such expenses incurred by a person acting as an insolvency practitioner as are payable under this subsection by virtue of section 432;

    (b)   second, they must be applied in making any payments directed by the Crown Court;

    (c)   third, they must be applied on the defendant's behalf towards satisfaction of the confiscation order by being paid to the Director on account of the amount payable under it.

(3)   If the amount payable under the confiscation order has been fully paid and any sums remain in the receiver's hands he must distribute them—

    (a)   among such persons who held (or hold) interests in the property concerned as the Crown Court directs, and

    (b)   in such proportions as it directs.

(4)   Before making a direction under subsection (3) the court must give persons who held (or hold) interests in the property concerned a reasonable opportunity to make representations to it.

(5)   For the purposes of subsections (3) and (4) the property concerned is—
    (a)   the property represented by the proceeds mentioned in subsection (1)(a);
    (b)   the sums mentioned in subsection (1)(b).

Definitions   For "confiscation order", see s 88(6)(a), (7); for "defendant", see s 88(3), (7); for "the Director", see s 1(2); for "interest" in relation to property other than land, see ss 84(2)(h), 88(7); for "property", see ss 84(1), 88(7).
References   See para 3.139.

57 Sums received by Director

(1)   This section applies if the Director receives sums on account of the amount payable under a confiscation order (whether the sums are received under section 56 or otherwise).

(2)   The Director's receipt of the sums reduces the amount payable under the order, but he must apply the sums received as follows.

(3)   First he must apply them in payment of such expenses incurred by a person acting as an insolvency practitioner as—
    (a)   are payable under this subsection by virtue of section 432, but
    (b)   are not already paid under section 56(2)(a).

(4)   If the Director received the sums under section 56 he must next apply them—
    (a)   first, in payment of the remuneration and expenses of a receiver appointed under section 48, to the extent that they have not been met by virtue of the exercise by that receiver of a power conferred under section 49(2)(d);
    (b)   second, in payment of the remuneration and expenses of the receiver appointed under section 52.

(5)   If a direction was made under section 13(6) for an amount of compensation to be paid out of sums recovered under the confiscation order, the Director must next apply the sums in payment of that amount.

(6)   Subsection (4) does not apply if the receiver is a member of the staff of the Agency or a person providing services under arrangements made by the Director.

Definitions   For "the Agency", see s 1(1); for "confiscation order", see s 88(6)(a), (7); for "the Director", see s 1(2).
References   See paras 3.140–3.142.

Restrictions

58 Restraint orders

(1)   Subsections (2) to (4) apply if a court makes a restraint order.

(2)   No distress may be levied against any realisable property to which the order applies except with the leave of the Crown Court and subject to any terms the Crown Court may impose.

(3)   If the order applies to a tenancy of any premises, no landlord or other person to whom rent is payable may exercise a right within subsection (4) except with the leave of the Crown Court and subject to any terms the Crown Court may impose.

(4)   A right is within this subsection if it is a right of forfeiture by peaceable re-entry in relation to the premises in respect of any failure by the tenant to comply with any term or condition of the tenancy.

(5)   If a court in which proceedings are pending in respect of any property is satisfied that a restraint order has been applied for or made in respect of the property, the court may either stay the proceedings or allow them to continue on any terms it thinks fit.

(6)   Before exercising any power conferred by subsection (5), the court must give an opportunity to be heard to—
    (a)   the applicant for the restraint order, and
    (b)   any receiver appointed in respect of the property under section 48, 50 or 52.

Definitions   For "property", see ss 84(1), 88(7); for "realisable property", see ss 83, 88(7); for "restraint order", see s 88(6)(b), (7).
References   See para 3.143.

59 Enforcement receivers

(1)   Subsections (2) to (4) apply if a court makes an order under section 50 appointing a receiver in respect of any realisable property.

(2)   No distress may be levied against the property except with the leave of the Crown Court and subject to any terms the Crown Court may impose.

(3)   If the receiver is appointed in respect of a tenancy of any premises, no landlord or other person to whom rent is payable may exercise a right within subsection (4) except with the leave of the Crown Court and subject to any terms the Crown Court may impose.

(4)   A right is within this subsection if it is a right of forfeiture by peaceable re-entry in relation to the premises in respect of any failure by the tenant to comply with any term or condition of the tenancy.

(5)   If a court in which proceedings are pending in respect of any property is satisfied that an order under section 50 appointing a receiver in respect of the property has been applied for or made, the court may either stay the proceedings or allow them to continue on any terms it thinks fit.

(6)   Before exercising any power conferred by subsection (5), the court must give an opportunity to be heard to—
    (a)   the prosecutor, and
    (b)   the receiver (if the order under section 50 has been made).

Definitions   For "property", see ss 84(1), 88(7); for "realisable property", see ss 83, 88(7).
References   See para 3.144.

60 Director's receivers

(1)   Subsections (2) to (4) apply if—
    (a)   the Crown Court has made an order under section 52 for the appointment of a receiver in respect of any realisable property, and
    (b)   the order has taken effect.

(2)   No distress may be levied against the property except with the leave of the Crown Court and subject to any terms the Crown Court may impose.

(3)   If the order is for the appointment of a receiver in respect of a tenancy of any premises, no landlord or other person to whom rent is payable may exercise a right within subsection (4) except with the leave of the Crown Court and subject to any terms the Crown Court may impose.

(4)   A right is within this subsection if it is a right of forfeiture by peaceable re-entry in relation to the premises in respect of any failure by the tenant to comply with any term or condition of the tenancy.

(5)   If a court (whether the Crown Court or any other court) in which proceedings are pending in respect of any property is satisfied that an order under section 52 for the appointment of a receiver in respect of the property has taken effect, the court may either stay the proceedings or allow them to continue on any terms it thinks fit.

(6)   Before exercising any power conferred by subsection (5), the court must give an opportunity to be heard to—
      (a)   the Director, and
      (b)   the receiver.

Definitions   For "the Director", see s 1(2); for "property", see ss 84(1), 88(7); for "realisable property", see ss 83, 88(7).
References   See para 3.144.

Receivers: further provisions

61 Protection

If a receiver appointed under section 48, 50 or 52—
      (a)   takes action in relation to property which is not realisable property,
      (b)   would be entitled to take the action if it were realisable property, and
      (c)   believes on reasonable grounds that he is entitled to take the action,

he is not liable to any person in respect of any loss or damage resulting from the action, except so far as the loss or damage is caused by his negligence.

Definitions   For "property", see ss 84(1), 88(7); for "realisable property", see ss 83, 88(7).
References   see para 3.145.

62 Further applications

(1)   This section applies to a receiver appointed under section 48, 50 or 52.

(2)   The receiver may apply to the Crown Court for an order giving directions as to the exercise of his powers.

(3)   The following persons may apply to the Crown Court—
      (a)   any person affected by action taken by the receiver;
      (b)   any person who may be affected by action the receiver proposes to take.

(4)   On an application under this section the court may make such order as it believes is appropriate.

References   See para 3.146.

63 Discharge and variation

(1)   The following persons may apply to the Crown Court to vary or discharge an order made under any of sections 48 to 53—

(a)   the receiver;

(b)   the person who applied for the order or (if the order was made under section 52 or 53) the Director;

(c)   any person affected by the order.

(2)   On an application under this section the court—

(a)   may discharge the order;

(b)   may vary the order.

(3)   But in the case of an order under section 48 or 49—

(a)   if the condition in section 40 which was satisfied was that proceedings were started or an application was made, the court must discharge the order on the conclusion of the proceedings or of the application (as the case may be);

(b)   if the condition which was satisfied was that an investigation was started or an application was to be made, the court must discharge the order if within a reasonable time proceedings for the offence are not started or the application is not made (as the case may be).

Definitions   For "the Director", see s 1(2); for "proceedings concluded", see ss 85(3)–(8), 88(7); for "proceedings started", see ss 85(1), (2), 88(7).
References   See para 3.147.

64 Management receivers: discharge

(1)   This section applies if—

(a)   a receiver stands appointed under section 48 in respect of realisable property (the management receiver), and

(b)   the court appoints a receiver under section 50 or makes an order for the appointment of a receiver under section 52.

(2)   The court must order the management receiver to transfer to the other receiver all property held by the management receiver by virtue of the powers conferred on him by section 49.

(3)   But in a case where the court makes an order under section 52 its order under subsection (2) above does not take effect until the order under section 52 takes effect.

(4)   Subsection (2) does not apply to property which the management receiver holds by virtue of the exercise by him of his power under section 49(2)(d).

(5)   If the management receiver complies with an order under subsection (2) he is discharged—

(a)   from his appointment under section 48;

(b)   from any obligation under this Act arising from his appointment.

(6)   If this section applies the court may make such a consequential or incidental order as it believes is appropriate.

Definitions   For "property", see ss 84(1), 88(7); for "property held", see ss 84(2)(a), (d), 88(7); for "realisable property", see ss 83, 88(7).
References   see para 3.148.

65 Appeal to Court of Appeal

(1)   If on an application for an order under any of sections 48 to 51 or section 53 the court decides not to make one, the person who applied for the order may appeal to the Court of Appeal against the decision.

(2)   If the court makes an order under any of sections 48 to 51 or section 53, the following persons may appeal to the Court of Appeal in respect of the court's decision—
  (a)   the person who applied for the order;
  (b)   any person affected by the order.

(3)   If on an application for an order under section 62 the court decides not to make one, the person who applied for the order may appeal to the Court of Appeal against the decision.

(4)   If the court makes an order under section 62, the following persons may appeal to the Court of Appeal in respect of the court's decision—
  (a)   the person who applied for the order;
  (b)   any person affected by the order;
  (c)   the receiver.

(5)   The following persons may appeal to the Court of Appeal against a decision of the court on an application under section 63—
  (a)   the person who applied for the order in respect of which the application was made or (if the order was made under section 52 or 53) the Director;
  (b)   any person affected by the court's decision;
  (c)   the receiver.

(6)   On an appeal under this section the Court of Appeal may—
  (a)   confirm the decision, or
  (b)   make such order as it believes is appropriate.

Definitions   For "the Director", see s 1(2).
References   See para 3.149.

66 Appeal to House of Lords

(1)   An appeal lies to the House of Lords from a decision of the Court of Appeal on an appeal under section 65.

(2)   An appeal under this section lies at the instance of any person who was a party to the proceedings before the Court of Appeal.

(3)   On an appeal under this section the House of Lords may—
  (a)   confirm the decision of the Court of Appeal, or
  (b)   make such order as it believes is appropriate.

References   See para 3.150.

Seized money

67 Seized money

(1)   This section applies to money which—
  (a)   is held by a person, and

        (b)   is held in an account maintained by him with a bank or a building society.

(2)   This section also applies to money which is held by a person and which—
        (a)   has been seized by a constable under section 19 of the Police and Criminal Evidence Act 1984 (c 60) (general power of seizure etc), and
        (b)   is held in an account maintained by a police force with a bank or a building society.

(3)   This section also applies to money which is held by a person and which—
        (a)   has been seized by a customs officer under section 19 of the 1984 Act as applied by order made under section 114(2) of that Act, and
        (b)   is held in an account maintained by the Commissioners of Customs and Excise with a bank or a building society.

(4)   This section applies if the following conditions are satisfied—
        (a)   a restraint order has effect in relation to money to which this section applies;
        (b)   a confiscation order is made against the person by whom the money is held;
        (c)   the Director has not been appointed as the enforcement authority for the confiscation order;
        (d)   a receiver has not been appointed under section 50 in relation to the money;
        (e)   any period allowed under section 11 for payment of the amount ordered to be paid under the confiscation order has ended.

(5)   In such a case a magistrates' court may order the bank or building society to pay the money to the justices' chief executive for the court on account of the amount payable under the confiscation order.

(6)   If a bank or building society fails to comply with an order under subsection (5)—
        (a)   the magistrates' court may order it to pay an amount not exceeding £5,000, and
        (b)   for the purposes of the Magistrates' Courts Act 1980 (c 43) the sum is to be treated as adjudged to be paid by a conviction of the court.

(7)   In order to take account of changes in the value of money the Secretary of State may by order substitute another sum for the sum for the time being specified in subsection (6)(a).

(8)   For the purposes of this section—
        (a)   a bank is a deposit-taking business within the meaning of the Banking Act 1987 (c 22);
        (b)   "building society" has the same meaning as in the Building Societies Act 1986 (c 53).

Definitions   For "confiscation order", see s 88(6)(a), (7); for "customs officer", see s 454; for "the Director", see s 1(2); for "restraint order", see s 88(6)(b), (7).
References   See paras 3.151–3.154.

Financial investigators

68 Applications and appeals

(1)   Subsections (2) and (3) apply to—
     (a)   an application under section 41, 42, 48, 49 or 63;
     (b)   an appeal under section 43, 44, 65 or 66.

(2)   An accredited financial investigator must not make such an application or bring such an appeal unless he falls within subsection (3).

(3)   An accredited financial investigator falls within this subsection if he is one of the following or is authorised for the purposes of this section by one of the following—
     (a)   a police officer who is not below the rank of superintendent,
     (b)   a customs officer who is not below such grade as is designated by the Commissioners of Customs and Excise as equivalent to that rank,
     (c)   an accredited financial investigator who falls within a description specified in an order made for the purposes of this paragraph by the Secretary of State under section 453.

(4)   If such an application is made or appeal brought by an accredited financial investigator any subsequent step in the application or appeal or any further application or appeal relating to the same matter may be taken, made or brought by a different accredited financial investigator who falls within subsection (3).

(5)   If—
     (a)   an application for a restraint order is made by an accredited financial investigator, and
     (b)   a court is required under section 58(6) to give the applicant for the order an opportunity to be heard,

the court may give the opportunity to a different accredited financial investigator who falls within subsection (3).

Definitions   For "accredited financial investigator", see s 3(5); for "customs officer", see s 454; for "restraint order", see s 88(6)(b), (7).
References   See paras 3.155, 3.156.

Exercise of powers

69 Powers of court and receiver

(1)   This section applies to—
     (a)   the powers conferred on a court by sections 41 to 60 and sections 62 to 67;
     (b)   the powers of a receiver appointed under section 48, 50 or 52.

(2)   The powers—
     (a)   must be exercised with a view to the value for the time being of realisable property being made available (by the property's realisation) for satisfying any confiscation order that has been or may be made against the defendant;
     (b)   must be exercised, in a case where a confiscation order has not been made, with a view to securing that there is no diminution in the value of realisable property;

(c) must be exercised without taking account of any obligation of the defendant or a recipient of a tainted gift if the obligation conflicts with the object of satisfying any confiscation order that has been or may be made against the defendant;

(d) may be exercised in respect of a debt owed by the Crown.

(3) Subsection (2) has effect subject to the following rules—

(a) the powers must be exercised with a view to allowing a person other than the defendant or a recipient of a tainted gift to retain or recover the value of any interest held by him;

(b) in the case of realisable property held by a recipient of a tainted gift, the powers must be exercised with a view to realising no more than the value for the time being of the gift;

(c) in a case where a confiscation order has not been made against the defendant, property must not be sold if the court so orders under subsection (4).

(4) If on an application by the defendant, or by the recipient of a tainted gift, the court decides that property cannot be replaced it may order that it must not be sold.

(5) An order under subsection (4) may be revoked or varied.

Definitions   For "confiscation order", see s 88(6)(a), (7); for "defendant", see s 88(3), (7); for "interest" in relation to land, see ss 84(2)(f), (g), 88(7); for "interest" in relation to property other than land, see ss 84(2)(h), 88(7); for "property", see ss 84(1), 88(7); for "realisable property", see ss 83, 88(7); for "recipient of a tainted gift", see ss 78(3), 88(7); for "satisfied", see ss 87(1), 88(7); for "tainted gift", see ss 77, 88(7).
References   See paras 3.157–3.159.

Committal

70 Committal by magistrates' court

(1) This section applies if—

(a) a defendant is convicted of an offence by a magistrates' court, and

(b) the prosecutor asks the court to commit the defendant to the Crown Court with a view to a confiscation order being considered under section 6.

(2) In such a case the magistrates' court—

(a) must commit the defendant to the Crown Court in respect of the offence, and

(b) may commit him to the Crown Court in respect of any other offence falling within subsection (3).

(3) An offence falls within this subsection if—

(a) the defendant has been convicted of it by the magistrates' court or any other court, and

(b) the magistrates' court has power to deal with him in respect of it.

(4) If a committal is made under this section in respect of an offence or offences—

(a) section 6 applies accordingly, and

(b) the committal operates as a committal of the defendant to be dealt with by the Crown Court in accordance with section 71.

(5)   If a committal is made under this section in respect of an offence for which (apart from this section) the magistrates' court could have committed the defendant for sentence under section 3(2) of the Sentencing Act (offences triable either way) the court must state whether it would have done so.

(6)   A committal under this section may be in custody or on bail.

Definitions   For "confiscation order", see s 88(6)(a), (7); for "defendant", see s 88(3), (7); for "Sentencing Act", see s 88(5), (7); for "sentencing the defendant for an offence", see s 88(4), (7).
References   See paras 3.160, 3.161.

71 Sentencing by Crown Court

(1)   If a defendant is committed to the Crown Court under section 70 in respect of an offence or offences, this section applies (whether or not the court proceeds under section 6).

(2)   In the case of an offence in respect of which the magistrates' court has stated under section 70(5) that it would have committed the defendant for sentence, the Crown Court—
   (a)   must inquire into the circumstances of the case, and
   (b)   may deal with the defendant in any way in which it could deal with him if he had just been convicted of the offence on indictment before it.

(3)   In the case of any other offence the Crown Court—
   (a)   must inquire into the circumstances of the case, and
   (b)   may deal with the defendant in any way in which the magistrates' court could deal with him if it had just convicted him of the offence.

Definitions   For "defendant", see s 88(3), (7); for "sentencing the defendant for an offence", see s 88(4), (7).
References   See para 3.162.

Compensation

72 Serious default

(1)   If the following three conditions are satisfied the Crown Court may order the payment of such compensation as it believes is just.

(2)   The first condition is satisfied if a criminal investigation has been started with regard to an offence and proceedings are not started for the offence.

(3)   The first condition is also satisfied if proceedings for an offence are started against a person and—
   (a)   they do not result in his conviction for the offence, or
   (b)   he is convicted of the offence but the conviction is quashed or he is pardoned in respect of it.

(4)   If subsection (2) applies the second condition is that—
   (a)   in the criminal investigation there has been a serious default by a person mentioned in subsection (9), and
   (b)   the investigation would not have continued if the default had not occurred.

(5) If subsection (3) applies the second condition is that—

    (a) in the criminal investigation with regard to the offence or in its prosecution there has been a serious default by a person who is mentioned in subsection (9), and

    (b) the proceedings would not have been started or continued if the default had not occurred.

(6) The third condition is that an application is made under this section by a person who held realisable property and has suffered loss in consequence of anything done in relation to it by or in pursuance of an order under this Part.

(7) The offence referred to in subsection (2) may be one of a number of offences with regard to which the investigation is started.

(8) The offence referred to in subsection (3) may be one of a number of offences for which the proceedings are started.

(9) Compensation under this section is payable to the applicant and—

    (a) if the person in default was or was acting as a member of a police force, the compensation is payable out of the police fund from which the expenses of that force are met;

    (b) if the person in default was a member of the Crown Prosecution Service or was acting on its behalf, the compensation is payable by the Director of Public Prosecutions;

    (c) if the person in default was a member of the Serious Fraud Office, the compensation is payable by the Director of that Office;

    (d) if the person in default was a customs officer, the compensation is payable by the Commissioners of Customs and Excise;

    (e) if the person in default was an officer of the Commissioners of Inland Revenue, the compensation is payable by those Commissioners.

Definitions   For "criminal investigation", see s 88(2), (7); for "customs officer", see s 454; for "proceedings started", see ss 85(1), (2), 88(7); for "property", see ss 84(1), 88(7); for "property held", see ss 84(2)(a), (d), 88(7); for "realisable property", see ss 83, 88(7).
References   See paras 3.163–3.168.

73 Order varied or discharged

(1) This section applies if—

    (a) the court varies a confiscation order under section 29 or discharges one under section 30, and

    (b) an application is made to the Crown Court by a person who held realisable property and has suffered loss as a result of the making of the order.

(2) The court may order the payment of such compensation as it believes is just.

(3) Compensation under this section is payable—

    (a) to the applicant;

    (b) by the Lord Chancellor.

Definitions   For "confiscation order", see s 88(6)(a), (7); for "property", see ss 84(1), 88(7); for "property held", see ss 84(2)(a), (d), 88(7); for "realisable property", see ss 83, 88(7).
References   See paras 3.169–3.171.

Enforcement abroad

74 Enforcement abroad

(1)   This section applies if—
  (a)   any of the conditions in section 40 is satisfied,
  (b)   the prosecutor or the Director believes that realisable property is situated in a country or territory outside the United Kingdom (the receiving country), and
  (c)   the prosecutor or the Director (as the case may be) sends a request for assistance to the Secretary of State with a view to it being forwarded under this section.

(2)   In a case where no confiscation order has been made, a request for assistance is a request to the government of the receiving country to secure that any person is prohibited from dealing with realisable property.

(3)   In a case where a confiscation order has been made and has not been satisfied, discharged or quashed, a request for assistance is a request to the government of the receiving country to secure that—
  (a)   any person is prohibited from dealing with realisable property;
  (b)   realisable property is realised and the proceeds are applied in accordance with the law of the receiving country.

(4)   No request for assistance may be made for the purposes of this section in a case where a confiscation order has been made and has been satisfied, discharged or quashed.

(5)   If the Secretary of State believes it is appropriate to do so he may forward the request for assistance to the government of the receiving country.

(6)   If property is realised in pursuance of a request under subsection (3) the amount ordered to be paid under the confiscation order must be taken to be reduced by an amount equal to the proceeds of realisation.

(7)   A certificate purporting to be issued by or on behalf of the requested government is admissible as evidence of the facts it states if it states—
  (a)   that property has been realised in pursuance of a request under subsection (3),
  (b)   the date of realisation, and
  (c)   the proceeds of realisation.

(8)   If the proceeds of realisation made in pursuance of a request under subsection (3) are expressed in a currency other than sterling, they must be taken to be the sterling equivalent calculated in accordance with the rate of exchange prevailing at the end of the day of realisation.

Definitions   For "confiscation order", see s 88(6)(a), (7); for "the Director", see s 1(2); for "property", see ss 84(1), 88(7); for "realisable property", see ss 83, 88(7); for "satisfied", see ss 87(1), 88(7).
References   See paras 3.172–3.177.

Interpretation

75 Criminal lifestyle

(1)   A defendant has a criminal lifestyle if (and only if) the following condition is satisfied.

(2) The condition is that the offence (or any of the offences) concerned satisfies any of these tests—
> (a) it is specified in Schedule 2;
> (b) it constitutes conduct forming part of a course of criminal activity;
> (c) it is an offence committed over a period of at least six months and the defendant has benefited from the conduct which constitutes the offence.

(3) Conduct forms part of a course of criminal activity if the defendant has benefited from the conduct and—
> (a) in the proceedings in which he was convicted he was convicted of three or more other offences, each of three or more of them constituting conduct from which he has benefited, or
> (b) in the period of six years ending with the day when those proceedings were started (or, if there is more than one such day, the earliest day) he was convicted on at least two separate occasions of an offence constituting conduct from which he has benefited.

(4) But an offence does not satisfy the test in subsection (2)(b) or (c) unless the defendant obtains relevant benefit of not less than £5000.

(5) Relevant benefit for the purposes of subsection (2)(b) is—
> (a) benefit from conduct which constitutes the offence;
> (b) benefit from any other conduct which forms part of the course of criminal activity and which constitutes an offence of which the defendant has been convicted;
> (c) benefit from conduct which constitutes an offence which has been or will be taken into consideration by the court in sentencing the defendant for an offence mentioned in paragraph (a) or (b).

(6) Relevant benefit for the purposes of subsection (2)(c) is—
> (a) benefit from conduct which constitutes the offence;
> (b) benefit from conduct which constitutes an offence which has been or will be taken into consideration by the court in sentencing the defendant for the offence mentioned in paragraph (a).

(7) The Secretary of State may by order amend Schedule 2.

(8) The Secretary of State may by order vary the amount for the time being specified in subsection (4).

Definitions   For "benefits from conduct", see ss 76(4), (7), 88(7); for "defendant", see ss 40(9)(a), 88(3), (7); for "offence concerned", see ss 6(9), 88(1), (7); for "offences concerned", see ss 6(9), 88(1), (7); for "proceedings started", see ss 85(1), (2), 88(7); for "sentencing the defendant for an offence", see s 88(4), (7).
References   See paras 3.179–3.188.

76 Conduct and benefit

(1) Criminal conduct is conduct which—
> (a) constitutes an offence in England and Wales, or
> (b) would constitute such an offence if it occurred in England and Wales.

(2) General criminal conduct of the defendant is all his criminal conduct, and it is immaterial—
> (a) whether conduct occurred before or after the passing of this Act;

(b)   whether property constituting a benefit from conduct was obtained before or after the passing of this Act.

(3)   Particular criminal conduct of the defendant is all his criminal conduct which falls within the following paragraphs—

(a)   conduct which constitutes the offence or offences concerned;

(b)   conduct which constitutes offences of which he was convicted in the same proceedings as those in which he was convicted of the offence or offences concerned;

(c)   conduct which constitutes offences which the court will be taking into consideration in deciding his sentence for the offence or offences concerned.

(4)   A person benefits from conduct if he obtains property as a result of or in connection with the conduct.

(5)   If a person obtains a pecuniary advantage as a result of or in connection with conduct, he is to be taken to obtain as a result of or in connection with the conduct a sum of money equal to the value of the pecuniary advantage.

(6)   References to property or a pecuniary advantage obtained in connection with conduct include references to property or a pecuniary advantage obtained both in that connection and some other.

(7)   If a person benefits from conduct his benefit is the value of the property obtained.

Definitions   For "defendant", see ss 40(9)(a), 88(3), (7); for "offence concerned", see ss 6(9), 88(1), (7); for "offences concerned", see ss 6(9), 88(1), (7); for "property", see ss 84(1), 88(7); for "property obtained", see ss 84(2)(b), 88(7); for "sentencing the defendant for an offence", see s 88(4), (7).
References   See paras 3.189–3.199.

77 Tainted gifts

(1)   Subsections (2) and (3) apply if—

(a)   no court has made a decision as to whether the defendant has a criminal lifestyle, or

(b)   a court has decided that the defendant has a criminal lifestyle.

(2)   A gift is tainted if it was made by the defendant at any time after the relevant day.

(3)   A gift is also tainted if it was made by the defendant at any time and was of property—

(a)   which was obtained by the defendant as a result of or in connection with his general criminal conduct, or

(b)   which (in whole or part and whether directly or indirectly) represented in the defendant's hands property obtained by him as a result of or in connection with his general criminal conduct.

(4)   Subsection (5) applies if a court has decided that the defendant does not have a criminal lifestyle.

(5)   A gift is tainted if it was made by the defendant at any time after—

(a)   the date on which the offence concerned was committed, or

(b)   if his particular criminal conduct consists of two or more offences and they were committed on different dates, the date of the earliest.

(6)   For the purposes of subsection (5) an offence which is a continuing offence is committed on the first occasion when it is committed.

(7)   For the purposes of subsection (5) the defendant's particular criminal conduct includes any conduct which constitutes offences which the court has taken into consideration in deciding his sentence for the offence or offences concerned.

(8)   A gift may be a tainted gift whether it was made before or after the passing of this Act.

(9)   The relevant day is the first day of the period of six years ending with—
>   (a)   the day when proceedings for the offence concerned were started against the defendant, or
>   (b)   if there are two or more offences and proceedings for them were started on different days, the earliest of those days.

Definitions   For "criminal conduct", see ss 76(1), 88(7); for "criminal lifestyle", see ss 75, 88(7), Sch 2; for "defendant", see ss 40(9)(a), 88(3), (7); for "general criminal conduct", see ss 76(2), 88(7); for "making a gift", see ss 78(1), (2), 88(7); for "offence concerned", see ss 6(9), 88(1), (7); for "particular criminal conduct", see ss 76(3), 88(7); for "proceedings started", see ss 85(1), (2), 88(7); for "property", see ss 84(1), 88(7); for "property obtained", see ss 84(2)(b), 88(7); for "property obtained in connection with conduct", see ss 76(6), 88(7); for "sentencing the defendant for an offence", see s 88(4), (7).
References   See paras 3.200, 3.201.

78 Gifts and their recipients

(1)   If the defendant transfers property to another person for a consideration whose value is significantly less than the value of the property at the time of the transfer, he is to be treated as making a gift.

(2)   If subsection (1) applies the property given is to be treated as such share in the property transferred as is represented by the fraction—
>   (a)   whose numerator is the difference between the two values mentioned in subsection (1), and
>   (b)   whose denominator is the value of the property at the time of the transfer.

(3)   References to a recipient of a tainted gift are to a person to whom the defendant has made the gift.

Definitions   For "defendant", see ss 40(9)(a), 88(3), (7); for "property", see ss 84(1), 88(7); for "property transferred", see ss 84(2)(c), 88(7).
References   See paras 3.202–3.204.

79 Value: the basic rule

(1)   This section applies for the purpose of deciding the value at any time of property then held by a person.

(2)   Its value is the market value of the property at that time.

(3)   But if at that time another person holds an interest in the property its value, in relation to the person mentioned in subsection (1), is the market value of his interest at that time, ignoring any charging order under a provision listed in subsection (4).

(4)   The provisions are—
   (a)   section 9 of the Drug Trafficking Offences Act 1986 (c 32);
   (b)   section 78 of the Criminal Justice Act 1988 (c 33);
   (c)   Article 14 of the Criminal Justice (Confiscation) (Northern Ireland) Order 1990 (SI 1990/2588 (NI 17));
   (d)   section 27 of the Drug Trafficking Act 1994 (c 37);
   (e)   Article 32 of the Proceeds of Crime (Northern Ireland) Order 1996 (SI 1996/1299 (NI 9)).

(5)   This section has effect subject to sections 80 and 81.

Definitions   For "interest" in relation to land, see ss 84(2)(f), (g), 88(7); for "interest" in relation to property other than land, see ss 84(2)(h), 88(7); for "property", see ss 84(1), 88(7); for "property held", see ss 84(2)(a), (d), 88(7).
References   See paras 3.205, 3.206.

---

80 Value of property obtained from conduct

(1)   This section applies for the purpose of deciding the value of property obtained by a person as a result of or in connection with his criminal conduct; and the material time is the time the court makes its decision.

(2)   The value of the property at the material time is the greater of the following—
   (a)   the value of the property (at the time the person obtained it) adjusted to take account of later changes in the value of money;
   (b)   the value (at the material time) of the property found under subsection (3).

(3)   The property found under this subsection is as follows—
   (a)   if the person holds the property obtained, the property found under this subsection is that property;
   (b)   if he holds no part of the property obtained, the property found under this subsection is any property which directly or indirectly represents it in his hands;
   (c)   if he holds part of the property obtained, the property found under this subsection is that part and any property which directly or indirectly represents the other part in his hands.

(4)   The references in subsection (2)(a) and (b) to the value are to the value found in accordance with section 79.

Definitions   For "criminal conduct", see ss 76(1), 88(7); for "property", see ss 84(1), 88(7); for "property held", see ss 84(2)(a), (d), 88(7); for "property obtained", see ss 84(2)(b), 88(7).
References   See paras 3.207–3.210.

---

81 Value of tainted gifts

(1)   The value at any time (the material time) of a tainted gift is the greater of the following—
   (a)   the value (at the time of the gift) of the property given, adjusted to take account of later changes in the value of money;
   (b)   the value (at the material time) of the property found under subsection (2).

271

(2)   The property found under this subsection is as follows—

    (a)   if the recipient holds the property given, the property found under this subsection is that property;

    (b)   if the recipient holds no part of the property given, the property found under this subsection is any property which directly or indirectly represents it in his hands;

    (c)   if the recipient holds part of the property given, the property found under this subsection is that part and any property which directly or indirectly represents the other part in his hands.

(3)   The references in subsection (1)(a) and (b) to the value are to the value found in accordance with section 79.

Definitions   For "property", see ss 84(1), 88(7); for "property held", see ss 84(2)(a), (d), 88(7); for "tainted gift", see ss 77, 88(7).
References   See paras 3.207–3.210.

82 Free property

Property is free unless an order is in force in respect of it under any of these provisions—

    (a)   section 27 of the Misuse of Drugs Act 1971 (c 38) (forfeiture orders);

    (b)   Article 11 of the Criminal Justice (Northern Ireland) Order 1994 (SI 1994/2795 (NI 15)) (deprivation orders);

    (c)   Part 2 of the Proceeds of Crime (Scotland) Act 1995 (c 43) (forfeiture of property used in crime);

    (d)   section 143 of the Sentencing Act (deprivation orders);

    (e)   section 23 or 111 of the Terrorism Act 2000 (c 11) (forfeiture orders);

    (f)   section 246, 266, 295(2) or 298(2) of this Act.

Definitions   For "property", see ss 84(1), 88(7); for "Sentencing Act", see s 88(5), (7).
References   See paras 3.211, 3.212.

83 Realisable property

Realisable property is—

    (a)   any free property held by the defendant;

    (b)   any free property held by the recipient of a tainted gift.

Definitions   For "defendant", see ss 40(9)(a), 88(3), (7); for "free property", see ss 82, 88(7); for "property", see ss 84(1), 88(7); for "property held", see ss 84(2)(a), (d), 88(7); for "recipient of a tainted gift", see ss 78(3), 88(7); for "tainted gift", see ss 77, 88(7).
References   See paras 3.211, 3.212.

84 Property: general provisions

(1)   Property is all property wherever situated and includes—

    (a)   money;

    (b)   all forms of real or personal property;

    (c)   things in action and other intangible or incorporeal property.

(2)   The following rules apply in relation to property—

    (a)   property is held by a person if he holds an interest in it;

    (b)   property is obtained by a person if he obtains an interest in it;

(c) property is transferred by one person to another if the first one transfers or grants an interest in it to the second;

(d) references to property held by a person include references to property vested in his trustee in bankruptcy, permanent or interim trustee (within the meaning of the Bankruptcy (Scotland) Act 1985 (c 66)) or liquidator;

(e) references to an interest held by a person beneficially in property include references to an interest which would be held by him beneficially if the property were not so vested;

(f) references to an interest, in relation to land in England and Wales or Northern Ireland, are to any legal estate or equitable interest or power;

(g) references to an interest, in relation to land in Scotland, are to any estate, interest, servitude or other heritable right in or over land, including a heritable security;

(h) references to an interest, in relation to property other than land, include references to a right (including a right to possession).

References   See paras 3.213–3.215.

---

85 Proceedings

(1) Proceedings for an offence are started—
  (a) when a justice of the peace issues a summons or warrant under section 1 of the Magistrates' Courts Act 1980 (c 43) in respect of the offence;
  (b) when a person is charged with the offence after being taken into custody without a warrant;
  (c) when a bill of indictment is preferred under section 2 of the Administration of Justice (Miscellaneous Provisions) Act 1933 (c 36) in a case falling within subsection (2)(b) of that section (preferment by Court of Appeal or High Court judge).

(2) If more than one time is found under subsection (1) in relation to proceedings they are started at the earliest of them.

(3) If the defendant is acquitted on all counts in proceedings for an offence, the proceedings are concluded when he is acquitted.

(4) If the defendant is convicted in proceedings for an offence and the conviction is quashed or the defendant is pardoned before a confiscation order is made, the proceedings are concluded when the conviction is quashed or the defendant is pardoned.

(5) If a confiscation order is made against the defendant in proceedings for an offence (whether the order is made by the Crown Court or the Court of Appeal) the proceedings are concluded—
  (a) when the order is satisfied or discharged, or
  (b) when the order is quashed and there is no further possibility of an appeal against the decision to quash the order.

(6) If the defendant is convicted in proceedings for an offence but the Crown Court decides not to make a confiscation order against him, the following rules apply—

(a) if an application for leave to appeal under section 31(2) is refused, the proceedings are concluded when the decision to refuse is made;

(b) if the time for applying for leave to appeal under section 31(2) expires without an application being made, the proceedings are concluded when the time expires;

(c) if on appeal under section 31(2) the Court of Appeal confirms the Crown Court's decision, and an application for leave to appeal under section 33 is refused, the proceedings are concluded when the decision to refuse is made;

(d) if on appeal under section 31(2) the Court of Appeal confirms the Crown Court's decision, and the time for applying for leave to appeal under section 33 expires without an application being made, the proceedings are concluded when the time expires;

(e) if on appeal under section 31(2) the Court of Appeal confirms the Crown Court's decision, and on appeal under section 33 the House of Lords confirms the Court of Appeal's decision, the proceedings are concluded when the House of Lords confirms the decision;

(f) if on appeal under section 31(2) the Court of Appeal directs the Crown Court to reconsider the case, and on reconsideration the Crown Court decides not to make a confiscation order against the defendant, the proceedings are concluded when the Crown Court makes that decision;

(g) if on appeal under section 33 the House of Lords directs the Crown Court to reconsider the case, and on reconsideration the Crown Court decides not to make a confiscation order against the defendant, the proceedings are concluded when the Crown Court makes that decision.

(7) In applying subsection (6) any power to extend the time for making an application for leave to appeal must be ignored.

(8) In applying subsection (6) the fact that a court may decide on a later occasion to make a confiscation order against the defendant must be ignored.

Definitions For "confiscation order", see s 88(6)(a), (7); for "defendant", see ss 40(9)(a), 88(3), (7).
References See para 3.216.

86 Applications

(1) An application under section 19, 20, 27 or 28 is concluded—

(a) in a case where the court decides not to make a confiscation order against the defendant, when it makes the decision;

(b) in a case where a confiscation order is made against him as a result of the application, when the order is satisfied or discharged, or when the order is quashed and there is no further possibility of an appeal against the decision to quash the order;

(c) in a case where the application is withdrawn, when the person who made the application notifies the withdrawal to the court to which the application was made.

(2) An application under section 21 or 22 is concluded—

(a) in a case where the court decides not to vary the confiscation order concerned, when it makes the decision;

> (b) in a case where the court varies the confiscation order as a result of the application, when the order is satisfied or discharged, or when the order is quashed and there is no further possibility of an appeal against the decision to quash the order;
>
> (c) in a case where the application is withdrawn, when the person who made the application notifies the withdrawal to the court to which the application was made.

Definitions For "confiscation order", see s 88(6)(a), (7); for "defendant", see s 88(3), (7); for "satisfied", see ss 87(1), 88(7).
References See para 3.216.

87 Confiscation orders

(1) A confiscation order is satisfied when no amount is due under it.

(2) A confiscation order is subject to appeal until there is no further possibility of an appeal on which the order could be varied or quashed; and for this purpose any power to grant leave to appeal out of time must be ignored.

Definitions For "confiscation order", see s 88(6)(a), (7).
References see para 3.216.

88 Other interpretative provisions

(1) A reference to the offence (or offences) concerned must be construed in accordance with section 6(9).

(2) A criminal investigation is an investigation which police officers or other persons have a duty to conduct with a view to it being ascertained whether a person should be charged with an offence.

(3) A defendant is a person against whom proceedings for an offence have been started (whether or not he has been convicted).

(4) A reference to sentencing the defendant for an offence includes a reference to dealing with him otherwise in respect of the offence.

(5) The Sentencing Act is the Powers of Criminal Courts (Sentencing) Act 2000 (c 6).

(6) The following paragraphs apply to references to orders—
>
> (a) a confiscation order is an order under section 6;
>
> (b) a restraint order is an order under section 41.

(7) Sections 75 to 87 and this section apply for the purposes of this Part.

Definitions For "proceedings started", see ss 85(1), (2).
References See para 3.217.

General

89 Procedure on appeal to the Court of Appeal

(1) An appeal to the Court of Appeal under this Part lies only with the leave of that Court.

(2)   Subject to rules of court made under section 53(1) of the Supreme Court Act 1981 (c 54) (distribution of business between civil and criminal divisions) the criminal division of the Court of Appeal is the division—

    (a)   to which an appeal to that Court under this Part is to lie, and

    (b)   which is to exercise that Court's jurisdiction under this Part.

(3)   In relation to appeals to the Court of Appeal under this Part, the Secretary of State may make an order containing provision corresponding to any provision in the Criminal Appeal Act 1968 (c 19) (subject to any specified modifications).

References   See paras 3.218, 3.219.

90 Procedure on appeal to the House of Lords

(1)   Section 33(3) of the Criminal Appeal Act 1968 (limitation on appeal from criminal division of the Court of Appeal) does not prevent an appeal to the House of Lords under this Part.

(2)   In relation to appeals to the House of Lords under this Part, the Secretary of State may make an order containing provision corresponding to any provision in the Criminal Appeal Act 1968 (subject to any specified modifications).

References   See para 3.220.

91 Crown Court Rules

In relation to—

    (a)   proceedings under this Part, or

    (b)   receivers appointed under this Part,

Crown Court Rules may make provision corresponding to provision in Civil Procedure Rules.

References   see para 3.221.

PART 3
CONFISCATION: SCOTLAND

Confiscation orders

92 Making of order

(1)   The court must act under this section where the following three conditions are satisfied.

(2)   The first condition is that an accused falls within either of the following paragraphs—

    (a)   he is convicted of an offence or offences, whether in solemn or summary proceedings, or

    (b)   in the case of summary proceedings in respect of an offence (without proceeding to conviction) an order is made discharging him absolutely.

(3)   The second condition is that the prosecutor asks the court to act under this section.

(4)   The third condition is that the court decides to order some disposal in respect of the accused; and an absolute discharge is a disposal for the purpose of this subsection.

(5)   If the court acts under this section it must proceed as follows—
  (a)   it must decide whether the accused has a criminal lifestyle;
  (b)   if it decides that he has a criminal lifestyle it must decide whether he has benefited from his general criminal conduct;
  (c)   if it decides that he does not have a criminal lifestyle it must decide whether he has benefited from his particular criminal conduct.

(6)   If the court decides under subsection (5)(b) or (c) that the accused has benefited from the conduct referred to—
  (a)   it must decide the recoverable amount, and
  (b)   it must make an order (a confiscation order) requiring him to pay that amount.

(7)   But the court must treat the duty in subsection (6) as a power if it believes that any victim of the conduct has at any time started or intends to start proceedings against the accused in respect of loss, injury or damage sustained in connection with the conduct.

(8)   Before making an order under this section the court must take into account any representations made to it by any person whom the court thinks is likely to be affected by the order.

(9)   The standard of proof required to decide any question arising under subsection (5) or (6) is the balance of probabilities.

(10) The first condition is not satisfied if the accused is unlawfully at large (but section 111 may apply).

(11) For the purposes of any appeal or review, an order under this section is a sentence.

(12) References in this Part to the offence (or offences) concerned are to the offence (or offences) mentioned in subsection (2).

(13) In this section and sections 93 to 118 "the court" means the High Court of Justiciary or the sheriff.

Definitions   For "accused", see s 154(1); for "benefits from conduct", see s 143(4)–(7); for "conviction", see s 154(1); for "criminal conduct", see s 143(1); for "criminal lifestyle", see s 142, Sch 2; for "general criminal conduct", see s 143(2); for "particular criminal conduct", see s 143(3); for "recoverable amount", see s 93(1)–(3).
References   See paras 4.2, 4.3.

93 Recoverable amount

(1)   The recoverable amount for the purposes of section 92 is an amount equal to the accused's benefit from the conduct concerned.

(2)   But if the accused shows that the available amount is less than that benefit the recoverable amount is—
  (a)   the available amount, or

(b)   a nominal amount, if the available amount is nil.

(3)   But if section 92(7) applies the recoverable amount is such amount as—
    (a)   the court believes is just, but
    (b)   does not exceed the amount found under subsection (1) or (2) (as the case may be).

(4)   In calculating the accused's benefit from the conduct concerned for the purposes of subsection (1), any property in respect of which—
    (a)   a recovery order is in force under section 266, or
    (b)   a forfeiture order is in force under section 298(2),
must be ignored.

(5)   If the court decides the available amount, it must include in the confiscation order a statement of its findings as to the matters relevant for deciding that amount.

Definitions   For "accused", see s 154(1); for "benefits from conduct", see s 143(4)–(7); for "confiscation order", see s 154(1); for "the court", see s 92(13); for "property", see s 150.
References   See para 4.1.

---

94 Accused's benefit

(1)   If the court is acting under section 92 this section applies for the purpose of—
    (a)   deciding whether the accused has benefited from conduct, and
    (b)   deciding his benefit from the conduct.

(2)   The court must take account of—
    (a)   conduct occurring up to the time it makes its decision;
    (b)   property obtained up to that time.

(3)   Subsection (4) applies if—
    (a)   the conduct concerned is general criminal conduct,
    (b)   a confiscation order mentioned in subsection (5) has at an earlier time been made against the accused, and
    (c)   his benefit for the purposes of that order was benefit from his general criminal conduct.

(4)   His benefit found at the time the last confiscation order mentioned in subsection (3)(c) was made against him must be taken for the purposes of this section to be his benefit from his general criminal conduct at that time.

(5)   If the conduct concerned is general criminal conduct the court must deduct the aggregate of the following amounts—
    (a)   the amount ordered to be paid under each confiscation order previously made against the accused;
    (b)   the amount ordered to be paid under each confiscation order previously made against him under—
      (i)   the Drug Trafficking Offences Act 1986 (c 32);
      (ii)   Part 1 of the Criminal Justice (Scotland) Act 1987 (c 41);
      (iii)   Part 6 of the Criminal Justice Act 1988 (c 33);
      (iv)   the Criminal Justice (Confiscation) (Northern Ireland) Order 1990 (SI 1990/2588 (NI 17));
      (v)   Part 1 of the Drug Trafficking Act 1994 (c 37);
      (vi)   Part 1 of the Proceeds of Crime (Scotland) Act 1995 (c 43);

(vii) the Proceeds of Crime (Northern Ireland) Order 1996 (SI 1996/1299 (NI 9)); or

(viii) Part 2 or 4 of this Act.

(6) But subsection (5) does not apply to an amount which has been taken into account for the purposes of a deduction under that subsection on any earlier occasion.

(7) The reference to general criminal conduct in the case of a confiscation order made under any of the provisions listed in subsection (5)(b) is a reference to conduct in respect of which a court is required or entitled to make one or more assumptions for the purpose of assessing a person's benefit from the conduct.

Definitions   For "accused", see s 154(1); for "benefits from conduct", see s 143(4)–(7); for "confiscation order", see s 154(1); for "the court", see s 92(13); for "general criminal conduct", see s 143(2); for "property", see s 150.
References   See para 4.1.

95 Available amount

(1)   For the purposes of deciding the recoverable amount, the available amount is the aggregate of—

    (a)   the total of the values (at the time the confiscation order is made) of all the free property then held by the accused minus the total amount payable in pursuance of obligations which then have priority, and

    (b)   the total of the values (at that time) of all tainted gifts.

(2)   An obligation has priority if—

    (a)   it is an obligation of the accused to pay an amount due in respect of a fine or other order of a court which was imposed or made on conviction for an offence and at any time before the confiscation order is made, or

    (b)   it is an obligation of the accused to pay a sum which would be—

        (i)   a preferred debt if the accused's estate were sequestrated on the date of the confiscation order, or

        (ii)   a preferential debt if his winding up were ordered on that date.

(3)   In subsection (2)—

"preferred debt" has the meaning given by section 51(2) of the Bankruptcy (Scotland) Act 1985 (c 66);

"preferential debt" has the meaning given by section 386 of the Insolvency Act 1986 (c 45).

Definitions   For "accused", see s 154(1); for "confiscation order", see s 154(1); for "conviction", see s 154(1); for "free property", see s 148; for "property", see s 150; for "value . . . tainted gifts", see s 147.
References   See para 4.1.

96 Assumptions to be made in case of criminal lifestyle

(1)   Where the court decides under section 92 that the accused has a criminal lifestyle it must make the following four assumptions for the purpose of—

    (a)   deciding whether he has benefited from his general criminal conduct, and

    (b)   deciding his benefit from the conduct.

(2)   The first assumption is that any property transferred to the accused at any time after the relevant day was obtained by him—

    (a)   as a result of his general criminal conduct, and

    (b)   at the earliest time he appears to have held it.

(3)   The second assumption is that any property held by the accused at any time after the date of conviction was obtained by him—

    (a)   as a result of his general criminal conduct, and

    (b)   at the earliest time he appears to have held it.

(4)   The third assumption is that any expenditure incurred by the accused at any time after the relevant day was met from property obtained by him as a result of his general criminal conduct.

(5)   The fourth assumption is that, for the purpose of valuing any property obtained (or assumed to have been obtained) by the accused, he obtained it free of any other interests in it.

(6)   But the court must not make any of those assumptions in relation to particular property or expenditure if—

    (a)   the assumption is shown to be incorrect, or

    (b)   there would be a serious risk of injustice if the assumption were made.

(7)   If the court does not make one or more of those assumptions it must state its reasons.

(8)   The relevant day is the first day of the period of six years ending with—

    (a)   the day when proceedings for the offence concerned were instituted against the accused, or

    (b)   if there are two or more offences and proceedings for them were instituted on different days, the earliest of those days.

(9)   But if a confiscation order mentioned in section 94(3)(c) has been made against the accused at any time during the period mentioned in subsection (8)—

    (a)   the relevant day is the day when the accused's benefit was calculated for the purposes of the last such confiscation order;

    (b)   the second assumption does not apply to any property which was held by him on or before the relevant day.

(10)   The date of conviction is—

    (a)   the date on which the accused was convicted of the offence concerned, or

    (b)   if there are two or more offences and the convictions are on different dates, the date of the latest.

Definitions   For "accused", see s 154(1); for "benefits from conduct", see s 143(4)–(7); for "confiscation order", see s 154(1); for "conviction", see s 154(1); for "the court", see s 92(13); for "criminal lifestyle", see s 142; for "general criminal conduct", see s 143(2); for "offence concerned", see s 92(12); for "proceedings", see s 151; for "property", see s 150.
References   See para 4.1.

---

97 Effect of order on court's other powers

(1)   If the court decides to make a confiscation order it must act as mentioned in subsections (2) and (4) in respect of the offence or offences concerned.

(2) The court must take account of the confiscation order before—
  (a) it imposes a fine on the accused, or
  (b) it makes an order falling within subsection (3).

(3) These orders fall within this subsection—
  (a) an order involving payment by the accused, other than a compensation order under section 249 of the Procedure Act (compensation orders);
  (b) an order under section 27 of the Misuse of Drugs Act 1971 (c 38) (forfeiture orders);
  (c) an order under Part 2 of the Proceeds of Crime (Scotland) Act 1995 (c 43) (forfeiture orders);
  (d) an order under section 23 of the Terrorism Act 2000 (c 11) (forfeiture orders).

(4) Subject to subsection (2), the court must leave the confiscation order out of account in deciding the appropriate sentence for the accused.

(5) Subsection (6) applies if—
  (a) a court makes both a confiscation order and a compensation order under section 249 of the Procedure Act against the same person in the same proceedings, and
  (b) the court believes he will not have sufficient means to satisfy both the orders in full.

(6) In such a case the court must direct that so much of the compensation as it specifies is to be paid out of any sums recovered under the confiscation order; and the amount it specifies must be the amount it believes will not be recoverable because of the insufficiency of the person's means.

Definitions   For "accused", see s 154(1); for "confiscation order", see s 154(1); for "the court", see s 92(13); for "offence concerned", see s 92(12); for "the Procedure Act", see s 154(1).
References   See para 4.1.

98 Disposal of family home

(1) This section applies where a confiscation order has been made in relation to any person and the prosecutor has not satisfied the court that the person's interest in his family home has been acquired as a benefit from his criminal conduct.

(2) Where this section applies, then, before the administrator disposes of any right or interest in the person's family home he shall—
  (a) obtain the relevant consent; or
  (b) where he is unable to do so, apply to the court for authority to carry out the disposal.

(3) On an application being made to it under subsection (2)(b), the court, after having regard to all the circumstances of the case including—
  (a) the needs and financial resources of the spouse or former spouse of the person concerned;
  (b) the needs and financial resources of any child of the family;
  (c) the length of the period during which the family home has been used as a residence by any of the persons referred to in paragraph (a) or (b),

may refuse to grant the application or may postpone the granting of the application for such period (not exceeding 12 months) as it may consider reasonable in the circumstances or may grant the application subject to such conditions as it may prescribe.

(4)   Subsection (3) shall apply—
    (a)   to an action for division and sale of the family home of the person concerned; or
    (b)   to an action for the purpose of obtaining vacant possession of that home,

brought by the administrator as it applies to an application under subsection (2)(b) and, for the purposes of this subsection, any reference in subsection (3) to the granting of the application shall be construed as a reference to the granting of decree in the action.

(5)   In this section—
    "family home", in relation to any person (in this subsection referred to as "the relevant person") means any property in which the relevant person has or had (whether alone or in common with any other person) a right or interest, being property which is occupied as a residence by the relevant person and his or her spouse or by the relevant person's spouse or former spouse (in any case with or without a child of the family) or by the relevant person with a child of the family;
    "child of the family" includes any child or grandchild of either the relevant person or his or her spouse or former spouse, and any person who has been treated by either the relevant person or his or her spouse or former spouse as if he or she were a child of the relevant person, spouse or former spouse, whatever the age of such a child, grandchild or person may be; and
    "relevant consent" means in relation to the disposal of any right or interest in a family home—
        (a)   in a case where the family home is occupied by the spouse or former spouse of the relevant person, the consent of the spouse or, as the case may be, of the former spouse, whether or not the family home is also occupied by the relevant person;
        (b)   where paragraph (a) does not apply, in a case where the family home is occupied by the relevant person with a child of the family, the consent of the relevant person.

Definitions   For "benefit from conduct", see s 143(4)–(7); for "confiscation order", see s 154(1); for "the court", see s 92(13); for "criminal conduct", see s 143(1); for "property", see s 150.
References   See paras 4.8–4.10.

Procedural matters

99 Postponement

(1)   The court may—
    (a)   proceed under section 92 before it sentences the accused for the offence (or any of the offences concerned), or
    (b)   postpone proceedings under section 92 for a specified period.

(2)   A period of postponement may be extended.

(3)   A period of postponement (including one as extended) must not end after the permitted period ends.

(4) But subsection (3) does not apply if there are exceptional circumstances or if the accused has failed to comply with an order under section 102(1).

(5) The permitted period is the period of two years starting with the date of conviction.

(6) But if—
  (a) the accused appeals against his conviction for the offence (or any of the offences) concerned, and
  (b) the period of three months (starting with the day when the appeal is determined or otherwise disposed of) ends after the period found under subsection (5),
the permitted period is that period of three months.

(7) A postponement or extension may be made—
  (a) on application by the accused;
  (b) on application by the prosecutor;
  (c) by the court of its own motion.

(8) If—
  (a) proceedings are postponed for a period, and
  (b) an application to extend the period is made before it ends,
the application may be granted even after the period ends.

(9) The date of conviction is—
  (a) the date on which the accused was convicted of the offence concerned, or
  (b) if there are two or more offences and the convictions were on different dates, the date of the latest.

(10) A confiscation order must not be quashed only on the ground that there was a defect or omission in the procedure connected with the application for or the granting of a postponement.

(11) But subsection (10) does not apply if before it made the confiscation order the court has—
  (a) imposed a fine on the accused;
  (b) made an order falling within section 97(3);
  (c) made an order under section 249 of the Procedure Act.

Definitions   For "accused", see s 154(1); for "confiscation order", see s 154(1); for "conviction", see s 154(1); for "the court", see s 92(13); for "offence concerned", see s 92(12); for "the Procedure Act", see s 154(1).
References   See para 4.11.

---

100 Effect of postponement

(1) If the court postpones proceedings under section 92 it may proceed to sentence the accused for the offence (or any of the offences) concerned.

(2) Subsection (1) is without prejudice to sections 201 and 202 of the Procedure Act.

(3) In sentencing the accused for the offence (or any of the offences) concerned in the postponement period the court must not—
  (a) impose a fine on him,
  (b) make an order falling within section 97(3), or

    (c)   make an order for the payment of compensation under section 249 of the Procedure Act.

(4)   If the court sentences the accused for the offence (or any of the offences) concerned in the postponement period, after that period ends it may vary the sentence by—

    (a)   imposing a fine on him,

    (b)   making an order falling within section 97(3), or

    (c)   making an order for the payment of compensation under section 249 of the Procedure Act.

(5)   But the court may proceed under subsection (4) only within the period of 28 days which starts with the last day of the postponement period.

(6)   Where the court postpones proceedings under section 92 following conviction on indictment, section 109(1) of the Procedure Act (intimation of intention to appeal against conviction or conviction and sentence) has effect as if the reference to the final determination of the proceedings were a reference to the relevant day.

(7)   Despite subsection (6), the accused may appeal under section 106 of the Procedure Act against any confiscation order made, or any other sentence passed, after the end of the postponement period, in respect of the conviction.

(8)   Where the court postpones proceedings under section 92 following conviction on complaint—

    (a)   section 176(1) of the Procedure Act (stated case: manner and time of appeal) has effect in relation to an appeal under section 175(2)(a) or (d) as if the reference to the final determination of the proceedings were a reference to the relevant day, and

    (b)   the draft stated case in such an appeal must be prepared and issued within 3 weeks of the relevant day.

(9)   Despite subsection (8), the accused may appeal under section 175(2)(b), and the prosecutor may appeal under section 175(3)(b), of the Procedure Act against any confiscation order made, or any other sentence passed, after the end of the postponement period, in respect of the conviction.

(10)   The relevant day is—

    (a)   in the case of an appeal against conviction where the court has sentenced the accused under subsection (1), the day on which the postponement period commenced;

    (b)   in any other case, the day on which sentence is passed in open court.

(11)   The postponement period is the period for which proceedings under section 92 are postponed.

Definitions   For "accused", see s 154(1); for "confiscation order", see s 154(1); for "conviction", see s 154(1); for "the court", see s 92(13); for "offence concerned", see s 92(12); for "the Procedure Act", see s 154(1); for "sentence the accused", see s 154(3).
References   See para 4.1.

101 Statement of information

(1)   When the court is proceeding under section 92 the prosecutor must, within such period as the court may order, give the court a statement of information.

(2)   If the prosecutor believes the accused has a criminal lifestyle the statement of information is a statement of matters the prosecutor believes are relevant in connection with deciding these issues—

(a)   whether the accused has a criminal lifestyle;

(b)   whether he has benefited from his general criminal conduct;

(c)   his benefit from the conduct.

(3)   A statement under subsection (2) must include information the prosecutor believes is relevant—

(a)   in connection with the making by the court of a required assumption under section 96;

(b)   for the purpose of enabling the court to decide if the circumstances are such that it must not make such an assumption.

(4)   If the prosecutor does not believe the accused has a criminal lifestyle the statement of information is a statement of matters the prosecutor believes are relevant in connection with deciding these issues—

(a)   whether the accused has benefited from his particular criminal conduct;

(b)   his benefit from the conduct.

(5)   If the prosecutor gives the court a statement of information—

(a)   he may at any time give the court a further statement of information;

(b)   he must give the court a further statement of information if it orders him to do so, and he must give it within the period the court orders.

(6)   If the court makes an order under this section it may at any time vary it by making another one.

Definitions   For "accused", see s 154(1); for "benefits from conduct", see s 143(4)–(7); for "the court", see s 92(13); for "criminal conduct", see s 143(1); for "criminal lifestyle", see s 142, Sch 2; for "general criminal conduct", see s 143(2); for "particular criminal conduct", see s 143(3).
References   See para 4.1.

102 Accused's response to statement of information

(1)   When the prosecutor gives the court a statement of information and the court is satisfied that he has served a copy on the accused, the court shall order the accused—

(a)   to indicate the extent to which he accepts each allegation in the statement, and

(b)   so far as he does not accept such an allegation, to give particulars of any matters he proposes to rely on,

within the period it orders.

(2)   Where by virtue of section 99 the court postpones proceedings under section 92, the period ordered by the court under subsection (1) shall be a period ending not less than six months before the end of the permitted period mentioned in section 99.

(3)   If the accused accepts to any extent an allegation in a statement of information the court may treat his acceptance as conclusive of the matters to which it relates for the purpose of deciding the issues referred to in section 101(2) or (4) (as the case may be).

(4)   If the accused fails in any respect to comply with an order under subsection (1) he may be treated for the purposes of subsection (3) as accepting every allegation in the statement of information apart from—

(a)   any allegation in respect of which he has complied with the requirement;

(b)   any allegation that he has benefited from his general or particular criminal conduct.

(5)   Where—

(a)   an allegation in a statement of information is challenged by the accused, or

(b)   the matters referred to in subsection (1)(b) are challenged by the prosecutor,

the court must consider the matters being challenged at a hearing.

(6)   The judge presiding at the hearing may, if he is not the trial judge and he considers it in the interests of justice to do so, adjourn the hearing to a date when the trial judge is available.

(7)   If the court makes an order under this section it may at any time vary it by making another one.

(8)   No acceptance under this section that the accused has benefited from conduct is admissible in evidence in proceedings for an offence.

Definitions   For "accused", see s 154(1); for "benefits from conduct", see s 143(4)–(7); for "the court", see s 92(13); for "criminal conduct", see s 143(1); for "general criminal conduct", see s 143(2); for "particular criminal conduct", see s 143(3).
References   See paras 4.12–4.15.

---

103 Provision of information by accused

(1)   For the purpose of obtaining information to help it in carrying out its functions under section 92 the court may at any time order the accused to give it information specified in the order.

(2)   An order under this section may require all or a specified part of the information to be given in a specified manner and before a specified date.

(3)   If the accused fails without reasonable excuse to comply with an order under this section the court may draw such inference as it thinks appropriate.

(4)   Subsection (3) does not affect any power of the court to deal with the accused in respect of a failure to comply with an order under this section.

(5)   If the prosecutor accepts to any extent an allegation made by the accused—

(a)   in giving information required by an order under this section, or

(b)   in any other statement given to the court in relation to any matter relevant to deciding the available amount under section 95,

the court may treat the acceptance as conclusive of the matters to which it relates.

(6)   For the purposes of this section an allegation may be accepted in a manner ordered by the court.

(7)   If the court makes an order under this section it may at any time vary it by making another order.

(8)   No information given under this section which amounts to an admission by the accused that he has benefited from criminal conduct is admissible in evidence in proceedings for an offence.

Definitions   For "accused", see s 154(1); for "benefits from conduct", see s 143(4)–(7); for "the court", see s 92(13); for "criminal conduct", see s 143(1).
References   See para 4.1.

Reconsideration

104 No order made: reconsideration of case

(1)   This section applies if—
  (a)   the first condition in section 92 is satisfied but no court has proceeded under that section,
  (b)   the prosecutor has evidence which was not available to him on the relevant date,
  (c)   before the end of the period of six years starting with the date of conviction the prosecutor applies to the court to consider the evidence, and
  (d)   after considering the evidence the court thinks it is appropriate for it to proceed under section 92.

(2)   The court must proceed under section 92, and when it does so subsections (3) to (8) below apply.

(3)   If the court has already sentenced the accused for the offence (or any of the offences) concerned section 92(4) does not apply.

(4)   Section 94(2) does not apply, and the rules applying instead are that the court must take account of—
  (a)   conduct occurring before the relevant date;
  (b)   property obtained before that date;
  (c)   property obtained on or after that date if it was obtained as a result of or in connection with conduct occurring before that date.

(5)   In relation to the assumptions that the court must make under section 96—
  (a)   the first and second assumptions do not apply with regard to property first held by the accused on or after the relevant date;
  (b)   the third assumption does not apply with regard to expenditure incurred by him on or after that date;
  (c)   the fourth assumption does not apply with regard to property obtained (or assumed to have been obtained) by him on or after that date.

(6)   The recoverable amount for the purposes of section 92 is such amount as—
  (a)   the court believes is just, but
  (b)   does not exceed the amount found under section 93.

(7)   In arriving at the just amount the court must have regard in particular to—
  (a)   the amount found under section 93;
  (b)   any fine imposed on the accused in respect of the offence (or any of the offences) concerned;
  (c)   any order which falls within section 97(3) and has been made against him in respect of the offence (or any of the offences) concerned and

has not already been taken into account by a court in deciding what is the free property held by the accused for the purposes of section 95;

    (d)   any compensation order which has been made against him in respect of the offence (or any of the offences) concerned under section 249 of the Procedure Act.

(8)   If an order for payment of compensation under section 249 of the Procedure Act has been made against the accused in respect of the offence or offences concerned, section 97(5) and (6) do not apply.

(9)   The relevant date is—

    (a)   if the court made a decision not to proceed under section 92, the date of the decision;

    (b)   if the court did not make such a decision, the date of the conviction.

(10)   The date of conviction is—

    (a)   the date on which the accused was convicted of the offence concerned, or

    (b)   if there are two or more offences and the convictions were on different dates, the date of the latest.

(11)   In this section references to the court are to the court which had jurisdiction in respect of the offence or offences concerned to make a confiscation order.

Definitions   For "accused", see s 154(1); for "confiscation order", see s 154(1); for "conviction", see s 154(1); for "the court", see s 92(13); for "free property", see s 148; for "offence concerned", see s 92(12); for "Procedure Act", see s 154(1); for "property", see s 150(1); for "property held", see s 150(2)(a), (d); for "property obtained", see s 150(2)(b); for "property obtained . . . in connection with conduct", see s 143(6); for "sentenced the accused", see s 154(3).
References   See para 4.1.

---

105 No order made: reconsideration of benefit

(1)   This section applies if the following two conditions are satisfied.

(2)   The first condition is that in proceeding under section 92 the court has decided that—

    (a)   the accused has a criminal lifestyle but has not benefited from his general criminal conduct, or

    (b)   the accused does not have a criminal lifestyle and has not benefited from his particular criminal conduct.

(3)   The second condition is that—

    (a)   the prosecutor has evidence which was not available to him when the court decided that the accused had not benefited from his general or particular criminal conduct,

    (b)   before the end of the period of six years starting with the date of conviction the prosecutor applies to the court to consider the evidence, and

    (c)   after considering the evidence the court concludes that it would have decided that the accused had benefited from his general or particular criminal conduct (as the case may be) if the evidence had been available to it.

(4)   If this section applies the court—
- (a)   must make a fresh decision under section 92(5)(b) or (c) as to whether the accused has benefited from his general or particular criminal conduct (as the case may be);
- (b)   may make a confiscation order under that section.

(5)   Subsections (6) to (11) below apply if the court proceeds under section 92 in pursuance of this section.

(6)   If the court has already sentenced the accused for the offence (or any of the offences) concerned section 92(4) does not apply.

(7)   Section 94(2) does not apply, and the rules applying instead are that the court must take account of—
- (a)   conduct occurring before the date of the original decision that the accused had not benefited from his general or particular criminal conduct;
- (b)   property obtained before that date;
- (c)   property obtained on or after that date if it was obtained as a result of or in connection with conduct occurring before that date.

(8)   In relation to the assumptions that the court must make under section 96—
- (a)   the first and second assumptions do not apply with regard to property first held by the accused on or after the date of the original decision that the accused had not benefited from his general or particular criminal conduct;
- (b)   the third assumption does not apply with regard to expenditure incurred by him on or after that date;
- (c)   the fourth assumption does not apply with regard to property obtained (or assumed to have been obtained) by him on or after that date.

(9)   The recoverable amount for the purposes of section 92 is such amount as—
- (a)   the court believes is just, but
- (b)   does not exceed the amount found under section 93.

(10) In arriving at the just amount the court must have regard in particular to—
- (a)   the amount found under section 93;
- (b)   any fine imposed on the accused in respect of the offence (or any of the offences) concerned;
- (c)   any order which falls within section 97(3) and has been made against him in respect of the offence (or any of the offences) concerned and has not already been taken into account by a court in deciding what is the free property held by the accused for the purposes of section 95;
- (d)   any compensation order which has been made against him in respect of the offence (or any of the offences) concerned under section 249 of the Procedure Act.

(11) If an order for the payment of compensation under section 249 of the Procedure Act has been made against the accused in respect of the offence or offences concerned, section 97(5) and (6) do not apply.

(12) The date of conviction is the date found by applying section 104(10).

(13) In this section references to the court are to the court which had jurisdiction in respect of the offence or offences concerned to make a confiscation order.

Definitions   For "accused", see s 154(1); for "benefits from conduct", see s 143(4)–(7); for "confiscation order", see s 154(1); for "conviction", see s 154(1); for "the court", see s 92(13); for "criminal conduct", see s 143(1); for "criminal lifestyle", see s 142; for "free property", see s 148; for "general criminal conduct", see s 143(2); for "offence concerned", see s 92(12); for "particular criminal conduct", see s 143(3); for "Procedure Act", see s 154(1); for "property", see s 150(1); for "property held", see s 150(2)(a), (d); for "property obtained", see s 150(2)(b); for "property obtained . . . in connection with conduct", see s 143(6).
References   See para 4.1.

106 Order made: reconsideration of benefit

(1)   This section applies if—
- (a)   a court has made a confiscation order,
- (b)   there is evidence which was not available to the prosecutor at the relevant time,
- (c)   the prosecutor believes that if the court were to find the amount of the accused's benefit in pursuance of this section it would exceed the relevant amount,
- (d)   before the end of the period of six years starting with the date of conviction the prosecutor applies to the court to consider the evidence, and
- (e)   after considering the evidence the court thinks it is appropriate for it to proceed under this section.

(2)   The court must make a new calculation of the accused's benefit from the conduct concerned, and when it does so subsections (3) to (5) below apply.

(3)   Section 94(2) does not apply, and the rules applying instead are that the court must take account of—
- (a)   conduct occurring up to the time it decided the accused's benefit for the purposes of the confiscation order;
- (b)   property obtained up to that time;
- (c)   property obtained after that time if it was obtained as a result of or in connection with conduct occurring before that time.

(4)   In applying section 94(3) the confiscation order must be ignored.

(5)   In relation to the assumptions that the court must make under section 96—
- (a)   the first and second assumptions do not apply with regard to property first held by the accused after the time the court decided his benefit for the purposes of the confiscation order;
- (b)   the third assumption does not apply with regard to expenditure incurred by him after that time;
- (c)   the fourth assumption does not apply with regard to property obtained (or assumed to have been obtained) by him after that time.

(6)   If the amount found under the new calculation of the accused's benefit exceeds the relevant amount the court—
- (a)   must make a new calculation of the recoverable amount for the purposes of section 92, and
- (b)   if it exceeds the amount required to be paid under the confiscation order, may vary the order by substituting for the amount required to be paid such amount as it believes just.

(7)   In applying subsection (6)(a) the court must—
- (a)   take the new calculation of the accused's benefit;

    (b)   apply section 95 as if references to the time the confiscation order is made were to the time of the new calculation of the recoverable amount and as if references to the date of the confiscation order were to the date of that new calculation.

(8)   In applying subsection (6)(b) the court must have regard in particular to—
    (a)   any fine imposed on the accused for the offence (or any of the offences) concerned;
    (b)   any order which falls within section 97(3) and has been made against him in respect of the offence (or any of the offences) concerned and has not already been taken into account by a court in deciding what is the free property held by the accused for the purposes of section 95;
    (c)   any order which has been made against him in respect of the offence (or any of the offences) concerned under section 249 of the Procedure Act.

(9)   But in applying subsection (6)(b) the court must not have regard to an order falling within subsection (8)(c) if a court has made a direction under section 97(6).

(10) In deciding under this section whether one amount exceeds another the court must take account of any change in the value of money.

(11) The relevant time is—
    (a)   when the court calculated the accused's benefit for the purposes of the confiscation order, if this section has not applied previously;
    (b)   when the court last calculated the accused's benefit in pursuance of this section, if this section has applied previously.

(12) The relevant amount is—
    (a)   the amount found as the accused's benefit for the purposes of the confiscation order, if this section has not applied previously;
    (b)   the amount last found as the accused's benefit in pursuance of this section, if this section has applied previously.

(13) The date of conviction is the date found by applying section 104(10).

Definitions   For "accused", see s 154(1); for "benefits from conduct", see s 143(4)–(7); for "confiscation order", see s 154(1); for "conviction", see s 154(1); for "the court", see s 92(13); for "free property", see s 148; for "offence concerned", see s 92(12); for "Procedure Act", see s 154(1); for "property", see s 150(1); for "property held", see s 150(2)(a), (d); for "property obtained", see s 150(2)(b); for "property obtained . . . in connection with conduct", see s 143(6).
References   See para 4.1.

107 Order made: reconsideration of available amount

(1)   This section applies if—
    (a)   a court has made a confiscation order,
    (b)   the amount required to be paid was the amount found under section 93(2), and
    (c)   the prosecutor applies to the court to make a new calculation of the available amount.

(2)   In a case where this section applies the court must make the new calculation, and in doing so it must apply section 95 as if references to the time the confiscation order is made were to the time of the new calculation and as if references to the date of the confiscation order were to the date of the new calculation.

(3)   If the amount found under the new calculation exceeds the relevant amount the court may vary the order by substituting for the amount required to be paid such amount as—
- (a)   it thinks is just, but
- (b)   does not exceed the amount found as the accused's benefit from the conduct concerned.

(4)   In arriving at the just amount the court must have regard in particular to—
- (a)   any fine imposed on the accused for the offence (or any of the offences) concerned;
- (b)   any order which falls within section 97(3) and has been made against him in respect of the offence (or any of the offences) concerned and has not already been taken into account by a court in deciding what is the free property held by the accused for the purposes of section 95;
- (c)   any order which has been made against him in respect of the offence (or any of the offences) concerned under section 249 of the Procedure Act.

(5)   But in deciding what is just the court must not have regard to an order falling within subsection (4)(c) if a court has made a direction under section 97(6).

(6)   In deciding under this section whether one amount exceeds another the court must take account of any change in the value of money.

(7)   The relevant amount is—
- (a)   the amount found as the available amount for the purposes of the confiscation order, if this section has not applied previously;
- (b)   the amount last found as the available amount in pursuance of this section, if this section has applied previously.

(8)   The amount found as the accused's benefit from the conduct concerned is—
- (a)   the amount so found when the confiscation order was made, or
- (b)   if one or more new calculations of the accused's benefit have been made under section 106 the amount found on the occasion of the last such calculation.

Definitions   For "accused", see s 154(1); for "benefits from conduct", see s 143(4)–(7); for "confiscation order", see s 154(1); for "the court", see s 92(13); for "free property", see s 148; for "offence concerned", see s 92(12); for "Procedure Act", see s 154(1).
References   See para 4.1.

---

108 Inadequacy of available amount: variation of order

(1)   This section applies if—
- (a)   a court has made a confiscation order, and
- (b)   the accused or the prosecutor applies to the court to vary the order under this section.

(2)   In such a case the court must calculate the available amount and in doing so it must apply section 95 as if references to the time the confiscation order is made were to the time of the calculation and as if references to the date of the confiscation order were to the date of the calculation.

(3)   If the court finds that the available amount (as so calculated) is inadequate to meet the amount remaining to be paid it may vary the order by substituting for the amount required to be paid such smaller amount as the court believes is just.

(4)   If a person's estate has been sequestrated or he has been adjudged bankrupt, or if an order for the winding up of a company has been made, the court must take into account the extent to which realisable property held by him or by the company may be distributed among creditors.

(5)   The court may disregard any inadequacy which it thinks is attributable (wholly or partly) to anything done by the accused for the purpose of preserving property held by the recipient of a tainted gift from any risk of realisation under this Part.

(6)   In subsection (4) "company" means any company which may be wound up under the Insolvency Act 1986 (c 45) or the Insolvency (Northern Ireland) Order 1989 (SI 1989/2405 (NI 19)).

Definitions   For "accused", see s 154(1); for "confiscation order", see s 154(1); for "the court", see s 92(13); for "property", see s 150; for "tainted gifts", see s 144.
References   See paras 4.16, 4.17.

109 Inadequacy of available amount: discharge of order

(1)   This section applies if—
- (a)   a court has made a confiscation order,
- (b)   the prosecutor applies to the court to discharge the order under this section, and
- (c)   the amount remaining to be paid under the order is less than £1,000.

(2)   In such a case the court must calculate the available amount, and in doing so it must apply section 95 as if references to the time the confiscation order is made were to the time of the calculation and as if references to the date of the confiscation order were to the date of the calculation.

(3)   If the court—
- (a)   finds that the available amount (as so calculated) is inadequate to meet the amount remaining to be paid, and
- (b)   is satisfied that the inadequacy is due wholly to a specified reason or a combination of specified reasons,

it may discharge the confiscation order.

(4)   The specified reasons are—
- (a)   in a case where any of the realisable property consists of money in a currency other than sterling, that fluctuations in currency exchange rates have occurred;
- (b)   any reason specified by the Scottish Ministers.

(5)   The Scottish Ministers may by order vary the amount for the time being specified in subsection (1)(c).

Definitions   For "confiscation order", see s 154(1); for "the court", see s 92(13); for "realisable property", see s 149.
References   See para 4.18.

110 Information

(1)   This section applies if—
    (a)   the court proceeds under section 92 in pursuance of section 104 or 105, or
    (b)   the prosecutor applies under section 106.

(2)   In such a case—
    (a)   the prosecutor must give the court a statement of information within such period as the court may specify;
    (b)   section 101 applies accordingly (with appropriate modifications where the prosecutor applies under section 106);
    (c)   sections 102 and 103 apply accordingly.

Definitions   For "the court", see s 92(13).
References   See para 4.1.

Accused unlawfully at large

111 Conviction or other disposal of accused

(1)   This section applies if an accused is unlawfully at large after—
    (a)   he is convicted of an offence or offences, whether in solemn or summary proceedings, or
    (b)   in the case of summary proceedings in respect of an offence (without proceeding to conviction) an order is made discharging him absolutely.

(2)   If this section applies the court may, on the application of the prosecutor and if it believes it is appropriate for it to do so, proceed under section 92 in the same way as it must proceed if the conditions there mentioned are satisfied; but this is subject to subsection (3).

(3)   If the court proceeds under section 92 as applied by this section, this Part has effect with these modifications—
    (a)   any person the court believes is likely to be affected by an order under section 92 is entitled to appear before the court and make representations;
    (b)   the court must not make an order under section 92 unless the prosecutor has taken reasonable steps to contact the accused;
    (c)   section 92(12) applies as if the reference to subsection (2) were to subsection (1) of this section;
    (d)   sections 96, 101(3), 102 and 103 do not apply;
    (e)   sections 104, 105 and 106 do not apply while the accused is still unlawfully at large.

(4)   Once the accused has ceased to be unlawfully at large, section 104 has effect as if subsection (1)(a) read—
    "(a)   in a case where section 111 applies the court did not proceed under section 92,".

Definitions   For "accused", see s 154(1); for "conviction", see s 154(1).
References   See para 4.1.

112 Accused neither convicted nor acquitted

(1)   This section applies if—
  (a)   proceedings for an offence or offences are instituted against an accused but are not concluded,
  (b)   he is unlawfully at large, and
  (c)   the period of two years (starting with the day the court believes he first became unlawfully at large) has ended.

(2)   If this section applies the court may, on an application by the prosecutor and if it believes it is appropriate for it to do so, proceed under section 92 in the same way as it must proceed if the conditions there mentioned are satisfied; but this is subject to subsection (3).

(3)   If the court proceeds under section 92 as applied by this section, this Part has effect with these modifications—
  (a)   any person the court believes is likely to be affected by an order under section 92 is entitled to appear before the court and make representations;
  (b)   the court must not make an order under section 92 unless the prosecutor has taken reasonable steps to contact the accused;
  (c)   section 92(12) applies as if the reference to subsection (2) were to subsection (1) of this section;
  (d)   sections 96, 101(3), 102, 103, 104 and 105 do not apply;
  (e)   section 106 does not apply while the accused is still unlawfully at large.

(4)   Once the accused has ceased to be unlawfully at large, section 106 has effect as if references to the date of conviction were to—
  (a)   the day when proceedings for the offence were instituted against the accused, or
  (b)   if there are two or more offences and proceedings for them were instituted on different days, the earliest of those days.

(5)   If—
  (a)   the court makes an order under section 92 as applied by this section, and
  (b)   the accused is later convicted of the offence (or any of the offences) concerned,

section 92 does not apply so far as that conviction is concerned.

Definitions   For "accused", see s 154(1); for "the court", see s 92(13); for "offence concerned", see s 92(12); for "proceedings ... concluded", see s 151; for "proceedings ... instituted", see s 151.
References   See para 4.1.

113 Variation of order

(1)   This section applies if—
  (a)   the court makes a confiscation order under section 92 as applied by section 112,
  (b)   the accused ceases to be unlawfully at large,
  (c)   he is convicted of an offence (or any of the offences) mentioned in section 112(1)(a),

(d)　he believes that the amount required to be paid was too large (taking the circumstances prevailing when the amount was found for the purposes of the order), and

(e)　before the end of the relevant period he applies to the court to consider the evidence on which his belief is based.

(2)　If (after considering the evidence) the court concludes that the accused's belief is well founded—

(a)　it must find the amount which should have been the amount required to be paid (taking the circumstances prevailing when the amount was found for the purposes of the order), and

(b)　it may vary the order by substituting for the amount required to be paid such amount as it believes is just.

(3)　The relevant period is the period of 28 days starting with—

(a)　the date on which the accused was convicted of the offence mentioned in section 112(1)(a), or

(b)　if there are two or more offences and the convictions were on different dates, the date of the latest.

(4)　But in a case where section 112(1)(a) applies to more than one offence the court must not make an order under this section unless it is satisfied that there is no possibility of any further proceedings being taken or continued in relation to any such offence in respect of which the accused has not been convicted.

Definitions　For "accused", see s 154(1); for "confiscation order", see s 154(1); for "conviction", see s 154(1); for "the court", see s 92(13).
References　See para 4.1.

---

114 Discharge of order

(1)　Subsection (2) applies if—

(a)　the court makes a confiscation order under section 92 as applied by section 112,

(b)　the accused is later tried for the offence or offences concerned and acquitted of the offence or offences, and

(c)　he applies to the court to discharge the order.

(2)　In such a case the court must discharge the order.

(3)　Subsection (4) applies if—

(a)　the court makes a confiscation order under section 92 as applied by section 112,

(b)　the accused ceases to be unlawfully at large,

(c)　subsection (1)(b) does not apply, and

(d)　he applies to the court to discharge the order.

(4)　In such a case the court may discharge the order if it finds that—

(a)　there has been undue delay in continuing the proceedings mentioned in section 112(1), or

(b)　the prosecutor does not intend to proceed with the prosecution.

(5)　If the court discharges a confiscation order under this section it may make such a consequential or incidental order as it thinks is appropriate.

Definitions   For "accused", see s 154(1); for "confiscation order", see s 154(1); for "the court", see s 92(13); for "offence concerned", see s 92(12).
References   See para 4.1.

Appeals

115 Appeal by prosecutor

(1)   Section 108 of the Procedure Act (Lord Advocate's right of appeal in solemn proceedings) is amended as provided in subsections (2) to (4).

(2)   In subsection (1), after paragraph (c) insert—
  "(ca) a decision under section 92 of the Proceeds of Crime Act 2002 not to make a confiscation order;".

(3)   In subsection (2)(b)(ii), for the words "or (c)" substitute ", (c) or (ca)".

(4)   After subsection (2) insert—

  "(3) For the purposes of subsection (2)(b)(i) above in its application to a confiscation order by virtue of section 92(11) of the Proceeds of Crime Act 2002, the reference to the disposal being unduly lenient is a reference to the amount required to be paid by the order being unduly low."

(5)   Section 175 of the Procedure Act (right of appeal in summary proceedings) is amended as provided in subsections (6) to (8).

(6)   In subsection (4), after paragraph (c) insert—
  "(ca) a decision under section 92 of the Proceeds of Crime Act 2002 not to make a confiscation order;".

(7)   In subsection (4A)(b)(ii), for the words "or (c)" substitute ", (c) or (ca)".

(8)   After subsection (4A) insert—

  "(4B) For the purposes of subsection (4A)(b)(i) above in its application to a confiscation order by virtue of section 92(11) of the Proceeds of Crime Act 2002, the reference to the disposal being unduly lenient is a reference to the amount required to be paid by the order being unduly low."

Definitions   For "Procedure Act", see s 154(1).
References   See para 4.19.

Payment and enforcement

116 Time for payment

(1)   The amount ordered to be paid under a confiscation order must be paid on the making of the order; but this is subject to the following provisions of this section.

(2)   If the accused shows that he needs time to pay the amount ordered to be paid, the court making the confiscation order may make an order allowing payment to be made in a specified period.

(3)   The specified period—
>   (a)   must start with the day on which the confiscation order is made, and
>   (b)   must not exceed six months.

(4)   If within the specified period the accused applies to the sheriff court for the period to be extended and the court, after giving the prosecutor an opportunity of being heard, believes there are exceptional circumstances, it may make an order extending the period.

(5)   The extended period—
>   (a)   must start with the day on which the confiscation order is made, and
>   (b)   must not exceed 12 months.

(6)   An order under subsection (4)—
>   (a)   may be made after the end of the specified period, but
>   (b)   must not be made after the end of the period of twelve months starting with the day on which the confiscation order is made.

(7)   The court must not make an order under subsection (2) or (4) unless it gives the prosecutor an opportunity to make representations.

Definitions   For "accused", see s 154(1); for "confiscation order", see s 154(1); for "the court", see s 92(13).
References   See para 4.20.

117 Interest on unpaid sums

(1)   If the amount required to be paid by a person under a confiscation order is not paid when it is required to be paid (whether when the order is made or within a period specified under section 116), he must pay interest on the amount for the period for which it remains unpaid.

(2)   The rate of interest is the rate payable under a decree of the Court of Session.

(3)   For the purposes of this section no amount is required to be paid under a confiscation order if—
>   (a)   an application has been made under section 116(4),
>   (b)   the application has not been determined by the court, and
>   (c)   the period of 12 months starting with the day on which the confiscation order was made has not ended.

(4)   In applying this Part the amount of the interest must be treated as part of the amount to be paid under the confiscation order.

Definitions   For "confiscation order", see s 154(1); for "court", see s 92(13).
References   See para 4.21.

118 Application of provisions about fine enforcement

(1)   The provisions of the Procedure Act specified in subsection (2) apply, with the qualifications mentioned in that subsection, in relation to a confiscation order as if the amount ordered to be paid were a fine imposed on the accused by the court making the confiscation order.

(2)   Those provisions are—
- (a)   section 211(3) to (6);
- (b)   section 214(4) to (6), but as if the references in subsection (4) to payment by instalments were omitted;
- (c)   section 216, but as if subsection (1)—
  - (i)   gave the prosecutor an opportunity to be heard at any enquiry under that subsection; and
  - (ii)   applied whether the offender was in prison or not;
- (d)   section 217;
- (e)   section 218(2) and (3);
- (f)   section 219, provided that—
  - (i)   where a court imposes a period of imprisonment in respect of both a fine and a confiscation order the amounts in respect of which the period is imposed must, for the purposes of subsection (2), be aggregated;
  - (ii)   before imposing a period of imprisonment by virtue of that section the court must require a report from any administrator appointed in relation to the confiscation order as to whether and how he is likely to exercise his powers and duties under this Part and must take that report into account; and the court may, pending such exercise, postpone any decision as to such imposition; and
  - (iii)   where an administrator has not been appointed in relation to the confiscation order, or where the accused does not ask under section 116 for time for payment of any confiscation order imposed by the court, the prosecutor may apply to the court to postpone the imposition of any period of imprisonment for a period not exceeding 3 months to enable the prosecutor to apply to the court for the appointment of an administrator;
- (g)   section 220, but as if the reference in subsection (1) to payment of a sum by the person included a reference to payment of the sum in respect of the person by an administrator appointed in relation to the confiscation order;
- (h)   section 221, except where an administrator is appointed in relation to the confiscation order;
- (i)   section 222, except that for the purposes of that section "confiscation order" in subsection (1) above must be construed as including such an order within the meaning of the Drug Trafficking Act 1994 (c 37), the Criminal Justice (Confiscation) (Northern Ireland) Order 1990 (SI 1990/2588 (NI 17)), the Proceeds of Crime (Northern Ireland) Order 1996 (SI 1996/1299 (NI 9)) or of Part 2 or 4 of this Act;
- (j)   section 223;
- (k)   section 224.

(3)   Where a court, by virtue of subsection (1), orders the amount ordered to be paid under a confiscation order to be recovered by civil diligence under section 221 of the Procedure Act, any arrestment executed by a prosecutor under subsection (3) of section 124 of this Act is to be treated as having been executed by the court as if that subsection authorised such execution.

(4)   Subsection (5) applies where—
- (a)   a warrant for apprehension of the accused is issued for a default in payment of the amount ordered to be paid under a confiscation order in respect of an offence or offences, and

(b) at the time the warrant is issued the accused is liable to serve a period of imprisonment or detention (other than one of life imprisonment or detention for life) in respect of the offence (or any of the offences).

(5) In such a case any period of imprisonment or detention to which the accused is liable by virtue of section 219 of the Procedure Act runs from the expiry of the period of imprisonment or detention mentioned in subsection (4)(b).

Definitions For "accused", see s 154(1); for "confiscation order", see s 154(1); for "the court", see s 92(13); for "Procedure Act", see s 154(1).
References See para 4.22.

Restraint orders etc

119 Conditions for exercise of powers

(1) The court may exercise the powers conferred by section 120 if any of the following conditions is satisfied.

(2) The first condition is that—
   (a) a criminal investigation has been instituted in Scotland with regard to an offence, and
   (b) there is reasonable cause to believe that the alleged offender has benefited from his criminal conduct.

(3) The second condition is that—
   (a) proceedings for an offence have been instituted in Scotland and not concluded, and
   (b) there is reasonable cause to believe that the accused has benefited from his criminal conduct.

(4) The third condition is that—
   (a) an application by the prosecutor has been made under section 104, 105, 111 or 112 and not concluded, or the court believes that such an application is to be made, and
   (b) there is reasonable cause to believe that the accused has benefited from his criminal conduct.

(5) The fourth condition is that—
   (a) an application by the prosecutor has been made under section 106 and not concluded, or the court believes that such an application is to be made, and
   (b) there is reasonable cause to believe that the court will decide under that section that the amount found under the new calculation of the accused's benefit exceeds the relevant amount (as defined in that section).

(6) The fifth condition is that—
   (a) an application by the prosecutor has been made under section 107 and not concluded, or the court believes that such an application is to be made, and

    (b)   there is reasonable cause to believe that the court will decide under that section that the amount found under the new calculation of the available amount exceeds the relevant amount (as defined in that section).

(7)   The second condition is not satisfied if the court believes that—
    (a)   there has been undue delay in continuing the proceedings, or
    (b)   the prosecutor does not intend to proceed.

(8)   If an application mentioned in the third, fourth or fifth condition has been made the condition is not satisfied if the court believes that—
    (a)   there has been undue delay in continuing the application, or
    (b)   the prosecutor does not intend to proceed.

(9)   If the first condition is satisfied—
    (a)   references in this Part to the accused are to the alleged offender;
    (b)   references in this Part to the prosecutor are to the person the court believes is to have conduct of any proceedings for the offence;
    (c)   section 144(8) has effect as if proceedings for the offence had been instituted against the accused when the investigation was instituted.

(10) In this section, sections 120 to 140 and Schedule 3 "the court" means—
    (a)   the Court of Session, where a trial diet or a diet fixed for the purposes of section 76 of the Procedure Act in proceedings for the offence or offences concerned is to be, is being or has been held in the High Court of Justiciary;
    (b)   the sheriff exercising his civil jurisdiction, where a diet referred to in paragraph (a) is to be, is being or has been held in the sheriff court.

Definitions   For "accused", see s 154(1); for "benefits from conduct", see s 143(4)–(7); for "criminal conduct", see s 143(1); for "criminal investigation", see s 154(1); for "Procedure Act", see s 154(1); for "proceedings . . . concluded", see s 151; for "proceedings . . . instituted", see s 151.
References   See para 4.1.

---

120 Restraint orders etc

(1)   If any condition set out in section 119 is satisfied the court may make an order (a restraint order) interdicting any specified person from dealing with any realisable property held by him.

(2)   A restraint order may provide that it applies—
    (a)   to all realisable property held by the specified person whether or not the property is described in the order;
    (b)   to realisable property transferred to the specified person after the order is made.

(3)   A restraint order may be made subject to exceptions, and an exception may in particular—
    (a)   make provision for reasonable living expenses and reasonable legal expenses;
    (b)   make provision for the purpose of enabling any person to carry on any trade, business, profession or occupation;
    (c)   be made subject to conditions.

(4)   But an exception to a restraint order may not make provision for any legal expenses which—

> (a) relate to an offence which falls within subsection (5), and
> (b) are incurred by a person against whom proceedings for the offence have been instituted or by a recipient of a tainted gift.

(5) These offences fall within this subsection—
> (a) the offence mentioned in section 119(2) or (3), if the first or second condition (as the case may be) is satisfied;
> (b) the offence (or any of the offences) concerned, if the third, fourth or fifth condition is satisfied.

(6) The court may make such order as it believes is appropriate for the purpose of ensuring that the restraint order is effective.

(7) A restraint order does not affect property subject to a charge under—
> (a) section 9 of the Drug Trafficking Offences Act 1986 (c 32),
> (b) Part 6 of the Criminal Justice Act 1988 (c 33),
> (c) Article 14 of the Criminal Justice (Confiscation) (Northern Ireland) Order 1990 (SI 1990/2588 (NI 17)),
> (d) section 27 of the Drug Trafficking Act 1994 (c 37), or
> (e) Article 32 of the Proceeds of Crime (Northern Ireland) Order 1996 (SI 1996/1299 (NI 9)).

(8) Dealing with property includes removing the property from Scotland.

Definitions   For "accused", see s 154(1); for "the court", see s 119(10); for "offence", see s 92(12); for "proceedings . . . instituted", see s 151; for "property", see s 150(1); for "property held", see s 150(2)(a), (d); for "realisable property", see s 149; for "recipient of a tainted gift", see s 144(11); for "tainted gift", see s 144.
References   See para 4.1.

---

121 Application, recall and variation

(1) This section applies to a restraint order.

(2) An order may be made on an ex parte application by the prosecutor, which may be heard in chambers.

(3) The prosecutor must intimate an order to every person affected by it.

(4) Subsection (3) does not affect the time when the order becomes effective.

(5) The prosecutor and any other person affected by the order may apply to the court to recall an order or to vary it; and subsections (6) to (9) apply in such a case.

(6) If an application under subsection (5) in relation to an order has been made but not determined, realisable property to which the order applies must not be realised.

(7) The court may—
> (a) recall the order;
> (b) vary the order.

(8) In the case of a restraint order, if the condition in section 119 which was satisfied was that proceedings were instituted or an application was made, the court must recall the order on the conclusion of the proceedings or of the application (as the case may be).

(9) In the case of a restraint order, if the condition in section 119 which was satisfied was that an investigation was instituted or an application was to be made,

the court must recall the order if within a reasonable time proceedings for the offence are not instituted or the application is not made (as the case may be).

Definitions   For "the court", see s 119(10); for "proceedings . . . concluded", see s 151; for "proceedings . . . instituted", see s 151; for "property", see s 150(1); for "realisable property", see s 149; for "restraint order", see s 154(1).
References   See para 4.23.

122 Appeals

(1)   If on an application for a restraint order the court decides not to make one, the prosecutor may reclaim or appeal to the Court of Session against the decision.

(2)   The prosecutor and any person affected by the order may reclaim or appeal to the Court of Session against the decision of the court on an application under section 121(5).

Definitions   For "the court", see s 119(10); for "restraint order", see s 154(1).
References   See para 4.24.

123 Inhibition of property affected by order

(1)   On the application of the Lord Advocate, the Court of Session may, in relation to the property mentioned in subsection (2), grant warrant for inhibition against any person specified in a restraint order.

(2)   That property is the heritable realisable property to which the restraint order applies (whether generally or such of it as is specified in the application).

(3)   The warrant for inhibition—
   (a)   has effect as if granted on the dependence of an action for debt by the Lord Advocate against the person and may be executed, recalled, loosed or restricted accordingly, and
   (b)   has the effect of letters of inhibition and must forthwith be registered by the Lord Advocate in the Register of Inhibitions and Adjudications.

(4)   Section 155 of the Titles to Land Consolidation (Scotland) Act 1868 (c 101) (effective date of inhibition) applies in relation to an inhibition for which warrant is granted under subsection (1) as it applies to an inhibition by separate letters or contained in a summons.

(5)   The execution of an inhibition under this section in respect of property does not prejudice the exercise of an administrator's powers under or for the purposes of this Part in respect of that property.

(6)   An inhibition executed under this section ceases to have effect when, or in so far as, the restraint order ceases to apply in respect of the property in relation to which the warrant for inhibition was granted.

(7)   If an inhibition ceases to have effect to any extent by virtue of subsection (6) the Lord Advocate must—
   (a)   apply for the recall or, as the case may be, the restriction of the inhibition, and
   (b)   ensure that the recall or restriction is reflected in the Register of Inhibitions and Adjudications.

Definitions For "property", see s 150(1); for "realisable property", see s 149; for "restraint order", see s 154(1).
References See paras 4.25, 4.26.

124 Arrestment of property affected by order

(1)   On the application of the prosecutor the court may, in relation to moveable realisable property to which a restraint order applies (whether generally or such of it as is specified in the application), grant warrant for arrestment.

(2)   Such a warrant for arrestment may be granted only if the property would be arrestable if the person entitled to it were a debtor.

(3)   A warrant under subsection (1) has effect as if granted on the dependence of an action for debt at the instance of the prosecutor against the person and may be executed, recalled, loosed or restricted accordingly.

(4)   The execution of an arrestment under this section in respect of property does not prejudice the exercise of an administrator's powers under or for the purposes of this Part in respect of that property.

(5)   An arrestment executed under this section ceases to have effect when, or in so far as, the restraint order ceases to apply in respect of the property in relation to which the warrant for arrestment was granted.

(6)   If an arrestment ceases to have effect to any extent by virtue of subsection (5) the prosecutor must apply to the court for an order recalling, or as the case may be, restricting the arrestment.

Definitions For "the court", see s 119(10); for "property", see s 150(1); for "realisable property", see s 149; for "restraint order", see s 154(1).
References See para 4.27.

125 Management administrators

(1)   If the court makes a restraint order it may at any time, on the application of the prosecutor—

(a)   appoint an administrator to take possession of any realisable property to which the order applies and (in accordance with the court's directions) to manage or otherwise deal with the property;

(b)   order a person who has possession of property in respect of which an administrator is appointed to give him possession of it.

(2)   An appointment of an administrator may be made subject to conditions or exceptions.

(3)   Where the court makes an order under subsection (1)(b), the clerk of court must notify the accused and any person subject to the order of the making of the order.

(4)   Any dealing of the accused or any such person in relation to property to which the order applies is of no effect in a question with the administrator unless the accused or, as the case may be, that person had no knowledge of the administrator's appointment.

(5)   The court—

  (a)   may order a person holding an interest in realisable property to which the restraint order applies to make to the administrator such payment as the court specifies in respect of a beneficial interest held by the accused or the recipient of a tainted gift;

  (b)   may (on the payment being made) by order transfer, grant or extinguish any interest in the property.

(6)   The court must not—

  (a)   confer the power mentioned in subsection (1) to manage or otherwise deal with the property, or

  (b)   exercise the power conferred on it by subsection (5),

unless it gives persons holding interests in the property a reasonable opportunity to make representations to it.

(7)   The court may order that a power conferred by an order under this section is subject to such conditions and exceptions as it specifies.

(8)   Managing or otherwise dealing with property includes—

  (a)   selling the property or any part of it or interest in it;

  (b)   carrying on or arranging for another person to carry on any trade or business the assets of which are or are part of the property;

  (c)   incurring capital expenditure in respect of the property.

(9)   Subsections (1)(b) and (5) do not apply to property for the time being subject to a charge under—

  (a)   section (9) of the Drug Trafficking Offences Act 1986 (c 32);

  (b)   section 78 of the Criminal Justice Act 1988 (c 33);

  (c)   Article 14 of the Criminal Justice (Confiscation) (Northern Ireland) Order 1990 (SI 1990/2588 (NI 17));

  (d)   section 27 of the Drug Trafficking Act 1994 (c 37);

  (e)   Article 32 of the Proceeds of Crime (Northern Ireland) Order 1996 (SI 1996/1299 (NI 9)).

Definitions   For "accused", see s 154(1); for "clerk of court", see s 154(1); for "the court", see s 119(10); for "property", see s 150(1); for "realisable property", see s 149; for "recipient of a tainted gift", see s 144(11); for "restraint order", see s 154(1); for "tainted gift", see s 144.
References   See para 4.28.

126 Seizure

(1)   If a restraint order is in force a constable or a customs officer may seize any realisable property to which it applies to prevent its removal from Scotland.

(2)   Property seized under subsection (1) must be dealt with in accordance with the directions of the court which made the order.

Definitions   For "the court", see s 119(10); for "property", see s 150(1); for "realisable property", see s 149; for "restraint order", see s 154(1).
References   See para 4.30.

127 Restraint orders: restriction on proceedings and remedies

(1)   While a restraint order has effect, the court may sist any action, execution or any legal process in respect of the property to which the order applies.

(2)   If a court (whether the Court of Session or any other court) in which proceedings are pending in respect of any property is satisfied that a restraint order has been made or applied for or made in respect of the property, the court may either sist the proceedings or allow them to continue on any terms it thinks fit.

(3)   Before exercising any power conferred by subsection (2), the court must give an opportunity to be heard to—

     (a)   the applicant for the restraint order;

     (b)   any administrator appointed under section 125.

Definitions   For "the court", see s 119(10); for "property", see s 150(1); for "restraint order", see
s 154(1).
References   See para 4.31.

Realisation of property: general

128 Enforcement administrators

(1)   This section applies if—

     (a)   a confiscation order is made,

     (b)   it is not satisfied, and

     (c)   it is not subject to appeal.

(2)   In such a case the court may on the application of the prosecutor exercise the powers conferred on it by this section.

(3)   The court may appoint an administrator in respect of realisable property.

(4)   An appointment of an administrator may be made subject to conditions or exceptions.

(5)   The court may confer the powers mentioned in subsection (6) on an administrator appointed under subsection (3) above.

(6)   Those powers are—

     (a)   power to take possession of any realisable property;

     (b)   power to manage or otherwise deal with the property;

     (c)   power to realise any realisable property, in such manner as the court may specify.

(7)   The court may order any person who has possession of realisable property to give possession of it to an administrator referred to in subsection (5).

(8)   The clerk of court must notify the accused and any person subject to an order under subsection (7) of the making of the order.

(9)   Any dealing of the accused or any such person in relation to property to which the order applies is of no effect in a question with the administrator unless the accused or, as the case may be, that person had no knowledge of the administrator's appointment.

(10)   The court—

     (a)   may order a person holding an interest in realisable property to make to the administrator such payment as the court specifies in respect of a beneficial interest held by the accused or the recipient of a tainted gift;

(b)   may (on the payment being made) by order transfer, grant or extinguish any interest in the property.

(11) The court must not—
- (a)   confer the power mentioned in subsection (6)(b) or (c) in respect of property, or
- (b)   exercise the power conferred on it by subsection (10) in respect of property,

unless it gives persons holding interests in the property a reasonable opportunity to make representations to it.

(12) Managing or otherwise dealing with property includes—
- (a)   selling the property or any part of it or interest in it;
- (b)   carrying on or arranging for another person to carry on any trade or business the assets of which are or are part of the property;
- (c)   incurring capital expenditure in respect of the property.

(13) The court may order that a power conferred by an order under this section is subject to such conditions and exceptions as it specifies.

(14) Subsection (6) does not apply to property for the time being subject to a charge under—
- (a)   section 9 of the Drug Trafficking Offences Act 1986 (c 32);
- (b)   section 78 of the Criminal Justice Act 1988 (c 33);
- (c)   Article 14 of the Criminal Justice (Confiscation) (Northern Ireland) Order 1990 (SI 199/2588 (NI 17));
- (d)   section 27 of the Drug Trafficking Act 1994 (c 37);
- (e)   Article 32 of the Proceeds of Crime (Northern Ireland) Order 1996 (SI 1996/1299 (NI 9)).

Definitions   For "accused", see s 154(1); for "clerk of court", see s 154(1); for "confiscation order", see s 154(1); for "the court", see s 119(10); for "property", see s 150(1); for "realisable property", see s 149; for "recipient of a tainted gift", see s 144(11); for "tainted gift", see s 144.
References   See para 4.32.

129 Management administrators: discharge

(1)   This section applies if—
- (a)   an administrator stands appointed under section 125 in respect of realisable property (the management administrator), and
- (b)   the court appoints an administrator under section 128.

(2)   The court must order the management administrator to transfer to the other administrator all property held by him by virtue of the powers conferred on him by section 125.

(3) If the management administrator complies with an order under subsection (2) he is discharged—
- (a)   from his appointment under that section,
- (b)   from any obligation under this Act arising from his appointment.

Definitions   For "the court", see s 119(10); for "property", see s 150(1); for "realisable property", see s 149.
References   See para 4.33.

130 Application of sums by enforcement administrator

(1) This section applies to sums which—
    (a) are in the hands of an administrator appointed under section 128(3), and
    (b) fall within subsection (2).

(2) These sums fall within this subsection—
    (a) the proceeds of the realisation of property under section 128(6)(c);
    (b) any sums (other than those mentioned in paragraph (a)) in which the accused holds an interest.

(3) The sums must be applied as follows—
    (a) first, they must be applied in payment of such expenses incurred by a person acting as an insolvency practitioner as are payable under this subsection by virtue of section 432;
    (b) second, they must be applied in making any payments as directed by the court;
    (c) third, they must be applied on the accused's behalf towards satisfaction of the confiscation order.

(4) If the amount payable under any confiscation order has been fully paid and any sums remain in the administrator's hands he must distribute them—
    (a) among such persons who held (or hold) interests in the property concerned as the court directs, and
    (b) in such proportions as it directs.

(5) Before making a direction under subsection (4) the court must give persons who held (or hold) interests in the property concerned a reasonable opportunity to make representations to it.

(6) For the purposes of subsections (4) and (5) the property concerned is—
    (a) the property represented by the proceeds mentioned in subsection (2)(a);
    (b) the sums mentioned in subsection (2)(b).

(7) The administrator applies sums as mentioned in subsection (3)(c) by paying them to the appropriate clerk of court on account of the amount payable under the order.

(8) The appropriate clerk of court is the sheriff clerk of the sheriff court responsible for enforcing the confiscation order under section 211 of the Procedure Act as applied by section 118(1) of this Act.

Definitions   For "clerk of court", see s 154(1); for "confiscation order", see s 154(1); for "the court", see s 119(10); for "Procedure Act", see s 154(1); for "property", see s 150(1).
References   See para 4.34.

131 Sums received by clerk of court

(1) This section applies if a clerk of court receives sums on account of the amount payable under a confiscation order (whether the sums are received under section 130 or otherwise).

(2) The clerk of court's receipt of the sums reduces the amount payable under the order, but he must apply the sums received as follows.

(3)   First he must apply them in payment of such expenses incurred by a person acting as an insolvency practitioner as—

    (a)   are payable under this subsection by virtue of section 432, but

    (b)   are not already paid under section 130(3)(a).

(4)   If the Lord Advocate has reimbursed the administrator in respect of remuneration or expenses under section 133 the clerk of court must next apply the sums in reimbursing the Lord Advocate.

(5)   If the clerk of court received the sums under section 130 he must next apply them in payment of the administrator's remuneration and expenses.

(6)   If a direction was made under section 97(6) for an amount of compensation to be paid out of sums recovered under the confiscation order, the clerk of court must next apply the sums in payment of that amount.

(7)   If any amount remains after the clerk of court makes any payments required by the preceding provisions of this section, the amount must be disposed of in accordance with section 211(5) or (6) of the Procedure Act as applied by section 118(1) of this Act.

Definitions   For "clerk of court", see s 154(1); for "confiscation order", see s 154(1); for "Procedure Act", see s 154(1).
References   See para 4.34.

Exercise of powers

132 Powers of court and administrator

(1)   This section applies to—

    (a)   the powers conferred on a court by sections 119 to 131, 134 to 136 and Schedule 3;

    (b)   the powers of an administrator appointed under section 125 or 128(3).

(2)   The powers—

    (a)   must be exercised with a view to the value for the time being of realisable property being made available (by the property's realisation) for satisfying any confiscation order that has been or may be made against the accused;

    (b)   must be exercised, in a case where a confiscation order has not been made, with a view to securing that there is no diminution in the value of realisable property or of the proceeds of realisation;

    (c)   must be exercised without taking account of any obligation of the accused or a recipient of a tainted gift if the obligation conflicts with the object of satisfying any confiscation order that has been or may be made against the accused;

    (d)   may be exercised in respect of a debt owed by the Crown.

(3)   Subsection (2) has effect subject to the following rules—

    (a)   the powers must be exercised with a view to allowing a person other than the accused or a recipient of a tainted gift to retain or recover the value of any interest held by him;

    (b)   in the case of realisable property held by a recipient of a tainted gift, the powers must be exercised with a view to realising no more than the value for the time being of the gift;

(c) in a case where a confiscation order has not been made against the accused, property must not be realised if the court so orders under subsection (4).

(4) If on an application by the accused or by the recipient of a tainted gift the court decides that property cannot be replaced it may order that it must not be sold.

(5) An order under subsection (4) may be revoked or varied.

Definitions For "accused", see s 154(1); for "confiscation order", see s 154(1); for "the court", see s 119(10); for "realisable property", see s 149; for "property", see s 150(1); for "recipient of a tainted gift", see s 144(11); for "tainted gift", see s 144; for "value", see s 145.
References See para 4.1.

Administrators: general

133 Protection of administrators

(1) If an administrator appointed under section 125 or 128(3)—
  (a) takes action in relation to property which is not realisable property,
  (b) would be entitled to take the action if it were realisable property, and
  (c) believes on reasonable grounds that he is entitled to take the action,

he is not liable to any person in respect of any loss or damage resulting from the action, except so far as the loss or damage is caused by his negligence.

(2) Subsection (3) applies if an administrator incurs expenses in the exercise of his functions at a time when—
  (a) a confiscation order has not been made, or
  (b) a confiscation order has been made but the administrator has recovered no money.

(3) As soon as is practicable after they have been incurred the expenses must be reimbursed by the Lord Advocate.

(4) Subsection (5) applies if—
  (a) an amount is due in respect of the administrator's remuneration and expenses, but
  (b) nothing (or not enough) is available to be applied in payment of them under section 131(4).

(5) The remuneration and expenses must be paid (or must be paid to the extent of the shortfall) by the Lord Advocate.

Definitions For "confiscation order", see s 154(1); for "property", see s 150(1); for "realisable property", see s 149.
References See para 4.35.

134 Protection of persons affected

(1) This section applies where an administrator is appointed under section 125 or 128(3).

(2) The following persons may apply to the court—
  (a) any person affected by action taken by the administrator;
  (b) any person who may be affected by action the administrator proposes to take.

(3)   On an application under this section the court may make such order as it thinks appropriate.

Definitions   For "the court", see s 119(10).
References   See para 4.36.

135 Recall and variation of order

(1)   The prosecutor, an administrator and any other person affected by an order made under section 125 or 128 may apply to the court to vary or recall the order.

(2)   On an application under this section the court—
    (a)   may vary the order;
    (b)   may recall the order.

(3)   But in the case of an order under section 125—
    (a)   if the condition in section 119 which was satisfied was that proceedings were started or an application was made, the court must recall the order on the conclusion of the proceedings or of the application (as the case may be);
    (b)   if the condition which was satisfied was that an investigation was started or an application was to be made, the court must recall the order if within a reasonable time proceedings for the offence are not started or the application is not made (as the case may be).

Definitions   For "the court", see s 119(10); for "proceedings . . . started", see s 151.
References   See paras 4.37, 4.38.

136 Appeals

(1)   If on an application for an order under section 125 or 128 the court decides not to make one, the prosecutor may appeal to the Court of Session against the decision.

(2)   If the court makes an order under section 125 or 128 the following persons may appeal to the Court of Session in respect of the court's decision—
    (a)   the prosecutor;
    (b)   any person affected by the order.

(3)   If on an application for an order under section 134 the court decides not to make one, the person who applied for the order may appeal to the Court of Session against the decision.

(4)   If the court makes an order under section 134, the following persons may appeal to the Court of Session in respect of the court's decision—
    (a)   the person who applied for the order;
    (b)   any person affected by the order;
    (c)   the administrator.

(5)   The following persons may appeal to the Court of Session against a decision of the court on an application under section 135—
    (a)   the person who applied for the order in respect of which the application was made;
    (b)   any person affected by the court's decision;
    (c)   the administrator.

(6) On an appeal under this section the Court of Session may—
    (a) confirm the decision, or
    (b) make such order as it believes is appropriate.

Definitions For "the court", see s 119(10).
References See para 4.39.

137 Administrators: further provision

Schedule 3, which makes further provision about administrators appointed under section 125 and 128(3), has effect.

References See para 4.40.

138 Administrators: restriction on proceedings and remedies

(1) Where an administrator is appointed under section 128, the court may sist any action, execution or other legal process in respect of the property to which the order appointing the administrator relates.

(2) If a court (whether the Court of Session or any other court) in which proceedings are pending in respect of any property is satisfied that an application has been made for the appointment of an administrator or that an administrator has been appointed in relation to that property, the court may either sist the proceedings or allow them to continue on any terms it thinks fit.

(3) Before exercising any power conferred by subsection (2) the court must give an opportunity to be heard to—
    (a) the prosecutor;
    (b) if appointed, the administrator.

Definitions For "the court", see s 119(10); for "property", see s 150(1).
References See para 4.41.

Compensation

139 Serious default

(1) If the following three conditions are satisfied the court may order the payment of such compensation as it thinks is just.

(2) The first condition is satisfied if a criminal investigation has been instituted with regard to an offence and proceedings are not instituted for the offence.

(3) The first condition is also satisfied if proceedings for an offence are instituted against a person and—
    (a) they do not result in his conviction for the offence, or
    (b) he is convicted of the offence but the conviction is quashed or he is pardoned in respect of it.

(4) If subsection (2) applies the second condition is that—
    (a) in the criminal investigation there has been a serious default by a person mentioned in subsection (9), and

    (b)   the investigation would not have continued if the default had not occurred.

(5)   If subsection (3) applies the second condition is that—
    (a)   in the criminal investigation with regard to the offence or in its prosecution there has been a serious default by a person mentioned in subsection (9), and
    (b)   the proceedings would not have been instituted or continued if the default had not occurred.

(6)   The third condition is that an application is made under this section by a person who held realisable property and has suffered loss in consequence of anything done in relation to it by or in pursuance of an order under this Part.

(7)   The offence referred to in subsection (2) may be one of a number of offences with regard to which the investigation is instituted.

(8)   The offence referred to in subsection (3) may be one of a number of offences for which the proceedings are instituted.

(9)   Compensation under this section is payable to the applicant and—
    (a)   if the person in default was a constable of a police force (within the meaning of the Police (Scotland) Act 1967 (c 77)), the compensation is payable by the police authority or joint police board for the police area for which that force is maintained;
    (b)   if the person in default was a constable not falling within paragraph (a), the compensation is payable by the body under whose authority he acts;
    (c)   if the person in default was a procurator fiscal or was acting on behalf of the Lord Advocate, the compensation is payable by the Lord Advocate;
    (d)   if the person in default was a customs officer, the compensation is payable by the Commissioners of Customs and Excise;
    (e)   if the person in default was an officer of the Commissioners of Inland Revenue, the compensation is payable by those Commissioners.

(10) Nothing in this section affects any delictual liability in relation to a serious default.

Definitions   For "conviction", see s 154(1); for "the court", see s 119(10); for "criminal investigation", see s 154(1); for "proceedings . . . instituted", see s 151; for "realisable property", see s 149.
References   see paras 4.42, 4.43.

140 Confiscation order varied or discharged

(1)   This section applies if—
    (a)   the court varies a confiscation order under section 113 or discharges one under section 114, and
    (b)   an application is made to the court by a person who held realisable property and has suffered loss as a result of the making of the order.

(2)   The court may order the payment to the applicant of such compensation as it believes is just.

(3)   Compensation payable under this section is payable by the Lord Advocate.

Definitions   For "confiscation order", see s 154(1); for "the court", see s 119(10); for "realisable property", see s 149.
References   See para 4.44.

Enforcement abroad

141 Enforcement abroad

(1)   This section applies if—
  (a)   any of the conditions in section 119 are satisfied,
  (b)   the prosecutor believes that realisable property is situated in a country or territory outside the United Kingdom (the receiving country), and
  (c)   the prosecutor sends a request for assistance to the Secretary of State with a view to it being forwarded under this section.

(2)   In a case where no confiscation order has been made, a request for assistance is a request to the government of the receiving country to secure that any person is prohibited from dealing with realisable property.

(3)   In a case where a confiscation order has been made and has not been satisfied, discharged or quashed, a request for assistance is a request to the government of the receiving country to secure that—
  (a)   any person is prohibited from dealing with realisable property,
  (b)   realisable property is realised and the proceeds are applied in accordance with the law of the receiving country.

(4)   No request for assistance may be made for the purposes of this section in a case where a confiscation order has been made and has been satisfied, discharged or quashed.

(5)   If the Secretary of State believes it is appropriate to do so he may forward the request for assistance to the government of the receiving country.

(6)   If property is realised in pursuance of a request under subsection (3) the amount ordered to be paid under the confiscation order must be taken to be reduced by an amount equal to the proceeds of the realisation.

(7)   A certificate purporting to be issued by or on behalf of the requested government is sufficient evidence of the facts it states if it states—
  (a)   that the property has been realised in pursuance of a request under subsection (3),
  (b)   the date of realisation, and
  (c)   the proceeds of realisation.

(8)   If the proceeds of realisation made in pursuance of a request under subsection (3) are expressed in a currency other than sterling, they must be taken to be the sterling equivalent calculated in accordance with the rate of exchange prevailing at the end of the day of realisation.

Definitions   For "confiscation order", see s 154(1); for "property", see s 150(1); for "realisable property", see s 149.
References   See para 4.1.

Interpretation

142 Criminal lifestyle

(1)   An accused has a criminal lifestyle if (and only if) the offence (or any of the offences) concerned satisfies any of these tests—
- (a)   it is specified in Schedule 4;
- (b)   it constitutes conduct forming part of a course of criminal activity;
- (c)   it is an offence committed over a period of at least six months and the accused has benefited from the conduct which constitutes the offence.

(2)   Conduct forms part of a course of criminal activity if the accused has benefited from the conduct and—
- (a)   in the proceedings in which he was convicted he was convicted of three or more other offences, each of three or more of them constituting conduct from which he has benefited, or
- (b)   in the period of six years ending with the day when those proceedings were instituted (or, if there is more than one such day, the earliest day) he was convicted on at least two separate occasions of an offence constituting conduct from which he has benefited.

(3)   But an offence does not satisfy the test in subsection (1)(b) or (c) unless the accused obtains relevant benefit of not less than £5000.

(4)   Relevant benefit for the purposes of subsection (1)(b) is—
- (a)   benefit from conduct which constitutes the offence;
- (b)   benefit from any other conduct which forms part of the course of criminal activity and which constitutes an offence of which the accused has been convicted.

(5)   Relevant benefit for the purposes of subsection (1)(c) is benefit from conduct which constitutes the offence.

(6)   The Scottish Ministers may by order amend Schedule 4.

(7)   The Scottish Ministers may by order vary the amount for the time being specified in subsection (3).

Definitions   For "accused", see s 154(1); for "benefits from conduct", see s 143(4)–(7); for "offence concerned", see s 92(12); for "proceedings . . . instituted", see s 151.
References   See para 4.45.

143 Conduct and benefit

(1)   Criminal conduct is conduct which—
- (a)   constitutes an offence in Scotland, or
- (b)   would constitute such an offence if it had occurred in Scotland.

(2)   General criminal conduct of the accused is all his criminal conduct, and it is immaterial—
- (a)   whether conduct occurred before or after the passing of this Act;
- (b)   whether property constituting a benefit from conduct was obtained before or after the passing of this Act.

(3)   Particular criminal conduct of the accused is all his criminal conduct which falls within the following paragraphs—

> (a) conduct which constitutes the offence or offences concerned;
> (b) conduct which constitutes offences of which he was convicted in the same proceedings as those in which he was convicted of the offence or offences concerned.

(4) A person benefits from conduct if he obtains property as a result of or in connection with the conduct.

(5) If a person obtains a pecuniary advantage as a result of or in connection with conduct, he is to be taken to obtain as a result of or in connection with the conduct a sum of money equal to the value of the pecuniary advantage.

(6) References to property or a pecuniary advantage obtained in connection with conduct include references to property or a pecuniary advantage obtained both in that connection and in some other.

(7) If a person benefits from conduct his benefit is the value of the property obtained.

Definitions   For "accused", see s 154(1); for "offence concerned", see s 92(12); for "property", see s 150(1); for "property obtained", see s 150(2)(b).
References   See para 4.1.

---

144 Tainted gifts and their recipients

(1) Subsections (2) and (3) apply if—
> (a) no court has made a decision as to whether the accused has a criminal lifestyle, or
> (b) a court has decided that the accused has a criminal lifestyle.

(2) A gift is tainted if it was made by the accused at any time after the relevant day.

(3) A gift is also tainted if it was made by the accused at any time and was of property—
> (a) which was obtained by the accused as a result of or in connection with his general criminal conduct, or
> (b) which (in whole or part and whether directly or indirectly) represented in the accused's hands property obtained by him as a result of or in connection with his general criminal conduct.

(4) Subsection (5) applies if a court has decided that an accused does not have a criminal lifestyle.

(5) A gift is tainted if it was made by the accused at any time after—
> (a) the date on which the offence concerned was committed, or
> (b) if his particular criminal conduct consists of two or more offences and they were committed on different dates, the earliest of those dates.

(6) For the purposes of subsection (5) an offence which is a continuing offence is committed on the first occasion when it is committed.

(7) A gift may be a tainted gift whether it was made before or after the passing of this Act.

(8) The relevant day is the first day of the period of six years ending with—

    (a) the day when proceedings for the offence concerned were instituted against the accused, or

    (b) if there are two or more offences and proceedings for them were instituted on different days, the earliest of those days.

(9) If the accused transfers property to another person (whether directly or indirectly) for a consideration whose value is significantly less than the value of the property at the time of the transfer, he is to be treated as making a gift.

(10) If subsection (9) applies the property given is to be treated as such share in the property transferred as is represented by the fraction—

    (a) whose numerator is the difference between the two values mentioned in subsection (9), and

    (b) whose denominator is the value of the property at the time of the transfer.

(11) References to a recipient of a tainted gift are to a person to whom the accused has (whether directly or indirectly) made the gift.

Definitions   For "accused", see s 154(1); for "criminal lifestyle", see s 142; for "general criminal conduct", see s 143(2); for "offence concerned", see s 92(12); for "particular criminal conduct", see s 143(3); for "proceedings . . . instituted", see s 151; for "property", see s 150(1); for "property obtained", see s 150(2)(b).
References   See para 4.1.

145 Value: the basic rule

(1) This section applies for the purpose of deciding the value at any time of property then held by a person.

(2) Its value is the market value of the property at that time.

(3) But if at that time another person holds an interest in the property its value, in relation to the person mentioned in subsection (1), is the market value of his interest at that time ignoring any charging order under a provision listed in subsection (4).

(4) The provisions are—

    (a) section 9 of the Drug Trafficking Offences Act 1986 (c 32);

    (b) section 78 of the Criminal Justice Act 1988 (c 33);

    (c) Article 14 of the Criminal Justice (Confiscation) (Northern Ireland) Order 1990 (SI 199/2588 (NI 17));

    (d) section 27 of the Drug Trafficking Act 1994 (c 37);

    (e) Article 32 of the Proceeds of Crime (Northern Ireland) Order 1996 (SI 1996/1299 (NI 9)).

(5) This section has effect subject to sections 146 and 147.

Definitions   For "interest" in relation to land, see s 150(2)(f), (g); for "interest" in relation to property other than land, see s 150(2)(h); for "property", see s 150(1); for "property held", see s 150(2)(a), (d).
References   See para 4.1.

146 Value of property obtained from conduct

(1) This section applies for the purpose of deciding the value of property obtained by a person as a result of or in connection with his criminal conduct; and the material time is the time the court makes its decision.

(2) The value of the property at the material time is the greater of the following—
  (a) the value of the property (at the time the person obtained it) adjusted to take account of later changes in the value of money;
  (b) the value (at the material time) of the property found under subsection (3).

(3) The property found under this subsection is—
  (a) if the person holds the property obtained, that property;
  (b) if he holds no part of the property obtained, any property which directly or indirectly represents it in his hands;
  (c) if he holds part of the property obtained, that part and any property which directly or indirectly represents the other part in his hands.

(4) The references in subsection (2)(a) and (b) to the value are to the value found in accordance with section 145.

Definitions   For "criminal conduct", see s 143(1); for "property", see s 150(1); for "property held", see s 150(2)(a), (d); for "property obtained", see s 150(2)(b).
References   See para 4.1.

147 Value of tainted gifts

(1) The value at any time (the material time) of a tainted gift is the greater of the following—
  (a) the value (at the time of the gift) of the property given, adjusted to take account of later changes in the value of money;
  (b) the value (at the material time) of the property found under subsection (2).

(2) The property found under this subsection is—
  (a) if the recipient holds the property given, that property;
  (b) if the recipient holds no part of the property given, any property which directly or indirectly represents it in his hands;
  (c) if the recipient holds part of the property given, that part and any property which directly or indirectly represents the other part in his hands.

(3) The references in subsection (1)(a) and (b) to the value are to the value found in accordance with section 145.

Definitions   For "property", see s 150(1); for "property held", see s 150(2)(a), (d); for "tainted gift", see s 144.
References   See para 4.1.

148 Free property

Property is free unless an order is in force in respect of it under—
  (a) section 27 of the Misuse of Drugs Act 1971 (c 38) (forfeiture orders),

318

    (b)   Article 11 of the Criminal Justice (Northern Ireland) Order 1994 (SI 1994/2795 (NI 15) (deprivation orders),

    (c)   Part 2 of the Proceeds of Crime (Scotland) Act 1995 (c 43) (forfeiture of property used in crime),

    (d)   section 143 of the Powers of Criminal Courts (Sentencing) Act 2000 (c 6) (deprivation orders),

    (e)   section 23 or 111 of the Terrorism Act 2000 (c 11) (forfeiture orders), or

    (f)   section 246, 266, 295(2) or 298(2) of this Act.

Definitions   For "property", see s 150(1).
References   See para 4.1.

149 Realisable property

Realisable property is—

    (a)   any free property held by the accused;

    (b)   any free property held by the recipient of a tainted gift.

Definitions   For "accused", see s 154(1); for "free property", see s 148; for "property", see s 150(1); for "property held", see s 150(2)(a), (d); for "recipient of a tainted gift", see s 144(11); for "tainted gift", see s 144.
References   See para 4.1.

150 Property: general provisions

(1)   Property is all property wherever situated and includes—

    (a)   money;

    (b)   all forms of property whether heritable or moveable and whether corporeal or incorporeal.

(2)   The following rules apply in relation to property—

    (a)   property is held by a person if he holds an interest in it;

    (b)   property is obtained by a person if he obtains an interest in it;

    (c)   property is transferred by one person to another if the first one transfers or grants an interest in it to the second;

    (d)   references to property held by a person include references to his property vested in his permanent or interim trustee (within the meaning of the Bankruptcy (Scotland) Act 1985 (c 66)), trustee in bankruptcy or liquidator;

    (e)   references to an interest held by a person beneficially in property include references to an interest which would be held by him beneficially if the property were not so vested;

    (f)   references to an interest, in relation to land in England, Wales or Northern Ireland, are to any legal estate or equitable interest or power;

    (g)   references to an interest, in relation to land in Scotland, are to any estate, interest, servitude or other heritable right in or over land, including a heritable security;

    (h)   references to an interest, in relation to property other than land, include references to a right (including a right to possession).

References   See para 4.1.

151 Proceedings

(1) Proceedings for an offence are instituted against a person—
    (a) on his arrest without warrant;
    (b) when he is charged with the offence without being arrested;
    (c) when a warrant to arrest him is granted;
    (d) when a warrant to cite him is granted;
    (e) when he first appears on petition or when an indictment or complaint is served on him.

(2) If more than one time is found under subsection (1) in relation to proceedings they are instituted at the earliest of those times.

(3) Proceedings for an offence are concluded when—
    (a) the trial diet is deserted simpliciter,
    (b) the accused is acquitted or, under section 65 or 147 of the Procedure Act, discharged or liberated,
    (c) the court sentences the accused without making a confiscation order and without postponing a decision as regards making such an order,
    (d) the court decides, after such a postponement, not to make a confiscation order,
    (e) the accused's conviction is quashed, or
    (f) the accused is pardoned.

(4) If a confiscation order is made against the accused in proceedings for an offence, the proceedings are concluded—
    (a) when the order is satisfied or discharged, or
    (b) when the order is quashed and there is no further possibility of an appeal against the decision to quash the order.

(5) If—
    (a) the accused is convicted in proceedings for an offence but the court decides not to make a confiscation order against him, and
    (b) on appeal under section 108(1)(ca) or 175(4)(ca) of the Procedure Act, the High Court of Justiciary refuses the appeal,

the proceedings are concluded on the determination of the appeal.

Definitions   For "accused", see s 154(1); for "confiscation order", see s 154(1); for "Procedure Act", see s 154(1); for "sentences the accused", see s 154(2); for "satisfied", see s 153.
References   See para 4.1.

152 Applications

(1) An application under section 104, 105, 111 or 112 is concluded—
    (a) in a case where the court decides not to make a confiscation order against the accused, when it makes the decision;
    (b) in a case where a confiscation order is made against him as a result of the application, when the order is satisfied or discharged, or when the order is quashed and there is no further possibility of an appeal against the decision to quash the order;
    (c) in a case where the application is withdrawn, when the prosecutor notifies the withdrawal to the court to which the application was made.

(2)   An application under section 106 or 107 is concluded—
   (a)   in a case where the court decides not to vary the confiscation order concerned, when it makes the decision;
   (b)   in a case where the court varies the confiscation order as a result of the application, when the order is satisfied or discharged, or when the order is quashed and there is no further possibility of an appeal against the decision to quash the order;
   (c)   in a case where the application is withdrawn, when the prosecutor notifies the withdrawal to the court to which the application was made.

Definitions   For "accused", see s 154(1); for "confiscation order", see s 154(1); for "satisfied", see s 153.
References   See para 4.1.

153 Satisfaction of confiscation orders

(1)   A confiscation order is satisfied—
   (a)   when no amount is due under it;
   (b)   where the accused against whom it was made serves a term of imprisonment or detention in default of payment of the amount due under the order, on the completion of that term of imprisonment or detention.

(2)   A confiscation order is subject to appeal until there is no further possibility of an appeal on which the order could be varied or quashed; and for this purpose any power to grant leave to appeal out of time must be ignored.

Definitions   For "accused", see s 154(1); for "confiscation order", see s 154(1).
References   See para 4.1.

154 Other interpretative provisions

(1)   In this Part—
   "accused" means a person against whom proceedings for an offence have been instituted (whether or not he has been convicted);
   "clerk of court" includes the sheriff clerk;
   "confiscation order" means an order under section 92;
   "conviction", in relation to an offence, includes a finding that the offence has been committed;
   "court" must be construed in accordance with sections 92(13) and 119(10);
   "criminal investigation" means an investigation which police officers or other persons have a duty to conduct with a view to it being ascertained whether a person should be charged with an offence;
   "the Procedure Act" means the Criminal Procedure (Scotland) Act 1995 (c 46);
   "restraint order" means an order under section 120.

(2)   A reference to the offence (or offences) concerned must be construed in accordance with section 92(12).

(3)   A reference to sentencing the accused for an offence includes a reference to dealing with him otherwise in respect of the offence.

Definitions For "proceedings", see s 151.
References See para 4.1.

General

155 Rules of court

(1) Provision may be made by act of sederunt as to—
  (a) giving notice or serving any document for the purposes of this Part;
  (b) the accountant of court's functions under Schedule 3;
  (c) the accounts to be kept by the administrator in relation to the exercise of his functions.

(2) Subsection (1) is without prejudice to section 32 of the Sheriff Courts (Scotland) Act 1971 (c 58) or section 5 of the Court of Session Act 1988 (c 36).

References See para 4.46.

PART 4
CONFISCATION: NORTHERN IRELAND

Confiscation orders

156 Making of order

(1) The Crown Court must proceed under this section if the following two conditions are satisfied.

(2) The first condition is that a defendant falls within either of the following paragraphs—
  (a) he is convicted of an offence or offences in proceedings before the Crown Court;
  (b) he is committed to the Crown Court in respect of an offence or offences under section 218 below (committal with a view to a confiscation order being considered).

(3) The second condition is that—
  (a) the prosecutor or the Director asks the court to proceed under this section, or
  (b) the court believes it is appropriate for it to do so.

(4) The court must proceed as follows—
  (a) it must decide whether the defendant has a criminal lifestyle;
  (b) if it decides that he has a criminal lifestyle it must decide whether he has benefited from his general criminal conduct;
  (c) if it decides that he does not have a criminal lifestyle it must decide whether he has benefited from his particular criminal conduct.

(5) If the court decides under subsection (4)(b) or (c) that the defendant has benefited from the conduct referred to it must—
  (a) decide the recoverable amount, and
  (b) make an order (a confiscation order) requiring him to pay that amount.

(6)   But the court must treat the duty in subsection (5) as a power if it believes that any victim of the conduct has at any time started or intends to start proceedings against the defendant in respect of loss, injury or damage sustained in connection with the conduct.

(7)   The court must decide any question arising under subsection (4) or (5) on a balance of probabilities.

(8)   The first condition is not satisfied if the defendant absconds (but section 177 may apply).

(9)   References in this Part to the offence (or offences) concerned are to the offence (or offences) mentioned in subsection (2).

Definitions   For "benefits from conduct", see ss 224(4), (7), 236(6); for "criminal conduct", see ss 224(1), 236(6); for "criminal lifestyle", see ss 223, 236(6), Sch 5; for "defendant", see s 236(3), (6); for "the Director", see s 1(2); for "general criminal conduct", see ss 224(2), 236(6); for "particular criminal conduct", see ss 224(3), 236(6).
References   See paras 5.1, 5.2.

157 Recoverable amount

(1)   The recoverable amount for the purposes of section 156 is an amount equal to the defendant's benefit from the conduct concerned.

(2)   But if the defendant shows that the available amount is less than that benefit the recoverable amount is—
    (a)   the available amount, or
    (b)   a nominal amount, if the available amount is nil.

(3)   But if section 156(6) applies the recoverable amount is such amount as—
    (a)   the court believes is just, but
    (b)   does not exceed the amount found under subsection (1) or (2) (as the case may be).

(4)   In calculating the defendant's benefit from the conduct concerned for the purposes of subsection (1), any property in respect of which—
    (a)   a recovery order is in force under section 266, or
    (b)   a forfeiture order is in force under section 298(2),
must be ignored.

(5)   If the court decides the available amount, it must include in the confiscation order a statement of its findings as to the matters relevant for deciding that amount.

Definitions   For "benefits from conduct", see ss 224(4), (7), 236(6); for "confiscation order", see s 236(5)(a), (6); for "defendant", see s 236(3), (6); for "property", see ss 232(1), 236(6).
References   See para 5.1.

158 Defendant's benefit

(1)   If the court is proceeding under section 156 this section applies for the purpose of—
    (a)   deciding whether the defendant has benefited from conduct, and
    (b)   deciding his benefit from the conduct.

(2)   The court must—
  (a)   take account of conduct occurring up to the time it makes its decision;
  (b)   take account of property obtained up to that time.

(3)   Subsection (4) applies if—
  (a)   the conduct concerned is general criminal conduct,
  (b)   a confiscation order mentioned in subsection (5) has at an earlier time been made against the defendant, and
  (c)   his benefit for the purposes of that order was benefit from his general criminal conduct.

(4)   His benefit found at the time the last confiscation order mentioned in subsection (3)(c) was made against him must be taken for the purposes of this section to be his benefit from his general criminal conduct at that time.

(5)   If the conduct concerned is general criminal conduct the court must deduct the aggregate of the following amounts—
  (a)   the amount ordered to be paid under each confiscation order previously made against the defendant;
  (b)   the amount ordered to be paid under each confiscation order previously made against him under any of the provisions listed in subsection (7).

(6)   But subsection (5) does not apply to an amount which has been taken into account for the purposes of a deduction under that subsection on any earlier occasion.

(7)   These are the provisions—
  (a)   the Drug Trafficking Offences Act 1986 (c 32);
  (b)   Part 1 of the Criminal Justice (Scotland) Act 1987 (c 41);
  (c)   Part 6 of the Criminal Justice Act 1988 (c 33);
  (d)   the Criminal Justice (Confiscation) (Northern Ireland) Order 1990 (SI 1990/2588 (NI 17));
  (e)   Part 1 of the Drug Trafficking Act 1994 (c 37);
  (f)   Part 1 of the Proceeds of Crime (Scotland) Act 1995 (c 43);
  (g)   the Proceeds of Crime (Northern Ireland) Order 1996 (SI 1996/1299 (NI 9));
  (h)   Part 2 or 3 of this Act.

(8)   The reference to general criminal conduct in the case of a confiscation order made under any of the provisions listed in subsection (7) is a reference to conduct in respect of which a court is required or entitled to make one or more assumptions for the purpose of assessing a person's benefit from the conduct.

Definitions   For "benefits from conduct", see ss 224(4), (7), 236(6); for "confiscation order", see s 236(5)(a), (6); for "criminal conduct", see ss 224(1), 236(6); for "defendant", see s 236(3), (6); for "general criminal conduct", see ss 224(2), 236(6); for "property", see ss 232(1), 236(6); for "property held", see ss 232(2)(a), (d), 236(6); for "property obtained in connection with conduct", see ss 224(6), 236(6).
References   See para 5.1.

159 Available amount

(1)   For the purposes of deciding the recoverable amount, the available amount is the aggregate of—

> (a) the total of the values (at the time the confiscation order is made) of all the free property then held by the defendant minus the total amount payable in pursuance of obligations which then have priority, and
> (b) the total of the values (at that time) of all tainted gifts.

(2) An obligation has priority if it is an obligation of the defendant—
> (a) to pay an amount due in respect of a fine or other order of a court which was imposed or made on conviction of an offence and at any time before the time the confiscation order is made, or
> (b) to pay a sum which would be included among the preferential debts if the defendant's bankruptcy had commenced on the date of the confiscation order or his winding up had been ordered on that date.

(3) "Preferential debts" has the meaning given by Article 346 of the Insolvency (Northern Ireland) Order 1989 (SI 1989/2405 (NI 19)).

Definitions   For "confiscation order", see s 236(5)(a), (6); for "defendant", see s 236(3), (6); for "free property", see ss 230, 236(6); for "property", see ss 232(1), 236(6); for "property held", see ss 232(2)(a), (d), 236(6); for "tainted gift", see ss 225, 236(6).
References   See para 5.3.

---

160 Assumptions to be made in case of criminal lifestyle

(1) If the court decides under section 156 that the defendant has a criminal lifestyle it must make the following four assumptions for the purpose of—
> (a) deciding whether he has benefited from his general criminal conduct, and
> (b) deciding his benefit from the conduct.

(2) The first assumption is that any property transferred to the defendant at any time after the relevant day was obtained by him—
> (a) as a result of his general criminal conduct, and
> (b) at the earliest time he appears to have held it.

(3) The second assumption is that any property held by the defendant at any time after the date of conviction was obtained by him—
> (a) as a result of his general criminal conduct, and
> (b) at the earliest time he appears to have held it.

(4) The third assumption is that any expenditure incurred by the defendant at any time after the relevant day was met from property obtained by him as a result of his general criminal conduct.

(5) The fourth assumption is that, for the purpose of valuing any property obtained (or assumed to have been obtained) by the defendant, he obtained it free of any other interests in it.

(6) But the court must not make a required assumption in relation to particular property or expenditure if—
> (a) the assumption is shown to be incorrect, or
> (b) there would be a serious risk of injustice if the assumption were made.

(7) If the court does not make one or more of the required assumptions it must state its reasons.

(8)　The relevant day is the first day of the period of six years ending with—

    (a)　the day when proceedings for the offence concerned were started against the defendant, or

    (b)　if there are two or more offences and proceedings for them were started on different days, the earliest of those days.

(9)　But if a confiscation order mentioned in section 158(3)(c) has been made against the defendant at any time during the period mentioned in subsection (8)—

    (a)　the relevant day is the day when the defendant's benefit was calculated for the purposes of the last such confiscation order;

    (b)　the second assumption does not apply to any property which was held by him on or before the relevant day.

(10)　The date of conviction is—

    (a)　the date on which the defendant was convicted of the offence concerned, or

    (b)　if there are two or more offences and the convictions were on different dates, the date of the latest.

Definitions　For "benefits from conduct", see ss 224(4), (7), 236(6); for "criminal conduct", see ss 224(1), 236(6); for "criminal lifestyle", see ss 223, 236(6), Sch 5; for "defendant", see s 236(3), (6); for "general criminal conduct", see ss 224(2), 236(6); for "interest" in relation to land, see ss 232(2)(f), (g), 236(6); for "interest" in relation to property other than land, see ss 232(2)(h), 236(6); for "offence concerned", see ss 156(9), 236(1), (6); for "offences concerned", see ss 156(9), 236(1), (6); for "proceedings started", see ss 233(1), (2), 236(6); for "property", see ss 232(1), 236(6); for "property held", see ss 232(2)(a), (d), 236(6); for "property obtained", see ss 232(2)(b), 236(6); for "property obtained in connection with conduct", see ss 224(6), 236(6); for "property transferred", see ss 232(2)(c), 236(6).
References　See para 5.1.

161　Time for payment

(1)　The amount ordered to be paid under a confiscation order must be paid on the making of the order; but this is subject to the following provisions of this section.

(2)　If the defendant shows that he needs time to pay the amount ordered to be paid, the court making the confiscation order may make an order allowing payment to be made in a specified period.

(3)　The specified period—

    (a)　must start with the day on which the confiscation order is made, and

    (b)　must not exceed six months.

(4)　If within the specified period the defendant applies to the Crown Court for the period to be extended and the court believes there are exceptional circumstances, it may make an order extending the period.

(5)　The extended period—

    (a)　must start with the day on which the confiscation order is made, and

    (b)　must not exceed 12 months.

(6)　An order under subsection (4)—

    (a)　may be made after the end of the specified period, but

    (b)　must not be made after the end of the period of 12 months starting with the day on which the confiscation order is made.

(7)   The court must not make an order under subsection (2) or (4) unless it gives—

(a)   the prosecutor, or

(b)   if the Director was appointed as the enforcement authority for the order under section 184, the Director,

an opportunity to make representations.

Definitions   For "confiscation order", see s 236(5)(a), (6); for "defendant", see s 236(3), (6); for "the Director", see s 1(2).
References   See para 5.1.

162 Interest on unpaid sums

(1)   If the amount required to be paid by a person under a confiscation order is not paid when it is required to be paid, he must pay interest on the amount for the period for which it remains unpaid.

(2)   The rate of interest is the same rate as that for the time being applying to a money judgment of the High Court.

(3)   For the purposes of this section no amount is required to be paid under a confiscation order if—

(a)   an application has been made under section 161(4),

(b)   the application has not been determined by the court, and

(c)   the period of 12 months starting with the day on which the confiscation order was made has not ended.

(4)   In applying this Part the amount of the interest must be treated as part of the amount to be paid under the confiscation order.

Definitions   For "confiscation order", see s 236(5)(a), (6).
References   See para 5.1.

163 Effect of order on court's other powers

(1)   If the court makes a confiscation order it must proceed as mentioned in subsections (2) and (4) in respect of the offence or offences concerned.

(2)   The court must take account of the confiscation order before—

(a)   it imposes a fine on the defendant, or

(b)   it makes an order falling within subsection (3).

(3)   These orders fall within this subsection—

(a)   an order involving payment by the defendant, other than an order under Article 14 of the Criminal Justice (Northern Ireland) Order 1994 (SI 1994/2795 (NI 15)) (compensation orders);

(b)   an order under section 27 of the Misuse of Drugs Act 1971 (c 38) (forfeiture orders);

(c)   an order under Article 11 of the Criminal Justice (Northern Ireland) Order 1994 (SI 1994/2795 (NI 15)) (deprivation orders);

(d)   an order under section 23 or 111 of the Terrorism Act 2000 (c 11) (forfeiture orders).

(4)   Subject to subsection (2), the court must leave the confiscation order out of account in deciding the appropriate sentence for the defendant.

    (5)   Subsection (6) applies if—

        (a)   a court makes both a confiscation order and an order for the payment of compensation under Article 14 of the Criminal Justice (Northern Ireland) Order 1994 (SI 1994/2795 (NI 15)) against the same person in the same proceedings, and

        (b)   the court believes he will not have sufficient means to satisfy both the orders in full.

    (6)   In such a case the court must direct that so much of the compensation as it specifies is to be paid out of any sums recovered under the confiscation order; and the amount it specifies must be the amount it believes will not be recoverable because of the insufficiency of the person's means.

Definitions   For "confiscation order", see s 236(5)(a), (6); for "defendant", see s 236(3), (6); for "offence concerned", see ss 156(9), 236(1), (6); for "offences concerned", see ss 156(9), 236(1), (6).
References   See para 5.1.

Procedural matters

164 Postponement

    (1)   The court may—

        (a)   proceed under section 161 before it sentences the defendant for the offence (or any of the offences) concerned, or

        (b)   postpone proceedings under section 161 for a specified period.

    (2)   A period of postponement may be extended.

    (3)   A period of postponement (including one as extended) must not end after the permitted period ends.

    (4)   But subsection (3) does not apply if there are exceptional circumstances.

    (5)   The permitted period is the period of two years starting with the date of conviction.

    (6)   But if—

        (a)   the defendant appeals against his conviction for the offence (or any of the offences) concerned, and

        (b)   the period of three months (starting with the day when the appeal is determined or otherwise disposed of) ends after the period found under subsection (5),

the permitted period is that period of three months.

    (7)   A postponement or extension may be made—

        (a)   on application by the defendant;

        (b)   on application by the prosecutor or the Director (as the case may be);

        (c)   by the court of its own motion.

    (8)   If—

        (a)   proceedings are postponed for a period, and

        (b)   an application to extend the period is made before it ends,

the application may be granted even after the period ends.

(9)   The date of conviction is—
  (a)   the date on which the defendant was convicted of the offence concerned, or
  (b)   if there are two or more offences and the convictions were on different dates, the date of the latest.

(10)   References to appealing include references to applying under Article 146 of the Magistrates' Courts (Northern Ireland) Order 1981 (SI 1981/1675 (NI 26)) (statement of case).

(11)   A confiscation order must not be quashed only on the ground that there was a defect or omission in the procedure connected with the application for or the granting of a postponement.

(12)   But subsection (11) does not apply if before it made the confiscation order the court—
  (a)   imposed a fine on the defendant;
  (b)   made an order falling within section 163(3);
  (c)   made an order under Article 14 of the Criminal Justice (Northern Ireland) Order 1994 (SI 1994/2795 (NI 15)) (compensation orders).

Definitions   For "confiscation order", see s 236(5)(a), (6); for "defendant", see s 236(3), (6); for "the Director", see s 1(2); for "offence concerned", see ss 156(9), 236(1), (6); for "offences concerned", see ss 156(9), 236(1), (6).
References   See para 5.1.

165 Effect of postponement

(1)   If the court postpones proceedings under section 156 it may proceed to sentence the defendant for the offence (or any of the offences) concerned.

(2)   In sentencing the defendant for the offence (or any of the offences) concerned in the postponement period the court must not—
  (a)   impose a fine on him,
  (b)   make an order falling within section 163(3), or
  (c)   make an order for the payment of compensation under Article 14 of the Criminal Justice (Northern Ireland) Order 1994 (SI 1994/2795 (NI 15)).

(3)   If the court sentences the defendant for the offence (or any of the offences) concerned in the postponement period, after that period ends it may vary the sentence by—
  (a)   imposing a fine on him,
  (b)   making an order falling within section 163(3), or
  (c)   making an order for the payment of compensation under Article 14 of the Criminal Justice (Northern Ireland) Order 1994.

(4)   But the court may proceed under subsection (3) only within the period of 28 days which starts with the last day of the postponement period.

(5)   For the purposes of—
  (a)   section 16(1) of the Criminal Appeal (Northern Ireland) Act 1980 (c 47) (time limit for notice of appeal or of application for leave to appeal), and

(b) paragraph 1 of Schedule 3 to the Criminal Justice Act 1988 (c 33) (time limit for notice of application for leave to refer a case under section 36 of that Act),

the sentence must be regarded as imposed or made on the day on which it is varied under subsection (3).

(6) If the court proceeds to sentence the defendant under subsection (1), section 156 has effect as if the defendant's particular criminal conduct included conduct which constitutes offences which the court has taken into consideration in deciding his sentence for the offence or offences concerned.

(7) The postponement period is the period for which proceedings under section 156 are postponed.

Definitions For "criminal conduct", see ss 224(1), 236(6); for "defendant", see s 236(3), (6); for "offence concerned", see ss 156(9), 236(1), (6); for "offences concerned", see ss 156(9), 236(1), (6); for "particular criminal conduct", see ss 224(3), 236(6); for "sentencing the defendant for an offence", see s 236(4), (6).
References See para 5.1.

166 Statement of information

(1) If the court is proceeding under section 156 in a case where section 156(3)(a) applies, the prosecutor or the Director (as the case may be) must give the court a statement of information within the period the court orders.

(2) If the court is proceeding under section 156 in a case where section 156(3)(b) applies and it orders the prosecutor to give it a statement of information, the prosecutor must give it such a statement within the period the court orders.

(3) If the prosecutor or the Director (as the case may be) believes the defendant has a criminal lifestyle the statement of information is a statement of matters the prosecutor or the Director believes are relevant in connection with deciding these issues—

(a) whether the defendant has a criminal lifestyle;
(b) whether he has benefited from his general criminal conduct;
(c) his benefit from the conduct.

(4) A statement under subsection (3) must include information the prosecutor or Director believes is relevant—

(a) in connection with the making by the court of a required assumption under section 160;
(b) for the purpose of enabling the court to decide if the circumstances are such that it must not make such an assumption.

(5) If the prosecutor or the Director (as the case may be) does not believe the defendant has a criminal lifestyle the statement of information is a statement of matters the prosecutor or the Director believes are relevant in connection with deciding these issues—

(a) whether the defendant has benefited from his particular criminal conduct;
(b) his benefit from the conduct.

(6) If the prosecutor or the Director gives the court a statement of information—

(a) he may at any time give the court a further statement of information;

    (b)   he must give the court a further statement of information if it orders him to do so, and he must give it within the period the court orders.

(7)   If the court makes an order under this section it may at any time vary it by making another one.

Definitions   For "benefits from conduct", see ss 224(4), (7), 236(6); for "criminal conduct", see ss 224(1), 236(6); for "criminal lifestyle", see ss 223, 236(6), Sch 5; for "defendant", see s 236(3), (6); for "the Director", see s 1(2); for "general criminal conduct", see ss 224(2), 236(6); for "particular criminal conduct", see ss 224(3), 236(6).
References   See paras 5.1, 5.3.

167 Defendant's response to statement of information

(1)   If the prosecutor or the Director gives the court a statement of information and a copy is served on the defendant, the court may order the defendant—
    (a)   to indicate (within the period it orders) the extent to which he accepts each allegation in the statement, and
    (b)   so far as he does not accept such an allegation, to give particulars of any matters he proposes to rely on.

(2)   If the defendant accepts to any extent an allegation in a statement of information the court may treat his acceptance as conclusive of the matters to which it relates for the purpose of deciding the issues referred to in section 166(3) or (5) (as the case may be).

(3)   If the defendant fails in any respect to comply with an order under subsection (1) he may be treated for the purposes of subsection (2) as accepting every allegation in the statement of information apart from—
    (a)   any allegation in respect of which he has complied with the requirement;
    (b)   any allegation that he has benefited from his general or particular criminal conduct.

(4)   For the purposes of this section an allegation may be accepted or particulars may be given in a manner ordered by the court.

(5)   If the court makes an order under this section it may at any time vary it by making another one.

(6)   No acceptance under this section that the defendant has benefited from conduct is admissible in evidence in proceedings for an offence.

Definitions   For "benefits from conduct", see ss 224(4), (7), 236(6); for "criminal conduct", see ss 224(1), 236(6); for "defendant", see s 236(3), (6); for "the Director", see s 1(2); for "general criminal conduct", see ss 224(2), 236(6); for "particular criminal conduct", see ss 224(3), 236(6).
References   See para 5.1.

168 Provision of information by defendant

(1)   This section applies if—
    (a)   the court is proceeding under section 156 in a case where section 156(3)(a) applies, or
    (b)   it is proceeding under section 156 in a case where section 156(3)(b) applies or it is considering whether to proceed.

(2)   For the purpose of obtaining information to help it in carrying out its functions the court may at any time order the defendant to give it information specified in the order.

(3)   An order under this section may require all or a specified part of the information to be given in a specified manner and before a specified date.

(4)   If the defendant fails without reasonable excuse to comply with an order under this section the court may draw such inference as it believes is appropriate.

(5)   Subsection (4) does not affect any power of the court to deal with the defendant in respect of a failure to comply with an order under this section.

(6)   If the prosecutor or the Director (as the case may be) accepts to any extent an allegation made by the defendant—
  (a)   in giving information required by an order under this section, or
  (b)   in any other statement given to the court in relation to any matter relevant to deciding the available amount under section 159,
the court may treat the acceptance as conclusive of the matters to which it relates.

(7)   For the purposes of this section an allegation may be accepted in a manner ordered by the court.

(8)   If the court makes an order under this section it may at any time vary it by making another one.

(9)   No information given under this section which amounts to an admission by the defendant that he has benefited from criminal conduct is admissible in evidence in proceedings for an offence.

Definitions For "defendant", see s 236(3), (6); for "the Director", see s 1(2).
References See para 5.1.

Reconsideration

169 No order made: reconsideration of case

(1)   This section applies if—
  (a)   the first condition in section 156 is satisfied but no court has proceeded under that section,
  (b)   there is evidence which was not available to the prosecutor on the relevant date,
  (c)   before the end of the period of six years starting with the date of conviction the prosecutor or the Director applies to the Crown Court to consider the evidence, and
  (d)   after considering the evidence the court believes it is appropriate for it to proceed under section 156.

(2)   If this section applies the court must proceed under section 156, and when it does so subsections (3) to (8) below apply.

(3)   If the court has already sentenced the defendant for the offence (or any of the offences) concerned, section 156 has effect as if his particular criminal conduct included conduct which constitutes offences which the court has taken into consideration in deciding his sentence for the offence or offences concerned.

(4)   Section 158(2) does not apply, and the rules applying instead are that the court must—
  (a)   take account of conduct occurring before the relevant date;
  (b)   take account of property obtained before that date;
  (c)   take account of property obtained on or after that date if it was obtained as a result of or in connection with conduct occurring before that date.

(5)   In section 160—
  (a)   the first and second assumptions do not apply with regard to property first held by the defendant on or after the relevant date;
  (b)   the third assumption does not apply with regard to expenditure incurred by him on or after that date;
  (c)   the fourth assumption does not apply with regard to property obtained (or assumed to have been obtained) by him on or after that date.

(6)   The recoverable amount for the purposes of section 156 is such amount as—
  (a)   the court believes is just, but
  (b)   does not exceed the amount found under section 157.

(7)   In arriving at the just amount the court must have regard in particular to—
  (a)   the amount found under section 157;
  (b)   any fine imposed on the defendant in respect of the offence (or any of the offences) concerned;
  (c)   any order which falls within section 163(3) and has been made against him in respect of the offence (or any of the offences) concerned and has not already been taken into account by the court in deciding what is the free property held by him for the purposes of section 159;
  (d)   any order which has been made against him in respect of the offence (or any of the offences) concerned under Article 14 of the Criminal Justice (Northern Ireland) Order 1994 (SI 1994/2795 (NI 15)) (compensation orders).

(8)   If an order for the payment of compensation under Article 14 of the Criminal Justice (Northern Ireland) Order 1994 has been made against the defendant in respect of the offence or offences concerned, section 163(5) and (6) above do not apply.

(9)   The relevant date is—
  (a)   if the court made a decision not to proceed under section 156, the date of the decision;
  (b)   if the court did not make such a decision, the date of conviction.

(10)   The date of conviction is—
  (a)   the date on which the defendant was convicted of the offence concerned, or
  (b)   if there are two or more offences and the convictions were on different dates, the date of the latest.

Definitions   For "benefits from conduct", see ss 224(4), (7), 236(6); for "criminal conduct", see ss 224(1), 236(6); for "defendant", see s 236(3), (6); for "the Director", see s 1(2); for "free property", see ss 230, 236(6); for "offence concerned", see ss 156(9), 236(1), (6); for "offences concerned", see ss 156(9), 236(1), (6); for "particular criminal conduct", see ss 224(3), 236(6); for "property", see ss 232(1), 236(6); for "property held", see ss 232(2)(a), (d), 236(6); for "property obtained", see ss 232(2)(b), 236(6); for "property obtained in connection with conduct", see ss 224(6), 236(6); for "sentencing the defendant for an offence", see s 236(4), (6).
References   See para 5.1.

170 No order made: reconsideration of benefit

(1)   This section applies if the following two conditions are satisfied.

(2)   The first condition is that in proceeding under section 156 the court has decided that—

    (a)   the defendant has a criminal lifestyle but has not benefited from his general criminal conduct, or

    (b)   the defendant does not have a criminal lifestyle and has not benefited from his particular criminal conduct.

(3)   If the court proceeded under section 156 because the Director asked it to, the second condition is that—

    (a)   the Director has evidence which was not available to him when the court decided that the defendant had not benefited from his general or particular criminal conduct,

    (b)   before the end of the period of six years starting with the date of conviction the Director applies to the Crown Court to consider the evidence, and

    (c)   after considering the evidence the court concludes that it would have decided that the defendant had benefited from his general or particular criminal conduct (as the case may be) if the evidence had been available to it.

(4)   If the court proceeded under section 156 because the prosecutor asked it to or because it believed it was appropriate for it to do so, the second condition is that—

    (a)   there is evidence which was not available to the prosecutor when the court decided that the defendant had not benefited from his general or particular criminal conduct,

    (b)   before the end of the period of six years starting with the date of conviction the prosecutor or the Director applies to the Crown Court to consider the evidence, and

    (c)   after considering the evidence the court concludes that it would have decided that the defendant had benefited from his general or particular criminal conduct (as the case may be) if the evidence had been available to it.

(5)   If this section applies the court—

    (a)   must make a fresh decision under section 156(4)(b) or (c) whether the defendant has benefited from his general or particular criminal conduct (as the case may be);

    (b)   may make a confiscation order under that section.

(6)   Subsections (7) to (12) below apply if the court proceeds under section 156 in pursuance of this section.

(7)   If the court has already sentenced the defendant for the offence (or any of the offences) concerned, section 156 has effect as if his particular criminal conduct included conduct which constitutes offences which the court has taken into consideration in deciding his sentence for the offence or offences concerned.

(8)   Section 158(2) does not apply, and the rules applying instead are that the court must—

    (a)   take account of conduct occurring before the date of the original decision that the defendant had not benefited from his general or particular criminal conduct;

    (b)   take account of property obtained before that date;

    (c)   take account of property obtained on or after that date if it was obtained as a result of or in connection with conduct occurring before that date.

(9)   In section 160—

    (a)   the first and second assumptions do not apply with regard to property first held by the defendant on or after the date of the original decision that the defendant had not benefited from his general or particular criminal conduct;

    (b)   the third assumption does not apply with regard to expenditure incurred by him on or after that date;

    (c)   the fourth assumption does not apply with regard to property obtained (or assumed to have been obtained) by him on or after that date.

(10)   The recoverable amount for the purposes of section 156 is such amount as—

    (a)   the court believes is just, but

    (b)   does not exceed the amount found under section 157.

(11)   In arriving at the just amount the court must have regard in particular to—

    (a)   the amount found under section 157;

    (b)   any fine imposed on the defendant in respect of the offence (or any of the offences) concerned;

    (c)   any order which falls within section 163(3) and has been made against him in respect of the offence (or any of the offences) concerned and has not already been taken into account by the court in deciding what is the free property held by him for the purposes of section 159;

    (d)   any order which has been made against him in respect of the offence (or any of the offences) concerned under Article 14 of the Criminal Justice (Northern Ireland) Order 1994 (SI 1994/2795 (NI 15)) (compensation orders).

(12)   If an order for the payment of compensation under Article 14 of the Criminal Justice (Northern Ireland) Order 1994 has been made against the defendant in respect of the offence or offences concerned, section 163(5) and (6) above do not apply.

(13)   The date of conviction is the date found by applying section 169(10).

Definitions   For "benefits from conduct", see ss 224(4), (7), 236(6); for "confiscation order", see s 236(5)(a), (6); for "criminal conduct", see ss 224(1), 236(6); for "criminal lifestyle", see ss 223, 236(6), Sch 5; for "defendant", see s 236(3), (6); for "the Director", see s 1(2); for "free property", see ss 230, 236(6); for "general criminal conduct", see ss 224(2), 236(6); for "offence concerned", see ss 156(9), 236(1), (6); for "offences concerned", see ss 156(9), 236(1), (6); for "particular criminal conduct", see ss 224(3), 236(6); for "property", see ss 232(1), 236(6); for "property held", see ss 232(2)(a), (d), 236(6); for "property obtained", see ss 232(2)(b), 236(6); for "property obtained in connection with conduct", see ss 224(6), 236(6); for "sentencing the defendant for an offence", see s 236(4), (6).
References   See para 5.1.

171 Order made: reconsideration of benefit

(1)　This section applies if—
- (a)　a court has made a confiscation order,
- (b)　there is evidence which was not available to the prosecutor or the Director at the relevant time,
- (c)　the prosecutor or the Director believes that if the court were to find the amount of the defendant's benefit in pursuance of this section it would exceed the relevant amount,
- (d)　before the end of the period of six years starting with the date of conviction the prosecutor or the Director applies to the Crown Court to consider the evidence, and
- (e)　after considering the evidence the court believes it is appropriate for it to proceed under this section.

(2)　The court must make a new calculation of the defendant's benefit from the conduct concerned, and when it does so subsections (3) to (6) below apply.

(3)　If a court has already sentenced the defendant for the offence (or any of the offences) concerned section 156 has effect as if his particular criminal conduct included conduct which constitutes offences which the court has taken into consideration in deciding his sentence for the offence or offences concerned.

(4)　Section 158(2) does not apply, and the rules applying instead are that the court must—
- (a)　take account of conduct occurring up to the time it decided the defendant's benefit for the purposes of the confiscation order;
- (b)　take account of property obtained up to that time;
- (c)　take account of property obtained after that time if it was obtained as a result of or in connection with conduct occurring before that time.

(5)　In applying section 158(5) the confiscation order must be ignored.

(6)　In section 160—
- (a)　the first and second assumptions do not apply with regard to property first held by the defendant after the time the court decided his benefit for the purposes of the confiscation order;
- (b)　the third assumption does not apply with regard to expenditure incurred by him after that time;
- (c)　the fourth assumption does not apply with regard to property obtained (or assumed to have been obtained) by him after that time.

(7)　If the amount found under the new calculation of the defendant's benefit exceeds the relevant amount the court—
- (a)　must make a new calculation of the recoverable amount for the purposes of section 156, and
- (b)　if it exceeds the amount required to be paid under the confiscation order, may vary the order by substituting for the amount required to be paid such amount as it believes is just.

(8)　In applying subsection (7)(a) the court must—
- (a)　take the new calculation of the defendant's benefit;
- (b)　apply section 159 as if references to the time the confiscation order is made were to the time of the new calculation of the recoverable amount and as if references to the date of the confiscation order were to the date of that new calculation.

(9)   In applying subsection (7)(b) the court must have regard in particular to—

   (a)   any fine imposed on the defendant for the offence (or any of the offences) concerned;

   (b)   any order which falls within section 163(3) and has been made against him in respect of the offence (or any of the offences) concerned and has not already been taken into account by the court in deciding what is the free property held by him for the purposes of section 159;

   (c)   any order which has been made against him in respect of the offence (or any of the offences) concerned under Article 14 of the Criminal Justice (Northern Ireland) Order 1994 (SI 1994/2795 (NI 15)) (compensation orders).

(10) But in applying subsection (7)(b) the court must not have regard to an order falling within subsection (9)(c) if a court has made a direction under section 163(6).

(11) In deciding under this section whether one amount exceeds another the court must take account of any change in the value of money.

(12) The relevant time is—

   (a)   when the court calculated the defendant's benefit for the purposes of the confiscation order, if this section has not applied previously;

   (b)   when the court last calculated the defendant's benefit in pursuance of this section, if this section has applied previously.

(13) The relevant amount is—

   (a)   the amount found as the defendant's benefit for the purposes of the confiscation order, if this section has not applied previously;

   (b)   the amount last found as the defendant's benefit in pursuance of this section, if this section has applied previously.

(14) The date of conviction is the date found by applying section 169(10).

Definitions   For "benefits from conduct", see ss 224(4), (7), 236(6); for "confiscation order", see s 236(5)(a), (6); for "criminal conduct", see ss 224(1), 236(6); for "defendant", see s 236(3), (6); for "the Director", see s 1(2); for "free property", see ss 230, 236(6); for "offence concerned", see ss 156(9), 236(1), (6); for "offences concerned", see ss 156(9), 236(1), (6); for "particular criminal conduct", see ss 224(3), 236(6); for "property", see ss 232(1), 236(6); for "property held", see ss 232(2)(a), (d), 236(6); for "property obtained", see ss 232(2)(b), 236(6); for "property obtained in connection with conduct", see ss 224(6), 236(6); for "sentencing the defendant for an offence", see s 236(4), (6).
References   See para 5.1.

---

172 Order made: reconsideration of available amount

(1)   This section applies if—

   (a)   a court has made a confiscation order,

   (b)   the amount required to be paid was the amount found under section 157(2), and

   (c)   an applicant falling within subsection (2) applies to the Crown Court to make a new calculation of the available amount.

(2)   These applicants fall within this subsection—

   (a)   the prosecutor;

   (b)   the Director;

   (c)   a receiver appointed under section 198 or 200.

(3)   In a case where this section applies the court must make the new calculation, and in doing so it must apply section 159 as if references to the time the confiscation order is made were to the time of the new calculation and as if references to the date of the confiscation order were to the date of the new calculation.

(4)   If the amount found under the new calculation exceeds the relevant amount the court may vary the order by substituting for the amount required to be paid such amount as—

    (a)   it believes is just, but
    (b)   does not exceed the amount found as the defendant's benefit from the conduct concerned.

(5)   In deciding what is just the court must have regard in particular to—

    (a)   any fine imposed on the defendant for the offence (or any of the offences) concerned;
    (b)   any order which falls within section 163(3) and has been made against him in respect of the offence (or any of the offences) concerned and has not already been taken into account by the court in deciding what is the free property held by him for the purposes of section 159;
    (c)   any order which has been made against him in respect of the offence (or any of the offences) concerned under Article 14 of the Criminal Justice (Northern Ireland) Order 1994 (SI 1994/2795 (NI 15)) (compensation orders).

(6)   But in deciding what is just the court must not have regard to an order falling within subsection (5)(c) if a court has made a direction under section 163(6).

(7)   In deciding under this section whether one amount exceeds another the court must take account of any change in the value of money.

(8)   The relevant amount is—

    (a)   the amount found as the available amount for the purposes of the confiscation order, if this section has not applied previously;
    (b)   the amount last found as the available amount in pursuance of this section, if this section has applied previously.

(9)   The amount found as the defendant's benefit from the conduct concerned is—

    (a)   the amount so found when the confiscation order was made, or
    (b)   if one or more new calculations of the defendant's benefit have been made under section 171 the amount found on the occasion of the last such calculation.

Definitions   For "benefits from conduct", see ss 224(4), (7), 236(6); for "confiscation order", see s 236(5)(a), (6); for "defendant", see s 236(3), (6); for "the Director", see s 1(2); for "free property", see ss 230, 236(6); for "offence concerned", see ss 156(9), 236(1), (6); for "offences concerned", see ss 156(9), 236(1), (6); for "property", see ss 232(1), 236(6).
References   See para 5.1.

---

173 Inadequacy of available amount: variation of order

(1)   This section applies if—

    (a)   a court has made a confiscation order, and

(b) the defendant, or a receiver appointed under section 198 or 200, applies to the Crown Court to vary the order under this section.

(2) In such a case the court must calculate the available amount, and in doing so it must apply section 159 as if references to the time the confiscation order is made were to the time of the calculation and as if references to the date of the confiscation order were to the date of the calculation.

(3) If the court finds that the available amount (as so calculated) is inadequate for the payment of any amount remaining to be paid under the confiscation order it may vary the order by substituting for the amount required to be paid such smaller amount as the court believes is just.

(4) If a person has been adjudged bankrupt or his estate has been sequestrated, or if an order for the winding up of a company has been made, the court must take into account the extent to which realisable property held by that person or that company may be distributed among creditors.

(5) The court may disregard any inadequacy which it believes is attributable (wholly or partly) to anything done by the defendant for the purpose of preserving property held by the recipient of a tainted gift from any risk of realisation under this Part.

(6) In subsection (4) "company" means any company which may be wound up under the Insolvency (Northern Ireland) Order 1989 (SI 1989/2405 (NI 19)) or the Insolvency Act 1986 (c 45).

Definitions   For "confiscation order", see s 236(5)(a), (6); for "defendant", see s 236(3), (6); for "property", see ss 232(1), 236(6); for "property held", see ss 232(2)(a), (d), 236(6); for "realisable property", see ss 231, 236(6); for "recipient of a tainted gift", see ss 226(3), 236(6); for "tainted gift", see ss 225, 236(6).
References   See para 5.1.

174 Inadequacy of available amount: discharge of order

(1) This section applies if—
(a) a court has made a confiscation order,
(b) the prosecutor applies to the Crown Court for the discharge of the order, and
(c) the amount remaining to be paid under the order is less than £1,000.

(2) In such a case the court must calculate the available amount, and in doing so it must apply section 159 as if references to the time the confiscation order is made were to the time of the calculation and as if references to the date of the confiscation order were to the date of the calculation.

(3) If the court—
(a) finds that the available amount (as so calculated) is inadequate to meet the amount remaining to be paid, and
(b) is satisfied that the inadequacy is due wholly to a specified reason or a combination of specified reasons,
it may discharge the confiscation order.

(4) The specified reasons are—
(a) in a case where any of the realisable property consists of money in a currency other than sterling, that fluctuations in currency exchange rates have occurred;

(b)   any reason specified by the Secretary of State by order.

(5)   The Secretary of State may by order vary the amount for the time being specified in subsection (1)(c).

Definitions   For "confiscation order", see s 236(5)(a), (6); for "property", see ss 232(1), 236(6); for "realisable property", see ss 231, 236(6).
References   See para 5.1.

---

175 Small amount outstanding: discharge of order

(1)   This section applies if—
- (a)   a court has made a confiscation order,
- (b)   a chief clerk applies to the Crown Court for the discharge of the order, and
- (c)   the amount remaining to be paid under the order is £50 or less.

(2)   In such a case the court may discharge the order.

(3)   The Secretary of State may by order vary the amount for the time being specified in subsection (1)(c).

Definitions   For "confiscation order", see s 236(5)(a), (6).
References   See para 5.1.

---

176 Information

(1)   This section applies if—
- (a)   the court proceeds under section 156 in pursuance of section 169 or 170, or
- (b)   the prosecutor or the Director applies under section 171.

(2)   In such a case—
- (a)   the prosecutor or the Director (as the case may be) must give the court a statement of information within the period the court orders;
- (b)   section 166 applies accordingly (with appropriate modifications where the prosecutor or the Director applies under section 171);
- (c)   section 167 applies accordingly;
- (d)   section 168 applies as it applies in the circumstances mentioned in section 168(1).

Definitions   For "the Director", see s 1(2).
References   See para 5.1.

Defendant absconds

177 Defendant convicted or committed

(1)   This section applies if the following two conditions are satisfied.

(2)   The first condition is that a defendant absconds after—
- (a)   he is convicted of an offence or offences in proceedings before the Crown Court, or

    (b)   he is committed to the Crown Court in respect of an offence or offences under section 218 below (committal with a view to a confiscation order being considered).

(3)   The second condition is that—
    (a)   the prosecutor or the Director applies to the Crown Court to proceed under this section, and
    (b)   the court believes it is appropriate for it to do so.

(4)   If this section applies the court must proceed under section 156 in the same way as it must proceed if the two conditions there mentioned are satisfied; but this is subject to subsection (5).

(5)   If the court proceeds under section 156 as applied by this section, this Part has effect with these modifications—
    (a)   any person the court believes is likely to be affected by an order under section 156 is entitled to appear before the court and make representations;
    (b)   the court must not make an order under section 156 unless the prosecutor or the Director (as the case may be) has taken reasonable steps to contact the defendant;
    (c)   section 156(9) applies as if the reference to subsection (2) were to subsection (2) of this section;
    (d)   sections 160, 166(4), 167 and 168 must be ignored;
    (e)   sections 169, 170 and 171 must be ignored while the defendant is still an absconder.

(6)   Once the defendant has ceased to be an absconder section 169 has effect as if subsection (1)(a) read—
    "(a)   at a time when the first condition in section 177 was satisfied the court did not proceed under section 156,".

(7)   If the court does not believe it is appropriate for it to proceed under this section, once the defendant ceases to be an absconder section 169 has effect as if subsection (1)(b) read—
    "(b)   there is evidence which was not available to the prosecutor or the Director on the relevant date,".

Definitions   For "defendant", see s 236(3), (6); for "the Director", see s 1(2).
References   See para 5.4.

178 Defendant neither convicted nor acquitted

(1)   This section applies if the following two conditions are satisfied.

(2)   The first condition is that—
    (a)   proceedings for an offence or offences are started against a defendant but are not concluded,
    (b)   he absconds, and
    (c)   the period of two years (starting with the day the court believes he absconded) has ended.

(3)   The second condition is that—
    (a)   the prosecutor or the Director applies to the Crown Court to proceed under this section, and
    (b)   the court believes it is appropriate for it to do so.

(4)   If this section applies the court must proceed under section 156 in the same way as it must proceed if the two conditions there mentioned are satisfied; but this is subject to subsection (5).

(5)   If the court proceeds under section 156 as applied by this section, this Part has effect with these modifications—

> (a)   any person the court believes is likely to be affected by an order under section 156 is entitled to appear before the court and make representations;
>
> (b)   the court must not make an order under section 156 unless the prosecutor or the Director (as the case may be) has taken reasonable steps to contact the defendant;
>
> (c)   section 156(9) applies as if the reference to subsection (2) were to subsection (2) of this section;
>
> (d)   sections 160, 166(4) and 167 to 170 must be ignored;
>
> (e)   section 171 must be ignored while the defendant is still an absconder.

(6)   Once the defendant has ceased to be an absconder section 171 has effect as if references to the date of conviction were to—

> (a)   the day when proceedings for the offence concerned were started against the defendant, or
>
> (b)   if there are two or more offences and proceedings for them were started on different days, the earliest of those days.

(7)   If—

> (a)   the court makes an order under section 156 as applied by this section, and
>
> (b)   the defendant is later convicted in proceedings before the Crown Court of the offence (or any of the offences) concerned,

section 156 does not apply so far as that conviction is concerned.

Definitions   For "defendant", see s 236(3), (6); for "the Director", see s 1(2); for "offence concerned", see ss 156(9), 236(1), (6); for "offences concerned", see ss 156(9), 236(1), (6); for "proceedings concluded", see ss 233(3)–(8), 236(6); for "proceedings started", see ss 233(1), (2), 236(6).
References   See para 5.1.

---

179 Variation of order

(1)   This section applies if—

> (a)   the court makes a confiscation order under section 156 as applied by section 178,
>
> (b)   the defendant ceases to be an absconder,
>
> (c)   he is convicted of an offence (or any of the offences) mentioned in section 178(2)(a),
>
> (d)   he believes that the amount required to be paid was too large (taking the circumstances prevailing when the amount was found for the purposes of the order), and
>
> (e)   before the end of the relevant period he applies to the Crown Court to consider the evidence on which his belief is based.

(2)   If (after considering the evidence) the court concludes that the defendant's belief is well founded—

    (a)   it must find the amount which should have been the amount required to be paid (taking the circumstances prevailing when the amount was found for the purposes of the order), and

    (b)   it may vary the order by substituting for the amount required to be paid such amount as it believes is just.

(3)   The relevant period is the period of 28 days starting with—

    (a)   the date on which the defendant was convicted of the offence mentioned in section 178(2)(a), or

    (b)   if there are two or more offences and the convictions were on different dates, the date of the latest.

(4)   But in a case where section 178(2)(a) applies to more than one offence the court must not make an order under this section unless it is satisfied that there is no possibility of any further proceedings being taken or continued in relation to any such offence in respect of which the defendant has not been convicted.

Definitions   For "confiscation order", see s 236(5)(a), (6); for "defendant", see s 236(3), (6).
References   See para 5.1.

180 Discharge of order

(1)   Subsection (2) applies if—

    (a)   the court makes a confiscation order under section 156 as applied by section 178,

    (b)   the defendant is later tried for the offence or offences concerned and acquitted on all counts, and

    (c)   he applies to the Crown Court to discharge the order.

(2)   In such a case the court must discharge the order.

(3)   Subsection (4) applies if—

    (a)   the court makes a confiscation order under section 156 as applied by section 178,

    (b)   the defendant ceases to be an absconder,

    (c)   subsection (1)(b) does not apply, and

    (d)   he applies to the Crown Court to discharge the order.

(4)   In such a case the court may discharge the order if it finds that—

    (a)   there has been undue delay in continuing the proceedings mentioned in section 178(2), or

    (b)   the prosecutor does not intend to proceed with the prosecution.

(5)   If the court discharges a confiscation order under this section it may make such a consequential or incidental order as it believes is appropriate.

Definitions   For "confiscation order", see s 236(5)(a), (6); for "defendant", see s 236(3), (6); for "offence concerned", see ss 156(9), 236(1), (6); for "offences concerned", see ss 156(9), 236(1), (6).
References   See para 5.1.

Appeals

181 Appeal by prosecutor or Director

(1)   If the Crown Court makes a confiscation order the prosecutor or the Director may appeal to the Court of Appeal in respect of the order.

(2)   If the Crown Court decides not to make a confiscation order the prosecutor or the Director may appeal to the Court of Appeal against the decision.

(3)   Subsections (1) and (2) do not apply to an order or decision made by virtue of section 169, 170, 177 or 178.

182 Court's powers on appeal

(1)   On an appeal under section 181(1) the Court of Appeal may confirm, quash or vary the confiscation order.

(2)   On an appeal under section 181(2) the Court of Appeal may confirm the decision, or if it believes the decision was wrong it may—
      (a)   itself proceed under section 156 (ignoring subsections (1) to (3)), or
      (b)   direct the Crown Court to proceed afresh under section 156.

(3)   In proceeding afresh in pursuance of this section the Crown Court must comply with any directions the Court of Appeal may make.

(4)   If a court makes or varies a confiscation order under this section or in pursuance of a direction under this section it must—
      (a)   have regard to any fine imposed on the defendant in respect of the offence (or any of the offences) concerned;
      (b)   have regard to any order which falls within section 163(3) and has been made against him in respect of the offence (or any of the offences) concerned, unless the order has already been taken into account by a court in deciding what is the free property held by the defendant for the purposes of section 159.

(5)   If the Court of Appeal proceeds under section 156 or the Crown Court proceeds afresh under that section in pursuance of a direction under this section subsections (6) to (10) apply.

(6)   If a court has already sentenced the defendant for the offence (or any of the offences) concerned, section 156 has effect as if his particular criminal conduct included conduct which constitutes offences which the court has taken into consideration in deciding his sentence for the offence or offences concerned.

(7)   If an order has been made against the defendant in respect of the offence (or any of the offences) concerned under Article 14 of the Criminal Justice (Northern Ireland) Order 1994 (SI 1994/2795 (NI 15)) (compensation orders)—
      (a)   the court must have regard to it, and
      (b)   section 163(5) and (6) above do not apply.

(8)   Section 158(2) does not apply, and the rules applying instead are that the court must—
      (a)   take account of conduct occurring before the relevant date;
      (b)   take account of property obtained before that date;
      (c)   take account of property obtained on or after that date if it was obtained as a result of or in connection with conduct occurring before that date.

(9)   In section 160—
- (a)   the first and second assumptions do not apply with regard to property first held by the defendant on or after the relevant date;
- (b)   the third assumption does not apply with regard to expenditure incurred by him on or after that date;
- (c)   the fourth assumption does not apply with regard to property obtained (or assumed to have been obtained) by him on or after that date.

(10) Section 176 applies as it applies in the circumstances mentioned in subsection (1) of that section.

(11) The relevant date is the date on which the Crown Court decided not to make a confiscation order.

Definitions   For "confiscation order", see s 236(5)(a), (6); for "criminal conduct", see ss 224(1), 236(6); for "defendant", see s 236(3), (6); for "free property", see ss 230, 236(6); for "offence concerned", see ss 156(9), 236(1), (6); for "offences concerned", see ss 156(9), 236(1), (6); for "particular criminal conduct", see ss 224(3), 236(6); for "property", see ss 232(1), 236(6); for "property held", see ss 232(2)(a), (d), 236(6); for "property obtained", see ss 232(2)(b), 236(6); for "property obtained in connection with conduct", see ss 224(6), 236(6); for "sentencing the defendant for an offence", see s 236(4), (6).
References   See para 5.1.

183 Appeal to House of Lords

(1)   An appeal lies to the House of Lords from a decision of the Court of Appeal on an appeal under section 181.

(2)   An appeal under this section lies at the instance of—
- (a)   the defendant or the prosecutor (if the prosecutor appealed under section 181);
- (b)   the defendant or the Director (if the Director appealed under section 181).

(3)   On an appeal from a decision of the Court of Appeal to confirm, vary or make a confiscation order the House of Lords may confirm, quash or vary the order.

(4)   On an appeal from a decision of the Court of Appeal to confirm the decision of the Crown Court not to make a confiscation order or from a decision of the Court of Appeal to quash a confiscation order the House of Lords may—
- (a)   confirm the decision, or
- (b)   direct the Crown Court to proceed afresh under section 156 if it believes the decision was wrong.

(5)   In proceeding afresh in pursuance of this section the Crown Court must comply with any directions the House of Lords may make.

(6)   If a court varies a confiscation order under this section or makes a confiscation order in pursuance of a direction under this section it must—
- (a)   have regard to any fine imposed on the defendant in respect of the offence (or any of the offences) concerned;
- (b)   have regard to any order which falls within section 163(3) and has been made against him in respect of the offence (or any of the offences) concerned, unless the order has already been taken into

account by a court in deciding what is the free property held by the defendant for the purposes of section 159.

(7)   If the Crown Court proceeds afresh under section 156 in pursuance of a direction under this section subsections (8) to (12) apply.

(8)   If a court has already sentenced the defendant for the offence (or any of the offences) concerned, section 156 has effect as if his particular criminal conduct included conduct which constitutes offences which the court has taken into consideration in deciding his sentence for the offence or offences concerned.

(9)   If an order has been made against the defendant in respect of the offence (or any of the offences) concerned under Article 14 of the Criminal Justice (Northern Ireland) Order 1994 (SI 1994/2795 (NI 15)) (compensation orders)—
   (a)   the Crown Court must have regard to it, and
   (b)   section 163(5) and (6) above do not apply.

(10)   Section 158(2) does not apply, and the rules applying instead are that the Crown Court must—
   (a)   take account of conduct occurring before the relevant date;
   (b)   take account of property obtained before that date;
   (c)   take account of property obtained on or after that date if it was obtained as a result of or in connection with conduct occurring before that date.

(11)   In section 160—
   (a)   the first and second assumptions do not apply with regard to property first held by the defendant on or after the relevant date;
   (b)   the third assumption does not apply with regard to expenditure incurred by him on or after that date;
   (c)   the fourth assumption does not apply with regard to property obtained (or assumed to have been obtained) by him on or after that date.

(12)   Section 176 applies as it applies in the circumstances mentioned in subsection (1) of that section.

(13)   The relevant date is—
   (a)   in a case where the Crown Court made a confiscation order which was quashed by the Court of Appeal, the date on which the Crown Court made the order;
   (b)   in any other case, the date on which the Crown Court decided not to make a confiscation order.

Definitions   For "confiscation order", see s 236(5)(a), (6); for "criminal conduct", see ss 224(1), 236(6); for "defendant", see s 236(3), (6); for "the Director", see s 1(2); for "free property", see ss 230, 236(6); for "offence concerned", see ss 156(9), 236(1), (6); for "offences concerned", see ss 156(9), 236(1), (6); for "particular criminal conduct", see ss 224(3), 236(6); for "property", see ss 232(1), 236(6); for "property held", see ss 232(2)(a), (d), 236(6); for "property obtained", see ss 232(2)(b), 236(6); for "property obtained in connection with conduct", see ss 224(6), 236(6); for "sentencing the defendant for an offence", see s 236(4), (6).
References   See para 5.1.

Enforcement authority

184 Enforcement authority

(1)   Subsection (2) applies if a court makes a confiscation order and any of the following paragraphs applies—

(a)   the court proceeded under section 156 after being asked to do so by the Director;

(b)   the court proceeded under section 156 by virtue of an application by the Director under section 169, 170, 177 or 178;

(c)   the court proceeded under section 156 as a result of an appeal by the Director under section 181(2) or 183;

(d)   before the court made the order the Director applied to the court to appoint him as the enforcement authority for the order.

(2)   In any such case the court must appoint the Director as the enforcement authority for the order.

Definitions	For "confiscation order", see s 236(5)(a), (6); for "the Director", see s 1(2).
References	See para 5.1.

Enforcement as fines etc

185 Enforcement as fines etc

(1)   This section applies if a court makes a confiscation order.

(2)   Section 35(1)(c), (2), (4) and (5) of the Criminal Justice Act (Northern Ireland) 1945 (c 15) (functions of court as to fines) apply as if the amount ordered to be paid were a fine imposed on the defendant by the Crown Court.

(3)   An amount payable under a confiscation order is not a fine, costs, damages or compensation for the purposes of Article 35 of the Criminal Justice (Northern Ireland) Order 1998 (SI 1998/1504 (NI 9)) (parent or guardian to pay fine etc instead of child).

Definitions	For "confiscation order", see s 236(5)(a), (6).
References	See para 5.5.

186 Director's application for enforcement

(1)   If the Director believes that the conditions set out in subsection (2) are satisfied he may make an ex parte application to the Crown Court for the issue of a summons against the defendant.

(2)   The conditions are that—

(a)   a confiscation order has been made;

(b)   the Director has been appointed as the enforcement authority for the order;

(c)   the order is not satisfied;

(d)   the order is not subject to appeal;

(e)   the Director has done all that is practicable (apart from this section) to enforce the order.

(3)   If it appears to the Crown Court that the conditions are satisfied it may issue a summons ordering the defendant to appear before the court at the time and place specified in the summons.

(4)   If the defendant fails to appear before the Crown Court in pursuance of the summons the court may issue a warrant for his arrest.

(5)   If—
    (a)   the defendant appears before the Crown Court in pursuance of the summons or of a warrant issued under subsection (4), and
    (b)   the court is satisfied that the conditions set out in subsection (2) are satisfied,

it may issue a warrant committing the defendant to prison or to detention under section 5 of the Treatment of Offenders Act (Northern Ireland) 1968 (c 29 (NI)) for default in payment of the amount ordered to be paid by the confiscation order.

(6)   Subsection (7) applies if the amount remaining to be paid under the confiscation order when the warrant under subsection (5) is issued is less than the amount ordered to be paid.

(7)   In such a case the court must substitute for the term of imprisonment or detention fixed in respect of the order under section 35(1) of the Criminal Justice Act (Northern Ireland) 1945 (c 15 (NI)) such term as bears to the original term the same proportion as the amount remaining to be paid bears to the amount ordered to be paid.

Definitions   For "confiscation order", see s 236(5)(a), (6); for "defendant", see s 236(3), (6); for "the Director", see s 1(2); for "satisfied", see ss 235(1), 236(6); for "subject to appeal", see ss 235(2), 236(6). **References**   See para 5.6.

187 Provisions about imprisonment or detention

(1)   Subsection (2) applies if—
    (a)   a warrant committing the defendant to prison or detention is issued for a default in payment of an amount ordered to be paid under a confiscation order in respect of an offence or offences, and
    (b)   at the time the warrant is issued the defendant is liable to serve a term of custody in respect of the offence (or any of the offences).

(2)   In such a case the term of imprisonment or of detention to be served in default of payment of the amount does not begin to run until after the term mentioned in subsection (1)(b) above.

(3)   The reference in subsection (1)(b) to the term of custody the defendant is liable to serve in respect of the offence (or any of the offences) is a reference to the term of imprisonment, or detention under section 5 of the Treatment of Offenders Act (Northern Ireland) 1968 (c 29 (NI)), which he is liable to serve in respect of the offence (or any of the offences).

(4)   For the purposes of subsection (3) consecutive terms and terms which are wholly or partly concurrent must be treated as a single term and the following must be ignored—
    (a)   any sentence of imprisonment or order for detention suspended under section 18 of the Treatment of Offenders Act (Northern Ireland) 1968 which has not taken effect at the time the warrant is issued;

(b)   any term of imprisonment or detention fixed under section 35(1)(c) of the Criminal Justice Act (Northern Ireland) 1945 (c 15 (NI)) (term to be served in default of payment of fine etc) for which a warrant committing the defendant to prison or detention has not been issued at that time.

(5)   If the defendant serves a term of imprisonment or detention in default of paying any amount due under a confiscation order, his serving that term does not prevent the confiscation order from continuing to have effect so far as any other method of enforcement is concerned.

Definitions   For "confiscation order", see s 236(5)(a), (6); for "defendant", see s 236(3), (6).
References   See para 5.7.

188 Reconsideration etc: variation of prison term

(1)   Subsection (2) applies if—
  (a)   a court varies a confiscation order under section 171, 172, 173, 179, 182 or 183,
  (b)   the effect of the variation is to vary the maximum period applicable in relation to the order under section 35(2) of the Criminal Justice Act (Northern Ireland) 1945 (c 15 (NI)), and
  (c)   the result is that that maximum period is less than the term of imprisonment or detention fixed in respect of the order under section 35(1)(c) of that Act.

(2)   In such a case the court must fix a reduced term of imprisonment or detention in respect of the confiscation order under section 35(1)(c) of that Act in place of the term previously fixed.

(3)   Subsection (4) applies if paragraphs (a) and (b) of subsection (1) apply but paragraph (c) does not.

(4)   In such a case the court may amend the term of imprisonment or detention fixed in respect of the confiscation order under section 35(1)(c) of that Act.

(5)   If the effect of section 162 is to increase the maximum period applicable in relation to a confiscation order under section 35(2) of that Act, on the application of the appropriate person the Crown Court may amend the term of imprisonment or detention fixed in respect of the order under section 35(1)(c) of that Act.

(6)   The appropriate person is—
  (a)   the Director, if he was appointed as the enforcement authority for the order under section 184;
  (b)   the prosecutor, in any other case.

Definitions   For "confiscation order", see s 236(5)(a), (6); for "the Director", see s 1(2).
References   See para 5.1.

Restraint orders

189 Conditions for exercise of powers

(1)   The High Court may exercise the powers conferred by section 190 if any of the following conditions is satisfied.

(2)   The first condition is that—
    (a)   a criminal investigation has been started in Northern Ireland with regard to an offence, and
    (b)   there is reasonable cause to believe that the alleged offender has benefited from his criminal conduct.

(3)   The second condition is that—
    (a)   proceedings for an offence have been started in Northern Ireland and not concluded,
    (b)   there is reasonable cause to believe that the defendant has benefited from his criminal conduct.

(4)   The third condition is that—
    (a)   an application by the prosecutor or the Director has been made under section 169, 170, 177 or 178 and not concluded, or the court believes that such an application is to be made, and
    (b)   there is reasonable cause to believe that the defendant has benefited from his criminal conduct.

(5)   The fourth condition is that—
    (a)   an application by the prosecutor or the Director has been made under section 171 and not concluded, or the court believes that such an application is to be made, and
    (b)   there is reasonable cause to believe that the court will decide under that section that the amount found under the new calculation of the defendant's benefit exceeds the relevant amount (as defined in that section).

(6)   The fifth condition is that—
    (a)   an application by the prosecutor or the Director has been made under section 172 and not concluded, or the court believes that such an application is to be made, and
    (b)   there is reasonable cause to believe that the court will decide under that section that the amount found under the new calculation of the available amount exceeds the relevant amount (as defined in that section).

(7)   The second condition is not satisfied if the court believes that—
    (a)   there has been undue delay in continuing the proceedings, or
    (b)   the prosecutor does not intend to proceed.

(8)   If an application mentioned in the third, fourth or fifth condition has been made the condition is not satisfied if the court believes that—
    (a)   there has been undue delay in continuing the application, or
    (b)   the prosecutor or the Director (as the case may be) does not intend to proceed.

(9)   If the first condition is satisfied—
    (a)   references in this Part to the defendant are to the alleged offender;
    (b)   references in this Part to the prosecutor are to the person the court believes is to have conduct of any proceedings for the offence;
    (c)   section 225(9) has effect as if proceedings for the offence had been started against the defendant when the investigation was started.

Definitions   For "application under s 169, 170, 177 or 178 concluded", see ss 234(1), 236(6); for "application under s 171 or 172 concluded", see ss 234(2), 236(6); for "benefits from conduct", see ss 224(4), (7), 236(6); for "confiscation order", see s 236(5)(a), (6); for "criminal conduct", see ss 224(1), 236(6); for "defendant", see s 236(3), (6) (and sub-s (9)(a) above); for "the Director", see s 1(2); for "proceedings concluded", see ss 233(3)–(8), 236(6); for "proceedings started", see ss 233(1), (2), 236(6).
References   See para 5.1.

190 Restraint orders

(1)   If any condition set out in section 189 is satisfied the High Court may make an order (a restraint order) prohibiting any specified person from dealing with any realisable property held by him.

(2)   A restraint order may provide that it applies—
- (a)   to all realisable property held by the specified person whether or not the property is described in the order;
- (b)   to realisable property transferred to the specified person after the order is made.

(3)   A restraint order may be made subject to exceptions, and an exception may in particular—
- (a)   make provision for reasonable living expenses and reasonable legal expenses;
- (b)   make provision for the purpose of enabling any person to carry on any trade, business, profession or occupation;
- (c)   be made subject to conditions.

(4)   But an exception to a restraint order may not make provision for any legal expenses which—
- (a)   relate to an offence which falls within subsection (5), and
- (b)   are incurred by the defendant or by a recipient of a tainted gift.

(5)   These offences fall within this subsection—
- (a)   the offence mentioned in section 189(2) or (3), if the first or second condition (as the case may be) is satisfied;
- (b)   the offence (or any of the offences) concerned, if the third, fourth or fifth condition is satisfied.

(6)   Subsection (7) applies if—
- (a)   the court makes a restraint order, and
- (b)   the applicant for the order applies to the court to proceed under subsection (7) (whether as part of the application for the restraint order or at any time afterwards).

(7)   The court may make such order as it believes is appropriate for the purpose of ensuring that the restraint order is effective.

(8)   A restraint order does not affect property for the time being subject to a charge under any of these provisions—
- (a)   section 9 of the Drug Trafficking Offences Act 1986 (c 32);
- (b)   section 78 of the Criminal Justice Act 1988 (c 33);
- (c)   Article 14 of the Criminal Justice (Confiscation) (Northern Ireland) Order 1990 (SI 1990/2588 (NI 17));
- (d)   section 27 of the Drug Trafficking Act 1994 (c 37);

(e) Article 32 of the Proceeds of Crime (Northern Ireland) Order 1996 (SI 1996/1299 (NI 9)).

(9) Dealing with property includes removing it from Northern Ireland.

Definitions For "offence concerned", see ss 156(9), 236(1), (6); for "offences concerned", see ss 156(9), 236(1), (6); for "property held", see ss 232(2)(a), (d), 236(6); for "property obtained", see ss 232(2)(b), 236(6); for "property transferred", see ss 232(2)(c), 236(6); for "realisable property", see ss 231, 236(6); for "recipient of a tainted gift", see ss 226(3), 236(6); for "tainted gift", see ss 225, 236(6). **References** See para 5.1.

---

191 Application, discharge and variation

(1) A restraint order—
    (a) may be made only on an application by an applicant falling within subsection (2);
    (b) may be made on an ex parte application to a judge in chambers.

(2) These applicants fall within this subsection—
    (a) the prosecutor;
    (b) the Director;
    (c) an accredited financial investigator.

(3) An application to discharge or vary a restraint order or an order under section 190(7) may be made to the High Court by—
    (a) the person who applied for the order;
    (b) any person affected by the order.

(4) Subsections (5) to (7) apply to an application under subsection (3).

(5) The court—
    (a) may discharge the order;
    (b) may vary the order.

(6) If the condition in section 189 which was satisfied was that proceedings were started or an application was made, the court must discharge the order on the conclusion of the proceedings or of the application (as the case may be).

(7) If the condition in section 189 which was satisfied was that an investigation was started or an application was to be made, the court must discharge the order if within a reasonable time proceedings for the offence are not started or the application is not made (as the case may be).

Definitions For "accredited financial investigator", see s 3(5); for "the Director", see s 1(2); for "proceedings concluded", see ss 233(3)–(8), 236(6); for "proceedings started", see ss 233(1), (2), 236(6); for "the prosecutor", see s 189(9)(b); for "restraint order", see s 236(5)(b), (6). **References** See para 5.1.

---

192 Appeal to Court of Appeal

(1) If on an application for a restraint order the court decides not to make one, the person who applied for the order may appeal to the Court of Appeal against the decision.

(2) If an application is made under section 191(3) in relation to a restraint order or an order under section 190(7) the following persons may appeal to the Court of Appeal in respect of the High Court's decision on the application—

    (a)   the person who applied for the order;

    (b)   any person affected by the order.

(3)   On an appeal under subsection (1) or (2) the Court of Appeal may—

    (a)   confirm the decision, or

    (b)   make such order as it believes is appropriate.

Definitions   For "restraint order", see s 236(5)(b), (6).
References   See para 5.1.

---

193 Appeal to House of Lords

(1)   An appeal lies to the House of Lords from a decision of the Court of Appeal on an appeal under section 192.

(2)   An appeal under this section lies at the instance of any person who was a party to the proceedings before the Court of Appeal.

(3)   On an appeal under this section the House of Lords may—

    (a)   confirm the decision of the Court of Appeal, or

    (b)   make such order as it believes is appropriate.

References   See para 5.1.

---

194 Seizure

(1)   If a restraint order is in force a constable or a customs officer may seize any realisable property to which it applies to prevent its removal from Northern Ireland.

(2)   Property seized under subsection (1) must be dealt with in accordance with the directions of the court which made the order.

Definitions   For "customs officer", see s 454; for "property", see ss 232(1), 236(6); for "realisable property", see ss 231, 236(6); for "restraint order", see s 236(5)(b), (6).
References   See para 5.1.

---

195 Supplementary

(1)   The person applying for a restraint order must be treated for the purposes of section 66 of the Land Registration Act (Northern Ireland) 1970 (c 18 (NI)) (cautions) as a person interested in relation to any registered land to which—

    (a)   the application relates, or

    (b)   a restraint order made in pursuance of the application relates.

(2)   Upon being served with a copy of a restraint order, the Registrar shall, in respect of any registered land to which a restraint order or an application for a restraint order relates, make an entry inhibiting any dealing with the land without the consent of the High Court.

(3)   Subsections (2) and (4) of section 67 of the Land Registration Act (Northern Ireland) 1970 (inhibitions) shall apply to an entry made under subsection (2) as they apply to an entry made on the application of any person interested in the registered land under subsection (1) of that section.

(4)   Where a restraint order has been protected by an entry registered under the Land Registration Act (Northern Ireland) 1970 or the Registration of Deeds Acts, an order discharging the restraint order may require that the entry be vacated.

(5)   In this section—

"Registrar" and "entry" have the same meanings as in the Land Registration Act (Northern Ireland) 1970; and

"Registration of Deeds Acts" has the meaning given by section 46(2) of the Interpretation Act (Northern Ireland) 1954 (c 33 (NI)).

Definitions   For "restraint order", see s 236(5)(b), (6).
References   See para 5.8.

Management receivers

196 Appointment

(1)   Subsection (2) applies if—

(a)   the High Court makes a restraint order, and

(b)   the applicant for the restraint order applies to the court to proceed under subsection (2) (whether as part of the application for the restraint order or at any time afterwards).

(2)   The High Court may by order appoint a receiver in respect of any realisable property to which the restraint order applies.

Definitions   For "property", see ss 232(1), 236(6); for "realisable property", see ss 231, 236(6); for "restraint order", see s 236(5)(b), (6).
References   See para 5.1.

197 Powers

(1)   If the court appoints a receiver under section 196 it may act under this section on the application of the person who applied for the restraint order.

(2)   The court may by order confer on the receiver the following powers in relation to any realisable property to which the restraint order applies—

(a)   power to take possession of the property;

(b)   power to manage or otherwise deal with the property;

(c)   power to start, carry on or defend any legal proceedings in respect of the property;

(d)   power to realise so much of the property as is necessary to meet the receiver's remuneration and expenses.

(3)   The court may by order confer on the receiver power to enter any premises in Northern Ireland and to do any of the following—

(a)   search for or inspect anything authorised by the court;

(b)   make or obtain a copy, photograph or other record of anything so authorised;

(c)   remove anything which the receiver is required or authorised to take possession of in pursuance of an order of the court.

(4)   The court may by order authorise the receiver to do any of the following for the purpose of the exercise of his functions—

(a)   hold property;

    (b)   enter into contracts;

    (c)   sue and be sued;

    (d)   employ agents;

    (e)   execute powers of attorney, deeds or other instruments;

    (f)   take any other steps the court thinks appropriate.

(5)   The court may order any person who has possession of realisable property to which the restraint order applies to give possession of it to the receiver.

(6)   The court—

    (a)   may order a person holding an interest in realisable property to which the restraint order applies to make to the receiver such payment as the court specifies in respect of a beneficial interest held by the defendant or the recipient of a tainted gift;

    (b)   may (on the payment being made) by order transfer, grant or extinguish any interest in the property.

(7)   Subsections (2), (5) and (6) do not apply to property for the time being subject to a charge under any of these provisions—

    (a)   section 9 of the Drug Trafficking Offences Act 1986 (c 32);

    (b)   section 78 of the Criminal Justice Act 1988 (c 33);

    (c)   Article 14 of the Criminal Justice (Confiscation) (Northern Ireland) Order 1990 (SI 1990/2588 (NI 17));

    (d)   section 27 of the Drug Trafficking Act 1994 (c 37);

    (e)   Article 32 of the Proceeds of Crime (Northern Ireland) Order 1996 (SI 1996/1299 (NI 9)).

(8)   The court must not—

    (a)   confer the power mentioned in subsection (2)(b) or (d) in respect of property, or

    (b)   exercise the power conferred on it by subsection (6) in respect of property,

unless it gives persons holding interests in the property a reasonable opportunity to make representations to it.

(9)   The court may order that a power conferred by an order under this section is subject to such conditions and exceptions as it specifies.

(10)   Managing or otherwise dealing with property includes—

    (a)   selling the property or any part of it or interest in it;

    (b)   carrying on or arranging for another person to carry on any trade or business the assets of which are or are part of the property;

    (c)   incurring capital expenditure in respect of the property.

Definitions   For "defendant", see ss 189(9)(a), 239(3), (6); for "interest" in relation to land, see ss 232(2)(f), (g), 236(6); for "interest" in relation to property other than land, see ss 232(2)(h), 236(6); for "interest held by a person beneficially in property", see ss 232(2)(e), 236(6); for "property", see ss 232(1), 236(6); for "realisable property", see ss 231, 236(6); for "recipient of a tainted gift", see ss 226(3), 236(6); for "restraint order", see s 236(5)(b), (6); for "tainted gift", see ss 225, 236(6).
References   See para 5.1.

Enforcement receivers

198 Appointment

(1)   This section applies if—

(a) a confiscation order is made,
(b) it is not satisfied, and
(c) it is not subject to appeal.

(2)   On the application of the prosecutor the Crown Court may by order appoint a receiver in respect of realisable property.

Definitions   For "confiscation order", see s 236(5)(a), (6); for "property", see ss 232(1), 236(6); for "realisable property", see ss 231, 236(6); for "satisfied", see ss 235(1), 236(6); for "subject to appeal", see ss 235(2), 236(6).
References   See para 5.1.

199 Powers

(1)   If the court appoints a receiver under section 198 it may act under this section on the application of the prosecutor.

(2)   The court may by order confer on the receiver the following powers in relation to the realisable property—
(a) power to take possession of the property;
(b) power to manage or otherwise deal with the property;
(c) power to realise the property, in such manner as the court may specify;
(d) power to start, carry on or defend any legal proceedings in respect of the property.

(3)   The court may by order confer on the receiver power to enter any premises in Northern Ireland and to do any of the following—
(a) search for or inspect anything authorised by the court;
(b) make or obtain a copy, photograph or other record of anything so authorised;
(c) remove anything which the receiver is required or authorised to take possession of in pursuance of an order of the court.

(4)   The court may by order authorise the receiver to do any of the following for the purpose of the exercise of his functions—
(a) hold property;
(b) enter into contracts;
(c) sue and be sued;
(d) employ agents;
(e) execute powers of attorney, deeds or other instruments;
(f) take any other steps the court thinks appropriate.

(5)   The court may order any person who has possession of realisable property to give possession of it to the receiver.

(6)   The court—
(a) may order a person holding an interest in realisable property to make to the receiver such payment as the court specifies in respect of a beneficial interest held by the defendant or the recipient of a tainted gift;
(b) may (on the payment being made) by order transfer, grant or extinguish any interest in the property.

(7)   Subsections (2), (5) and (6) do not apply to property for the time being subject to a charge under any of these provisions—
(a) section 9 of the Drug Trafficking Offences Act 1986 (c 32);

    (b)   section 78 of the Criminal Justice Act 1988 (c 33);

    (c)   Article 14 of the Criminal Justice (Confiscation) (Northern Ireland) Order 1990 (SI 1990/2588 (NI 17));

    (d)   section 27 of the Drug Trafficking Act 1994 (c 37);

    (e)   Article 32 of the Proceeds of Crime (Northern Ireland) Order 1996 (SI 1996/1299 (NI 9)).

(8)   The court must not—

    (a)   confer the power mentioned in subsection (2)(b) or (c) in respect of property, or

    (b)   exercise the power conferred on it by subsection (6) in respect of property,

unless it gives persons holding interests in the property a reasonable opportunity to make representations to it.

(9)   The court may order that a power conferred by an order under this section is subject to such conditions and exceptions as it specifies.

(10) Managing or otherwise dealing with property includes—

    (a)   selling the property or any part of it or interest in it;

    (b)   carrying on or arranging for another person to carry on any trade or business the assets of which are or are part of the property;

    (c)   incurring capital expenditure in respect of the property.

Definitions   For "defendant", see s 236(3), (6); for "interest" in relation to land, see ss 232(2)(f), (g), 236(6); for "interest" in relation to property other than land, see ss 232(2)(h), 236(6); for "interest held by a person beneficially in property", see ss 232(2)(e), 236(6); for "property", see ss 232(1), 236(6); for "realisable property", see ss 231, 236(6); for "recipient of a tainted gift", see ss 226(3), 236(6); for "tainted gift", see ss 225, 236(6).
References   See para 5.1.

Director's receivers

200 Appointment

(1)   This section applies if—

    (a)   a confiscation order is made, and

    (b)   the Director is appointed as the enforcement authority for the order under section 184.

(2)   But this section does not apply if—

    (a)   the confiscation order was made by the Court of Appeal, and

    (b)   when the Crown Court comes to proceed under this section the confiscation order has been satisfied.

(3)   If this section applies the Crown Court must make an order for the appointment of a receiver in respect of realisable property.

(4)   An order under subsection (3)—

    (a)   must confer power on the Director to nominate the person who is to be the receiver, and

    (b)   takes effect when the Director nominates that person.

(5)   The Director must not nominate a person under subsection (4) unless at the time he does so the confiscation order—

    (a)   is not satisfied, and

    (b)   is not subject to appeal.

(6)   A person nominated to be the receiver under subsection (4) may be—
    (a)   a member of the staff of the Agency;
    (b)   a person providing services under arrangements made by the Director.

(7)   If this section applies section 198 does not apply.

Definitions   For "the Agency", see s 1(1); for "confiscation order", see s 236(5)(a), (6); for "the Director", see s 1(2); for "property", see ss 232(1), 236(6); for "realisable property", see ss 231, 236(6); for "satisfied", see ss 235(1), 236(6); for "subject to appeal", see ss 235(2), 236(6).
References   See para 5.1.

---

201 Powers

(1)   If the court makes an order for the appointment of a receiver under section 200 it may act under this section on the application of the Director.

(2)   The court may by order confer on the receiver the following powers in relation to the realisable property—
    (a)   power to take possession of the property;
    (b)   power to manage or otherwise deal with the property;
    (c)   power to realise the property, in such manner as the court may specify;
    (d)   power to start, carry on or defend any legal proceedings in respect of the property.

(3)   The court may by order confer on the receiver power to enter any premises in Northern Ireland and to do any of the following—
    (a)   search for or inspect anything authorised by the court;
    (b)   make or obtain a copy, photograph or other record of anything so authorised;
    (c)   remove anything which the receiver is required or authorised to take possession of in pursuance of an order of the court.

(4)   The court may by order authorise the receiver to do any of the following for the purpose of the exercise of his functions—
    (a)   hold property;
    (b)   enter into contracts;
    (c)   sue and be sued;
    (d)   employ agents;
    (e)   execute powers of attorney, deeds or other instruments;
    (f)   take any other steps the court thinks appropriate.

(5)   The court may order any person who has possession of realisable property to give possession of it to the receiver.

(6)   The court—
    (a)   may order a person holding an interest in realisable property to make to the receiver such payment as the court specifies in respect of a beneficial interest held by the defendant or the recipient of a tainted gift;
    (b)   may (on the payment being made) by order transfer, grant or extinguish any interest in the property.

(7)   Subsections (2), (5) and (6) do not apply to property for the time being subject to a charge under any of these provisions—
    (a)   section 9 of the Drug Trafficking Offences Act 1986 (c 32);

(b) section 78 of the Criminal Justice Act 1988 (c 33);
(c) Article 14 of the Criminal Justice (Confiscation) (Northern Ireland) Order 1990 (SI 1990/2588 (NI 17));
(d) section 27 of the Drug Trafficking Act 1994 (c 37);
(e) Article 32 of the Proceeds of Crime (Northern Ireland) Order 1996 (SI 1996/1299 (NI 9)).

(8) The court must not—
(a) confer the power mentioned in subsection (2)(b) or (c) in respect of property, or
(b) exercise the power conferred on it by subsection (6) in respect of property,

unless it gives persons holding interests in the property a reasonable opportunity to make representations to it.

(9) The court may order that a power conferred by an order under this section is subject to such conditions and exceptions as it specifies.

(10) Managing or otherwise dealing with property includes—
(a) selling the property or any part of it or interest in it;
(b) carrying on or arranging for another person to carry on any trade or business the assets of which are or are part of the property;
(c) incurring capital expenditure in respect of the property.

Definitions   For "defendant", see s 236(3), (6); for "the Director", see s 1(2); for "interest" in relation to land, see ss 232(2)(f), (g), 236(6); for "interest" in relation to property other than land, see ss 232(2)(h), 236(6); for "interest held by a person beneficially in property", see ss 232(2)(e), 236(6); for "property", see ss 232(1), 236(6); for "realisable property", see ss 231, 236(6); for "recipient of a tainted gift", see ss 226(3), 236(6); for "tainted gift", see ss 225, 236(6).
References   See para 5.1.

Application of sums

202 Enforcement receivers

(1) This section applies to sums which are in the hands of a receiver appointed under section 198 if they are—
(a) the proceeds of the realisation of property under section 199;
(b) sums (other than those mentioned in paragraph (a)) in which the defendant holds an interest.

(2) The sums must be applied as follows—
(a) first, they must be applied in payment of such expenses incurred by a person acting as an insolvency practitioner as are payable under this subsection by virtue of section 432;
(b) second, they must be applied in making any payments directed by the Crown Court;
(c) third, they must be applied on the defendant's behalf towards satisfaction of the confiscation order.

(3) If the amount payable under the confiscation order has been fully paid and any sums remain in the receiver's hands he must distribute them—
(a) among such persons who held (or hold) interests in the property concerned as the Crown Court directs, and
(b) in such proportions as it directs.

(4)   Before making a direction under subsection (3) the court must give persons who held (or hold) interests in the property concerned a reasonable opportunity to make representations to it.

(5)   For the purposes of subsections (3) and (4) the property concerned is—
      (a)   the property represented by the proceeds mentioned in subsection (1)(a);
      (b)   the sums mentioned in subsection (1)(b).

(6)   The receiver applies sums as mentioned in subsection (2)(c) by paying them to the appropriate chief clerk on account of the amount payable under the order.

(7)   The appropriate chief clerk is the chief clerk of the court at the place where the confiscation order was made.

Definitions   For "confiscation order", see s 236(5)(a), (6); for "defendant", see s 236(3), (6); for "interest" in relation to property other than land, see ss 232(2)(h), 236(6); for "property", see ss 232(1), 236(6).
References   See para 5.1.

203 Sums received by chief clerk

(1)   This section applies if a chief clerk receives sums on account of the amount payable under a confiscation order (whether the sums are received under section 202 or otherwise).

(2)   The chief clerk's receipt of the sums reduces the amount payable under the order, but he must apply the sums received as follows.

(3)   First he must apply them in payment of such expenses incurred by a person acting as an insolvency practitioner as—
      (a)   are payable under this subsection by virtue of section 432, but
      (b)   are not already paid under section 202(2)(a).

(4)   If the chief clerk received the sums under section 202 he must next apply them—
      (a)   first, in payment of the remuneration and expenses of a receiver appointed under section 196, to the extent that they have not been met by virtue of the exercise by that receiver of a power conferred under section 197(2)(d);
      (b)   second, in payment of the remuneration and expenses of the receiver appointed under section 198.

(5)   If a direction was made under section 163(6) for an amount of compensation to be paid out of sums recovered under the confiscation order, the chief clerk must next apply the sums in payment of that amount.

(6)   If any amount remains after the chief clerk makes any payments required by the preceding provisions of this section, the amount must be treated for the purposes of section 20 of the Administration of Justice Act (Northern Ireland) 1954 (c 9 (NI)) (application of fines) as if it were a fine.

(7)   Subsection (4) does not apply if the receiver is a member of the staff of the Director of Public Prosecutions for Northern Ireland or of the Commissioners of Customs and Excise; and it is immaterial whether he is a permanent or temporary member or he is on secondment from elsewhere.

204 Director's receivers

(1)   This section applies to sums which are in the hands of a receiver appointed under section 200 if they are—
    (a)   the proceeds of the realisation of property under section 201;
    (b)   sums (other than those mentioned in paragraph (a)) in which the defendant holds an interest.

(2)   The sums must be applied as follows—
    (a)   first, they must be applied in payment of such expenses incurred by a person acting as an insolvency practitioner as are payable under this subsection by virtue of section 432;
    (b)   second, they must be applied in making any payments directed by the Crown Court;
    (c)   third, they must be applied on the defendant's behalf towards satisfaction of the confiscation order by being paid to the Director on account of the amount payable under it.

(3)   If the amount payable under the confiscation order has been fully paid and any sums remain in the receiver's hands he must distribute them—
    (a)   among such persons who held (or hold) interests in the property concerned as the Crown Court directs, and
    (b)   in such proportions as it directs.

(4)   Before making a direction under subsection (3) the court must give persons who held (or hold) interests in the property concerned a reasonable opportunity to make representations to it.

(5)   For the purposes of subsections (3) and (4) the property concerned is—
    (a)   the property represented by the proceeds mentioned in subsection (1)(a);
    (b)   the sums mentioned in subsection (1)(b).

205 Sums received by Director

(1)   This section applies if the Director receives sums on account of the amount payable under a confiscation order (whether the sums are received under section 204 or otherwise).

(2)   The Director's receipt of the sums reduces the amount payable under the order, but he must apply the sums received as follows.

(3)   First he must apply them in payment of such expenses incurred by a person acting as an insolvency practitioner as—
    (a)   are payable under this subsection by virtue of section 432, but
    (b)   are not already paid under section 204(2)(a).

(4) If the Director received the sums under section 204 he must next apply them—

  (a) first, in payment of the remuneration and expenses of a receiver appointed under section 196, to the extent that they have not been met by virtue of the exercise by that receiver of a power conferred under section 197(2)(d);

  (b) second, in payment of the remuneration and expenses of the receiver appointed under section 200.

(5) If a direction was made under section 163(6) for an amount of compensation to be paid out of sums recovered under the confiscation order, the Director must next apply the sums in payment of that amount.

(6) Subsection (4) does not apply if the receiver is a member of the staff of the Agency or a person providing services under arrangements made by the Director.

Definitions   For "the Agency", see s 1(1); for "confiscation order", see s 236(5)(a), (6); for "the Director", see s 1(2).
References   See para 5.1.

Restrictions

206 Restraint orders

(1) Subsections (2) and (3) apply if a court makes a restraint order.

(2) If the order applies to a tenancy of any premises, no landlord or other person to whom rent is payable may exercise a right within subsection (3) except with the leave of the High Court and subject to any terms the High Court may impose.

(3) A right is within this subsection if it is a right of forfeiture by peaceable re-entry in relation to the premises in respect of any failure by the tenant to comply with any term or condition of the tenancy.

(4) If a court in which proceedings are pending in respect of any property is satisfied that a restraint order has been applied for or made in respect of the property, the court may either stay the proceedings or allow them to continue on any terms it thinks fit.

(5) Before exercising any power conferred by subsection (4), the court must give an opportunity to be heard to—

  (a) the applicant for the restraint order, and

  (b) any receiver appointed in respect of the property under section 196, 198 or 200.

Definitions   For "property", see ss 232(1), 236(6); for "realisable property", see ss 231, 236(6); for "restraint order", see s 236(5)(b), (6).
References   See para 5.9.

207 Enforcement receivers

(1) Subsections (2) and (3) apply if a court makes an order under section 198 appointing a receiver in respect of any realisable property.

(2)   If the receiver is appointed in respect of a tenancy of any premises, no landlord or other person to whom rent is payable may exercise a right within subsection (3) except with the leave of the Crown Court and subject to any terms the Crown Court may impose.

(3)   A right is within this subsection if it is a right of forfeiture by peaceable re-entry in relation to the premises in respect of any failure by the tenant to comply with any term or condition of the tenancy.

(4)   If a court in which proceedings are pending in respect of any property is satisfied that an order under section 198 appointing a receiver in respect of the property has been applied for or made, the court may either stay the proceedings or allow them to continue on any terms it thinks fit.

(5)   Before exercising any power conferred by subsection (4), the court must give an opportunity to be heard to—
(a)   the prosecutor, and
(b)   the receiver (if the order under section 198 has been made).

Definitions   For "property", see ss 232(1), 236(6); for "realisable property", see ss 231, 236(6).
References   See para 5.9.

208 Director's receivers

(1)   Subsections (2) and (3) apply if—
(a)   the Crown Court has made an order under section 200 for the appointment of a receiver in respect of any realisable property, and
(b)   the order has taken effect.

(2)   If the order is for the appointment of a receiver in respect of a tenancy of any premises, no landlord or other person to whom rent is payable may exercise a right within subsection (3) except with the leave of the Crown Court and subject to any terms the Crown Court may impose.

(3)   A right is within this subsection if it is a right of forfeiture by peaceable re-entry in relation to the premises in respect of any failure by the tenant to comply with any term or condition of the tenancy.

(4)   If a court (whether the Crown Court or any other court) in which proceedings are pending in respect of any property is satisfied that an order under section 200 for the appointment of a receiver in respect of the property has taken effect, the court may either stay the proceedings or allow them to continue on any terms it thinks fit.

(5)   Before exercising any power conferred by subsection (4), the court must give an opportunity to be heard to—
(a)   the Director, and
(b)   the receiver.

Definitions   For "the Director", see s 1(2); for "property", see ss 232(1), 236(6); for "realisable property", see ss 231, 236(6).
References   See para 5.9.

Receivers: further provisions

209 Protection

If a receiver appointed under section 196, 198 or 200—
  (a) takes action in relation to property which is not realisable property,
  (b) would be entitled to take the action if it were realisable property, and
  (c) believes on reasonable grounds that he is entitled to take the action,

he is not liable to any person in respect of any loss or damage resulting from the action, except so far as the loss or damage is caused by his negligence.

Definitions   For "property", see ss 232(1), 236(6); for "realisable property", see ss 231, 236(6).
References   See para 5.1.

210 Further applications

(1) This section applies to a receiver appointed under section 196, 198 or 200.

(2) The receiver may apply—
  (a) to the High Court if he is appointed under section 196;
  (b) to the Crown Court if he is appointed under section 198 or 200,

for an order giving directions as to the exercise of his powers.

(3) The following persons may apply to the High Court if the receiver is appointed under section 196 or to the Crown Court if the receiver is appointed under section 198 or 200—
  (a) any person affected by action taken by the receiver;
  (b) any person who may be affected by action the receiver proposes to take.

(4) On an application under this section the court may make such order as it believes is appropriate.

References   See para 5.10.

211 Discharge and variation

(1) The following persons may apply to the High Court to vary or discharge an order made under section 196 or 197 or to the Crown Court to vary or discharge an order made under any of sections 198 to 201—
  (a) the receiver;
  (b) the person who applied for the order or (if the order was made under section 200 or 201) the Director;
  (c) any person affected by the order.

(2) On an application under this section the court—
  (a) may discharge the order;
  (b) may vary the order.

(3) But in the case of an order under section 196 or 197—
  (a) if the condition in section 189 which was satisfied was that proceedings were started or an application was made, the court must discharge the order on the conclusion of the proceedings or of the application (as the case may be);

    (b)   if the condition which was satisfied was that an investigation was started or an application was to be made, the court must discharge the order if within a reasonable time proceedings for the offence are not started or the application is not made (as the case may be).

Definitions   For "the Director", see s 1(2); for "proceedings concluded", see ss 233(3)–(8), 236(6); for "proceedings started", see ss 233(1), (2), 236(6).
References   See para 5.1.

212 Management receivers: discharge

(1)   This section applies if—
    (a)   a receiver stands appointed under section 196 in respect of realisable property (the management receiver), and
    (b)   the court appoints a receiver under section 198 or makes an order for the appointment of a receiver under section 200.

(2)   The court must order the management receiver to transfer to the other receiver all property held by the management receiver by virtue of the powers conferred on him by section 197.

(3)   But in a case where the court makes an order under section 200 its order under subsection (2) above does not take effect until the order under section 200 takes effect.

(4)   Subsection (2) does not apply to property which the management receiver holds by virtue of the exercise by him of his power under section 197(2)(d).

(5)   If the management receiver complies with an order under subsection (2) he is discharged—
    (a)   from his appointment under section 196;
    (b)   from any obligation under this Act arising from his appointment.

(6)   If this section applies the court may make such a consequential or incidental order as it believes is appropriate.

Definitions   For "property", see ss 232(1), 236(6); for "property held", see ss 232(2)(a), (d), 236(6); for "realisable property", see ss 231, 236(6).
References   See para 5.1.

213 Appeal to Court of Appeal

(1)   If on an application for an order under any of sections 196 to 199 or section 201 the court decides not to make one, the person who applied for the order may appeal to the Court of Appeal against the decision.

(2)   If the court makes an order under any of sections 196 to 199 or section 201, the following persons may appeal to the Court of Appeal in respect of the court's decision—
    (a)   the person who applied for the order;
    (b)   any person affected by the order.

(3)   If on an application for an order under section 210 the court decides not to make one, the person who applied for the order may appeal to the Court of Appeal against the decision.

(4)   If the court makes an order under section 210, the following persons may appeal to the Court of Appeal in respect of the court's decision—

    (a)   the person who applied for the order;

    (b)   any person affected by the order;

    (c)   the receiver.

(5)   The following persons may appeal to the Court of Appeal against a decision of the court on an application under section 211—

    (a)   the person who applied for the order in respect of which the application was made or (if the order was made under section 200 or 201) the Director;

    (b)   any person affected by the court's decision;

    (c)   the receiver.

(6)   On an appeal under this section the Court of Appeal may—

    (a)   confirm the decision, or

    (b)   make such order as it believes if appropriate.

Definitions   For "the Director", see s 1(2).
References   See para 5.1.

214 Appeal to House of Lords

(1)   An appeal lies to the House of Lords from a decision of the Court of Appeal on an appeal under section 213.

(2)   An appeal under this section lies at the instance of any person who was a party to the proceedings before the Court of Appeal.

(3)   On an appeal under this section the House of Lords may—

    (a)   confirm the decision of the Court of Appeal, or

    (b)   make such order as it believes is appropriate.

References   See para 5.1.

Seized money

215 Seized money

(1)   This section applies to money which—

    (a)   is held by a person, and

    (b)   is held in an account maintained by him with a bank or a building society.

(2)   This section also applies to money which is held by a person and which—

    (a)   has been seized by a constable under Article 21 of the Police and Criminal Evidence (Northern Ireland) Order 1989 (SI 1989/1341 (NI 12)) (general power of seizure etc), and

    (b)   is held in an account maintained by a police force with a bank or a building society.

(3)   This section also applies to money which is held by a person and which—

    (a)   has been seized by a customs officer under Article 21 of the 1989 Order as applied by order made under Article 85(1) of that Order, and

366

(b) is held in an account maintained by the Commissioners of Customs and Excise with a bank or a building society.

(4) This section applies if the following conditions are satisfied—
 (a) a restraint order has effect in relation to money to which this section applies;
 (b) a receiver has not been appointed under section 198 in relation to the money;
 (c) a confiscation order is made against the person by whom the money is held;
 (d) the Director has not been appointed as the enforcement authority for the confiscation order;
 (e) any period allowed under section 161 for payment of the amount ordered to be paid under the confiscation order has ended.

(5) In such a case on the application of the prosecutor a magistrates' court may order the bank or building society to pay the money to the appropriate chief clerk on account of the amount payable under the confiscation order.

(6) If a bank or building society fails to comply with an order under subsection (5)—
 (a) the magistrates' court may order it to pay an amount not exceeding £5,000, and
 (b) for the purposes of the Magistrates' Courts (Northern Ireland) Order 1981 (SI 1981/1675 (NI 26)) the sum is to be treated as adjudged to be paid by a conviction of the magistrates' court.

(7) In order to take account of changes in the value of money the Secretary of State may by order substitute another sum for the sum for the time being specified in subsection (6)(a).

(8) For the purposes of this section—
 (a) a bank is a deposit-taking business within the meaning of the Banking Act 1987 (c 22);
 (b) "building society" has the same meaning as in the Building Societies Act 1986 (c 53);
 (c) "appropriate chief clerk" has the same meaning as in section 202(7).

Definitions For "confiscation order", see s 236(5)(a), (6); for "customs officer", see s 454; for "the Director", see s 1(2); for "restraint order", see s 236(5)(b), (6).
References See para 5.1.

Financial investigators

216 Applications and appeals

(1) This section applies to—
 (a) an application under section 190, 191, 196, 197 or 211;
 (b) an appeal under section 192, 193, 213 or 214.

(2) An accredited financial investigator must not make such an application or bring such an appeal unless he falls within subsection (3).

(3) An accredited financial investigator falls within this subsection if he is one of the following or is authorised for the purposes of this section by one of the following—

    (a)   a police officer who is not below the rank of superintendent,

    (b)   a customs officer who is not below such grade as is designated by the Commissioners of Customs and Excise as equivalent to that rank,

    (c)   an accredited financial investigator who falls within a description specified in an order made for the purposes of this paragraph by the Secretary of State under section 453.

(4)   If such an application is made or appeal brought by an accredited financial investigator any subsequent step in the application or appeal or any further application or appeal relating to the same matter may be taken, made or brought by a different accredited financial investigator who falls within subsection (3).

(5)   If—

    (a)   an application for a restraint order is made by an accredited financial investigator, and

    (b)   a court is required under section 206(5) to give the applicant for the order an opportunity to be heard,

the court may give the opportunity to a different accredited financial investigator who falls within subsection (3).

Definitions   For "accredited financial investigator", see s 3(5); for "customs officer", see s 454; for "restraint order", see s 236(5)(b), (6).
References   See para 5.1.

Exercise of powers

217 Powers of court and receiver

(1)   This section applies to—

    (a)   the powers conferred on a court by sections 189 to 208 and sections 210 to 215;

    (b)   the powers of a receiver appointed under section 196, 198 or 200.

(2)   The powers—

    (a)   must be exercised with a view to the value for the time being of realisable property being made available (by the property's realisation) for satisfying any confiscation order that has been or may be made against the defendant;

    (b)   must be exercised, in a case where a confiscation order has not been made, with a view to securing that there is no diminution in the value of realisable property;

    (c)   must be exercised without taking account of any obligation of the defendant or a recipient of a tainted gift if the obligation conflicts with the object of satisfying any confiscation order that has been or may be made against the defendant;

    (d)   may be exercised in respect of a debt owed by the Crown.

(3)   Subsection (2) has effect subject to the following rules—

    (a)   the powers must be exercised with a view to allowing a person other than the defendant or a recipient of a tainted gift to retain or recover the value of any interest held by him;

    (b)   in the case of realisable property held by a recipient of a tainted gift, the powers must be exercised with a view to realising no more than the value for the time being of the gift;

(c) in a case where a confiscation order has not been made against the defendant, property must not be realised if the court so orders under subsection (4).

(4) If on an application by the defendant, or by the recipient of a tainted gift, the court decides that property cannot be replaced it may order that it must not be sold.

(5) An order under subsection (4) may be revoked or varied.

Definitions   For "confiscation order", see s 236(5)(a), (6); for "defendant", see s 236(3), (6); for "interest" in relation to land, see ss 232(2)(f), (g), 236(6); for "interest" in relation to property other than land, see ss 232(2)(h), 236(6); for "property", see ss 232(1), 236(6); for "realisable property", see ss 231, 236(6); for "recipient of a tainted gift", see ss 226(3), 236(6); for "satisfied", see ss 235(1), 236(6); for "tainted gift", see ss 225, 236(6).
References   See para 5.1.

Committal

218 Committal by magistrates' court

(1) This section applies if—
    (a) a defendant is convicted of an offence by a magistrates' court, and
    (b) the prosecutor asks the court to commit the defendant to the Crown Court with a view to a confiscation order being considered under section 156.

(2) In such a case the magistrates' court—
    (a) must commit the defendant to the Crown Court in respect of the offence, and
    (b) may commit him to the Crown Court in respect of any other offence falling within subsection (3).

(3) An offence falls within this subsection if—
    (a) the defendant has been convicted of it by the magistrates' court or any other court, and
    (b) the magistrates' court has power to deal with him in respect of it.

(4) If a committal is made under this section in respect of an offence or offences—
    (a) section 156 applies accordingly, and
    (b) the committal operates as a committal of the defendant to be dealt with by the Crown Court in accordance with section 219.

(5) A committal under this section may be in custody or on bail.

Definitions   For "confiscation order", see s 236(5)(a), (6); for "defendant", see s 236(3), (6).
References   See para 5.12.

---

219 Sentencing by Crown Court

(1) If a defendant is committed to the Crown Court under section 218 in respect of an offence or offences, this section applies (whether or not the court proceeds under section 156).

(2)   The Crown Court—
    (a)   must inquire into the circumstances of the case, and
    (b)   may deal with the defendant in any way in which the magistrates' court could deal with him if it had just convicted him of the offence.

Definitions   For "defendant", see s 236(3), (6).
References   See para 5.12.

Compensation

220 Serious default

(1)   If the following three conditions are satisfied the Crown Court may order the payment of such compensation as it believes is just.

(2)   The first condition is satisfied if a criminal investigation has been started with regard to an offence and proceedings are not started for the offence.

(3)   The first condition is also satisfied if proceedings for an offence are started against a person and—
    (a)   they do not result in his conviction for the offence, or
    (b)   he is convicted of the offence but the conviction is quashed or he is pardoned in respect of it.

(4)   If subsection (2) applies the second condition is that—
    (a)   in the criminal investigation there has been a serious default by a person mentioned in subsection (9), and
    (b)   the investigation would not have continued if the default had not occurred.

(5)   If subsection (3) applies the second condition is that—
    (a)   in any criminal investigation with regard to the offence or in its prosecution there has been a serious default by a person who is mentioned in subsection (9), and
    (b)   the proceedings would not have been started or continued if the default had not occurred.

(6)   The third condition is that an application is made under this section by a person who held realisable property and has suffered loss in consequence of anything done in relation to it by or in pursuance of an order under this Part.

(7)   The offence referred to in subsection (2) may be one of a number of offences with regard to which the investigation is started.

(8)   The offence referred to in subsection (3) may be one of a number of offences for which the proceedings are started.

(9)   Compensation under this section is payable to the applicant and—
    (a)   if the person in default was or was acting as a police officer within the meaning of the Police (Northern Ireland) Act 2000 (c 32), the compensation is payable by the Chief Constable;
    (b)   if the person in default was a member of the Director of Public Prosecutions for Northern Ireland or was acting on his behalf, the compensation is payable by the Director of Public Prosecutions for Northern Ireland;

(c) if the person in default was a member of the Serious Fraud Office, the compensation is payable by the Director of that Office;

(d) if the person in default was a customs officer, the compensation is payable by the Commissioners of Customs and Excise;

(e) if the person in default was an officer of the Commissioners of Inland Revenue, the compensation is payable by those Commissioners.

Definitions   For "criminal investigation", see s 236(2), (6); for "customs officer", see s 454; for "proceedings started", see ss 233(1), (2), 236(6); for "property", see ss 232(1), 236(6); for "property held", see ss 232(2)(a), (d), 236(6); for "realisable property", see ss 231, 236(6).
References   See para 5.12.

---

221 Order varied or discharged

(1) This section applies if—

    (a) the court varies a confiscation order under section 179 or discharges one under section 180, and

    (b) an application is made to the Crown Court by a person who held realisable property and has suffered loss as a result of the making of the order.

(2) The court may order the payment of such compensation as it believes is just.

(3) Compensation under this section is payable—

    (a) to the applicant;

    (b) by the Lord Chancellor.

Definitions   For "confiscation order", see s 236(5)(a), (6); for "property", see ss 232(1), 236(6); for "property held", see ss 232(2)(a), (d), 236(6); for "realisable property", see ss 231, 236(6).
References   See para 5.1.

Enforcement abroad

222 Enforcement abroad

(1) This section applies if—

    (a) any of the conditions in section 189 is satisfied,

    (b) the prosecutor or the Director believes that realisable property is situated in a country or territory outside the United Kingdom (the receiving country), and

    (c) the prosecutor or the Director (as the case may be) sends a request for assistance to the Secretary of State with a view to it being forwarded under this section.

(2) In a case where no confiscation order has been made, a request for assistance is a request to the government of the receiving country to secure that any person is prohibited from dealing with realisable property.

(3) In a case where a confiscation order has been made and has not been satisfied, discharged or quashed, a request for assistance is a request to the government of the receiving country to secure that—

    (a) any person is prohibited from dealing with realisable property;

    (b) realisable property is realised and the proceeds are applied in accordance with the law of the receiving country.

(4)   No request for assistance may be made for the purposes of this section in a case where a confiscation order has been made and has been satisfied, discharged or quashed.

(5)   If the Secretary of State believes it is appropriate to do so he may forward the request for assistance to the government of the receiving country.

(6)   If property is realised in pursuance of a request under subsection (3) the amount ordered to be paid under the confiscation order must be taken to be reduced by an amount equal to the proceeds of realisation.

(7)   A certificate purporting to be issued by or on behalf of the requested government is admissible as evidence of the facts it states if it states—

    (a)   that property has been realised in pursuance of a request under subsection (3),

    (b)   the date of realisation, and

    (c)   the proceeds of realisation.

(8)   If the proceeds of realisation made in pursuance of a request under subsection (3) are expressed in a currency other than sterling, they must be taken to be the sterling equivalent calculated in accordance with the rate of exchange prevailing at the end of the day of realisation.

Definitions   For "confiscation order", see s 236(5)(a), (6); for "the Director", see s 1(2); for "property", see ss 232(1), 236(6); for "realisable property", see ss 231, 236(6); for "satisfied", see ss 235(1), 236(6).
References   See para 5.1.

Interpretation

223 Criminal lifestyle

(1)   A defendant has a criminal lifestyle if (and only if) the following condition is satisfied.

(2)   The condition is that the offence (or any of the offences) concerned satisfies any of these tests—

    (a)   it is specified in Schedule 5;

    (b)   it constitutes conduct forming part of a course of criminal activity;

    (c)   it is an offence committed over a period of at least six months and the defendant has benefited from the conduct which constitutes the offence.

(3)   Conduct forms part of a course of criminal activity if the defendant has benefited from the conduct and—

    (a)   in the proceedings in which he was convicted he was convicted of three or more other offences, each of three or more of them constituting conduct from which he has benefited, or

    (b)   in the period of six years ending with the day when those proceedings were started (or, if there is more than one such day, the earliest day) he was convicted on at least two separate occasions of an offence constituting conduct from which he has benefited.

(4)   But an offence does not satisfy the test in subsection (2)(b) or (c) unless the defendant obtains relevant benefit of not less than £5000.

(5)   Relevant benefit for the purposes of subsection (2)(b) is—

   (a)   benefit from conduct which constitutes the offence;

   (b)   benefit from any other conduct which forms part of the course of criminal activity and which constitutes an offence of which the defendant has been convicted;

   (c)   benefit from conduct which constitutes an offence which has been or will be taken into consideration by the court in sentencing the defendant for an offence mentioned in paragraph (a) or (b).

(6)   Relevant benefit for the purposes of subsection (2)(c) is—

   (a)   benefit from conduct which constitutes the offence;

   (b)   benefit from conduct which constitutes an offence which has been or will be taken into consideration by the court in sentencing the defendant for the offence mentioned in paragraph (a).

(7)   The Secretary of State may by order amend Schedule 5.

(8)   The Secretary of State may by order vary the amount for the time being specified in subsection (4).

Definitions   For "benefits from conduct", see ss 224(4), (7), 236(6); for "defendant", see ss 189(9)(a), 236(3), (6); for "offence concerned", see ss 156(9), 236(1), (6); for "offences concerned", see ss 156(9), 236(1), (6); for "proceedings started", see ss 233(1), (2), 236(6); for "sentencing the defendant for an offence", see s 236(4), (6).
References   See para 5.13.

---

224 Conduct and benefit

(1)   Criminal conduct is conduct which—

   (a)   constitutes an offence in Northern Ireland, or

   (b)   would constitute such an offence if it occurred in Northern Ireland.

(2)   General criminal conduct of the defendant is all his criminal conduct, and it is immaterial—

   (a)   whether conduct occurred before or after the passing of this Act;

   (b)   whether property constituting a benefit from conduct was obtained before or after the passing of this Act.

(3)   Particular criminal conduct of the defendant is all his criminal conduct which falls within the following paragraphs—

   (a)   conduct which constitutes the offence or offences concerned;

   (b)   conduct which constitutes offences of which he was convicted in the same proceedings as those in which he was convicted of the offence or offences concerned;

   (c)   conduct which constitutes offences which the court will be taking into consideration in deciding his sentence for the offence or offences concerned.

(4)   A person benefits from conduct if he obtains property as a result of or in connection with the conduct.

(5)   If a person obtains a pecuniary advantage as a result of or in connection with conduct, he is to be taken to obtain as a result of or in connection with the conduct a sum of money equal to the value of the pecuniary advantage.

(6) References to property or a pecuniary advantage obtained in connection with conduct include references to property or a pecuniary advantage obtained both in that connection and some other.

(7) If a person benefits from conduct his benefit is the value of the property obtained.

Definitions For "defendant", see ss 189(9)(a), 236(3), (6); for "offence concerned", see ss 156(9), 236(1), (6); for "offences concerned", see ss 156(9), 236(1), (6); for "property", see ss 232(1), 236(6); for "property obtained", see ss 232(2)(b), 236(6); for "sentencing the defendant for an offence", see s 236(4), (6).
References See para 5.1.

---

225 Tainted gifts

(1) Subsections (2) and (3) apply if—
  (a) no court has made a decision as to whether the defendant has a criminal lifestyle, or
  (b) a court has decided that the defendant has a criminal lifestyle.

(2) A gift is tainted if it was made by the defendant at any time after the relevant day.

(3) A gift is also tainted if it was made by the defendant at any time and was of property—
  (a) which was obtained by the defendant as a result of or in connection with his general criminal conduct, or
  (b) which (in whole or part and whether directly or indirectly) represented in the defendant's hands property obtained by him as a result of or in connection with his general criminal conduct.

(4) Subsection (5) applies if a court has decided that the defendant does not have a criminal lifestyle.

(5) A gift is tainted if it was made by the defendant at any time after—
  (a) the date on which the offence concerned was committed, or
  (b) if his particular criminal conduct consists of two or more offences and they were committed on different dates, the date of the earliest.

(6) For the purposes of subsection (5) an offence which is a continuing offence is committed on the first occasion when it is committed.

(7) For the purposes of subsection (5) the defendant's particular criminal conduct includes any conduct which constitutes offences which the court has taken into consideration in deciding his sentence for the offence or offences concerned.

(8) A gift may be a tainted gift whether it was made before or after the passing of this Act.

(9) The relevant day is the first day of the period of six years ending with—
  (a) the day when proceedings for the offence concerned were started against the defendant, or
  (b) if there are two or more offences and proceedings for them were started on different days, the earliest of those days.

Definitions   For "criminal conduct", see ss 224(1), 236(6); for "criminal lifestyle", see ss 223, 236(6), Sch 5; for "defendant", see ss 189(9)(a), 236(3), (6); for "general criminal conduct", see ss 224(2), 236(6); for "making a gift", see ss 226(1), (2), 236(6); for "offence concerned", see ss 156(9), 236(1), (6); for "particular criminal conduct", see ss 224(3), 236(6); for "proceedings started", see ss 233(1), (2), 236(6); for "property", see ss 232(1), 236(6); for "property obtained", see ss 232(2)(b), 236(6); for "property obtained in connection with conduct", see ss 224(6), 236(6); for "sentencing the defendant for an offence", see s 236(4), (6).
References   See para 5.1.

226 Gifts and their recipients

(1)   If the defendant transfers property to another person for a consideration whose value is significantly less than the value of the property at the time of the transfer, he is to be treated as making a gift.

(2)   If subsection (1) applies the property given is to be treated as such share in the property transferred as is represented by the fraction—

    (a)   whose numerator is the difference between the two values mentioned in subsection (1), and

    (b)   whose denominator is the value of the property at the time of the transfer.

(3)   References to a recipient of a tainted gift are to a person to whom the defendant has made the gift.

Definitions   For "defendant", see ss 189(9)(a), 236(3), (6); for "property", see ss 232(1), 236(6); for "property transferred", see ss 232(2)(c), 236(6).
References   See para 5.1.

227 Value: the basic rule

(1)   This section applies for the purpose of deciding the value at any time of property then held by a person.

(2)   Its value is the market value of the property at that time.

(3)   But if at that time another person holds an interest in the property its value, in relation to the person mentioned in subsection (1), is the market value of his interest at that time, ignoring any charging order under a provision listed in subsection (4).

(4)   The provisions are—

    (a)   section 9 of the Drug Trafficking Offences Act 1986 (c 32);

    (b)   section 78 of the Criminal Justice Act 1988 (c 33);

    (c)   Article 14 of the Criminal Justice (Confiscation) (Northern Ireland) Order 1990 (SI 1990/2588 (NI 17));

    (d)   section 27 of the Drug Trafficking Act 1994 (c 37);

    (e)   Article 32 of the Proceeds of Crime (Northern Ireland) Order 1996 (SI 1996/1299 (NI 9)).

(5)   This section has effect subject to sections 228 and 229.

Definitions   For "interest" in relation to land, see ss 232(2)(f), (g), 236(6); for "interest" in relation to property other than land, see ss 232(2)(h), 236(6); for "property", see ss 232(1), 236(6); for "property held", see ss 232(2)(a), (d), 236(6).
References   See para 5.1.

228 Value of property obtained from conduct

(1)   This section applies for the purpose of deciding the value of property obtained by a person as a result of or in connection with his criminal conduct; and the material time is the time the court makes its decision.

(2)   The value of the property at the material time is the greater of the following—

    (a)   the value of the property (at the time the person obtained it) adjusted to take account of later changes in the value of money;

    (b)   the value (at the material time) of the property found under subsection (3).

(3)   The property found under this subsection is as follows—

    (a)   if the person holds the property obtained, the property found under this subsection is that property;

    (b)   if he holds no part of the property obtained, the property found under this subsection is any property which directly or indirectly represents it in his hands;

    (c)   if he holds part of the property obtained, the property found under this subsection is that part and any property which directly or indirectly represents the other part in his hands.

(4)   The references in subsection (2)(a) and (b) to the value are to the value found in accordance with section 227.

Definitions   For "criminal conduct", see ss 224(1), 236(6); for "property", see ss 232(1), 236(6); for "property held", see ss 232(2)(a), (d), 236(6); for "property obtained", see ss 232(2)(b), 236(6).
References   See para 5.1.

229 Value of tainted gifts

(1)   The value at any time (the material time) of a tainted gift is the greater of the following—

    (a)   the value (at the time of the gift) of the property given, adjusted to take account of later changes in the value of money;

    (b)   the value (at the material time) of the property found under subsection (2).

(2)   The property found under this subsection is as follows—

    (a)   if the recipient holds the property given, the property found under this subsection is that property;

    (b)   if the recipient holds no part of the property given, the property found under this subsection is any property which directly or indirectly represents it in his hands;

    (c)   if the recipient holds part of the property given, the property found under this subsection is that part and any property which directly or indirectly represents the other part in his hands.

(3)   The references in subsection (1)(a) and (b) to the value are to the value found in accordance with section 227.

Definitions   For "property", see ss 232(1), 236(6); for "property held", see ss 232(2)(a), (d), 236(6); for "tainted gift", see ss 225, 236(6).
References   See para 5.1.

230 Free property

Property is free unless an order is in force in respect of it under any of these provisions—

    (a)   section 27 of the Misuse of Drugs Act 1971 (c 38) (forfeiture orders);

    (b)   Article 11 of the Criminal Justice (Northern Ireland) Order 1994 (SI 1994/2795 (NI 15)) (deprivation orders);

    (c)   Part 2 of the Proceeds of Crime (Scotland) Act 1995 (c 43) (forfeiture of property used in crime);

    (d)   section 143 of the Powers of Criminal Courts (Sentencing) Act 2000 (c 6) (deprivation orders);

    (e)   section 23 or 111 of the Terrorism Act 2000 (c 11) (forfeiture orders);

    (f)   section 246, 266, 295(2) or 298(2) of this Act.

Definitions   For "property", see ss 232(1), 236(6).
References   See para 5.1.

231 Realisable property

Realisable property is—

    (a)   any free property held by the defendant;

    (b)   any free property held by the recipient of a tainted gift.

Definitions   For "defendant", see ss 189(9)(a), 236(3), (6); for "free property", see ss 230, 236(6); for "property", see ss 232(1), 236(6); for "property held", see ss 232(2)(a), (d), 236(6); for "recipient of a tainted gift", see ss 226(3), 236(6); for "tainted gift", see ss 225, 236(6).

232 Property: general provisions

    (1)   Property is all property wherever situated and includes—

        (a)   money;

        (b)   all forms of real or personal property;

        (c)   things in action and other intangible or incorporeal property.

    (2)   The following rules apply in relation to property—

        (a)   property is held by a person if he holds an interest in it;

        (b)   property is obtained by a person if he obtains an interest in it;

        (c)   property is transferred by one person to another if the first one transfers or grants an interest in it to the second;

        (d)   references to property held by a person include references to property vested in his trustee in bankruptcy, permanent or interim trustee (within the meaning of the Bankruptcy (Scotland) Act 1985 (c 66)) or liquidator;

        (e)   references to an interest held by a person beneficially in property include references to an interest which would be held by him beneficially if the property were not so vested;

        (f)   references to an interest, in relation to land in Northern Ireland or England and Wales, are to any legal estate or equitable interest or power;

        (g)   references to an interest, in relation to land in Scotland, are to any estate, interest, servitude or other heritable right in or over land, including a heritable security;

(h) references to an interest, in relation to property other than land, include references to a right (including a right to possession).

References See para 5.1.

---

233 Proceedings

(1) Proceedings for an offence are started—
  (a) when a justice of the peace issues a summons or warrant under Article 20 of the Magistrates' Courts (Northern Ireland) Order 1981 (SI 1981/ 1675 (NI 26)) in respect of the offence;
  (b) when a person is charged with the offence after being taken into custody without a warrant;
  (c) when an indictment is preferred under section 2(2)(c), (e) or (f) of the Grand Jury (Abolition) Act (Northern Ireland) 1969 (c 15 (NI)).

(2) If more than one time is found under subsection (1) in relation to proceedings they are started at the earliest of them.

(3) If the defendant is acquitted on all counts in proceedings for an offence, the proceedings are concluded when he is acquitted.

(4) If the defendant is convicted in proceedings for an offence and the conviction is quashed or the defendant is pardoned before a confiscation order is made, the proceedings are concluded when the conviction is quashed or the defendant is pardoned.

(5) If a confiscation order is made against the defendant in proceedings for an offence (whether the order is made by the Crown Court or the Court of Appeal) the proceedings are concluded—
  (a) when the order is satisfied or discharged, or
  (b) when the order is quashed and there is no further possibility of an appeal against the decision to quash the order.

(6) If the defendant is convicted in proceedings for an offence but the Crown Court decides not to make a confiscation order against him, the following rules apply—
  (a) if an application for leave to appeal under section 181(2) is refused, the proceedings are concluded when the decision to refuse is made;
  (b) if the time for applying for leave to appeal under section 181(2) expires without an application being made, the proceedings are concluded when the time expires;
  (c) if on an appeal under section 181(2) the Court of Appeal confirms the Crown Court's decision and an application for leave to appeal under section 183 is refused, the proceedings are concluded when the decision to refuse is made;
  (d) if on appeal under section 181(2) the Court of Appeal confirms the Crown Court's decision, and the time for applying for leave to appeal under section 183 expires without an application being made, the proceedings are concluded when the time expires;
  (e) if on appeal under section 181(2) the Court of Appeal confirms the Crown Court's decision, and on appeal under section 183 the House of Lords confirms the Court of Appeal's decision, the proceedings are concluded when the House of Lords confirms the decision;

    (f)   if on appeal under section 181(2) the Court of Appeal directs the Crown Court to reconsider the case, and on reconsideration the Crown Court decides not to make a confiscation order against the defendant, the proceedings are concluded when the Crown Court makes that decision;

    (g)   if on appeal under section 183 the House of Lords directs the Crown Court to reconsider the case, and on reconsideration the Crown Court decides not to make a confiscation order against the defendant, the proceedings are concluded when the Crown Court makes that decision.

(7)   In applying subsection (6) any power to extend the time for making an application for leave to appeal must be ignored.

(8)   In applying subsection (6) the fact that a court may decide on a later occasion to make a confiscation order against the defendant must be ignored.

Definitions   For "defendant", see ss 189(9)(a), 236(3), (6); for "confiscation order", see s 236(5)(a), (6).
References   See para 5.1.

234 Applications

(1)   An application under section 169, 170, 177 or 178 is concluded—
    (a)   in a case where the court decides not to make a confiscation order against the defendant, when it makes the decision;
    (b)   in a case where a confiscation order is made against him as a result of the application, when the order is satisfied or discharged, or when the order is quashed and there is no further possibility of an appeal against the decision to quash the order;
    (c)   in a case where the application is withdrawn, when the person who made the application notifies the withdrawal to the court to which the application was made.

(2)   An application under section 171 or 172 is concluded—
    (a)   in a case where the court decides not to vary the confiscation order concerned, when it makes the decision;
    (b)   in a case where the court varies the confiscation order as a result of the application, when the order is satisfied or discharged, or when the order is quashed and there is no further possibility of an appeal against the decision to quash the order;
    (c)   in a case where the application is withdrawn, when the person who made the application notifies the withdrawal to the court to which the application was made.

Definitions   For "confiscation order", see s 236(5)(a), (6); for "defendant", see s 236(3), (6); for "satisfied", see ss 235(1), 236(6).
References   See para 5.1.

235 Confiscation orders

(1)   A confiscation order is satisfied when no amount is due under it.

(2)   A confiscation order is subject to appeal until there is no further possibility of an appeal on which the order could be varied or quashed; and for this purpose any power to grant leave to appeal out of time must be ignored.

Definitions   For "confiscation order", see s 236(5)(a), (6).
References   See para 5.1.

---

236 Other interpretative provisions

(1)   A reference to the offence (or offences) concerned must be construed in accordance with section 156(9).

(2)   A criminal investigation is an investigation which police officers or other persons have a duty to conduct with a view to it being ascertained whether a person should be charged with an offence.

(3)   A defendant is a person against whom proceedings for an offence have been started (whether or not he has been convicted).

(4)   A reference to sentencing the defendant for an offence includes a reference to dealing with him otherwise in respect of the offence.

(5)   The following paragraphs apply to references to orders—
    (a)   a confiscation order is an order under section 156;
    (b)   a restraint order is an order under section 190.

(6)   Sections 223 to 235 and this section apply for the purposes of this Part.

Definitions   For "proceedings started", see ss 233(1), (2), 236(6).
References   See para 5.1.

General

237 Procedure on appeal to the Court of Appeal

(1)   An appeal to the Court of Appeal under this Part lies only with the leave of that Court.

(2)   In relation to appeals to the Court of Appeal under this Part, the Secretary of State may make an order containing provision corresponding to any provision in the Criminal Appeal (Northern Ireland) Act 1980 (c 47) (subject to any specified modifications).

References   See para 5.1.

---

238 Procedure on appeal to the House of Lords

In relation to appeals to the House of Lords under this Part, the Secretary of State may make an order containing provision corresponding to any provision in the Criminal Appeal (Northern Ireland) Act 1980 (subject to any specified modifications).

References   See para 5.1.

---

239 Crown Court Rules

In relation to—
- (a) proceedings under this Part, or
- (b) receivers appointed under this Part,

Crown Court Rules may make provision corresponding to provision in rules of court (within the meaning of section 120(1) of the Judicature (Northern Ireland) Act 1978 (c 23)).

References See para 5.1.

PART 5
CIVIL RECOVERY OF THE PROCEEDS ETC OF UNLAWFUL CONDUCT

CHAPTER 1
INTRODUCTORY

240 General purpose of this Part

(1) This Part has effect for the purposes of—
- (a) enabling the enforcement authority to recover, in civil proceedings before the High Court or Court of Session, property which is, or represents, property obtained through unlawful conduct,
- (b) enabling cash which is, or represents, property obtained through unlawful conduct, or which is intended to be used in unlawful conduct, to be forfeited in civil proceedings before a magistrates' court or (in Scotland) the sheriff.

(2) The powers conferred by this Part are exercisable in relation to any property (including cash) whether or not any proceedings have been brought for an offence in connection with the property.

Definitions For "cash", see ss 289(6), (7), 316(1); for "enforcement authority", see s 316(1); for "property", see s 316(2), (4)–(7); for "property obtained through unlawful conduct", see s 242; for "unlawful conduct", see s 241.
References See para 6.10.

241 "Unlawful conduct"

(1) Conduct occurring in any part of the United Kingdom is unlawful conduct if it is unlawful under the criminal law of that part.

(2) Conduct which—
- (a) occurs in a country outside the United Kingdom and is unlawful under the criminal law of that country, and
- (b) if it occurred in a part of the United Kingdom, would be unlawful under the criminal law of that part,

is also unlawful conduct.

(3) The court or sheriff must decide on a balance of probabilities whether it is proved—
- (a) that any matters alleged to constitute unlawful conduct have occurred, or
- (b) that any person intended to use any cash in unlawful conduct.

Definitions   For "cash", see ss 289(6), (7), 316(1); for "country", see s 316(1); for "the court", see
s 316(1).
References   See paras 6.12–6.14.

242 "Property obtained through unlawful conduct"

(1)   A person obtains property through unlawful conduct (whether his own conduct or another's) if he obtains property by or in return for the conduct.

(2)   In deciding whether any property was obtained through unlawful conduct—

(a)   it is immaterial whether or not any money, goods or services were provided in order to put the person in question in a position to carry out the conduct,

(b)   it is not necessary to show that the conduct was of a particular kind if it is shown that the property was obtained through conduct of one of a number of kinds, each of which would have been unlawful conduct.

Definitions   For "property", see s 316(2), (4)–(7); for "unlawful conduct", see s 241
References   See paras 6.15–6.17.

CHAPTER 2
CIVIL RECOVERY IN THE HIGH COURT OR COURT OF SESSION

Proceedings for recovery orders

243 Proceedings for recovery orders in England and Wales or Northern Ireland

(1)   Proceedings for a recovery order may be taken by the enforcement authority in the High Court against any person who the authority thinks holds recoverable property.

(2)   The enforcement authority must serve the claim form—

(a)   on the respondent, and

(b)   unless the court dispenses with service, on any other person who the authority thinks holds any associated property which the authority wishes to be subject to a recovery order,

wherever domiciled, resident or present.

(3)   If any property which the enforcement authority wishes to be subject to a recovery order is not specified in the claim form it must be described in the form in general terms; and the form must state whether it is alleged to be recoverable property or associated property.

(4)   The references above to the claim form include the particulars of claim, where they are served subsequently.

Definitions   For "associated property", see s 245; for "enforcement authority", see s 316(1); for
"property", see s 316(2), (4)–(7); for "recoverable property", see s 316(1); for "recovery order", see
s 316(1); for "respondent", see s 316(1).
References   See para 6.18.

244 Proceedings for recovery orders in Scotland

(1)   Proceedings for a recovery order may be taken by the enforcement authority in the Court of Session against any person who the authority thinks holds recoverable property.

(2)   The enforcement authority must serve the application—
     (a)   on the respondent, and
     (b)   unless the court dispenses with service, on any other person who the authority thinks holds any associated property which the authority wishes to be subject to a recovery order,

wherever domiciled, resident or present.

(3)   If any property which the enforcement authority wishes to be subject to a recovery order is not specified in the application it must be described in the application in general terms; and the application must state whether it is alleged to be recoverable property or associated property.

Definitions   For "associated property", see s 245; for "enforcement authority", see s 316(1); for "property", see s 316(2), (4)–(7); for "recoverable property", see s 316(1); for "recovery order", see s 316(1); for "respondent", see s 316(1).
References   See para 6.18.

245 "Associated property"

(1)   "Associated property" means property of any of the following descriptions (including property held by the respondent) which is not itself the recoverable property—
     (a)   any interest in the recoverable property,
     (b)   any other interest in the property in which the recoverable property subsists,
     (c)   if the recoverable property is a tenancy in common, the tenancy of the other tenant,
     (d)   if (in Scotland) the recoverable property is owned in common, the interest of the other owner,
     (e)   if the recoverable property is part of a larger property, but not a separate part, the remainder of that property.

(2)   References to property being associated with recoverable property are to be read accordingly.

(3)   No property is to be treated as associated with recoverable property consisting of rights under a pension scheme (within the meaning of sections 273 to 275).

Definitions   For "interest" in relation to land, see s 316(1); for "interest" in relation to property other than land", see s 316(1); for "part" in relation to property, see s 316(1); for "property", see s 316(2), (4)–(7); for "recoverable property", see s 316(1); for "respondent", see s 316(1).
References   See paras 6.18–6.20.

Interim receiving orders (England and Wales and Northern Ireland)

246 Application for interim receiving order

(1)   Where the enforcement authority may take proceedings for a recovery order in the High Court, the authority may apply to the court for an interim receiving order (whether before or after starting the proceedings).

(2)   An interim receiving order is an order for—
    (a)   the detention, custody or preservation of property, and
    (b)   the appointment of an interim receiver.

(3)   An application for an interim receiving order may be made without notice if the circumstances are such that notice of the application would prejudice any right of the enforcement authority to obtain a recovery order in respect of any property.

(4)   The court may make an interim receiving order on the application if it is satisfied that the conditions in subsections (5) and, where applicable, (6) are met.

(5)   The first condition is that there is a good arguable case—
    (a)   that the property to which the application for the order relates is or includes recoverable property, and
    (b)   that, if any of it is not recoverable property, it is associated property.

(6)   The second condition is that, if—
    (a)   the property to which the application for the order relates includes property alleged to be associated property, and
    (b)   the enforcement authority has not established the identity of the person who holds it,
the authority has taken all reasonable steps to do so.

(7)   In its application for an interim receiving order, the enforcement authority must nominate a suitably qualified person for appointment as interim receiver, but the nominee may not be a member of the staff of the Agency.

(8)   The extent of the power to make an interim receiving order is not limited by sections 247 to 255.

Definitions   For "the Agency", see s 1(1); for "associated property", see s 245; for "the court", see s 316(1); for "enforcement authority", see s 316(1); for "property", see s 316(2), (4)–(7); for "recoverable property", see s 316(1); for "recovery order", see s 316(1).
References   See paras 6.22–6.25.

---

247 Functions of interim receiver

(1)   An interim receiving order may authorise or require the interim receiver—
    (a)   to exercise any of the powers mentioned in Schedule 6,
    (b)   to take any other steps the court thinks appropriate,
for the purpose of securing the detention, custody or preservation of the property to which the order applies or of taking any steps under subsection (2).

(2)   An interim receiving order must require the interim receiver to take any steps which the court thinks necessary to establish—
    (a)   whether or not the property to which the order applies is recoverable property or associated property,
    (b)   whether or not any other property is recoverable property (in relation to the same unlawful conduct) and, if it is, who holds it.

(3)   If—
    (a)   the interim receiver deals with any property which is not property to which the order applies, and
    (b)   at the time he deals with the property he believes on reasonable grounds that he is entitled to do so in pursuance of the order,

the interim receiver is not liable to any person in respect of any loss or damage resulting from his dealing with the property except so far as the loss or damage is caused by his negligence.

Definitions   For "associated property", see s 245; for "the court", see s 316(1); for "dealing", see s 316(1); for "interim receiving order", see s 246(2); for "property", see s 316(2), (4)–(7); for "recoverable property", see s 316(1); for "unlawful conduct", see s 241.
References   See paras 6.26–6.29.

248 Registration

(1)   The registration Acts—
    (a)   apply in relation to interim receiving orders as they apply in relation to orders which affect land and are made by the court for the purpose of enforcing judgements or recognisances,
    (b)   apply in relation to applications for interim receiving orders as they apply in relation to other pending land actions.

(2)   The registration Acts are—
    (a)   the Land Registration Act 1925 (c 21),
    (b)   the Land Charges Act 1972 (c 61), and
    (c)   the Land Registration Act 2002 (c 9).

(3)   But no notice may be entered in the register of title under the Land Registration Act 2002 in respect of an interim receiving order.

(4)   A person applying for an interim receiving order must be treated for the purposes of section 57 of the Land Registration Act 1925 (inhibitions) as a person interested in relation to any registered land to which—
    (a)   the application relates, or
    (b)   an interim receiving order made in pursuance of the application relates.

Prospective repeal   Sub-ss (2)(a), (4): repealed by s 457, Sch 12, as from a day to be appointed under s 458 post.
Definitions   For "the court", see s 316(1); for "interim receiving order", see s 246(2).
References   See paras 6.34, 6.35.

249 Registration (Northern Ireland)

(1)   A person applying for an interim receiving order must be treated for the purposes of section 66 of the Land Registration Act (Northern Ireland) 1970 (c 18 (NI)) (cautions) as a person interested in relation to any registered land to which—
    (a)   the application relates, or
    (b)   an interim receiving order made in pursuance of the application relates.

(2)   Upon being served with a copy of an interim receiving order, the Registrar must, in respect of any registered land to which an interim receiving order or an application for an interim receiving order relates, make an entry inhibiting any dealing with the land without the consent of the High Court.

(3)   Subsections (2) and (4) of section 67 of the Land Registration Act (Northern Ireland) 1970 (inhibitions) apply to an entry made under subsection (2) as they apply to an entry made on the application of any person interested in the registered land under subsection (1) of that section.

(4)   Where an interim receiving order has been protected by an entry registered under the Land Registration Act (Northern Ireland) 1970 or the Registration of Deeds Acts, an order setting aside the interim receiving order may require that entry to be vacated.

(5)   In this section—
>   "Registrar" and "entry" have the same meanings as in the Land Registration Act (Northern Ireland) 1970, and
>   "Registration of Deeds Acts" has the meaning given by section 46(2) of the Interpretation Act (Northern Ireland) 1954 (c 33 (NI)).

Definitions   For "interim receiving order", see s 246(2).
References   See para 6.36.

---

250 Duties of respondent etc

(1)   An interim receiving order may require any person to whose property the order applies—
>   (a)   to bring the property to a place (in England and Wales or, as the case may be, Northern Ireland) specified by the interim receiver or place it in the custody of the interim receiver (if, in either case, he is able to do so),
>   (b)   to do anything he is reasonably required to do by the interim receiver for the preservation of the property.

(2)   An interim receiving order may require any person to whose property the order applies to bring any documents relating to the property which are in his possession or control to a place (in England and Wales or, as the case may be, Northern Ireland) specified by the interim receiver or to place them in the custody of the interim receiver.

"Document" means anything in which information of any description is recorded.

Definitions   For "interim receiving order", see s 246(2); for "property", see s 316(2), (4)–(7).
References   See para 6.37.

---

251 Supervision of interim receiver and variation of order

(1)   The interim receiver, any party to the proceedings and any person affected by any action taken by the interim receiver, or who may be affected by any action proposed to be taken by him, may at any time apply to the court for directions as to the exercise of the interim receiver's functions.

(2)   Before giving any directions under subsection (1), the court must (as well as giving the parties to the proceedings an opportunity to be heard) give such an opportunity to the interim receiver and to any person who may be interested in the application.

(3)   The court may at any time vary or set aside an interim receiving order.

(4)   Before exercising any power under this Chapter to vary or set aside an interim receiving order, the court must (as well as giving the parties to the proceedings an opportunity to be heard) give such an opportunity to the interim receiver and to any person who may be affected by the court's decision.

Definitions   For "the court", see s 316(1).
References   See para 6.38.

252 Restrictions on dealing etc with property

(1)   An interim receiving order must, subject to any exclusions made in accordance with this section, prohibit any person to whose property the order applies from dealing with the property.

(2)   Exclusions may be made when the interim receiving order is made or on an application to vary the order.

(3)   An exclusion may, in particular, make provision for the purpose of enabling any person—

(a)   to meet his reasonable living expenses, or

(b)   to carry on any trade, business, profession or occupation,

and may be made subject to conditions.

(4)   But an exclusion may not be made for the purpose of enabling any person to meet any legal expenses in respect of proceedings under this Part.

(5)   If the excluded property is not specified in the order it must be described in the order in general terms.

(6)   The power to make exclusions must be exercised with a view to ensuring, so far as practicable, that the satisfaction of any right of the enforcement authority to recover the property obtained through unlawful conduct is not unduly prejudiced.

Definitions   For "dealing", see s 316(1); for "enforcement authority", see s 316(1); for "interim receiving order", see s 246(2); for "property", see s 316(2), (4)–(7); for "property obtained through unlawful conduct", see s 242; for "satisfaction of the enforcement authority's right to recover property obtained through unlawful conduct", see ss 279, 316(2), (8); for "unlawful conduct", see s 241.
References   See para 6.39.

253 Restriction on proceedings and remedies

(1)   While an interim receiving order has effect—

(a)   the court may stay any action, execution or other legal process in respect of the property to which the order applies,

(b)   no distress may be levied against the property to which the order applies except with the leave of the court and subject to any terms the court may impose.

(2)   If a court (whether the High Court or any other court) in which proceedings are pending in respect of any property is satisfied that an interim receiving order has been applied for or made in respect of the property, the court may either stay the proceedings or allow them to continue on any terms it thinks fit.

(3)   If the interim receiving order applies to a tenancy of any premises, no landlord or other person to whom rent is payable may exercise any right of forfeiture by peaceable re-entry in relation to the premises in respect of any failure by the tenant to comply with any term or condition of the tenancy, except with the leave of the court and subject to any terms the court may impose.

(4) Before exercising any power conferred by this section, the court must (as well as giving the parties to any of the proceedings in question an opportunity to be heard) give such an opportunity to the interim receiver (if appointed) and any person who may be affected by the court's decision.

Definitions For "the court", see s 316(1); for "enforcement authority", see s 316(1); for "interim receiving order", see s 246(2); for "premises", see s 316(1); for "property", see s 316(2), (4)–(7).
References See paras 6.40, 6.41.

254 Exclusion of property which is not recoverable etc

(1) If the court decides that any property to which an interim receiving order applies is neither recoverable property nor associated property, it must vary the order so as to exclude it.

(2) The court may vary an interim receiving order so as to exclude from the property to which the order applies any property which is alleged to be associated property if the court thinks that the satisfaction of any right of the enforcement authority to recover the property obtained through unlawful conduct will not be prejudiced.

(3) The court may exclude any property within subsection (2) on any terms or conditions, applying while the interim receiving order has effect, which the court thinks necessary or expedient.

Definitions For "associated property", see s 245; for "the court", see s 316(1); for "enforcement authority", see s 316(1); for "interim receiving order", see s 246(2); for "property", see s 316(2), (4)–(7); for "property obtained through unlawful conduct", see s 242; for "recoverable property", see s 316(1); for "satisfaction of the enforcement authority's right to recover property obtained through unlawful conduct", see ss 279, 316(2), (8); for "unlawful conduct", see s 241.
References See para 6.42.

255 Reporting

(1) An interim receiving order must require the interim receiver to inform the enforcement authority and the court as soon as reasonably practicable if he thinks that—

(a) any property to which the order applies by virtue of a claim that it is recoverable property is not recoverable property,

(b) any property to which the order applies by virtue of a claim that it is associated property is not associated property,

(c) any property to which the order does not apply is recoverable property (in relation to the same unlawful conduct) or associated property, or

(d) any property to which the order applies is held by a person who is different from the person it is claimed holds it,

or if he thinks that there has been any other material change of circumstances.

(2) An interim receiving order must require the interim receiver—

(a) to report his findings to the court,

(b) to serve copies of his report on the enforcement authority and on any person who holds any property to which the order applies or who may otherwise be affected by the report.

Definitions   For "associated property", see s 245; for "the court", see s 316(1); for "enforcement authority", see s 316(1); for "interim receiving order", see s 246(2); for "property", see s 316(2), (4)–(7); for "recoverable property", see s 316(1); for "unlawful conduct", see s 241.
References   See paras 6.43, 6.44.

Interim administration orders (Scotland)

256 Application for interim administration order

(1)   Where the enforcement authority may take proceedings for a recovery order in the Court of Session, the authority may apply to the court for an interim administration order (whether before or after starting the proceedings).

(2)   An interim administration order is an order for—
  (a)   the detention, custody or preservation of property, and
  (b)   the appointment of an interim administrator.

(3)   An application for an interim administration order may be made without notice if the circumstances are such that notice of the application would prejudice any right of the enforcement authority to obtain a recovery order in respect of any property.

(4)   The court may make an interim administration order on the application if it is satisfied that the conditions in subsections (5) and, where applicable, (6) are met.

(5)   The first condition is that there is a probabilis causa litigandi—
  (a)   that the property to which the application for the order relates is or includes recoverable property, and
  (b)   that, if any of it is not recoverable property, it is associated property.

(6)   The second condition is that, if—
  (a)   the property to which the application for the order relates includes property alleged to be associated property, and
  (b)   the enforcement authority has not established the identity of the person who holds it,
the authority has taken all reasonable steps to do so.

(7)   In its application for an interim administration order, the enforcement authority must nominate a suitably qualified person for appointment as interim administrator, but the nominee may not be a member of the staff of the Scottish Administration.

(8)   The extent of the power to make an interim administration order is not limited by sections 257 to 264.

Definitions   For "associated property", see s 245; for "the court", see s 316(1); for "enforcement authority", see s 316(1); for "property", see s 316(2), (4)–(7); for "recoverable property", see s 316(1); for "recovery order", see s 316(1).
References   See paras 6.45, 6.46.

257 Functions of interim administrator

(1)   An interim administration order may authorise or require the interim administrator—
  (a)   to exercise any of the powers mentioned in Schedule 6,
  (b)   to take any other steps the court thinks appropriate,

for the purpose of securing the detention, custody or preservation of the property to which the order applies or of taking any steps under subsection (2).

(2)   An interim administration order must require the interim administrator to take any steps which the court thinks necessary to establish—

      (a)   whether or not the property to which the order applies is recoverable property or associated property,

      (b)   whether or not any other property is recoverable property (in relation to the same unlawful conduct) and, if it is, who holds it.

(3)   If—

      (a)   the interim administrator deals with any property which is not property to which the order applies, and

      (b)   at the time he deals with the property he believes on reasonable grounds that he is entitled to do so in pursuance of the order,

the interim administrator is not liable to any person in respect of any loss or damage resulting from his dealing with the property except so far as the loss or damage is caused by his negligence.

Definitions   For "associated property", see s 245; for "the court", see s 316(1); for "dealing", see s 316(1); for "interim administration order", see s 256(2); for "property", see s 316(2), (4)–(7); for "recoverable property", see s 316(1); for "unlawful conduct", see s 241.

---

258 Inhibition of property affected by order

(1)   On the application of the enforcement authority, the Court of Session may, in relation to the property mentioned in subsection (2), grant warrant for inhibition against any person specified in an interim administration order.

(2)   That property is heritable property situated in Scotland to which the interim administration order applies (whether generally or such of it as is specified in the application).

(3)   The warrant for inhibition—

      (a)   has effect as if granted on the dependence of an action for debt by the enforcement authority against the person and may be executed, recalled, loosed or restricted accordingly, and

      (b)   has the effect of letters of inhibition and must forthwith be registered by the enforcement authority in the register of inhibitions and adjudications.

(4)   Section 155 of the Titles to Land Consolidation (Scotland) Act 1868 (c 101) (effective date of inhibition) applies in relation to an inhibition for which warrant is granted under subsection (1) as it applies to an inhibition by separate letters or contained in a summons.

(5)   The execution of an inhibition under this section in respect of property does not prejudice the exercise of an interim administrator's powers under or for the purposes of this Part in respect of that property.

(6)   An inhibition executed under this section ceases to have effect when, or in so far as, the interim administration order ceases to apply in respect of the property in relation to which the warrant for inhibition was granted.

(7)   If an inhibition ceases to have effect to any extent by virtue of subsection (6) the enforcement authority must—

    (a)   apply for the recall or, as the case may be, the restriction of the inhibition, and

    (b)   ensure that the recall or restriction is reflected in the register of inhibitions and adjudications.

Definitions   For "enforcement authority", see s 316(1); for "interim administration order", see s 256(2); for "property", see s 316(2), (4)–(7).
References   See para 6.47.

259 Duties of respondent etc

(1)   An interim administration order may require any person to whose property the order applies—

    (a)   to bring the property to a place (in Scotland) specified by the interim administrator or place it in the custody of the interim administrator (if, in either case, he is able to do so),

    (b)   to do anything he is reasonably required to do by the interim administrator for the preservation of the property.

(2)   An interim administration order may require any person to whose property the order applies to bring any documents relating to the property which are in his possession or control to a place (in Scotland) specified by the interim administrator or to place them in the custody of the interim administrator.

"Document" means anything in which information of any description is recorded.

Definitions   For "interim administration order", see s 256(2); for "property", see s 316(2), (4)–(7).

260 Supervision of interim administrator and variation of order

(1)   The interim administrator, any party to the proceedings and any person affected by any action taken by the interim administrator, or who may be affected by any action proposed to be taken by him, may at any time apply to the court for directions as to the exercise of the interim administrator's functions.

(2)   Before giving any directions under subsection (1), the court must (as well as giving the parties to the proceedings an opportunity to be heard) give such an opportunity to the interim administrator and to any person who may be interested in the application.

(3)   The court may at any time vary or recall an interim administration order.

(4)   Before exercising any power under this Chapter to vary or set aside an interim administration order, the court must (as well as giving the parties to the proceedings an opportunity to be heard) give such an opportunity to the interim administrator and to any person who may be affected by the court's decision.

Definitions   For "the court", see s 316(1).

261 Restrictions on dealing etc with property

(1)   An interim administration order must, subject to any exclusions made in accordance with this section, prohibit any person to whose property the order applies from dealing with the property.

(2)   Exclusions may be made when the interim administration order is made or on an application to vary the order.

(3)   An exclusion may, in particular, make provision for the purpose of enabling any person—

      (a)   to meet his reasonable living expenses, or

      (b)   to carry on any trade, business, profession or occupation,

and may be made subject to conditions.

(4)   But an exclusion may not be made for the purpose of enabling any person to meet any legal expenses in respect of proceedings under this Part.

(5)   If the excluded property is not specified in the order it must be described in the order in general terms.

(6)   The power to make exclusions must be exercised with a view to ensuring, so far as practicable, that the satisfaction of any right of the enforcement authority to recover the property obtained through unlawful conduct is not unduly prejudiced.

Definitions   For "dealing", see s 316(1); for "enforcement authority", see s 316(1); for "interim administration order", see s 256(2); for "property", see s 316(2), (4)–(7); for "property obtained through unlawful conduct", see s 242; for "satisfaction of the enforcement authority's right to recover property obtained through unlawful conduct", see ss 279, 316(2), (8); for "unlawful conduct", see s 241.

262 Restriction on proceedings and remedies

(1)   While an interim administration order has effect, the court may sist any action, execution or other legal process in respect of the property to which the order applies.

(2)   If a court (whether the Court of Session or any other court) in which proceedings are pending in respect of any property is satisfied that an interim administration order has been applied for or made in respect of the property, the court may either sist the proceedings or allow them to continue on any terms it thinks fit.

(3)   Before exercising any power conferred by this section, the court must (as well as giving the parties to any of the proceedings in question an opportunity to be heard) give such an opportunity to the interim administrator (if appointed) and any person who may be affected by the court's decision.

Definitions   For "the court", see s 316(1); for "interim administration order", see s 256(2); for "property", see s 316(2), (4)–(7).
References   See para 6.48.

263 Exclusion of property which is not recoverable etc

(1)   If the court decides that any property to which an interim administration order applies is neither recoverable property nor associated property, it must vary the order so as to exclude it.

(2)   The court may vary an interim administration order so as to exclude from the property to which the order applies any property which is alleged to be associated property if the court thinks that the satisfaction of any right of the enforcement authority to recover the property obtained through unlawful conduct will not be prejudiced.

(3)   The court may exclude any property within subsection (2) on any terms or conditions, applying while the interim administration order has effect, which the court thinks necessary or expedient.

Definitions   For "associated property", see s 245; for "the court", see s 316(1); for "enforcement authority", see s 316(1); for "interim administration order", see s 256(2); for "property", see s 316(2), (4)–(7); for "property obtained through unlawful conduct", see s 242; for "recoverable property", see s 316(1); for "satisfaction of the enforcement authority's right to recover property obtained through unlawful conduct", see ss 279, 316(2), (8); for "unlawful conduct", see s 241.

264 Reporting

(1)   An interim administration order must require the interim administrator to inform the enforcement authority and the court as soon as reasonably practicable if he thinks that—
  (a)   any property to which the order applies by virtue of a claim that it is recoverable property is not recoverable property,
  (b)   any property to which the order applies by virtue of a claim that it is associated property is not associated property,
  (c)   any property to which the order does not apply is recoverable property (in relation to the same unlawful conduct) or associated property, or
  (d)   any property to which the order applies is held by a person who is different from the person it is claimed holds it,

or if he thinks that there has been any other material change of circumstances.

(2)   An interim administration order must require the interim administrator—
  (a)   to report his findings to the court,
  (b)   to serve copies of his report on the enforcement authority and on any person who holds any property to which the order applies or who may otherwise be affected by the report.

Definitions   For "associated property", see s 245; for "the court", see s 316(1); for "enforcement authority", see s 316(1); for "interim administration order", see s 256(2); for "property", see s 316(2), (4)–(7); for "recoverable property", see s 316(1); for "unlawful conduct", see s 241.

265 Arrestment of property affected by interim administration order

(1)   On the application of the enforcement authority or the interim administrator the Court of Session may, in relation to moveable recoverable property to which an interim administration order applies (whether generally or such of it as is specified in the application), grant warrant for arrestment.

(2)   An application by the enforcement authority under subsection (1) may be made at the same time as the application for the interim administration order or at any time thereafter.

(3)   Such a warrant for arrestment may be granted only if the property would be arrestable if the person entitled to it were a debtor.

(4)   A warrant under subsection (1) has effect as if granted on the dependence of an action for debt at the instance of the enforcement authority or, as the case may be, the interim administrator against the person and may be executed, recalled, loosed or restricted accordingly.

(5)   The execution of an arrestment under this section in respect of property does not prejudice the exercise of an interim administrator's powers under or for the purposes of this Part in respect of that property.

(6)   An arrestment executed under this section ceases to have effect when, or in so far as, the interim administration order ceases to apply in respect of the property in relation to which the warrant for arrestment was granted.

(7)   If an arrestment ceases to have effect to any extent by virtue of subsection (6) the enforcement authority or, as the case may be, the interim administrator must apply to the Court of Session for an order recalling or, as the case may be, restricting the arrestment.

Definitions   For "enforcement authority", see s 316(1); for "interim administration order", see s 256(2); for "property", see s 316(2), (4)–(7); for "recoverable property", see s 316(1).
References   See para 6.49.

Vesting and realisation of recoverable property

266 Recovery orders

(1)   If in proceedings under this Chapter the court is satisfied that any property is recoverable, the court must make a recovery order.

(2)   The recovery order must vest the recoverable property in the trustee for civil recovery.

(3)   But the court may not make in a recovery order—
    (a)   any provision in respect of any recoverable property if each of the conditions in subsection (4) or (as the case may be) (5) is met and it would not be just and equitable to do so, or
    (b)   any provision which is incompatible with any of the Convention rights (within the meaning of the Human Rights Act 1998 (c 42)).

(4)   In relation to a court in England and Wales or Northern Ireland, the conditions referred to in subsection (3)(a) are that—
    (a)   the respondent obtained the recoverable property in good faith,
    (b)   he took steps after obtaining the property which he would not have taken if he had not obtained it or he took steps before obtaining the property which he would not have taken if he had not believed he was going to obtain it,

(c)   when he took the steps, he had no notice that the property was recoverable,

(d)   if a recovery order were made in respect of the property, it would, by reason of the steps, be detrimental to him.

(5)   In relation to a court in Scotland, the conditions referred to in subsection (3)(a) are that—

(a)   the respondent obtained the recoverable property in good faith,

(b)   he took steps after obtaining the property which he would not have taken if he had not obtained it or he took steps before obtaining the property which he would not have taken if he had not believed he was going to obtain it,

(c)   when he took the steps, he had no reasonable grounds for believing that the property was recoverable,

(d)   if a recovery order were made in respect of the property, it would, by reason of the steps, be detrimental to him.

(6)   In deciding whether it would be just and equitable to make the provision in the recovery order where the conditions in subsection (4) or (as the case may be) (5) are met, the court must have regard to—

(a)   the degree of detriment that would be suffered by the respondent if the provision were made,

(b)   the enforcement authority's interest in receiving the realised proceeds of the recoverable property.

(7)   A recovery order may sever any property.

(8)   A recovery order may impose conditions as to the manner in which the trustee for civil recovery may deal with any property vested by the order for the purpose of realising it.

(9)   This section is subject to sections 270 to 278.

Definitions   For "the court", see s 316(1); for "dealing", see s 316(1); for "enforcement authority", see s 316(1); for "property", see s 316(2), (4)–(7); for "recoverable property", see s 316(1); for "respondent", see s 316(1).
References   See para 6.50.

267 Functions of the trustee for civil recovery

(1)   The trustee for civil recovery is a person appointed by the court to give effect to a recovery order.

(2)   The enforcement authority must nominate a suitably qualified person for appointment as the trustee.

(3)   The functions of the trustee are—

(a)   to secure the detention, custody or preservation of any property vested in him by the recovery order,

(b)   in the case of property other than money, to realise the value of the property for the benefit of the enforcement authority, and

(c)   to perform any other functions conferred on him by virtue of this Chapter.

(4)   In performing his functions, the trustee acts on behalf of the enforcement authority and must comply with any directions given by the authority.

(5)   The trustee is to realise the value of property vested in him by the recovery order, so far as practicable, in the manner best calculated to maximise the amount payable to the enforcement authority.

(6)   The trustee has the powers mentioned in Schedule 7.

(7)   References in this section to a recovery order include an order under section 276 and references to property vested in the trustee by a recovery order include property vested in him in pursuance of an order under section 276.

Definitions   For "the court", see s 316(1); for "enforcement authority", see s 316(1); for "property", see s 316(2), (4)–(7); for "recovery order", see s 316(1) (and sub-s (7) above); for "value", see s 316(1).
References   See para 6.51, 6.52.

---

268 Recording of recovery order (Scotland)

(1)   The clerk of the court must immediately after the making of a recovery order which relates to heritable property situated in Scotland send a certified copy of it to the keeper of the register of inhibitions and adjudications for recording in that register.

(2)   Recording under subsection (1) is to have the effect, as from the date of the recovery order, of an inhibition at the instance of the trustee for civil recovery against the person in whom the heritable property was vest prior to that date.

Definitions   For "property", see s 316(2), (4)–(7); for "recovery order", see s 316(1).
References   See para 6.53.

---

269 Rights of pre-emption, etc

(1)   A recovery order is to have effect in relation to any property despite any provision (of whatever nature) which would otherwise prevent, penalise or restrict the vesting of the property.

(2)   A right of pre-emption, right of irritancy, right of return or other similar right does not operate or become exercisable as a result of the vesting of any property under a recovery order.

A right of return means any right under a provision for the return or reversion of property in specified circumstances.

(3)   Where property is vested under a recovery order, any such right is to have effect as if the person in whom the property is vested were the same person in law as the person who held the property and as if no transfer of the property had taken place.

(4)   References to rights in subsections (2) and (3) do not include any rights in respect of which the recovery order was made.

(5)   This section applies in relation to the creation of interests, or the doing of anything else, by a recovery order as it applies in relation to the vesting of property.

Definitions   For "interest" in relation to land, see s 316(1); for "interest" in relation to property other than land", see s 316(1); for "property", see s 316(2), (4)–(7); for "recovery order", see s 316(1).
References   See para 6.54.

---

270 Associated and joint property

(1)   Sections 271 and 272 apply if the court makes a recovery order in respect of any recoverable property in a case within subsection (2) or (3).

(2)   A case is within this subsection if—
    (a)   the property to which the proceedings relate includes property which is associated with the recoverable property and is specified or described in the claim form or (in Scotland) application, and
    (b)   if the associated property is not the respondent's property, the claim form or application has been served on the person whose property it is or the court has dispensed with service.

(3)   A case is within this subsection if—
    (a)   the recoverable property belongs to joint tenants, and
    (b)   one of the tenants is an excepted joint owner.

(4)   An excepted joint owner is a person who obtained the property in circumstances in which it would not be recoverable as against him; and references to the excepted joint owner's share of the recoverable property are to so much of the recoverable property as would have been his if the joint tenancy had been severed.

(5)   Subsections (3) and (4) do not extend to Scotland.

Definitions   For "associated property", see s 245; for "the court", see s 316(1); for "property", see s 316(2), (4)–(7); for "property associated with recoverable property", see s 245(2), (3); for "recoverable property", see s 316(1); for "recovery order", see s 316(1); for "respondent", see s 316(1).
References   See para 6.56.

---

271 Agreements about associated and joint property

(1)   Where—
    (a)   this section applies, and
    (b)   the enforcement authority (on the one hand) and the person who holds the associated property or who is the excepted joint owner (on the other) agree,
the recovery order may, instead of vesting the recoverable property in the trustee for civil recovery, require the person who holds the associated property or who is the excepted joint owner to make a payment to the trustee.

(2)   A recovery order which makes any requirement under subsection (1) may, so far as required for giving effect to the agreement, include provision for vesting, creating or extinguishing any interest in property.

(3)   The amount of the payment is to be the amount which the enforcement authority and that person agree represents—
    (a)   in a case within section 270(2), the value of the recoverable property,
    (b)   in a case within section 270(3), the value of the recoverable property less the value of the excepted joint owner's share.

(4)   But if—
    (a)   an interim receiving order or interim administration order applied at any time to the associated property or joint tenancy, and
    (b)   the enforcement authority agrees that the person has suffered loss as a result of the interim receiving order or interim administration order,

the amount of the payment may be reduced by any amount the enforcement authority and that person agree is reasonable, having regard to that loss and to any other relevant circumstances.

(5)   If there is more than one such item of associated property or excepted joint owner, the total amount to be paid to the trustee, and the part of that amount which is to be provided by each person who holds any such associated property or who is an excepted joint owner, is to be agreed between both (or all) of them and the enforcement authority.

(6)   A recovery order which makes any requirement under subsection (1) must make provision for any recoverable property to cease to be recoverable.

272 Associated and joint property: default of agreement

(1)   Where this section applies, the court may make the following provision if—
   (a)   there is no agreement under section 271, and
   (b)   the court thinks it just and equitable to do so.

(2)   The recovery order may provide—
   (a)   for the associated property to vest in the trustee for civil recovery or (as the case may be) for the excepted joint owner's interest to be extinguished, or
   (b)   in the case of an excepted joint owner, for the severance of his interest.

(3)   A recovery order making any provision by virtue of subsection (2)(a) may provide—
   (a)   for the trustee to pay an amount to the person who holds the associated property or who is an excepted joint owner, or
   (b)   for the creation of interests in favour of that person, or the imposition of liabilities or conditions, in relation to the property vested in the trustee,

or for both.

(4)   In making any provision in a recovery order by virtue of subsection (2) or (3), the court must have regard to—
   (a)   the rights of any person who holds the associated property or who is an excepted joint owner and the value to him of that property or, as the case may be, of his share (including any value which cannot be assessed in terms of money),
   (b)   the enforcement authority's interest in receiving the realised proceeds of the recoverable property.

(5)   If—
   (a)   an interim receiving order or interim administration order applied at any time to the associated property or joint tenancy, and

(b)   the court is satisfied that the person who holds the associated property or who is an excepted joint owner has suffered loss as a result of the interim receiving order or interim administration order,

a recovery order making any provision by virtue of subsection (2) or (3) may require the enforcement authority to pay compensation to that person.

(6)   The amount of compensation to be paid under subsection (5) is the amount the court thinks reasonable, having regard to the person's loss and to any other relevant circumstances.

Definitions   For "associated property", see s 245; for "the court", see s 316(1); for "enforcement authority", see s 316(1); for "excepted joint owner", see s 270(4); for "interest" in relation to land, see s 316(1); for "interest" in relation to property other than land", see s 316(1); for "interim administration order", see s 256(2); for "interim receiving order", see s 246(2); for "property", see s 316(2), (4)–(7); for "recoverable property", see s 316(1); for "recovery order", see s 316(1); for "share" in relation to an excepted joint owner, see s 270(4); for "value", see s 316(1).
References   See paras 6.59–6.61.

---

273 Payments in respect of rights under pension schemes

(1)   This section applies to recoverable property consisting of rights under a pension scheme.

(2)   A recovery order in respect of the property must, instead of vesting the property in the trustee for civil recovery, require the trustees or managers of the pension scheme—

(a)   to pay to the trustee for civil recovery within a prescribed period the amount determined by the trustees or managers to be equal to the value of the rights, and

(b)   to give effect to any other provision made by virtue of this section and the two following sections in respect of the scheme.

This subsection is subject to sections 276 to 278.

(3)   A recovery order made by virtue of subsection (2) overrides the provisions of the pension scheme to the extent that they conflict with the provisions of the order.

(4)   A recovery order made by virtue of subsection (2) may provide for the recovery by the trustees or managers of the scheme (whether by deduction from any amount which they are required to pay to the trustee for civil recovery or otherwise) of costs incurred by them in—

(a)   complying with the recovery order, or

(b)   providing information, before the order was made, to the enforcement authority, interim receiver or interim administrator.

(5)   None of the following provisions applies to a court making a recovery order by virtue of subsection (2)—

(a)   any provision of section 159 of the Pension Schemes Act 1993 (c 48), section 155 of the Pension Schemes (Northern Ireland) Act 1993 (c 49), section 91 of the Pensions Act 1995 (c 26) or Article 89 of the Pensions (Northern Ireland) Order 1995 (SI 1995/3213 (NI 22)) (which prevent assignment and the making of orders that restrain a person from receiving anything which he is prevented from assigning),

(b) any provision of any enactment (whenever passed or made) corresponding to any of the provisions mentioned in paragraph (a),

(c) any provision of the pension scheme in question corresponding to any of those provisions.

Definitions   For "enforcement authority", see s 316(1); for "pension scheme", see s 275(4), (6), (8); for "prescribed", see s 275(3); for "property", see s 316(2), (4)–(7); for "recoverable property", see s 316(1); for "recovery order", see s 316(1); for "trustees or managers", see s 275(5), (7), (8); for "value", see s 316(1).
References   See para 6.62.

---

274 Consequential adjustment of liabilities under pension schemes

(1) A recovery order made by virtue of section 273(2) must require the trustees or managers of the pension scheme to make such reduction in the liabilities of the scheme as they think necessary in consequence of the payment made in pursuance of that subsection.

(2) Accordingly, the order must require the trustees or managers to provide for the liabilities of the pension scheme in respect of the respondent's recoverable property to which section 273 applies to cease.

(3) So far as the trustees or managers are required by the recovery order to provide for the liabilities of the pension scheme in respect of the respondent's recoverable property to which section 273 applies to cease, their powers include (in particular) power to reduce the amount of—

(a) any benefit or future benefit to which the respondent is or may be entitled under the scheme,

(b) any future benefit to which any other person may be entitled under the scheme in respect of that property.

Definitions   For "pension scheme", see s 275(4), (6), (8); for "recovery order", see s 316(1); for "respondent", see s 316(1); for "trustees or managers", see s 275(5), (7), (8).
References   See paras 6.63, 6.64.

---

275 Pension schemes: supplementary

(1) Regulations may make provision as to the exercise by trustees or managers of their powers under sections 273 and 274, including provision about the calculation and verification of the value at any time of rights or liabilities.

(2) The power conferred by subsection (1) includes power to provide for any values to be calculated or verified—

(a) in a manner which, in the particular case, is approved by a prescribed person, or

(b) in accordance with guidance from time to time prepared by a prescribed person.

(3) Regulations means regulations made by the Secretary of State after consultation with the Scottish Ministers; and prescribed means prescribed by regulations.

(4) A pension scheme means an occupational pension scheme or a personal pension scheme; and those expressions have the same meaning as in the Pension Schemes Act 1993 (c 48) or, in relation to Northern Ireland, the Pension Schemes (Northern Ireland) Act 1993 (c 49).

(5)   In relation to an occupational pension scheme or a personal pension scheme, the trustees or managers means—
  (a)   in the case of a scheme established under a trust, the trustees,
  (b)   in any other case, the managers.

(6)   References to a pension scheme include—
  (a)   a retirement annuity contract (within the meaning of Part 3 of the Welfare Reform and Pensions Act 1999 (c 30) or, in relation to Northern Ireland, Part 4 of the Welfare Reform and Pensions (Northern Ireland) Order 1999),
  (b)   an annuity or insurance policy purchased, or transferred, for the purpose of giving effect to rights under an occupational pension scheme or a personal pension scheme,
  (c)   an annuity purchased, or entered into, for the purpose of discharging any liability in respect of a pension credit under section 29(1)(b) of the Welfare Reform and Pensions Act 1999 (c 30) or, in relation to Northern Ireland, Article 26(1)(b) of the Welfare Reform and Pensions (Northern Ireland) Order 1999.

(7)   References to the trustees or managers—
  (a)   in relation to a retirement annuity contract or other annuity, are to the provider of the annuity,
  (b)   in relation to an insurance policy, are to the insurer.

(8)   Subsections (3) to (7) have effect for the purposes of this group of sections (that is, sections 273 and 274 and this section).

Definitions   For "value", see s 316(1).
References   See para 6.65.

276 Consent orders

(1)   The court may make an order staying (in Scotland, sisting) any proceedings for a recovery order on terms agreed by the parties for the disposal of the proceedings if each person to whose property the proceedings, or the agreement, relates is a party both to the proceedings and the agreement.

(2)   An order under subsection (1) may, as well as staying (or sisting) the proceedings on terms—
  (a)   make provision for any property which may be recoverable property to cease to be recoverable,
  (b)   make any further provision which the court thinks appropriate.

(3)   Section 280 applies to property vested in the trustee for civil recovery, or money paid to him, in pursuance of the agreement as it applies to property vested in him by a recovery order or money paid under section 271.

Definitions   For "the court", see s 316(1); for "property", see s 316(2), (4)–(7); for "recoverable property", see s 316(1); for "recovery order", see s 316(1).
References   See para 6.66.

277 Consent orders: pensions

(1)   This section applies where recoverable property to which proceedings under this Chapter relate includes rights under a pension scheme.

(2) An order made under section 276—
    (a) may not stay (in Scotland, sist) the proceedings on terms that the rights are vested in any other person, but
    (b) may include provision imposing the following requirement, if the trustees or managers of the scheme are parties to the agreement by virtue of which the order is made.

(3) The requirement is that the trustees or managers of the pension scheme—
    (a) make a payment in accordance with the agreement, and
    (b) give effect to any other provision made by virtue of this section in respect of the scheme.

(4) The trustees or managers of the pension scheme have power to enter into an agreement in respect of the proceedings on any terms on which an order made under section 276 may stay (in Scotland, sist) the proceedings.

(5) The following provisions apply in respect of an order under section 276, so far as it includes the requirement mentioned in subsection (3).

(6) The order overrides the provisions of the pension scheme to the extent that they conflict with the requirement.

(7) The order may provide for the recovery by the trustees or managers of the scheme (whether by deduction from any amount which they are required to pay in pursuance of the agreement or otherwise) of costs incurred by them in—
    (a) complying with the order, or
    (b) providing information, before the order was made, to the enforcement authority, interim receiver or interim administrator.

(8) Sections 273(5) and 274 (read with section 275) apply as if the requirement were included in an order made by virtue of section 273(2).

(9) Section 275(4) to (7) has effect for the purposes of this section.

Definitions   For "enforcement authority", see s 316(1); for "pension scheme", see s 275(4), (6) (by virtue of sub-s (9) above); for "property", see s 316(2), (4)–(7); for "recoverable property", see s 316(1); for "trustees or managers", see s 275(5), (7) (by virtue of sub-s (9) above).
References   See paras 6.67–6.69.

278 Limit on recovery

(1) This section applies if the enforcement authority seeks a recovery order—
    (a) in respect of both property which is or represents property obtained through unlawful conduct and related property, or
    (b) in respect of property which is or represents property obtained through unlawful conduct where such an order, or an order under section 276, has previously been made in respect of related property.

(2) For the purposes of this section—
    (a) the original property means the property obtained through unlawful conduct,
    (b) the original property, and any items of property which represent the original property, are to be treated as related to each other.

(3) The court is not to make a recovery order if it thinks that the enforcement authority's right to recover the original property has been satisfied by a previous recovery order or order under section 276.

(4)   Subject to subsection (3), the court may act under subsection (5) if it thinks that—

(a)   a recovery order may be made in respect of two or more related items of recoverable property, but

(b)   the making of a recovery order in respect of both or all of them is not required in order to satisfy the enforcement authority's right to recover the original property.

(5)   The court may in order to satisfy that right to the extent required make a recovery order in respect of—

(a)   only some of the related items of property, or

(b)   only a part of any of the related items of property,

or both.

(6)   Where the court may make a recovery order in respect of any property, this section does not prevent the recovery of any profits which have accrued in respect of the property.

(7)   If—

(a)   an order is made under section 298 for the forfeiture of recoverable property, and

(b)   the enforcement authority subsequently seeks a recovery order in respect of related property,

the order under section 298 is to be treated for the purposes of this section as if it were a recovery order obtained by the enforcement authority in respect of the forfeited property.

(8)   If—

(a)   in pursuance of a judgment in civil proceedings (whether in the United Kingdom or elsewhere), the claimant has obtained property from the defendant ("the judgment property"),

(b)   the claim was based on the defendant's having obtained the judgment property or related property through unlawful conduct, and

(c)   the enforcement authority subsequently seeks a recovery order in respect of property which is related to the judgment property,

the judgment is to be treated for the purposes of this section as if it were a recovery order obtained by the enforcement authority in respect of the judgment property.

In relation to Scotland, "claimant" and "defendant" are to be read as "pursuer" and "defender".

(9)   If—

(a)   property has been taken into account in deciding the amount of a person's benefit from criminal conduct for the purpose of making a confiscation order, and

(b)   the enforcement authority subsequently seeks a recovery order in respect of related property,

the confiscation order is to be treated for the purposes of this section as if it were a recovery order obtained by the enforcement authority in respect of the property referred to in paragraph (a).

(10)   In subsection (9), a confiscation order means—

(a)   an order under section 6, 92 or 156, or

(b)   an order under a corresponding provision of an enactment mentioned in section 8(7)(a) to (g),

and, in relation to an order mentioned in paragraph (b), the reference to the amount of a person's benefit from criminal conduct is to be read as a reference to the corresponding amount under the enactment in question.

Definitions   For "the court", see s 316(1); for "enactment", see s 455; for "enforcement authority", see s 316(1); for "property", see s 316(2), (4)–(7); for "property obtained through unlawful conduct", see s 242; for "recoverable property", see s 316(1); for "recovery order", see s 316(1); for "unlawful conduct", see s 241.
References   See paras 6.70–6.72.

279 Section 278: supplementary

(1)   Subsections (2) and (3) give examples of the satisfaction of the enforcement authority's right to recover the original property.

(2)   If—
    (a)   there is a disposal, other than a part disposal, of the original property, and
    (b)   other property (the representative property) is obtained in its place,

the enforcement authority's right to recover the original property is satisfied by the making of a recovery order in respect of either the original property or the representative property.

(3)   If—
    (a)   there is a part disposal of the original property, and
    (b)   other property (the representative property) is obtained in place of the property disposed of,

the enforcement authority's right to recover the original property is satisfied by the making of a recovery order in respect of the remainder of the original property together with either the representative property or the property disposed of.

(4)   In this section—
    (a)   a part disposal means a disposal to which section 314(1) applies,
    (b)   the original property has the same meaning as in section 278.

Definitions   For "enforcement authority", see s 316(1); for "property", see s 316(2), (4)–(7); for "recovery order", see s 316(1).
References   See para 6.73.

280 Applying realised proceeds

(1)   This section applies to—
    (a)   sums which represent the realised proceeds of property which was vested in the trustee for civil recovery by a recovery order or which he obtained in pursuance of a recovery order,
    (b)   sums vested in the trustee by a recovery order or obtained by him in pursuance of a recovery order.

(2)   The trustee is to make out of the sums—
    (a)   first, any payment required to be made by him by virtue of section 272,

    (b)   second, any payment of expenses incurred by a person acting as an insolvency practitioner which are payable under this subsection by virtue of section 432(10),

and any sum which remains is to be paid to the enforcement authority.

Definitions   For "enforcement authority", see s 316(1); for "property", see s 316(2), (4)–(7); for "recovery order", see s 316(1).
References   See para 6.74.

Exemptions etc

281 Victims of theft, etc

(1)   In proceedings for a recovery order, a person who claims that any property alleged to be recoverable property, or any part of the property, belongs to him may apply for a declaration under this section.

(2)   If the applicant appears to the court to meet the following condition, the court may make a declaration to that effect.

(3)   The condition is that—
    (a)   the person was deprived of the property he claims, or of property which it represents, by unlawful conduct,
    (b)   the property he was deprived of was not recoverable property immediately before he was deprived of it, and
    (c)   the property he claims belongs to him.

(4)   Property to which a declaration under this section applies is not recoverable property.

Definitions   For "the court", see s 316(1); for "part" in relation to property, see s 316(1); for "property", see s 316(2), (4)–(7); for "recoverable property", see s 316(1); for "recovery order", see s 316(1); for "unlawful conduct", see s 241.
References   See paras 6.75, 6.76.

---

282 Other exemptions

(1)   Proceedings for a recovery order may not be taken against any person in circumstances of a prescribed description; and the circumstances may relate to the person himself or to the property or to any other matter.

In this subsection, prescribed means prescribed by an order made by the Secretary of State after consultation with the Scottish Ministers.

(2)   Proceedings for a recovery order may not be taken in respect of cash found at any place in the United Kingdom unless the proceedings are also taken in respect of property other than cash which is property of the same person.

(3)   Proceedings for a recovery order may not be taken against the Financial Services Authority in respect of any recoverable property held by the authority.

(4)   Proceedings for a recovery order may not be taken in respect of any property which is subject to any of the following charges—
    (a)   a collateral security charge, within the meaning of the Financial Markets and Insolvency (Settlement Finality) Regulations 1999 (SI 1999/2979),

    (b)   a market charge, within the meaning of Part 7 of the Companies Act 1989 (c 40),

    (c)   a money market charge, within the meaning of the Financial Markets and Insolvency (Money Market) Regulations 1995 (SI 1995/2049),

    (d)   a system charge, within the meaning of the Financial Markets and Insolvency Regulations 1996 (SI 1996/1469) or the Financial Markets and Insolvency Regulations (Northern Ireland) 1996 (SR 1996/252).

(5)   Proceedings for a recovery order may not be taken against any person in respect of any recoverable property which he holds by reason of his acting, or having acted, as an insolvency practitioner.

Acting as an insolvency practitioner has the same meaning as in section 433.

Definitions   For "associated property", see s 245; for "cash", see ss 289(6), (7), 316(1); for "property", see s 316(2), (4)–(7); for "recoverable property", see s 316(1); for "recovery order", see s 316(1).
References   See para 6.77.

Miscellaneous

283 Compensation

(1)   If, in the case of any property to which an interim receiving order or interim administration order has at any time applied, the court does not in the course of the proceedings decide that the property is recoverable property or associated property, the person whose property it is may make an application to the court for compensation.

(2)   Subsection (1) does not apply if the court—

    (a)   has made a declaration in respect of the property by virtue of section 281, or

    (b)   makes an order under section 276.

(3)   If the court has made a decision by reason of which no recovery order could be made in respect of the property, the application for compensation must be made within the period of three months beginning—

    (a)   in relation to a decision of the High Court in England and Wales, with the date of the decision or, if any application is made for leave to appeal, with the date on which the application is withdrawn or refused or (if the application is granted) on which any proceedings on appeal are finally concluded,

    (b)   in relation to a decision of the Court of Session or of the High Court in Northern Ireland, with the date of the decision or, if there is an appeal against the decision, with the date on which any proceedings on appeal are finally concluded.

(4)   If, in England and Wales or Northern Ireland, the proceedings in respect of the property have been discontinued, the application for compensation must be made within the period of three months beginning with the discontinuance.

(5)   If the court is satisfied that the applicant has suffered loss as a result of the interim receiving order or interim administration order, it may require the enforcement authority to pay compensation to him.

(6)   If, but for section 269(2), any right mentioned there would have operated in favour of, or become exercisable by, any person, he may make an application to the court for compensation.

(7)   The application for compensation under subsection (6) must be made within the period of three months beginning with the vesting referred to in section 269(2).

(8)   If the court is satisfied that, in consequence of the operation of section 269, the right in question cannot subsequently operate in favour of the applicant or (as the case may be) become exercisable by him, it may require the enforcement authority to pay compensation to him.

(9)   The amount of compensation to be paid under this section is the amount the court thinks reasonable, having regard to the loss suffered and any other relevant circumstances.

Definitions   For "associated property", see s 245; for "the court", see s 316(1); for "enforcement authority", see s 316(1); for "interim administration order", see s 256(2); for "interim receiving order", see s 246(2); for "property", see s 316(2), (4)–(7); for "recoverable property", see s 316(1); for "recovery order", see s 316(1).
References   See paras 6.78–6.80.

284 Payment of interim administrator or trustee (Scotland)

Any fees or expenses incurred by an interim administrator, or a trustee for civil recovery appointed by the Court of Session, in the exercise of his functions are to be reimbursed by the Scottish Ministers as soon as is practicable after they have been incurred.

References   See para 6.81.

285 Effect on diligence of recovery order (Scotland)

(1)   An arrestment or poinding of any recoverable property executed on or after the appointment of the trustee for civil recovery is ineffectual in a question with the trustee.

(2)   Any recoverable property so arrested or poinded, or (if the property has been sold) the proceeds of sale, must be handed over to the trustee for civil recovery.

(3)   A poinding of the ground in respect of recoverable property on or after such an appointment is ineffectual in a question with the trustee for civil recovery except for the interest mentioned in subsection (4).

(4)   That interest is—
   (a)   interest on the debt of a secured creditor for the current half yearly term, and
   (b)   arrears of interest on that debt for one year immediately before the commencement of that term.

(5)   On and after such appointment no other person may raise or insist in an adjudication against recoverable property or be confirmed as an executor-creditor on that property.

(6)   An inhibition on recoverable property shall cease to have effect in relation to any heritable property comprised in the recoverable property on such appointment.

(7)   The provisions of this section apply in relation to—
      (a)   an action of maills and duties, and
      (b)   an action for sequestration of rent,
as they apply in relation to an arrestment or poinding.

Definitions   For "property", see s 316(2), (4)–(7); for "recoverable property", see s 316(1).
References   See para 6.82.

---

286 Scope of powers (Scotland)

(1)   Orders under this Chapter may be made by the Court of Session in respect of a person wherever domiciled, resident or present.

(2)   Such an order may be made by the Court of Session in respect of moveable property wherever situated.

(3)   But such an order in respect of a person's moveable property may not be made by the Court of Session where—
      (a)   the person is not domiciled, resident or present in Scotland, and
      (b)   the property is not situated in Scotland,
unless the unlawful conduct took place in Scotland.

Definitions   For "property", see s 316(2), (4)–(7); for "unlawful conduct", see s 241.
References   See para 6.83.

---

287 Financial threshold

(1)   At any time when an order specifying an amount for the purposes of this section has effect, the enforcement authority may not start proceedings for a recovery order unless the authority reasonably believes that the aggregate value of the recoverable property which the authority wishes to be subject to a recovery order is not less than the specified amount.

(2)   The power to make an order under subsection (1) is exercisable by the Secretary of State after consultation with the Scottish Ministers.

(3)   If the authority applies for an interim receiving order or interim administration order before starting the proceedings, subsection (1) applies to the application instead of to the start of the proceedings.

(4)   This section does not affect the continuation of proceedings for a recovery order which have been properly started or the making or continuing effect of an interim receiving order or interim administration order which has been properly applied for.

Definitions   For "enforcement authority", see s 316(1); for "interim administration order", see s 256(2); for "interim receiving order", see s 246(2); for "property", see s 316(2), (4)–(7); for "recoverable property", see s 316(1); for "recovery order", see s 316(1); for "value", see s 316(1).
References   See para 6.84.

---

288 Limitation

(1)   After section 27 of the Limitation Act 1980 (c 58) there is inserted—

"27A Actions for recovery of property obtained through unlawful conduct etc

(1)   None of the time limits given in the preceding provisions of this Act applies to any proceedings under Chapter 2 of Part 5 of the Proceeds of Crime Act 2002 (civil recovery of proceeds of unlawful conduct).

(2)   Proceedings under that Chapter for a recovery order in respect of any recoverable property shall not be brought after the expiration of the period of twelve years from the date on which the Director's cause of action accrued.

(3)   Proceedings under that Chapter are brought when—
    (a) a claim form is issued, or
    (b) an application is made for an interim receiving order,
whichever is the earlier.

(4)   The Director's cause of action accrues in respect of any recoverable property—
    (a) in the case of proceedings for a recovery order in respect of property obtained through unlawful conduct, when the property is so obtained,
    (b) in the case of proceedings for a recovery order in respect of any other recoverable property, when the property obtained through unlawful conduct which it represents is so obtained.

(5)   If—
    (a) a person would (but for the preceding provisions of this Act) have a cause of action in respect of the conversion of a chattel, and
    (b) proceedings are started under that Chapter for a recovery order in respect of the chattel,
section 3(2) of this Act does not prevent his asserting on an application under section 281 of that Act that the property belongs to him, or the court making a declaration in his favour under that section.

(6)   If the court makes such a declaration, his title to the chattel is to be treated as not having been extinguished by section 3(2) of this Act.

(7)   Expressions used in this section and Part 5 of that Act have the same meaning in this section as in that Part."

(2)   After section 19A of the Prescription and Limitation (Scotland) Act 1973 (c 52) there is inserted—

"19B Actions for recovery of property obtained through unlawful conduct etc

(1)   None of the time limits given in the preceding provisions of this Act applies to any proceedings under Chapter 2 of Part 5 of the Proceeds of Crime Act 2002 (civil recovery of proceeds of unlawful conduct).

(2)   Proceedings under that Chapter for a recovery order in respect of any recoverable property shall not be commenced after the expiration of the period of twelve years from the date on which the Scottish Ministers' right of action accrued.

(3)   Proceedings under that Chapter are commenced when—
(a) the proceedings are served, or
(b) an application is made for an interim administration order,
whichever is the earlier.

(4)   The Scottish Ministers' right of action accrues in respect of any recoverable property—
(a) in the case of proceedings for a recovery order in respect of property obtained through unlawful conduct, when the property is so obtained,
(b) in the case of proceedings for a recovery order in respect of any other recoverable property, when the property obtained through unlawful conduct which it represents is so obtained.

(5)   Expressions used in this section and Part 5 of that Act have the same meaning in this section as in that Part."

(3)   After Article 72 of the Limitation (Northern Ireland) Order 1989 (SI 1989/1339 (NI 11)) there is inserted—

"72A Actions for recovery of property obtained through unlawful conduct etc

(1)   None of the time limits fixed by Parts II and III applies to any proceedings under Chapter 2 of Part 5 of the Proceeds of Crime Act 2002 (civil recovery of proceeds of unlawful conduct).

(2)   Proceedings under that Chapter for a recovery order in respect of any recoverable property shall not be brought after the expiration of the period of twelve years from the date on which the Director's cause of action accrued.

(3)   Proceedings under that Chapter are brought when—
(a) a claim form is issued, or
(b) an application is made for an interim receiving order,
whichever is the earlier.

(4)   The Director's cause of action accrues in respect of any recoverable property—
(a) in the case of proceedings for a recovery order in respect of property obtained through unlawful conduct, when the property is so obtained,
(b) in the case of proceedings for a recovery order in respect of any other recoverable property, when the property obtained through unlawful conduct which it represents is so obtained.

(5)   If—
(a) a person would (but for a time limit fixed by this Order) have a cause of action in respect of the conversion of a chattel, and
(b) proceedings are started under that Chapter for a recovery order in respect of the chattel,
Article 17(2) does not prevent his asserting on an application under section 281 of that Act that the property belongs to him, or the court making a declaration in his favour under that section.

(6)   If the court makes such a declaration, his title to the chattel is to be treated as not having been extinguished by Article 17(2).

(7)   Expressions used in this Article and Part 5 of that Act have the same meaning in this Article as in that Part."

Definitions   In the Limitation Act 1980: for "the Director", see s 1(2) (by virtue of Limitation Act 1980, s 27A(7), as inserted by sub-s (1) above); for "interim receiving order", see s 246(2) (by virtue of Limitation Act 1980, s 27A(7), as inserted by sub-s (1) above); for "property", see s 316(2), (4)–(7) (by virtue of Limitation Act 1980, s 27A(7), as inserted by sub-s (1) above); for "property obtained through unlawful conduct", see s 242 (by virtue of Limitation Act 1980, s 27A(7), as inserted by sub-s (1) above); for "recoverable property", see s 316(1) (by virtue of Limitation Act 1980, s 27A(7), as inserted by sub-s (1) above); for "recovery order", see s 316(1) (by virtue of Limitation Act 1980, s 27A(7), as inserted by sub-s (1) above); for "unlawful conduct", see s 241 (by virtue of Limitation Act 1980, s 27A(7), as inserted by sub-s (1) above).
References   See para 6.85.

CHAPTER 3
RECOVERY OF CASH IN SUMMARY PROCEEDINGS

Searches

289 Searches

(1)   If a customs officer or constable who is lawfully on any premises has reasonable grounds for suspecting that there is on the premises cash—
>   (a)   which is recoverable property or is intended by any person for use in unlawful conduct, and
>   (b)   the amount of which is not less than the minimum amount,

he may search for the cash there.

(2)   If a customs officer or constable has reasonable grounds for suspecting that a person (the suspect) is carrying cash—
>   (a)   which is recoverable property or is intended by any person for use in unlawful conduct, and
>   (b)   the amount of which is not less than the minimum amount,

he may exercise the following powers.

(3)   The officer or constable may, so far as he thinks it necessary or expedient, require the suspect—
>   (a)   to permit a search of any article he has with him,
>   (b)   to permit a search of his person.

(4)   An officer or constable exercising powers by virtue of subsection (3)(b) may detain the suspect for so long as is necessary for their exercise.

(5)   The powers conferred by this section—
>   (a)   are exercisable only so far as reasonably required for the purpose of finding cash,
>   (b)   are exercisable by a customs officer only if he has reasonable grounds for suspecting that the unlawful conduct in question relates to an assigned matter (within the meaning of the Customs and Excise Management Act 1979 (c 2)).

(6)   Cash means—
>   (a)   notes and coins in any currency,
>   (b)   postal orders,
>   (c)   cheques of any kind, including travellers' cheques,

>   (d)   bankers' drafts,
>   (e)   bearer bonds and bearer shares,

found at any place in the United Kingdom.

(7)   Cash also includes any kind of monetary instrument which is found at any place in the United Kingdom, if the instrument is specified by the Secretary of State by an order made after consultation with the Scottish Ministers.

(8)   This section does not require a person to submit to an intimate search or strip search (within the meaning of section 164 of the Customs and Excise Management Act 1979 (c 2)).

Definitions   For "constable", see s 316(1); for "customs officer", see s 454; for "the minimum amount", see s 303; for "premises", see s 316(1); for "recoverable property", see s 316(1); for "unlawful conduct", see s 241.
References   See paras 6.89–6.92.

---

290 Prior approval

(1)   The powers conferred by section 289 may be exercised only with the appropriate approval unless, in the circumstances, it is not practicable to obtain that approval before exercising the power.

(2)   The appropriate approval means the approval of a judicial officer or (if that is not practicable in any case) the approval of a senior officer.

(3)   A judicial officer means—
>   (a)   in relation to England and Wales and Northern Ireland, a justice of the peace,
>   (b)   in relation to Scotland, the sheriff.

(4)   A senior officer means—
>   (a)   in relation to the exercise of the power by a customs officer, a customs officer of a rank designated by the Commissioners of Customs and Excise as equivalent to that of a senior police officer,
>   (b)   in relation to the exercise of the power by a constable, a senior police officer.

(5)   A senior police officer means a police officer of at least the rank of inspector.

(6)   If the powers are exercised without the approval of a judicial officer in a case where—
>   (a)   no cash is seized by virtue of section 294, or
>   (b)   any cash so seized is not detained for more than 48 hours,

the customs officer or constable who exercised the powers must give a written report to the appointed person.

(7)   The report must give particulars of the circumstances which led him to believe that—
>   (a)   the powers were exercisable, and
>   (b)   it was not practicable to obtain the approval of a judicial officer.

(8)   In this section and section 291, the appointed person means—
>   (a)   in relation to England and Wales and Northern Ireland, a person appointed by the Secretary of State,
>   (b)   in relation to Scotland, a person appointed by the Scottish Ministers.

(9)   The appointed person must not be a person employed under or for the purposes of a government department or of the Scottish Administration; and the terms and conditions of his appointment, including any remuneration or expenses to be paid to him, are to be determined by the person appointing him.

Definitions   For "cash", see ss 289(6), (7), 316(1); for "constable", see s 316(1); for "customs officer", see s 454.
References   See paras 6.89–6.92.

291 Report on exercise of powers

(1)   As soon as possible after the end of each financial year, the appointed person must prepare a report for that year.
"Financial year" means—
- (a)   the period beginning with the day on which this section comes into force and ending with the next 31 March (which is the first financial year), and
- (b)   each subsequent period of twelve months beginning with 1 April.

(2)   The report must give his opinion as to the circumstances and manner in which the powers conferred by section 289 are being exercised in cases where the customs officer or constable who exercised them is required to give a report under section 290(6).

(3)   In the report, he may make any recommendations he considers appropriate.

(4)   He must send a copy of his report to the Secretary of State or, as the case may be, the Scottish Ministers, who must arrange for it to be published.

(5)   The Secretary of State must lay a copy of any report he receives under this section before Parliament; and the Scottish Ministers must lay a copy of any report they receive under this section before the Scottish Parliament.

Definitions   For "the appointed person", see s 290(8); for "constable", see s 316(1); for "customs officer", see s 454.
References   See paras 6.89–6.92.

292 Code of practice

(1)   The Secretary of State must make a code of practice in connection with the exercise by customs officers and (in relation to England and Wales and Northern Ireland) constables of the powers conferred by virtue of section 289.

(2)   Where he proposes to issue a code of practice he must—
- (a)   publish a draft,
- (b)   consider any representations made to him about the draft by the Scottish Ministers or any other person,
- (c)   if he thinks it appropriate, modify the draft in the light of any such representations.

(3)   He must lay a draft of the code before Parliament.

(4)   When he has laid a draft of the code before Parliament he may bring it into operation by order.

(5)   He may revise the whole or any part of the code issued by him and issue the code as revised; and subsections (2) to (4) apply to such a revised code as they apply to the original code.

(6)   A failure by a customs officer or constable to comply with a provision of the code does not of itself make him liable to criminal or civil proceedings.

(7)   The code is admissible in evidence in criminal or civil proceedings and is to be taken into account by a court or tribunal in any case in which it appears to the court or tribunal to be relevant.

Definitions   For "constable", see s 316(1); for "customs officer", see s 454.
References   See para 6.93.

293 Code of practice (Scotland)

(1)   The Scottish Ministers must make a code of practice in connection with the exercise by constables in relation to Scotland of the powers conferred by virtue of section 289.

(2)   Where they propose to issue a code of practice they must—
  (a)   publish a draft,
  (b)   consider any representations made to them about the draft,
  (c)   if they think it appropriate, modify the draft in the light of any such representations.

(3)   They must lay a draft of the code before the Scottish Parliament.

(4)   When they have laid a draft of the code before the Scottish Parliament they may bring it into operation by order.

(5)   They may revise the whole or any part of the code issued by them and issue the code as revised; and subsections (2) to (4) apply to such a revised code as they apply to the original code.

(6)   A failure by a constable to comply with a provision of the code does not of itself make him liable to criminal or civil proceedings.

(7)   The code is admissible in evidence in criminal or civil proceedings and is to be taken into account by a court or tribunal in any case in which it appears to the court or tribunal to be relevant.

References   See para 6.93.

Seizure and detention

294 Seizure of cash

(1)   A customs officer or constable may seize any cash if he has reasonable grounds for suspecting that it is—
  (a)   recoverable property, or
  (b)   intended by any person for use in unlawful conduct.

(2)   A customs officer or constable may also seize cash part of which he has reasonable grounds for suspecting to be—
  (a)   recoverable property, or

(b) intended by any person for use in unlawful conduct,

if it is not reasonably practicable to seize only that part.

(3) This section does not authorise the seizure of an amount of cash if it or, as the case may be, the part to which his suspicion relates, is less than the minimum amount.

Definitions   For "cash", see ss 289(6), (7), 316(1); for "constable", see s 316(1); for "customs officer", see s 454; for "the minimum amount", see s 303; for "recoverable property", see s 316(1); for "unlawful conduct", see s 241.
References   See paras 6.94–6.96.

295 Detention of seized cash

(1) While the customs officer or constable continues to have reasonable grounds for his suspicion, cash seized under section 294 may be detained initially for a period of 48 hours.

(2) The period for which the cash or any part of it may be detained may be extended by an order made by a magistrates' court or (in Scotland) the sheriff; but the order may not authorise the detention of any of the cash—
- (a) beyond the end of the period of three months beginning with the date of the order,
- (b) in the case of any further order under this section, beyond the end of the period of two years beginning with the date of the first order.

(3) A justice of the peace may also exercise the power of a magistrates' court to make the first order under subsection (2) extending the period.

(4) An application for an order under subsection (2)—
- (a) in relation to England and Wales and Northern Ireland, may be made by the Commissioners of Customs and Excise or a constable,
- (b) in relation to Scotland, may be made by the Scottish Ministers in connection with their functions under section 298 or by a procurator fiscal,

and the court, sheriff or justice may make the order if satisfied, in relation to any cash to be further detained, that either of the following conditions is met.

(5) The first condition is that there are reasonable grounds for suspecting that the cash is recoverable property and that either—
- (a) its continued detention is justified while its derivation is further investigated or consideration is given to bringing (in the United Kingdom or elsewhere) proceedings against any person for an offence with which the cash is connected, or
- (b) proceedings against any person for an offence with which the cash is connected have been started and have not been concluded.

(6) The second condition is that there are reasonable grounds for suspecting that the cash is intended to be used in unlawful conduct and that either—
- (a) its continued detention is justified while its intended use is further investigated or consideration is given to bringing (in the United Kingdom or elsewhere) proceedings against any person for an offence with which the cash is connected, or
- (b) proceedings against any person for an offence with which the cash is connected have been started and have not been concluded.

(7)   An application for an order under subsection (2) may also be made in respect of any cash seized under section 294(2), and the court, sheriff or justice may make the order if satisfied that—

(a)   the condition in subsection (5) or (6) is met in respect of part of the cash, and

(b)   it is not reasonably practicable to detain only that part.

(8)   An order under subsection (2) must provide for notice to be given to persons affected by it.

Definitions   For "cash", see ss 289(6), (7), 316(1); for "constable", see s 316(1); for "customs officer", see s 454; for "proceedings concluded", see s 316(2), (9); for "recoverable property", see s 316(1); for "unlawful conduct", see s 241.
References   See paras 6.97–6.100.

296 Interest

(1)   If cash is detained under section 295 for more than 48 hours, it is at the first opportunity to be paid into an interest-bearing account and held there; and the interest accruing on it is to be added to it on its forfeiture or release.

(2)   In the case of cash detained under section 295 which was seized under section 294(2), the customs officer or constable must, on paying it into the account, release the part of the cash to which the suspicion does not relate.

(3)   Subsection (1) does not apply if the cash or, as the case may be, the part to which the suspicion relates is required as evidence of an offence or evidence in proceedings under this Chapter.

Definitions   For "cash", see ss 289(6), (7), 316(1); for "constable", see s 316(1); for "customs officer", see s 454.
References   See para 6.101.

297 Release of detained cash

(1)   This section applies while any cash is detained under section 295.

(2)   A magistrates' court or (in Scotland) the sheriff may direct the release of the whole or any part of the cash if the following condition is met.

(3)   The condition is that the court or sheriff is satisfied, on an application by the person from whom the cash was seized, that the conditions in section 295 for the detention of the cash are no longer met in relation to the cash to be released.

(4)   A customs officer, constable or (in Scotland) procurator fiscal may, after notifying the magistrates' court, sheriff or justice under whose order cash is being detained, release the whole or any part of it if satisfied that the detention of the cash to be released is no longer justified.

Definitions   For "cash", see ss 289(6), (7), 316(1); for "constable", see s 316(1); for "customs officer", see s 454.
References   See paras 6.102–6.104.

Forfeiture

298 Forfeiture

(1)   While cash is detained under section 295, an application for the forfeiture of the whole or any part of it may be made—

    (a)   to a magistrates' court by the Commissioners of Customs and Excise or a constable,

    (b)   (in Scotland) to the sheriff by the Scottish Ministers.

(2)   The court or sheriff may order the forfeiture of the cash or any part of it if satisfied that the cash or part—

    (a)   is recoverable property, or

    (b)   is intended by any person for use in unlawful conduct.

(3)   But in the case of recoverable property which belongs to joint tenants, one of whom is an excepted joint owner, the order may not apply to so much of it as the court thinks is attributable to the excepted joint owner's share.

(4)   Where an application for the forfeiture of any cash is made under this section, the cash is to be detained (and may not be released under any power conferred by this Chapter) until any proceedings in pursuance of the application (including any proceedings on appeal) are concluded.

Definitions   For "cash", see ss 289(6), (7), 316(1); for "constable", see s 316(1); for "excepted joint owner", see s 270(4); for "proceedings concluded", see s 316(2), (9); for "recoverable property", see s 316(1); for "share" in relation to an excepted joint owner, see s 270(4); for "unlawful conduct", see s 241.
References   See para 6.105.

299 Appeal against forfeiture

(1)   Any party to proceedings in which an order is made under section 298 for the forfeiture of cash who is aggrieved by the order may appeal—

    (a)   in relation to England and Wales, to the Crown Court,

    (b)   in relation to Scotland, to the Court of Session,

    (c)   in relation to Northern Ireland, to a county court.

(2)   An appeal under subsection (1) must be made within the period of 30 days beginning with the date on which the order is made.

(3)   The appeal is to be by way of a rehearing.

(4)   The court hearing the appeal may make any order it thinks appropriate.

(5)   If the court upholds the appeal, it may order the release of the cash.

Definitions   For "cash", see ss 289(6), (7), 316(1).
References   See para 6.106.

300 Application of forfeited cash

(1)   Cash forfeited under this Chapter, and any accrued interest on it—

    (a)   if forfeited by a magistrates' court in England and Wales or Northern Ireland, is to be paid into the Consolidated Fund,

    (b)   if forfeited by the sheriff, is to be paid into the Scottish Consolidated Fund.

(2)   But it is not to be paid in—
     (a)   before the end of the period within which an appeal under section 299 may be made, or
     (b)   if a person appeals under that section, before the appeal is determined or otherwise disposed of.

Definitions   For "cash", see ss 289(6), (7), 316(1).

Supplementary

301 Victims and other owners

(1)   A person who claims that any cash detained under this Chapter, or any part of it, belongs to him may apply to a magistrates' court or (in Scotland) the sheriff for the cash or part to be released to him.

(2)   The application may be made in the course of proceedings under section 295 or 298 or at any other time.

(3)   If it appears to the court or sheriff concerned that—
     (a)   the applicant was deprived of the cash to which the application relates, or of property which it represents, by unlawful conduct,
     (b)   the property he was deprived of was not, immediately before he was deprived of it, recoverable property, and
     (c)   that cash belongs to him,

the court or sheriff may order the cash to which the application relates to be released to the applicant.

(4)   If—
     (a)   the applicant is not the person from whom the cash to which the application relates was seized,
     (b)   it appears to the court or sheriff that that cash belongs to the applicant,
     (c)   the court or sheriff is satisfied that the conditions in section 295 for the detention of that cash are no longer met or, if an application has been made under section 298, the court or sheriff decides not to make an order under that section in relation to that cash, and
     (d)   no objection to the making of an order under this subsection has been made by the person from whom that cash was seized,

the court or sheriff may order the cash to which the application relates to be released to the applicant or to the person from whom it was seized.

Definitions   For "cash", see ss 289(6), (7), 316(1); for "property", see s 316(2), (4)–(7); for "recoverable property", see s 316(1); for "unlawful conduct", see s 241.
References   See para 6.108.

---

302 Compensation

(1)   If no forfeiture order is made in respect of any cash detained under this Chapter, the person to whom the cash belongs or from whom it was seized may make an application to the magistrates' court or (in Scotland) the sheriff for compensation.

(2)   If, for any period beginning with the first opportunity to place the cash in an interest-bearing account after the initial detention of the cash for 48 hours, the cash was not held in an interest-bearing account while detained, the court or sheriff may order an amount of compensation to be paid to the applicant.

(3)   The amount of compensation to be paid under subsection (2) is the amount the court or sheriff thinks would have been earned in interest in the period in question if the cash had been held in an interest-bearing account.

(4)   If the court or sheriff is satisfied that, taking account of any interest to be paid under section 296 or any amount to be paid under subsection (2), the applicant has suffered loss as a result of the detention of the cash and that the circumstances are exceptional, the court or sheriff may order compensation (or additional compensation) to be paid to him.

(5)   The amount of compensation to be paid under subsection (4) is the amount the court or sheriff thinks reasonable, having regard to the loss suffered and any other relevant circumstances.

(6)   If the cash was seized by a customs officer, the compensation is to be paid by the Commissioners of Customs and Excise.

(7)   If the cash was seized by a constable, the compensation is to be paid as follows—

(a)   in the case of a constable of a police force in England and Wales, it is to be paid out of the police fund from which the expenses of the police force are met,

(b)   in the case of a constable of a police force in Scotland, it is to be paid by the police authority or joint police board for the police area for which that force is maintained,

(c)   in the case of a police officer within the meaning of the Police (Northern Ireland) Act 2000 (c 32), it is to be paid out of money provided by the Chief Constable.

(8)   If a forfeiture order is made in respect only of a part of any cash detained under this Chapter, this section has effect in relation to the other part.

Definitions   For "cash", see ss 289(6), (7), 316(1); for "constable", see s 316(1); for "customs officer", see s 454.
References   See para 6.109.

303 "The minimum amount"

(1)   In this Chapter, the minimum amount is the amount in sterling specified in an order made by the Secretary of State after consultation with the Scottish Ministers.

(2)   For that purpose the amount of any cash held in a currency other than sterling must be taken to be its sterling equivalent, calculated in accordance with the prevailing rate of exchange.

Definitions   For "cash", see ss 289(6), (7), 316(1).
References   See para 6.110.

CHAPTER 4
GENERAL

Recoverable property

304 Property obtained through unlawful conduct

(1)   Property obtained through unlawful conduct is recoverable property.

(2)   But if property obtained through unlawful conduct has been disposed of (since it was so obtained), it is recoverable property only if it is held by a person into whose hands it may be followed.

(3)   Recoverable property obtained through unlawful conduct may be followed into the hands of a person obtaining it on a disposal by—
      (a)   the person who through the conduct obtained the property, or
      (b)   a person into whose hands it may (by virtue of this subsection) be followed.

Definitions   For "disposal", see s 314(1)–(3); for "disposed", see s 314(1)–(3); for "property", see s 316(2), (4)–(7); for "property obtained through unlawful conduct", see s 242; for "unlawful conduct", see s 241.
References   See paras 6.111, 6.112.

305 Tracing property, etc

(1)   Where property obtained through unlawful conduct ("the original property") is or has been recoverable, property which represents the original property is also recoverable property.

(2)   If a person enters into a transaction by which—
      (a)   he disposes of recoverable property, whether the original property or property which (by virtue of this Chapter) represents the original property, and
      (b)   he obtains other property in place of it,
the other property represents the original property.

(3)   If a person disposes of recoverable property which represents the original property, the property may be followed into the hands of the person who obtains it (and it continues to represent the original property).

Definitions   For "disposes", see s 314(1)–(3); for "property", see s 316(2), (4)–(7); for "property obtained through unlawful conduct", see s 242; for "unlawful conduct", see s 241.
References   See paras 6.111, 6.112.

306 Mixing property

(1)   Subsection (2) applies if a person's recoverable property is mixed with other property (whether his property or another's).

(2)   The portion of the mixed property which is attributable to the recoverable property represents the property obtained through unlawful conduct.

(3)   Recoverable property is mixed with other property if (for example) it is used—
      (a)   to increase funds held in a bank account,

   (b)   in part payment for the acquisition of an asset,
   (c)   for the restoration or improvement of land,
   (d)   by a person holding a leasehold interest in the property to acquire the freehold.

Definitions   For "property", see s 316(2), (4)–(7); for "property obtained through unlawful conduct", see s 242; for "unlawful conduct", see s 241.
References   See paras 6.111, 6.112.

307 Recoverable property: accruing profits

   (1)   This section applies where a person who has recoverable property obtains further property consisting of profits accruing in respect of the recoverable property.

   (2)   The further property is to be treated as representing the property obtained through unlawful conduct.

Definitions   For "property", see s 316(2), (4)–(7); for "property obtained through unlawful conduct", see s 242; for "unlawful conduct", see s 241.
References   See paras 6.111, 6.112.

308 General exceptions

   (1)   If—
   (a)   a person disposes of recoverable property, and
   (b)   the person who obtains it on the disposal does so in good faith, for value and without notice that it was recoverable property,

the property may not be followed into that person's hands and, accordingly, it ceases to be recoverable.

   (2)   If recoverable property is vested, forfeited or otherwise disposed of in pursuance of powers conferred by virtue of this Part, it ceases to be recoverable.

   (3)   If—
   (a)   in pursuance of a judgment in civil proceedings (whether in the United Kingdom or elsewhere), the defendant makes a payment to the claimant or the claimant otherwise obtains property from the defendant,
   (b)   the claimant's claim is based on the defendant's unlawful conduct, and
   (c)   apart from this subsection, the sum received, or the property obtained, by the claimant would be recoverable property,

the property ceases to be recoverable.

   In relation to Scotland, "claimant" and "defendant" are to be read as "pursuer" and "defender".

   (4)   If—
   (a)   a payment is made to a person in pursuance of a compensation order under Article 14 of the Criminal Justice (Northern Ireland) Order 1994 (SI 1994/2795 (NI 15)), section 249 of the Criminal Procedure (Scotland) Act 1995 (c 46) or section 130 of the Powers of Criminal Courts (Sentencing) Act 2000 (c 6), and
   (b)   apart from this subsection, the sum received would be recoverable property,

the property ceases to be recoverable.

(5)   If—

    (a)   a payment is made to a person in pursuance of a restitution order under section 27 of the Theft Act (Northern Ireland) 1969 (c 16 (NI)) or section 148(2) of the Powers of Criminal Courts (Sentencing) Act 2000 or a person otherwise obtains any property in pursuance of such an order, and

    (b)   apart from this subsection, the sum received, or the property obtained, would be recoverable property,

the property ceases to be recoverable.

(6)   If—

    (a)   in pursuance of an order made by the court under section 382(3) or 383(5) of the Financial Services and Markets Act 2000 (c 8) (restitution orders), an amount is paid to or distributed among any persons in accordance with the court's directions, and

    (b)   apart from this subsection, the sum received by them would be recoverable property,

the property ceases to be recoverable.

(7)   If—

    (a)   in pursuance of a requirement of the Financial Services Authority under section 384(5) of the Financial Services and Markets Act 2000 (power of authority to require restitution), an amount is paid to or distributed among any persons, and

    (b)   apart from this subsection, the sum received by them would be recoverable property,

the property ceases to be recoverable.

(8)   Property is not recoverable while a restraint order applies to it, that is—

    (a)   an order under section 41, 120 or 190, or

    (b)   an order under any corresponding provision of an enactment mentioned in section 8(7)(a) to (g).

(9)   Property is not recoverable if it has been taken into account in deciding the amount of a person's benefit from criminal conduct for the purpose of making a confiscation order, that is—

    (a)   an order under section 6, 92 or 156, or

    (b)   an order under a corresponding provision of an enactment mentioned in section 8(7)(a) to (g),

and, in relation to an order mentioned in paragraph (b), the reference to the amount of a person's benefit from criminal conduct is to be read as a reference to the corresponding amount under the enactment in question.

(10) Where—

    (a)   a person enters into a transaction to which section 305(2) applies, and

    (b)   the disposal is one to which subsection (1) or (2) applies,

this section does not affect the recoverability (by virtue of section 305(2)) of any property obtained on the transaction in place of the property disposed of.

Definitions   For "disposal", see s 314(1)–(3); for "disposes", see s 314(1)–(3); for "enactment", see s 455; for "obtained for value", see s 314(4); for "property", see s 316(2), (4)–(7); for "unlawful conduct", see s 241.
References   See paras 6.113–6.115.

---

309 Other exemptions

(1)   An order may provide that property is not recoverable or (as the case may be) associated property if—

   (a)   it is prescribed property, or

   (b)   it is disposed of in pursuance of a prescribed enactment or an enactment of a prescribed description.

(2)   An order may provide that if property is disposed of in pursuance of a prescribed enactment or an enactment of a prescribed description, it is to be treated for the purposes of section 278 as if it had been disposed of in pursuance of a recovery order.

(3)   An order under this section may be made so as to apply to property, or a disposal of property, only in prescribed circumstances; and the circumstances may relate to the property or disposal itself or to a person who holds or has held the property or to any other matter.

(4)   In this section, an order means an order made by the Secretary of State after consultation with the Scottish Ministers, and prescribed means prescribed by the order.

Definitions   For "associated property", see s 245; for "disposal", see s 314(1)–(3); for "disposes", see s 314(1)–(3); for "enactment", see s 455; for "property", see s 316(2), (4)–(7); for "recovery order", see s 316(1).

---

310 Granting interests

(1)   If a person grants an interest in his recoverable property, the question whether the interest is also recoverable is to be determined in the same manner as it is on any other disposal of recoverable property.

(2)   Accordingly, on his granting an interest in the property ("the property in question")—

   (a)   where the property in question is property obtained through unlawful conduct, the interest is also to be treated as obtained through that conduct,

   (b)   where the property in question represents in his hands property obtained through unlawful conduct, the interest is also to be treated as representing in his hands the property so obtained.

Definitions   For "disposal", see s 314(1)–(3); for "interest" in relation to land, see s 316(1); for "interest" in relation to property other than land", see s 316(1); for "property", see s 316(2), (4)–(7); for "property obtained through unlawful conduct", see s 242; for "unlawful conduct", see s 241.
References   See para 6.116.

Insolvency

311 Insolvency

(1)   Proceedings for a recovery order may not be taken or continued in respect of property to which subsection (3) applies unless the appropriate court gives leave and the proceedings are taken or (as the case may be) continued in accordance with any terms imposed by that court.

(2)   An application for an order for the further detention of any cash to which subsection (3) applies may not be made under section 295 unless the appropriate court gives leave.

(3)   This subsection applies to recoverable property, or property associated with it, if—

    (a)   it is an asset of a company being wound up in pursuance of a resolution for voluntary winding up,

    (b)   it is an asset of a company and a voluntary arrangement under Part 1 of the 1986 Act, or Part 2 of the 1989 Order, has effect in relation to the company,

    (c)   an order under section 2 of the 1985 Act, section 286 of the 1986 Act or Article 259 of the 1989 Order (appointment of interim trustee or interim receiver) has effect in relation to the property,

    (d)   it is an asset comprised in the estate of an individual who has been adjudged bankrupt or, in relation to Scotland, of a person whose estate has been sequestrated,

    (e)   it is an asset of an individual and a voluntary arrangement under Part 8 of the 1986 Act, or Part 8 of the 1989 Order, has effect in relation to him, or

    (f)   in relation to Scotland, it is property comprised in the estate of a person who has granted a trust deed within the meaning of the 1985 Act.

(4)   An application under this section, or under any provision of the 1986 Act or the 1989 Order, for leave to take proceedings for a recovery order may be made without notice to any person.

(5)   Subsection (4) does not affect any requirement for notice of an application to be given to any person acting as an insolvency practitioner or to the official receiver (whether or not acting as an insolvency practitioner).

(6)   References to the provisions of the 1986 Act in sections 420 and 421 of that Act, or to the provisions of the 1989 Order in Articles 364 or 365 of that Order, (insolvent partnerships and estates of deceased persons) include subsections (1) to (3) above.

(7)   In this section—

    (a)   the 1985 Act means the Bankruptcy (Scotland) Act 1985 (c 66),

    (b)   the 1986 Act means the Insolvency Act 1986 (c 45),

    (c)   the 1989 Order means the Insolvency (Northern Ireland) Order 1989 (SI 1989/2405 (NI 19)),

and in subsection (8) "the applicable enactment" means whichever enactment mentioned in paragraphs (a) to (c) is relevant to the resolution, arrangement, order or trust deed mentioned in subsection (3).

(8)   In this section—

    (a)   an asset means any property within the meaning of the applicable enactment or, where the 1985 Act is the applicable enactment, any property comprised in an estate to which the 1985 Act applies,

    (b)   the appropriate court means the court which, in relation to the resolution, arrangement, order or trust deed mentioned in subsection (3), is the court for the purposes of the applicable enactment or, in relation to Northern Ireland, the High Court,

(c) acting as an insolvency practitioner has the same meaning as in section 433,

(d) other expressions used in this section and in the applicable enactment have the same meaning as in that enactment.

Definitions For "cash", see ss 289(6), (7), 316(1); for "enactment", see s 455; for "property", see s 316(2), (4)–(7); for "property associated with recoverable property", see s 245(2), (3); for "recoverable property", see s 316(1); for "recovery order", see s 316(1).
References See paras 6.117, 6.118.

Delegation of enforcement functions

312 Performance of functions of Scottish Ministers by constables in Scotland

(1) In Scotland, a constable engaged in temporary service with the Scottish Ministers in connection with their functions under this Part may perform functions, other than those specified in subsection (2), on behalf of the Scottish Ministers.

(2) The specified functions are the functions conferred on the Scottish Ministers by—

(a) sections 244(1) and (2) and 256(1) and (7) (proceedings in the Court of Session),

(b) section 267(2) (trustee for civil recovery),

(c) sections 271(3) and (4) and 272(5) (agreements about associated and joint property),

(d) section 275(3) (pension schemes),

(e) section 282(1) (exemptions),

(f) section 283(5) and (8) (compensation),

(g) section 287(2) (financial threshold),

(h) section 293(1) (code of practice),

(i) section 298(1) (forfeiture),

(j) section 303(1) (minimum amount).

References See para 6.119.

---

313 Restriction on performance of Director's functions by police

(1) In spite of section 1(6), nothing which the Director is authorised or required to do for the purposes of this Part may be done by—

(a) a member of a police force,

(b) a member of the Police Service of Northern Ireland,

(c) a person appointed as a police member of the National Criminal Intelligence Service under section 9(1)(b) of the Police Act 1997 (c 50),

(d) a person appointed as a police member of the National Crime Squad under section 55(1)(b) of that Act.

(2) In this section—

(a) "member of a police force" has the same meaning as in the Police Act 1996 (c 16) and includes a person who would be a member of a police force but for section 97(3) of that Act (police officers engaged on service outside their force),

(b)   "member of the Police Service of Northern Ireland" includes a person who would be a member of the Police Service of Northern Ireland but for section 27(3) of the Police (Northern Ireland) Act 1998 (c 32) (members of that service engaged on other police service).

Definitions   For "the Director", see s 1(2).
References   See para 6.119.

Interpretation

314 Obtaining and disposing of property

(1)   References to a person disposing of his property include a reference—
  (a)   to his disposing of a part of it, or
  (b)   to his granting an interest in it,
(or to both); and references to the property disposed of are to any property obtained on the disposal.

(2)   A person who makes a payment to another is to be treated as making a disposal of his property to the other, whatever form the payment takes.

(3)   Where a person's property passes to another under a will or intestacy or by operation of law, it is to be treated as disposed of by him to the other.

(4)   A person is only to be treated as having obtained his property for value in a case where he gave unexecuted consideration if the consideration has become executed consideration.

Definitions   For "interest" in relation to land, see s 316(1); for "interest" in relation to property other than land", see s 316(1); for "property", see s 316(2), (4)–(7).
References   See para 6.120.

---

315 Northern Ireland courts

In relation to the practice and procedure of courts in Northern Ireland, expressions used in this Part are to be read in accordance with rules of court.

References   See para 6.121.

---

316 General interpretation

(1)   In this Part—
  "associated property" has the meaning given by section 245,
  "cash" has the meaning given by section 289(6) or (7),
  "constable", in relation to Northern Ireland, means a police officer within the meaning of the Police (Northern Ireland) Act 2000 (c 32),
  "country" includes territory,
  "the court" (except in sections 253(2) and (3) and 262(2) and (3) and Chapter 3) means the High Court or (in relation to proceedings in Scotland) the Court of Session,
  "dealing" with property includes disposing of it, taking possession of it or removing it from the United Kingdom,

"enforcement authority"—

    (a)   in relation to England and Wales and Northern Ireland, means the Director,

    (b)   in relation to Scotland, means the Scottish Ministers,

"excepted joint owner" has the meaning given by section 270(4),

"interest", in relation to land—

    (a)   in the case of land in England and Wales or Northern Ireland, means any legal estate and any equitable interest or power,

    (b)   in the case of land in Scotland, means any estate, interest, servitude or other heritable right in or over land, including a heritable security,

"interest", in relation to property other than land, includes any right (including a right to possession of the property),

"interim administration order" has the meaning given by section 256(2),

"interim receiving order" has the meaning given by section 246(2),

"the minimum amount" (in Chapter 3) has the meaning given by section 303,

"part", in relation to property, includes a portion,

"premises" has the same meaning as in the Police and Criminal Evidence Act 1984 (c 60),

"property obtained through unlawful conduct" has the meaning given by section 242,

"recoverable property" is to be read in accordance with sections 304 to 310,

"recovery order" means an order made under section 266,

"respondent" means—

    (a)   where proceedings are brought by the enforcement authority by virtue of Chapter 2, the person against whom the proceedings are brought,

    (b)   where no such proceedings have been brought but the enforcement authority has applied for an interim receiving order or interim administration order, the person against whom he intends to bring such proceedings,

"share", in relation to an excepted joint owner, has the meaning given by section 270(4),

"unlawful conduct" has the meaning given by section 241,

"value" means market value.

(2)   The following provisions apply for the purposes of this Part.

(3)   For the purpose of deciding whether or not property was recoverable at any time (including times before commencement), it is to be assumed that this Part was in force at that and any other relevant time.

(4)   Property is all property wherever situated and includes—

    (a)   money,

    (b)   all forms of property, real or personal, heritable or moveable,

    (c)   things in action and other intangible or incorporeal property.

(5)   Any reference to a person's property (whether expressed as a reference to the property he holds or otherwise) is to be read as follows.

(6)   In relation to land, it is a reference to any interest which he holds in the land.

(7) In relation to property other than land, it is a reference—
  (a) to the property (if it belongs to him), or
  (b) to any other interest which he holds in the property.

(8) References to the satisfaction of the enforcement authority's right to recover property obtained through unlawful conduct are to be read in accordance with section 279.

(9) Proceedings against any person for an offence are concluded when—
  (a) the person is convicted or acquitted,
  (b) the prosecution is discontinued or, in Scotland, the trial diet is deserted simpliciter, or
  (c) the jury is discharged without a finding.

Definitions For "the Director", see s 1(2); for "disposing", see s 314(1)–(3).
References See para 6.122.

PART 6
REVENUE FUNCTIONS

General functions

317 Director's general Revenue functions

(1) For the purposes of this section the qualifying condition is that the Director has reasonable grounds to suspect that—
  (a) income arising or a gain accruing to a person in respect of a chargeable period is chargeable to income tax or is a chargeable gain (as the case may be) and arises or accrues as a result of the person's or another's criminal conduct (whether wholly or partly and whether directly or indirectly), or
  (b) a company is chargeable to corporation tax on its profits arising in respect of a chargeable period and the profits arise as a result of the company's or another person's criminal conduct (whether wholly or partly and whether directly or indirectly).

(2) If the qualifying condition is satisfied the Director may serve on the Commissioners of Inland Revenue (the Board) a notice which—
  (a) specifies the person or the company (as the case may be) and the period, and
  (b) states that the Director intends to carry out, in relation to the person or the company (as the case may be) and in respect of the period, such of the general Revenue functions as are specified in the notice.

(3) Service of a notice under subsection (2) vests in the Director, in relation to the person or the company (as the case may be) and in respect of the period, such of the general Revenue functions as are specified in the notice; but this is subject to section 318.

(4) The Director—
  (a) may at any time serve on the Board a notice of withdrawal of the notice under subsection (2);
  (b) must serve such a notice of withdrawal on the Board if the qualifying condition ceases to be satisfied.

(5)   A notice under subsection (2) and a notice of withdrawal under subsection (4) may be in respect of one or more periods.

(6)   Service of a notice under subsection (4) divests the Director of the functions concerned in relation to the person or the company (as the case may be) and in respect of the period or periods specified in the notice.

(7)   The vesting of a function in the Director under this section does not divest the Board or an officer of the Board of the function.

(8)   If—
    (a)   apart from this section the Board's authorisation would be required for the exercise of a function, and
    (b)   the function is vested in the Director under this section,

the authorisation is not required in relation to the function as so vested.

(9)   It is immaterial whether a chargeable period or any part of it falls before or after the passing of this Act.

Definitions   For "chargeable gain", see Income and Corporation Taxes Act 1988, s 832(1), title Taxation (by virtue of s 326(12), (13)); for "chargeable period", see Income and Corporation Taxes Act 1988, s 832(1), (by virtue of s 326(12), (13)); for "company", see Income and Corporation Taxes Act 1988, s 832(1), (2), (by virtue of s 326(12), (13)); for "criminal conduct", see s 326(1)–(3), (13); for "the Director", see s 1(2); for "general Revenue functions", see s 323(1), (3)–(5); for "notice", see Income and Corporation Taxes Act 1988, s 832(1), (by virtue of s 326(12), (13)); for "officer of the Board", see s 326(11), (13).
References   See paras 7.5–7.111.

---

318 Revenue functions regarding employment

(1)   Subsection (2) applies if—
    (a)   the Director serves a notice or notices under section 317(2) in relation to a company and in respect of a period or periods, and
    (b)   the company is an employer.

(2)   The general Revenue functions vested in the Director do not include functions relating to any requirement which—
    (a)   is imposed on the company in its capacity as employer, and
    (b)   relates to a year of assessment which does not fall wholly within the period or periods.

(3)   Subsection (4) applies if—
    (a)   the Director serves a notice or notices under section 317(2) in relation to an individual and in respect of a year or years of assessment, and
    (b)   the individual is a self-employed earner.

(4)   The general Revenue functions vested in the Director do not include functions relating to any liability to pay Class 2 contributions in respect of a period which does not fall wholly within the year or years of assessment.

(5)   In this section in its application to Great Britain—
    (a)   "self-employed earner" has the meaning given by section 2(1)(b) of the Social Security Contributions and Benefits Act 1992 (c 4);
    (b)   "Class 2 contributions" must be construed in accordance with section 1(2)(c) of that Act.

(6)   In this section in its application to Northern Ireland—

(a)   "self-employed earner" has the meaning given by section 2(1)(b) of the Social Security Contributions and Benefits (Northern Ireland) Act 1992 (c 7);

(b)   "Class 2 contributions" must be construed in accordance with section 1(2)(c) of that Act.

Definitions   For "company", see Income and Corporation Taxes Act 1988, s 832(1), (2), (by virtue of s 326(12), (13)); for "the Director", see s 1(2); for "general Revenue functions", see s 323(1), (3)–(5); for "notice", see Income and Corporation Taxes Act 1988, s 832(1), (by virtue of s 326(12), (13)); for "year of assessment", see Income and Corporation Taxes Act 1988, s 832(1), (by virtue of s 326(12), (13)).
References   See para 7.12.

319 Source of income

(1)   For the purpose of the exercise by the Director of any function vested in him by virtue of this Part it is immaterial that he cannot identify a source for any income.

(2)   An assessment made by the Director under section 29 of the Taxes Management Act 1970 (c 9) (assessment where loss of tax discovered) in respect of income charged to tax under Case 6 of Schedule D must not be reduced or quashed only because it does not specify (to any extent) the source of the income.

(3)   If the Director serves on the Board a notice of withdrawal under section 317(4), any assessment made by him under section 29 of the Taxes Management Act 1970 is invalid to the extent that it does not specify a source for the income.

(4)   Subsections (2) and (3) apply in respect of years of assessment whenever occurring.

Definitions   For "the Board", see s 317(2); for "the Director", see s 1(2); for "notice", see Income and Corporation Taxes Act 1988, s 832(1), (by virtue of s 326(12), (13)); for "year of assessment", see Income and Corporation Taxes Act 1988, s 832(1), (by virtue of s 326(12), (13)).
References   See para 7.13.

320 Appeals

(1)   An appeal in respect of the exercise by the Director of general Revenue functions shall be to the Special Commissioners.

(2)   The Presiding Special Commissioner may nominate one or more assessors to assist the Special Commissioners in any appeal to be heard by them in respect of the exercise by the Director of any of his Revenue functions.

(3)   An assessor nominated under subsection (2)—

(a)   must have special knowledge and experience of the matter to which the appeal relates, and

(b)   must be selected from a panel of persons appointed for the purposes of this section by the Lord Chancellor after consultation with the Scottish Ministers.

(4)   Regulations made under section 56B of the Taxes Management Act 1970 may include provision as to the manner in which an assessor nominated under subsection (2) is to assist the Special Commissioners.

(5)   The remuneration of an assessor nominated under subsection (2) must be paid by the Lord Chancellor and must be at such rate as he decides.

Definitions   For "the Director", see s 1(2); for "general Revenue functions", see s 323(1), (3)–(5); for "Special Commissioners", see Taxes Management Act 1970, s 4(1), (by virtue of s 326(12), (13).
References   See para 7.14.

Inheritance tax functions

321 Director's functions: transfers of value

(1)   For the purposes of this section the qualifying condition is that the Director has reasonable grounds to suspect that—
  (a) there has been a transfer of value within the meaning of the Inheritance Tax Act 1984 (c 51), and
  (b) the value transferred by it is attributable (in whole or part) to criminal property.

(2)   If the qualifying condition is satisfied the Director may serve on the Board a notice which—
  (a) specifies the transfer of value, and
  (b) states that the Director intends to carry out the Revenue inheritance tax functions in relation to the transfer.

(3)   Service of a notice under subsection (2) vests in the Director the Revenue inheritance tax functions in relation to the transfer.

(4)   The Director—
  (a) may at any time serve on the Board a notice of withdrawal of the notice under subsection (2);
  (b) must serve such a notice of withdrawal on the Board if the qualifying condition ceases to be satisfied.

(5)   Service of a notice under subsection (4) divests the Director of the Revenue inheritance tax functions in relation to the transfer.

(6)   The vesting of a function in the Director under this section does not divest the Board or an officer of the Board of the function.

(7)   It is immaterial whether a transfer of value is suspected to have occurred before or after the passing of this Act.

Definitions   For "the Board", see s 317(2); for "criminal property", see s 326(4), (13); for "the Director", see s 1(2); for "notice", see Income and Corporation Taxes Act 1988, s 832(1), (by virtue of s 326(12), (13)); for "officer of the Board", see s 326(11), (13); for "property", see s 326(9), (13); for "Revenue inheritance tax functions", see s 323(2), (3).
References   See paras 7.15, 716.

322 Director's functions: certain settlements

(1)   For the purposes of this section the qualifying condition is that the Director has reasonable grounds to suspect that—

(a) all or part of the property comprised in a settlement is relevant property for the purposes of Chapter 3 of Part 3 of the Inheritance Tax Act 1984 (settlements without interest in possession), and

(b) the relevant property is (in whole or part) criminal property.

(2) If the qualifying condition is satisfied the Director may serve on the Board a notice which—

(a) specifies the settlement concerned,

(b) states that the Director intends to carry out the Revenue inheritance tax functions in relation to the settlement, and

(c) states the period for which he intends to carry them out.

(3) Service of a notice under subsection (2) vests in the Director the Revenue inheritance tax functions in relation to the settlement for the period.

(4) The Director—

(a) may at any time serve on the Board a notice of withdrawal of the notice under subsection (2);

(b) must serve such a notice of withdrawal on the Board if the qualifying condition ceases to be satisfied.

(5) Service of a notice under subsection (4) divests the Director of the Revenue inheritance tax functions in relation to the settlement for the period.

(6) The vesting of a function in the Director under this section does not divest the Board or an officer of the Board of the function.

(7) It is immaterial whether the settlement is commenced or a charge to tax arises or a period or any part of it falls before or after the passing of this Act.

Definitions   For "the Board", see s 317(2); for "criminal property", see s 326(4), (13); for "the Director", see s 1(2); for "notice", see Income and Corporation Taxes Act 1988, s 832(1), (by virtue of s 326(12), (13)); for "officer of the Board", see s 326(11), (13); for "property", see s 326(9), (13); for "Revenue inheritance tax functions", see s 323(2), (3).
References   See para 7.18.

General

323 Functions

(1) The general Revenue functions are such of the functions vested in the Board or in an officer of the Board as relate to any of the following matters—

(a) income tax;

(b) capital gains tax;

(c) corporation tax;

(d) national insurance contributions;

(e) statutory sick pay;

(f) statutory maternity pay;

(g) statutory paternity pay;

(h) statutory adoption pay;

(i) student loans.

(2) The Revenue inheritance tax functions are such functions vested in the Board or in an officer of the Board as relate to inheritance tax.

(3) But the general Revenue functions and the Revenue inheritance tax functions do not include any of the following functions—

(a)   functions relating to the making of subordinate legislation (within the meaning given by section 21(1) of the Interpretation Act 1978 (c 30));
(b)   the function of the prosecution of offences;
(c)   the function of authorising an officer for the purposes of section 20BA of the Taxes Management Act 1970 (c 9) (orders for delivery of documents);
(d)   the function of giving information under that section;
(e)   the function of approving an officer's application for the purposes of section 20C of the Taxes Management Act 1970 (warrant to enter and search premises);
(f)   the function of applying under that section.

(4)   For the purposes of this section in its application to Great Britain—
(a)   national insurance contributions are contributions payable under Part 1 of the Social Security Contributions and Benefits Act 1992 (c 4);
(b)   "statutory sick pay" must be construed in accordance with section 151(1) of that Act;
(c)   "statutory maternity pay" must be construed in accordance with section 164(1) of that Act;
(d)   "statutory paternity pay" must be construed in accordance with section 171ZA of that Act;
(e)   "statutory adoption pay" must be construed in accordance with section 171ZL of that Act;
(f)   "student loans" must be construed in accordance with the Education (Student Loans) (Repayment) Regulations 2000 (SI 2000/944).

(5)   For the purposes of this section in its application to Northern Ireland—
(a)   national insurance contributions are contributions payable under Part 1 of the Social Security Contributions and Benefits (Northern Ireland) Act 1992 (c 7);
(b)   "statutory sick pay" must be construed in accordance with section 147(1) of that Act;
(c)   "statutory maternity pay" must be construed in accordance with section 160(1) of that Act;
(d)   "statutory paternity pay" must be construed in accordance with any Northern Ireland legislation which corresponds to Part 12ZA of the Social Security Contributions and Benefits Act 1992;
(e)   "statutory adoption pay" must be construed in accordance with any Northern Ireland legislation which corresponds to Part 12ZB of that Act;
(f)   "student loans" must be construed in accordance with the Education (Student Loans) (Repayment) Regulations (Northern Ireland) 2000 (S.R.2000/121).

Definitions   For "the Board", see s 317(2); for "officer of the Board", see s 326(11), (13).
References   See para 7.19.

324 Exercise of Revenue functions

(1)   This section applies in relation to the exercise by the Director of—
(a)   general Revenue functions;
(b)   Revenue inheritance tax functions.

(2)   Paragraph (b) of section 1(6) does not apply.

(3) The Director must apply—
  (a) any interpretation of the law which has been published by the Board;
  (b) any concession which has been published by the Board and which is available generally to any person falling within its terms.

(4) The Director must also take account of any material published by the Board which does not fall within subsection (3).

(5) The Director must provide the Board with such documents and information as they consider appropriate.

(6) "Concession" includes any practice, interpretation or other statement in the nature of a concession.

Definitions For "the Board", see s 317(2); for "the Director", see s 1(2); for "general Revenue functions", see s 323(1), (3)–(5); for "Revenue inheritance tax functions", see s 323(2), (3).
References See para 7.20.

325 Declarations

(1) As soon as practicable after the appointment of a person as the Director he must make a declaration in the form set out in Schedule 8 before a member of the Board.

(2) Every member of the staff of the Agency who is authorised under section 1(6)(a) to carry out any of the functions of the Director under this Part must, as soon as practicable after being so authorised, make a declaration in the form set out in Schedule 8 before a person nominated by the Director for the purpose.

Definitions For "the Agency", see s 1(1); for "the Board", see s 317(2); for "the Director", see s 1(2).
References See para 7.21.

326 Interpretation

(1) Criminal conduct is conduct which—
  (a) constitutes an offence in any part of the United Kingdom, or
  (b) would constitute an offence in any part of the United Kingdom if it occurred there.

(2) But criminal conduct does not include conduct constituting an offence relating to a matter under the care and management of the Board.

(3) In applying subsection (1) it is immaterial whether conduct occurred before or after the passing of this Act.

(4) Property is criminal property if it constitutes a person's benefit from criminal conduct or it represents such a benefit (in whole or part and whether directly or indirectly); and it is immaterial—
  (a) who carried out the conduct;
  (b) who benefited from it.

(5) A person benefits from conduct if he obtains property as a result of or in connection with the conduct.

(6) If a person obtains a pecuniary advantage as a result of or in connection with conduct, he is to be taken to obtain as a result of or in connection with the conduct a sum of money equal to the value of the pecuniary advantage.

(7) References to property or a pecuniary advantage obtained in connection with conduct include references to property or a pecuniary advantage obtained in both that connection and some other.

(8) If a person benefits from conduct his benefit is the property obtained as a result of or in connection with the conduct.

(9) Property is all property wherever situated and includes—
    (a) money;
    (b) all forms of property, real or personal, heritable or moveable;
    (c) things in action and other intangible or incorporeal property.

(10) The following rules apply in relation to property—
    (a) property is obtained by a person if he obtains an interest in it;
    (b) references to an interest, in relation to land in England and Wales or Northern Ireland, are to any legal estate or equitable interest or power;
    (c) references to an interest, in relation to land in Scotland, are to any estate, interest, servitude or other heritable right in or over land, including a heritable security;
    (d) references to an interest, in relation to property other than land, include references to a right (including a right to possession).

(11) Any reference to an officer of the Board includes a reference to—
    (a) a collector of taxes;
    (b) an inspector of taxes.

(12) Expressions used in this Part and in the Taxes Acts have the same meaning as in the Taxes Acts (within the meaning given by section 118 of the Taxes Management Act 1970 (c 9)).

(13) This section applies for the purposes of this Part.

Definitions For "the Board", see s 317(2).
References See para 7.22.

PART 7
MONEY LAUNDERING

Offences

327 Concealing etc

(1) A person commits an offence if he—
    (a) conceals criminal property;
    (b) disguises criminal property;
    (c) converts criminal property;
    (d) transfers criminal property;
    (e) removes criminal property from England and Wales or from Scotland or from Northern Ireland.

(2) But a person does not commit such an offence if—
    (a) he makes an authorised disclosure under section 338 and (if the disclosure is made before he does the act mentioned in subsection (1)) he has the appropriate consent;

(b) he intended to make such a disclosure but had a reasonable excuse for not doing so;

(c) the act he does is done in carrying out a function he has relating to the enforcement of any provision of this Act or of any other enactment relating to criminal conduct or benefit from criminal conduct.

(3) Concealing or disguising criminal property includes concealing or disguising its nature, source, location, disposition, movement or ownership or any rights with respect to it.

Definitions For "benefits from conduct", see s 340(1), (4), (5), (8); for "criminal conduct", see s 340(1), (2), (4); for "criminal property", see s 340(1), (3); for "enactment", see s 455; for "property", see s 340(1), (9).
References See paras 8.6–8.9.

328 Arrangements

(1) A person commits an offence if he enters into or becomes concerned in an arrangement which he knows or suspects facilitates (by whatever means) the acquisition, retention, use or control of criminal property by or on behalf of another person.

(2) But a person does not commit such an offence if—

(a) he makes an authorised disclosure under section 338 and (if the disclosure is made before he does the act mentioned in subsection (1)) he has the appropriate consent;

(b) he intended to make such a disclosure but had a reasonable excuse for not doing so;

(c) the act he does is done in carrying out a function he has relating to the enforcement of any provision of this Act or of any other enactment relating to criminal conduct or benefit from criminal conduct.

Definitions For "benefits from conduct", see s 340(1), (4), (5), (8); for "criminal conduct", see s 340(1), (2), (4); for "criminal property", see s 340(1), (3); for "enactment", see s 455; for "property", see s 340(1), (9).
References See paras 810, 8.11.

329 Acquisition, use and possession

(1) A person commits an offence if he—

(a) acquires criminal property;

(b) uses criminal property;

(c) has possession of criminal property.

(2) But a person does not commit such an offence if—

(a) he makes an authorised disclosure under section 338 and (if the disclosure is made before he does the act mentioned in subsection (1)) he has the appropriate consent;

(b) he intended to make such a disclosure but had a reasonable excuse for not doing so;

(c) he acquired or used or had possession of the property for adequate consideration;

(d)   the act he does is done in carrying out a function he has relating to the enforcement of any provision of this Act or of any other enactment relating to criminal conduct or benefit from criminal conduct.

(3)   For the purposes of this section—
   (a)   a person acquires property for inadequate consideration if the value of the consideration is significantly less than the value of the property;
   (b)   a person uses or has possession of property for inadequate consideration if the value of the consideration is significantly less than the value of the use or possession;
   (c)   the provision by a person of goods or services which he knows or suspects may help another to carry out criminal conduct is not consideration.

Definitions   For "benefits from conduct", see s 340(1), (4), (5), (8); for "criminal conduct", see s 340(1), (2), (4); for "criminal property", see s 340(1), (3); for "enactment", see s 455; for "property", see s 340(1), (9).
References   See paras 8.12–8.15.

330 Failure to disclose: regulated sector

(1)   A person commits an offence if each of the following three conditions is satisfied.

(2)   The first condition is that he—
   (a)   knows or suspects, or
   (b)   has reasonable grounds for knowing or suspecting,
that another person is engaged in money laundering.

(3)   The second condition is that the information or other matter—
   (a)   on which his knowledge or suspicion is based, or
   (b)   which gives reasonable grounds for such knowledge or suspicion,
came to him in the course of a business in the regulated sector.

(4)   The third condition is that he does not make the required disclosure as soon as is practicable after the information or other matter comes to him.

(5)   The required disclosure is a disclosure of the information or other matter—
   (a)   to a nominated officer or a person authorised for the purposes of this Part by the Director General of the National Criminal Intelligence Service;
   (b)   in the form and manner (if any) prescribed for the purposes of this subsection by order under section 339.

(6)   But a person does not commit an offence under this section if—
   (a)   he has a reasonable excuse for not disclosing the information or other matter;
   (b)   he is a professional legal adviser and the information or other matter came to him in privileged circumstances;
   (c)   subsection (7) applies to him.

(7)   This subsection applies to a person if—
   (a)   he does not know or suspect that another person is engaged in money laundering, and

(b)　he has not been provided by his employer with such training as is specified by the Secretary of State by order for the purposes of this section.

(8)　In deciding whether a person committed an offence under this section the court must consider whether he followed any relevant guidance which was at the time concerned—

(a)　issued by a supervisory authority or any other appropriate body,

(b)　approved by the Treasury, and

(c)　published in a manner it approved as appropriate in its opinion to bring the guidance to the attention of persons likely to be affected by it.

(9)　A disclosure to a nominated officer is a disclosure which—

(a)　is made to a person nominated by the alleged offender's employer to receive disclosures under this section, and

(b)　is made in the course of the alleged offender's employment and in accordance with the procedure established by the employer for the purpose.

(10)　Information or other matter comes to a professional legal adviser in privileged circumstances if it is communicated or given to him—

(a)　by (or by a representative of) a client of his in connection with the giving by the adviser of legal advice to the client,

(b)　by (or by a representative of) a person seeking legal advice from the adviser, or

(c)　by a person in connection with legal proceedings or contemplated legal proceedings.

(11)　But subsection (10) does not apply to information or other matter which is communicated or given with the intention of furthering a criminal purpose.

(12)　Schedule 9 has effect for the purpose of determining what is—

(a)　a business in the regulated sector;

(b)　a supervisory authority.

(13)　An appropriate body is any body which regulates or is representative of any trade, profession, business or employment carried on by the alleged offender.

Definitions　For "employer", see s 340(1), (12); for "employment", see s 340(1), (12); for "money laundering", see s 340(1), (11).
References　See paras 8.16–8.32.

---

331 Failure to disclose: nominated officers in the regulated sector

(1)　A person nominated to receive disclosures under section 330 commits an offence if the conditions in subsections (2) to (4) are satisfied.

(2)　The first condition is that he—

(a)　knows or suspects, or

(b)　has reasonable grounds for knowing or suspecting,

that another person is engaged in money laundering.

(3)　The second condition is that the information or other matter—

(a)　on which his knowledge or suspicion is based, or

(b)　which gives reasonable grounds for such knowledge or suspicion,

came to him in consequence of a disclosure made under section 330.

(4)   The third condition is that he does not make the required disclosure as soon as is practicable after the information or other matter comes to him.

(5)   The required disclosure is a disclosure of the information or other matter—
  (a)   to a person authorised for the purposes of this Part by the Director General of the National Criminal Intelligence Service;
  (b)   in the form and manner (if any) prescribed for the purposes of this subsection by order under section 339.

(6)   But a person does not commit an offence under this section if he has a reasonable excuse for not disclosing the information or other matter.

(7)   In deciding whether a person committed an offence under this section the court must consider whether he followed any relevant guidance which was at the time concerned—
  (a)   issued by a supervisory authority or any other appropriate body,
  (b)   approved by the Treasury, and
  (c)   published in a manner it approved as appropriate in its opinion to bring the guidance to the attention of persons likely to be affected by it.

(8)   Schedule 9 has effect for the purpose of determining what is a supervisory authority.

(9)   An appropriate body is a body which regulates or is representative of a trade, profession, business or employment.

Definitions   For "employment", see s 340(1), (12); for "money laundering", see s 340(1), (11).
References   See para 8.33.

332 Failure to disclose: other nominated officers

(1)   A person nominated to receive disclosures under section 337 or 338 commits an offence if the conditions in subsections (2) to (4) are satisfied.

(2)   The first condition is that he knows or suspects that another person is engaged in money laundering.

(3)   The second condition is that the information or other matter on which his knowledge or suspicion is based came to him in consequence of a disclosure made under section 337 or 338.

(4)   The third condition is that he does not make the required disclosure as soon as is practicable after the information or other matter comes to him.

(5)   The required disclosure is a disclosure of the information or other matter—
  (a)   to a person authorised for the purposes of this Part by the Director General of the National Criminal Intelligence Service;
  (b)   in the form and manner (if any) prescribed for the purposes of this subsection by order under section 339.

(6)   But a person does not commit an offence under this section if he has a reasonable excuse for not disclosing the information or other matter.

Definitions   For "money laundering", see s 340(1), (11).
References   See para 8.34.

333 Tipping off

(1)   A person commits an offence if—
    (a)   he knows or suspects that a disclosure falling within section 337 or 338 has been made, and
    (b)   he makes a disclosure which is likely to prejudice any investigation which might be conducted following the disclosure referred to in paragraph (a).

(2)   But a person does not commit an offence under subsection (1) if—
    (a)   he did not know or suspect that the disclosure was likely to be prejudicial as mentioned in subsection (1);
    (b)   the disclosure is made in carrying out a function he has relating to the enforcement of any provision of this Act or of any other enactment relating to criminal conduct or benefit from criminal conduct;
    (c)   he is a professional legal adviser and the disclosure falls within subsection (3).

(3)   A disclosure falls within this subsection if it is a disclosure—
    (a)   to (or to a representative of) a client of the professional legal adviser in connection with the giving by the adviser of legal advice to the client, or
    (b)   to any person in connection with legal proceedings or contemplated legal proceedings.

(4)   But a disclosure does not fall within subsection (3) if it is made with the intention of furthering a criminal purpose.

Definitions   For "benefits from conduct", see s 340(1), (4), (5), (8); for "criminal conduct", see s 340(1), (2), (4); for "enactment", see s 455.
References   See paras 8.35–8.37.

---

334 Penalties

(1)   A person guilty of an offence under section 327, 328 or 329 is liable—
    (a)   on summary conviction, to imprisonment for a term not exceeding six months or to a fine not exceeding the statutory maximum or to both, or
    (b)   on conviction on indictment, to imprisonment for a term not exceeding 14 years or to a fine or to both.

(2)   A person guilty of an offence under section 330, 331, 332 or 333 is liable—
    (a)   on summary conviction, to imprisonment for a term not exceeding six months or to a fine not exceeding the statutory maximum or to both, or
    (b)   on conviction on indictment, to imprisonment for a term not exceeding five years or to a fine or to both.

References   See para 8.38.

Consent

335 Appropriate consent

(1)   The appropriate consent is—
- (a)   the consent of a nominated officer to do a prohibited act if an authorised disclosure is made to the nominated officer;
- (b)   the consent of a constable to do a prohibited act if an authorised disclosure is made to a constable;
- (c)   the consent of a customs officer to do a prohibited act if an authorised disclosure is made to a customs officer.

(2)   A person must be treated as having the appropriate consent if—
- (a)   he makes an authorised disclosure to a constable or a customs officer, and
- (b)   the condition in subsection (3) or the condition in subsection (4) is satisfied.

(3)   The condition is that before the end of the notice period he does not receive notice from a constable or customs officer that consent to the doing of the act is refused.

(4)   The condition is that—
- (a)   before the end of the notice period he receives notice from a constable or customs officer that consent to the doing of the act is refused, and
- (b)   the moratorium period has expired.

(5)   The notice period is the period of seven working days starting with the first working day after the person makes the disclosure.

(6)   The moratorium period is the period of 31 days starting with the day on which the person receives notice that consent to the doing of the act is refused.

(7)   A working day is a day other than a Saturday, a Sunday, Christmas Day, Good Friday or a day which is a bank holiday under the Banking and Financial Dealings Act 1971 (c 80) in the part of the United Kingdom in which the person is when he makes the disclosure.

(8)   References to a prohibited act are to an act mentioned in section 327(1), 328(1) or 329(1) (as the case may be).

(9)   A nominated officer is a person nominated to receive disclosures under section 338.

(10) Subsections (1) to (4) apply for the purposes of this Part.

Definitions   For "constable", see s 340(1), (13); for "customs officer", see s 454.
References   See para 8.39.

336 Nominated officer: consent

(1)   A nominated officer must not give the appropriate consent to the doing of a prohibited act unless the condition in subsection (2), the condition in subsection (3) or the condition in subsection (4) is satisfied.

(2) The condition is that—

    (a) he makes a disclosure that property is criminal property to a person authorised for the purposes of this Part by the Director General of the National Criminal Intelligence Service, and

    (b) such a person gives consent to the doing of the act.

(3) The condition is that—

    (a) he makes a disclosure that property is criminal property to a person authorised for the purposes of this Part by the Director General of the National Criminal Intelligence Service, and

    (b) before the end of the notice period he does not receive notice from such a person that consent to the doing of the act is refused.

(4) The condition is that—

    (a) he makes a disclosure that property is criminal property to a person authorised for the purposes of this Part by the Director General of the National Criminal Intelligence Service,

    (b) before the end of the notice period he receives notice from such a person that consent to the doing of the act is refused, and

    (c) the moratorium period has expired.

(5) A person who is a nominated officer commits an offence if—

    (a) he gives consent to a prohibited act in circumstances where none of the conditions in subsections (2), (3) and (4) is satisfied, and

    (b) he knows or suspects that the act is a prohibited act.

(6) A person guilty of such an offence is liable—

    (a) on summary conviction, to imprisonment for a term not exceeding six months or to a fine not exceeding the statutory maximum or to both, or

    (b) on conviction on indictment, to imprisonment for a term not exceeding five years or to a fine or to both.

(7) The notice period is the period of seven working days starting with the first working day after the nominated officer makes the disclosure.

(8) The moratorium period is the period of 31 days starting with the day on which the nominated officer is given notice that consent to the doing of the act is refused.

(9) A working day is a day other than a Saturday, a Sunday, Christmas Day, Good Friday or a day which is a bank holiday under the Banking and Financial Dealings Act 1971 (c 80) in the part of the United Kingdom in which the nominated officer is when he gives the appropriate consent.

(10) References to a prohibited act are to an act mentioned in section 327(1), 328(1) or 329(1) (as the case may be).

(11) A nominated officer is a person nominated to receive disclosures under section 338.

Definitions   For "criminal property", see s 340(1), (3); for "property", see s 340(1), (9).
References   See para 8.40–8.43.

Disclosures

337 Protected disclosures

(1)   A disclosure which satisfies the following three conditions is not to be taken to breach any restriction on the disclosure of information (however imposed).

(2)   The first condition is that the information or other matter disclosed came to the person making the disclosure (the discloser) in the course of his trade, profession, business or employment.

(3)   The second condition is that the information or other matter—
    (a)   causes the discloser to know or suspect, or
    (b)   gives him reasonable grounds for knowing or suspecting,

that another person is engaged in money laundering.

(4)   The third condition is that the disclosure is made to a constable, a customs officer or a nominated officer as soon as is practicable after the information or other matter comes to the discloser.

(5)   A disclosure to a nominated officer is a disclosure which—
    (a)   is made to a person nominated by the discloser's employer to receive disclosures under this section, and
    (b)   is made in the course of the discloser's employment and in accordance with the procedure established by the employer for the purpose.

Definitions   For "constable", see s 340(1), (13); for "customs officer", see s 454; for "employer", see s 340(1), (12); for "employment", see s 340(1), (12); for "money laundering", see s 340(1), (11).
References   See para 8.44.

338 Authorised disclosures

(1)   For the purposes of this Part a disclosure is authorised if—
    (a)   it is a disclosure to a constable, a customs officer or a nominated officer by the alleged offender that property is criminal property,
    (b)   it is made in the form and manner (if any) prescribed for the purposes of this subsection by order under section 339, and
    (c)   the first or second condition set out below is satisfied.

(2)   The first condition is that the disclosure is made before the alleged offender does the prohibited act.

(3)   The second condition is that—
    (a)   the disclosure is made after the alleged offender does the prohibited act,
    (b)   there is a good reason for his failure to make the disclosure before he did the act, and
    (c)   the disclosure is made on his own initiative and as soon as it is practicable for him to make it.

(4)   An authorised disclosure is not to be taken to breach any restriction on the disclosure of information (however imposed).

(5)   A disclosure to a nominated officer is a disclosure which—
  (a)   is made to a person nominated by the alleged offender's employer to receive authorised disclosures, and
  (b)   is made in the course of the alleged offender's employment and in accordance with the procedure established by the employer for the purpose.

(6)   References to the prohibited act are to an act mentioned in section 327(1), 328(1) or 329(1) (as the case may be).

Definitions   For "constable", see s 340(1), (13); for "criminal property", see s 340(1), (3); for "customs officer", see s 454; for "employer", see s 340(1), (12); for "employment", see s 340(1), (12); for "property", see s 340(1), (9).
References   See para 8.46.

339 Form and manner of disclosures

(1)   The Secretary of State may by order prescribe the form and manner in which a disclosure under section 330, 331, 332 or 338 must be made.

(2)   An order under this section may also provide that the form may include a request to the discloser to provide additional information specified in the form.

(3)   The additional information must be information which is necessary to enable the person to whom the disclosure is made to decide whether to start a money laundering investigation.

(4)   A disclosure made in pursuance of a request under subsection (2) is not to be taken to breach any restriction on the disclosure of information (however imposed).

(5)   The discloser is the person making a disclosure mentioned in subsection (1).

(6)   Money laundering investigation must be construed in accordance with section 341(4).

(7)   Subsection (2) does not apply to a disclosure made to a nominated officer.

References   See para 8.47.

Interpretation

340 Interpretation

(1)   This section applies for the purposes of this Part.

(2)   Criminal conduct is conduct which—
  (a)   constitutes an offence in any part of the United Kingdom, or
  (b)   would constitute an offence in any part of the United Kingdom if it occurred there.

(3)   Property is criminal property if—
  (a)   it constitutes a person's benefit from criminal conduct or it represents such a benefit (in whole or part and whether directly or indirectly), and
  (b)   the alleged offender knows or suspects that it constitutes or represents such a benefit.

(4)   It is immaterial—
    (a)   who carried out the conduct;
    (b)   who benefited from it;
    (c)   whether the conduct occurred before or after the passing of this Act.

(5)   A person benefits from conduct if he obtains property as a result of or in connection with the conduct.

(6)   If a person obtains a pecuniary advantage as a result of or in connection with conduct, he is to be taken to obtain as a result of or in connection with the conduct a sum of money equal to the value of the pecuniary advantage.

(7)   References to property or a pecuniary advantage obtained in connection with conduct include references to property or a pecuniary advantage obtained in both that connection and some other.

(8)   If a person benefits from conduct his benefit is the property obtained as a result of or in connection with the conduct.

(9)   Property is all property wherever situated and includes—
    (a)   money;
    (b)   all forms of property, real or personal, heritable or moveable;
    (c)   things in action and other intangible or incorporeal property.

(10)   The following rules apply in relation to property—
    (a)   property is obtained by a person if he obtains an interest in it;
    (b)   references to an interest, in relation to land in England and Wales or Northern Ireland, are to any legal estate or equitable interest or power;
    (c)   references to an interest, in relation to land in Scotland, are to any estate, interest, servitude or other heritable right in or over land, including a heritable security;
    (d)   references to an interest, in relation to property other than land, include references to a right (including a right to possession).

(11)   Money laundering is an act which—
    (a)   constitutes an offence under section 327, 328 or 329,
    (b)   constitutes an attempt, conspiracy or incitement to commit an offence specified in paragraph (a),
    (c)   constitutes aiding, abetting, counselling or procuring the commission of an offence specified in paragraph (a), or
    (d)   would constitute an offence specified in paragraph (a), (b) or (c) if done in the United Kingdom.

(12)   For the purposes of a disclosure to a nominated officer—
    (a)   references to a person's employer include any body, association or organisation (including a voluntary organisation) in connection with whose activities the person exercises a function (whether or not for gain or reward), and
    (b)   references to employment must be construed accordingly.

(13)   References to a constable include references to a person authorised for the purposes of this Part by the Director General of the National Criminal Intelligence Service.

References   See para 8.48–8.50.

PART 8
INVESTIGATIONS

CHAPTER 1
INTRODUCTION

341 Investigations

(1)   For the purposes of this Part a confiscation investigation is an investigation into—

> (a)   whether a person has benefited from his criminal conduct, or
> (b)   the extent or whereabouts of his benefit from his criminal conduct.

(2)   For the purposes of this Part a civil recovery investigation is an investigation into—

> (a)   whether property is recoverable property or associated property,
> (b)   who holds the property, or
> (c)   its extent or whereabouts.

(3)   But an investigation is not a civil recovery investigation if—

> (a)   proceedings for a recovery order have been started in respect of the property in question,
> (b)   an interim receiving order applies to the property in question,
> (c)   an interim administration order applies to the property in question, or
> (d)   the property in question is detained under section 295.

(4)   For the purposes of this Part a money laundering investigation is an investigation into whether a person has committed a money laundering offence.

Definitions   For "associated property", see ss 245, 414(2), 416(9); for "benefits from conduct", see ss 413(2), (4), (5), 416(9); for "criminal conduct", see ss 413(1), (5), 416(9); for "interim receiving order", see ss 246(2), 416(7), (9); for "money laundering offence", see ss 415, 416(9); for "property", see ss 414(1), 416(9); for "recoverable property", see ss 316(1), 414(2), 416(9), for "recovery order", see ss 316(1), 416(7), (9).
References   See paras 9.3, 9.4.

---

342 Offences of prejudicing investigation

(1)   This section applies if a person knows or suspects that an appropriate officer or (in Scotland) a proper person is acting (or proposing to act) in connection with a confiscation investigation, a civil recovery investigation or a money laundering investigation which is being or is about to be conducted.

(2)   The person commits an offence if—

> (a)   he makes a disclosure which is likely to prejudice the investigation, or
> (b)   he falsifies, conceals, destroys or otherwise disposes of, or causes or permits the falsification, concealment, destruction or disposal of, documents which are relevant to the investigation.

(3)   A person does not commit an offence under subsection (2)(a) if—

> (a)   he does not know or suspect that the disclosure is likely to prejudice the investigation,

    (b)   the disclosure is made in the exercise of a function under this Act or any other enactment relating to criminal conduct or benefit from criminal conduct or in compliance with a requirement imposed under or by virtue of this Act, or

    (c)   he is a professional legal adviser and the disclosure falls within subsection (4).

(4)   A disclosure falls within this subsection if it is a disclosure—

    (a)   to (or to a representative of) a client of the professional legal adviser in connection with the giving by the adviser of legal advice to the client, or

    (b)   to any person in connection with legal proceedings or contemplated legal proceedings.

(5)   But a disclosure does not fall within subsection (4) if it is made with the intention of furthering a criminal purpose.

(6)   A person does not commit an offence under subsection (2)(b) if—

    (a)   he does not know or suspect that the documents are relevant to the investigation, or

    (b)   he does not intend to conceal any facts disclosed by the documents from any appropriate officer or (in Scotland) proper person carrying out the investigation.

(7)   A person guilty of an offence under subsection (2) is liable—

    (a)   on summary conviction, to imprisonment for a term not exceeding six months or to a fine not exceeding the statutory maximum or to both, or

    (b)   on conviction on indictment, to imprisonment for a term not exceeding five years or to a fine or to both.

(8)   For the purposes of this section—

    (a)   "appropriate officer" must be construed in accordance with section 378;

    (b)   "proper person" must be construed in accordance with section 412.

Definitions   For "appropriate officer" in relation to a civil recovery investigation, see ss 378(3), 416(2), (9); for "appropriate officers" in relation to a confiscation investigation, see ss 378(1), 416(2), (9); for "appropriate officers" in relation to a money laundering investigation, see ss 378(4), (7), 416(2), (9); for "benefits from conduct", see ss 413(2), (4), (5), 416(9); for "civil recovery investigation", see ss 341(2), (3), 416(1), (9); for "confiscation investigation", see ss 341(1), 416(1), (9); for "criminal conduct", see ss 413(1), (5), 416(9); for "document", see ss 379, 416(2), (9); for "enactment", see s 455; for "money laundering investigation", see ss 341(4), 416(1), (9).
References   See paras 9.5, 9.6.

CHAPTER 2
ENGLAND AND WALES AND NORTHERN IRELAND

Judges and courts

343 Judges

(1)   In this Chapter references to a judge in relation to an application must be construed in accordance with this section.

(2)　In relation to an application for the purposes of a confiscation investigation or a money laundering investigation a judge is—

    (a)　in England and Wales, a judge entitled to exercise the jurisdiction of the Crown Court;

    (b)　in Northern Ireland, a Crown Court judge.

(3)　In relation to an application for the purposes of a civil recovery investigation a judge is a judge of the High Court.

Definitions　For "civil recovery investigation", see ss 341(2), (3), 416(1), (9); for "confiscation investigation", see ss 341(1), 416(1), (9); for "money laundering investigation", see ss 341(4), 416(1), (9).
References　See para 9.7.

344　Courts

In this Chapter references to the court are to—

    (a)　the Crown Court, in relation to an order for the purposes of a confiscation investigation or a money laundering investigation;

    (b)　the High Court, in relation to an order for the purposes of a civil recovery investigation.

Definitions　For "civil recovery investigation", see ss 341(2), (3), 416(1), (9); for "confiscation investigation", see ss 341(1), 416(1), (9); for "money laundering investigation", see ss 341(4), 416(1), (9).
References　See para 9.7.

Production orders

345　Production orders

(1)　A judge may, on an application made to him by an appropriate officer, make a production order if he is satisfied that each of the requirements for the making of the order is fulfilled.

(2)　The application for a production order must state that—

    (a)　a person specified in the application is subject to a confiscation investigation or a money laundering investigation, or

    (b)　property specified in the application is subject to a civil recovery investigation.

(3)　The application must also state that—

    (a)　the order is sought for the purposes of the investigation;

    (b)　the order is sought in relation to material, or material of a description, specified in the application;

    (c)　a person specified in the application appears to be in possession or control of the material.

(4)　A production order is an order either—

    (a)　requiring the person the application for the order specifies as appearing to be in possession or control of material to produce it to an appropriate officer for him to take away, or

    (b)　requiring that person to give an appropriate officer access to the material,

within the period stated in the order.

(5)   The period stated in a production order must be a period of seven days beginning with the day on which the order is made, unless it appears to the judge by whom the order is made that a longer or shorter period would be appropriate in the particular circumstances.

Definitions   For "appropriate officer" in relation to a civil recovery investigation, see ss 378(3), 416(2), (9); for "appropriate officers" in relation to a confiscation investigation, see ss 378(1), 416(2), (9); for "appropriate officers" in relation to a money laundering investigation, see ss 378(4), (7), 416(2), (9); for "civil recovery investigation", see ss 341(2), (3), 416(1), (9); for "confiscation investigation", see ss 341(1), 416(1), (9); for "judge" in relation to an application for the purposes of a civil recovery investigation, see s 343(1), (3); for "judge" in relation to an application for the purposes of a confiscation investigation or a money laundering investigation, see s 343(1), (2); for "money laundering investigation", see ss 341(4), 416(1), (9); for "property", see ss 414(1), 416(9).
References   See para 9.8.

346 Requirements for making of production order

(1)   These are the requirements for the making of a production order.

(2)   There must be reasonable grounds for suspecting that—
   (a)   in the case of a confiscation investigation, the person the application for the order specifies as being subject to the investigation has benefited from his criminal conduct;
   (b)   in the case of a civil recovery investigation, the property the application for the order specifies as being subject to the investigation is recoverable property or associated property;
   (c)   in the case of a money laundering investigation, the person the application for the order specifies as being subject to the investigation has committed a money laundering offence.

(3)   There must be reasonable grounds for believing that the person the application specifies as appearing to be in possession or control of the material so specified is in possession or control of it.

(4)   There must be reasonable grounds for believing that the material is likely to be of substantial value (whether or not by itself) to the investigation for the purposes of which the order is sought.

(5)   There must be reasonable grounds for believing that it is in the public interest for the material to be produced or for access to it to be given, having regard to—
   (a)   the benefit likely to accrue to the investigation if the material is obtained;
   (b)   the circumstances under which the person the application specifies as appearing to be in possession or control of the material holds it.

Definitions   For "associated property", see ss 245, 414(2), 416(9); for "benefits from conduct", see ss 413(2), (4), (5), 416(9); for "civil recovery investigation", see ss 341(2), (3), 416(1), (9); for "confiscation investigation", see ss 341(1), 416(1), (9); for "criminal conduct", see ss 413(1), (5), 416(9); for "money laundering investigation", see ss 341(4), 416(1), (9); for "money laundering offence", see ss 415, 416(9); for "production order", see ss 345(4), 416(2), (9); for "property", see ss 414(1), 416(9); for "recoverable property", see ss 316(1), 414(2), 416(9).
References   See paras 9.9, 9.10.

347 Order to grant entry

(1)   This section applies if a judge makes a production order requiring a person to give an appropriate officer access to material on any premises.

(2)   The judge may, on an application made to him by an appropriate officer and specifying the premises, make an order to grant entry in relation to the premises.

(3)   An order to grant entry is an order requiring any person who appears to an appropriate officer to be entitled to grant entry to the premises to allow him to enter the premises to obtain access to the material.

Definitions   For "appropriate officer" in relation to a civil recovery investigation, see ss 378(3), 416(2), (9); for "appropriate officers" in relation to a confiscation investigation, see ss 378(1), 416(2), (9); for "appropriate officers" in relation to a money laundering investigation, see ss 378(4), (7), 416(2), (9); for "judge" in relation to an application for the purposes of a civil recovery investigation, see s 343(1), (3); for "judge" in relation to an application for the purposes of a confiscation investigation or a money laundering investigation, see s 343(1), (2); for "premises", see s 379; for "production order", see ss 345(4), 416(2), (9).
References   See para 9.11.

---

348 Further provisions

(1)   A production order does not require a person to produce, or give access to, privileged material.

(2)   Privileged material is any material which the person would be entitled to refuse to produce on grounds of legal professional privilege in proceedings in the High Court.

(3)   A production order does not require a person to produce, or give access to, excluded material.

(4)   A production order has effect in spite of any restriction on the disclosure of information (however imposed).

(5)   An appropriate officer may take copies of any material which is produced, or to which access is given, in compliance with a production order.

(6)   Material produced in compliance with a production order may be retained for so long as it is necessary to retain it (as opposed to copies of it) in connection with the investigation for the purposes of which the order was made.

(7)   But if an appropriate officer has reasonable grounds for believing that—
>   (a)   the material may need to be produced for the purposes of any legal proceedings, and
>   (b)   it might otherwise be unavailable for those purposes,

it may be retained until the proceedings are concluded.

Definitions   For "appropriate officer" in relation to a civil recovery investigation, see ss 378(3), 416(2), (9); for "appropriate officers" in relation to a confiscation investigation, see ss 378(1), 416(2), (9); for "appropriate officers" in relation to a money laundering investigation, see ss 378(4), (7), 416(2), (9); for "excluded material", see s 379; for "production order", see ss 345(4), 416(2), (9).
References   See para 9.12.

---

349 Computer information

(1)   This section applies if any of the material specified in an application for a production order consists of information contained in a computer.

(2)   If the order is an order requiring a person to produce the material to an appropriate officer for him to take away, it has effect as an order to produce the material in a form in which it can be taken away by him and in which it is visible and legible.

(3)   If the order is an order requiring a person to give an appropriate officer access to the material, it has effect as an order to give him access to the material in a form in which it is visible and legible.

Definitions   For "appropriate officer" in relation to a civil recovery investigation, see ss 378(3), 416(2), (9); for "appropriate officers" in relation to a confiscation investigation, see ss 378(1), 416(2), (9); for "appropriate officers" in relation to a money laundering investigation, see ss 378(4), (7), 416(2), (9); for "production order", see ss 345(4), 416(2), (9).
References   See para 9.13.

350 Government departments

(1)   A production order may be made in relation to material in the possession or control of an authorised government department.

(2)   An order so made may require any officer of the department (whether named in the order or not) who may for the time being be in possession or control of the material to comply with it.

(3)   An order containing such a requirement must be served as if the proceedings were civil proceedings against the department.

(4)   If an order contains such a requirement—
   (a)   the person on whom it is served must take all reasonable steps to bring it to the attention of the officer concerned;
   (b)   any other officer of the department who is in receipt of the order must also take all reasonable steps to bring it to the attention of the officer concerned.

(5)   If the order is not brought to the attention of the officer concerned within the period stated in the order (in pursuance of section 345(4)) the person on whom it is served must report the reasons for the failure to—
   (a)   a judge entitled to exercise the jurisdiction of the Crown Court or (in Northern Ireland) a Crown Court judge, in the case of an order made for the purposes of a confiscation investigation or a money laundering investigation;
   (b)   a High Court judge, in the case of an order made for the purposes of a civil recovery investigation.

(6)   An authorised government department is a government department, or a Northern Ireland department, which is an authorised department for the purposes of the Crown Proceedings Act 1947 (c 44).

Definitions   For "civil recovery investigation", see ss 341(2), (3), 416(1), (9); for "confiscation investigation", see ss 341(1), 416(1), (9); for "money laundering investigation", see ss 341(4), 416(1), (9); for "production order", see ss 345(4), 416(2), (9).
References   See para 9.14.

351 Supplementary

(1)   An application for a production order or an order to grant entry may be made ex parte to a judge in chambers.

(2)   Rules of court may make provision as to the practice and procedure to be followed in connection with proceedings relating to production orders and orders to grant entry.

(3)   An application to discharge or vary a production order or an order to grant entry may be made to the court by—
    (a)   the person who applied for the order;
    (b)   any person affected by the order.

(4)   The court—
    (a)   may discharge the order;
    (b)   may vary the order.

(5)   If an accredited financial investigator, a constable or a customs officer applies for a production order or an order to grant entry, an application to discharge or vary the order need not be by the same accredited financial investigator, constable or customs officer.

(6)   References to a person who applied for a production order or an order to grant entry must be construed accordingly.

(7)   Production orders and orders to grant entry have effect as if they were orders of the court.

(8)   Subsections (2) to (7) do not apply to orders made in England and Wales for the purposes of a civil recovery investigation.

Definitions   For "accredited financial investigator", see s 3(5); for "civil recovery investigation", see ss 341(2), (3), 416(1), (9); for "the court" in relation to an order for the purposes of a civil recovery investigation, see s 344(b); for "the court" in relation to an order for the purposes of a confiscation investigation or a money laundering investigation, see s 344(a); for "customs officer", see s 454; for "judge" in relation to an application for the purposes of a civil recovery investigation, see s 343(1), (3); for "judge" in relation to an application for the purposes of a confiscation investigation or a money laundering investigation, see s 343(1), (2); for "order to grant entry", see ss 347(3), 416(2), (9); for "production order", see ss 345(4), 416(2), (9).
References   See paras 9.15–9.17.

Search and seizure warrants

352 Search and seizure warrants

(1)   A judge may, on an application made to him by an appropriate officer, issue a search and seizure warrant if he is satisfied that either of the requirements for the issuing of the warrant is fulfilled.

(2)   The application for a search and seizure warrant must state that—
    (a)   a person specified in the application is subject to a confiscation investigation or a money laundering investigation, or
    (b)   property specified in the application is subject to a civil recovery investigation.

(3)   The application must also state—
    (a)   that the warrant is sought for the purposes of the investigation;

(b)   that the warrant is sought in relation to the premises specified in the application;

(c)   that the warrant is sought in relation to material specified in the application, or that there are reasonable grounds for believing that there is material falling within section 353(6), (7) or (8) on the premises.

(4)   A search and seizure warrant is a warrant authorising an appropriate person—

(a)   to enter and search the premises specified in the application for the warrant, and

(b)   to seize and retain any material found there which is likely to be of substantial value (whether or not by itself) to the investigation for the purposes of which the application is made.

(5)   An appropriate person is—

(a)   a constable or a customs officer, if the warrant is sought for the purposes of a confiscation investigation or a money laundering investigation;

(b)   a named member of the staff of the Agency, if the warrant is sought for the purposes of a civil recovery investigation.

(6)   The requirements for the issue of a search and seizure warrant are—

(a)   that a production order made in relation to material has not been complied with and there are reasonable grounds for believing that the material is on the premises specified in the application for the warrant, or

(b)   that section 353 is satisfied in relation to the warrant.

Definitions   For "the Agency", see s 1(1); for "appropriate officer" in relation to a civil recovery investigation, see ss 378(3), 416(2), (9); for "appropriate officers" in relation to a confiscation investigation, see ss 378(1), 416(2), (9); for "appropriate officers" in relation to a money laundering investigation, see ss 378(4), (7), 416(2), (9); for "civil recovery investigation", see ss 341(2), (3), 416(1), (9); for "confiscation investigation", see ss 341(1), 416(1), (9); for "customs officer", see s 454; for "judge" in relation to an application for the purposes of a civil recovery investigation, see s 343(1), (3); for "judge" in relation to an application for the purposes of a confiscation investigation or a money laundering investigation, see s 343(1), (2); for "money laundering investigation", see ss 341(4), 416(1), (9); for "premises", see s 379; for "production order", see ss 345(4), 416(2), (9).
References   See para 9.20.

---

353 Requirements where production order not available

(1)   This section is satisfied in relation to a search and seizure warrant if—

(a)   subsection (2) applies, and

(b)   either the first or the second set of conditions is complied with.

(2)   This subsection applies if there are reasonable grounds for suspecting that—

(a)   in the case of a confiscation investigation, the person specified in the application for the warrant has benefited from his criminal conduct;

(b)   in the case of a civil recovery investigation, the property specified in the application for the warrant is recoverable property or associated property;

(c)   in the case of a money laundering investigation, the person specified in the application for the warrant has committed a money laundering offence.

(3)   The first set of conditions is that there are reasonable grounds for believing that—

- (a)   any material on the premises specified in the application for the warrant is likely to be of substantial value (whether or not by itself) to the investigation for the purposes of which the warrant is sought,
- (b)   it is in the public interest for the material to be obtained, having regard to the benefit likely to accrue to the investigation if the material is obtained, and
- (c)   it would not be appropriate to make a production order for any one or more of the reasons in subsection (4).

(4)   The reasons are—

- (a)   that it is not practicable to communicate with any person against whom the production order could be made;
- (b)   that it is not practicable to communicate with any person who would be required to comply with an order to grant entry to the premises;
- (c)   that the investigation might be seriously prejudiced unless an appropriate person is able to secure immediate access to the material.

(5)   The second set of conditions is that—

- (a)   there are reasonable grounds for believing that there is material on the premises specified in the application for the warrant and that the material falls within subsection (6), (7) or (8),
- (b)   there are reasonable grounds for believing that it is in the public interest for the material to be obtained, having regard to the benefit likely to accrue to the investigation if the material is obtained, and
- (c)   any one or more of the requirements in subsection (9) is met.

(6)   In the case of a confiscation investigation, material falls within this subsection if it cannot be identified at the time of the application but it—

- (a)   relates to the person specified in the application, the question whether he has benefited from his criminal conduct or any question as to the extent or whereabouts of his benefit from his criminal conduct, and
- (b)   is likely to be of substantial value (whether or not by itself) to the investigation for the purposes of which the warrant is sought.

(7)   In the case of a civil recovery investigation, material falls within this subsection if it cannot be identified at the time of the application but it—

- (a)   relates to the property specified in the application, the question whether it is recoverable property or associated property, the question as to who holds any such property, any question as to whether the person who appears to hold any such property holds other property which is recoverable property, or any question as to the extent or whereabouts of any property mentioned in this paragraph, and
- (b)   is likely to be of substantial value (whether or not by itself) to the investigation for the purposes of which the warrant is sought.

(8)   In the case of a money laundering investigation, material falls within this subsection if it cannot be identified at the time of the application but it—

- (a)   relates to the person specified in the application or the question whether he has committed a money laundering offence, and

    (b)   is likely to be of substantial value (whether or not by itself) to the investigation for the purposes of which the warrant is sought.

(9)   The requirements are—
    (a)   that it is not practicable to communicate with any person entitled to grant entry to the premises;
    (b)   that entry to the premises will not be granted unless a warrant is produced;
    (c)   that the investigation might be seriously prejudiced unless an appropriate person arriving at the premises is able to secure immediate entry to them.

(10)   An appropriate person is—
    (a)   a constable or a customs officer, if the warrant is sought for the purposes of a confiscation investigation or a money laundering investigation;
    (b)   a member of the staff of the Agency, if the warrant is sought for the purposes of a civil recovery investigation.

Definitions   For "the Agency", see s 1(1); for "associated property", see ss 245, 414(2), 416(9); for "benefits from conduct", see ss 413(2), (4), (5), 416(9); for "civil recovery investigation", see ss 341(2), (3), 416(1), (9); for "confiscation investigation", see ss 341(1), 416(1), (9); for "criminal conduct", see ss 413(1), (5), 416(9); for "customs officer", see s 454; for "money laundering investigation", see ss 341(4), 416(1), (9); for "money laundering offence", see ss 415, 416(9); for "order to grant entry", see ss 347(3), 416(2), (9); for "premises", see s 379; for "production order", see ss 345(4), 416(2), (9); for "property", see ss 414(1), 416(9); for "recoverable property", see ss 316(1), 414(2), 416(9); for "search and seizure warrant", see ss 352(4), 416(2), (9).
References   See paras 9.21, 9.22.

354 Further provisions: general

(1)   A search and seizure warrant does not confer the right to seize privileged material.

(2)   Privileged material is any material which a person would be entitled to refuse to produce on grounds of legal professional privilege in proceedings in the High Court.

(3)   A search and seizure warrant does not confer the right to seize excluded material.

Definitions   For "excluded material", see s 379; for "search and seizure warrant", see ss 352(4), 416(2), (9).
References   See para 9.24.

355 Further provisions: confiscation and money laundering

(1)   This section applies to—
    (a)   search and seizure warrants sought for the purposes of a confiscation investigation or a money laundering investigation, and
    (b)   powers of seizure under them.

(2)   In relation to such warrants and powers, the Secretary of State may make an order which applies the provisions to which subsections (3) and (4) apply subject to any specified modifications.

(3)   This subsection applies to the following provisions of the Police and Criminal Evidence Act 1984 (c 60)—

    (a)   section 15 (search warrants – safeguards);
    (b)   section 16 (execution of warrants);
    (c)   section 21 (access and copying);
    (d)   section 22 (retention).

(4)   This subsection applies to the following provisions of the Police and Criminal Evidence (Northern Ireland) Order 1989 (SI 1989/1341 (NI 12))—

    (a)   Article 17 (search warrants -safeguards);
    (b)   Article 18 (execution of warrants);
    (c)   Article 23 (access and copying);
    (d)   Article 24 (retention).

Definitions   For "confiscation investigation", see ss 341(1), 416(1), (9); for "money laundering investigation", see ss 341(4), 416(1), (9); for "search and seizure warrant", see ss 352(4), 416(2), (9).
References   See para 9.25.

356 Further provisions: civil recovery

(1)   This section applies to search and seizure warrants sought for the purposes of civil recovery investigations.

(2)   An application for a warrant may be made ex parte to a judge in chambers.

(3)   A warrant may be issued subject to conditions.

(4)   A warrant continues in force until the end of the period of one month starting with the day on which it is issued.

(5)   A warrant authorises the person it names to require any information which is held in a computer and is accessible from the premises specified in the application for the warrant, and which the named person believes relates to any matter relevant to the investigation, to be produced in a form—

    (a)   in which it can be taken away, and
    (b)   in which it is visible and legible.

(6)   If—

    (a)   the Director gives written authority for members of staff of the Agency to accompany the person a warrant names when executing it, and
    (b)   a warrant is issued,

the authorised members have the same powers under it as the person it names.

(7)   A warrant may include provision authorising a person who is exercising powers under it to do other things which—

    (a)   are specified in the warrant, and
    (b)   need to be done in order to give effect to it.

(8)   Copies may be taken of any material seized under a warrant.

(9)   Material seized under a warrant may be retained for so long as it is necessary to retain it (as opposed to copies of it) in connection with the investigation for the purposes of which the warrant was issued.

(10) But if the Director has reasonable grounds for believing that—
- (a) the material may need to be produced for the purposes of any legal proceedings, and
- (b) it might otherwise be unavailable for those purposes,

it may be retained until the proceedings are concluded.

Definitions For "the Agency", see s 1(1); for "civil recovery investigation", see ss 341(2), (3), 416(1), (9); for "the Director", see s 1(2); for "judge" in relation to an application for the purposes of a civil recovery investigation, see s 343(1), (3); for "premises", see s 379; for "search and seizure warrant", see ss 352(4), 416(2), (9).
References See para 9.26.

Disclosure orders

357 Disclosure orders

(1) A judge may, on an application made to him by the Director, make a disclosure order if he is satisfied that each of the requirements for the making of the order is fulfilled.

(2) No application for a disclosure order may be made in relation to a money laundering investigation.

(3) The application for a disclosure order must state that—
- (a) a person specified in the application is subject to a confiscation investigation which is being carried out by the Director and the order is sought for the purposes of the investigation, or
- (b) property specified in the application is subject to a civil recovery investigation and the order is sought for the purposes of the investigation.

(4) A disclosure order is an order authorising the Director to give to any person the Director considers has relevant information notice in writing requiring him to do, with respect to any matter relevant to the investigation for the purposes of which the order is sought, any or all of the following—
- (a) answer questions, either at a time specified in the notice or at once, at a place so specified;
- (b) provide information specified in the notice, by a time and in a manner so specified;
- (c) produce documents, or documents of a description, specified in the notice, either at or by a time so specified or at once, and in a manner so specified.

(5) Relevant information is information (whether or not contained in a document) which the Director considers to be relevant to the investigation.

(6) A person is not bound to comply with a requirement imposed by a notice given under a disclosure order unless evidence of authority to give the notice is produced to him.

Definitions For "civil recovery investigation", see ss 341(2), (3), 416(1), (9); for "confiscation investigation", see ss 341(1), 416(1), (9); for "the Director", see s 1(2); for "document", see s 379, 416(2), (9); for "judge" in relation to an application for the purposes of a civil recovery investigation, see s 343(1), (3); for "judge" in relation to an application for the purposes of a confiscation investigation or a money laundering investigation, see s 343(1), (2); for "money laundering investigation", see ss 341(4), 416(1), (9); for "notice in writing", see s 416(8), (9); for "property", see ss 414(1), 416(9).
References See paras 9.27–9.30.

358 Requirements for making of disclosure order

(1)   These are the requirements for the making of a disclosure order.

(2)   There must be reasonable grounds for suspecting that—
   (a)   in the case of a confiscation investigation, the person specified in the application for the order has benefited from his criminal conduct;
   (b)   in the case of a civil recovery investigation, the property specified in the application for the order is recoverable property or associated property.

(3)   There must be reasonable grounds for believing that information which may be provided in compliance with a requirement imposed under the order is likely to be of substantial value (whether or not by itself) to the investigation for the purposes of which the order is sought.

(4)   There must be reasonable grounds for believing that it is in the public interest for the information to be provided, having regard to the benefit likely to accrue to the investigation if the information is obtained.

Definitions   For "associated property", see ss 245, 414(2), 416(9); for "benefits from conduct", see ss 413(2), (4), (5), 416(9); for "civil recovery investigation", see ss 341(2), (3), 416(1), (9); for "confiscation investigation", see ss 341(1), 416(1), (9); for "criminal conduct", see ss 413(1), (5), 416(9); for "disclosure order", see ss 357(4), 416(2), (9); for "property", see ss 414(1), 416(9); for "recoverable property", see ss 316(1), 414(2), 416(9).
References   See paras 9.31, 9.32.

359 Offences

(1)   A person commits an offence if without reasonable excuse he fails to comply with a requirement imposed on him under a disclosure order.

(2)   A person guilty of an offence under subsection (1) is liable on summary conviction to—
   (a)   imprisonment for a term not exceeding six months,
   (b)   a fine not exceeding level 5 on the standard scale, or
   (c)   both.

(3)   A person commits an offence if, in purported compliance with a requirement imposed on him under a disclosure order, he—
   (a)   makes a statement which he knows to be false or misleading in a material particular, or
   (b)   recklessly makes a statement which is false or misleading in a material particular.

(4)   A person guilty of an offence under subsection (3) is liable—
   (a)   on summary conviction, to imprisonment for a term not exceeding six months or to a fine not exceeding the statutory maximum or to both, or
   (b)   on conviction on indictment, to imprisonment for a term not exceeding two years or to a fine or to both.

Definitions   For "disclosure order", see ss 357(4), 416(2), (9).
References   See para 9.33.

360 Statements

(1)   A statement made by a person in response to a requirement imposed on him under a disclosure order may not be used in evidence against him in criminal proceedings.

(2)   But subsection (1) does not apply—

    (a)   in the case of proceedings under Part 2 or 4,

    (b)   on a prosecution for an offence under section 359(1) or (3),

    (c)   on a prosecution for an offence under section 5 of the Perjury Act 1911 (c 6) or Article 10 of the Perjury (Northern Ireland) Order 1979 (SI 1979/1714 (NI 19)) (false statements), or

    (d)   on a prosecution for some other offence where, in giving evidence, the person makes a statement inconsistent with the statement mentioned in subsection (1).

(3)   A statement may not be used by virtue of subsection (2)(d) against a person unless—

    (a)   evidence relating to it is adduced, or

    (b)   a question relating to it is asked,

by him or on his behalf in the proceedings arising out of the prosecution.

Definitions   For "disclosure order", see ss 357(4), 416(2), (9).
References   See para 9.34.

---

361 Further provisions

(1)   A disclosure order does not confer the right to require a person to answer any privileged question, provide any privileged information or produce any privileged document, except that a lawyer may be required to provide the name and address of a client of his.

(2)   A privileged question is a question which the person would be entitled to refuse to answer on grounds of legal professional privilege in proceedings in the High Court.

(3)   Privileged information is any information which the person would be entitled to refuse to provide on grounds of legal professional privilege in proceedings in the High Court.

(4)   Privileged material is any material which the person would be entitled to refuse to produce on grounds of legal professional privilege in proceedings in the High Court.

(5)   A disclosure order does not confer the right to require a person to produce excluded material.

(6)   A disclosure order has effect in spite of any restriction on the disclosure of information (however imposed).

(7)   The Director may take copies of any documents produced in compliance with a requirement to produce them which is imposed under a disclosure order.

(8)   Documents so produced may be retained for so long as it is necessary to retain them (as opposed to a copy of them) in connection with the investigation for the purposes of which the order was made.

(9)   But if the Director has reasonable grounds for believing that—
    (a)   the documents may need to be produced for the purposes of any legal proceedings, and
    (b)   they might otherwise be unavailable for those purposes,

they may be retained until the proceedings are concluded.

Definitions   For "the Director", see s 1(2); for "disclosure order", see ss 357(4), 416(2), (9); for "document", see ss 379, 416(2), (9); for "excluded material", see s 379.
References   See para 9.35.

---

362 Supplementary

(1)   An application for a disclosure order may be made ex parte to a judge in chambers.

(2)   Rules of court may make provision as to the practice and procedure to be followed in connection with proceedings relating to disclosure orders.

(3)   An application to discharge or vary a disclosure order may be made to the court by—
    (a)   the Director;
    (b)   any person affected by the order.

(4)   The court—
    (a)   may discharge the order;
    (b)   may vary the order.

(5)   Subsections (2) to (4) do not apply to orders made in England and Wales for the purposes of a civil recovery investigation.

Definitions   For "civil recovery investigation", see ss 341(2), (3), 416(1), (9); for "the court" in relation to an order for the purposes of a civil recovery investigation, see s 344(b); for "the court" in relation to an order for the purposes of a confiscation investigation or a money laundering investigation, see s 344(a); for "the Director", see s 1(2); for "disclosure order", see ss 357(4), 416(2), (9); for "judge" in relation to an application for the purposes of a civil recovery investigation, see s 343(1), (3); for "judge" in relation to an application for the purposes of a confiscation investigation or a money laundering investigation, see s 343(1), (2).
References   See paras 9.36, 9.37.

Customer information orders

363 Customer information orders

(1)   A judge may, on an application made to him by an appropriate officer, make a customer information order if he is satisfied that each of the requirements for the making of the order is fulfilled.

(2)   The application for a customer information order must state that—
    (a)   a person specified in the application is subject to a confiscation investigation or a money laundering investigation, or
    (b)   property specified in the application is subject to a civil recovery investigation and a person specified in the application appears to hold the property.

(3)   The application must also state that—
    (a)   the order is sought for the purposes of the investigation;

(b) the order is sought against the financial institution or financial institutions specified in the application.

(4) An application for a customer information order may specify—
    (a) all financial institutions,
    (b) a particular description, or particular descriptions, of financial institutions, or
    (c) a particular financial institution or particular financial institutions.

(5) A customer information order is an order that a financial institution covered by the application for the order must, on being required to do so by notice in writing given by an appropriate officer, provide any such customer information as it has relating to the person specified in the application.

(6) A financial institution which is required to provide information under a customer information order must provide the information to an appropriate officer in such manner, and at or by such time, as an appropriate officer requires.

(7) If a financial institution on which a requirement is imposed by a notice given under a customer information order requires the production of evidence of authority to give the notice, it is not bound to comply with the requirement unless evidence of the authority has been produced to it.

Definitions For "appropriate officer" in relation to a civil recovery investigation, see ss 378(3), 416(2), (9); for "appropriate officers" in relation to a confiscation investigation, see ss 378(1), 416(2), (9); for "appropriate officers" in relation to a money laundering investigation, see ss 378(4), (7), 416(2), (9); for "civil recovery investigation", see ss 341(2), (3), 416(1), (9); for "confiscation investigation", see ss 341(1), 416(1), (9); for "customer information", see ss 364, 416(2), (9); for "financial institution", see s 416(4), (5), (9); for "judge" in relation to an application for the purposes of a civil recovery investigation, see s 343(1), (3); for "judge" in relation to an application for the purposes of a confiscation investigation or a money laundering investigation, see s 343(1), (2); for "money laundering investigation", see ss 341(4), 416(1), (9); for "notice in writing", see s 416(8), (9); for "property", see ss 414(1), 416(9).
References See para 9.38.

364 Meaning of customer information

(1) "Customer information", in relation to a person and a financial institution, is information whether the person holds, or has held, an account or accounts at the financial institution (whether solely or jointly with another) and (if so) information as to—
    (a) the matters specified in subsection (2) if the person is an individual;
    (b) the matters specified in subsection (3) if the person is a company or limited liability partnership or a similar body incorporated or otherwise established outside the United Kingdom.

(2) The matters referred to in subsection (1)(a) are—
    (a) the account number or numbers;
    (b) the person's full name;
    (c) his date of birth;
    (d) his most recent address and any previous addresses;
    (e) the date or dates on which he began to hold the account or accounts and, if he has ceased to hold the account or any of the accounts, the date or dates on which he did so;
    (f) such evidence of his identity as was obtained by the financial institution under or for the purposes of any legislation relating to money laundering;

     (g)   the full name, date of birth and most recent address, and any previous addresses, of any person who holds, or has held, an account at the financial institution jointly with him;

     (h)   the account number or numbers of any other account or accounts held at the financial institution to which he is a signatory and details of the person holding the other account or accounts.

(3)   The matters referred to in subsection (1)(b) are—

     (a)   the account number or numbers;

     (b)   the person's full name;

     (c)   a description of any business which the person carries on;

     (d)   the country or territory in which it is incorporated or otherwise established and any number allocated to it under the Companies Act 1985 (c 6) or the Companies (Northern Ireland) Order 1986 (SI 1986/ 1032 (NI 6)) or corresponding legislation of any country or territory outside the United Kingdom;

     (e)   any number assigned to it for the purposes of value added tax in the United Kingdom;

     (f)   its registered office, and any previous registered offices, under the Companies Act 1985 or the Companies (Northern Ireland) Order 1986 (SI 1986/1032 (NI 6)) or anything similar under corresponding legislation of any country or territory outside the United Kingdom;

     (g)   its registered office, and any previous registered offices, under the Limited Liability Partnerships Act 2000 (c 12) or anything similar under corresponding legislation of any country or territory outside Great Britain;

     (h)   the date or dates on which it began to hold the account or accounts and, if it has ceased to hold the account or any of the accounts, the date or dates on which it did so;

     (i)   such evidence of its identity as was obtained by the financial institution under or for the purposes of any legislation relating to money laundering;

     (j)   the full name, date of birth and most recent address and any previous addresses of any person who is a signatory to the account or any of the accounts.

(4)   The Secretary of State may by order provide for information of a description specified in the order—

     (a)   to be customer information, or

     (b)   no longer to be customer information.

(5)   Money laundering is an act which—

     (a)   constitutes an offence under section 327, 328 or 329 of this Act or section 18 of the Terrorism Act 2000 (c 11), or

     (b)   would constitute an offence specified in paragraph (a) if done in the United Kingdom.

Definitions   For "financial institution", see s 416(4), (5), (9).
References   See para 9.39.

---

365 Requirements for making of customer information order

(1)   These are the requirements for the making of a customer information order.

(2)   In the case of a confiscation investigation, there must be reasonable grounds for suspecting that the person specified in the application for the order has benefited from his criminal conduct.

(3)   In the case of a civil recovery investigation, there must be reasonable grounds for suspecting that—
  (a)   the property specified in the application for the order is recoverable property or associated property;
  (b)   the person specified in the application holds all or some of the property.

(4)   In the case of a money laundering investigation, there must be reasonable grounds for suspecting that the person specified in the application for the order has committed a money laundering offence.

(5)   In the case of any investigation, there must be reasonable grounds for believing that customer information which may be provided in compliance with the order is likely to be of substantial value (whether or not by itself) to the investigation for the purposes of which the order is sought.

(6)   In the case of any investigation, there must be reasonable grounds for believing that it is in the public interest for the customer information to be provided, having regard to the benefit likely to accrue to the investigation if the information is obtained.

Definitions   For "associated property", see ss 245, 414(2), 416(9); for "benefits from conduct", see ss 413(2), (4), (5), 416(9); for "civil recovery investigation", see ss 341(2), (3), 416(1), (9); for "confiscation investigation", see ss 341(1), 416(1), (9); for "criminal conduct", see ss 413(1), (5), 416(9); for "customer information", see ss 364, 416(2), (9); for "customer information order", see ss 363(5), 416(2), (9); for "money laundering investigation", see ss 341(4), 416(1), (9); for "money laundering offence", see ss 415, 416(9); for "property", see ss 414(1), 416(9); for "recoverable property", see ss 316(1), 414(2), 416(9).
References   See para 9.40.

366 Offences

(1)   A financial institution commits an offence if without reasonable excuse it fails to comply with a requirement imposed on it under a customer information order.

(2)   A financial institution guilty of an offence under subsection (1) is liable on summary conviction to a fine not exceeding level 5 on the standard scale.

(3)   A financial institution commits an offence if, in purported compliance with a customer information order, it—
  (a)   makes a statement which it knows to be false or misleading in a material particular, or
  (b)   recklessly makes a statement which is false or misleading in a material particular.

(4)   A financial institution guilty of an offence under subsection (3) is liable—
  (a)   on summary conviction, to a fine not exceeding the statutory maximum, or
  (b)   on conviction on indictment, to a fine.

Definitions   For "customer information order", see ss 363(5), 416(2), (9); for "financial institution", see s 416(4), (5), (9).
References   See para 9.41.

367 Statements

(1)   A statement made by a financial institution in response to a customer information order may not be used in evidence against it in criminal proceedings.

(2)   But subsection (1) does not apply—
    (a)   in the case of proceedings under Part 2 or 4,
    (b)   on a prosecution for an offence under section 366(1) or (3), or
    (c)   on a prosecution for some other offence where, in giving evidence, the financial institution makes a statement inconsistent with the statement mentioned in subsection (1).

(3)   A statement may not be used by virtue of subsection (2)(c) against a financial institution unless—
    (a)   evidence relating to it is adduced, or
    (b)   a question relating to it is asked,
by or on behalf of the financial institution in the proceedings arising out of the prosecution.

Definitions   For "customer information order", see ss 363(5), 416(2), (9); for "financial institution", see s 416(4), (5), (9).
References   See para 9.42.

368 Disclosure of information

A customer information order has effect in spite of any restriction on the disclosure of information (however imposed).

Definitions   For "customer information order", see ss 363(5), 416(2), (9).
References   See para 9.43.

369 Supplementary

(1)   An application for a customer information order may be made ex parte to a judge in chambers.

(2)   Rules of court may make provision as to the practice and procedure to be followed in connection with proceedings relating to customer information orders.

(3)   An application to discharge or vary a customer information order may be made to the court by—
    (a)   the person who applied for the order;
    (b)   any person affected by the order.

(4)   The court—
    (a)   may discharge the order;
    (b)   may vary the order.

(5)   If an accredited financial investigator, a constable or a customs officer applies for a customer information order, an application to discharge or vary the order need not be by the same accredited financial investigator, constable or customs officer.

(6)   References to a person who applied for a customer information order must be construed accordingly.

(7)   An accredited financial investigator, a constable or a customs officer may not make an application for a customer information order or an application to vary such an order unless he is a senior appropriate officer or he is authorised to do so by a senior appropriate officer.

(8)   Subsections (2) to (6) do not apply to orders made in England and Wales for the purposes of a civil recovery investigation.

Definitions   For "accredited financial investigator", see s 3(5); for "civil recovery investigation", see ss 341(2), (3), 416(1), (9); for "the court" in relation to an order for the purposes of a civil recovery investigation, see s 344(b); for "the court" in relation to an order for the purposes of a confiscation investigation or a money laundering investigation, see s 344(a); for "customer information order", see ss 363(5), 416(2), (9); for "customs officer", see s 454; for "judge" in relation to an application for the purposes of a civil recovery investigation, see s 343(1), (3); for "judge" in relation to an application for the purposes of a confiscation investigation or a money laundering investigation, see s 343(1), (2); for "senior appropriate officer" in relation to a civil recovery investigation, see ss 378(3), 416(2), (9); for "senior appropriate officers" in relation to a confiscation investigation, see ss 378(2), 416(2), (9); for "senior appropriate officers" in relation to a money laundering investigation, see ss 378(6), (7), 416(2), (9).
References   See paras 9.44–9.48.

Account monitoring orders

370 Account monitoring orders

(1)   A judge may, on an application made to him by an appropriate officer, make an account monitoring order if he is satisfied that each of the requirements for the making of the order is fulfilled.

(2)   The application for an account monitoring order must state that—
- (a)   a person specified in the application is subject to a confiscation investigation or a money laundering investigation, or
- (b)   property specified in the application is subject to a civil recovery investigation and a person specified in the application appears to hold the property.

(3)   The application must also state that—
- (a)   the order is sought for the purposes of the investigation;
- (b)   the order is sought against the financial institution specified in the application in relation to account information of the description so specified.

(4)   Account information is information relating to an account or accounts held at the financial institution specified in the application by the person so specified (whether solely or jointly with another).

(5)   The application for an account monitoring order may specify information relating to—
- (a)   all accounts held by the person specified in the application for the order at the financial institution so specified,

(b)   a particular description, or particular descriptions, of accounts so held, or

(c)   a particular account, or particular accounts, so held.

(6)   An account monitoring order is an order that the financial institution specified in the application for the order must, for the period stated in the order, provide account information of the description specified in the order to an appropriate officer in the manner, and at or by the time or times, stated in the order.

(7)   The period stated in an account monitoring order must not exceed the period of 90 days beginning with the day on which the order is made.

Definitions   For "appropriate officer" in relation to a civil recovery investigation, see ss 378(3), 416(2), (9); for "appropriate officers" in relation to a confiscation investigation, see ss 378(1), 416(2), (9); for "appropriate officers" in relation to a money laundering investigation, see ss 378(4), (7), 416(2), (9); for "civil recovery investigation", see ss 341(2), (3), 416(1), (9); for "confiscation investigation", see ss 341(1), 416(1), (9); for "financial institution", see s 416(4), (5), (9); for "judge" in relation to an application for the purposes of a civil recovery investigation, see s 343(1), (3); for "judge" in relation to an application for the purposes of a confiscation investigation or a money laundering investigation, see s 343(1), (2); for "money laundering investigation", see ss 341(4), 416(1), (9); for "property", see ss 414(1), 416(9).
References   See paras 9.49–9.51.

371 Requirements for making of account monitoring order

(1)   These are the requirements for the making of an account monitoring order.

(2)   In the case of a confiscation investigation, there must be reasonable grounds for suspecting that the person specified in the application for the order has benefited from his criminal conduct.

(3)   In the case of a civil recovery investigation, there must be reasonable grounds for suspecting that—

(a)   the property specified in the application for the order is recoverable property or associated property;

(b)   the person specified in the application holds all or some of the property.

(4)   In the case of a money laundering investigation, there must be reasonable grounds for suspecting that the person specified in the application for the order has committed a money laundering offence.

(5)   In the case of any investigation, there must be reasonable grounds for believing that account information which may be provided in compliance with the order is likely to be of substantial value (whether or not by itself) to the investigation for the purposes of which the order is sought.

(6)   In the case of any investigation, there must be reasonable grounds for believing that it is in the public interest for the account information to be provided, having regard to the benefit likely to accrue to the investigation if the information is obtained.

Definitions   For "account information", see ss 370(4), 416(2), (9); for "account monitoring order", see ss 370(6), 416(2), (9); for "associated property", see ss 245, 414(2), 416(9); for "benefits from conduct", see ss 413(2), (4), (5), 416(9); for "civil recovery investigation", see ss 341(2), (3), 416(1), (9); for "confiscation investigation", see ss 341(1), 416(1), (9); for "criminal conduct", see ss 413(1), (5), 416(9); for "money laundering investigation", see ss 341(4), 416(1), (9); for "money laundering offence", see ss 415, 416(9); for "property", see ss 414(1), 416(9); for "recoverable property", see ss 316(1), 414(2), 416(9).
References   See para 9.52.

372 Statements

(1)   A statement made by a financial institution in response to an account monitoring order may not be used in evidence against it in criminal proceedings.

(2)   But subsection (1) does not apply—
    (a)   in the case of proceedings under Part 2 or 4,
    (b)   in the case of proceedings for contempt of court, or
    (c)   on a prosecution for an offence where, in giving evidence, the financial institution makes a statement inconsistent with the statement mentioned in subsection (1).

(3)   A statement may not be used by virtue of subsection (2)(c) against a financial institution unless—
    (a)   evidence relating to it is adduced, or
    (b)   a question relating to it is asked,

by or on behalf of the financial institution in the proceedings arising out of the prosecution.

Definitions   For "account monitoring order", see ss 370(6), 416(2), (9); for "financial institution", see s 416(4), (5), (9).
References   See para 9.53.

373 Applications

An application for an account monitoring order may be made ex parte to a judge in chambers.

Definitions   For "account monitoring order", see ss 370(6), 416(2), (9); for "judge" in relation to an application for the purposes of a civil recovery investigation, see s 343(1), (3); for "judge" in relation to an application for the purposes of a confiscation investigation or a money laundering investigation, see s 343(1), (2).
References   See para 9.54.

374 Disclosure of information

An account monitoring order has effect in spite of any restriction on the disclosure of information (however imposed).

Definitions   For "account monitoring order", see ss 370(6), 416(2), (9).
References   See para 9.55.

375 Supplementary

(1)   Rules of court may make provision as to the practice and procedure to be followed in connection with proceedings relating to account monitoring orders.

(2)   An application to discharge or vary an account monitoring order may be made to the court by—
    (a)   the person who applied for the order;
    (b)   any person affected by the order.

(3)   The court—
    (a)   may discharge the order;
    (b)   may vary the order.

(4)   If an accredited financial investigator, a constable or a customs officer applies for an account monitoring order, an application to discharge or vary the order need not be by the same accredited financial investigator, constable or customs officer.

(5)   References to a person who applied for an account monitoring order must be construed accordingly.

(6)   Account monitoring orders have effect as if they were orders of the court.

(7)   This section does not apply to orders made in England and Wales for the purposes of a civil recovery investigation.

Definitions   For "account monitoring order", see ss 370(6), 416(2), (9); for "accredited financial investigator", see s 3(5); for "civil recovery investigation", see ss 341(2), (3), 416(1), (9); for "the court" in relation to an order for the purposes of a civil recovery investigation, see s 344(b); for "the court" in relation to an order for the purposes of a confiscation investigation or a money laundering investigation, see s 344(a); for "customs officer", see s 454.
References   See para 9.56, 9.57

Evidence overseas

376 Evidence overseas

(1)   This section applies if the Director is carrying out a confiscation investigation.

(2)   A judge on the application of the Director or a person subject to the investigation may issue a letter of request if he thinks that there is evidence in a country or territory outside the United Kingdom—
  (a)   that such a person has benefited from his criminal conduct, or
  (b)   of the extent or whereabouts of that person's benefit from his criminal conduct.

(3)   The Director may issue a letter of request if he thinks that there is evidence in a country or territory outside the United Kingdom—
  (a)   that a person subject to the investigation has benefited from his criminal conduct, or
  (b)   of the extent or whereabouts of that person's benefit from his criminal conduct.

(4)   A letter of request is a letter requesting assistance in obtaining outside the United Kingdom such evidence as is specified in the letter for use in the investigation.

(5)   The person issuing a letter of request must send it to the Secretary of State.

(6)   If the Secretary of State believes it is appropriate to do so he may forward a letter received under subsection (5)—
  (a)   to a court or tribunal which is specified in the letter and which exercises jurisdiction in the place where the evidence is to be obtained, or
  (b)   to an authority recognised by the government of the country or territory concerned as the appropriate authority for receiving letters of request.

(7)   But in a case of urgency the person issuing the letter of request may send it directly to the court or tribunal mentioned in subsection (6)(a).

(8)   Evidence obtained in pursuance of a letter of request must not be used—

(a)   by any person other than the Director or a person subject to the investigation;

(b)   for any purpose other than that for which it is obtained.

(9)   Subsection (8) does not apply if the authority mentioned in subsection (6)(b) consents to the use.

(10) Evidence includes documents and other articles.

(11) Rules of court may make provision as to the practice and procedure to be followed in connection with proceedings relating to the issue of letters of request by a judge under this section.

Definitions   For "benefits from conduct", see ss 413(2), (4), (5), 416(9); for "confiscation investigation", see ss 341(1), 416(1), (9); for "criminal conduct", see ss 413(1), (5), 416(9); for "the Director", see s 1(2); for "document", see ss 379, 416(2), (9); for "judge" in relation to an application for the purposes of a confiscation investigation or a money laundering investigation, see s 343(1), (2).
References   See para 9.58.

Code of practice

377 Code of practice

(1)   The Secretary of State must prepare a code of practice as to the exercise by all of the following of functions they have under this Chapter—

(a)   the Director;

(b)   members of the staff of the Agency;

(c)   accredited financial investigators;

(d)   constables;

(e)   customs officers.

(2)   After preparing a draft of the code the Secretary of State—

(a)   must publish the draft;

(b)   must consider any representations made to him about the draft;

(c)   may amend the draft accordingly.

(3)   After the Secretary of State has proceeded under subsection (2) he must lay the code before Parliament.

(4)   When he has done so the Secretary of State may bring the code into operation on such day as he may appoint by order.

(5)   A person specified in subsection (1)(a) to (e) must comply with a code of practice which is in operation under this section in the exercise of any function he has under this Chapter.

(6)   If such a person fails to comply with any provision of such a code of practice he is not by reason only of that failure liable in any criminal or civil proceedings.

(7)   But the code of practice is admissible in evidence in such proceedings and a court may take account of any failure to comply with its provisions in determining any question in the proceedings.

(8)   The Secretary of State may from time to time revise a code previously brought into operation under this section; and the preceding provisions of this section apply to a revised code as they apply to the code as first prepared.

(9)   The following provisions do not apply to an appropriate officer in the exercise of any function he has under this Chapter—

(a)   section 67(9) of the Police and Criminal Evidence Act 1984 (c 60) (application of codes of practice under that Act to persons other than police officers);

(b)   Article 66(8) of the Police and Criminal Evidence (Northern Ireland) Order 1989 (SI 1989/1341 (NI 12)) (which makes similar provision for Northern Ireland).

Definitions   For "accredited financial investigator", see s 3(5); for "the Agency", see s 1(1); for "customs officer", see s 454; for "the Director", see s 1(2).
References   See para 9.59.

Interpretation

378 Officers

(1)   In relation to a confiscation investigation these are appropriate officers—

(a)   the Director;

(b)   an accredited financial investigator;

(c)   a constable;

(d)   a customs officer.

(2)   In relation to a confiscation investigation these are senior appropriate officers—

(a)   the Director;

(b)   a police officer who is not below the rank of superintendent;

(c)   a customs officer who is not below such grade as is designated by the Commissioners of Customs and Excise as equivalent to that rank;

(d)   an accredited financial investigator who falls within a description specified in an order made for the purposes of this paragraph by the Secretary of State under section 453.

(3)   In relation to a civil recovery investigation the Director (and only the Director) is—

(a)   an appropriate officer;

(b)   a senior appropriate officer.

(4)   In relation to a money laundering investigation these are appropriate officers—

(a)   an accredited financial investigator;

(b)   a constable;

(c)   a customs officer.

(5)   For the purposes of section 342, in relation to a money laundering investigation a person authorised for the purposes of money laundering investigations by the Director General of the National Criminal Intelligence Service is also an appropriate officer.

(6)   In relation to a money laundering investigation these are senior appropriate officers—

(a)   a police officer who is not below the rank of superintendent;

(b)   a customs officer who is not below such grade as is designated by the Commissioners of Customs and Excise as equivalent to that rank;

(c)   an accredited financial investigator who falls within a description specified in an order made for the purposes of this paragraph by the Secretary of State under section 453.

(7)   But a person is not an appropriate officer or a senior appropriate officer in relation to a money laundering investigation if he is—

(a)   a member of the staff of the Agency, or

(b)   a person providing services under arrangements made by the Director.

Definitions   For "accredited financial investigator", see s 3(5); for "the Agency", see s 1(1); for "civil recovery investigation", see ss 341(2), (3), 416(1), (9); for "confiscation investigation", see ss 341(1), 416(1), (9); for "customs officer", see s 454; for "the Director", see s 1(2); for "money laundering investigation", see ss 341(4), 416(1), (9).
References   See paras 9.60, 9.61.

379 Miscellaneous

"Document", "excluded material" and "premises" have the same meanings as in the Police and Criminal Evidence Act 1984 (c 60) or (in relation to Northern Ireland) the Police and Criminal Evidence (Northern Ireland) Order 1989 (SI 1989/1341 (NI 12)).

References   See para 9.62.

CHAPTER 3
SCOTLAND

Production orders

380 Production orders

(1)   The sheriff may, on an application made to him by the appropriate person, make a production order if he is satisfied that each of the requirements for the making of the order is fulfilled.

(2)   In making a production order in relation to property subject to a civil recovery investigation, the sheriff shall act in the exercise of his civil jurisdiction.

(3)   The application for a production order must state that—

(a)   a person specified in the application is subject to a confiscation investigation or a money laundering investigation, or

(b)   property specified in the application is subject to a civil recovery investigation.

(4)   The application must also state that—

(a)   the order is sought for the purposes of the investigation;

(b)   the order is sought in relation to material, or material of a description, specified in the application;

(c)   a person specified in the application appears to be in possession or control of the material.

(5) A production order is an order either—

    (a) requiring the person the application for the order specifies as appearing to be in possession or control of material to produce it to a proper person for him to take away, or

    (b) requiring that person to give a proper person access to the material,

within the period stated in the order.

(6) The period stated in a production order must be a period of seven days beginning with the day on which the order is made, unless it appears to the sheriff that a longer or shorter period would be appropriate in the particular circumstances.

Definitions   For "appropriate person", see s 412; for "civil recovery investigation", see ss 341(2), (3), 416(1), (9); for "confiscation investigation", see ss 341(1), 416(1), (9); for "money laundering investigation", see ss 341(4), 416(1), (9); for "proper person", see ss 412, 416(3), (9); for "property", see ss 414(1), 416(9).
References   See para 9.63.

---

381 Requirements for making of production order

(1) These are the requirements for the making of a production order.

(2) There must be reasonable grounds for suspecting that—

    (a) in the case of a confiscation investigation, the person the application for the order specifies as being subject to the investigation has benefited from his criminal conduct;

    (b) in the case of a civil recovery investigation, the property the application for the order specifies as being subject to the investigation is recoverable property or associated property;

    (c) in the case of a money laundering investigation, the person the application for the order specifies as being subject to the investigation has committed a money laundering offence.

(3) There must be reasonable grounds for believing that the person the application specifies as appearing to be in possession or control of the material so specified is in possession or control of it.

(4) There must be reasonable grounds for believing that the material is likely to be of substantial value (whether or not by itself) to the investigation for the purposes of which the order is sought.

(5) There must be reasonable grounds for believing that it is in the public interest for the material to be produced or for access to it to be given, having regard to—

    (a) the benefit likely to accrue to the investigation if the material is obtained,

    (b) the circumstances under which the person the application specifies as appearing to be in possession or control of the material holds it.

Definitions   For "associated property", see ss 245, 414(2), 416(9); for "benefits from conduct", see ss 413(2), (4), (5), 416(9); for "civil recovery investigation", see ss 341(2), (3), 416(1), (9); for "confiscation investigation", see ss 341(1), 416(1), (9); for "criminal conduct", see ss 413(1), (5), 416(9); for "money laundering investigation", see ss 341(4), 416(1), (9); for "money laundering offence", see ss 415, 416(9); for "production order", see ss 380(5), 416(3), (9); for "property", see ss 414(1), 416(9); for "recoverable property", see ss 316(1), 414(2), 416(9).
References   See para 9.63.

382 Order to grant entry

(1)   This section applies if a sheriff makes a production order requiring a person to give a proper person access to material on any premises.

(2)   The sheriff may, on an application made to him by the appropriate person and specifying the premises, make an order to grant entry in relation to the premises.

(3)   An order to grant entry is an order requiring any person who appears to the appropriate person to be entitled to grant entry to the premises to allow a proper person to enter the premises to obtain access to the material.

Definitions   For "appropriate person", see s 412; for "premises", see s 412; for "production order", see ss 380(5), 416(3), (9); for "proper person", see ss 412, 416(3), (9).
References   See para 9.63.

383 Further provisions

(1)   A production order does not require a person to produce, or give access to, any items subject to legal privilege.

(2)   A production order has effect in spite of any restriction on the disclosure of information (however imposed).

(3)   A proper person may take copies of any material which is produced, or to which access is given, in compliance with a production order.

(4)   Material produced in compliance with a production order may be retained for so long as it is necessary to retain it (as opposed to copies of it) in connection with the investigation for the purposes of which the order was made.

(5)   But if a proper person has reasonable grounds for believing that—
    (a)   the material may need to be produced for the purposes of any legal proceedings, and
    (b)   it might otherwise be unavailable for those purposes,
it may be retained until the proceedings are concluded.

Definitions   For "legal privilege", see s 412; for "production order", see ss 380(5), 416(3), (9); for "proper person", see ss 412, 416(3), (9).
References   See para 9.63.

384 Computer information

(1)   This section applies if any of the material specified in an application for a production order consists of information contained in a computer.

(2)   If the order is an order requiring a person to produce the material to a proper person for him to take away, it has effect as an order to produce the material in a form in which it can be taken away by him and in which it is visible and legible.

(3)   If the order is an order requiring a person to give a proper person access to the material, it has effect as an order to give him access to the material in a form in which it is visible and legible.

Definitions   For "production order", see ss 380(5), 416(3), (9); for "proper person", see ss 412, 416(3), (9).
References   See para 9.63.

385 Government departments

(1)   A production order may be made in relation to material in the possession or control of an authorised government department.

(2)   An order so made may require any officer of the department (whether named in the order or not) who may for the time being be in possession or control of the material to comply with it.

(3)   If an order contains such a requirement—
   (a)   the person on whom it is served must take all reasonable steps to bring it to the attention of the officer concerned;
   (b)   any other officer of the department who is in receipt of the order must also take all reasonable steps to bring it to the attention of the officer concerned.

(4)   If the order is not brought to the attention of the officer concerned within the period stated in the order (in pursuance of section 380(5)) the person on whom it is served must report the reasons for the failure to—
   (a)   the sheriff in the case of an order made for the purposes of a confiscation investigation or a money laundering investigation;
   (b)   the sheriff exercising a civil jurisdiction in the case of an order made for the purposes of a civil recovery investigation.

(5)   In this section, "authorised government department" includes a government department which is an authorised department for the purposes of the Crown Proceedings Act 1947 (c 44) and the Scottish Administration.

Definitions   For "civil recovery investigation", see ss 341(2), (3), 416(1), (9); for "confiscation investigation", see ss 341(1), 416(1), (9); for "money laundering investigation", see ss 341(4), 416(1), (9); for "production order", see ss 380(5), 416(3), (9).
References   See para 9.63.

386 Supplementary

(1)   An application for a production order or an order to grant entry may be made ex parte to a sheriff in chambers.

(2)   Provision may be made by rules of court as to the discharge and variation of production orders and orders to grant entry.

(3)   Rules of court under subsection (2) relating to production orders and orders to grant entry—
   (a)   made in a confiscation investigation or a money laundering investigation shall, without prejudice to section 305 of the Criminal Procedure (Scotland) Act 1995 (c 46) be made by act of adjournal;
   (b)   made in a civil recovery investigation shall, without prejudice to section 32 of the Sheriff Courts (Scotland) Act 1971 (c 58) be made by act of sederunt.

(4)   An application to discharge or vary a production order or an order to grant entry may be made to the sheriff by—
   (a)   the person who applied for the order;
   (b)   any person affected by the order.

(5) The sheriff may—
    (a) discharge the order;
    (b) vary the order.

Definitions For "civil recovery investigation", see ss 341(2), (3), 416(1), (9); for "confiscation investigation", see ss 341(1), 416(1), (9); for "money laundering investigation", see ss 341(4), 416(1), (9); for "production order", see ss 380(5), 416(3), (9).
References See para 9.63.

Search warrants

387 Search warrants

(1) The sheriff may, on an application made to him by the appropriate person, issue a search warrant if he is satisfied that either of the requirements for the issuing of the warrant is fulfilled.

(2) In issuing a search warrant in relation to property subject to a civil recovery investigation, the sheriff shall act in the exercise of his civil jurisdiction.

(3) The application for a search warrant must state that—
    (a) a person specified in the application is subject to a confiscation investigation or a money laundering investigation, or
    (b) property specified in the application is subject to a civil recovery investigation.

(4) A search warrant is a warrant authorising a proper person—
    (a) to enter and search the premises specified in the application for the warrant, and
    (b) to seize and retain any material specified in the warrant which is found there and which is likely to be of substantial value (whether or not by itself) to the investigation for the purposes of which the application is made.

(5) The requirements for the issue of a search warrant are—
    (a) that a production order made in relation to material has not been complied with and there are reasonable grounds for believing that the material is on the premises specified in the application for the warrant, or
    (b) that section 388 is satisfied in relation to the warrant.

(6) An application for a search warrant may be made ex parte to a sheriff in chambers.

Definitions For "appropriate person", see s 412; for "civil recovery investigation", see ss 341(2), (3), 416(1), (9); for "confiscation investigation", see ss 341(1), 416(1), (9); for "money laundering investigation", see s 341(4), 416(1), (9); for "production order", see ss 380(5), 416(3), (9); for "proper person", see ss 412, 416(3), (9); for "property", see ss 414(1), 416(9).
References See para 9.64.

---

388 Requirements where production order not available

(1) This section is satisfied in relation to a search warrant if—
    (a) subsection (2) applies, and
    (b) either the first or the second set of conditions is complied with.

(2) This subsection applies if there are reasonable grounds for suspecting that—
 (a) in the case of a confiscation investigation, the person specified in the application for the warrant has benefited from his criminal conduct;
 (b) in the case of a civil recovery investigation, the property specified in the application for the warrant is recoverable property or associated property;
 (c) in the case of a money laundering investigation, the person specified in the application for the warrant has committed a money laundering offence.

(3) The first set of conditions is that there are reasonable grounds for believing that—
 (a) any material on the premises specified in the application for the warrant is likely to be of substantial value (whether or not by itself) to the investigation for the purposes of which the warrant is sought,
 (b) it is in the public interest for the material to be obtained, having regard to the benefit likely to accrue to the investigation if the material is obtained, and
 (c) it would not be appropriate to make a production order for any one or more of the reasons in subsection (4).

(4) The reasons are—
 (a) that it is not practicable to communicate with any person against whom the production order could be made;
 (b) that it is not practicable to communicate with any person who would be required to comply with an order to grant access to the material or to grant entry to the premises on which the material is situated;
 (c) that the investigation might be seriously prejudiced unless a proper person is able to secure immediate access to the material.

(5) The second set of conditions is that—
 (a) there are reasonable grounds for believing that there is material on the premises specified in the application for the warrant and that the material falls within subsection (6), (7) or (8),
 (b) there are reasonable grounds for believing that it is in the public interest for the material to be obtained, having regard to the benefit likely to accrue to the investigation if the material is obtained, and
 (c) any one or more of the requirements in subsection (9) is met.

(6) In the case of a confiscation investigation, material falls within this subsection if it cannot be identified at the time of the application but it—
 (a) relates to the person specified in the application, the question whether he has benefited from his criminal conduct or any question as to the extent or whereabouts of his benefit from his criminal conduct, and
 (b) is likely to be of substantial value (whether or not by itself) to the investigation for the purposes of which the warrant is sought.

(7) In the case of a civil recovery investigation, material falls within this subsection if it cannot be identified at the time of the application but it—
 (a) relates to the property specified in the application, the question whether it is recoverable property or associated property, the question as to who holds any such property, any question as to whether the person who appears to hold any such property holds

other property which is recoverable property, or any question as to the extent or whereabouts of any property mentioned in this paragraph, and

(b) is likely to be of substantial value (whether or not by itself) to the investigation for the purposes of which the warrant is sought.

(8) In the case of a money laundering investigation, material falls within this subsection if it cannot be identified at the time of the application but it—

(a) relates to the person specified in the application or the question whether he has committed a money laundering offence, and

(b) is likely to be of substantial value (whether or not by itself) to the investigation for the purposes of which the warrant is sought.

(9) The requirements are—

(a) that it is not practicable to communicate with any person entitled to grant entry to the premises;

(b) that entry to the premises will not be granted unless a warrant is produced;

(c) that the investigation might be seriously prejudiced unless a proper person arriving at the premises is able to secure immediate entry to them.

Definitions For "associated property", see ss 245, 414(2), 416(9); for "benefits from conduct", see ss 413(2), (4), (5), 416(9); for "civil recovery investigation", see ss 341(2), (3), 416(1), (9); for "confiscation investigation", see ss 341(1), 416(1), (9); for "criminal conduct", see ss 413(1), (5), 416(9); for "money laundering investigation", see ss 341(4), 416(1), (9); for "money laundering offence", see ss 415, 416(9); for "premises", see s 412; for "production order", see s 380(5), 416(3), (9); for "proper person", see ss 412, 416(3), (9); for "property", see ss 414(1), 416(9); for "recoverable property", see ss 316(1), 414(2), 416(9); for "search warrant", see ss 387(4), 416(3), (9).
References See para 9.64.

389 Further provisions: general

A search warrant does not confer the right to seize any items subject to legal privilege.

Definitions For "legal privilege", see s 412; for "search warrant", see ss 387(4), 416(3), (9).
References See para 9.64.

390 Further provisions: confiscation, civil recovery and money laundering

(1) This section applies to search warrants sought for the purposes of confiscation investigations, civil recovery investigations or money laundering investigations.

(2) A warrant continues in force until the end of the period of one month starting with the day on which it is issued.

(3) A warrant authorises the person executing it to require any information which is held in a computer and is accessible from the premises specified in the application for the warrant, and which the proper person believes relates to any matter relevant to the investigation, to be produced in a form—

(a) in which it can be taken away, and

(b) in which it is visible and legible.

(4) Copies may be taken of any material seized under a warrant.

(5)   A warrant issued in relation to a civil recovery investigation may be issued subject to conditions.

(6)   A warrant issued in relation to a civil recovery investigation may include provision authorising the person executing it to do other things which—
    (a)   are specified in the warrant, and
    (b)   need to be done in order to give effect to it.

(7)   Material seized under a warrant issued in relation to a civil recovery investigation may be retained for so long as it is necessary to retain it (as opposed to copies of it) in connection with the investigation for the purposes of which the warrant was issued.

(8)   But if the Scottish Ministers have reasonable grounds for believing that—
    (a)   the material may need to be produced for the purposes of any legal proceedings, and
    (b)   it might otherwise be unavailable for those purposes,
it may be retained until the proceedings are concluded.

Definitions   For "civil recovery investigation", see ss 341(2), (3), 416(1), (9); for "confiscation investigation", see ss 341(1), 416(1), (9); for "money laundering investigation", see ss 341(4), 416(1), (9); for "premises", see s 412; for "proper person", see ss 412, 416(3), (9); for "search warrant", see ss 387(4), 416(3), (9).
References   See para 9.64.

Disclosure orders

391 Disclosure orders

(1)   The High Court of Justiciary, on an application made to it by the Lord Advocate in relation to confiscation investigations, or the Court of Session, on an application made to it by the Scottish Ministers in relation to civil recovery investigations, may make a disclosure order if it is satisfied that each of the requirements for the making of the order is fulfilled.

(2)   No application for a disclosure order may be made in relation to a money laundering investigation.

(3)   The application for a disclosure order must state that—
    (a)   a person specified in the application is subject to a confiscation investigation and the order is sought for the purposes of the investigation, or
    (b)   property specified in the application is subject to a civil recovery investigation and the order is sought for the purposes of the investigation.

(4)   A disclosure order is an order authorising the Lord Advocate or the Scottish Ministers to give to any person the Lord Advocate considers or the Scottish Ministers consider has relevant information, notice in writing requiring him to do, with respect to any matter relevant to the investigation for the purposes of which the order is sought, any or all of the following—
    (a)   answer questions, either at a time specified in the notice or at once, at a place so specified;
    (b)   provide information specified in the notice, by a time and in a manner so specified;

(c)   produce documents, or documents of a description, specified in the notice, either at or by a time so specified or at once, and in a manner so specified.

(5)   Relevant information is information (whether or not contained in a document) which the Lord Advocate considers or the Scottish Ministers consider to be relevant to the investigation.

(6)   A person is not bound to comply with a requirement imposed by a notice given under a disclosure order unless evidence of authority to give the notice is produced to him.

Definitions   For "civil recovery investigation", see ss 341(2), (3), 416(1), (9); for "confiscation investigation", see ss 341(1), 416(1), (9); for "money laundering investigation", see ss 341(4), 416(1), (9); for "notice in writing", see s 416(8), (9); for "property", see ss 414(1), 416(9).
References   See para 9.64.

392 Requirements for making of disclosure order

(1)   These are the requirements for the making of a disclosure order.

(2)   There must be reasonable grounds for suspecting that—
    (a)   in the case of a confiscation investigation, the person specified in the application for the order has benefited from his criminal conduct;
    (b)   in the case of a civil recovery investigation, the property specified in the application for the order is recoverable property or associated property.

(3)   There must be reasonable grounds for believing that information which may be provided in compliance with a requirement imposed under the order is likely to be of substantial value (whether or not by itself) to the investigation for the purposes of which the order is sought.

(4)   There must be reasonable grounds for believing that it is in the public interest for the information to be provided, having regard to the benefit likely to accrue to the investigation if the information is obtained.

Definitions   For "associated property", see ss 245, 414(2), 416(9); for "benefits from conduct", see ss 413(2), (4), (5), 416(9); for "civil recovery investigation", see ss 341(2), (3), 416(1), (9); for "confiscation investigation", see ss 341(1), 416(1), (9); for "criminal conduct", see ss 413(1), (5), 416(9); for "disclosure order", see ss 391(4), 416(3), (9); for "property", see ss 414(1), 416(9); for "recoverable property", see ss 316(1), 414(2), 416(9).
References   See para 9.65.

393 Offences

(1)   A person commits an offence if without reasonable excuse he fails to comply with a requirement imposed on him under a disclosure order.

(2)   A person guilty of an offence under subsection (1) is liable on summary conviction to—
    (a)   imprisonment for a term not exceeding six months,
    (b)   a fine not exceeding level 5 on the standard scale, or
    (c)   both.

(3)   A person commits an offence if, in purported compliance with a requirement imposed on him under a disclosure order, he—

    (a)   makes a statement which he knows to be false or misleading in a material particular, or

    (b)   recklessly makes a statement which is false or misleading in a material particular.

(4)   A person guilty of an offence under subsection (3) is liable—

    (a)   on summary conviction, to imprisonment for a term not exceeding six months or to a fine not exceeding the statutory maximum or to both, or

    (b)   on conviction on indictment, to imprisonment for a term not exceeding two years or to a fine or to both.

Definitions   For "disclosure order", see ss 391(4), 416(3), (9).
References   See para 9.65.

394 Statements

(1)   A statement made by a person in response to a requirement imposed on him under a disclosure order may not be used in evidence against him in criminal proceedings.

(2)   But subsection (1) does not apply—

    (a)   in the case of proceedings under Part 3,

    (b)   on a prosecution for an offence under section 393(1) or (3),

    (c)   on a prosecution for perjury, or

    (d)   on a prosecution for some other offence where, in giving evidence, the person makes a statement inconsistent with the statement mentioned in subsection (1).

(3)   A statement may not be used by virtue of subsection (2)(d) against a person unless—

    (a)   evidence relating to it is adduced, or

    (b)   a question relating to it is asked,

by him or on his behalf in the proceedings arising out of the prosecution.

Definitions   For "disclosure order", see ss 391(4), 416(3), (9).
References   See para 9.65.

395 Further provisions

(1)   A disclosure order does not confer the right to require a person to answer any question, provide any information or produce any document which he would be entitled to refuse to answer, provide or produce on grounds of legal privilege.

(2)   A disclosure order has effect in spite of any restriction on the disclosure of information (however imposed).

(3)   The Lord Advocate and the Scottish Ministers may take copies of any documents produced in compliance with a requirement to produce them which is imposed under a disclosure order.

(4)   Documents so produced may be retained for so long as it is necessary to retain them (as opposed to a copy of them) in connection with the investigation for the purposes of which the order was made.

(5) But if the Lord Advocate has, or the Scottish Ministers have, reasonable grounds for believing that—

    (a) the documents may need to be produced for the purposes of any legal proceedings, and

    (b) they might otherwise be unavailable for those purposes,

they may be retained until the proceedings are concluded.

Definitions For "disclosure order", see ss 391(4), 416(3), (9); for "legal privilege", see s 412.
References See para 9.65.

396 Supplementary

(1) An application for a disclosure order may be made ex parte to—

    (a) in the case of an order made in a confiscation investigation, a judge of the High Court of Justiciary;

    (b) in the case of an order made in a civil recovery investigation, a judge of the Court of Session,

in chambers.

(2) Provision may be made by rules of court as to the discharge and variation of disclosure orders.

(3) Rules of court under subsection (2) relating to disclosure orders—

    (a) made in a confiscation investigation shall, without prejudice to section 305 of the Criminal Procedure (Scotland) Act 1995 (c 46) be made by act of adjournal;

    (b) made in a civil recovery investigation shall, without prejudice to section 5 of the Court of Session Act 1988 (c 36), be made by act of sederunt.

(4) An application to discharge or vary a disclosure order may be made to a judge of the court which made the order by—

    (a) the Lord Advocate or the Scottish Ministers;

    (b) any person affected by the order.

(5) The court may—

    (a) discharge the order;

    (b) vary the order.

Definitions For "civil recovery investigation", see s 341(2), (3), 416(1), (9); for "confiscation investigation", see ss 341(1), 416(1), (9); for "disclosure order", see ss 391(4), 416(3), (9).
References See para 9.65.

Customer information orders

397 Customer information orders

(1) The sheriff may, on an application made to him by the appropriate person, make a customer information order if he is satisfied that each of the requirements for the making of the order is fulfilled.

(2) In making a customer information order in relation to property subject to a civil recovery investigation the sheriff shall act in the exercise of his civil jurisdiction.

(3) The application for a customer information order must state that—
  (a) a person specified in the application is subject to a confiscation investigation or a money laundering investigation, or
  (b) property specified in the application is subject to a civil recovery investigation and a person specified in the application appears to hold the property.

(4) The application must also state that—
  (a) the order is sought for the purposes of the investigation;
  (b) the order is sought against the financial institution or financial institutions specified in the application.

(5) An application for a customer information order may specify—
  (a) all financial institutions,
  (b) a particular description, or particular descriptions, of financial institutions, or
  (c) a particular financial institution or particular financial institutions.

(6) A customer information order is an order that a financial institution covered by the application for the order must, on being required to do so by notice in writing given by the appropriate person, provide any such customer information as it has relating to the person specified in the application.

(7) A financial institution which is required to provide information under a customer information order must provide the information to a proper person in such manner, and at or by such time, as that person requires.

(8) If a financial institution on which a requirement is imposed by a notice given under a customer information order requires the production of evidence of authority to give the notice, it is not bound to comply with the requirement unless evidence of the authority has been produced to it.

Definitions   For "appropriate person", see s 412; for "civil recovery investigation", see ss 341(2), (3), 416(1), (9); for "confiscation investigation", see ss 341(1), 416(1), (9); for "customer information", see ss 398, 416(3), (9); for "financial institution", see s 416(4), (5), (9); for "money laundering investigation", see ss 341(4), 416(1), (9); for "notice in writing", see s 416(8), (9); for "proper person", see ss 412, 416(3), (9); for "property", see ss 414(1), 416(9).
References   See para 9.66.

398 Meaning of customer information

(1) "Customer information", in relation to a person and a financial institution, is information whether the person holds, or has held, an account or accounts at the financial institution (whether solely or jointly with another) and (if so) information as to—
  (a) the matters specified in subsection (2) if the person is an individual;
  (b) the matters specified in subsection (3) if the person is a company or limited liability partnership or a similar body incorporated or otherwise established outside the United Kingdom.

(2) The matters referred to in subsection (1)(a) are—
  (a) the account number or numbers;
  (b) the person's full name;
  (c) his date of birth;
  (d) his most recent address and any previous addresses;

(e) the date or dates on which he began to hold the account or accounts and, if he has ceased to hold the account or any of the accounts, the date or dates on which he did so;

(f) such evidence of his identity as was obtained by the financial institution under or for the purposes of any legislation relating to money laundering;

(g) the full name, date of birth and most recent address, and any previous addresses, of any person who holds, or has held, an account at the financial institution jointly with him;

(h) the account number or numbers of any other account or accounts held at the financial institution to which he is a signatory and details of the person holding the other account or accounts.

(3) The matters referred to in subsection (1)(b) are—

(a) the account number or numbers;

(b) the person's full name;

(c) a description of any business which the person carries on;

(d) the country or territory in which it is incorporated or otherwise established and any number allocated to it under the Companies Act 1985 (c 6) or the Companies (Northern Ireland) Order 1986 (SI 1986/1032 (NI 6)) or corresponding legislation of any country or territory outside the United Kingdom;

(e) any number assigned to it for the purposes of value added tax in the United Kingdom;

(f) its registered office, and any previous registered offices, under the Companies Act 1985 or the Companies (Northern Ireland) Order 1986 (SI 1986/1032 (NI 6)) or anything similar under corresponding legislation of any country or territory outside the United Kingdom;

(g) its registered office, and any previous registered offices, under the Limited Liability Partnerships Act 2000 (c 12) or anything similar under corresponding legislation of any country or territory outside Great Britain;

(h) the date or dates on which it began to hold the account or accounts and, if it has ceased to hold the account or any of the accounts, the date or dates on which it did so;

(i) such evidence of its identity as was obtained by the financial institution under or for the purposes of any legislation relating to money laundering;

(j) the full name, date of birth and most recent address and any previous addresses of any person who is a signatory to the account or any of the accounts.

(4) The Scottish Ministers may by order provide for information of a description specified in the order—

(a) to be customer information, or

(b) no longer to be customer information.

(5) Money laundering is an act which—

(a) constitutes an offence under section 327, 328 or 329 of this Act or section 18 of the Terrorism Act 2000 (c 11), or

(b) would constitute an offence specified in paragraph (a) if done in the United Kingdom.

Definitions   For "financial institution", see s 416(4), (5), (9).
References   See para 9.66.

399 Requirements for making of customer information order

(1)   These are the requirements for the making of a customer information order.

(2)   In the case of a confiscation investigation, there must be reasonable grounds for suspecting that the person specified in the application for the order has benefited from his criminal conduct.

(3)   In the case of a civil recovery investigation, there must be reasonable grounds for suspecting that—
  (a)   the property specified in the application for the order is recoverable property or associated property;
  (b)   the person specified in the application holds all or some of the property.

(4)   In the case of a money laundering investigation, there must be reasonable grounds for suspecting that the person specified in the application for the order has committed a money laundering offence.

(5)   In the case of any investigation, there must be reasonable grounds for believing that customer information which may be provided in compliance with the order is likely to be of substantial value (whether or not by itself) to the investigation for the purposes of which the order is sought.

(6)   In the case of any investigation there must be reasonable grounds for believing that it is in the public interest for the customer information to be provided, having regard to the benefit likely to accrue to the investigation if the information is obtained.

Definitions   For "associated property", see ss 245, 414(2), 416(9); for "benefits from conduct", see ss 413(2), (4), (5), 416(9); for "civil recovery investigation", see ss 341(2), (3), 416(1), (9); for "confiscation investigation", see ss 341(1), 416(1), (9); for "criminal conduct", see ss 413(1), (5), 416(9); for "customer information", see ss 398, 416(3), (9); for "customer information order", see ss 397(6), 416(3), (9); for "money laundering investigation", see ss 341(4), 416(1), (9); for "money laundering offence", see ss 415, 416(9); for "property", see ss 414(1), 416(9); for "recoverable property", see ss 316(1), 414(2), 416(9).
References   See para 9.66.

400 Offences

(1)   A financial institution commits an offence if without reasonable excuse it fails to comply with a requirement imposed on it under a customer information order.

(2)   A financial institution guilty of an offence under subsection (1) is liable on summary conviction to a fine not exceeding level 5 on the standard scale.

(3)   A financial institution commits an offence if, in purported compliance with a customer information order, it—
  (a)   makes a statement which it knows to be false or misleading in a material particular, or
  (b)   recklessly makes a statement which is false or misleading in a material particular.

(4)   A financial institution guilty of an offence under subsection (3) is liable—

    (a)   on summary conviction, to a fine not exceeding the statutory maximum, or

    (b)   on conviction on indictment, to a fine.

Definitions   For "customer information order", see ss 397(6), 416(3), (9); for "financial institution", see s 416(4), (5), (9).
References   See para 9.66.

401 Statements

(1)   A statement made by a financial institution in response to a customer information order may not be used in evidence against it in criminal proceedings.

(2)   But subsection (1) does not apply—

    (a)   in the case of proceedings under Part 3,

    (b)   on a prosecution for an offence under section 400(1) or (3), or

    (c)   on a prosecution for some other offence where, in giving evidence, the financial institution makes a statement inconsistent with the statement mentioned in subsection (1).

(3)   A statement may not be used by virtue of subsection (2)(c) against a financial institution unless—

    (a)   evidence relating to it is adduced, or

    (b)   a question relating to it is asked,

by or on behalf of the financial institution in the proceedings arising out of the prosecution.

Definitions   For "customer information order", see ss 397(6), 416(3), (9); for "financial institution", see s 416(4), (5), (9).
References   See para 9.66.

402 Further provisions

A customer information order has effect in spite of any restriction on the disclosure of information (however imposed).

Definitions   For "customer information order", see ss 397(6), 416(3), (9).
References   See para 9.66.

403 Supplementary

(1)   An application for a customer information order may be made ex parte to a sheriff in chambers.

(2)   Provision may be made by rules of court as to the discharge and variation of customer information orders.

(3)   Rules of court under subsection (2) relating to customer information orders—

    (a)   made in a confiscation investigation or a money laundering investigation shall, without prejudice to section 305 of the Criminal Procedure (Scotland) Act 1995 (c 46), be made by act of adjournal;

> (b) made in a civil recovery investigation shall, without prejudice to section 32 of the Sheriff Courts (Scotland) Act 1971 (c 58), be made by act of sederunt.

(4) An application to discharge or vary a customer information order may be made to the sheriff by—

> (a) the person who applied for the order;
> (b) any person affected by the order.

(5) The sheriff may—

> (a) discharge the order;
> (b) vary the order.

Definitions For "confiscation investigation", see ss 341(1), 416(1), (9); for "customer information order", see ss 397(6), 416(3), (9); for "money laundering investigation", see ss 341(4), 416(1), (9).
References See para 9.66.

Account monitoring orders

404 Account monitoring orders

(1) The sheriff may, on an application made to him by the appropriate person, make an account monitoring order if he is satisfied that each of the requirements for the making of the order is fulfilled.

(2) In making an account monitoring order in relation to property subject to a civil recovery investigation, the sheriff shall act in the exercise of his civil jurisdiction.

(3) The application for an account monitoring order must state that—

> (a) a person specified in the application is subject to a confiscation investigation or a money laundering investigation, or
> (b) property specified in the application is subject to a civil recovery investigation and a person specified in the application appears to hold the property.

(4) The application must also state that—

> (a) the order is sought for the purposes of the investigation;
> (b) the order is sought against the financial institution specified in the application in relation to account information of the description so specified.

(5) Account information is information relating to an account or accounts held at the financial institution specified in the application by the person so specified (whether solely or jointly with another).

(6) The application for an account monitoring order may specify information relating to—

> (a) all accounts held by the person specified in the application for the order at the financial institution so specified,
> (b) a particular description, or particular descriptions, of accounts so held, or
> (c) a particular account, or particular accounts, so held.

(7) An account monitoring order is an order that the financial institution specified in the application for the order must, for the period stated in the order,

provide account information of the description specified in the order to the proper person in the manner, and at or by the time or times, stated in the order.

(8)   The period stated in an account monitoring order must not exceed the period of 90 days beginning with the day on which the order is made.

Definitions   For "civil recovery investigation", see ss 341(2), (3), 416(1), (9); for "confiscation investigation", see ss 341(1), 416(1), (9); for "financial institution", see s 416(4), (5), (9); for "money laundering investigation", see ss 341(4), 416(1), (9); for "proper person", see ss 412, 416(3), (9); for "property", see ss 414(1), 416(9).
References   See para 9.67.

405 Requirements for making of account monitoring order

(1)   These are the requirements for the making of an account monitoring order.

(2)   In the case of a confiscation investigation, there must be reasonable grounds for suspecting that the person specified in the application for the order has benefited from his criminal conduct.

(3)   In the case of a civil recovery investigation, there must be reasonable grounds for suspecting that—
    (a)   the property specified in the application for the order is recoverable property or associated property;
    (b)   the person specified in the application holds all or some of the property.

(4)   In the case of a money laundering investigation, there must be reasonable grounds for suspecting that the person specified in the application for the order has committed a money laundering offence.

(5)   In the case of any investigation, there must be reasonable grounds for believing that account information which may be provided in compliance with the order is likely to be of substantial value (whether or not by itself) to the investigation for the purposes of which the order is sought.

(6)   In the case of any investigation, there must be reasonable grounds for believing that it is in the public interest for the account information to be provided, having regard to the benefit likely to accrue to the investigation if the information is obtained.

Definitions   For "account information", see ss 404(5), 416(3), (9); for "account monitoring order", see ss 404(7), 416(3), (9); for "associated property", see ss 245, 414(2), 416(9); for "benefits from conduct", see ss 413(2), (4), (5), 416(9); for "civil recovery investigation", see ss 341(2), (3), 416(1), (9); for "confiscation investigation", see ss 341(1), 416(1), (9); for "criminal conduct", see ss 413(1), (5), 416(9); for "money laundering investigation", see ss 341(4), 416(1), (9); for "money laundering offence", see ss 415, 416(9); for "property", see ss 414(1), 416(9); for "recoverable property", see ss 316(1), 414(2), 416(9).
References   See para 9.67.

406 Statements

(1)   A statement made by a financial institution in response to an account monitoring order may not be used in evidence against it in criminal proceedings.

(2)   But subsection (1) does not apply—
    (a)   in the case of proceedings under Part 3;
    (b)   in the case of proceedings for contempt of court, or

(c) on a prosecution for an offence where, in giving evidence, the financial institution makes a statement inconsistent with the statement mentioned in subsection (1).

(3) A statement may not be used by virtue of subsection (2)(c) against a financial institution unless—

(a) evidence relating to it is adduced, or

(b) a question relating to it is asked,

by or on behalf of the financial institution in the proceedings arising out of the prosecution.

Definitions For "account monitoring order", see ss 404(7), 416(3), (9); for "financial institution", see s 416(4), (5), (9).
References See para 9.67.

407 Further provisions

An account monitoring order has effect in spite of any restriction on the disclosure of information (however imposed).

Definitions For "account monitoring order", see ss 404(7), 416(3), (9).
References See para 9.67.

408 Supplementary

(1) An application for an account monitoring order may be made ex parte to a sheriff in chambers.

(2) Provision may be made by rules of court as to the discharge and variation of account monitoring orders.

(3) Rules of court under subsection (2) relating to account monitoring orders—

(a) made in a confiscation investigation or a money laundering investigation shall, without prejudice to section 305 of the Criminal Procedure (Scotland) Act 1995 (c 46), be made by act of adjournal;

(b) made in a civil recovery investigation shall, without prejudice to section 32 of the Sheriff Courts (Scotland) Act 1971 (c 58), be made by act of sederunt.

(4) An application to discharge or vary an account monitoring order may be made to the sheriff by—

(a) the person who applied for the order;

(b) any person affected by the order.

(5) The sheriff may—

(a) discharge the order;

(b) vary the order.

Definitions For "account monitoring order", see ss 404(7), 416(3), (9).
References See para 9.67.

General

409 Jurisdiction of sheriff

(1)　A sheriff may grant a production order, search warrant, customer information order or account monitoring order under this Act in relation to property situated in any area of Scotland notwithstanding that it is outside the area of that sheriff.

(2)　Any such order or warrant may, without being backed or endorsed by another sheriff, be executed throughout Scotland in the same way as it may be executed within the sheriffdom of the sheriff who granted it.

(3)　This section is without prejudice to any existing rule of law or to any other provision of this Act.

Definitions　For "account monitoring order", see ss 404(7), 416(3), (9); for "customer information order", see ss 397(6), 416(3), (9); for "production order", see ss 380(5), 416(3), (9); for "property", see ss 414(1), 416(9); for "search warrant", see ss 387(4), 416(3), (9).
References　See para 9.68.

410 Code of practice

(1)　The Scottish Ministers must prepare a code of practice as to the exercise by proper persons of functions they have under this Chapter.

(2)　After preparing a draft of the code the Scottish Ministers—
    (a)　must publish the draft;
    (b)　must consider any representations made to them about the draft;
    (c)　may amend the draft accordingly.

(3)　After the Scottish Ministers have proceeded under subsection (2) they must lay the code before the Scottish Parliament.

(4)　When they have done so, the Scottish Ministers may bring the code into operation on such day as they may appoint by order.

(5)　A proper person must compy with a code of practice which is in operation under this section in the exercise of any function he has under this Chapter.

(6)　If a proper person fails to comply with any provision of a code of practice issued under this section he is not by reason only of that failure liable in any criminal or civil proceedings.

(7)　But the code of practice is admissible in evidence in such proceedings and a court may take account of any failure to comply with its provisions in determining any questions in the proceedings.

(8)　The Scottish Ministers may from time to time revise a code previously brought into operation under this section; and the preceding provisions of this section apply to a revised code as they apply to the code as first prepared.

Definitions　For "proper person", see ss 412, 416(3), (9).
References　See para 9.69.

411 Performance of functions of Scottish Ministers by constables in Scotland

(1)　In Scotland, a constable engaged in temporary service with the Scottish Ministers in connection with their functions under this Part may perform functions, other than those specified in subsection (2), on behalf of the Scottish Ministers.

(2)　The specified functions are the functions conferred on the Scottish Ministers by—

(a)　section 380(1) (production orders),
(b)　section 382(2) (entry orders),
(c)　section 386(4) (supplementary to production and entry orders),
(d)　section 387(1) (search warrants),
(e)　section 391(1) (disclosure orders),
(f)　section 396(4) (supplementary to disclosure orders),
(g)　section 397(1) (customer information orders),
(h)　section 403(4) (supplementary to customer information orders),
(i)　section 404(1) (account monitoring orders),
(j)　section 408(4) (supplementary to account monitoring orders).

Definitions　For "constable", see s 412.
References　See para 9.70.

412 Interpretation

In this Chapter, unless the context otherwise requires—
"appropriate person" means—

(a)　the procurator fiscal, in relation to a confiscation investigation or a money laundering investigation,
(b)　the Scottish Ministers, in relation to a civil recovery investigation;
references to a "constable" include references to a customs and excise officer;
"legal privilege" means protection in legal proceedings from disclosure, by virtue of any rule of law relating to the confidentiality of communications; and "items subject to legal privilege" are—

(a)　communications between a professional legal adviser and his client, or
(b)　communications made in connection with or in contemplation of legal proceedings and for the purposes of those proceedings,
which would be so protected.
"premises" include any place and, in particular, include—

(a)　any vehicle, vessel, aircraft or hovercraft;
(b)　any offshore installation within the meaning of section 1 of the Mineral Workings (Offshore Installations) Act 1971 (c 61) and any tent or movable structure;
"proper person" means—

(a)　a constable, in relation to a confiscation investigation or a money laundering investigation;
(b)　the Scottish Ministers or a person named by them, in relation to a civil recovery investigation.

Definitions　For "civil recovery investigation", see ss 341(2), (3), 416(1), (9); for "confiscation investigation", see ss 341(1), 416(1), (9); for "money laundering investigation", see ss 341(4), 416(1), (9).
References　See para 9.71.

CHAPTER 4
INTERPRETATION

413 Criminal conduct

(1) Criminal conduct is conduct which—
  (a) constitutes an offence in any part of the United Kingdom, or
  (b) would constitute an offence in any part of the United Kingdom if it occurred there.

(2) A person benefits from conduct if he obtains property or a pecuniary advantage as a result of or in connection with the conduct.

(3) References to property or a pecuniary advantage obtained in connection with conduct include references to property or a pecuniary advantage obtained in both that connection and some other.

(4) If a person benefits from conduct his benefit is the property or pecuniary advantage obtained as a result of or in connection with the conduct.

(5) It is immaterial—
  (a) whether conduct occurred before or after the passing of this Act, and
  (b) whether property or a pecuniary advantage constituting a benefit from conduct was obtained before or after the passing of this Act.

Definitions For "property", see ss 414(1), 416(9); for "property obtained", see ss 414(3)(a), 416(9).
References See para 9.72.

414 Property

(1) Property is all property wherever situated and includes—
  (a) money;
  (b) all forms of property, real or personal, heritable or moveable;
  (c) things in action and other intangible or incorporeal property.

(2) "Recoverable property" and "associated property" have the same meanings as in Part 5.

(3) The following rules apply in relation to property—
  (a) property is obtained by a person if he obtains an interest in it;
  (b) references to an interest, in relation to land in England and Wales or Northern Ireland, are to any legal estate or equitable interest or power;
  (c) references to an interest, in relation to land in Scotland, are to any estate, interest, servitude or other heritable right in or over land, including a heritable security;
  (d) references to an interest, in relation to property other than land, include references to a right (including a right to possession).

References See para 9.74.

415 Money laundering offences

(1) An offence under section 327, 328 or 329 is a money laundering offence.

(2)   Each of the following is a money laundering offence—
    (a)   an attempt, conspiracy or incitement to commit an offence specified in subsection (1);
    (b)   aiding, abetting, counselling or procuring the commission of an offence specified in subsection (1).

References   See para 9.75.

---

416 Other interpretative provisions

(1)   These expressions are to be construed in accordance with these provisions of this Part—
    civil recovery investigation: section 341(2) and (3)
    confiscation investigation: section 341(1)
    money laundering investigation: section 341(4).

(2)   In the application of this Part to England and Wales and Northern Ireland, these expressions are to be construed in accordance with these provisions of this Part—
    account information: section 370(4)
    account monitoring order: section 370(6)
    appropriate officer: section 378
    customer information: section 364
    customer information order: section 363(5)
    disclosure order: section 357(4)
    document: section 379
    order to grant entry: section 347(3)
    production order: section 345(4)
    search and seizure warrant: section 352(4)
    senior appropriate officer: section 378.

(3)   In the application of this Part to Scotland, these expressions are to be construed in accordance with these provisions of this Part—
    account information: section 404(5)
    account monitoring order: section 404(7)
    customer information: section 398
    customer information order: section 397(6)
    disclosure order: section 391(4)
    production order: section 380(5)
    proper person: section 412
    search warrant: section 387(4).

(4)   "Financial institution" means a person carrying on a business in the regulated sector.

(5)   But a person who ceases to carry on a business in the regulated sector (whether by virtue of paragraph 5 of Schedule 9 or otherwise) is to continue to be treated as a financial institution for the purposes of any requirement under—
    (a)   a customer information order, or
    (b)   an account monitoring order,
to provide information which relates to a time when the person was a financial institution.

(6)   References to a business in the regulated sector must be construed in accordance with Schedule 9.

(7)   "Recovery order", "interim receiving order" and "interim administration order" have the same meanings as in Part 5.

(8)   References to notice in writing include references to notice given by electronic means.

(9)   This section and sections 413 to 415 apply for the purposes of this Part.

References   See para 9.76.

PART 9
INSOLVENCY ETC

Bankruptcy in England and Wales

417 Modifications of the 1986 Act

(1)   This section applies if a person is adjudged bankrupt in England and Wales.

(2)   The following property is excluded from his estate for the purposes of Part 9 of the 1986 Act—

   (a)   property for the time being subject to a restraint order which was made under section 41, 120 or 190 before the order adjudging him bankrupt;

   (b)   any property in respect of which an order under section 50 or 52 is in force;

   (c)   any property in respect of which an order under section 128(3) is in force;

   (d)   any property in respect of which an order under section 198 or 200 is in force.

(3)   Subsection (2)(a) applies to heritable property in Scotland only if the restraint order is recorded in the General Register of Sasines or registered in the Land Register of Scotland before the order adjudging the person bankrupt.

(4)   If in the case of a debtor an interim receiver stands at any time appointed under section 286 of the 1986 Act and any property of the debtor is then subject to a restraint order made under section 41, 120 or 190 the powers conferred on the receiver by virtue of that Act do not apply to property then subject to the restraint order.

Definitions   For "the 1986 Act", see s 434(1), (3).
References   See para 10.2.

418 Restriction of powers

(1)   If a person is adjudged bankrupt in England and Wales the powers referred to in subsection (2) must not be exercised in relation to the property referred to in subsection (3).

(2)   These are the powers—
    (a)   the powers conferred on a court by sections 41 to 67 and the powers of a receiver appointed under section 48, 50 or 52;
    (b)   the powers conferred on a court by sections 120 to 136 and Schedule 3 and the powers of an administrator appointed under section 125 or 128(3);
    (c)   the powers conferred on a court by sections 190 to 215 and the powers of a receiver appointed under section 196, 198 or 200.

(3)   This is the property—
    (a)   property which is for the time being comprised in the bankrupt's estate for the purposes of Part 9 of the 1986 Act;
    (b)   property in respect of which his trustee in bankruptcy may (without leave of the court) serve a notice under section 307, 308 or 308A of the 1986 Act (after-acquired property, tools, tenancies etc);
    (c)   property which is to be applied for the benefit of creditors of the bankrupt by virtue of a condition imposed under section 280(2)(c) of the 1986 Act;
    (d)   in a case where a confiscation order has been made under section 6 or 156 of this Act, any sums remaining in the hands of a receiver appointed under section 50, 52, 198 or 200 of this Act after the amount required to be paid under the confiscation order has been fully paid;
    (e)   in a case where a confiscation order has been made under section 92 of this Act, any sums remaining in the hands of an administrator appointed under section 128 of this Act after the amount required to be paid under the confiscation order has been fully paid.

(4)   But nothing in the 1986 Act must be taken to restrict (or enable the restriction of) the powers referred to in subsection (2).

(5)   In a case where a petition in bankruptcy was presented or a receiving order or adjudication in bankruptcy was made before 29 December 1986 (when the 1986 Act came into force) this section has effect with these modifications—
    (a)   for the reference in subsection (3)(a) to the bankrupt's estate for the purposes of Part 9 of that Act substitute a reference to the property of the bankrupt for the purposes of the 1914 Act;
    (b)   omit subsection (3)(b);
    (c)   for the reference in subsection (3)(c) to section 280(2)(c) of the 1986 Act substitute a reference to section 26(2) of the 1914 Act;
    (d)   for the reference in subsection (4) to the 1986 Act substitute a reference to the 1914 Act.

Definitions   For "the 1914 Act", see s 434(1), (3); for "the 1986 Act", see s 434(1), (3).
References   See paras 10.2–10.4.

419 Tainted gifts

(1)   This section applies if a person who is adjudged bankrupt in England and Wales has made a tainted gift (whether directly or indirectly).

(2)   No order may be made under section 339, 340 or 423 of the 1986 Act (avoidance of certain transactions) in respect of the making of the gift at any time when—

(a) any property of the recipient of the tainted gift is subject to a restraint order under section 41, 120 or 190, or

(b) there is in force in respect of such property an order under section 50, 52, 128(3), 198 or 200.

(3) Any order made under section 339, 340 or 423 of the 1986 Act after an order mentioned in subsection (2)(a) or (b) is discharged must take into account any realisation under Part 2, 3 or 4 of this Act of property held by the recipient of the tainted gift.

(4) A person makes a tainted gift for the purposes of this section if he makes a tainted gift within the meaning of Part 2, 3 or 4.

(5) In a case where a petition in bankruptcy was presented or a receiving order or adjudication in bankruptcy was made before 29 December 1986 (when the 1986 Act came into force) this section has effect with the substitution for a reference to section 339, 340 or 423 of the 1986 Act of a reference to section 27, 42 or 44 of the 1914 Act.

Definitions For "the 1914 Act", see s 434(1), (3); for "the 1986 Act", see s 434(1), (3).
References See paras 10.2–10.4.

Sequestration in Scotland

420 Modifications of the 1985 Act

(1) This section applies if an award of sequestration is made in Scotland.

(2) The following property is excluded from the debtor's estate for the purposes of the 1985 Act—

(a) property for the time being subject to a restraint order which was made under section 41, 120 or 190 before the award of sequestration;

(b) any property in respect of which an order under section 50 or 52 is in force;

(c) any property in respect of which an order under section 128(3) is in force;

(d) any property in respect of which an order under section 198 or 200 is in force.

(3) Subsection (2)(a) applies to heritable property in Scotland only if the restraint order is recorded in the General Register of Sasines or registered in the Land Register of Scotland before the award of sequestration.

(4) It shall not be competent to submit a claim in relation to a confiscation order to the permanent trustee in accordance with section 48 of the 1985 Act; and the reference here to a confiscation order is to any confiscation order that has been or may be made against the debtor under Part 2, 3 or 4 of this Act.

(5) If at any time in the period before the award of sequestration is made an interim trustee stands appointed under section 2(5) of the 1985 Act and any property in the debtor's estate is at that time subject to a restraint order made under section 41, 120 or 190, the powers conferred on the trustee by virtue of that Act do not apply to property then subject to the restraint order.

References See para 10.5.

421 Restriction of powers

(1)   If an award of sequestration is made in Scotland the powers referred to in subsection (2) must not be exercised in relation to the property referred to in subsection (3).

(2)   These are the powers—
  (a)   the powers conferred on a court by sections 41 to 67 and the powers of a receiver appointed under section 48, 50 or 52;
  (b)   the powers conferred on a court by sections 120 to 136 and Schedule 3 and the powers of an administrator appointed under section 125 or 128(3);
  (c)   the powers conferred on a court by sections 190 to 215 and the powers of a receiver appointed under section 196, 198 or 200.

(3)   This is the property—
  (a)   property which is for the time being comprised in the whole estate of the debtor within the meaning of section 31(8) of the 1985 Act;
  (b)   any income of the debtor which has been ordered under section 32(2) of that Act to be paid to the permanent trustee;
  (c)   any estate which under section 31(10) or 32(6) of that Act vests in the permanent trustee;
  (d)   in a case where a confiscation order has been made under section 6 or 156 of this Act, any sums remaining in the hands of a receiver appointed under section 50, 52, 198 or 200 of this Act after the amount required to be paid under the confiscation order has been fully paid;
  (e)   in a case where a confiscation order has been made under section 92 of this Act, any sums remaining in the hands of an administrator appointed under section 128 of this Act after the amount required to be paid under the confiscation order has been fully paid.

(4)   But nothing in the 1985 Act must be taken to restrict (or enable the restriction of) the powers referred to in subsection (2).

(5)   In a case where (despite the coming into force of the 1985 Act) the 1913 Act applies to a sequestration, subsection (3) above has effect as if for paragraphs (a) to (c) there were substituted—
  "(a) property which is for the time being comprised in the whole property of the debtor which vests in the trustee under section 97 of the 1913 Act;
  (b) any income of the bankrupt which has been ordered under section 98(2) of that Act to be paid to the trustee;
  (c) any estate which under section 98(1) of that Act vests in the trustee."

(6)   In a case where subsection (5) applies, subsection (4) has effect as if for the reference to the 1985 Act there were substituted a reference to the 1913 Act.

References   See para 10.5.

422 Tainted gifts

(1)   This section applies if a person whose estate is sequestrated in Scotland has made a tainted gift (whether directly or indirectly).

(2)   No decree may be granted under the Bankruptcy Act 1621 (c 18) or section 34 or 36 of the 1985 Act (gratuitous alienations and unfair preferences), or otherwise, in respect of the making of the gift at any time when—

(a)   any property of the recipient of the tainted gift is subject to a restraint order under section 41, 120 or 190, or

(b)   there is in force in respect of such property an order under section 50, 52, 128(3), 198 or 200.

(3)   Any decree made under the Bankruptcy Act 1621 (c 18) or section 34 or 36 of the 1985 Act, or otherwise, after an order mentioned in subsection (2)(a) or (b) is discharged must take into account any realisation under Part 2, 3 or 4 of this Act of property held by the recipient of the tainted gift.

(4)   A person makes a tainted gift for the purposes of this section if he makes a tainted gift within the meaning of Part 2, 3 or 4.

References   See para 10.5.

Bankruptcy in Northern Ireland

423 Modifications of the 1989 Order

(1)   This section applies if a person is adjudged bankrupt in Northern Ireland.

(2)   The following property is excluded from his estate for the purposes of Part 9 of the 1989 Order—

(a)   property for the time being subject to a restraint order which was made under section 41, 120 or 190 before the order adjudging him bankrupt;

(b)   any property in respect of which an order under section 50 or 52 is in force;

(c)   any property in respect of which an order under section 128(3) is in force;

(d)   any property in respect of which an order under section 198 or 200 is in force.

(3)   Subsection (2)(a) applies to heritable property in Scotland only if the restraint order is recorded in the General Register of Sasines or registered in the Land Register of Scotland before the order adjudging the person bankrupt.

(4)   If in the case of a debtor an interim receiver stands at any time appointed under Article 259 of the 1989 Order and any property of the debtor is then subject to a restraint order made under section 41, 120 or 190, the powers conferred on the receiver by virtue of that Order do not apply to property then subject to the restraint order.

Definitions   For "the 1989 Order", see s 434(1), (3).
References   See para 10.5.

424 Restriction of powers

(1)   If a person is adjudged bankrupt in Northern Ireland the powers referred to in subsection (2) must not be exercised in relation to the property referred to in subsection (3).

(2)   These are the powers—

   (a)   the powers conferred on a court by sections 41 to 67 and the powers of a receiver appointed under section 48, 50 or 52;

   (b)   the powers conferred on a court by sections 120 to 136 and Schedule 3 and the powers of an administrator appointed under section 125 or 128(3);

   (c)   the powers conferred on a court by sections 190 to 215 and the powers of a receiver appointed under section 196, 198 or 200.

(3)   This is the property—

   (a)   property which is for the time being comprised in the bankrupt's estate for the purposes of Part 9 of the 1989 Order;

   (b)   property in respect of which his trustee in bankruptcy may (without leave of the court) serve a notice under Article 280 or 281 of the 1989 Order (after-acquired property etc);

   (c)   property which is to be applied for the benefit of creditors of the bankrupt by virtue of a condition imposed under Article 254(2)(c) of the 1989 Order;

   (d)   in a case where a confiscation order has been made under section 6 or 156 of this Act, any sums remaining in the hands of a receiver appointed under section 50, 52, 198 or 200 of this Act after the amount required to be paid under the confiscation order has been fully paid;

   (e)   in a case where a confiscation order has been made under section 92 of this Act, any sums remaining in the hands of an administrator appointed under section 128 of this Act after the amount required to be paid under the confiscation order has been fully paid.

(4)   But nothing in the 1989 Order must be taken to restrict (or enable the restriction of) the powers mentioned in subsection (2).

(5)   In a case where a petition in bankruptcy was presented or an adjudication in bankruptcy was made before 1 October 1991 (when the 1989 Order came into force) this section has effect with these modifications—

   (a)   for the reference in subsection (3)(a) to the bankrupt's estate for the purposes of Part 9 of that Order substitute a reference to the property of the bankrupt for the purposes of the Bankruptcy Acts (Northern Ireland) 1857 to 1980;

   (b)   omit subsection (3)(b);

   (c)   for the reference in subsection (3)(c) to Article 254(2)(c) of the 1989 Order substitute a reference to Articles 28(4), (5)(c) and (11) and 30(6)(c) of the Bankruptcy Amendment (Northern Ireland) Order 1980 (SI 1980/561 (NI 4));

   (d)   for the reference in subsection (4) to the 1989 Order substitute a reference to the Bankruptcy Acts (Northern Ireland) 1857 to 1980.

Definitions   For "the 1989 Order", see s 434(1), (3).
References   See para 10.5.

425 Tainted gifts

(1)   This section applies if a person who is adjudged bankrupt in Northern Ireland has made a tainted gift (whether directly or indirectly).

(2)   No order may be made under Article 312, 313 or 367 of the 1989 Order (avoidance of certain transactions) in respect of the making of the gift at any time when—

    (a)   any property of the recipient of the tainted gift is subject to a restraint order under section 41, 120 or 190, or

    (b)   there is in force in respect of such property an order under section 50, 52, 128(3), 198 or 200.

(3)   Any order made under Article 312, 313 or 367 of the 1989 Order after an order mentioned in subsection (2)(a) or (b) is discharged must take into account any realisation under Part 2, 3 or 4 of this Act of property held by the recipient of the tainted gift.

(4)   A person makes a tainted gift for the purposes of this section if he makes a tainted gift within the meaning of Part 2, 3 or 4.

(5)   In a case where a petition in bankruptcy was presented or an adjudication in bankruptcy was made before 1 October 1991 (when the 1989 Order came into force) this section has effect with these modifications—

    (a)   for a reference to Article 312 of the 1989 Order substitute a reference to section 12 of the Bankruptcy Amendment Act (Northern Ireland) 1929 (c 1 (NI));

    (b)   for a reference to Article 367 of the 1989 Order substitute a reference to section 10 of the Conveyancing Act (Ireland) 1634 (c 3).

Definitions   For "the 1989 Order", see s 434(1), (3).
References   See para 10.5.

Winding up in England and Wales and Scotland

426 Winding up under the 1986 Act

(1)   In this section "company" means any company which may be wound up under the 1986 Act.

(2)   If an order for the winding up of a company is made or it passes a resolution for its voluntary winding up, the functions of the liquidator (or any provisional liquidator) are not exercisable in relation to the following property—

    (a)   property for the time being subject to a restraint order which was made under section 41, 120 or 190 before the relevant time;

    (b)   any property in respect of which an order under section 50 or 52 is in force;

    (c)   any property in respect of which an order under section 128(3) is in force;

    (d)   any property in respect of which an order under section 198 or 200 is in force.

(3)   Subsection (2)(a) applies to heritable property in Scotland only if the restraint order is recorded in the General Register of Sasines or registered in the Land Register of Scotland before the relevant time.

(4)   If an order for the winding up of a company is made or it passes a resolution for its voluntary winding up the powers referred to in subsection (5) must not be exercised in the way mentioned in subsection (6) in relation to any property—

    (a)   which is held by the company, and

    (b)   in relation to which the functions of the liquidator are exercisable.

(5)   These are the powers—
  (a)   the powers conferred on a court by sections 41 to 67 and the powers of a receiver appointed under section 48, 50 or 52;
  (b)   the powers conferred on a court by sections 120 to 136 and Schedule 3 and the powers of an administrator appointed under section 125 or 128(3);
  (c)   the powers conferred on a court by sections 190 to 215 and the powers of a receiver appointed under section 196, 198 or 200.

(6)   The powers must not be exercised—
  (a)   so as to inhibit the liquidator from exercising his functions for the purpose of distributing property to the company's creditors;
  (b)   so as to prevent the payment out of any property of expenses (including the remuneration of the liquidator or any provisional liquidator) properly incurred in the winding up in respect of the property.

(7)   But nothing in the 1986 Act must be taken to restrict (or enable the restriction of) the exercise of the powers referred to in subsection (5).

(8)   For the purposes of the application of Parts 4 and 5 of the 1986 Act (winding up) to a company which the Court of Session has jurisdiction to wind up, a person is not a creditor in so far as any sum due to him by the company is due in respect of a confiscation order made under section 6, 92 or 156.

(9)   The relevant time is—
  (a)   if no order for the winding up of the company has been made, the time of the passing of the resolution for voluntary winding up;
  (b)   if such an order has been made, but before the presentation of the petition for the winding up of the company by the court such a resolution has been passed by the company, the time of the passing of the resolution;
  (c)   if such an order has been made, but paragraph (b) does not apply, the time of the making of the order.

(10)   In a case where a winding up of a company commenced or is treated as having commenced before 29 December 1986, this section has effect with the following modifications—
  (a)   in subsections (1) and (7) for "the 1986 Act" substitute "the Companies Act 1985";
  (b)   in subsection (8) for "Parts 4 and 5 of the 1986 Act" substitute "Parts 20 and 21 of the Companies Act 1985".

Definitions   For "the 1986 Act", see s 434(1), (3); for "company", see s 431.
References   See para 10.6.

427 Tainted gifts

(1)   In this section "company" means any company which may be wound up under the 1986 Act.

(2)   This section applies if—
  (a)   an order for the winding up of a company is made or it passes a resolution for its voluntary winding up, and
  (b)   it has made a tainted gift (whether directly or indirectly).

(3)   No order may be made under section 238, 239 or 423 of the 1986 Act (avoidance of certain transactions) and no decree may be granted under section 242 or 243 of that Act (gratuitous alienations and unfair preferences), or otherwise, in respect of the making of the gift at any time when—

(a)   any property of the recipient of the tainted gift is subject to a restraint order under section 41, 120 or 190, or

(b)   there is in force in respect of such property an order under section 50, 52, 128(3), 198 or 200.

(4)   Any order made under section 238, 239 or 423 of the 1986 Act or decree granted under section 242 or 243 of that Act, or otherwise, after an order mentioned in subsection (3)(a) or (b) is discharged must take into account any realisation under Part 2, 3 or 4 of this Act of property held by the recipient of the tainted gift.

(5)   A person makes a tainted gift for the purposes of this section if he makes a tainted gift within the meaning of Part 2, 3 or 4.

(6)   In a case where the winding up of a company commenced or is treated as having commenced before 29 December 1986 this section has effect with the substitution—

(a)   for references to section 239 of the 1986 Act of references to section 615 of the Companies Act 1985 (c 6);

(b)   for references to section 242 of the 1986 Act of references to section 615A of the Companies Act 1985;

(c)   for references to section 243 of the 1986 Act of references to section 615B of the Companies Act 1985.

Definitions   For "the 1986 Act", see s 434(1), (3); for "company", see s 431.
References   See para 10.6.

Winding up in Northern Ireland

428 Winding up under the 1989 Order

(1)   In this section "company" means any company which may be wound up under the 1989 Order.

(2)   If an order for the winding up of a company is made or it passes a resolution for its voluntary winding up, the functions of the liquidator (or any provisional liquidator) are not exercisable in relation to the following property—

(a)   property for the time being subject to a restraint order which was made under section 41, 120 or 190 before the relevant time;

(b)   any property in respect of which an order under section 50 or 52 is in force;

(c)   any property in respect of which an order under section 128(3) is in force;

(d)   any property in respect of which an order under section 198 or 200 is in force.

(3)   Subsection (2)(a) applies to heritable property in Scotland only if the restraint order is recorded in the General Register of Sasines or registered in the Land Register of Scotland before the relevant time.

(4)   If an order for the winding up of a company is made or it passes a resolution for its voluntary winding up the powers referred to in subsection (5) must not be exercised in the way mentioned in subsection (6) in relation to any property—

    (a)   which is held by the company, and

    (b)   in relation to which the functions of the liquidator are exercisable.

(5)   These are the powers—

    (a)   the powers conferred on a court by sections 41 to 67 and the powers of a receiver appointed under section 48, 50 or 52;

    (b)   the powers conferred on a court by sections 120 to 136 and Schedule 3 and the powers of an administrator appointed under section 125 or 128(3);

    (c)   the powers conferred on a court by sections 190 to 215 and the powers of a receiver appointed under section 196, 198 or 200.

(6)   The powers must not be exercised—

    (a)   so as to inhibit the liquidator from exercising his functions for the purpose of distributing property to the company's creditors;

    (b)   so as to prevent the payment out of any property of expenses (including the remuneration of the liquidator or any provisional liquidator) properly incurred in the winding up in respect of the property.

(7)   But nothing in the 1989 Order must be taken to restrict (or enable the restriction of) the exercise of the powers referred to in subsection (5).

(8)   The relevant time is—

    (a)   if no order for the winding up of the company has been made, the time of the passing of the resolution for voluntary winding up;

    (b)   if such an order has been made, but before the presentation of the petition for the winding up of the company by the court such a resolution has been passed by the company, the time of the passing of the resolution;

    (c)   if such an order has been made, but paragraph (b) does not apply, the time of the making of the order.

(9)   In a case where a winding up of a company commenced or is treated as having commenced before 1 October 1991, this section has effect with the substitution for references to the 1989 Order of references to the Companies (Northern Ireland) Order 1986 (SI 1986/1032 (NI 6)).

Definitions   For "the 1989 Order", see s 434(1), (3).
References   See para 10.6.

---

429 Tainted gifts

(1)   In this section "company" means any company which may be wound up under the 1989 Order.

(2)   This section applies if—

    (a)   an order for the winding up of a company is made or it passes a resolution for its voluntary winding up, and

    (b)   it has made a tainted gift (whether directly or indirectly).

(3)   No order may be made under Article 202, 203 or 367 of the 1989 Order (avoidance of certain transactions) in respect of the making of the gift at any time when—

(a)   any property of the recipient of the tainted gift is subject to a restraint order under section 41, 120 or 190, or

(b)   there is in force in respect of such property an order under section 50, 52, 128(3), 198 or 200.

(4)   Any order made under Article 202, 203 or 367 of the 1989 Order after an order mentioned in subsection (3)(a) or (b) is discharged must take into account any realisation under Part 2, 3 or 4 of this Act of property held by the recipient of the tainted gift.

(5)   A person makes a tainted gift for the purposes of this section if he makes a tainted gift within the meaning of Part 2, 3 or 4.

Definitions   For "the 1989 Order", see s 434(1), (3).
References   See para 10.6.

Floating charges

430 Floating charges

(1)   In this section "company" means a company which may be wound up under

(a)   the 1986 Act, or

(b)   the 1989 Order.

(2)   If a company holds property which is subject to a floating charge, and a receiver has been appointed by or on the application of the holder of the charge, the functions of the receiver are not exercisable in relation to the following property—

(a)   property for the time being subject to a restraint order which was made under section 41, 120 or 190 before the appointment of the receiver;

(b)   any property in respect of which an order under section 50 or 52 is in force;

(c)   any property in respect of which an order under section 128(3) is in force;

(d)   any property in respect of which an order under section 198 or 200 is in force.

(3)   Subsection (2)(a) applies to heritable property in Scotland only if the restraint order is recorded in the General Register of Sasines or registered in the Land Register of Scotland before the appointment of the receiver.

(4)   If a company holds property which is subject to a floating charge, and a receiver has been appointed by or on the application of the holder of the charge, the powers referred to in subsection (5) must not be exercised in the way mentioned in subsection (6) in relation to any property—

(a)   which is held by the company, and

(b)   in relation to which the functions of the receiver are exercisable.

(5)   These are the powers—
    (a)   the powers conferred on a court by sections 41 to 67 and the powers of a receiver appointed under section 48, 50 or 52;
    (b)   the powers conferred on a court by sections 120 to 136 and Schedule 3 and the powers of an administrator appointed under section 125 or 128(3);
    (c)   the powers conferred on a court by sections 190 to 215 and the powers of a receiver appointed under section 196, 198 or 200.

(6)   The powers must not be exercised—
    (a)   so as to inhibit the receiver from exercising his functions for the purpose of distributing property to the company's creditors;
    (b)   so as to prevent the payment out of any property of expenses (including the remuneration of the receiver) properly incurred in the exercise of his functions in respect of the property.

(7)   But nothing in the 1986 Act or the 1989 Order must be taken to restrict (or enable the restriction of) the exercise of the powers referred to in subsection (5).

(8)   In this section "floating charge" includes a floating charge within the meaning of section 462 of the Companies Act 1985 (c 6).

Definitions   For "the 1986 Act", see s 434(1), (3).; for "the 1989 Order", see s 434(1), (3); for "company", see s 431.
References   See para 10.7.

Limited liability partnerships

431 Limited liability partnerships

(1)   In sections 426, 427 and 430 "company" includes a limited liability partnership which may be wound up under the 1986 Act.

(2)   A reference in those sections to a company passing a resolution for its voluntary winding up is to be construed in relation to a limited liability partnership as a reference to the partnership making a determination for its voluntary winding up.

Definitions   For "the 1986 Act", see s 434(1), (3).
References   See para 10.8.

Insolvency practitioners

432 Insolvency practitioners

(1)   Subsections (2) and (3) apply if a person acting as an insolvency practitioner seizes or disposes of any property in relation to which his functions are not exercisable because—
    (a)   it is for the time being subject to a restraint order made under section 41, 120 or 190, or
    (b)   it is for the time being subject to an interim receiving order made under section 246 or an interim administration order made under section 256,

and at the time of the seizure or disposal he believes on reasonable grounds that he is entitled (whether in pursuance of an order of a court or otherwise) to seize or dispose of the property.

(2)   He is not liable to any person in respect of any loss or damage resulting from the seizure or disposal, except so far as the loss or damage is caused by his negligence.

(3)   He has a lien on the property or the proceeds of its sale—
- (a)   for such of his expenses as were incurred in connection with the liquidation, bankruptcy, sequestration or other proceedings in relation to which he purported to make the seizure or disposal, and
- (b)   for so much of his remuneration as may reasonably be assigned to his acting in connection with those proceedings.

(4)   Subsection (2) does not prejudice the generality of any provision of the 1985 Act, the 1986 Act, the 1989 Order or any other Act or Order which confers protection from liability on him.

(5)   Subsection (7) applies if—
- (a)   property is subject to a restraint order made under section 41, 120 or 190,
- (b)   a person acting as an insolvency practitioner incurs expenses in respect of property subject to the restraint order, and
- (c)   he does not know (and has no reasonable grounds to believe) that the property is subject to the restraint order.

(6)   Subsection (7) also applies if—
- (a)   property is subject to a restraint order made under section 41, 120 or 190,
- (b)   a person acting as an insolvency practitioner incurs expenses which are not ones in respect of property subject to the restraint order, and
- (c)   the expenses are ones which (but for the effect of the restraint order) might have been met by taking possession of and realising property subject to it.

(7)   Whether or not he has seized or disposed of any property, he is entitled to payment of the expenses under—
- (a)   section 54(2), 55(3), 56(2) or 57(3) if the restraint order was made under section 41;
- (b)   section 130(3) or 131(3) if the restraint order was made under section 120;
- (c)   section 202(2), 203(3), 204(2) or 205(3) if the restraint order was made under section 190.

(8)   Subsection (10) applies if—
- (a)   property is subject to an interim receiving order made under section 246 or an interim administration order made under section 256,
- (b)   a person acting as an insolvency practitioner incurs expenses in respect of property subject to the order, and
- (c)   he does not know (and has no reasonable grounds to believe) that the property is subject to the order.

(9) Subsection (10) also applies if—

    (a) property is subject to an interim receiving order made under section 246 or an interim administration order made under section 256,

    (b) a person acting as an insolvency practitioner incurs expenses which are not ones in respect of property subject to the order, and

    (c) the expenses are ones which (but for the effect of the order) might have been met by taking possession of and realising property subject to it.

(10) Whether or not he has seized or disposed of any property, he is entitled to payment of the expenses under section 280.

Definitions   For "the 1985 Act", see s 434(1), (3); for "the 1986 Act", see s 434(1), (3); for "the 1989 Order", see s 434(1), (3); for "insolvency practitioner", see s 433.
References   See para 10.9.

---

433 Meaning of insolvency practitioner

(1) This section applies for the purposes of section 432.

(2) A person acts as an insolvency practitioner if he so acts within the meaning given by section 388 of the 1986 Act or Article 3 of the 1989 Order; but this is subject to subsections (3) to (5).

(3) The expression "person acting as an insolvency practitioner" includes the official receiver acting as receiver or manager of the property concerned.

(4) In applying section 388 of the 1986 Act under subsection (2) above—

    (a) the reference in section 388(2)(a) to a permanent or interim trustee in sequestration must be taken to include a reference to a trustee in sequestration;

    (b) section 388(5) (which includes provision that nothing in the section applies to anything done by the official receiver or the Accountant in Bankruptcy) must be ignored.

(5) In applying Article 3 of the 1989 Order under subsection (2) above, paragraph (5) (which includes provision that nothing in the Article applies to anything done by the official receiver) must be ignored.

Definitions   For "the 1986 Act", see s 434(1), (3); for "the 1989 Order", see s 434(1), (3).
References   See para 10.9.

Interpretation

434 Interpretation

(1) The following paragraphs apply to references to Acts or Orders—

    (a) the 1913 Act is the Bankruptcy (Scotland) Act 1913 (c 20);

    (b) the 1914 Act is the Bankruptcy Act 1914 (c 59);

    (c) the 1985 Act is the Bankruptcy (Scotland) Act 1985 (c 66);

    (d) the 1986 Act is the Insolvency Act 1986 (c 45);

    (e) the 1989 Order is the Insolvency (Northern Ireland) Order 1989 (SI 1989/2405 (NI 19)).

(2)   An award of sequestration is made on the date of sequestration within the meaning of section 12(4) of the 1985 Act.

(3)   This section applies for the purposes of this Part.

PART 10
INFORMATION

England and Wales and Northern Ireland

435 Use of information by Director

Information obtained by or on behalf of the Director in connection with the exercise of any of his functions may be used by him in connection with his exercise of any of his other functions.

Definitions   For "the Director", see s 1(2).
References   See para 11.2.

---

436 Disclosure of information to Director

(1)   Information which is held by or on behalf of a permitted person (whether it was obtained before or after the coming into force of this section) may be disclosed to the Director for the purpose of the exercise by the Director of his functions.

(2)   A disclosure under this section is not to be taken to breach any restriction on the disclosure of information (however imposed).

(3)   But nothing in this section authorises the making of a disclosure—
    (a)   which contravenes the Data Protection Act 1998 (c 29);
    (b)   which is prohibited by Part 1 of the Regulation of Investigatory Powers Act 2000 (c 23).

(4)   This section does not affect a power to disclose which exists apart from this section.

(5)   These are permitted persons—
    (a)   a constable;
    (b)   the Director General of the National Criminal Intelligence Service;
    (c)   the Director General of the National Crime Squad;
    (d)   the Director of the Serious Fraud Office;
    (e)   the Commissioners of Inland Revenue;
    (f)   the Commissioners of Customs and Excise;
    (g)   the Director of Public Prosecutions;
    (h)   the Director of Public Prosecutions for Northern Ireland.

(6)   The Secretary of State may by order designate as permitted persons other persons who exercise functions which he believes are of a public nature.

(7)   But an order under subsection (6) must specify the functions in respect of which the designation is made.

(8)   Information must not be disclosed under this section on behalf of the Commissioners of Inland Revenue or on behalf of the Commissioners of Customs and Excise unless the Commissioners concerned authorise the disclosure.

(9)   The power to authorise a disclosure under subsection (8) may be delegated (either generally or for a specified purpose)—

    (a)   in the case of the Commissioners of Inland Revenue, to an officer of the Board of Inland Revenue;

    (b)   in the case of the Commissioners of Customs and Excise, to a customs officer.

Definitions   For "customs officer", see s 454; for "the Director", see s 1(2).
References   See para 11.3.

437 Further disclosure

(1)   Subsection (2) applies to information obtained under section 436 from the Commissioners of Inland Revenue or from the Commissioners of Customs and Excise or from a person acting on behalf of either of them.

(2)   Such information must not be further disclosed except—

    (a)   for a purpose connected with the exercise of the Director's functions, and

    (b)   with the consent of the Commissioners concerned.

(3)   Consent under subsection (2) may be given—

    (a)   in relation to a particular disclosure;

    (b)   in relation to disclosures made in circumstances specified or described in the consent.

(4)   The power to consent to further disclosure under subsection (2)(b) may be delegated (either generally or for a specified purpose)—

    (a)   in the case of the Commissioners of Inland Revenue, to an officer of the Board of Inland Revenue;

    (b)   in the case of the Commissioners of Customs and Excise, to a customs officer.

(5)   Subsection (6) applies to information obtained under section 436 from a permitted person other than the Commissioners of Inland Revenue or the Commissioners of Customs and Excise or a person acting on behalf of either of them.

(6)   A permitted person who discloses such information to the Director may make the disclosure subject to such conditions as to further disclosure by the Director as the permitted person thinks appropriate; and the information must not be further disclosed in contravention of the conditions.

Definitions   For "customs officer", see s 454; for "the Director", see s 1(2).
References   See para 11.8.

438 Disclosure of information by Director

(1)   Information obtained by or on behalf of the Director in connection with the exercise of any of his functions may be disclosed by him if the disclosure is for the purposes of any of the following—

(a) any criminal investigation which is being or may be carried out, whether in the United Kingdom or elsewhere;

(b) any criminal proceedings which have been or may be started, whether in the United Kingdom or elsewhere;

(c) the exercise of the Director's functions;

(d) the exercise by the prosecutor of functions under Parts 2, 3 and 4;

(e) the exercise by the Scottish Ministers of their functions under Part 5;

(f) the exercise by a customs officer or a constable of his functions under Chapter 3 of Part 5;

(g) safeguarding national security;

(h) investigations or proceedings outside the United Kingdom which have led or may lead to the making of an external order within the meaning of section 447;

(i) the exercise of a designated function.

(2) Subsection (1) does not apply to information obtained by the Director or on his behalf in connection with the exercise of his functions under Part 6.

(3) But such information may be disclosed by the Director—

(a) to the Commissioners of Inland Revenue;

(b) to the Lord Advocate for the purpose of the exercise by the Lord Advocate of his functions under Part 3.

(4) Information disclosed to the Lord Advocate under subsection (3)(b) may be further disclosed by him only to the Scottish Ministers for the purpose of the exercise by them of their functions under Part 5.

(5) If the Director makes a disclosure of information for a purpose specified in subsection (1) he may make any further disclosure of the information by the person to whom he discloses it subject to such conditions as he thinks fit.

(6) Such a person must not further disclose the information in contravention of the conditions.

(7) A disclosure under this section is not to be taken to breach any restriction on the disclosure of information (however imposed).

(8) But nothing in this section authorises the making of a disclosure—

(a) which contravenes the Data Protection Act 1998 (c 29);

(b) which is prohibited by Part 1 of the Regulation of Investigatory Powers Act 2000 (c 23).

(9) A designated function is a function which the Secretary of State thinks is a function of a public nature and which he designates by order.

Definitions For "customs officer", see s 454; for "the Director", see s 1(2).
References See paras 11.9–11.14.

Scotland

439 Disclosure of information to Lord Advocate and to Scottish Ministers

(1) Information which is held by or on behalf of a permitted person (whether it was obtained before or after the coming into force of this section) may be disclosed to the Lord Advocate in connection with the exercise of any of his functions under

Part 3 or to the Scottish Ministers in connection with the exercise of any of their functions under Part 5.

(2)   A disclosure under this section is not to be taken to breach any restriction on the disclosure of information (however imposed).

(3)   But nothing in this section authorises the making of a disclosure—
- (a)   which contravenes the Data Protection Act 1998;
- (b)   which is prohibited by Part 1 of the Regulation of Investigatory Powers Act 2000.

(4)   This section does not affect a power to disclose which exists apart from this section.

(5)   These are permitted persons—
- (a)   a constable;
- (b)   the Director General of the National Criminal Intelligence Service;
- (c)   the Director General of the National Crime Squad;
- (d)   the Director of the Serious Fraud Office;
- (e)   the Commissioners of Inland Revenue;
- (f)   the Commissioners of Customs and Excise;
- (g)   the Director of Public Prosecutions;
- (h)   the Director of Public Prosecutions for Northern Ireland.

(6)   The Scottish Ministers may by order designate as permitted persons other persons who exercise functions which they believe are of a public nature.

(7)   But an order under subsection (6) must specify the functions in respect of which the designation is made.

(8)   Information must not be disclosed under this section on behalf of the Commissioners of Inland Revenue or on behalf of the Commissioners of Customs and Excise unless the Commissioners concerned authorise the disclosure.

(9)   The power to authorise a disclosure under subsection (8) may be delegated (either generally or for a specified purpose)—
- (a)   in the case of the Commissioners of Inland Revenue, to an officer of the Board of Inland Revenue;
- (b)   in the case of the Commissioners of Customs and Excise, to a customs officer.

Definitions   For "customs officer", see s 454.
References   See para 11.15.

440 Further disclosure

(1)   Subsection (2) applies to information obtained under section 439 from the Commissioners of Inland Revenue or from the Commissioners of Customs and Excise or from a person acting on behalf of either of them.

(2)   Such information must not be further disclosed except—
- (a)   for a purpose connected with the exercise of the functions of the Lord Advocate under Part 3 and of the Scottish Ministers under Part 5, and
- (b)   with the consent of the Commissioners concerned.

(3)   Consent under subsection (2) may be given—
    (a)   in relation to a particular disclosure;
    (b)   in relation to disclosures made in circumstances specified or described in the consent.

(4)   The power to consent to further disclosure under subsection (2)(b) may be delegated (either generally or for a specified purpose)—
    (a)   in the case of the Commissioners of Inland Revenue, to an officer of the Board of Inland Revenue;
    (b)   in the case of the Commissioners of Customs and Excise, to a customs officer.

(5)   Subsection (6) applies to information obtained under section 439 from a permitted person other than the Commissioners of Inland Revenue or the Commissioners of Customs and Excise or a person acting on behalf of either of them.

(6)   A permitted person who discloses such information to the Lord Advocate or to the Scottish Ministers may make the disclosure subject to such conditions as to further disclosure by the Lord Advocate or by the Scottish Ministers as the permitted person thinks appropriate; and the information must not be further disclosed in contravention of the conditions.

Definitions   For "customs officer", see s 454.
References   See para 11.16.

---

441 Disclosure of information by Lord Advocate and by Scottish Ministers

(1)   Information obtained by or on behalf of the Lord Advocate in connection with the exercise of any of his functions under Chapter 3 of Part 5 may be disclosed to the Scottish Ministers in connection with the exercise of any of their functions under that Part.

(2)   Information obtained by or on behalf of the Lord Advocate in connection with the exercise of any of his functions under Part 3 or by or on behalf of the Scottish Ministers in connection with the exercise of any of their functions under Part 5 may be disclosed by him or by them if the disclosure is for the purposes of any of the following—
    (a)   any criminal investigation which is being or may be carried out whether in the United Kingdom or elsewhere;
    (b)   any criminal proceedings which have been or may be started, whether in the United Kingdom or elsewhere;
    (c)   the exercise of the functions of the Lord Advocate under Part 3;
    (d)   the exercise of the functions of the Scottish Ministers under Part 5;
    (e)   the exercise by the prosecutor of functions under Parts 2, 3 and 4;
    (f)   the exercise of the Director's functions;
    (g)   the exercise by a customs officer or a constable of his functions under Chapter 3 of Part 5;
    (h)   safeguarding national security;
    (i)   investigations or proceedings outside the United Kingdom which have led or may lead to the making of an external order within the meaning of section 447;
    (j)   the exercise of a designated function.

(3) If the Lord Advocate makes a disclosure of information for a purpose specified in subsection (2) he may make any further disclosure of the information by the person to whom he discloses it subject to such conditions as he thinks fit.

(4) If the Scottish Ministers make a disclosure of information for a purpose specified in subsection (2) they may make any further disclosure of the information by the person to whom they disclose it subject to such conditions as they think fit.

(5) A person mentioned in subsection (3) or (4) must not further disclose the information in contravention of the conditions.

(6) A disclosure under this section is not to be taken to breach any restriction on the disclosure of information (however imposed).

(7) But nothing in this section authorises the making of a disclosure—
  (a) which contravenes the Data Protection Act 1998 (c 29);
  (b) which is prohibited by Part 1 of the Regulation of Investigatory Powers Act 2000 (c 23).

(8) This section does not affect a power to disclose which exists apart from this section.

(9) A designated function is a function which the Scottish Ministers think is a function of a public nature and which they designate by order.

Definitions   For "customs officer", see s 454; for "the Director", see s 1(2).
References   See para 11.17.

Overseas purposes

442 Restriction on disclosure for overseas purposes

(1) Section 18 of the Anti-terrorism, Crime and Security Act 2001 (c 24) (restrictions on disclosure of information for overseas purposes) applies to a disclosure of information authorised by section 438(1)(a) or (b) or 441(2)(a) or (b).

(2) In the application of section 18 of the Anti-terrorism, Crime and Security Act 2001 by virtue of subsection (1) section 20 of that Act must be ignored and the following subsection is substituted for subsection (2) of section 18 of that Act—

  "(2) In subsection (1) the reference, in relation to a direction, to a relevant disclosure is a reference to a disclosure which—
    (a) is made for a purpose authorised by section 438(1)(a) or (b) or 441(2)(a) or (b) of the Proceeds of Crime Act 2002, and
    (b) is of any such information as is described in the direction.".

References   See para 11.18.

PART 11
CO-OPERATION

443 Enforcement in different parts of the United Kingdom

(1) Her Majesty may by Order in Council make provision—
  (a) for an order made by a court under Part 2 to be enforced in Scotland or Northern Ireland;

- (b) for an order made by a court under Part 3 to be enforced in England and Wales or Northern Ireland;
- (c) for an order made by a court under Part 4 to be enforced in England and Wales or Scotland;
- (d) for an order made under Part 8 in one part of the United Kingdom to be enforced in another part;
- (e) for a warrant issued under Part 8 in one part of the United Kingdom to be executed in another part.

(2) Her Majesty may by Order in Council make provision—
- (a) for a function of a receiver appointed in pursuance of Part 2 to be exercisable in Scotland or Northern Ireland;
- (b) for a function of an administrator appointed in pursuance of Part 3 to be exercisable in England and Wales or Northern Ireland;
- (c) for a function of a receiver appointed in pursuance of Part 4 to be exercisable in England and Wales or Scotland.

(3) An Order under this section may include—
- (a) provision conferring and imposing functions on the prosecutor and the Director;
- (b) provision about the registration of orders and warrants;
- (c) provision allowing directions to be given in one part of the United Kingdom about the enforcement there of an order made or warrant issued in another part;
- (d) provision about the authentication in one part of the United Kingdom of an order made or warrant issued in another part.

(4) An Order under this section may—
- (a) amend an enactment;
- (b) apply an enactment (with or without modifications).

Definitions For "the Director", see s 1(2); for "enactment", see s 455.
References See para 12.3.

444 External requests and orders

(1) Her Majesty may by Order in Council—
- (a) make provision for a prohibition on dealing with property which is the subject of an external request;
- (b) make provision for the realisation of property for the purpose of giving effect to an external order.

(2) An Order under this section may include provision which (subject to any specified modifications) corresponds to any provision of Part 2, 3 or 4 or Part 5 except Chapter 3.

(3) An Order under this section may include—
- (a) provision about the functions of the Secretary of State, the Lord Advocate, the Scottish Ministers and the Director in relation to external requests and orders;
- (b) provision about the registration of external orders;
- (c) provision about the authentication of any judgment or order of an overseas court, and of any other document connected with such a judgment or order or any proceedings relating to it;

    (d)   provision about evidence (including evidence required to establish whether proceedings have been started or are likely to be started in an overseas court);

    (e)   provision to secure that any person affected by the implementation of an external request or the enforcement of an external order has an opportunity to make representations to a court in the part of the United Kingdom where the request is being implemented or the order is being enforced.

Definitions   For "the Director", see s 1(2); for "external order", see s 447(2), (12); for "external request", see s 447(1), (12); for "overseas court", see s 447(10), (12); for "property", see s 447(4), (12).
References   See paras 12.4–12.10.

445 External investigations

(1)   Her Majesty may by Order in Council make—

    (a)   provision to enable orders equivalent to those under Part 8 to be made, and warrants equivalent to those under Part 8 to be issued, for the purposes of an external investigation;

    (b)   provision creating offences in relation to external investigations which are equivalent to offences created by Part 8.

(2)   An Order under this section may include—

    (a)   provision corresponding to any provision of Part 8 (subject to any specified modifications);

    (b)   provision about the functions of the Secretary of State, the Lord Advocate, the Scottish Ministers, the Director, the Director General of the National Criminal Intelligence Service, the Director of the Serious Fraud Office, constables and customs officers;

    (c)   provision about evidence (including evidence required to establish whether an investigation is being carried out in a country or territory outside the United Kingdom).

(3)   But an Order under this section must not provide for a disclosure order to be made for the purposes of an external investigation into whether a money laundering offence has been committed.

Definitions   For "customs officer", see s 454; for "the Director", see s 1(2); for "external investigation", see s 447(3), (12); for "money laundering offence", see s 447(9), (12).
References   See paras 12.11–12.14.

446 Rules of court

Rules of court may make such provision as is necessary or expedient to give effect to an Order in Council made under this Part (including provision about the exercise of functions of a judge conferred or imposed by the Order).

References   See para 12.15.

447 Interpretation

(1)   An external request is a request by an overseas authority to prohibit dealing with relevant property which is identified in the request.

(2)   An external order is an order which—
    (a)   is made by an overseas court where property is found or believed to have been obtained as a result of or in connection with criminal conduct, and
    (b)   is for the recovery of specified property or a specified sum of money.

(3)   An external investigation is an investigation by an overseas authority into—
    (a)   whether property has been obtained as a result of or in connection with criminal conduct, or
    (b)   whether a money laundering offence has been committed.

(4)   Property is all property wherever situated and includes—
    (a)   money;
    (b)   all forms of property, real or personal, heritable or moveable;
    (c)   things in action and other intangible or incorporeal property.

(5)   Property is obtained by a person if he obtains an interest in it.

(6)   References to an interest, in relation to property other than land, include references to a right (including a right to possession).

(7)   Property is relevant property if there are reasonable grounds to believe that it may be needed to satisfy an external order which has been or which may be made.

(8)   Criminal conduct is conduct which—
    (a)   constitutes an offence in any part of the United Kingdom, or
    (b)   would constitute an offence in any part of the United Kingdom if it occurred there.

(9)   A money laundering offence is conduct carried out in a country or territory outside the United Kingdom and which if carried out in the United Kingdom would constitute any of the following offences—
    (a)   an offence under section 327, 328 or 329;
    (b)   an attempt, conspiracy or incitement to commit an offence specified in paragraph (a);
    (c)   aiding, abetting, counselling or procuring the commission of an offence specified in paragraph (a).

(10) An overseas court is a court of a country or territory outside the United Kingdom.

(11) An overseas authority is an authority which has responsibility in a country or territory outside the United Kingdom—
    (a)   for making a request to an authority in another country or territory (including the United Kingdom) to prohibit dealing with relevant property,
    (b)   for carrying out an investigation into whether property has been obtained as a result of or in connection with criminal conduct, or
    (c)   for carrying out an investigation into whether a money laundering offence has been committed.

(12) This section applies for the purposes of this Part.

References   See para 12.16.

PART 12
MISCELLANEOUS AND GENERAL

Miscellaneous

448 Tax

Schedule 10 contains provisions about tax.

<hr>

References   See para 13.1.

449 Agency staff: pseudonyms

(1)   This section applies to a member of the staff of the Agency if—
- (a)   he is authorised (generally or specifically) by the Director to do anything for the purposes of this Act, and
- (b)   it is necessary or expedient for the purpose of doing the thing for the member of the staff of the Agency to identify himself by name.

(2)   The Director may direct that such a member of the staff of the Agency may for that purpose identify himself by means of a pseudonym.

(3)   For the purposes of any proceedings or application under this Act a certificate signed by the Director which sufficiently identifies the member of the staff of the Agency by reference to the pseudonym is conclusive evidence that that member of the staff of the Agency is authorised to use the pseudonym.

(4)   In any proceedings or application under this Act a member of the staff of the Agency in respect of whom a direction under this section is in force must not be asked (and if asked is not required to answer) any question which is likely to reveal his true identity.

(5)   Section 1(6) does not apply to anything done by the Director under this section.

<hr>

Definitions   For "the Agency", see s 1(1); for "the Director", see s 1(2).
References   See para 13.8.

450 Pseudonyms: Scotland

(1)   This section applies to—
- (a)   any person named by the Scottish Ministers for the purpose of a civil recovery investigation under Part 8, or
- (b)   any person authorised by the Scottish Ministers for the purpose of such a civil recovery investigation to receive relevant information under section 391,

if it is necessary or expedient for the person to identify himself by name for that purpose.

(2)   The Scottish Ministers may direct that such a person may for that purpose identify himself by means of a pseudonym.

(3)   For the purposes of any proceedings or application under this Act, a certificate signed by the Scottish Ministers which sufficiently identifies the person by reference to the pseudonym is conclusive evidence that the person is authorised to use the pseudonym.

(4)   In any proceedings or application under this Act a person in respect of whom a direction under this section is in force must not be asked (and if asked is not required to answer) any question which is likely to reveal his true identity.

References   See para 13.8.

---

451 Customs and Excise prosecutions

(1)   Proceedings for a specified offence may be started by order of the Commissioners of Customs and Excise (the Commissioners).

(2)   Such proceedings must be brought in the name of a customs officer.

(3)   If the customs officer in whose name the proceedings are brought—
  (a)   dies,
  (b)   is removed or discharged, or
  (c)   is absent,
the proceedings may be continued by a different customs officer.

(4)   If the Commissioners investigate, or propose to investigate, any matter to help them to decide—
  (a)   whether there are grounds for believing that a specified offence has been committed, or
  (b)   whether a person is to be prosecuted for such an offence,
the matter must be treated as an assigned matter within the meaning of the Customs and Excise Management Act 1979 (c 2).

(5)   This section—
  (a)   does not prevent any person (including a customs officer) who has power to arrest, detain or prosecute a person for a specified offence from doing so;
  (b)   does not prevent a court from dealing with a person brought before it following his arrest by a customs officer for a specified offence, even if the proceedings were not started by an order under subsection (1).

(6)   The following are specified offences—
  (a)   an offence under Part 7;
  (b)   an offence under section 342;
  (c)   an attempt, conspiracy or incitement to commit an offence specified in paragraph (a) or (b);
  (d)   aiding, abetting, counselling or procuring the commission of an offence specified in paragraph (a) or (b).

(7)   This section does not apply to proceedings on indictment in Scotland.

Definitions   For "customs officer", see s 454.
References   See paras 13.9, 13.10.

---

452 Crown servants

(1)   The Secretary of State may by regulations provide that any of the following provisions apply to persons in the public service of the Crown.

(2)   The provisions are—
      (a)   the provisions of Part 7;
      (b)   section 342.

453 References to financial investigators

(1)   The Secretary of State may by order provide that a specified reference in this Act to an accredited financial investigator is a reference to such an investigator who falls within a specified description.

(2)   A description may be framed by reference to a grade designated by a specified person.

Definitions   For "accredited financial investigator", see s 3(5).

---

454 Customs officers

For the purposes of this Act a customs officer is a person commissioned by the Commissioners of Customs and Excise under section 6(3) of the Customs and Excise Management Act 1979 (c 2).

455 Enactment

In this Act (except in section 460(1)) a reference to an enactment includes a reference to—
      (a)   an Act of the Scottish Parliament;
      (b)   Northern Ireland legislation.

General

456 Amendments

Schedule 11 contains miscellaneous and consequential amendments.

References   See paras 13.11–13.16.

---

457 Repeals and revocations

Schedule 12 contains repeals and revocations.

References   See para 13.16.

---

458 Commencement

(1)   The preceding provisions of this Act (except the provisions specified in subsection (3)) come into force in accordance with provision made by the Secretary of State by order.

(2)   But no order may be made which includes provision for the commencement of Part 5, 8 or 10 unless the Secretary of State has consulted the Scottish Ministers.

(3)   The following provisions come into force in accordance with provision made by the Scottish Ministers by order after consultation with the Secretary of State—

    (a)   Part 3;

    (b)   this Part, to the extent that it relates to Part 3.

References   See para 13.17.

---

459 Orders and regulations

(1)   References in this section to subordinate legislation are to—

    (a)   any Order in Council under this Act;

    (b)   any order under this Act (other than one falling to be made by a court);

    (c)   any regulations under this Act.

(2)   Subordinate legislation—

    (a)   may make different provision for different purposes;

    (b)   may include supplementary, incidental, saving or transitional provisions.

(3)   Any power to make subordinate legislation is exercisable by statutory instrument.

(4)   A statutory instrument is subject to annulment in pursuance of a resolution of either House of Parliament if it contains subordinate legislation other than—

    (a)   an order under section 75(7) or (8), 223(7) or (8), 282, 292(4), 309, 364(4), 377(4), 436(6), 438(9) or 458;

    (b)   subordinate legislation made by the Scottish Ministers;

    (c)   an Order in Council made under section 443 which makes provision only in relation to Scotland.

(5)   A statutory instrument is subject to annulment in pursuance of a resolution of the Scottish Parliament if it contains—

    (a)   subordinate legislation made by the Scottish Ministers other than an order under section 142(6) or (7), 293(4), 398(4), 410(4), 439(6), 441(9) or 458;

    (b)   an Order in Council made under section 443 which makes provision only in relation to Scotland.

(6)   No order may be made—

    (a)   by the Secretary of State under section 75(7) or (8), 223(7) or (8), 282, 292(4), 309, 364(4), 377(4), 436(6) or 438(9) unless a draft of the order has been laid before Parliament and approved by a resolution of each House;

    (b)   by the Scottish Ministers under section 142(6) or (7), 293(4), 398(4), 410(4), 439(6) or 441(9) unless a draft of the order has been laid before and approved by a resolution of the Scottish Parliament.

(7)   The Scottish Ministers must lay before the Scottish Parliament a copy of every statutory instrument containing an Order in Council made under section 444 or 445.

460 Finance

(1)   The following are to be paid out of money provided by Parliament—

    (a)   any expenditure incurred by any Minister of the Crown under this Act;

    (b)   any increase attributable to this Act in the sums payable out of money so provided under any other enactment.

(2)   Any sums received by the Secretary of State in consequence of this Act are to be paid into the Consolidated Fund.

Definitions   For "enactment", see s 455.

---

461 Extent

(1)   Part 2 extends to England and Wales only.

(2)   In Part 8, Chapter 2 extends to England and Wales and Northern Ireland only.

(3)   These provisions extend to Scotland only—

    (a)   Part 3;

    (b)   in Part 8, Chapter 3.

(4)   Part 4 extends to Northern Ireland only.

(5)   The amendments in Schedule 11 have the same extent as the provisions amended.

(6)   The repeals and revocations in Schedule 12 have the same extent as the provisions repealed or revoked.

462 Short title

This Act may be cited as the Proceeds of Crime Act 2002.

SCHEDULE 1

Section 1

ASSETS RECOVERY AGENCY

Director's terms of appointment

1.—(1) The Director holds office for the period determined by the Secretary of State on his appointment (or re-appointment) to the office.

(2) But—
- (a) the Director may at any time resign by giving notice to the Secretary of State;
- (b) the Secretary of State may at any time remove the Director from office if satisfied that he is unable or unfit to exercise his functions.

2. Subject to that, the Director holds office on the terms determined by the Secretary of State with the approval of the Minister for the Civil Service.

Staff

3.—(1) The members of staff of the Agency must include—
- (a) a deputy to the Director who is to act as Director during any vacancy in that office or if the Director is absent, subject to suspension or unable to act, and
- (b) an assistant to the Director with responsibilities in relation to the exercise of the Director's functions in Northern Ireland.

(2) But the Director must not appoint a person under sub-paragraph (1)(b) unless he first consults the Secretary of State.

4. The members of staff of the Agency hold office on the terms determined by the Director with the approval of the Minister for the Civil Service.

Finances

5.—(1) These amounts are to be paid out of money provided by Parliament—
- (a) the remuneration of the Director and the staff of the Agency;
- (b) any expenses incurred by the Director or any of the staff in the exercise of his or their functions.

(2) Subject to anything in this Act any sums received by the Director are to be paid into the Consolidated Fund.

Annual plan

6.—(1) The Director must, before the beginning of each financial year apart from the first, prepare a plan setting out how he intends to exercise his functions during the financial year (an annual plan).

(2) The annual plan must, in particular, set out how the Director intends to exercise his functions in Northern Ireland.

(3) The annual plan must also include a statement of—
- (a) the Director's objectives for the financial year;
- (b) any performance targets which he has for the financial year (whether or not relating to his objectives);
- (c) his priorities for the financial year;
- (d) the financial resources expected to be available to him for the financial year;
- (e) his proposed allocation of those resources.

(4) Once the annual plan has been prepared the Director must send a copy to the Secretary of State for his approval.

(5) If the Secretary of State does not approve the annual plan—
- (a) he must give the Director his reasons for not approving it, and
- (b) he may require the Director to revise it in the manner specified by the Secretary of State.

(6)   The Director must revise the annual plan, but if sub-paragraph (5)(b) applies he must do so in the manner specified by the Secretary of State.

(7)   The Director must send a copy of the revised annual plan to the Secretary of State for his approval.

Annual report

7.—(1) The Director must, as soon as possible after the end of each financial year, prepare a report on how he has exercised his functions during the financial year.

(2)   The report for any financial year apart from the first must include—
      (a)   the Director's annual plan for the financial year, and
      (b)   an assessment of the extent to which it has been carried out.

(3)   The Director must send a copy of each report to the Secretary of State who must—
      (a)   lay a copy of it before each House of Parliament, and
      (b)   arrange for it to be published.

Meaning of "financial year"

8. In this Schedule "financial year" means—
      (a)   the period beginning with the day on which section 1 comes into force and ending with the next 31 March (which is the first financial year), and
      (b)   each subsequent period of twelve months beginning with 1 April.

Definitions   For "the Agency", see s 1(1); for "the Director", see s 1(2).
References   See ch 2.

SCHEDULE 2

Section 75

LIFESTYLE OFFENCES: ENGLAND AND WALES

Drug trafficking

1.—(1) An offence under any of the following provisions of the Misuse of Drugs Act 1971 (c 38)—
      (a)   section 4(2) or (3) (unlawful production or supply of controlled drugs);
      (b)   section 5(3) (possession of controlled drug with intent to supply);
      (c)   section 8 (permitting certain activities relating to controlled drugs);
      (d)   section 20 (assisting in or inducing the commission outside the UK of an offence punishable under a corresponding law).

(2)   An offence under any of the following provisions of the Customs and Excise Management Act 1979 (c 2) if it is committed in connection with a prohibition or restriction on importation or exportation which has effect by virtue of section 3 of the Misuse of Drugs Act 1971—
      (a)   section 50(2) or (3) (improper importation of goods);
      (b)   section 68(2) (exploration of prohibited or restricted goods);
      (c)   section 170 (fraudulent evasion).

(3)   An offence under either of the following provisions of the Criminal Justice (International Co-operation) Act 1990 (c 5)—
      (a)   section 12 (manufacture or supply of a substance for the time being specified in Schedule 2 to that Act);
      (b)   section 19 (using a ship for illicit traffic in controlled drugs).

Money laundering

2. An offence under either of the following provisions of this Act—
      (a)   section 327 (concealing etc criminal property);
      (b)   section 328 (assisting another to retain criminal property).

Directing terrorism

3. An offence under section 56 of the Terrorism Act 2000 (c 11) (directing the activities of a terrorist organisation).

People trafficking

4. An offence under section 25(1) of the Immigration Act 1971 (c 77) (assisting illegal entry etc).

Arms trafficking

5.—(1) An offence under either of the following provisions of the Customs and Excise Management Act 1979 if it is committed in connection with a firearm or ammunition—

    (a)   section 68(2) (exportation of prohibited goods);

    (b)   section 170 (fraudulent evasion).

    (2)   An offence under section 3(1) of the Firearms Act 1968 (c 27) (dealing in firearms or ammunition by way of trade or business).

    (3)   In this paragraph "firearm" and "ammunition" have the same meanings as in section 57 of the Firearms Act 1968 (c 27).

Counterfeiting

6. An offence under any of the following provisions of the Forgery and Counterfeiting Act 1981 (c 45)—

    (a)   section 14 (making counterfeit notes or coins);

    (b)   section 15 (passing etc counterfeit notes or coins);

    (c)   section 16 (having counterfeit notes or coins);

    (d)   section 17 (making or possessing materials or equipment for counterfeiting).

Intellectual property

7.—(1) An offence under any of the following provisions of the Copyright, Designs and Patents Act 1988 (c 48)—

    (a)   section 107(1) (making or dealing in an article which infringes copyright);

    (b)   section 107(2) (making or possessing an article designed or adapted for making a copy of a copyright work);

    (c)   section 198(1) (making or dealing in an illicit recording);

    (d)   section 297A (making or dealing in unauthorised decoders).

    (2)   An offence under section 92(1), (2) or (3) of the Trade Marks Act 1994 (c 26) (unauthorised use etc of trade mark).

Pimps and brothels

8.—(1) An offence under any of the following provisions of the Sexual Offences Act 1956 (c 69)—

    (a)   section 2 (procuring a woman by threats);

    (b)   section 3 (procuring a woman by false pretences);

    (c)   section 9 (procuring a defective woman to have sexual intercourse);

    (d)   section 22 (procuring a woman for prostitution);

    (e)   section 24 (detaining a woman in a brothel);

    (f)   section 28 (causing or encouraging prostitution etc of girl under 16);

    (g)   section 29 (causing or encouraging prostitution of defective woman);

    (h)   section 30 (man living on earnings of prostitution);

    (i)   section 31 (woman exercising control over prostitute);

    (j)   section 33 (keeping a brothel);

    (k)   section 34 (letting premises for use as brothel).

    (2)   An offence under section 5 of the Sexual Offences Act 1967 (c 60) (living on the earnings of male prostitute).

Blackmail

9. An offence under section 21 of the Theft Act 1968 (c 60) (blackmail).

Inchoate offences

10.—(1) An offence of attempting, conspiring or inciting the commission of an offence specified in this Schedule.

(2) An offence of aiding, abetting, counselling or procuring the commission of such an offence.

References   See ch 3.

SCHEDULE 3

Section 137

ADMINISTRATORS: FURTHER PROVISION

General

1. In this Schedule, unless otherwise expressly provided—
    (a) references to an administrator are to an administrator appointed under section 125 or 128(3);
    (b) references to realisable property are to the realisable property in respect of which the administrator is appointed.

Appointment etc

2.—(1) If the office of administrator is vacant, for whatever reason, the court must appoint a new administrator.

(2) Any property vested in the previous administrator by virtue of paragraph 5(4) vests in the new administrator.

(3) Any order under section 125 or 128(7) in relation to the previous administrator applies in relation to the new administrator when he gives written notice of his appointment to the person subject to the order.

(4) The administration of property by an administrator must be treated as continuous despite any temporary vacancy in that office.

(5) The appointment of an administrator is subject to such conditions as to caution as the accountant of court may impose.

(6) The premium of any bond of caution or other security required by such conditions must be treated as part of the administrator's expenses in the exercise of his functions.

Functions

3.—(1) An administrator—
    (a) may, if appointed under section 125, and
    (b) must, if appointed under section 128(3),
as soon as practicable take possession of the realisable property and of the documents mentioned in sub-paragraph (2).

(2) Those documents are any document which—
    (a) is in the possession or control of the person ("A") in whom the property is vested (or would be vested but for an order made under paragraph 5(4)), and
    (b) relates to the property or to A's assets, business or financial affairs.

(3) An administrator is entitled to have access to, and to copy, any document relating to the property or to A's assets, business or financial affairs and not falling within sub-paragraph (2)(a).

(4)   An administrator may bring, defend or continue any legal proceedings relating to the property.

(5)   An administrator may borrow money so far as it is necessary to do so to safeguard the property and may for the purposes of such borrowing create a security over any part of the property.

(6)   An administrator may, if he considers that it would be beneficial for the management or realisation of the property—

      (a)   carry on any business of A;
      (b)   exercise any right of A as holder of securities in a company;
      (c)   grant a lease of the property or take on lease any other property;
      (d)   enter into any contract, or execute any deed, as regards the property or as regards A's business.

(7)   An administrator may, where any right, option or other power forms part of A's estate, make payments or incur liabilities with a view to—

      (a)   obtaining property which is the subject of, or
      (b)   maintaining,

the right, option or power.

(8)   An administrator may effect or maintain insurance policies as regards the property on A's business.

(9)   An administrator may, if appointed under section 128(3), complete any uncompleted title which A has to any heritable estate; but completion of title in A's name does not validate by accretion any unperfected right in favour of any person other than the administrator.

(10)   An administrator may sell, purchase or exchange property or discharge any security for an obligation due to A; but it is incompetent for the administrator or an associate of his (within the meaning of section 74 of the Bankruptcy (Scotland) Act 1985 (c 66)) to purchase any of A's property in pursuance of this sub-paragraph.

(11)   An administrator may claim, vote and draw dividends in the sequestration of the estate (or bankruptcy or liquidation) of a debtor of A and may accede to a voluntary trust deed for creditors of such a debtor.

(12)   An administrator may discharge any of his functions through agents or employees, but is personally liable to meet the fees and expenses of any such agent or employee out of such remuneration as is payable to the administrator on a determination by the accountant of court.

(13)   An administrator may take such professional advice as he considers necessary in connection with the exercise of his functions.

(14)   An administrator may at any time apply to the court for directions as regards the exercise of his functions.

(15)   An administrator may exercise any power specifically conferred on him by the court, whether conferred on his appointment or subsequently.

(16)   An administrator may—

      (a)   enter any premises;
      (b)   search for or inspect anything authorised by the court;
      (c)   make or obtain a copy, photograph or other record of anything so authorised;
      (d)   remove anything which the administrator is required or authorised to take possession of in pursuance of an order of the court.

(17)   An administrator may do anything incidental to the powers and duties listed in the previous provisions of this paragraph.

Consent of accountant of court

4.   An administrator proposing to exercise any power conferred by paragraph 3(4) to (17) must first obtain the consent of the accountant of court.

Dealings in good faith with administrator

5.—(1) A person dealing with an administrator in good faith and for value is not concerned to enquire whether the administrator is acting within the powers mentioned in paragraph 3.

(2) Sub-paragraph (1) does not apply where the administrator or an associate purchases property in contravention of paragraph 3(10).

(3) The validity of any title is not challengeable by reason only of the administrator having acted outwith the powers mentioned in paragraph 3.

(4) The exercise of a power mentioned in paragraph 3(4) to (11) must be in A's name except where and in so far as an order made by the court under this sub-paragraph vests the property in the administrator (or in a previous administrator).

(5) The court may make an order under sub-paragraph (4) on the application of the administrator or on its own motion.

Money received by administrator

6.—(1) All money received by an administrator in the exercise of his functions must be deposited by him, in the name (unless vested in the administrator by virtue of paragraph 5(4)) of the holder of the property realised, in an appropriate bank or institution.

(2) But the administrator may at any time retain in his hands a sum not exceeding £200 or such other sum as may be prescribed by the Scottish Ministers by regulations.

(3) In sub-paragraph (1), "appropriate bank or institution" means a bank or institution mentioned in section 3(1) of the Banking Act 1987 (c 22) or for the time being specified in Schedule 2 to that Act.

Effect of appointment of administrator on diligence

7.—(1) An arrestment or poinding of realisable property executed on or after the appointment of an administrator does not create a preference for the arrester or poinder.

(2) Any realisable property so arrested or poinded, or (if the property has been sold) the proceeds of sale, must be handed over to the administrator.

(3) A poinding of the ground in respect of realisable property on or after such appointment is ineffectual in a question with the administrator except for the interest mentioned in sub-paragraph (4).

(4) That interest is—
 (a) interest on the debt of a secured creditor for the current half-yearly term, and
 (b) arrears of interest on that debt for one year immediately before the commencement of that term.

(5) On and after such appointment no other person may raise or insist in an adjudication against realisable property or be confirmed as executor-creditor on that property.

(6) An inhibition on realisable property which takes effect on or after such appointment does not create a preference for the inhibitor in a question with the administrator.

(7) This paragraph is without prejudice to sections 123 and 124.

(8) In this paragraph, the reference to an administrator is to an administrator appointed under section 128(3).

Supervision

8.—(1) If the accountant of court reports to the court that an administrator has failed to perform any duty imposed on him, the court may, after giving the administrator an opportunity to be heard as regards the matter—
 (a) remove him from office,
 (b) censure him, or
 (c) make such other order as it thinks fit.

(2)   Section 6 of the Judicial Factors (Scotland) Act 1889 (c 39) (supervision of judicial factors) does not apply in relation to an administrator.

Accounts and remuneration

9.—(1) Not later than two weeks after the issuing of any determination by the accountant of court as to the remuneration and expenses payable to the administrator, the administrator or the Lord Advocate may appeal against it to the court.

(2)   The amount of remuneration payable to the administrator must be determined on the basis of the value of the work reasonably undertaken by him, regard being had to the extent of the responsibilities involved.

(3)   The accountant of court may authorise the administrator to pay without taxation an account in respect of legal services incurred by the administrator.

Discharge of administrator

10.—(1) After an administrator has lodged his final accounts under paragraph 9(1), he may apply to the accountant of court to be discharged from office.

(2)   A discharge, if granted, frees the administrator from all liability (other than liability arising from fraud) in respect of any act or omission of his in exercising his functions as administrator.

SCHEDULE 4

Section 142

LIFESTYLE OFFENCES: SCOTLAND

Money laundering

1. An offence under either of the following provisions of this Act—
>   (a)   section 327 (concealing etc criminal property);
>   (b)   section 328 (assisting another person to retain criminal property).

Drug trafficking

2.—(1) An offence under any of the following provisions of the Misuse of Drugs Act 1971 (c 38)—
>   (a)   section 4(2) or (3) (unlawful production or supply of controlled drugs);
>   (b)   section 5(3) (possession of controlled drug with intent to supply);
>   (c)   section 8 (permitting certain activities relating to controlled drugs);
>   (d)   section 20 (assisting in or inducing the commission outside the UK of an offence punishable under a corresponding law).

(2)   An offence under any of the following provisions of the Customs and Excise Management Act 1979 (c 2) if it is committed in connection with a prohibition or restriction on importation or exportation which has effect by virtue of section 3 of the Misuse of Drugs Act 1971—
>   (a)   section 50(2) or (3) (improper importation of goods);
>   (b)   section 68(2) (exploration of prohibited or restricted goods);
>   (c)   section 170 (fraudulent evasion).

(3)   An offence under either of the following provisions of the Criminal Justice (International Co-operation) Act 1990 (c 5)—
>   (a)   section 12 (manufacture or supply of a substance for the time being specified in Schedule 2 to that Act);
>   (b)   section 19 (using a ship for illicit traffic in controlled drugs).

Directing terrorism

3. An offence under section 56 of the Terrorism Act 2000 (c 11) (directing the activities of a terrorist organisation).

People trafficking

4. An offence under section 25(1) of the Immigration Act 1971 (c 77) (assisting illegal entry etc).

Arms trafficking

5.—(1) An offence under either of the following provisions of the Customs and Excise Management Act 1979 if it is committed in connection with a firearm or ammunition—
    (a)   section 68(2) (exportation of prohibited goods);
    (b)   section 170 (fraudulent evasion).

   (2)   An offence under section 3(1) of the Firearms Act 1968 (c 27) (dealing in firearms or ammunition by way of trade or business).

   (3)   In this paragraph "firearm" and "ammunition" have the same meanings as in section 57 of the Firearms Act 1968 (c 27).

Counterfeiting

6. An offence under any of the following provisions of the Forgery and Counterfeiting Act 1981 (c 45)—
    (a)   section 14 (making counterfeit notes or coins);
    (b)   section 15 (passing etc counterfeit notes or coins);
    (c)   section 16 (having counterfeit notes or coins);
    (d)   section 17 (making or possessing materials or equipment for counterfeiting).

Intellectual property

7.—(1) An offence under any of the following provisions of the Copyright, Designs and Patents Act 1988 (c 48)—
    (a)   section 107(1) (making or dealing in an article which infringes copyright);
    (b)   section 107(2) (making or possessing an article designed or adapted for making a copy of a copyright work);
    (c)   section 198(1) (making or dealing in an illicit recording);
    (d)   section 297A (making or dealing in unauthorised decoders).

   (2)   An offence under section 92(1), (2), or (3) of the Trade Marks Act 1994 (c 26) (unauthorised use etc of trade mark).

Pimps and brothels

8. An offence under either of the following provisions of the Criminal Law (Consolidation) (Scotland) Act 1995 (c 39)—
    (a)   section 11(1) (living on earnings of prostitution or soliciting for immoral purposes);
    (b)   section 11(5) (running of brothels).

Blackmail

9. An offence of blackmail or extortion.

Inchoate offences

10.—(1) An offence of conspiring or inciting the commission of an offence specified in this Schedule.

   (2)   An offence of aiding, abetting, counselling or procuring the commission of such an offence.

References   See ch 4.

SCHEDULE 5

LIFESTYLE OFFENCES: NORTHERN IRELAND

Drug trafficking

1.—(1) An offence under any of the following provisions of the Misuse of Drugs Act 1971 (c 38)—

    (a)   section 4(2) or (3) (unlawful production or supply of controlled drugs);

    (b)   section 5(3) (possession of controlled drug with intent to supply);

    (c)   section 8 (permitting certain activities relating to controlled drugs);

    (d)   section 20 (assisting in or inducing the commission outside the UK of an offence punishable under a corresponding law).

(2) An offence under any of the following provisions of the Customs and Excise Management Act 1979 (c 2) if it is committed in connection with a prohibition or restriction on importation or exportation which has effect by virtue of section 3 of the Misuse of Drugs Act 1971—

    (a)   section 50(2) or (3) (improper importation of goods);

    (b)   section 68(2) (exportation of prohibited or restricted goods);

    (c)   section 170 (fraudulent evasion).

(3) An offence under either of the following provisions of the Criminal Justice (International Co-operation) Act 1990 (c 5)—

    (a)   section 12 (manufacture or supply of a substance for the time being specified in Schedule 2 to that Act);

    (b)   section 19 (using a ship for illicit traffic in controlled drugs).

Money laundering

2. An offence under either of the following provisions of this Act—

    (a)   section 327 (concealing etc criminal property);

    (b)   section 328 (assisting another to retain criminal property).

Directing terrorism

3. An offence under section 56 of the Terrorism Act 2000 (c 11) (directing the activities of a terrorist organisation).

People trafficking

4. An offence under section 25(1) of the Immigration Act 1971 (c 77) (assisting illegal entry etc).

Arms trafficking

5.—(1) An offence under either of the following provisions of the Customs and Excise Management Act 1979 if it is committed in connection with a firearm or ammunition—

    (a)   section 68(2) (exportation of prohibited goods);

    (b)   section 170 (fraudulent evasion).

(2) An offence under Article 4(1) of the Firearms (Northern Ireland) Order 1981 (SI 1981/155 (NI 2) (dealing in firearms or ammunition by way of trade or business).

(3) In this paragraph "firearm" and "ammunition" have the same meanings as in Article 2(2) of that Order.

Counterfeiting

6. An offence under any of the following provisions of the Forgery and Counterfeiting Act 1981 (c 45)—

    (a)   section 14 (making counterfeit notes or coins);

    (b)   section 15 (passing etc counterfeit notes or coins);

(c) section 16 (having counterfeit notes or coins);
(d) section 17 (making or possessing materials or equipment for counterfeiting).

Intellectual property

7.—(1)An offence under any of the following provisions of the Copyright, Designs and Patents Act 1988 (c 48)—

(a) section 107(1) (making or dealing in an article which infringes copyright);
(b) section 107(2) (making or possessing an article designed or adapted for making a copy of a copyright work);
(c) section 198(1) (making or dealing in an illicit recording);
(d) section 297A (making or dealing in unauthorised decoders).

(2) An offence under section 92(1), (2) or (3) of the Trade Marks Act 1994 (c 26) (unauthorised use etc of trade mark).

Pimps and brothels

8.—(1)An offence under any of the following provisions of the Criminal Law Amendment Act 1885 (c 69)—

(a) section 2 (procuring a woman or girl);
(b) section 3 (procuring a woman or girl by threats or false pretences);
(c) section 8 (detaining a woman in a brothel);
(d) section 13(3) (letting premises for use as a brothel).

(2) An offence under section 1(1) of the Vagrancy Act 1898 (c 39) (man living on the earnings of prostitution).

(3) An offence under that Act as extended by section 7(4) of the Criminal Law Amendment Act 1912 (c 20) (woman exercising control over prostitute).

(4) An offence under section 21 of the Children and Young Persons Act (Northern Ireland) 1968 (c 34) (causing or encouraging prostitution etc of girl under 17).

(5) An offence under Article 8 of the Homosexual Offences (Northern Ireland) Order 1982 (SI 1982/1536 (NI 19)) (living on the earnings of male prostitute).

(6) An offence under Article 122(1)(b) or (c) of the Mental Health (Northern Ireland) Order 1986 (SI 1986/595 (NI 4)) (procuring or causing prostitution by woman suffering from severe mental handicap).

(7) An offence of keeping a bawdy house.

Blackmail

9. An offence under section 20 of the Theft Act (Northern Ireland) 1969 (c 16) (blackmail).

Inchoate offences

10.—(1) An offence of attempting, conspiring or inciting the commission of an offence specified in this Schedule.

(2) An offence of aiding, abetting, counselling or procuring the commission of such an offence.

References   See ch 5.

SCHEDULE 6

Sections 247 and 257

POWERS OF INTERIM RECEIVER OR ADMINISTRATOR

Seizure

1. Power to seize property to which the order applies.

Information

2.—(1) Power to obtain information or to require a person to answer any question.

(2)   A requirement imposed in the exercise of the power has effect in spite of any restriction on the disclosure of information (however imposed).

(3)   An answer given by a person in pursuance of such a requirement may not be used in evidence against him in criminal proceedings.

(4)   Sub-paragraph (3) does not apply—
  (a)   on a prosecution for an offence under section 5 of the Perjury Act 1911, section 44(2) of the Criminal Law (Consolidation) (Scotland) Act 1995 or Article 10 of the Perjury (Northern Ireland) Order 1979 (false statements), or
  (b)   on a prosecution for some other offence where, in giving evidence, he makes a statement inconsistent with it.

(5)   But an answer may not be used by virtue of sub-paragraph (4)(b) against a person unless—
  (a)   evidence relating to it is adduced, or
  (b)   a question relating to it is asked,

by him or on his behalf in the proceedings arising out of the prosecution.

Entry, search, etc

3.—(1) Power to—
  (a)   enter any premises in the United Kingdom to which the interim order applies, and
  (b)   take any of the following steps.

(2)   Those steps are—
  (a)   to carry out a search for or inspection of anything described in the order,
  (b)   to make or obtain a copy, photograph or other record of anything so described,
  (c)   to remove anything which he is required to take possession of in pursuance of the order or which may be required as evidence in the proceedings under Chapter 2 of Part 5.

(3)   The order may describe anything generally, whether by reference to a class or otherwise.

Supplementary

4.—(1) An order making any provision under paragraph 2 or 3 must make provision in respect of legal professional privilege (in Scotland, legal privilege within the meaning of Chapter 3 of Part 8).

(2)   An order making any provision under paragraph 3 may require any person—
  (a)   to give the interim receiver or administrator access to any premises which he may enter in pursuance of paragraph 3,
  (b)   to give the interim receiver or administrator any assistance he may require for taking the steps mentioned in that paragraph.

Management

5.—(1) Power to manage any property to which the order applies.

(2)   Managing property includes—
  (a)   selling or otherwise disposing of assets comprised in the property which are perishable or which ought to be disposed of before their value diminishes,

     (b)   where the property comprises assets of a trade or business, carrying on, or arranging for another to carry on, the trade or business,

     (c)   incurring capital expenditure in respect of the property.

Definitions   For "disposing", see s 314(1)–(3); for "premises", see s 316(1); for "property", see s 316(2), (4)–(7); for "value", see s 316(1).
References   See ch 6.

SCHEDULE 7

Section 267

POWERS OF TRUSTEE FOR CIVIL RECOVERY

Sale

1. Power to sell the property or any part of it or interest in it.

Expenditure

2. Power to incur expenditure for the purpose of—

     (a)   acquiring any part of the property, or any interest in it, which is not vested in him,

     (b)   discharging any liabilities, or extinguishing any rights, to which the property is subject.

Management

3.—(1) Power to manage property.

  (2) Managing property includes doing anything mentioned in paragraph 5(2) of Schedule 6.

Legal proceedings

4. Power to start, carry on or defend any legal proceedings in respect of the property.

Compromise

5. Power to make any compromise or other arrangement in connection with any claim relating to the property.

Supplementary

6.—(1) For the purposes of, or in connection with, the exercise of any of his powers—

     (a)   power by his official name to do any of the things mentioned in sub-paragraph (2),

     (b)   power to do any other act which is necessary or expedient.

  (2) Those things are—

     (a)   holding property,

     (b)   entering into contracts,

     (c)   suing and being sued,

     (d)   employing agents,

     (e)   executing a power of attorney, deed or other instrument.

Definitions   For "interest" in relation to land, see s 316(1); for "interest" in relation to property other than land", see s 316(1); for "part" in relation to property, see s 316(1); for "property", see s 316(2), (4)–(7).
References   See ch 6.

SCHEDULE 8

Section 325

FORMS OF DECLARATIONS

The Director

"I, A.B., do solemnly declare that I will not disclose any information received by me in carrying out my functions under Part 6 of the Proceeds of Crime Act 2002 except for the purposes of those functions or for the purposes of any prosecution for an offence relating to inland revenue, or in such other cases as may be required or permitted by law."

Members Of The Staff Of The Agency

"I, A.B., do solemnly declare that I will not disclose any information received by me in carrying out the functions under Part 6 of the Proceeds of Crime Act 2002 which I may from time to time be authorised by the Director of the Assets Recovery Agency to carry out except for the purposes of those functions, or to the Director or in accordance with his instructions, or for the purposes of any prosecution for an offence relating to inland revenue, or in such other cases as may be required or permitted by law."

Definitions   For "the Agency", see s 1(1); for "the Director", see s 1(2).

SCHEDULE 9

Section 330

REGULATED SECTOR AND SUPERVISORY AUTHORITIES

PART 1
REGULATED SECTOR

Business in the regulated sector

1.—(1) A business is in the regulated sector to the extent that it engages in any of the following activities—
  (a) accepting deposits by a person with permission under Part 4 of the Financial Services and Markets Act 2000 (c 8) to accept deposits (including, in the case of a building society, the raising of money from members of the society by the issue of shares);
  (b) the business of the National Savings Bank;
  (c) business carried on by a credit union;
  (d) any home-regulated activity carried on by a European institution in respect of which the establishment conditions in paragraph 13 of Schedule 3 to the Financial Services and Markets Act 2000, or the service conditions in paragraph 14 of that Schedule, are satisfied;
  (e) any activity carried on for the purpose of raising money authorised to be raised under the National Loans Act 1968 (c 13) under the auspices of the Director of Savings;
  (f) the activity of operating a bureau de change, transmitting money (or any representation of monetary value) by any means or cashing cheques which are made payable to customers;
  (g) any activity falling within sub-paragraph (2);
  (h) any of the activities in points 1 to 12 or 14 of Annex 1 to the Banking Consolidation Directive, ignoring an activity described in any of sub-paragraphs (a) to (g) above;
  (i) business which consists of effecting or carrying out contracts of long term insurance by a person who has received official authorisation pursuant to Article 6 or 27 of the First Life Directive.

  (2)   An activity falls within this sub-paragraph if it constitutes any of the following kinds of regulated activity in the United Kingdom—
  (a) dealing in investments as principal or as agent;

    (b)   arranging deals in investments;
    (c)   managing investments;
    (d)   safeguarding and administering investments;
    (e)   sending dematerialised instructions;
    (f)   establishing (and taking other steps in relation to) collective investment schemes;
    (g)   advising on investments.

(3)   Paragraphs (a) and (i) of sub-paragraph (1) and sub-paragraph (2) must be read with section 22 of the Financial Services and Markets Act 2000, any relevant order under that section and Schedule 2 to that Act.

2.—(1)   This paragraph has effect for the purposes of paragraph 1.

(2)   "Building society" has the meaning given by the Building Societies Act 1986 (c 53).

(3)   "Credit union" has the meaning given by the Credit Unions Act 1979 (c 34) or the Credit Unions (Northern Ireland) Order 1985 (SI 1985/1205 (NI 12)).

(4)   "European institution" means an EEA firm of the kind mentioned in paragraph 5(b) or (c) of Schedule 3 to the Financial Services and Markets Act 2000 (c 8) which qualifies for authorisation for the purposes of that Act under paragraph 12 of that Schedule.

(5)   "Home-regulated activity" in relation to a European institution, means an activity—
    (a)   which is specified in Annex 1 to the Banking Consolidation Directive and in respect of which a supervisory authority in the home State of the institution has regulatory functions, and
    (b)   if the institution is an EEA firm of the kind mentioned in paragraph 5(c) of Schedule 3 to the Financial Services and Markets Act 2000, which the institution carries on in its home State.

(6)   "Home State", in relation to a person incorporated in or formed under the law of another member State, means that State.

(7)   The Banking Consolidation Directive is the Directive of the European Parliament and Council relating to the taking up and pursuit of the business of credit institutions (No 2000/12 EC).

(8)   The First Life Directive is the First Council Directive on the co-ordination of laws, regulations and administrative provisions relating to the taking up and pursuit of the business of direct life assurance (No 79/267/EEC).

Excluded activities

3.   A business is not in the regulated sector to the extent that it engages in any of the following activities—
    (a)   the issue of withdrawable share capital within the limit set by section 6 of the Industrial and Provident Societies Act 1965 (c 12) by a society registered under that Act;
    (b)   the acceptance of deposits from the public within the limit set by section 7(3) of that Act by such a society;
    (c)   the issue of withdrawable share capital within the limit set by section 6 of the Industrial and Provident Societies Act (Northern Ireland) 1969 by a society registered under that Act;
    (d)   the acceptance of deposits from the public within the limit set by section 7(3) of that Act by such a society;
    (e)   activities carried on by the Bank of England;
    (f)   any activity in respect of which an exemption order under section 38 of the Financial Services and Markets Act 2000 has effect if it is carried on by a person who is for the time being specified in the order or falls within a class of persons so specified.

PART 2
SUPERVISORY AUTHORITIES

4.—(1) Each of the following is a supervisory authority—

(a) the Bank of England;
(b) the Financial Services Authority;
(c) the Council of Lloyd's;
(d) the Director General of Fair Trading;
(e) a body which is a designated professional body for the purposes of Part 20 of the Financial Services and Markets Act 2000 (c 8).

(2) The Secretary of State is also a supervisory authority in the exercise, in relation to a person carrying on a business in the regulated sector, of his functions under the enactments relating to companies or insolvency or under the Financial Services and Markets Act 2000.

(3) The Treasury are also a supervisory authority in the exercise, in relation to a person carrying on a business in the regulated sector, of their functions under the enactments relating to companies or insolvency or under the Financial Services and Markets Act 2000.

PART 3
POWER TO AMEND

5. The Treasury may by order amend Part 1 or 2 of this Schedule.

Definitions For "enactment", see s 455.
References See ch 8.

SCHEDULE 10

Section 448

TAX

PART 1
GENERAL

1. Sections 75 and 77 of the Taxes Management Act 1970 (c 9) (receivers: income tax and capital gains tax) shall not apply in relation to—

(a) a receiver appointed under section 48, 50 or 52;
(b) an administrator appointed under section 125 or 128;
(c) a receiver appointed under section 196, 198 or 200;
(d) an interim receiver appointed under section 246;
(e) an interim administrator appointed under section 256.

PART 2
PROVISIONS RELATING TO PART 5

INTRODUCTORY

2.—(1) The vesting of property in the trustee for civil recovery or any other person by a recovery order or in pursuance of an order under section 276 is referred to as a Part 5 transfer.

(2) The person who holds the property immediately before the vesting is referred to as the transferor; and the person in whom the property is vested is referred to as the transferee.

(3) Any amount paid in respect of the transfer by the trustee for civil recovery, or another, to a person who holds the property immediately before the vesting is referred to (in relation to that person) as a compensating payment.

(4) If the recovery order provides or (as the case may be) the terms on which the order under section 276 is made provide for the creation of any interest in favour of a person who holds the property immediately before the vesting, he is to be treated instead as receiving (in

535

addition to any payment referred to in sub-paragraph (3)) a compensating payment of an amount equal to the value of the interest.

(5)   Where the property belongs to joint tenants immediately before the vesting and a compensating payment is made to one or more (but not both or all) of the joint tenants, this Part has effect separately in relation to each joint tenant.

(6)   Expressions used in this paragraph have the same meaning as in Part 5 of this Act.

(7)   "The Taxes Act 1988" means the Income and Corporation Taxes Act 1988 (c 1), and "the Allowances Act 2001" means the Capital Allowances Act 2001 (c 2).

(8)   This paragraph applies for the purposes of this Part.

CAPITAL GAINS TAX

3.—(1) If a gain attributable to a Part 5 transfer accrues to the transferor, it is not a chargeable gain.

(2)   But if a compensating payment is made to the transferor—
    (a)   sub-paragraph (1) does not apply, and
    (b)   the consideration for the transfer is the amount of the compensating payment.

(3)   If a gain attributable to the forfeiture under section 298 of property consisting of—
    (a)   notes or coins in any currency other than sterling,
    (b)   anything mentioned in section 289(6)(b) to (d), if expressed in any currency other than sterling, or
    (c)   bearer bonds or bearer shares,

accrues to the person who holds the property immediately before the forfeiture, it is not a chargeable gain.

(4)   This paragraph has effect as if it were included in Chapter 1 of Part 2 of the Taxation of Chargeable Gains Act 1992 (c 12).

INCOME TAX AND CORPORATION TAX

Accrued income scheme

4. If a Part 5 transfer is a transfer of securities within the meaning of sections 711 to 728 of the Taxes Act 1988 (transfers with or without accrued interest), sections 713(2) and (3) and 716 of that Act do not apply to the transfer.

Discounted securities

5. In the case of a Part 5 transfer of property consisting of a relevant discounted security (within the meaning of Schedule 13 to the Finance Act 1996 (c 8)), it is not to be treated as a transfer for the purposes of that Schedule.

Rights to receive amounts stated in certificates of deposit etc

6. In the case of a Part 5 transfer of property consisting of a right to which section 56(2) of the Taxes Act 1988 applies, or a right mentioned in section 56A(1) of that Act, (rights stated in certificates of deposit etc) it is not to be treated as a disposal of the right for the purposes of section 56(2) of that Act.

Non-qualifying offshore funds

7. In the case of a Part 5 transfer of property consisting of an asset mentioned in section 757(1)(a) or (b) of the Taxes Act 1988 (interests in non-qualifying offshore funds etc), it is not to be treated as a disposal for the purposes of that section.

Futures and options

8. In the case of a Part 5 transfer of property consisting of futures or options (within the meaning of paragraph 4 of Schedule 5AA to the Taxes Act 1988), it is not to be treated as a disposal of the futures or options for the purposes of that Schedule.

Loan relationships

9.—(1) Sub-paragraph (2) applies if, apart from this paragraph, a Part 5 transfer would be a related transaction for the purposes of section 84 of the Finance Act 1996 (c 8) (debits and credits brought into account for the purpose of taxing loan relationships under Chapter 2 of Part 4 of that Act).

(2) The Part 5 transfer is to be disregarded for the purposes of that Chapter, except for the purpose of identifying any person in whose case any debit or credit not relating to the transaction is to be brought into account.

Exception from paragraphs 4 to 9

10. Paragraphs 4 to 9 do not apply if a compensating payment is made to the transferor.

Trading stock

11.—(1) Sub-paragraph (2) applies, in the case of a Part 5 transfer of property consisting of the trading stock of a trade, for the purpose of computing any profits of the trade for tax purposes.

(2) If, because of the transfer, the trading stock is to be treated for that purpose as if it had been sold in the course of the trade, the amount realised on the sale is to be treated for that purpose as equal to its acquisition cost.

(3) Sub-paragraph (2) has effect in spite of anything in section 100 of the Taxes Act 1988 (valuation of trading stock at discontinuance).

(4) In this paragraph, trading stock and trade have the same meaning as in that section.

CAPITAL ALLOWANCES

Plant and machinery

12.—(1) If there is a Part 5 transfer of plant or machinery, Part 2 of the Allowances Act 2001 is to have effect as if a transferor who has incurred qualifying expenditure were required to bring the disposal value of the plant or machinery into account in accordance with section 61 of that Act for the chargeable period in which the transfer occurs.

(2) But the Part 5 transfer is not to be treated as a disposal event for the purposes of Part 2 of that Act other than by virtue of sub-paragraph (1).

13.—(1) If a compensating payment is made to the transferor, the disposal value to be brought into account is the amount of the payment.

(2) Otherwise, the disposal value to be brought into account is the amount which would give rise neither to a balancing allowance nor to a balancing charge.

14.—(1) Paragraph 13(2) does not apply if the qualifying expenditure has been allocated to the main pool or a class pool.

(2) Instead, the disposal value to be brought into account is the notional written-down value of the qualifying expenditure incurred by the transferor on the provision of the plant or machinery.

The notional written-down value is—

$$QE - A$$

where—

QE is the qualifying expenditure incurred by the transferor on the provision of the plant or machinery,

A is the total of all allowances which could have been made to the transferor in respect of the expenditure if—

  (a)   that expenditure had been the only expenditure that had ever been taken into account in determining his available qualifying expenditure, and

  (b)   all allowances had been made in full.

(4)   But if—

  (a)   the Part 5 transfer of the plant or machinery occurs in the same chargeable period as that in which the qualifying expenditure is incurred, and

  (b)   a first-year allowance is made in respect of an amount of the expenditure,

the disposal value to be brought into account is that which is equal to the balance left after deducting the first year allowance.

15.—(1) Paragraph 13 does not apply if—

  (a)   a qualifying activity is carried on in partnership,

  (b)   the Part 5 transfer is a transfer of plant or machinery which is partnership property, and

  (c)   compensating payments are made to one or more, but not both or all, of the partners.

(2)   Instead, the disposal value to be brought into account is the sum of—

  (a)   any compensating payments made to any of the partners, and

  (b)   in the case of each partner to whom a compensating payment has not been made, his share of the tax-neutral amount.

(3)   A partner's share of the tax-neutral amount is to be determined according to the profit-sharing arrangements for the twelve months ending immediately before the date of the Part 5 transfer.

16.—(1) Paragraph 13 does not apply if—

  (a)   a qualifying activity is carried on in partnership,

  (b)   the Part 5 transfer is a transfer of plant or machinery which is not partnership property but is owned by two or more of the partners ("the owners"),

  (c)   the plant or machinery is used for the purposes of the qualifying activity, and

  (d)   compensating payments are made to one or more, but not both or all, of the owners.

(2)   Instead, the disposal value to be brought into account is the sum of—

  (a)   any compensating payments made to any of the owners, and

  (b)   in the case of each owner to whom a compensating payment has not been made, his share of the tax-neutral amount.

(3)   An owner's share of the tax-neutral amount is to be determined in proportion to the value of his interest in the plant or machinery.

17.—(1) Paragraphs 12 to 16 have effect as if they were included in section 61 of the Allowances Act 2001.

(2)   In paragraphs 15 and 16, the tax-neutral amount is the amount that would be brought into account as the disposal value under paragraph 13(2) or (as the case may be) 14 if the provision in question were not disapplied.

Industrial buildings

18.—(1) If there is a Part 5 transfer of a relevant interest in an industrial building, Part 3 of the Allowances Act 2001 is to have effect as if the transfer were a balancing event within section 315(1) of that Act.

(2)   But the Part 5 transfer is not to be treated as a balancing event for the purposes of Part 3 of that Act other than by virtue of sub-paragraph (1).

19.—(1) If a compensating payment is made to the transferor, the proceeds from the balancing event are the amount of the payment.

538

(2)   Otherwise—
    (a)   the proceeds from the balancing event are the amount which is equal to the residue of qualifying expenditure immediately before the transfer, and
    (b)   no balancing adjustment is to be made as a result of the event under section 319 of the Allowances Act 2001.

20.—(1) Paragraph 19 does not apply to determine the proceeds from the balancing event if—
    (a)   the relevant interest in the industrial building is partnership property, and
    (b)   compensating payments are made to one or more, but not both or all, of the partners.

(2)   Instead, the proceeds from the balancing event are the sum of—
    (a)   any compensating payments made to any of the partners, and
    (b)   in the case of each partner to whom a compensating payment has not been made, his share of the amount which is equal to the residue of qualifying expenditure immediately before the Part 5 transfer.

(3)   A partner's share of that amount is to be determined according to the profit-sharing arrangements for the twelve months ending immediately before the date of the Part 5 transfer.

21. Paragraphs 18 to 20 have effect as if they were included in Part 3 of the Allowances Act 2001.

Flat conversion

22.—(1) If there is a Part 5 transfer of a relevant interest in a flat, Part 4A of the Allowances Act 2001 is to have effect as if the transfer were a balancing event within section 393N of that Act.

(2)   But the Part 5 transfer is not to be treated as a balancing event for the purposes of Part 4A of that Act other than by virtue of sub-paragraph (1).

23.—(1) If a compensating payment is made to the transferor, the proceeds from the balancing event are the amount of the payment.

(2)   Otherwise, the proceeds from the balancing event are the amount which is equal to the residue of qualifying expenditure immediately before the transfer.

24.—(1) Paragraph 23 does not apply to determine the proceeds from the balancing event if—
    (a)   the relevant interest in the flat is partnership property, and
    (b)   compensating payments are made to one or more, but not both or all, of the partners.

(2)   Instead, the proceeds from the balancing event are the sum of—
    (a)   any compensating payments made to any of the partners, and
    (b)   in the case of each partner to whom a compensating payment has not been made, his share of the amount which is equal to the residue of qualifying expenditure immediately before the transfer.

(3)   A partner's share of that amount is to be determined according to the profit-sharing arrangements for the twelve months ending immediately before the date of the transfer.

25. Paragraphs 22 to 24 have effect as if they were included in Part 4A of the Allowances Act 2001.

Research and development

26. If there is a Part 5 transfer of an asset representing qualifying expenditure incurred by a person, the disposal value he is required to bring into account under section 443(1) of the Allowances Act 2001 for any chargeable period is to be determined as follows (and not in accordance with subsection (4) of that section).

27.—(1) If a compensating payment is made to the transferor, the disposal value he is required to bring into account is the amount of the payment.

(2)   Otherwise, the disposal value he is required to bring into account is nil.

28.—(1) Paragraph 27 does not apply to determine the disposal value to be brought into account if—

      (a)   the asset is partnership property, and

      (b)   compensating payments are made to one or more, but not both or all, of the partners.

(2)   Instead, the disposal value to be brought into account is equal to the sum of any compensating payments.

29. Paragraphs 26 to 28 have effect as if they were included in Part 6 of the Allowances Act 2001.

EMPLOYEE ETC SHARE SCHEMES

Share options

30. Section 135(6) of the Taxes Act 1988 (gains by directors and employees) does not make any person chargeable to tax in respect of any gain realised by the trustee for civil recovery.

Conditional acquisition of shares

31. Section 140A(4) of the Taxes Act 1988 (disposal etc of shares) does not make the transferor chargeable to income tax in respect of a Part 5 transfer of shares or an interest in shares.

Shares acquired at an undervalue

32. Section 162(5) of the Taxes Act 1988 (employee shareholdings) does not make the transferor chargeable to income tax in respect of a Part 5 transfer of shares.

Shares in dependent subsidiaries

33. Section 79 of the Finance Act 1988 (c 39) (charge on increase in value of shares) does not make the transferor chargeable to income tax in respect of a Part 5 transfer of shares or an interest in shares.

Definitions   For "interest" in relation to land, see s 316(1) (by virtue of para 2(6), (9) above); for "interest" in relation to property other than land", see s 316(1) (by virtue of para 2(6), (9) above); for "property", see s 316(2), (4)–(7) (by virtue of para 2(6), (9) above); for "recovery order", see s 316(1) (by virtue of para 2(6), (9) above); for "value", see s 316(1) (by virtue of para 2(6), (9) above).

SCHEDULE 11

Section 456

AMENDMENTS

Introduction

1. The amendments specified in this Schedule shall have effect.

Parliamentary Commissioner Act 1967 (c 13)

2.—(1) The Parliamentary Commissioner Act 1967 is amended as follows.

(2)   In Schedule 2 (Departments etc subject to investigation) at the appropriate place insert—

"Director of the Assets Recovery Agency."

(3)   In the Notes to that Schedule before paragraph 1 insert—

"A1

In the case of the Director of the Assets Recovery Agency an investigation under this Act may be conducted only in respect of the exercise of functions vested in him by virtue of a notice served on the Commissioners of Inland Revenue under section 317(2), 321(2) or 322(2) of the Proceeds of Crime Act 2002 (Inland Revenue functions)."

Police (Scotland) Act 1967 (c 77)

3.—(1) The Police (Scotland) Act 1967 is amended as follows.

(2) In section 38(3B) (liability of Scottish Ministers for constables on central service) after "central service" insert "or on temporary service as mentioned in section 38A(1)(aa) of this Act".

(3) In section 38A(1) (meaning of "relevant service") after paragraph (a) insert—
"(aa) temporary service with the Scottish Ministers in connection with their functions under Part 5 or 8 of the Proceeds of Crime Act 2002, on which a person is engaged with the consent of the appropriate authority;".

Criminal Appeal Act 1968 (c 19)

4.—(1) The Criminal Appeal Act 1968 is amended as follows.

(2) In section 33 (appeal to House of Lords) after subsection (1) insert—

"(1A) In subsection (1) above the reference to the prosecutor includes a reference to the Director of the Assets Recovery Agency in a case where (and to the extent that) he is a party to the appeal to the Court of Appeal."

(3) In section 50(1) (meaning of sentence) after paragraph (c) insert—
"(ca) a confiscation order under Part 2 of the Proceeds of Crime Act 2002;
(cb) an order which varies a confiscation order made under Part 2 of the Proceeds of Crime Act 2002 if the varying order is made under section 21, 22 or 29 of that Act (but not otherwise);".

Misuse of Drugs Act 1971 (c 38)

5.—(1) Section 27 of the Misuse of Drugs Act 1971 (forfeiture) is amended as follows.

(2) In subsection (1) for "a drug trafficking offence, as defined in section 1(3) of the Drug Trafficking Act 1994" substitute "an offence falling within subsection (3) below".

(3) After subsection (2) insert—
"(3) An offence falls within this subsection if it is an offence which is specified in—
(a) paragraph 1 of Schedule 2 to the Proceeds of Crime Act 2002 (drug trafficking offences), or
(b) so far as it relates to that paragraph, paragraph 10 of that Schedule."

Immigration Act 1971 (c 77)

6. In section 28L of the Immigration Act 1971, in paragraph (c) for the words "33 of the Criminal Law (Consolidation) (Scotland) Act 1995" substitute "412 of the Proceeds of Crime Act 2002".

Rehabilitation of Offenders Act 1974 (c 53)

7. In section 1 of the Rehabilitation of Offenders Act 1974 (rehabilitated persons and spent convictions) after subsection (2A) insert—

"(2B) In subsection (2)(a) above the reference to a fine or other sum adjudged to be paid by or imposed on a conviction does not include a reference to an amount payable under a confiscation order made under Part 2 or 3 of the Proceeds of Crime Act 2002."

Rehabilitation of Offenders (Northern Ireland) Order 1978 (SI 1978/1908 (NI 27))

8. In Article 3 of the Rehabilitation of Offenders (Northern Ireland) Order 1978 (rehabilitated persons and spent convictions) after paragraph (2) insert—

"(2A) In paragraph (2)(a) the reference to a fine or other sum adjudged to be paid by or imposed on a conviction does not include a reference to an amount payable under a confiscation order made under Part 4 of the Proceeds of Crime Act 2002."

Criminal Appeal (Northern Ireland) Act 1980 (c 47)

9.—(1) The Criminal Appeal (Northern Ireland) Act 1980 is amended as follows.

(2) In section 30(3) (meaning of sentence) omit "and" after paragraph (b) and after paragraph (c) insert—

"(d) a confiscation order under Part 4 of the Proceeds of Crime Act 2002;
(e) an order which varies a confiscation order made under Part 4 of the Proceeds of Crime Act 2002 if the varying order is made under section 171, 172 or 179 of that Act (but not otherwise)."

(3) In section 31 (appeal to House of Lords) after subsection (1) insert—

"(1A) In subsection (1) above the reference to the prosecutor includes a reference to the Director of the Assets Recovery Agency in a case where (and to the extent that) he is a party to the appeal to the Court of Appeal."

Legal Aid, Advice and Assistance (Northern Ireland) Order 1981 (SI 1981/228 (NI 8))

10.—(1) Part I of Schedule 1 to the Legal Aid, Advice and Assistance (Northern Ireland) Order 1981 (proceedings for which legal aid may be given under Part II of the Order) is amended as follows.

(2) After paragraph 2 insert—

"2A.—(1) The following proceedings in the Crown Court under the Proceeds of Crime Act 2002—
(a) proceedings which relate to a direction under section 202(3) or 204(3) as to the distribution of funds in the hands of a receiver;
(b) applications under section 210 relating to action taken or proposed to be taken by a receiver;
(c) applications under section 211 to vary or discharge an order under any of sections 196 to 201 for the appointment of or conferring powers on a receiver;
(d) applications under section 220 or 221 for the payment of compensation;
(e) applications under sections 351(3), 362(3), 369(3) or 375(2) to vary or discharge certain orders made under Part 8.

(2) But sub-paragraph (1) does not apply in relation to a defendant (within the meaning of Part 4 of that Act) in the following proceedings—
(a) proceedings mentioned in head (b) of that sub-paragraph;
(b) an application under section 221 for the payment of compensation if the confiscation order was varied under section 179."

(3) In paragraph 3 (courts of summary jurisdiction), after sub-paragraph (i) insert—
"(j) proceedings under sections 295, 297, 298, 301 and 302 of the Proceeds of Crime Act 2002".

(4) The amendments made by this paragraph are without prejudice to the power to make regulations under Article 10(2) of the Legal Aid, Advice and Assistance (Northern Ireland) Order 1981 amending or revoking the provisions inserted by this paragraph.

Civil Jurisdiction and Judgments Act 1982 (c 27)

11. In section 18 of the Civil Jurisdiction and Judgments Act 1982 (enforcement of United Kingdom judgments in other parts of the United Kingdom) in subsection (3) (exceptions) insert after paragraph (c)—

"(d) an order made under Part 2, 3 or 4 of the Proceeds of Crime Act 2002 (confiscation).".

Civic Government (Scotland) Act 1982 (c 45)

12.—(1) The Civic Government (Scotland) Act 1982 is amended as follows.

(2) In section 86A(3) (application of Part VIIA) for "sections 21(2) and 28(1) of the Proceeds of Crime (Scotland) Act 1995" substitute "section 21(2) of the Proceeds of Crime (Scotland) Act 1995 and Part 3 of the Proceeds of Crime Act 2002".

(3) In paragraph 8 of Schedule 2A (interpretation) for the definition of "restraint order" substitute—

""restraint order" means a restraint order made under Part 3 of the Proceeds of Crime Act 2002".

Criminal Justice Act 1982 (c 48)

13. In Part 2 of Schedule 1 to the Criminal Justice Act 1982 (offences excluded from early release provisions) after the entry relating to the Drug Trafficking Act 1994 insert—

"PROCEEDS OF CRIME ACT 2002

Section 327 (concealing criminal property etc).

Section 328 (arrangements relating to criminal property).

Section 329 (acquisition, use and possession of criminal property)."

Police and Criminal Evidence Act 1984 (c 60)

14.—(1) The Police and Criminal Evidence Act 1984 is amended as follows.

(2) In section 56 (right to have someone informed when arrested) for subsection (5A) substitute—

"(5A) An officer may also authorise delay where he has reasonable grounds for believing that—
    (a) the person detained for the serious arrestable offence has benefited from his criminal conduct, and
    (b) the recovery of the value of the property constituting the benefit will be hindered by telling the named person of the arrest.

(5B) For the purposes of subsection (5A) above the question whether a person has benefited from his criminal conduct is to be decided in accordance with Part 2 of the Proceeds of Crime Act 2002."

(3) In section 58 (access to legal advice) for subsection (8A) substitute—

"(8A) An officer may also authorise delay where he has reasonable grounds for believing that—
    (a) the person detained for the serious arrestable offence has benefited from his criminal conduct, and
    (b) the recovery of the value of the property constituting the benefit will be hindered by the exercise of the right conferred by subsection (1) above.

(8B) For the purposes of subsection (8A) above the question whether a person has benefited from his criminal conduct is to be decided in accordance with Part 2 of the Proceeds of Crime Act 2002."

(4) In section 116 (meaning of serious arrestable offence) in subsection (2) for paragraph (c) and the word "and" immediately preceding it substitute—

"(c) any offence which is specified in paragraph 1 of Schedule 2 to the Proceeds of Crime Act 2002 (drug trafficking offences),
    (d) any offence under section 327, 328 or 329 of that Act (certain money laundering offences)."

Bankruptcy (Scotland) Act 1985 (c 66)

15.—(1) The Bankruptcy (Scotland) Act 1985 is amended as follows.

(2)　In section 5(4) (meaning of "qualified creditor") for the words from "has the meaning" to "1995" substitute "means a confiscation order under Part 2, 3 or 4 of the Proceeds of Crime Act 2002".

(3)　In section 7(1) (meaning of "apparent insolvency") for the words from "has the meaning assigned" where second occurring to "said Act of 1994" where second occurring substitute ""confiscation order" and "restraint order" mean a confiscation order or a restraint order made under Part 2, 3 or 4 of the Proceeds of Crime Act 2002".

(4)　After section 31 (vesting of estate at date of sequestration) insert—

"31A Property subject to restraint order

(1)　This section applies where—
　(a)　property is excluded from the debtor's estate by virtue of section 420(2)(a) of the Proceeds of Crime Act 2002 (property subject to a restraint order),
　(b)　an order under section 50, 52, 128, 198 or 200 of that Act has not been made in respect of the property, and
　(c)　the restraint order is discharged.

(2)　On the discharge of the restraint order the property vests in the permanent trustee as part of the debtor's estate.

(3)　But subsection (2) does not apply to the proceeds of property realised by a management receiver under section 49(2)(d) or 197(2)(d) of that Act (realisation of property to meet receiver's remuneration and expenses).

31B Property in respect of which receivership or administration order is made

(1)　This section applies where—
　(a)　property is excluded from the debtor's estate by virtue of section 420(2)(b), (c) or (d) of the Proceeds of Crime Act 2002 (property in respect of which an order for the appointment of a receiver or administrator under certain provisions of that Act is in force), and
　(b)　a confiscation order is made under section 6, 92 or 156 of that Act,
　(c)　the amount payable under the confiscation order is fully paid, and
　(d)　any of the property remains in the hands of the receiver or administrator (as the case may be).

(2)　The property vests in the permanent trustee as part of the debtor's estate.

31C Property subject to certain orders where confiscation order discharged or quashed

(1)　This section applies where—
　(a)　property is excluded from the debtor's estate by virtue of section 420(2)(a), (b), (c) or (d) of the Proceeds of Crime Act 2002 (property in respect of which a restraint order or an order for the appointment of a receiver or administrator under that Act is in force),
　(b)　a confiscation order is made under section 6, 92 or 156 of that Act, and
　(c)　the confiscation order is discharged under section 30, 114 or 180 of that Act (as the case may be) or quashed under that Act or in pursuance of any enactment relating to appeals against conviction or sentence.

(2)　Any property in the hands of a receiver appointed under Part 2 or 4 of that Act or an administrator appointed under Part 3 of that Act vests in the permanent trustee as part of the debtor's estate.

(3)　But subsection (2) does not apply to the proceeds of property realised by a management receiver under section 49(2)(d) or 197(2)(d) of that Act (realisation of property to meet receiver's remuneration and expenses)."

(5)   In section 55 (effect of discharge) after subsection (2) insert—

"(3)   In subsection (2)(a) above the reference to a fine or other penalty due to the Crown includes a reference to a confiscation order made under Part 2, 3 or 4 of the Proceeds of Crime Act 2002.".

Insolvency Act 1986 (c 45)

16.—(1) The Insolvency Act 1986 is amended as follows.

(2)   In section 281 (effect of discharge) after subsection (4) insert—

"(4A) In subsection (4) the reference to a fine includes a reference to a confiscation order under Part 2, 3 or 4 of the Proceeds of Crime Act 2002."

(3)   After section 306 insert—

"306A Property subject to restraint order

(1)   This section applies where—
    (a) property is excluded from the bankrupt's estate by virtue of section 417(2)(a) of the Proceeds of Crime Act 2002 (property subject to a restraint order),
    (b) an order under section 50, 52, 128, 198 or 200 of that Act has not been made in respect of the property, and
    (c) the restraint order is discharged.

(2)   On the discharge of the restraint order the property vests in the trustee as part of the bankrupt's estate.

(3)   But subsection (2) does not apply to the proceeds of property realised by a management receiver under section 49(2)(d) or 197(2)(d) of that Act (realisation of property to meet receiver's remuneration and expenses).

306B Property in respect of which receivership or administration order made

(1)   This section applies where—
    (a) property is excluded from the bankrupt's estate by virtue of section 417(2)(b), (c) or (d) of the Proceeds of Crime Act 2002 (property in respect of which an order for the appointment of a receiver or administrator under certain provisions of that Act is in force),
    (b) a confiscation order is made under section 6, 92 or 156 of that Act,
    (c) the amount payable under the confiscation order is fully paid, and
    (d) any of the property remains in the hands of the receiver or administrator (as the case may be).

(2)   The property vests in the trustee as part of the bankrupt's estate.

306C Property subject to certain orders where confiscation order discharged or quashed

(1)   This section applies where—
    (a) property is excluded from the bankrupt's estate by virtue of section 417(2)(a), (b), (c) or (d) of the Proceeds of Crime Act 2002 (property in respect of which a restraint order or an order for the appointment of a receiver or administrator under that Act is in force),
    (b) a confiscation order is made under section 6, 92 or 156 of that Act, and
    (c) the confiscation order is discharged under section 30, 114 or 180 of that Act (as the case may be) or quashed under that Act or in pursuance of any enactment relating to appeals against conviction or sentence.

(2)   Any such property in the hands of a receiver appointed under Part 2 or 4 of that Act or an administrator appointed under Part 3 of that Act vests in the trustee as part of the bankrupt's estate.

(3)   But subsection (2) does not apply to the proceeds of property realised by a management receiver under section 49(2)(d) or 197(2)(d) of that Act (realisation of property to meet receiver's remuneration and expenses)."

Criminal Justice Act 1988 (c 33)

17.—(1) The Criminal Justice Act 1988 is amended as follows.

(2)   The following provisions shall cease to have effect—
    (a)   sections 71 to 102;
    (b)   Schedule 4.

(3)   In section 151(4) (Customs and Excise power of arrest) omit "and" after paragraph (a), and after paragraph (b) insert—
    "(c) a money laundering offence;".

(4)   In section 151(5) for the words after "means" substitute

"any offence which is specified in—
    (a) paragraph 1 of Schedule 2 to the Proceeds of Crime Act 2002 (drug trafficking offences), or
    (b) so far as it relates to that paragraph, paragraph 10 of that Schedule.".

(5)   In section 151 after subsection (5) insert—

"(6)   In this section "money laundering offence" means any offence which by virtue of section 415 of the Proceeds of Crime Act 2002 is a money laundering offence for the purposes of Part 8 of that Act.".

(6)   In section 152(4) (remands of suspected drugs offenders to customs detention) for the words after "means" substitute

"any offence which is specified in—
    (a) paragraph 1 of Schedule 5 to the Proceeds of Crime Act 2002 (drug trafficking offences), or
    (b) so far as it relates to that paragraph, paragraph 10 of that Schedule.".

Extradition Act 1989 (c 33)

18.—(1) The Extradition Act 1989 is amended as follows.

(2)   In section 22 (extension of purposes of extradition for offences under Acts giving effect to international conventions) in subsection (4)(h)—
    (a)   for sub-paragraph (i) substitute—
      "(i)   any offence which is specified in—
        (a)   paragraph 1 of Schedule 2 to the Proceeds of Crime Act 2002 (drug trafficking offences), or
        (b)   so far as it relates to that paragraph, paragraph 10 of that Schedule;
      (ia) any offence which by virtue of section 415 of the Proceeds of Crime Act 2002 is a money laundering offence for the purposes of Part 8 of that Act;";
    (b)   for sub-paragraph (ii) substitute—
      "(ii) any offence which is specified in—
        (a)   paragraph 2 of Schedule 4 to the Proceeds of Crime Act 2002, or
        (b)   so far as it relates to that paragraph, paragraph 10 of that Schedule;
      (iia) any offence which by virtue of section 415 of the Proceeds of Crime Act 2002 is a money laundering offence for the purposes of Part 8 of that Act;";
    (c)   omit "and" after sub-paragraph (ii) and for sub-paragraph (iii) substitute—
      "(iii) any offence which is specified in—
        (a)   paragraph 1 of Schedule 5 to the Proceeds of Crime Act 2002 (drug trafficking offences), or

> > (b) so far as it relates to that paragraph, paragraph 10 of that Schedule; and
>
> > (iv) any offence which by virtue of section 415 of the Proceeds of Crime Act 2002 is a money laundering offence for the purposes of Part 8 of that Act;".

(3) In paragraph 15 of Schedule 1 (deemed extension of jurisdiction of foreign states)—

> (a) for paragraph (j) substitute—
>
> > "(j) any offence which is specified in—
> >
> > > (i) paragraph 1 of Schedule 2 to the Proceeds of Crime Act 2002 (drug trafficking offences), or
> > >
> > > (ii) so far as it relates to that paragraph, paragraph 10 of that Schedule;
> >
> > (ja) any offence which by virtue of section 415 of the Proceeds of Crime Act 2002 is a money laundering offence for the purposes of Part 8 of that Act;";
>
> (b) for paragraph (k) substitute—
>
> > "(k) any offence which is specified in—
> >
> > > (i) paragraph 2 of Schedule 4 to the Proceeds of Crime Act 2002, or
> > >
> > > (ii) so far as it relates to that paragraph, paragraph 10 of that Schedule;
> >
> > (ka) any offence which by virtue of section 415 of the Proceeds of Crime Act 2002 is a money laundering offence for the purposes of Part 8 of that Act;";
>
> (c) for paragraph (m) substitute—
>
> > "(m) any offence which is specified in—
> >
> > > (i) paragraph 1 of Schedule 5 to the Proceeds of Crime Act 2002 (drug trafficking offences), or
> > >
> > > (ii) so far as it relates to that paragraph, paragraph 10 of that Schedule;
> >
> > (ma) any offence which by virtue of section 415 of the Proceeds of Crime Act 2002 is a money laundering offence for the purposes of Part 8 of that Act;".

Police and Criminal Evidence (Northern Ireland) Order 1989 (SI 1989/1341 (NI 12))

19.—(1) The Police and Criminal Evidence (Northern Ireland) Order 1989 is amended as follows.

(2) In Article 57 (right to have someone informed when arrested) for paragraph (5A) substitute—

> "(5A) An officer may also authorise delay where he has reasonable grounds for believing that—
>
> > (a) the person detained for the serious arrestable offence has benefited from his criminal conduct, and
> >
> > (b) the recovery of the value of the property constituting the benefit will be hindered by telling the named person of the arrest.

> (5B) For the purposes of paragraph (5A) the question whether a person has benefited from his criminal conduct is to be decided in accordance with Part 4 of the Proceeds of Crime Act 2002.".

(3) In Article 59 (access to legal advice) for paragraph (8A) substitute—

> "(8A) An officer may also authorise delay where he has reasonable grounds for believing that—
>
> > (a) the person detained for the serious arrestable offence has benefited from his criminal conduct, and
> >
> > (b) the recovery of the value of the property constituting the benefit will be hindered by the exercise of the right conferred by paragraph (1).

> (8B) For the purposes of paragraph (8A) the question whether a person has benefited from his criminal conduct is to be decided in accordance with Part 4 of the Proceeds of Crime Act 2002.".

(4)   In Article 87 (meaning of serious arrestable offence) in paragraph (2) for sub-paragraph (aa) substitute—

> "(aa) any offence which is specified in paragraph 1 of Schedule 5 to the Proceeds of Crime Act 2002 (drug trafficking offences);
> (ab) any offence under section 327, 328 or 329 of that Act (certain money laundering offences);".

Insolvency (Northern Ireland) Order 1989 (SI 1989/2405 (NI 19))

20.—(1) The Insolvency (Northern Ireland) Order 1989 is amended as follows.

(2)   In Article 255 (effect of discharge) after paragraph (4) insert—

> "(4A) In paragraph (4) the reference to a fine includes a reference to a confiscation order under Part 2, 3 or 4 of the Proceeds of Crime Act 2002.".

(3)   After Article 279 insert—

"279A Property subject to restraint order

(1)   This Article applies where—
  (a) property is excluded from the bankrupt's estate by virtue of section 423(2)(a) of the Proceeds of Crime Act 2002 (property subject to a restraint order),
  (b) an order under section 50, 52, 128, 198 or 200 of that Act has not been made in respect of the property, and
  (c) the restraint order is discharged.

(2)   On the discharge of the restraint order the property vests in the trustee as part of the bankrupt's estate.

(3)   But paragraph (2) does not apply to the proceeds of property realised by a management receiver under section 49(2)(d) or 197(2)(d) of that Act (realisation of property to meet receiver's remuneration and expenses).

279B Property in respect of which receivership or administration order made

(1)   This Article applies where—
  (a) property is excluded from the bankrupt's estate by virtue of section 423(2)(b), (c) or (d) of the Proceeds of Crime Act 2002 (property in respect of which an order for the appointment of a receiver or administrator under certain provisions of that Act is in force),
  (b) a confiscation order is made under section 6, 92 or 156 of that Act,
  (c) the amount payable under the confiscation order is fully paid, and
  (d) any of the property remains in the hands of the receiver or administrator (as the case may be).

(2)   The property vests in the trustee as part of the bankrupt's estate.

279C Property subject to certain orders where confiscation order discharged or quashed

(1)   This Article applies where—
  (a) property is excluded from the bankrupt's estate by virtue of section 423(2)(a), (b), (c) or (d) of the Proceeds of Crime Act 2002 (property in respect of which a restraint order or an order for the appointment of a receiver or administrator under that Act is in force),
  (b) a confiscation order is made under section 6, 92 or 156 of that Act, and
  (c) the confiscation order is discharged under section 30, 114 or 180 of that Act (as the case may be) or quashed under that Act or in pursuance of any enactment relating to appeals against conviction or sentence.

(2)   Any such property in the hands of a receiver appointed under Part 2 or 4 of that Act or an administrator appointed under Part 3 of that Act vests in the trustee as part of the bankrupt's estate.

(3)   But paragraph (2) does not apply to the proceeds of property realised by a management receiver under section 49(2)(d) or 197(2)(d) of that Act (realisation of property to meet receiver's remuneration and expenses).".

Criminal Justice (International Co-operation) Act 1990 (c 5)

21. In section 13(6) of the Criminal Justice (International Co-operation) Act 1990 (information not to be disclosed except for certain purposes)—
> (a)   omit "the Drug Trafficking Act 1994 or the Criminal Justice (Scotland) Act 1987";
> (b)   at the end insert "or of proceedings under Part 2, 3 or 4 of the Proceeds of Crime Act 2002".

Pension Schemes Act 1993 (c 48)

22.—(1) The Pension Schemes Act 1993 is amended as follows.

(2)   In section 10 (protected rights and money purchase benefits), after subsection (5) insert—

> "(6)   Where, in the case of a scheme which makes such provision as is mentioned in subsection (2) or (3), any liability of the scheme in respect of a member's protected rights ceases by virtue of a civil recovery order, his protected rights are extinguished or reduced accordingly.".

(3)   In section 14 (earner's guaranteed minimum), after subsection (2) insert—

> "(2A) Where any liability of a scheme in respect of an earner's guaranteed minimum pension ceases by virtue of a civil recovery order, his guaranteed minimum in relation to the scheme is extinguished or reduced accordingly.".

(4)   In section 47 (further provisions relating to guaranteed minimum pensions), in subsection (6), after "but for" insert "section 14(2A) and".

(5)   In section 68B (safeguarded rights), at the end insert "including provision for such rights to be extinguished or reduced in consequence of a civil recovery order made in respect of such rights".

(6)   In section 181(1) (general interpretation), after the definition of "Category A retirement pension" insert—

> ""civil recovery order" means an order under section 266 of the Proceeds of Crime Act 2002 or an order under section 276 imposing the requirement mentioned in section 277(3).".

Pension Schemes (Northern Ireland) Act 1993 (c 49)

23.—(1) The Pension Schemes (Northern Ireland) Act 1993 is amended as follows.

(2)   In section 6 (protected rights and money purchase benefits), after subsection (5) insert—

> "(6)   Where, in the case of a scheme which makes such provision as is mentioned in subsection (2) or (3), any liability of the scheme in respect of a member's protected rights ceases by virtue of a civil recovery order, his protected rights are extinguished or reduced accordingly.".

(3)   In section 10 (earner's guaranteed minimum), after subsection (2) insert—

> "(2A) Where any liability of a scheme in respect of an earner's guaranteed minimum pension ceases by virtue of a civil recovery order, his guaranteed minimum in relation to the scheme is extinguished or reduced accordingly.".

(4)   In section 43 (further provisions relating to guaranteed minimum pensions), in subsection (6), after "but for" insert "section 10(2A) and".

(5)   In section 64B (safeguarded rights), at the end insert "including provision for such rights to be extinguished or reduced in consequence of a civil recovery order made in respect of such rights".

(6)   In section 176(1) (general interpretation), after the definition of "Category A retirement pension" insert—

>   ""civil recovery order" means an order under section 266 of the Proceeds of Crime Act 2002 or an order under section 276 imposing the requirement mentioned in section 277(3).".

Criminal Justice and Public Order Act 1994 (c 31)

24. In section 139(12) of the Criminal Justice and Public Order Act 1994 (search powers) in paragraph (b) of the definition of "items subject to legal privilege" for "section 40 of the Criminal Justice (Scotland) Act 1987" substitute "section 412 of the Proceeds of Crime Act 2002".

Drug Trafficking Act 1994 (c 37)

25.—(1) The Drug Trafficking Act 1994 is amended as follows.

(2)   The following provisions shall cease to have effect—

- (a)   sections 1 to 54;
- (b)   in sections 55(4)(a) (orders to make material available) and 56(3)(a) and (4)(a) (authority for search) the words "or has benefited from";
- (c)   in section 59 (disclosure of information held by government departments), subsections (1) to (10) and in subsection (11) the words "An order under subsection (1) above, and,";
- (d)   in section 60(6) (Customs and Excise prosecution powers), in the definition of "specified offence", in paragraph (a) the words "Part III or" and paragraph (c) and the word "or" immediately preceding it;
- (e)   in section 60(6) the words from "and references to the institution of proceedings" to the end;
- (f)   in section 60, subsections (7) and (8);
- (g)   in section 61 (extension of certain offences to the Crown), subsections (2) to (4);
- (h)   sections 62, 63(1), (2) and (3)(a) and 64 (interpretation);
- (i)   in section 68(2) (extent -Scotland), paragraphs (a) to (c) and in paragraph (g) the words "1, 41, 62" and "64";
- (j)   in section 68(3) (extent -Northern Ireland), paragraph (a) and in paragraph (d) the word "64".

(3)   In section 59(12)(b) for the words "referred to in subsection (1) above" substitute "specified in an order under section 55(2)".

(4)   After section 59 insert the following section—

"59A Construction of sections 55 to 59

(1)   This section has effect for the purposes of sections 55 to 59.

(2)   A reference to a constable includes a reference to a customs officer.

(3)   A customs officer is a person commissioned by the Commissioners of Customs and Excise under section 6(3) of the Customs and Excise Management Act 1979 (c 2).

(4)   Drug trafficking means doing or being concerned in any of the following (whether in England and Wales or elsewhere)—

- (a)   producing or supplying a controlled drug where the production or supply contravenes section 4(1) of the Misuse of Drugs Act 1971 or a corresponding law;
- (b)   transporting or storing a controlled drug where possession of the drug contravenes section 5(1) of that Act or a corresponding law;
- (c)   importing or exporting a controlled drug where the importation or exportation is prohibited by section 3(1) of that Act or a corresponding law;
- (d)   manufacturing or supplying a scheduled substance within the meaning of section 12 of the Criminal Justice (International Co-operation) Act 1990

where the manufacture or supply is an offence under that section or would be such an offence if it took place in England and Wales;

(e) using any ship for illicit traffic in controlled drugs in circumstances which amount to the commission of an offence under section 19 of that Act.

(5) In this section "corresponding law" has the same meaning as in the Misuse of Drugs Act 1971.".

(5) In section 60 after subsection (6) insert—

"(6A) Proceedings for an offence are instituted—

(a) when a justice of the peace issues a summons or warrant under section 1 of the Magistrates' Courts Act 1980 (issue of summons to, or warrant for arrest of, accused) in respect of the offence;

(b) when a person is charged with the offence after being taken into custody without a warrant;

(c) when a bill of indictment is preferred under section 2 of the Administration of Justice (Miscellaneous Provisions) Act 1933 in a case falling within paragraph (b) of subsection (2) of that section (preferment by direction of the criminal division of the Court of Appeal or by direction, or with the consent, of a High Court judge).

(6B) Where the application of subsection (6A) would result in there being more than one time for the institution of proceedings they must be taken to have been instituted at the earliest of those times.".

(6) In section 61(1) for "sections 49(2), 50 to 53 and 58" substitute "section 58".

(7) In section 68(2)(d), for "59(10)" substitute "59(11)".

Criminal Justice (Northern Ireland) Order 1994 (SI 1994/2795 (NI 15))

26. In Article 16 of the Criminal Justice (Northern Ireland) Order 1994 in paragraph (a) after "Proceeds of Crime (Northern Ireland) Order 1996" insert "or Part 4 of the Proceeds of Crime Act 2002".

Proceeds of Crime Act 1995 (c 11)

27. Section 15(2) and (3) of the Proceeds of Crime Act 1995 (investigation into benefit to be treated as the investigation of an offence for the purposes of sections 21 and 22 of the Police and Criminal Evidence Act 1984) shall cease to have effect.

Proceeds of Crime (Scotland) Act 1995 (c 43)

28.—(1) The Proceeds of Crime (Scotland) Act 1995 is amended as follows.

(2) The following provisions in the Act shall cease to have effect—

(a) Part I, except section 2(7);

(b) in section 28, subsections (1)(a) and (2) and in subsection (5) the words "(including a restraint order made under and within the meaning of the 1994 Act)";

(c) section 29;

(d) in section 31, subsection (2) and in subsection (4) the words "or (2)";

(e) sections 35 to 39;

(f) in section 40, subsections (1)(a), (2) and (4);

(g) in section 42, subsections (1)(a) and (b);

(h) in section 43, in subsection (1) the words ", confiscation order" and subsection (2);

(i) in section 45, subsection (1)(a);

(j) section 47;

(k) in section 49, in subsection (1) the definitions of "the 1988 Act", "the 1994 Act" and "confiscation order" and subsection (4).

(3)   The following provisions in Schedule 1 to the Act shall cease to have effect—
- (a)   in paragraph 1(1)(b) the words "or a confiscation order", in paragraph 1(2)(a) the words "subject to paragraph (b) below", paragraph 1(2)(b) and in paragraph 1(3)(a)(i) the words "or confiscation order";
- (b)   in paragraph 2(1)(a) the words ", and if appointed (or empowered) under paragraph 1(1)(b) above where a confiscation order has been made";
- (c)   paragraph 4;
- (d)   in paragraph 5(1) the words "Part I of";
- (e)   in paragraph 8(2) the words ", unless in a case where a confiscation order has been made there are sums available to be applied in payment of it under paragraph 4(4)(b) above,";
- (f)   in paragraph 10(1) the words "or the recipient of a gift caught by Part I of this Act or an implicative gift" and paragraphs 10(2) and 10(3);
- (g)   in paragraph 12(1)(a) the words "paragraph (a) or (b) of section 4(1) or".

(4)   The following provisions in Schedule 2 to the Act shall cease to have effect—
- (a)   in paragraph 1(2) the words "and 35 to 38";
- (b)   in paragraph 2, in sub-paragraph (1) the words "realisable or", in sub-paragraph (2) the words "and 35 to 38", sub-paragraph (5).
- (c)   in paragraph 3(2) the words "and 35 to 38" and paragraphs 3(4) and (5);
- (d)   in paragraph 4(2) the words "and 35 to 38";
- (e)   paragraph 6(2)(a).

(5)   In section 28(9) (restraint orders) for "Subsections (2)(a) and" substitute "Subsection".

(6)   In section 42 (enforcement) in subsections (2)(a), (c) and (d) for "Part I," substitute "Part".

Criminal Procedure (Scotland) Act 1995 (c 46)

29.—(1) The Criminal Procedure (Scotland) Act 1995 is amended as follows.

(2)   In section 109(1) (intimation of appeal) for "section 10 of the Proceeds of Crime (Scotland) Act 1995 (postponed confiscation orders)" substitute "section 99 of the Proceeds of Crime Act 2002 (postponement)".

(3)   In section 205B(5) (minimum sentence for third drug trafficking offence) for the definition of "drug trafficking offence" substitute—
> ""drug trafficking offence" means an offence specified in paragraph 2 or (so far as it relates to that paragraph) paragraph 10 of Schedule 4 to the Proceeds of Crime Act 2002;".

(4)   In section 219(8)(b) (fines: imprisonment for non-payment) for "14(2) of the Proceeds of Crime (Scotland) Act 1995" substitute "118(2) of the Proceeds of Crime Act 2002".

Police Act 1996 (c 16)

30.—(1) Section 97 of the Police Act 1996 (police officers engaged on service outside their force) is amended as follows.

(2)   In subsection (1) after paragraph (cc) insert—
> "(cd)   temporary service with the Assets Recovery Agency on which a person is engaged with the consent of the appropriate authority;".

(3)   In subsection (6)(a) after "(cc)" insert "(cd)".

(4)   In subsection (8) after "(cc)" insert "(cd)".

Proceeds of Crime (Northern Ireland) Order 1996 (SI 1996/1299 (NI 9)

31.—(1) The Proceeds of Crime (Northern Ireland) Order 1996 is amended as follows.

(2)   Parts II and III shall cease to have effect.

(3)   The following provisions shall also cease to have effect—
   (a)   in Article 2 (interpretation) in paragraph (2) from the definition of "charging order" to the definition of "external confiscation order" and from the definition of "modifications" to the definition of "restraint order" and paragraphs (3) to (10) and (12);
   (b)   Article 3 (definition of "property" etc);
   (c)   in Article 49 (additional investigation powers), in paragraph (1) sub-paragraph (c) and the word "and" immediately preceding it, in paragraph (1A) sub-paragraph (c) and the word "and" immediately preceding it, paragraph (4) and in paragraph (5) the definitions of "customs officer" and "relevant property";
   (d)   in Article 52 (supplementary provisions) in paragraph (2) sub-paragraph (b) and the word "and" immediately preceding it, and paragraph (3);
   (e)   in Article 54 (disclosure of information held by government departments) paragraphs (1) to (10) and (13) and in paragraph (11) the words "An order under paragraph (1) and,";
   (f)   in Article 55 (Customs and Excise prosecution powers), in paragraph (6) in the definition of "specified offence" in paragraph (a) the words "Part III or" and paragraph (c) and the word "or" immediately preceding it, and paragraph (7);
   (g)   Article 56(2) to (4) (extension of certain offences to the Crown);
   (h)   in Schedule 2 paragraph 3.

(4)   In Article 49(1) (additional investigation powers)—
   (a)   for "county court" substitute "Crown Court";
   (b)   in sub-paragraph (a) for the words from "an investigation" to the end of head (ii) substitute "a confiscation investigation";
   (c)   in sub-paragraph (b) after "and who is" insert "an accredited financial investigator".

(5)   In Article 49(1A)—
   (a)   after "application made by" insert "the Director of the Assets Recovery Agency or";
   (b)   for "county court" substitute "Crown Court";
   (c)   in sub-paragraph (a) for the words from "an investigation" to the end of head (ii) substitute "a confiscation investigation";
   (d)   in sub-paragraph (b) after "if" insert "the Director or";
   (e)   after "authorise" insert "the Director or";
   (f)for "paragraphs 3 and 3A" where it twice occurs substitute "paragraph 3A".

(6)   In Article 49(5) insert at the appropriate place in alphabetical order—
        ""accredited financial investigator" has the meaning given by section 3(5) of the Proceeds of Crime Act 2002;
        "confiscation investigation" has the same meaning as it has for the purposes of Part 8 of that Act by virtue of section 341(1);".

(7)   In Article 50(1) (order to make material available)—
   (a)   for sub-paragraphs (a) and (b) substitute "drug trafficking";
   (b)   for "county court" substitute "Crown Court".

(8)   In Article 50(4)(a), for heads (i) to (iii) substitute "has carried on drug trafficking".

(9)   In Article 50(8) for "county court" substitute "Crown Court".

(10)   In Article 51(1) (authority for search)—
   (a)   for sub-paragraphs (a) and (b) substitute "drug trafficking";
   (b)   for "county court" substitute "Crown Court".

(11)   In Article 51(3)(a) for heads (i) to (iii) substitute "has carried on drug trafficking".

(12)   In Article 51(4)—
   (a)   in sub-paragraph (a) for heads (i) to (iii) substitute "has carried on drug trafficking";

    (b)   in sub-paragraph (b)(i) for the words from "the question" to the end substitute "drug trafficking".

(13) In Article 52(1)(a) (supplementary provisions), for heads (i) to (ii) substitute "drug trafficking".

(14) In Article 54 (disclosure of information held by government departments) in paragraph (12)(b) for "referred to in paragraph (1)" substitute "specified in an order under Article 50(2)".

(15) After Article 54 insert the following Article—

"54A Construction of Articles 49 to 54

    (1)   This Article has effect for the purposes of Articles 49 to 54.

    (2)   A reference to a constable includes a reference to a customs officer.

    (3)   A customs officer is a person commissioned by the Commissioners of Customs and Excise under section 6(3) of the Customs and Excise Management Act 1979.

    (4)   Drug trafficking means doing or being concerned in any of the following (whether in Northern Ireland or elsewhere)—

        (a) producing or supplying a controlled drug where the production or supply contravenes section 4(1) of the Misuse of Drugs Act 1971 or a corresponding law;

        (b) transporting or storing a controlled drug where possession of the drug contravenes section 5(1) of that Act or a corresponding law;

        (c) importing or exporting a controlled drug where the importation or exportation is prohibited by section 3(1) of that Act or a corresponding law;

        (d) manufacturing or supplying a scheduled substance within the meaning of section 12 of the Criminal Justice (International Co-operation) Act 1990 where the manufacture or supply is an offence under that section or would be such an offence if it took place in Northern Ireland;

        (e) using any ship for illicit traffic in controlled drugs in circumstances which amount to the commission of an offence under section 19 of that Act.

    (5)   In this Article "corresponding law" has the same meaning as in the Misuse of Drugs Act 1971.".

(16) In Article 55 after paragraph (6) insert—

   "(6A) Proceedings for an offence are instituted—

        (a) when a summons or warrant is issued under Article 20 of the Magistrates' Courts (Northern Ireland) Order 1981 in respect of the offence;

        (b) when a person is charged with the offence after being taken into custody without a warrant;

        (c) when an indictment is preferred under section 2(2)(c), (e) or (f) of the Grand Jury (Abolition) Act (Northern Ireland) 1969.

   (6B) Where the application of paragraph (6A) would result in there being more than one time for the institution of proceedings they must be taken to have been instituted at the earliest of those times.".

(17) In Article 56(1) (extension of certain offences to the Crown), for "Articles 44, 45, 46, 47(2), 48 and" substitute "Article".

(18) In Schedule 2 (financial investigations) in paragraph 3A—

    (a)   in sub-paragraph (1) for "any conduct to which Article 49 applies" substitute "his criminal conduct";

(b)　　after that paragraph insert—

"(1A) For the purposes of sub-paragraph (1) the question whether a person has benefited from his criminal conduct is to be decided in accordance with Part 4 of the Proceeds of Crime Act 2002.".

Crime (Sentences) Act 1997 (c 43)

32.—(1)The Crime (Sentences) Act 1997 is amended as follows.

(2)　　In section 35 (fine defaulters) in subsection (1)(a) after "Drug Trafficking Act 1994" insert "or section 6 of the Proceeds of Crime Act 2002".

(3)　　In section 40 (fine defaulters) in subsection (1)(a) after "Drug Trafficking Act 1994" insert "or section 6 of the Proceeds of Crime Act 2002".

Crime and Punishment (Scotland) Act 1997 (c 48)

33. The following provisions of the Crime and Punishment (Scotland) Act 1997 shall cease to have effect—

(a)　　section 15(3),
(b)　　in Schedule 1, paragraph 20.

Police (Northern Ireland) Act 1998 (c 32)

34.—(1) Section 27 of the Police (Northern Ireland) Act 1998 (members of the Police Service engaged on other police service) is amended as follows.

(2)　　In subsection (1) after paragraph (c) insert—

"(ca)　temporary service with the Assets Recovery Agency on which a member of the Police Service of Northern Ireland is engaged with the consent of the Chief Constable;".

(3)　　In subsection (5)(b) after "(c)" insert "(ca)".

(4)　　In subsection (7) for "or (c)" there is substituted "(c) or (ca)".

Crime and Disorder Act 1998 (c 37)

35. In Schedule 8 to the Crime and Disorder Act 1998 paragraphs 115 and 116 shall cease to have effect.

Access to Justice Act 1999 (c 22)

36.—(1) Schedule 2 to the Access to Justice Act 1999 (services excluded from the Community Legal Service) is amended as follows.

(2)　　In paragraph 2(2), after paragraph (d) insert
　　　　　　"or
(e)　　under the Proceeds of Crime Act 2002 to the extent specified in paragraph 3,"

and omit the "or" at the end of paragraph (c).

(3)　　In paragraph 2(3) (magistrates courts), after "2001" insert—
　　　　　　"(l)　for an order or direction under section 295, 297, 298, 301 or 302 of the Proceeds of Crime Act 2002,"

and omit the "or" at the end of paragraph (j).

(4)　　After paragraph 2 insert—

"3.—(1) These are the proceedings under the Proceeds of Crime Act 2002—
(a)　　an application under section 42(3) to vary or discharge a restraint order or an order under section 41(7);
(b)　　proceedings which relate to a direction under section 54(3) or 56(3) as to the distribution of funds in the hands of a receiver;

    (c) an application under section 62 relating to action taken or proposed to be taken by a receiver;

    (d) an application under section 63 to vary or discharge an order under any of sections 48 to 53 for the appointment of or conferring powers on a receiver;

    (e) an application under section 72 or 73 for the payment of compensation;

    (f) proceedings which relate to an order under section 298 for the forfeiture of cash;

    (g) an application under section 351(3), 362(3), 369(3) or 375(2) to vary or discharge certain orders made under Part 8.

    (2)   But sub-paragraph (1) does not authorise the funding of the provision of services to a defendant (within the meaning of Part 1 of that Act) in relation to—

    (a) proceedings mentioned in paragraph (b);

    (b) an application under section 73 for the payment of compensation if the confiscation order was varied under section 29."

Powers of Criminal Courts (Sentencing) Act 2000 (c 6)

37.—(1) The Powers of Criminal Courts (Sentencing) Act 2000 is amended as follows.

    (2)   In section 110(5) (minimum sentence for third drug trafficking offence) for the definition of "drug trafficking offence" there is substituted—

    ""drug trafficking offence" means an offence which is specified in—

    (a)   paragraph 1 of Schedule 2 to the Proceeds of Crime Act 2002 (drug trafficking offences), or

    (b)   so far as it relates to that paragraph, paragraph 10 of that Schedule.".

    (3)   In section 133 (review of compensation orders) in subsection (3)(c) after "Criminal Justice Act 1988" insert ", or Part 2 of the Proceeds of Crime Act 2002,".

Financial Services and Markets Act 2000 (c 8)

38. In Schedule 1 to the Financial Services and Markets Act 2000 (provisions relating to the Financial Services Authority) after paragraph 19 insert—

    "19A.—For the purposes of this Act anything done by an accredited financial investigator within the meaning of the Proceeds of Crime Act 2002 who is—

    (a) a member of the staff of the Authority, or

    (b) a person appointed by the Authority under section 97, 167 or 168 to conduct an investigation,

must be treated as done in the exercise or discharge of a function of the Authority."

Terrorism Act 2000 (c 11)

39.—(1) Schedule 8 to the Terrorism Act 2000 (detention) is amended as follows.

    (2)   In paragraph 8 (authorisation of delay in exercise of detained person's rights) for sub-paragraph (5) substitute—

    "(5)   An officer may also give an authorisation under sub-paragraph (1) if he has reasonable grounds for believing that—

    (a) the detained person has benefited from his criminal conduct, and

    (b) the recovery of the value of the property constituting the benefit will be hindered by—

       (i) informing the named person of the detained person's detention (in the case of an authorisation under sub-paragraph (1)(a)), or

       (ii) the exercise of the right under paragraph 7 (in the case of an authorisation under sub-paragraph (1)(b)).

    (5A)   For the purposes of sub-paragraph (5) the question whether a person has benefited from his criminal conduct is to be decided in accordance with Part 2 of the Proceeds of Crime Act 2002.".

(3)   In paragraph 17(3) (grounds for authorising delay or requiring presence of senior officer), in paragraph (d) for "Part VI of the Criminal Justice Act 1988, Part I of the Proceeds of Crime (Scotland) Act 1995" substitute "Part 2 or 3 of the Proceeds of Crime Act 2002".

(4)   For paragraph 17(4) (further grounds for authorising delay in exercise of detained person's rights) substitute—

"(4)   This sub-paragraph applies where an officer mentioned in paragraph 16(4) or (7) has reasonable grounds for believing that—

(a)   the detained person has benefited from his criminal conduct, and
(b)   the recovery of the value of the property constituting the benefit will be hindered by—
(i)   informing the named person of the detained person's detention (in the case of an authorisation under paragraph 16(4)), or
(ii)   the exercise of the entitlement under paragraph 16(6) (in the case of an authorisation under paragraph 16(7)).

(4A)   For the purposes of sub-paragraph (4) the question whether a person has benefited from his criminal conduct is to be decided in accordance with Part 3 of the Proceeds of Crime Act 2002.".

(5)   In paragraph 34 (authorisation for withholding information from detained person) for sub-paragraph (3) substitute—

"(3)   A judicial authority may also make an order under sub-paragraph (1) in relation to specified information if satisfied that there are reasonable grounds for believing that—

(a)   the detained person has benefited from his criminal conduct, and
(b)   the recovery of the value of the property constituting the benefit would be hindered if the information were disclosed.

(3A)   For the purposes of sub-paragraph (3) the question whether a person has benefited from his criminal conduct is to be decided in accordance with Part 2 or 3 of the Proceeds of Crime Act 2002.".

Criminal Justice and Police Act 2001 (c 16)

40.—(1) The Criminal Justice and Police Act 2001 is amended as follows.

(2)   In section 55 (obligation to return excluded and special procedure material) in subsection (5) (powers in relation to which section does not apply as regards special procedure material) omit "and" after paragraph (b), and after paragraph (c) insert—
"and
(d)   section 352(4) of the Proceeds of Crime Act 2002,".

(3)   In section 60 (cases where duty to secure seized property arises) in subsection (4) (powers in relation to which duty does not arise as regards special procedure material) omit "or" after paragraph (b), and after paragraph (c) insert—
"or
(d)   section 352(4) of the Proceeds of Crime Act 2002,".

(4)   In section 64 (meaning of appropriate judicial authority) in subsection (3) after paragraph (a) omit "and" and insert—
"(aa)   the power of seizure conferred by section 352(4) of the Proceeds of Crime Act 2002, if the power is exercisable for the purposes of a civil recovery investigation (within the meaning of Part 8 of that Act);".

(5)   In section 65 (meaning of "legal privilege")—
(a)   in subsection (1)(b) for the words "33 of the Criminal Law (Consolidation) (Scotland) Act 1995 (c 39)" substitute "412 of the Proceeds of Crime Act 2002";
(b)   after subsection (3) insert—

"(3A) In relation to property which has been seized in exercise, or purported exercise, of—

(a) the power of seizure conferred by section 352(4) of the Proceeds of Crime Act 2002, or

(b) so much of any power of seizure conferred by section 50 as is exercisable by reference to that power,

references in this Part to an item subject to legal privilege shall be read as references to privileged material within the meaning of section 354(2) of that Act.".

(6) In Part 1 of Schedule 1 (powers of seizure to which section 50 applies) at the end add—

"Proceeds of Crime Act 2002 (c 29)

73A. The power of seizure conferred by section 352(4) of the Proceeds of Crime Act 2002 (seizure of material likely to be of substantial value to certain investigations).".

(7) In Part 3 of Schedule 1 (powers of seizure to which section 55 applies) at the end add—

"Proceeds of Crime Act 2002 (c 29)

110. The power of seizure conferred by section 352(4) of the Proceeds of Crime Act 2002 (seizure of material likely to be of substantial value to certain investigations).".

Definitions In the Police and Criminal Evidence Act 1984: for "serious arrestable offence", see s 116. In the Pension Schemes Act 1993: for "civil recovery order", see s 181(1) (as amended by para 22(1), (6) above); for "earner", see s 181(1); for "protected rights", see s 10. In the Terrorism Act 2000: for "property", see s 121.

SCHEDULE 12

Section 457

REPEALS AND REVOCATIONS

Short title and chapter	Extent of repeal or revocation
Misuse of Drugs Act 1971 (c 38)	In section 21 the words "or section 49 of the Drug Trafficking Act 1994". In section 23(3A) the words "or section 49 of the Drug Trafficking Act 1994".
Criminal Appeal (Northern Ireland) Act 1980 (c 47)	In section 30(3) the word "and" after paragraph (b).
Police and Criminal Evidence Act 1984 (c 60)	In section 65— (a) the definitions of "drug trafficking" and "drug trafficking offence"; (b) the words from "references in this Part" to "in accordance with the Drug Trafficking Act 1994".
Criminal Justice Act 1988 (c 33)	Sections 71 to 102. In section 151(4) the word "and" after paragraph (a). In section 172— (a) in subsection (2) the words from "section 76(3)" to "extending to Scotland"; (b) in subsection (4) the words from "sections 90" to "section 93E". Schedule 4.

Short title and chapter	Extent of repeal or revocation
Housing Act 1988 (c 50)	In Schedule 17, paragraphs 83 and 84.
Extradition Act 1989 (c 33)	In section 22(4)(h) the word "and" after sub-paragraph (ii).
Police and Criminal Evidence (Northern Ireland) Order 1989 (SI 1989/1341 (NI 12))	In Article 53— (a) the definitions of "drug trafficking" and "drug trafficking offence"; (b) the words from "References in this Part" to "Order 1996".
Criminal Justice (International Co-operation) Act 1990 (c 5)	In section 13(6) the words "the Drug Trafficking Act 1994 or". Section 14. In Schedule 4, paragraph 1.
Criminal Justice (Confiscation) (Northern Ireland) Order 1990 (SI 1990/2588 (NI 17))	In Article 37— (a) paragraph (2); (b) in paragraphs (3) and (4) sub-paragraph (b) and the word "and" before it; (c) paragraph (5).
Criminal Justice Act 1993 (c 36)	Section 21(3)(e) to (g). Sections 27 to 35. In Schedule 4, paragraph 3. In Schedule 5, paragraph 14.
Criminal Justice and Public Order Act 1994 (c 33)	In Schedule 9, paragraph 36.
Drug Trafficking Act 1994 (c 37)	Sections 1 to 54. In sections 55(4)(a) and 56(3)(a) and (4)(a) the words "or has benefited from". In section 59, subsections (1) to (10) and in subsection (11) the words "An order under subsection (1) above, and". In section 60(6), in the definition of "specified offence", in paragraph (a) the words "Part III or" and paragraph (c) and the word "or" immediately preceding it. In section 60(6), the words from "and references to the institution of proceedings" to the end. Section 60(7) and (8). Section 61(2) to (4). Sections 62, 63(1), (2) and (3)(a) and 64. In section 68(2), paragraphs (a) to (c) and in paragraph (g) the words "1, 41, 62" and "64". In section 68(3), paragraph (a) and in paragraph (d) the word "64". In Schedule 1, paragraphs 3, 4(a), 8, 21 and 26.
Proceeds of Crime Act 1995 (c 11)	Sections 1 to 13. Section 15(1) to (3). Section 16(2), (5) and (6). Schedule 1.

Short title and chapter	Extent of repeal or revocation
Criminal Law (Consolidation) (Scotland) Act 1995 (c 39)	Part V.
Criminal Procedure (Consequential Provisions) (Scotland) Act 1995 (c 40)	In Schedule 3, paragraph 4(2). In Schedule 4, paragraphs 69 and 94.
Private International Law (Miscellaneous Provisions) Act 1995 (c 42)	Section 4(3).
Proceeds of Crime (Scotland) Act 1995 (c 43)	Part I, except section 2(7).
	In section 28, subsections (1)(a) and (2) and in subsection (5) the words "(including a restraint order made under and within the meaning of the 1994 Act)".
	Section 29.
	In section 31, subsection (2), in subsection (4) the words "or (2)".
	Sections 35 to 39.
	In section 40, subsections (1)(a), (2) and (4).
	In section 42, subsections (1)(a) and (b).
	In section 43, in subsection (1) the words "confiscation order", subsection (2).
	Section 45(1)(a).
	Section 47.
	In section 49, in subsection (1) the definitions of "the 1988 Act", "the 1994 Act" and "confiscation order" and subsection (4).
	In Schedule 1, in paragraph 1, in sub-paragraph (1)(b) the words "or a confiscation order", in sub-paragraph (2)(a) the words "subject to paragraph (b) below", sub-paragraph (2)(b), in sub-paragraph (3)(a)(i) the words "or confiscation order".
	In Schedule 1, in paragraph 2, in sub-paragraph (1)(a) the words ", and if appointed (or empowered) under paragraph 1(1)(b) above where a confiscation order has been made", paragraph 4, in paragraph 5(1) the words "Part I of", in paragraph 8(2) the words from ", unless in a case where a confiscation order has been" to "4(4)(b) above,".
	In Schedule 1, in paragraph 10(1) the words "or the recipient of a gift caught by Part I of this Act or an implicative gift", paragraphs 10(2) and (3), in paragraph 12(1)(a) the words "paragraph (a) or (b) of section 4(1) or".
	In Schedule 2, in paragraph 1(2) the words "and 35 to 38", in paragraph 2(1) the words "realisable or", in paragraph 2(2) the words "and 35 to 38", paragraph 2(5), in

Short title and chapter	Extent of repeal or revocation
Proceeds of Crime (Scotland) Act 1995 (c 43)—*contd*	paragraph 3(2) the words "and 35 to 38", paragraphs 3(4) and (5), in paragraph 4(2) the words "and 35 to 38", paragraph 6(2)(a).
Proceeds of Crime (Northern Ireland) Order 1996 (SI 1996/1299 (NI 9))	Parts II and III.
	In Article 2 in paragraph (2) from the definition of "charging order" to the definition of "external confiscation order" and from the definition of "modifications" to the definition of "restraint order" and paragraphs (3) to (10) and (12).
	Article 3.
	In Article 49, in paragraph (1) sub-paragraph (c) and the word "and" immediately preceding it, in paragraph (1A) sub-paragraph (c) and the word "and" immediately preceding it, paragraph (4) and in paragraph (5) the definitions of "customs officer" and "relevant property".
	In Article 52 in paragraph (2) sub-paragraph (b) and the word "and" immediately preceding it, and paragraph (3).
	In Article 54 paragraphs (1) to (10) and (13) and in paragraph (11) the words "An order under paragraph (1) and,".
	In Article 55, in paragraph (6) in the definition of "specified offence" in paragraph (a) the words "Part III or" and paragraph (c) and the word "or" immediately preceding it, and paragraph (7).
	Article 56(2) to (4).
	In Schedule 2—
	(a) in paragraph 1(3) "3 or";
	(b) paragraph 3;
	(c) in paragraphs 4(2), 5(1) and 6(1) "3".
	In Schedule 3, paragraphs 1 to 3 and 18.
Justices of the Peace Act 1997 (c 25)	In Schedule 5, paragraphs 23 and 36.
Crime and Punishment (Scotland) Act 1997 (c 48)	Section 15(3). In Schedule 1, paragraph 20.
Crime and Disorder Act 1998 (c 37)	Section 83. In Schedule 1, paragraphs 115 and 116. In Schedule 8, paragraph 114. In Schedule 9, paragraph 8.
Access to Justice Act 1999 (c 22)	In Schedule 2—
	(a) in paragraph 2(2) the word "or" at the end of paragraph (c);
	(b) in paragraph 2(3) the word "or" at the end of paragraph (j).
	In Schedule 13, paragraphs 139 and 172.

Short title and chapter	Extent of repeal or revocation
Powers of Criminal Courts (Sentencing) Act 2000 (c 6)	In Schedule 9, paragraphs 105 to 113 and 163 to 173.
Terrorism Act 2000 (c 11)	In Schedule 15, paragraphs 6, 10 and 11(2).
Criminal Justice and Police Act 2001 (c 16)	In section 55(5) paragraph (a) and the word "and" after paragraph (b).
	In section 60(4) paragraph (a) and the word "or" after paragraph (b).
	In section 64(3) the word "and" after paragraph (a).
	In Schedule 1, paragraphs 47 and 105.
Financial Investigations (Northern Ireland) Order 2001 (SI 2001/1866 (NI 1))	Articles 3(2)(b) and 4(1)(a) and (c), (2), (3) and (5).
Land Registration Act 2002 (c 9)	In Schedule 11, paragraphs 22 and 32.
This Act	Section 248(2)(a) and (4).

Appendix 2

Money Laundering Regulations 1993

Money Laundering Regulations 2001

Council Directive 91/308/EC on prevention of the use of the financial system for the purpose of money laundering

European Parliament and Council Directive 2001/97/EC (amending Council Directive 91/308/EEC)

Money Laundering Regulations 1993

(SI 1993/1933)

Made   28 July 1993.
Authority   European Communities Act 1972, s 2(2).
Commencement   1 April 1994.

General

1 Citation and commencement

(1)   These Regulations may be cited as the Money Laundering Regulations 1993.

(2)   These Regulations shall come into force on 1st April 1994.

2 Interpretation

(1)   In these Regulations—

"applicant for business" means a person seeking to form a business relationship, or carry out a one-off transaction, with a person who is carrying out relevant financial business in the United Kingdom;

["the Banking Consolidation Directive" means Directive 2000/12/EC of the European Parliament and of the Council of 20 March 2000 relating to the taking up and pursuit of the business of credit institutions;]

"business relationship" has the meaning given by regulation 3 below;

"Case 1", "Case 2", "Case 3" and "Case 4" have the meanings given in regulation 7 below;

"constable" includes a person commissioned by the Commissioners of Customs and Excise;

["European institution" means an EEA firm of the kind mentioned in sub-paragraph (b) or (c) of paragraph 5 of Schedule 3 to the Financial Services and Markets Act 2000 which qualifies for authorisation for the purposes of that Act under paragraph 12 of that Schedule;]

["home regulated activity", in relation to a European institution, means any activity listed in Annex 1 to the banking consolidation directive (the text of which is, for convenience) set out in the Schedule to these Regulations)—

(a)   in relation to which a supervisory authority in its home state has regulatory functions, and

(b)   in the case of an EEA firm of the kind mentioned in paragraph 5(c) of Schedule 3 to the Financial Services and Markets Act 2000, it is carrying on in its home State;

"home state", in relation to a person incorporated in or formed under the law of another member State, means that State;]

["insurance business" means business which consists of effecting or carrying out contracts of long-term insurance"]

"the Money Laundering Directive" means the Council Directive on prevention of the use of the financial system for the purpose of money laundering (No 91/308/EEC);

565

"one-off transaction" means any transaction other than a transaction carried out in the course of an established business relationship formed by a person acting in the course of relevant financial business;

"relevant financial business" has the meaning given by regulation 4 below; and

"supervisory authority" has the meaning given by regulation 15 below.

[(1A) The definition of "insurance business" in paragraph (1) must be read with—
    (a)   section 22 of the Financial Services and Markets Act 2000;
    (b)   any relevant order that section
    (c)   Schedule 2 to that Act.]

(2)   In these Regulations "ecu" means the european currency unit as defined in article 1 of Council Regulation No 3180/78/EEC; and the exchange rates as between the ecu and the currencies of the member States to be applied for each year beginning on 31st December shall be the rates applicable on the last day of the preceding October for which rates for the currencies of all the member States were published in the Official Journal of the Communities.

(3)   In these Regulations, except in so far as the context otherwise requires, "money laundering" means doing any act which constitutes an offence under—
    (a)   section 23A or 24 of the Drug Trafficking Offences Act 1986 (which relate to the handling etc of proceeds of drug trafficking);
    (b)   section 42A or 43 of the Criminal Justice (Scotland) Act 1987 (which relate to the handling etc of proceeds of drug trafficking);
    (c)   section 93A, 93B or 93C of the Criminal Justice Act 1988 (which relate to the handling etc of proceeds of certain other criminal conduct);
    (d)   section 11 of the Prevention of Terrorism (Temporary Provisions) Act 1989 (which relates to financial assistance for terrorism);
    (e)   section 14 of the Criminal Justice (International Co-operation) Act 1990 (concealing or transferring proceeds of drug trafficking);
    (f)   Article 29 or 30 of the Criminal Justice (Confiscation) (Northern Ireland) Order 1990 (which relate to the handling etc of proceeds of drug trafficking);
    (g)   section 53 or 54 of the Northern Ireland (Emergency Provisions) Act 1991 (which relate to the handling etc of proceeds of terrorist-related activities); or
    (h)   any provision, whenever made, which has effect in Northern Ireland and corresponds to any of the provisions mentioned in sub-paragraph (a) or (c) above;

or, in the case of an act done otherwise than in England and Wales, Scotland or, as the case may be, Northern Ireland would constitute such an offence if done in England and Wales, Scotland or Northern Ireland.

(4)   The reference in paragraph (3) above to doing any act which would constitute an offence under the provisions mentioned in sub-paragraph (c) of that paragraph shall, for the purposes of these Regulations, be construed as a reference to doing any act which would constitute an offence under those provisions if, for the definition of "criminal conduct" in section 93A(7) of the Criminal Justice Act 1988, there were substituted—

      "(7)   In this Part of this Act "criminal conduct" means—
          (a)   conduct which constitutes an offence to which this Part of this Act applies; or

    (b) conduct which—
        (i)   would constitute such an offence if it had occurred in England and Wales or (as the case may be) Scotland; and
       (ii)   contravenes the law of the country in which it occurred.".

(5) For the purposes of these Regulations, any provision having effect in Northern Ireland which corresponds to the provisions referred to in paragraph (3)(c) above shall be construed as if it had been amended by a provision which corresponds to paragraph (4) above, with appropriate modifications.

(6) For the purposes of this regulation, a business relationship formed by any person acting in the course of relevant financial business is an established business relationship where that person has obtained, under procedures maintained by him in accordance with regulation 7 below, satisfactory evidence of the identity of the person who, in relation to the formation of that business relationship, was the applicant for business.

Para (1): definition "the Banking Consolidation Directive" inserted by SI 2000/2952, reg 11(1), (2); definitions "European institution" and "insurance business" substituted, and definitions "home regulated activity" and "home state" inserted, by the Financial Services and Markets Act 2000 (Consequential Amendments and Repeals) Order 2001, SI 2001/3649, art 438(1)–(4)
Para (1A): inserted by SI 2001/3649, art 438(1), (5).

---

3 Business relationships

(1)   Any reference in this regulation to an arrangement between two or more persons is a reference to an arrangement in which at least one person is acting in the course of a business.

(2)   For the purposes of these Regulations, "business relationship" means any arrangement between two or more persons where—
    (a) the purpose of the arrangement is to facilitate the carrying out of transactions between the persons concerned on a frequent, habitual or regular basis; and
    (b) the total amount of any payment or payments to be made by any person to any other in the course of that arrangement is not known or capable of being ascertained at the time the arrangement is made.

4 Relevant financial business

(1)   For the purposes of these Regulations, "relevant financial business" means, subject to paragraph (2) below, the business of engaging in one or more of the following—
    [(a) accepting deposits, by a person with permission under Part 4 of the Financial Services and Markets Act 2000 to accept deposits (including, in the case of a building society, the raising of money from members of the society by the issue of shares);]
    (b) . . .
    (c) business of the National Savings Bank;
    (d) business carried on by a credit union within the meaning of the Credit Unions Act 1979 or the Credit Unions (Northern Ireland) Order 1985;
    (e) any home regulated activity carried on by a European institution in respect of which [the establishment conditions in paragraph 13 of

Schedule 3 to the Financial Services and Markets Act 2000, or the service conditions in paragraph 14 of that Schedule, have been satisfied];

[(f) business which consists of carrying on one or more activities of the following kinds of regulated activity in the United Kingdom—
  (i) dealing in investments as principal or as agent,
  (ii) arranging deals in investments,
  (iii) managing investments,
  (iv) safeguarding and administering investments,
  (v) sending dematerialised instructions,
  (vi) establishing etc collective investment schemes,
  (vii) advising on investments];

(g) any activity carried on for the purpose of raising money authorised to be raised under the National Loans Act 1968 under the auspices of the Director of National Savings;

[(ga) the activity of—
  (i) operating a bureau de change;
  (ii) transmitting money, or any representation of monetary value, by any means; or
  (iii) cashing cheques which are made payable to customers;]

(h) any of the activities in points 1 to 12, or 14, of [Annex 1 to the Banking Consolidation Directive] (the text of which is, for convenience of reference, set out in the Schedule to these Regulations), other than an activity falling within sub-paragraphs (a) to [(ga)] above;

(i) insurance business carried on by a person who has received official authorisation pursuant to Article 6 or 27 of the First Life Directive.

(2) A business is not relevant financial business in so far as it consists of—
  (a) any of the following activities carried on by a society registered under the Industrial and Provident Societies Act 1965—
    (i) the issue of withdrawable share capital within the limit set by section 6 of that Act; or
    (ii) the acceptance of deposits from the public within the limit set by section 7(3) of that Act;
  (b) the issue of withdrawable share capital within the limit set by section 6 of the Industrial and Provident Societies Act (Northern Ireland) 1969 by a society registered under that Act;
  (c) activities carried on by the Bank of England;
  (d) . . .; or
  [(e) in relation to any person who is for the time being specified in any order made under section 38 of the Financial Services and Markets Act 2000 as an exempt person in respect of all or any regulated activities (within the meaning of that Act), those activities in respect of which he is exempt].

(3) . . .

(4) In this regulation—
  "building society" has the same meaning as in the Building Societies Act 1986;

. . . . .

  "the First Life Directive" means the First Council Directive on the coordination of laws, regulations and administrative provisions relating to the taking up and pursuit of the business of direct life assurance (No 79/ 267/EEC); and

. . . . .

[(5) Sub-paragraphs (a) and (f) of paragraph (1) must be read with—
    (a)   section 22 of the Financial Services and Markets Act 2000,
    (b)   any relevant order under that section; and
    (c)   Schedule 2 to that Act.]

Para (1): sub-paras (a), (f) substituted, sub-para (b) revoked, and words in square brackets in sub-para (e) substituted, by the Financial Services and Markets Act 2000 (Consequential Amendments and Repeals) Order 2001, SI 2001/3649, art 439(1)–(5); sub-para (ga) inserted, and reference to "(ga)" in square brackets in sub-para (h) substituted, by the Money Laundering Regulations 2001, SI 2001/3641, reg 3(1), (2)(a); words in first pair of square brackets in sub-para (h) substituted by the Banking Consolidation Directive (Consequential Amendments) Regulations 2000, SI 2000/2952, reg 11(1), (3).
Para (2): sub-para (d) revoked, and sub-para (e) substituted, by SI 2001/3649, art 439(1), (6).
Para (3): revoked by SI 2001/3649, art 439(1), (7).
Para (4): first definition omitted revoked by SI 2001/3649, art 439(1), (8); second definition omitted revoked by SI 2000/2952, reg 11(1), (4).
Para (5): added by SI 2001/3649, art 439(1), (9).

Systems and training to prevent money laundering

5 Systems and training to prevent money laundering

(1)   No person shall, in the course of relevant financial business carried on by him in the United Kingdom, form a business relationship, or carry out a one-off transaction, with or for another unless that person—
    (a)   maintains the following procedures established in relation to that business—
        (i) identification procedures in accordance with regulations 7 and 9 below;
        (ii) record-keeping procedures in accordance with regulation 12 below;
        (iii) except where the person concerned is an individual who in the course of relevant financial business does not employ or act in association with any other person, internal reporting procedures in accordance with regulation 14 below; and
        (iv) such other procedures of internal control and communication as may be appropriate for the purposes of forestalling and preventing money laundering;
    (b)   takes appropriate measures from time to time for the purposes of making employees whose duties include the handling of relevant financial business aware of—
        (i) the procedures under sub-paragraph (a) above which are maintained by him and which relate to the relevant financial business in question, and
        (ii) the enactments relating to money laundering; and
    (c)   provides such employees from time to time with training in the recognition and handling of transactions carried out by, or on behalf of, any person who is, or appears to be, engaged in money laundering.

(2)   Any person who contravenes this regulation shall be guilty of an offence and liable—

(a) on conviction on indictment, to imprisonment not exceeding a term of two years or a fine or both;

(b) on summary conviction, to a fine not exceeding the statutory maximum.

(3) In determining whether a person has complied with any of the requirements of paragraph (1) above, a court may take account of—

(a) any relevant supervisory or regulatory guidance which applies to that person;

(b) in a case where no guidance falling within sub-paragraph (a) above applies, any other relevant guidance issued by a body that regulates, or is representative of, any trade, profession, business or employment carried on by that person.

(4) In proceedings against any person for an offence under this regulation, it shall be a defence for that person to show that he took all reasonable steps and exercised all due diligence to avoid committing the offence.

(5) In this regulation—

"enactments relating to money laundering" means the enactments referred to in regulation 2(3) above and the provisions of these Regulations; and

"supervisory or regulatory guidance" means guidance issued, adopted or approved by a supervisory authority.

6 Offences by bodies corporate, partnerships and unincorporated associations

(1) Where an offence under regulation 5 above committed by a body corporate is proved to have been committed with the consent or connivance of, or to be attributable to any neglect on the part of, any director, manager, secretary or other similar officer of the body corporate or any person who was purporting to act in any such capacity he, as well as the body corporate, shall be guilty of that offence and shall be liable to be proceeded against and punished accordingly.

(2) Where the affairs of a body corporate are managed by the members, paragraph (1) above shall apply in relation to the acts and defaults of a member in connection with his functions of management as if he were a director of a body corporate.

(3) Where an offence under regulation 5 above committed by a partnership, or by an unincorporated association other than a partnership, is proved to have been committed with the consent or connivance of, or is attributable to any neglect on the part of, a partner in the partnership or (as the case may be) a person concerned in the management or control of the association, he, as well as the partnership or association, shall be guilty of that offence and shall be liable to be proceeded against and punished accordingly.

Identification procedures

7 Identification procedures; business relationships and transactions

(1) Subject to regulations 8 and 10 below, identification procedures maintained by a person are in accordance with this regulation if in Cases 1 to 4 set out below they require, as soon as is reasonably practicable after contact is first made between that person and an applicant for business concerning any particular business relationship or one-off transaction—

    (a)   the production by the applicant for business of satisfactory evidence of his identity; or

    (b)   the taking of such measures specified in the procedures as will produce satisfactory evidence of his identity;

and the procedures are, subject to paragraph (6) below, in accordance with this regulation if they require that where that evidence is not obtained the business relationship or one-off transaction in question shall not proceed any further.

(2)   Case 1 is any case where the parties form or resolve to form a business relationship between them.

(3)   Case 2 is any case where, in respect of any one-off transaction, any person handling the transaction knows or suspects that the applicant for business is engaged in money laundering, or that the transaction is carried out on behalf of another person engaged in money laundering.

(4)   Case 3 is any case where, in respect of any one-off transaction, payment is to be made by or to the applicant for business of the amount of ecu 15,000 or more.

(5)   Case 4 is any case where, in respect of two or more one-off transactions—

    (a)   it appears at the outset to a person handling any of the transactions—

        (i) that the transactions are linked, and

        (ii) that the total amount, in respect of all of the transactions, which is payable by or to the applicant for business is ecu 15,000 or more; or

    (b)   at any later stage, it comes to the attention of such a person that paragraphs (i) and (ii) of sub-paragraph (a) above are satisfied.

(6)   The procedures referred to in paragraph (1) above are in accordance with this regulation if, when a report is made in circumstances falling within Case 2 (whether in accordance with regulation 14 or directly to a constable), they provided for steps to be taken in relation to the one-off transaction in question in accordance with any directions that may be given by a constable.

(7)   In these Regulations references to satisfactory evidence of a person's identity shall be construed in accordance with regulation 11(1) below.

8 Payment by post etc

(1)   Where satisfactory evidence of the identity of an applicant for business would, apart from this paragraph, be required under identification procedures in accordance with regulation 7 above but—

    (a)   the circumstances are such that a payment is to be made by the applicant for business; and

    (b)   it is reasonable in all the circumstances—

        (i) for the payment to be sent by post or by any electronic means which is effective to transfer funds; or

        (ii) for the details of the payment to be sent by post, to be given on the telephone or to be given by any other electronic means;

then, subject to paragraph (2) below, the fact that the payment is debited from an account held in the applicant's name at an institution mentioned in paragraph (4) below (whether the account is held by the applicant alone or jointly with one or more other persons) shall be capable of constituting the required evidence of identity.

(2)   Paragraph (1) above shall not have effect to the event that—
  (a)   the circumstances of the payment fall within Case 2; or
  (b)   the payment is made by any person for the purpose of opening a relevant account with an institution falling within paragraph (4)(a) or (b) below.

(3)   For the purposes of paragraph (1)(b) above, it shall be immaterial whether the payment or its details are sent or given to a person who is bound by regulation 5(1) above or to some other person acting on his behalf.

(4)   The institutions referred to in paragraph (1) above are—
  [(a)   a person who for the time being has permission under Part 4 of the Financial Services and Markets Act 2000 to accept deposits;
  (b)   an EEA firm of the kind mentioned in paragraph 5(b) of Schedule 3 to the Financial Services and Markets Act 2000 which has permission under paragraph 15 of that Schedule (as a result of qualifying for authorisation under paragraph 12 of that Schedule) to accept deposits; or]
  (c)   any other institution which is an authorised credit institution.

(5)   For the purposes of this regulation—
  ["authorised credit institution" means a credit institution, as defined in Article 1 of the Banking Consolidation Directive, which is authorised to carry on the business of a credit institution by a competent authority of a member State;]
  "relevant account" means an account from which a payment may be made by any means to a person other than the applicant for business, whether such a payment—
    (a)   may be made directly to such a person from the account by or on behalf of the applicant for business; or
    (b)   may be made to such a person indirectly as a result of—
      (i)   a direct transfer of funds from an account from which no such direct payment may be made to another account, or
      (ii)   a change in any of the characteristics of the account.

Para (4): sub-paras (a), (b) substituted by the Financial Services and Markets Act 2000 (Consequential Amendments and Repeals) Order 2001, SI 2001/3649, art 440.
Para (5): definition "authorised credit institution" substituted by the Banking Consolidation Directive (Consequential Amendments) Regulations 2000, SI 2000/2952, reg 11(1), (5).

9 Identification procedures; transactions on behalf of another

(1)   This regulation applies where, in relation to a person who is bound by regulation 5(1) above, an applicant for business is or appears to be acting otherwise than as principal.

(2)   Subject to regulation 10 below, identification procedures maintained by a person are in accordance with this regulation if, in a case to which this regulation applies, they require reasonable measures to be taken for the purpose of establishing the identity of any person on whose behalf the applicant for business is acting.

(3)   In determining, for the purposes of paragraph (2) above, what constitutes reasonable measures in any particular case regard shall be had to all the circumstances of the case and, in particular, to best practice which, for the time being, is followed in the relevant field of business and which is applicable to those circumstances.

(4)   Without prejudice to the generality of paragraph (3) above, if the conditions mentioned in paragraph (5) below are fulfilled in relation to an applicant for business who is, or appears to be, acting as an agent for a principal (whether undisclosed or disclosed for reference purposes only) it shall be reasonable for a person bound by regulation 5(1) above to accept a written assurance from the applicant for business to the effect that evidence of the identity of any principal on whose behalf the applicant for business may act in relation to that person will have been obtained and recorded under procedures maintained by the applicant for business.

(5)   The conditions referred to in paragraph (4) above are that, in relation to the business relationship or transaction in question, there are reasonable grounds for believing that the applicant for business—
    (a)   acts in the course of a business in relation to which an overseas regulatory authority exercises regulatory functions; and
    (b)   is based or incorporated in, or formed under the law of, a country other than a member State in which there are in force provisions at least equivalent to those required by the Money Laundering Directive.

(6)   In paragraph (5) above, "overseas regulatory authority" and "regulatory functions" have the same meaning as in section 82 of the Companies Act 1989.

10 Identification procedures; exemptions

(1)   Subject to paragraph (2) below, identification procedures under regulations 7 and 9 above shall not require any steps to be taken to obtain evidence of any person's identity—
    [(a)   where there are reasonable grounds for believing that the applicant for business—
      (i)   is a person who is bound by the provisions of regulation 5(1) above, or
      (ii)   is otherwise a person who is covered by the Money Laundering Directive,
other than a person who is engaged in any of the activities mentioned in regulation 4(1)(ga) above;]
    (c)   where any one-off transaction is carried out with or for a third party pursuant to an introduction effected by a person who has provided an assurance that evidence of the identity of all third parties introduced by him will have been obtained and recorded under procedures maintained by him, where that person identifies the third party and where—
      (i)   that person falls within sub-paragraph (a) . . . above; or
      (ii)   there are reasonable grounds for believing that the conditions mentioned in regulation 9(5)(a) and (b) above are fulfilled in relation to him;
    (d)   where the person who would otherwise be required to be identified, in relation to a one-off transaction, is the person to whom the proceeds of that transaction are payable but to whom no payment is made because all of those proceeds are directly reinvested on his behalf in another transaction—
      (i)   of which a record is kept, and
      (ii)   which can result only in another reinvestment made on that person's behalf or in a payment made directly to that person;

    (e)   in relation to insurance business consisting of a policy of insurance in connection with a pension scheme taken out by virtue of a person's contract of employment or occupation where the policy—
        (i) contains no surrender clause, and
        (ii) may not be used as collateral for a loan;
    (f)   in relation to insurance business in respect of which a premium is payable in one instalment of an amount not exceeding ecu 2,500; or
    (g)   in relation to insurance business in respect of which a periodic premium is payable and where the total payable in respect of any calendar year does not exceed ecu 1,000.

(2)   Nothing in this regulation shall apply in circumstances falling within Case 2.

(3)   In this regulation "calendar year" means a period of twelve months beginning on 31st December.

Para (1): sub-para (a) substituted for original sub-paras (a), (b), words omitted from sub-para (c)(i) revoked, by the Money Laundering Regulations 2001, SI 2001/3641, reg 3(1), (3).

---

11 Identification procedures; supplementary provisions

(1)   For the purposes of these Regulations, [and subject to paragraph (1A) below,] evidence of identify is satisfactory if—
    (a)   it is reasonably capable of establishing that the applicant is the person he claims to be; and
    (b)   the person who obtains the evidence is satisfied, in accordance with the procedures maintained under these Regulations in relation to the relevant financial business concerned, that it does establish that fact.

[(1A)   Where the applicant is a person who is engaged in any of the activities mentioned in regulation 4(1)(ga) above, satisfactory evidence of identity shall also include the applicant's registered number within the meaning given by regulation 4(3) of the Money Laundering Regulations 2001.]

(2)   In determining for the purposes of regulation 7(1) above the time span in which satisfactory evidence of a person's identity has to be obtained, in relation to any particular business relationship or one-off transaction, all the circumstances shall be taken into account including, in particular—
    (a)   the nature of the business relationship or one-off transaction concerned;
    (b)   the geographical locations of the parties;
    (c)   whether it is practical to obtain the evidence before commitments are entered into between the parties or before money passes;
    (d)   in relation to Case 3 or 4, the earliest stage at which there are reasonable grounds for believing that the total amount payable by an applicant for business is ecu 15,000 or more.

Para (1): words in square brackets inserted by the Money Laundering Regulations 2001, SI 2001/3641, reg 3(1), (4).
Para (1A): inserted by SI 2001/3641, reg 3(1), (5).

Record-keeping procedures

12 Record-keeping procedures

(1)   Record-keeping procedures maintained by a person are in accordance with this regulation if they require the keeping, for the prescribed period, of the following records—

    (a)   in any case where, in relation to any business relationship that is formed or one-off transaction that is carried out, evidence of a person's identity is obtained under procedures maintained in accordance with regulation 7 or 9 above, a record that indicates the nature of the evidence and—

        (i)   comprises a copy of the evidence;

        (ii)   provides such information as would enable a copy of it to be obtained; or

        (iii)   in a case where it is not reasonably practicable to comply with paragraph (i) or (ii) above, provides sufficient information to enable the details as to a person's identity contained in the relevant evidence to be re-obtained; and

    (b)   a record containing details relating to all transactions carried out by that person in the course of relevant financial business.

(2)   For the purposes of paragraph (1) above, the prescribed period is, subject to paragraph (3) below, the period of at least five years commencing with—

    (a)   in relation to such records as are described in sub-paragraph (a), the date on which the relevant business was completed within the meaning of paragraph (4) below; and

    (b)   in relation to such records as are described in sub-paragraph (b), the date on which all activities taking place in the course of the transaction in question were completed.

(3)   Where a person who is bound by the provisions of regulation 5(1) above—

    (a)   forms a business relationship or carries out a one-off transaction with another person;

    (b)   has reasonable grounds for believing that that person has become insolvent; and

    (c)   after forming that belief, takes any step for the purpose of recovering all or part of the amount of any debt payable to him by that person which has fallen due;

the prescribed period for the purposes of paragraph (1) above is the period of at least five years commencing with the date on which the first such step is taken.

(4)   For the purposes of paragraph (2)(a) above, the date on which relevant business is completed is, as the case may be—

    (a)   in circumstances falling within Case 1, the date of the ending of the business relationship in respect of whose formation the record under paragraph (1)(a) above was compiled;

    (b)   in circumstances falling within Case 2 or 3, the date of the completion of all activities taking place in the course of the one-off transaction in respect of which the record under paragraph (1)(a) above was compiled;

    (c)   in circumstances falling within Case 4, the date of the completion of all activities taking place in the course of the last one-off transaction in respect of which the record under paragraph (1)(a) above was compiled;

and where the formalities necessary to end a business relationship have not been observed, but a period of five years has elapsed since the date on which the last transaction was carried out in the course of that relationship, then the date of the completion of all activities taking place in the course of that last transaction shall be treated as the date on which the relevant business was completed.

13 Record-keeping procedures; supplementary provisions

   (1)   For the purposes of regulation 12(3)(b) above, a person shall be taken to be insolvent if, but only if, in England and Wales—

    (a)   he has been adjudged bankrupt or has made a composition or arrangement with his creditors;

    (b)   an order has been made with respect to him under section 112, 112A or 112B of the County Courts Act 1984 (administration orders, orders restricting enforcement and administration orders with composition provisions);

    (c)   he has died and his estate falls to be administered in accordance with an order under section 421 of the Insolvency Act 1986 (insolvent estates of deceased persons); or

    (d)   where that person is a company, a winding up order or an administration order has been made or a resolution for voluntary winding up has been passed with respect to it, or a receiver or manager of its undertaking has been duly appointed, or possession has been taken, by or on behalf of the holders of any debentures secured by a floating charge, of any property of the company comprised in or subject to the charge, or a voluntary arrangement proposed for the purpose of Part I of the Insolvency Act 1986 has been approved under that Part, or a compromise or arrangement in accordance with section 425 of the Companies Act 1985 has taken effect.

   (2)   For the purposes of regulation 12(3)(b) above, a person shall be taken to be insolvent if, but only if, in Scotland—

    (a)   his estate has been sequestrated, he has granted a trust deed for the benefit of his creditors or he has made a composition or arrangement for the benefit of his creditors; or

    (b)   where that person is a company, a winding up order or an administration order has been made or a resolution for voluntary winding up has been passed with respect to it, or a receiver has been appointed under a floating charge over any property of the company, or a voluntary arrangement proposed for the purpose of Part I of the Insolvency Act 1986 has been approved under that Part, or a compromise or arrangement in accordance with section 425 of the Companies Act 1985 has taken effect.

   (3)   For the purposes of regulation 12(3)(b) above, a person shall be taken to be insolvent if, but only if, in Northern Ireland—

    (a)   he has been adjudged bankrupt or has made a composition or arrangement with his creditors;

(b)   an administration order has been made with respect to him under Article 80 of the Judgements Enforcement (Northern Ireland) Order 1981 (power to make administration order on application of debtor);

(c)   he has died and his estate falls to be administered in accordance with an order under Article 365 of the Insolvency (Northern Ireland) Order 1989 (insolvent estates of deceased persons); or

(d)   where that person is a company, a winding up order or an administration order has been made or a resolution for voluntary winding up has been passed with respect to it, or a receiver or manager of its undertaking has been duly appointed, or possession has been taken, by or on behalf of the holders of any debentures secured by a floating charge, of any property of the company comprised in or subject to the charge, or a voluntary arrangement proposed for the purpose of Part II of the Insolvency (Northern Ireland) Order 1988 has been approved under that Part, or a compromise or arrangement in accordance with Article 418 of the Companies (Northern Ireland) Order 1986 has taken effect.

(4)   [Where a person bound by regulation 5(1) above is an appointed representative] it shall be the responsibility of the appointed representative's principal to ensure that record-keeping procedures in accordance with regulation 12 above are maintained in respect of any relevant financial business carried out by the appointed representative . . . for which the principal has accepted responsibility in writing [under section 39 of the Financial Services and Markets Act 2000].

(5)   Where record-keeping procedures in accordance with regulation 12 above are not maintained in respect of business relationships formed, and one-off transactions carried out, in the course of such relevant financial business as is referred to in paragraph (4) above, an appointed representative's principal shall be regarded as having contravened regulation 5 in respect of those procedures and he, as well as the appointed representative, shall be guilty of an offence and shall be liable to be proceeded against and punished accordingly.

[(6) For the purposes of paragraphs (4) and (5) above, "appointed representative" has the same meaning as in section 39(2) of the Financial Services and Markets Act 2000, and "principal" (in relation to an appointed representative) has the same meaning as in section 39(1) of that Act.]

Para (4): words in square brackets substituted by the Financial Services and Markets Act 2000 (Consequential Amendments and Repeals) Order 2001, SI 2001/3649, art 441(1); words omitted revoked by the Financial Services and Markets Act 2000 (Consequential Amendments) Order 2002, SI 2002/1555, art 35.
Para (6): substituted by SI 2001/3649, art 441(2).

Internal reporting procedures

14 Internal reporting procedures

Internal reporting procedures maintained by a person are in accordance with this regulation if they include provision—

(a)   identifying a person ("the appropriate person") to whom a report is to be made of any information or other matter which comes to the attention of a person handling relevant financial business and which, in the opinion of the person handling that business, gives rise to a knowledge or suspicion that another person is engaged in money laundering;

(b)   requiring that any such report be considered in the light of all other relevant information by the appropriate person, or by another designated person, for the purpose of determining whether or not the information or other matter contained in the report does give rise to such a knowledge or suspicion;

(c)   for any person charged with considering a report in accordance with sub-paragraph (b) above to have reasonable access to other information which may be of assistance to him and which is available to the person responsible for maintaining the internal reporting procedures concerned; and

(d)   for securing that the information or other matter contained in a report is disclosed to a constable where the person who has considered the report under the procedures maintained in accordance with the preceding provisions of this regulation knows or suspects that another person is engaged in money laundering.

Duty of supervisory authorities to report evidence of money laundering

15 Supervisory authorities

(1)   References in these Regulations to supervisory authorities shall be construed in accordance with the following provisions.

(2)   For the purposes of these Regulations, each of the following is a supervisory authority—

(a)   the Bank of England;

[(aa)   the Financial Services Authority;]

(b)–(d)   . . .

[(e)   a designated professional body within the meaning of section 326(2) of the Financial Services and Markets Act 2000;]

(f), (g)   . . .

(h)   the Secretary of State;

(i)   the Treasury;

(j)   the Council of Lloyd's;

(k)   the Director General of Fair Trading;

(l)–(p)   . . .

[(3)   These Regulations apply to the Secretary of State and to the Treasury in the exercise, in relation to any person carrying on relevant financial business, of their respective functions under the enactments relating to companies or insolvency or under the Financial Services and Markets Act 2000.]

Para (2): sub-para (aa) inserted by the Bank of England Act 1998 (Consequential Amendments of Subordinate Legislation) Order 1998, SI 1998/1129, art 2, Sch 1, para 13(b); sub-paras (b)–(d), (f), (g), (l)–(p) revoked, and sub-para (e) substituted, by the Financial Services and Markets Act 2000 (Consequential Amendments and Repeals) Order 2001, SI 2001/3649, art 442(1).
Para (3): substituted by SI 2001/3649, art 442(2).

---

16 Supervisors etc to report evidence of money laundering

(1)   Subject to paragraph (2) below, where a supervisory authority—

    (a)   obtains any information; and
    (b)   is of the opinion that the information indicates that any person has or may have been engaged in money laundering,

the authority shall, as soon as is reasonably practicable, disclose that information to a constable.

    (2)   Where any person is a secondary recipient of information obtained by a supervisory authority, and that person forms such an opinion as is mentioned in paragraph (1)(b) above, that person may disclose the information to a constable.

    (3)   Where any person within paragraph (6) below—
    (a)   obtains any information whilst acting in the course of any investigation, or discharging any functions, to which his appointment or authorisation relates; and
    (b)   is of the opinion that the information indicates that any person has or may have been engaged in money laundering,

that person shall, as soon as is reasonably practicable, either disclose that information to a constable or disclose that information to the supervisory authority by whom he was appointed or authorised.

    (4)   Any disclosure made by virtue of the preceding provisions of this regulation shall not be treated as a breach of any restriction imposed by statute or otherwise.

    (5)   Any information—
    (a)   which has been disclosed to a constable by virtue of the preceding provisions of this regulation; and
    (b)   which would, apart from the provisions of paragraph (4) above, be subject to such a restriction as is mentioned in that paragraph;

may be disclosed by the constable, or any person obtaining the information directly or indirectly from him, in connection with the investigation of any criminal offence or for the purposes of any criminal proceedings, but not otherwise.

    (6)   Persons falling within this paragraph are—
    (a)   a person or inspector appointed under . . . section 65 or 66 of the Friendly Societies Act 1992;
    (b)   an inspector appointed under section 49 of the Industrial and Provident Societies Act 1965 or section 18 of the Credit Unions Act 1979;
    (c)   an inspector appointed under section 431, 432, 442 or 446 of the Companies Act 1985 or under Article 424, 425, 435 or 439 of the Companies (Northern Ireland) Order 1986;
    (d)   a person or inspector appointed under section 55 or 56 of the Building Societies Act 1986;
    [(e)   a person appointed under section 167, 168(3) or (5), or 169(1)(b) or 284 of the Financial Services and Markets Act 2000, or under regulations made as a result of section 262(2)(k) of that Act, to conduct an investigation, or;]
    (f), [(fa)]   . . .
    (g)   a person authorised to require the production of documents under . . . section 447 of the Companies Act 1985, . . . Article 440 of the Companies (Northern Ireland) Order 1986 or section 84 of the Companies Act 1989.

    (7)   In this regulation "secondary recipient", in relation to information obtained by a supervisory authority, means any person to whom that information has been passed by the authority.

Para (6): words omitted from sub-paras (a), (g) revoked, sub-para (e) substituted, and sub-paras (f), (fa) (as inserted in the case of sub-para (fa) by SI 1994/1696, reg 68, Sch 8, para 36) revoked, by the Financial Services and Markets Act 2000 (Consequential Amendments and Repeals) Order 2001, SI 2001/3649, art 443.

Transitional provisions

17 Transitional provisions

(1)   Nothing in these Regulations shall require a person who is bound by regulation 5(1) above to maintain procedures in accordance with regulations 7 and 9 which require evidence to be obtained, in respect of any business relationship formed by him before the date on which these Regulations come into force, as to the identity of the person with whom that relationship has been formed.

(2)   For the purposes of regulation 2(6) above, any business relationship referred to in paragraph (1) above shall be treated as if it were an established business relationship.

(3)   In regulation 10(1)(g), the reference to the total payable in respect of any calendar year not exceeding ecu 1,000 shall, for the period commencing with the coming into force of these regulations and ending with 30th December 1994, be construed as a reference to the total payable in respect of that period not exceeding ecu 750.

SCHEDULE
Regulation 4(1)

ANNEX
LIST OF ACTIVITIES SUBJECT TO MUTUAL RECOGNITION

1.   Acceptance of deposits and other repayable funds from the public.

2.   Lending.

3.   Financial leasing.

4.   Money transmission services.

5.   Issuing and administering means of payment (eg credit cards, travellers' cheques and bankers' drafts).

6.   Guarantees and commitments.

7.   Trading for own account or for account of customers in:
      (a)   money market instruments (cheques, bills, CDs, etc);
      (b)   foreign exchange;
      (c)   financial futures and options;
      (d)   exchange and interest rate instruments;
      (e)   transferable securities.

8.   Participation in securities issues and the provision of services related to such issues.

9.   Advice to undertakings on capital structure, industrial strategy and related questions and advice and services relating to mergers and the purchase of undertakings.

10. Money broking.

11. Portfolio management and advice.

12. Safekeeping and administration of securities.

13. Credit reference services.

14. Safe custody services.

Money Laundering Regulations 2001

(SI 2001/3641)

Made   9 November 2001.
Authority   European Communities Act 1972, s 2(2); Finance Act 1973, s 56.
Commencement   12 November 2001 (for the purposes of regs 1, 2, 3(1), (2), 4–20); 15 July 2002 (for the purposes of reg 3(3)–(5)).

PART I
GENERAL

1 Citation and commencement

(1)   These Regulations may be cited as the Money Laundering Regulations 2001.

(2)   These Regulations come into force—
      (a)   for the purposes of regulation 3(3) to (5), on 15th July 2002;
      (b)   for all other purposes, on 12th November 2001.

2 Interpretation

In these Regulations—
"applicant" means an applicant for registration as a money service operator under regulation 5;
"the appropriate judicial authority" means—
      (a)   in England and Wales, a magistrates' court,
      (b)   in Scotland, the sheriff,
      (c)   in Northern Ireland, a court of summary jurisdiction;
"the Commissioners" means the Commissioners of Customs and Excise;
"justice" means a justice of the peace or, in relation to Scotland, a justice within the meaning of section 307 of the Criminal Procedure (Scotland) Act 1995;
"money laundering offence" means an offence under the 1993 Regulations;
"money laundering reporting officer" means the appropriate person within the meaning of regulation 14 of the 1993 Regulations;
"money service business" means the business of engaging in any of the activities referred to in regulation 4(1)(ga) of the 1993 Regulations (so far as not excluded by regulation 4(2) of those Regulations);
"money service operator" means a person who carries on money service business other than a person who carries on relevant financial business falling within any of sub-paragraphs (a) to (g) or (i) of regulation 4(1) of the 1993 Regulations;
"officer" has the meaning given by section 1(1) of the Customs and Excise Management Act 1979;
"officer in overall charge of the investigation" means the person whose name and address are endorsed on the order concerned as being the officer so in charge;

581

"operator" means a money service operator;

"recorded information" includes information recorded in any form and any document of any nature whatsoever;

"registered number" has the meaning given by regulation 4(3);

"the 1993 Regulations" means the Money Laundering Regulations 1993;

"the review procedure" means the procedure under regulation 16;

"tribunal" means a VAT and duties tribunal.

3 *(Amends the Money Laundering Regulations 1993, SI 1993/1933, regs 4(1), 10(1), 11(1), and inserts reg 11(1A).)*

PART II
REGISTRATION

4 Register of money service operators

(1)   The Commissioners must maintain a register of money service operators.

(2)   The Commissioners may keep the register in any form they think fit.

(3)   The Commissioners must allocate to every registered money service operator a number, which is to be known as his registered number.

5 Requirement to be registered

(1)   A person who, on or after 1st June 2002, acts as a money service operator must be registered by the Commissioners.

(2)   Paragraph (1) does not apply to a person who, immediately before 1st June 2002, is acting as a money service operator, provided he has before that date made an application to be registered which has not been determined.

(3)   A person to whom this regulation applies must—

    (a)   make an application to be registered in such manner as the Commissioners may direct; and

    (b)   furnish the following information to the Commissioners, that is to say—

        (i)   the applicant's name and (if different) the name of the business;

        (ii)   the applicant's VAT registration number or, if he is not registered for VAT, any other reference number issued to him by the Commissioners;

        (iii)   the nature of the business;

        (iv)   the address of each of the premises at which the applicant carries on (or proposes to carry on) business;

        (v)   any agency or franchise agreement relating to the business, and the names and addresses of all relevant principals, agents, franchisors or franchisees;

        (vi)   the name of the relevant money laundering reporting officer (if any); and

(vii) whether any person concerned (or proposed to be concerned) in the management, control or operation of the business has been convicted of a money laundering offence or of money laundering within the meaning of regulation 2(3) of the 1993 Regulations.

(4) At any time after receiving an application to be registered and before determining it, the Commissioners may require the applicant to furnish them, within 21 days beginning with the date of being requested to do so, with such further information as they reasonably consider necessary to enable them to determine the application.

(5) Any information to be furnished to the Commissioners under this regulation must be in such form or verified in such manner as they may specify.

(6) In this regulation, "the business" means money service business which the applicant carries on or proposes to carry on.

6 Supplementary information

(1) If any at time after supplying the Commissioners with any information under regulation 5—
> (a) there is a change affecting any matter contained in that information; or
> (b) it becomes apparent that the information contains an inaccuracy;

the applicant or, as the case may be, the operator must supply the Commissioners with details of the change or, as the case may be, a correction of the inaccuracy (hereafter "supplementary information") within 30 days beginning with the date of the occurrence of the change or, as the case may be, the discovery of the inaccuracy.

(2) The supplementary information must be supplied in such manner as the Commissioners may direct.

(3) The obligation in paragraph (1) applies also to changes affecting any matter contained in any supplementary information supplied pursuant to this regulation.

7 Determination of application to register

(1) The Commissioners may refuse to register an applicant if, and only if—
> (a) any requirement of—
>> (i) paragraphs (3) to (5) of regulation 5 (requirement to be registered);
>> (ii) regulation 6 (supplementary information); or
>> (iii) regulation 9 (fees);
>
> has not been complied with; or
> (b) it appears to them that any information supplied pursuant to regulation 5 or 6 is false or misleading in a material particular.

(2)   The Commissioners must, by the end of the period of 45 days beginning with the date on which they receive the application or, where applicable, the date on which they receive any further information required under regulation 5(4), give notice in writing to the applicant of—

    (a)   his registered number; or

    (b)   the following matters, that is to say—

        (i)   their decision not to register the applicant;

        (ii)   the reasons for their decision;

        (iii)   the review procedure; and

        (iv)   the right to appeal to a tribunal.

8 Cancellation of registration

(1)   The Commissioners may cancel the registration of an operator if, at any time after registration, it appears to them that they would have had grounds to refuse registration under paragraph (1) of regulation 7 (determination of application to register).

(2)   Where the Commissioners decide to cancel the registration of an operator, they must forthwith inform him, in writing, of—

    (a)   their decision and the date from which the cancellation takes effect;

    (b)   the reasons for their decision;

    (c)   the review procedure; and

    (d)   the right to appeal to a tribunal.

9 Fees

(1)   The Commissioners may charge a fee—

    (a)   to an applicant; and

    (b)   to an operator annually on the anniversary of his registration by them under these Regulations.

(2)   The Commissioners may charge under paragraph (1) such fees as they consider will enable them to meet any expenses incurred by them in carrying out any of their functions under these Regulations or for any incidental purpose.

(3)   Without prejudice to the generality of paragraph (2), a fee may be charged in respect of each of the premises at which the operator or, as the case may be, the applicant carries on (or proposes to carry on) money service business.

PART III

POWERS OF THE COMMISSIONERS

10 Entry, inspection etc

(1)   Where an officer has reasonable cause to believe that any premises are used in connection with money service business, he may at any reasonable time enter and inspect the premises and inspect any recorded information or currency found on the premises.

(2)   A money service operator must—
    (a)   furnish to an officer, within such time and in such form as the officer may reasonably require, such information relating to the operator's business as the officer may reasonably specify; and
    (b)   upon demand made by the officer, produce or cause to be produced for inspection by the officer at such place, and at such time, as the officer may reasonably require, any recorded information relating to the operator's business.

11 Order for access to recorded information

(1)   Where, on an application by an officer, a justice is satisfied that there are reasonable grounds for believing—
    (a)   that a money laundering offence is being, has been or is about to be committed by a money service operator; and
    (b)   that any recorded information which may be required as evidence for the purpose of any proceedings in respect of such an offence is in the possession of any person;

he may make an order under this regulation.

(2)   An order under this regulation is an order that the person who appears to the justice to be in possession of the recorded information to which the application relates must—
    (a)   give an officer access to it;
    (b)   permit an officer to take copies of, or make extracts from, any information produced; and
    (c)   permit an officer to remove and take away any of it which he reasonably considers necessary;

not later than the end of the period of 7 days beginning with the date of the order or the end of such longer period as the order may specify.

(3)   Where the recorded information consists of information stored in any electronic form, an order under this regulation has effect as an order to produce the information in a form in which it is visible and legible, or from which it can readily be produced in a visible and legible form, and, if the officer wishes to remove it, in a form in which it can be removed.

12 Procedure where recorded information is removed

(1)   An officer who removes any recorded information in the exercise of a power conferred by regulation 11 must, if so requested by a person showing himself—
    (a)   to be the occupier of premises from which it was removed; or
    (b)   to have had custody or control of it immediately before the removal;

provide that person with a record of what he removed.

(2)   The officer must provide the record within a reasonable time from the making of the request for it.

(3)   Subject to paragraph (7), if a request for permission to be granted access to anything which—

    (a)   has been removed by an officer; and

    (b)   is retained by the Commissioners for the purposes of investigating an offence;

is made to the officer in overall charge of the investigation by a person who had custody or control of the thing immediately before it was so removed or by someone acting on behalf of such a person, that officer must allow the person who made the request access to it under the supervision of an officer.

(4)   Subject to paragraph (7), if a request for a photograph or copy of any such thing is made to the officer in overall charge of the investigation by a person who had custody or control of the thing immediately before it was so removed, or by someone acting on behalf of such a person, that officer must—

    (a)   allow the person who made the request access to it under the supervision of an officer for the purpose of photographing it or copying it; or

    (b)   photograph or copy it, or cause it to be photographed or copied.

(5)   Where anything is photographed or copied under sub-paragraph (4)(b), the photograph or copy must be supplied to the person who made the request.

(6)   The photograph or copy must be supplied within a reasonable time from the making of the request.

(7)   There is no duty under this regulation to grant access to, or supply a photograph or a copy of, anything if the officer in overall charge of the investigation for the purposes of which it was removed has reasonable grounds for believing that to do so would prejudice—

    (a)   that investigation;

    (b)   the investigation of an offence other than the offence for the purposes of the investigation of which the document was removed; or

    (c)   any criminal proceedings which may be brought as a result of—

        (i)   the investigation of which he is in charge; or

        (ii)   any such investigation as is mentioned in sub-paragraph (b).

13 Failure to comply with requirements under regulation 12

(1)   Where, on an application made as mentioned in paragraph (2), the appropriate judicial authority is satisfied that a person has failed to comply with a requirement imposed by regulation 12, the authority may order that person to comply with the requirement within such time and in such manner as may be specified in the order.

(2)   An application under paragraph (1) may only be made—

    (a)   in the case of a failure to comply with any of the requirements imposed by regulation 12(1) and (2), by the occupier of the premises from which the thing in question was removed or by the person who had custody or control of it immediately before it was so removed; and

    (b)   in any other case, by the person who had such custody or control.

(3)   In England and Wales and Northern Ireland, an application for an order under this regulation is to be made by complaint; and sections 21 and 42(2) of the Interpretation Act (Northern Ireland) 1954 apply as if any reference in those provisions to any enactment included a reference to this registration.

14 Entry, search etc

(1)   Where a justice is satisfied on information on oath that there is reasonable ground for suspecting that a money laundering offence is being, has been or is about to be committed by a money service operator on any premises or that evidence of the commission of such an offence is to be found there, he may issue a warrant in writing authorising any officer to enter those premises, if necessary by force, at any time within one month from the time of the issue of the warrant and search them.

(2)   A person who enters the premises under the authority of the warrant may—

    (a)   take with him such other persons as appear to him to be necessary;

    (b)   seize and remove any documents or other things whatsoever found on the premises which he has reasonable cause to believe may be required as evidence for the purpose of proceedings in respect of a money laundering offence; and

    (c)   search or cause to be searched any person found on the premises whom he has reasonable cause to believe to be in possession of any such documents or other such things;

but no woman or girl may be searched except by a woman.

(3)   The powers conferred by a warrant under this regulation may not be exercised—

    (a)   outside such times of day as may be specified in the warrant; or

    (b)   if the warrant so provides, otherwise than in the presence of a constable in uniform.

(4)   An officer seeking to exercise the powers conferred by a warrant under this regulation or, if there is more than one such officer, that one of them who is in charge of the search must provide a copy of the warrant endorsed with his name as follows—

    (a)   if the occupier of the premises concerned is present at the time the search is to begin, the copy must be supplied to the occupier;

    (b)   if at that time the occupier is not present but a person who appears to the officer to be in charge of the premises is present, the copy must be supplied to that person;

    (c)   if neither sub-paragraph (a) nor (b) applies, the copy must be left in a prominent place on the premises.

PART IV
PENALTIES, REVIEW AND APPEALS

15 Power to impose penalties

(1)   The Commissioners may impose a penalty of such amount as they consider appropriate, not exceeding £5,000, on a person to whom regulation 5 (requirement to be registered) applies, where that person fails to comply with any requirement in regulation 5, 6 (supplementary information), 9 (fees) or 10 (entry, inspection etc).

(2)   The Commissioners must not impose a penalty on a person where there are reasonable grounds for them to be satisfied that the person took all reasonable steps for securing that the requirement would be complied with.

(3)   Where the Commissioners decide to impose a penalty under this regulation, they must forthwith inform the person, in writing, of—
      (a)   their decision to impose the penalty and its amount;
      (b)   their reasons for imposing the penalty;
      (c)   the review procedure; and
      (d)   the right to appeal to a tribunal.

(4)   Where a person is liable to a penalty under this regulation, the Commissioners may reduce the penalty to such amount (including nil) as they think proper.

16 Review procedure

(1)   This regulation applies to the following decisions of the Commissioners, that is to say—
      (a)   a decision under regulation 7 to refuse to register an applicant;
      (b)   a decision under regulation 8 to cancel the registration of an operator;
      (c)   a decision under regulation 15 to impose a penalty.

(2)   Any person who is the subject of a decision as mentioned in paragraph (1) may by notice in writing to the Commissioners require them to review that decision.

(3)   The Commissioners need not review any decision unless the notice requiring the review is given before the end of the period of 45 days beginning with the date on which written notification of the decision was first given to the person requiring the review.

(4)   A person may give a notice under this regulation to require a decision to be reviewed for a second or subsequent time only if—
      (a)   the grounds on which he requires the further review are that the Commissioners did not, on any previous review, have the opportunity to consider certain facts or other matters; and
      (b)   he does not, on the further review, require the Commissioners to consider any facts or matters which were considered on a previous review except in so far as they are relevant to any issue to which the facts or matters not previously considered relate.

(5)   Where the Commissioners are required under this regulation to review any decision they must either—

(a)   confirm the decision; or

(b)   withdraw or vary the decision and take such further steps (if any) in consequence of the withdrawal or variation as they consider appropriate.

(6)   Where the Commissioners do not, within 45 days beginning with the date on which the review was required by a person, give notice to that person of their determination of the review, they are to be assumed for the purposes of these Regulations to have confirmed the decision.

17 *(Amends the Value Added Tax Act 1994, s 83.)*

18 Further provisions relating to appeals

On an appeal from any decision by the Commissioners, on a review under regulation 16, the tribunal have the power to—

(a)   quash or vary any decision of the Commissioners, including the power to reduce any penalty to such amount (including nil) as they think proper; and

(b)   substitute their own decision for any decision quashed on appeal.

PART V

MISCELLANEOUS

19 Prosecution of money laundering offences by the Commissioners

(1)   Proceedings for a money laundering offence may be instituted by order of the Commissioners.

(2)   Such proceedings may be instituted only against an operator or, where the operator is a body corporate, a partnership or an unincorporated association, against any person who is liable to be proceeded against under regulation 6 of the 1993 Regulations (offences by bodies corporate, partnerships and unincorporated associations).

(3)   Any such proceedings which are so instituted must be commenced in the name of an officer.

(4)   In the case of the death, removal, discharge or absence of the officer in whose name any such proceedings were commenced, those proceedings may be continued by another officer.

(5)   Where the Commissioners investigate, or propose to investigate, any matter with a view to determining—

(a)   whether there are grounds for believing that a money laundering offence has been committed by any person referred to in paragraph (2); or

(b)   whether such a person should be prosecuted for such an offence;

the matter is to be treated as an assigned matter within the meaning of the Customs and Excise Management Act 1979.

(6)   In exercising their power to institute proceedings for a money laundering offence, the Commissioners must comply with any conditions or restrictions imposed in writing by the Treasury.

(7)   Conditions or restrictions may be imposed under paragraph (6) in relation to—

    (a)   proceedings generally; or

    (b)   such proceedings, or categories of proceedings, as the Treasury may direct.

20 Recovery of fees and penalties through the court

Where any fee is charged, or any penalty is imposed, by virtue of these Regulations—

    (a)   if the person from whom it is recoverable resides in England and Wales or Northern Ireland, it is recoverable as a civil debt; and

    (b)   if that person resides in Scotland, it may be enforced in the same manner as an extract registered decree arbitral bearing a warrant for execution issued by the sheriff court of any sheriffdom in Scotland.

Council Directive

of 10 June 1991

on prevention of the use of the financial system for the purpose of money laundering

(91/308/EEC)

Date of publication in OJ: OJ L166, 28.6.1991, p 77.

THE COUNCIL OF THE EUROPEAN COMMUNITIES,

Having regard to the Treaty establishing the European Economic Community, and in particular Article 57(2), first and third sentences, and Article 100a thereof,

Having regard to the proposal from the Commission,[1]

In cooperation with the European Parliament,[2]

Having regard to the opinion of the Economic and Social Committee,[3]

Whereas when credit and financial institutions are used to launder proceeds from criminal activities (hereinafter referred to as 'money laundering'), the soundness and stability of the institution concerned and confidence in the financial system as a whole could be seriously jeopardised, thereby losing the trust of the public;

Whereas lack of Community action against money laundering could lead Member States, for the purpose of protecting their financial systems, to adopt measures which could be inconsistent with completion of the single market; whereas, in order to facilitate their criminal activities, launderers could try to take advantage of the freedom of capital movement and freedom to supply financial services which the integrated financial areas involves, if certain coordinating measures are not adopted at Community level;

Whereas money laundering has an evident influence on the rise of organised crime in general and drug trafficking in particular; whereas there is more and more awareness that combating money laundering is one of the most effective means of opposing this form of criminal activity, which constitutes a particular threat to Member States' societies;

Whereas money laundering must be combated mainly by penal means and within the framework of international cooperation among judicial and law enforcement authorities, as has been undertaken, in the field of drugs, by the United Nations Convention Against Illicit Traffic in Narcotic Drugs and Psychotropic Substances, adopted on 19 December 1988 in Vienna (hereinafter referred to as the 'Vienna Convention') and more generally in relation to all criminal activities, by the Council of Europe Convention on laundering, tracing, seizure and confiscation of proceeds of crime, opened for signature on 8 November 1990 in Strasbourg;

Whereas a penal approach should, however, not be the only way to combat money laundering, since the financial system can play a highly effective role; whereas reference must be made in this context to the recommendation of the Council of Europe of 27 June 1980 and to the declaration of principles adopted in December 1988 in Basle by the banking supervisory authorities of the Group of Ten, both of which constitute major steps towards preventing the use of the financial system for money laundering;

Whereas money laundering is usually carried out in an international context so that the criminal origin of the funds can be better disguised; whereas measures exclusively adopted at a national level, without taking account of international coordination and cooperation, would have very limited effects;

Council Directive 91/308/EEC

Whereas any measures adopted by the Community in this field should be consistent with other action undertaken in other international for a; whereas in this respect any Community action should take particular account of the recommendations adopted by the financial action task force on money laundering, set up in July 1989 by the Paris summit of the seven most developed countries;

Whereas the European Parliament has requested, in several resolutions, the establishment of a global Community programme to combat drug trafficking, including provisions on prevention of money laundering;

Whereas for the purposes of this Directive the definition of money laundering is taken from that adopted in the Vienna Convention; whereas, however, since money laundering occurs not only in relation to the proceeds of drug-related offences but also in relation to the proceeds of other criminal activities (such as organised crime and terrorism), the Member States should, within the meaning of their legislation, extend the effects of the Directive to include the proceeds of such activities, to the extent that they are likely to result in laundering operations Justifying sanctions on that basis;

Whereas prohibition of money laundering in Member States' legislation backed by appropriate measures and penalties is a necessary condition for combating this phenomenon;

Whereas ensuring that credit and financial institutions require identification of their customers when entering into business relations or conducting transactions, exceeding certain thresholds, are necessary to avoid launderers' taking advantage of anonymity to carry out their criminal activities; whereas such provisions must also be extended, as far as possible, to any beneficial owners;

Whereas credit and financial institutions must keep for at least five years copies or references of the identification documents required as well as supporting evidence and records consisting of documents relating to transactions or copies thereof similarly admissible in court proceedings under the applicable national legislation for use as evidence in any investigation into money laundering;

Whereas ensuring that credit and financial institutions examine with special attention any transaction which they regard as particularly likely, by its nature, to be related to money laundering is necessary in order to preserve the soundness and integrity of the financial system as well as to contribute to combating this phenomenon; whereas to this end they should pay special attention to transactions with third countries which do not apply comparable standards against money laundering to those established by the Community or to other equivalent standards set out by international fora and endorsed by the Community;

Whereas, for those purposes, Member States may ask credit and financial institutions to record in writing the results of the examination they are required to carry out and to ensure that those results are available to the authorities responsible for efforts to eliminate money laundering;

Whereas preventing the financial system from being used for money laundering is a task which cannot be carried out by the authorities responsible for combating this phenomenon without the cooperation of credit and financial institutions and their supervisory authorities; whereas banking secrecy must be lifted in such cases; whereas a mandatory system of reporting suspicious transactions which ensures that information is transmitted to the above mentioned authorities without alerting the customers concerned, is the most effective way to accomplish such cooperation; whereas a special protection clause is necessary to exempt credit and financial institutions, their employees and their directors from responsibility for breaching restrictions on disclosure of information;

Whereas the information received by the authorities pursuant to this Directive may be used only in connection with combating money laundering; whereas Member States may nevertheless provide that this information may be used for other purposes;

Whereas establishment by credit and financial institutions of procedures of internal control and training programmes in this field are complementary provisions without which the other measures contained in this Directive could become ineffective;

Whereas, since money laundering can be carried out not only through credit and financial institutions but also through other types of professions and categories of undertakings, Member States must extend the provisions of this Directive in whole or in part, to include those professions and undertakings whose activities are particularly likely to be used for money laundering purposes;

Whereas it is important that the Member States should take particular care to ensure that coordinated action is taken in the Community where there are strong grounds for believing that professions or activities the conditions governing the pursuit of which have been harmonised at Community level are being used for laundering money;

Whereas the effectiveness of efforts to eliminate money laundering is particularly dependent on the close coordination and harmonisation of national implementing measures; whereas such coordination and harmonisation which is being carried out in various international bodies requires, in the Community context, cooperation between Member States and the Commission in the framework of a contact committee;

Whereas it is for each Member State to adopt appropriate measures and to penalise infringement of such measures in an appropriate manner to ensure full application of this Directive,

---

[1]   OJ C106, 24.4.1990, p 6; and OJ C319, 19.12.1990, p 9.
[2]   OJ C324, 24.12.1990, p 264; and OJ C129, 20.5.1991.
[3]   OJ C332, 31.12.1990, p86.

HAS ADOPTED THIS DIRECTIVE—

[Article 1

For the purpose of this Directive—
—   (A) "Credit institution" means a credit institution, as defined in Article 1(1) first subparagraph of Directive 2000/12/EC[1] and includes branches within the meaning of Article 1(3) of that Directive and located in the Community, of credit institutions having their head offices inside or outside the Community.
—   (B) "Financial institution" means—
1.   an undertaking other than a credit institution whose principal activity is to carry out one or more of the operations included in numbers 2 to 12 and number 14 of the list set out in Annex I to Directive 2000/12/EC; these include the activities of currency exchange offices (bureaux de change) and of money transmission/remittance offices;
2.   an insurance company duly authorised in accordance with Directive 79/267/EEC,[2] insofar as it carries out activities covered by that Directive;
3.   an investment firm as defined in Article 1(2) of Directive 93/22/EEC;[3]
4.   a collective investment undertaking marketing its units or shares.

This definition of financial institution includes branches located in the Community of financial institutions, whose head offices are inside or outside the Community.
—   (C) "Money laundering" means the following conduct when committed intentionally—

— the conversion or transfer of property, knowing that such property is derived from criminal activity or from an act of participation in such activity, for the purpose of concealing or disguising the illicit origin of the property or of assisting any person who is involved in the commission of such activity to evade the legal consequences of his action;

— the concealment or disguise of the true nature, source, location, disposition, movement, rights with respect to, or ownership of property, knowing that such property is derived from criminal activity or from an act of participation in such activity;

— the acquisition, possession or use of property, knowing, at the time of receipt, that such property was derived from criminal activity or from an act of participation in such activity;

— participation in, association to commit, attempts to commit and aiding, abetting, facilitating and counselling the commission of any of the actions mentioned in the foregoing indents.

Knowledge, intent or purpose required as an element of the abovementioned activities may be inferred from objective factual circumstances.

Money laundering shall be regarded as such even where the activities which generated the property to be laundered were carried out in the territory of another Member State or in that of a third country.

— (D) "Property" means assets of every kind, whether corporeal or incorporeal, movable or immovable, tangible or intangible, and legal documents or instruments evidencing title to or interests in such assets.

— (E) "Criminal activity" means any kind of criminal involvement in the commission of a serious crime.

Serious crimes are, at least—

— any of the offences defined in Article 3(1)(a) of the Vienna Convention;

— the activities of criminal organisations as defined in Article 1 of Joint Action 98/733/JHA;[4]

— fraud, at least serious, as defined in Article 1(1) and Article 2 of the Convention on the protection of the European Communities' financial interests;[5]

— corruption;

— an offence which may generate substantial proceeds and which is punishable by a severe sentence of imprisonment in accordance with the penal law of the Member State.

Member States shall before 15 December 2004 amend the definition provided for in this indent in order to bring this definition into line with the definition of serious crime of Joint Action 98/699/JHA. The Council invites the Commission to present before 15 December 2004 a proposal for a Directive amending in that respect this Directive.

Member States may designate any other offence as a criminal activity for the purposes of this Directive.

— (F) "Competent authorities" means the national authorities empowered by law or regulation to supervise the activity of any of the institutions or persons subject to this Directive.]

Substituted by European Parliament and Council Directive 2001/97/EC of 4 December 2001, Art 1.1.
[1]   OJ L126, 26.5.2000, p. 1.
[2]   OJ L63, 13.3.1979, p. 1.
[3]   OJ L141, 11.6.1993, p. 27.
[4]   OJ L351, 29.12.1998, p. 1.
[5]   OJ C316, 27.11.1995, p. 48.

Article 2

Member States shall ensure that money laundering as defined in this Directive is prohibited.

[Article 2a

Member States shall ensure that the obligations laid down in this Directive are imposed on the following institutions—
1.   credit institutions as defined in point A of Article 1;
2.   financial institutions as defined in point B of Article 1;
     and on the following legal or natural persons acting in the exercise of their professional activities:
3.   auditors, external accountants and tax advisors;
4.   real estate agents;
5.   notaries and other independent legal professionals, when they participate, whether—
     (a)   by assisting in the planning or execution of transactions for their client concerning the
           (i)   buying and selling of real property or business entities;
           (ii) managing of client money, securities or other assets;
           (iii) opening or management of bank, savings or securities accounts;
           (iv) organisation of contributions necessary for the creation, operation or management of companies;
           (v)   creation, operation or management of trusts, companies or similar structures;
     (b)   or by acting on behalf of and for their client in any financial or real estate transaction;
6.   dealers in high-value goods, such as precious stones or metals, or works of art, auctioneers, whenever payment is made in cash, and in an amount of EUR 15000 or more;
7.   casinos.]

Inserted by European Parliament and Council Directive 2001/97/EC of 4 December 2001, Art 1.2.

[Article 3

1. Member States shall ensure that the institutions and persons subject to this Directive require identification of their customers by means of supporting evidence when entering into business relations, particularly, in the case of the institutions, when opening an account or savings accounts, or when offering safe custody facilities.

2. The identification requirement shall also apply for any transaction with customers other than those referred to in paragraph 1, involving a sum amounting

to EUR 15000 or more, whether the transaction is carried out in a single operation or in several operations which seem to be linked. Where the sum is not known at the time when the transaction is undertaken, the institution or person concerned shall proceed with identification as soon as it or he is apprised of the sum and establishes that the threshold has been reached.

3. By way of derogation from the preceding paragraphs, the identification requirements with regard to insurance policies written by insurance undertakings within the meaning of Council Directive 92/96/EEC of 10 November 1992 on the coordination of laws, regulations and administrative provisions relating to direct life assurance (third life assurance Directive),[1] where they perform activities which fall within the scope of that Directive shall not be required where the periodic premium amount or amounts to be paid in any given year does or do not exceed EUR 1000 or where a single premium is paid amounting to EUR 2500 or less. If the periodic premium amount or amounts to be paid in any given year is or are increased so as to exceed the EUR 1000 threshold, identification shall be required.

4. Member States may provide that the identification requirement is not compulsory for insurance policies in respect of pension schemes taken out by virtue of a contract of employment or the insured's occupation, provided that such policies contain no surrender clause and may not be used as collateral for a loan.

5. By way of derogation from the preceding paragraphs, all casino customers shall be identified if they purchase or sell gambling chips with a value of EUR 1000 or more.

6. Casinos subject to State supervision shall be deemed in any event to have complied with the identification requirement laid down in this Directive if they register and identify their customers immediately on entry, regardless of the number of gambling chips purchased.

7. In the event of doubt as to whether the customers referred to in the above paragraphs are acting on their own behalf, or where it is certain that they are not acting on their own behalf, the institutions and persons subject to this Directive shall take reasonable measures to obtain information as to the real identity of the persons on whose behalf those customers are acting.

8. The institutions and persons subject to this Directive shall carry out such identification, even where the amount of the transaction is lower than the threshold laid down, wherever there is suspicion of money laundering.

9. The institutions and persons subject to this Directive shall not be subject to the identification requirements provided for in this Article where the customer is a credit or financial institution covered by this Directive or a credit or financial institution situated in a third country which imposes, in the opinion of the relevant Member States, equivalent requirements to those laid down by this Directive.

10. Member States may provide that the identification requirements regarding transactions referred to in paragraphs 3 and 4 are fulfilled when it is established that the payment for the transaction is to be debited from an account opened in the customer's name with a credit institution subject to this Directive according to the requirements of paragraph 1.

11. Member States shall, in any case, ensure that the institutions and persons subject to this Directive take specific and adequate measures necessary to compensate for the greater risk of money laundering which arises when establishing business relations or entering into a transaction with a customer who

has not been physically present for identification purposes ('non-face to face' operations). Such measures shall ensure that the customer's identity is established, for example, by requiring additional documentary evidence, or supplementary measures to verify or certify the documents supplied, or confirmatory certification by an institution subject to this Directive, or by requiring that the first payment of the operations is carried out through an account opened in the customer's name with a credit institution subject to this Directive. The internal control procedures laid down in Article 11(1) shall take specific account of these measures.]

Substituted by European Parliament and Council Directive 2001/97/EC of 4 December 2001, Art 1.3.
[1]   OJ L360, 9.12.1992, p. 1.

Article 4

Member States shall ensure that [the institutions and persons subject to this Directive] keep the following for use as evidence in any investigation into money laundering—
—   in the case of identification, a copy or the references of the evidence required, for a period of at least five years after the relationship with their customer has ended,
—   in the case of transactions, the supporting evidence and records, consisting of the original documents or copies admissible in court proceedings under the applicable national legislation for a period of at least five years following execution of the transactions.

Words in square brackets substituted by European Parliament and Council Directive 2001/97/EC of 4 December 2001, Art 1.4.

Article 5

Member States shall ensure that [the institutions and persons subject to this Directive] examine with special attention any transaction which they regard as particularly likely, by its nature, to be related to money laundering.

Words in square brackets substituted by European Parliament and Council Directive 2001/97/EC of 4 December 2001, Art 1.4.

[Article 6

1. Member States shall ensure that the institutions and persons subject to this Directive and their directors and employees cooperate fully with the authorities responsible for combating money laundering—
(a)   by informing those authorities, on their own initiative, of any fact which might be an indication of money laundering;
(b)   by furnishing those authorities, at their request, with all necessary information, in accordance with the procedures established by the applicable legislation.

2.   The information referred to in paragraph 1 shall be forwarded to the authorities responsible for combating money laundering of the Member State in whose territory the institution or person forwarding the information is situated. The person or persons designated by the institutions and persons in accordance with the procedures provided for in Article 11(1)(a) shall normally forward the information.

3. In the case of the notaries and independent legal professionals referred to in Article 2a(5), Member States may designate an appropriate self-regulatory body of the profession concerned as the authority to be informed of the facts referred to in paragraph 1(a) and in such case shall lay down the appropriate forms of cooperation between that body and the authorities responsible for combating money laundering.

Member States shall not be obliged to apply the obligations laid down in paragraph 1 to notaries, independent legal professionals, auditors, external accountants and tax advisors with regard to information they receive from or obtain on one of their clients, in the course of ascertaining the legal position for their client or performing their task of defending or representing that client in, or concerning judicial proceedings, including advice on instituting or avoiding proceedings, whether such information is received or obtained before, during or after such proceedings.]

Substituted by European Parliament and Council Directive 2001/97/EC of 4 December 2001, Art 1.5.

[Article 7

Member States shall ensure that the institutions and persons subject to this Directive refrain from carrying out transactions which they know or suspect to be related to money laundering until they have apprised the authorities referred to in Article 6. Those authorities may, under conditions determined by their national legislation, give instructions not to execute the operation. Where such a transaction is suspected of giving rise to money laundering and where to refrain in such manner is impossible or is likely to frustrate efforts to pursue the beneficiaries of a suspected money-laundering operation, the institutions and persons concerned shall apprise the authorities immediately afterwards.]

Substituted by European Parliament and Council Directive 2001/97/EC of 4 December 2001, Art 1.6.

Article 8

[1.] [The institutions and persons subject to this Directive] and their directors and employees shall not disclose to the customer concerned nor to other third persons that information has been transmitted to the authorities in accordance with Articles 6 and 7 or that a money laundering investigation is being carried out.

[2. Member States shall not be obliged under this Directive to apply the obligation laid down in paragraph 1 to the professions mentioned in the second paragraph of Article 6(3).]

Para 1: numbered as such and words in square brackets substituted by European Parliament and Council Directive 2001/97/EC of 4 December 2001, Art 1.7, Art 1.4, respectively.
Para 2: added by European Parliament and Council Directive 2001/97/EC of 4 December 2001, Art 1.7.

[Article 9

The disclosure in good faith to the authorities responsible for combating money laundering by an institution or person subject to this Directive or by an employee or director of such an institution or person of the information referred to in Articles 6 and 7 shall not constitute a breach of any restriction on disclosure of information imposed by contract or by any legislative, regulatory or administrative provision, and shall not involve the institution or person or its directors or employees in liability of any kind.]

Substituted by European Parliament and Council Directive 2001/97/EC of 4 December 2001, Art 1.8.

Article 10

Member States shall ensure that if, in the course of inspections carried out in [the institutions and persons subject to this Directive] by the competent authorities, or in any other way, those authorities discover facts that could constitute evidence of money laundering, they inform the authorities responsible for combating money laundering.

[Member States shall ensure that supervisory bodies empowered by law or regulation to oversee the stock, foreign exchange and financial derivatives markets inform the authorities responsible for combating money laundering if they discover facts that could constitute evidence of money laundering.]

Words in first pair of square brackets substituted by European Parliament and Council Directive 2001/97/EC of 4 December 2001, Art 1.4.
Second paragraph added by European Parliament and Council Directive 2001/97/EC of 4 December 2001, Art 1.9.

[Article 11

1. Member States shall ensure that the institutions and persons subject to this Directive—
    (a)   establish adequate procedures of internal control and communication in order to forestall and prevent operations related to money laundering;
    (b)   take appropriate measures so that their employees are aware of the provisions contained in this Directive. These measures shall include participation of their relevant employees in special training programmes to help them recognise operations which may be related to money laundering as well as to instruct them as to how to proceed in such cases.

Where a natural person falling within any of Article 2a(3) to (7) undertakes his professional activities as an employee of a legal person, the obligations in this Article shall apply to that legal person rather than to the natural person.

2. Member States shall ensure that the institutions and persons subject to this Directive have access to up-to-date information on the practices of money launderers and on indications leading to the recognition of suspicious transactions.]

Substituted by European Parliament and Council Directive 2001/97/EC of 4 December 2001, Art 1.10.

Article 12

Member States shall ensure that the provisions of this Directive are extended in whole or in part to professions and to categories of undertakings, other than the [institutions and persons referred to in Article 2a.], which engage in activities which are particularly likely to be used for money-laundering purposes.

Words in square brackets substituted by European Parliament and Council Directive 2001/97/EC of 4 December 2001, Art 1.11.

Article 13

1.   A contact committee (hereinafter referred to as "the Committee") shall be set up under the aegis of the Commission. Its function shall be—

   (a)   without prejudice to Articles 169 and 170 of the Treaty, to facilitate harmonised implementation of this Directive through regular consultation on any practical problems arising from its application and on which exchanges of view are deemed useful;

   (b)   to facilitate consultation between the Member States on the more stringent or additional conditions and obligations which they may lay down at national level;

   (c)   to advise the Commission, if necessary, on any supplements or amendments to be made to this Directive or on any adjustments deemed necessary, in particular to harmonise the effects of Article 12;

   (d)   to examine whether a profession or a category of undertaking should be included in the scope of Article 12 where it has been established that such profession or category of undertaking has been used in a Member State for money laundering.

2.   It shall not be the function of the Committee to appraise the merits of decisions taken by the competent authorities in individual cases.

3.   The Committee shall be composed of persons appointed by the Member States and of representatives of the Commission. The secretariat shall be provided by the Commission. The chairman shall be a representative of the Commission. It shall be convened by its chairman, either on his own initiative or at the request of the delegation of a Member State.

Article 14

Each Member State shall take appropriate measures to ensure full application of all the provisions of this Directive and shall in particular determine the penalties to be applied for infringement of the measures adopted pursuant to this Directive.

Article 15

The Member States may adopt or retain in force stricter provisions in the field covered by this Directive to prevent money laundering.

Article 16

1.   Member States shall bring into force the laws, regulations and administrative decisions necessary to comply with this Directive before 1 January 1993 at the latest.

2.   Where Member States adopt these measures, they shall contain a reference to this Directive or shall be accompanied by such reference on the occasion of their official publication. The methods of making such a reference shall be laid down by the Member States.

3.   Member States shall communicate to the Commission the text of the main provisions of national law which they adopt in the field governed by this Directive.

Article 17

One year after 1 January 1993, whenever necessary and at least at three yearly intervals thereafter, the Commission shall draw up a report on the implementation of this Directive and submit it to the European Parliament and the Council.

Article 18

This Directive is addressed to the Member States.

Done at Luxembourg, 10 June 1991.

STATEMENT BY THE REPRESENTATIVES OF THE GOVERNMENTS OF THE MEMBER STATES MEETING WITHIN THE COUNCIL

The representatives of the Governments of the Member States, meeting within the Council,

Recalling that the Member States signed the United Nations Convention against illicit traffic in narcotic drugs and psychotropic substances, adopted on 19 December 1988 in Vienna;

Recalling also that most Member States have already signed the Council of Europe Convention on laundering, tracing, seizure and confiscation of proceeds of crime on 8 November 1990 in Strasbourg;

Conscious of the fact that the descriptions of money laundering contained in Article 1 of Council Directive 91/308/EEC[1] derives its wording from the relevant provisions of the aforementioned Conventions; Hereby undertake to take all necessary steps by 31 December 1992 at the latest to enact criminal legislation enabling them to comply with their obligations under the aforementioned instruments.

---

[1]   OJ L166, 28.6.1991, p 77.

Council Directive

of 4 December 2001
amending Council Directive 91/308/EEC on prevention of the use of the financial system for the purpose of money laundering

(2001/97/EC)

Date of publication in OJ: OJ L344, 28.12.2001, p 76.

THE EUROPEAN PARLIAMENT AND THE COUNCIL OF THE EUROPEAN UNION,

Having regard to the Treaty establishing the European Community, and in particular Article 47(2), first and third sentences, and Article 95 thereof,

Having regard to the proposal from the Commission,[1]

Having regard to the opinion of the Economic and Social Committee,[2]

Acting in accordance with the procedure laid down in Article 251 of the Treaty,[3] in the light of the joint text approved by the Conciliation Committee on 18 September 2001,

Whereas—

(1) It is appropriate that Directive 91/308/EEC,[4] hereinafter referred to as "the Directive", as one of the main international instruments in the fight against money laundering, should be updated in line with the conclusions of the Commission and the wishes expressed by the European Parliament and the Member States. In this way the Directive should not only reflect best international practice in this area but should also continue to set a high standard in protecting the financial sector and other vulnerable activities from the harmful effects of the proceeds of crime.

(2) The General Agreement on Trade in Services (GATS) allows Members to adopt measures necessary to protect public morals and to adopt measures for prudential reasons, including for ensuring the stability and integrity of the financial system. Such measures should not impose restrictions that go beyond what is necessary to achieve those objectives.

(3) The Directive does not establish clearly which Member State's authorities should receive suspicious transaction reports from branches of credit and financial institutions having their head office in another Member State nor which Member State's authorities are responsible for ensuring that such branches comply with the Directive. The authorities of the Member States in which the branch is located should receive such reports and exercise the above responsibilities.

(4) This allocation of responsibilities should be set out clearly in the Directive by means of an amendment to the definition of "credit institution" and "financial institution".

(5) The European Parliament has expressed concerns that the activities of currency exchange offices ("bureaux de change") and money transmitters (money remittance offices) are vulnerable to money laundering. These activities should already fall within the scope of the Directive. In order to dispel any doubt in this matter the Directive should clearly confirm that these activities are covered.

(6) To ensure the fullest possible coverage of the financial sector it should also be made clear that the Directive applies to the activities of investment firms as defined in Council Directive 93/22/EEC of 10 May 1993 on investment services in the securities field.[5]

(7) The Directive obliges Member States only to combat the laundering of the proceeds of drugs offences. There has been a trend in recent years towards a much wider definition of money laundering based on a broader range of predicate or underlying offences, as reflected for example in the 1996 revision of the 40 Recommendations of the Financial Action Task Force (FATF), the leading international body devoted to the fight against money laundering.

(8) A wider range of predicate offences facilitates suspicious transaction reporting and international cooperation in this area. Therefore, the Directive should be brought up to date in this respect.

(9) In Joint Action 98/699/JHA of 3 December 1998 adopted by the Council on money laundering, the identification, tracing, freezing, seizing and confiscation of instrumentalities and the proceeds from crime,[6] the Member States agreed to make all serious offences, as defined in the Joint Action, predicate offences for the purpose of the criminalisation of money laundering.

(10) The suppression of organised crime in particular is closely linked to measures to combat money laundering. The list of predicate offences should therefore be adapted accordingly.

(11) The Directive imposes obligations regarding in particular the reporting of suspicious transactions. It would be more appropriate and in line with the philosophy of the Action Plan to Combat Organised Crime[7] for the prohibition of money laundering under the Directive to be extended.

(12) On 21 December 1998 the Council adopted Joint Action 98/733/JHA on making it a criminal offence to participate in a criminal organisation in the Member States of the European Union.[8] This Joint Action reflects the Member States' agreement on the need for a common approach in this area.

(13) As required by the Directive, suspicious transaction reports are being made by the financial sector, and particularly by the credit institutions, in every Member State. There is

evidence that the tightening of controls in the financial sector has prompted money launderers to seek alternative methods for concealing the origin of the proceeds of crime.

(14) There is a trend towards the increased use by money launderers of non-financial businesses. This is confirmed by the work of the FATF on money laundering techniques and typologies.

(15) The obligations of the Directive concerning customer identification, record keeping and the reporting of suspicious transactions should be extended to a limited number of activities and professions which have been shown to be vulnerable to money laundering.

(16) Notaries and independent legal professionals, as defined by the Member States, should be made subject to the provisions of the Directive when participating in financial or corporate transactions, including providing tax advice, where there is the greatest risk of the services of those legal professionals being misused for the purpose of laundering the proceeds of criminal activity.

(17) However, where independent members of professions providing legal advice which are legally recognised and controlled, such as lawyers, are ascertaining the legal position of a client or representing a client in legal proceedings, it would not be appropriate under the Directive to put these legal professionals in respect of these activities under an obligation to report suspicions of money laundering. There must be exemptions from any obligation to report information obtained either before, during or after judicial proceedings, or in the course of ascertaining the legal position for a client. Thus, legal advice remains subject to the obligation of professional secrecy unless the legal counsellor is taking part in money laundering activities, the legal advice is provided for money laundering purposes, or the lawyer knows that the client is seeking legal advice for money laundering purposes.

(18) Directly comparable services need to be treated in the same manner when practised by any of the professions covered by the Directive. In order to preserve the rights laid down in the European Convention for the Protection of Human Rights and Fundamental Freedoms (ECHR) and the Treaty of the European Union, in the case of auditors, external accountants and tax advisors who, in some Member States, may defend or represent a client in the context of judicial proceedings or ascertain a client's legal position, the information they obtain in the performance of these tasks should not be subject to the reporting obligations in accordance with the Directive.

(19) The Directive makes reference to "the authorities responsible for combating money laundering" to which reports of suspicious operations must be made on the one hand, and to authorities empowered by law or regulation to supervise the activity of any of the institutions or persons subject to this Directive ("competent authorities") on the other hand. It is understood that the Directive does not oblige Member States to create such "competent authorities" where they do not exist, and that bar associations and other self-regulatory bodies for independent professionals do not fall under the term "competent authorities".

(20) In the case of notaries and independent legal professionals, Member States should be allowed, in order to take proper account of these professionals' duty of discretion owed to their clients, to nominate the bar association or other self-regulatory bodies for independent professionals as the body to which reports on possible money laundering cases may be addressed by these professionals. The rules governing the treatment of such reports and their possible onward transmission to the "authorities responsible for combating money laundering" and in general the appropriate forms of cooperation between the bar associations or professional bodies and these authorities should be determined by the Member States,

---

[1]   OJ C177 E, 27.6.2000, p. 14.
[2]   OJ C75, 15.3.2000, p. 22.
[3]   Opinion of the European Parliament of 5 July 2000 (OJ C 121, 24.4.2001, p. 133), Council Common Position of 30 November 2000 (OJ C36, 2.2.2001, p. 24) and Decision of the European Parliament of 5 April 2001 (not yet published in the Official Journal). Decision of the European Parliament of 13 November 2001 and Decision of the Council of 19 November 2001.
[4]   OJ L166, 28.6.1991, p. 77.
[5]   OJ L141, 11.6.1993, p. 27.
[6]   OJ L333, 9.12.1998, p. 1.
[7]   OJ C251, 15.8.1997, p. 1.
[8]   OJ L351, 29.12.1998, p. 1.

HAVE ADOPTED THIS DIRECTIVE—

Article 1 *(Amends the Council Directive on prevention of the use of the financial system for the purpose of money laundering (91/308/EEC).)*

Article 2

Within three years of the entry into force of this Directive, the Commission shall carry out a particular examination, in the context of the report provided for in Article 17 of Directive 91/308/EEC, of aspects relating to the implementation of the fifth indent of Article 1(E), the specific treatment of lawyers and other independent legal professionals, the identification of clients in non-face to face transactions and possible implications for electronic commerce.

Article 3

1. Member States shall bring into force the laws, regulations and administrative provisions necessary to comply with this Directive by 15 June 2003 at the latest. They shall forthwith inform the Commission thereof.

Where Member States adopt these measures, they shall contain a reference to this Directive or shall be accompanied by such reference on the occasion of their official publication. The methods of making such a reference shall be laid down by the Member States.

2. Member States shall communicate to the Commission the text of the main provisions of domestic law which they adopt in the field governed by this Directive.

Article 4

This Directive shall enter into force on the day of its publication in the Official Journal of the European Communities.

Article 5

This Directive is addressed to the Member States.

Done at Brussels, 4 December 2001.

Index